The Inventor's War

The Inventor's War

Craig Suter

Krieg Books USA   Tucson, Arizona

To contact the author or order
additional copies of this book
Krieg Books USA
P.O. Box 17833
Tucson, AZ 85731-7833
Copies available at:
theinventorswar.com

This edition was prepared for printing by
Ghost River Images
5350 East Fourth Street
Tucson, Arizona 85711
www.ghostriverimages.com

Cover design by
Diane and Craig Suter

Cover image: Testing the fusible link for the selenium rectifier. (NARA)

ISBN: 978-0-9835274-0-4

Library of Congress Control Number: 2011906760

Printed in the United States of America
First Printing: May, 2011
10 9 8 7 6 5 4 3 2 1

Contents

Acknowledgements

A book of this size, complexity, and age—this book has been underway since 1997—could not be accomplished without the assistance and input from many people. And it is to those that I owe a debt of gratitude.

First and foremost is my beautiful bride Diane. It was her quiet prodding that kept the process going when it could, and her loving patience when she knew I was not up to the task. It, too, was her invaluable assistance of finding material and information when all other sources failed. Lastly, it was to her credit that she provided the finances to see this project through to the end, and had the confidence in me to carry it there.

I could not go forward with this announcement without including the one other who was instrumental in its inception. To Brigit Murphy, I say thanks for the course assignment that started this project, and thanks for the A.

Thank you to some of my mentors who did not survive to see this in print:
Robert J. Serling and Kathy Curley. You are both missed

There are a number of instructors who willingly gave their time, despite pressures from their profession, to test read or to give advice. Don Roberts, Ray Sparks, Dr. Ford, and Dr. Karl Johnson.

I could not have attempted such a project without the help of the following:
Dr. John Meaney M.D., my good friend Dr. Doug Huestis M.D., and Dr. Jack Quick D.V.M. with oversight and expertise.

The experience and timely advice from my dear friend Elizabeth Ohm was always welcome. She steered me right more often than I can remember.

My test readers below, your opinions and comments were very helpful. I thank you one and all.

Mary Anne Facelli, David Hansen, Craig Bennett, Cindy Edwards, Joyce Martin, Judy Oakles, Steve Peiper, Ted Falter, Lorraine Falter, April Baer, Rod Rodriguez, Linda Ashburn, Steve Wallace, Barbara Tidd, and Janet McWhite.

And I am eternally grateful to my publishing advisor and new friend Mike White.

Finally, I thank the reader, for without whom this would just be a typing exercise. I fear readers are a dying breed. Let's not ever abandon the search for knowledge and truth. Live long and prosper.

To the Reader,

It is my intention to explore all the different facets of the history of the Second World War. My whole life has focused on learning everything I could about the war and to pass on the knowledge. To that end, I have made an honest effort to present the stories and facts in an entertaining and as accurate format as possible. That, however, does not preclude errors creeping in now and then. If there are substantial mistakes, I would appreciate a letter outlining the mistake and the source of your material. If that results in a correction, subsequent editions will include your name as a contributor.

I have also begun to collect the materials for a second volume of this series. If there are stories or facts that would lead to the inclusion of an entry, again, I would add your name as a contributor. Send copies (never send originals, I would not be certain that they would not get lost or damaged) of any documents or photos along with your written comments. Include as many details as possible along with the identity of your source. Keep in mind the selection criteria—time, use, durability—but I would rather get stories that may be usable than miss a great story. Any that are used will be given proper attribution.

Craig Suter
Spring 2011

Introduction

In the early pre-dawn hours of July 16, 1945, the remnant clouds of a New Mexican thunderstorm were suddenly illuminated by a burst of intense light from the desert floor. One hundred feet above the sand, which was instantly fused into glass, a growing ball of fire burned with temperatures that rivaled those at the sun's core. Simultaneously, a tremendous blast of pressure ripped across the landscape, flattening all plants and animals in its path. From six miles away, observers watched the first atomic bomb test in amazement and stunned awe. Within a few short weeks, two similar displays of pyrotechnic sorcery would provide the means to end the bloodiest war in history.

The atomic bomb is the ultimate example of the inventions of the Second World War. The enormity of its power lent both contemporary observers and future historians to label the post-war era as the Atomic Age. Remarkably, on the same day that American and British scientists were trying out their newly developed physics prowess in the desert, Allied technicians and scientists in Europe were busy arranging for the shipment of masses of scientific bounty from recently defeated Germany. This material consisted of "tens of thousands of tons,"[1] where entire cargo ships had to be set aside to transport the hundreds of thousands of boxes of captured papers, drawings, and reports. Larger technological samples such as revolutionary jet engines and crated V2 rockets were loaded onto a dedicated aircraft carrier for transport back to America. In addition, dozens of former enemy scientists, engineers and technicians were offered a chance to pursue their wartime work and as a bonus, escape from the obvious hardships that would be the hallmark of post-war life on the shattered Continent. They would add to the mass of scientific knowledge that the Allied scientists had gone into the war with and, through painstaking work, built upon to make the war end successfully in their favor.

None of the technologies of World War Two came out of a vacuum. They came from societies that both revered technology and feared its consequences. And most importantly, they came from thousands of brilliant minds seeking answers to questions few dared to ask in a time that offered unprecedented opportunities for such thought. But that time was only the culmination of advancements that, in 1939, extended back less than fifty years.

Since the turn of the century, science was taking on an importance in everyday life, politics, and the military. This was evident in the First World War by the introduction of radio, the automobile, the airplane, the armored tank, and blood transfusions. Although these technologies were still immature, the success with which they were fielded set the stage for more advancement. Radios were transformed from huge, complicated masses of wires and tubes to cabinet-sized units that fit neatly into the corner of a parlor. The automobile went from a novelty to a necessity in a few short years. Government programs to promote the use of the airplane for carrying mail made them all the more visible and commonplace. The tank had its roots in the little known development of the crawler tractor tread, and, in turn, the tank's universal success as cross-terrain vehicle ensured the future of heavy construction machinery companies such as Caterpillar. The marvelous findings that blood could be safely transfused from donor to patient set the horizon for new medical frontiers such as immunology, hematology and, eventually, organ transplants.

Societal, political, and military forces, in that order, led the demand for more progression in technology. Societal demand proved, in retrospect, to be the greatest force. Simply put, the post-World War Two population wanted modern gadgets. But therein lay an irony. As much as there was a demand for new technology, so too was there a fear of it. In the 1930s, scientists were considered on the margins of society. Their public image was hardly helped with the release of the classic *Frankenstein* movies where the evil creator, crazed by his zeal to push the limits of science, transgresses moral and social codes but gets his righteous comeuppance in the end. Such perceptions were further aggravated in reality when a little known physiologist from Harvard named Gregory Pincus announced that he had successfully produced viable rabbit embryos by fertilizing the eggs in a test tube. Pincus himself turned the heat up on the controversy when he glibly remarked to several reporters that "he was not interested in the implications of the work," implying that the process of discovery was the all-important goal. Furthermore, his attitude indicated that he never pondered the greater question; "Should we be doing this?"[2] Pincus weathered substantial public outrage and bad press only to go on to formulate the oral birth control pill in the 1950s.

Scientists of this era did not help their cause by their behavior outside of the laboratory. Most were unremarkable, no more identifiable in crowd than anyone else. But a few stood out and became the stereotype for all scientists. For example, in the early days of the Second World War, Winston Churchill told one of his aides to find all of Britain's best "scientific minds" so that they could be put to work on war projects. Some days later, upon reviewing the gathered academics—most of them unshaven, their hair universally in various stages of unkemptness and their clothes disheveled—the Prime Minister allegedly stated, "When I told you to leave no rock unturned, I didn't think you would take me so literally."[3]

Of all the countries actively pursuing new technology, Germany led the way, but not before they had gone through a period of strife. In the years between 1919 and 1933, Germany teetered on the edge of chaos. Rampant inflation drove the value of the German mark to dizzyingly low levels and unemployment was endemic. Starvation was, at the time, a real threat to the average German citizen. Most of the German technological and industrial base had been torn apart to satisfy the terms of the Versailles Treaty. And yet, German scientists managed to weather it out.

Once Hitler came to power, he saw to it that science got more financial support from the government. He did this not only through direct payment of grants, but by awarding government contracts to established companies that showed the greatest potential of generating breakthroughs. The end result was that Hitler had at his fingertips the greatest collection of industrial and scientific minds during the 1930s. This allowed Germany to begin rebuilding an industrial base that had stagnated after years of Depression. Special attention was given to the petrochemical industry with the aim of becoming totally self-sufficient in meeting the country's needs for fuels and rubber. Moreover, the military spent considerable amounts of currency on developing rocket technology. The Versailles Treaty had restricted Germany from possessing artillery but placed no limitations on rockets, since rocket technology only fifteen years earlier had been considered virtually unusable for a modern army.

But Hitler was personally impatient with technology and exhibited a short tolerance for scientists. This was due, in no small part to his limited education. Of all of the war leaders, Hitler was the only one not to have had at least some college. Furthermore, his secondary grades in mathematics and physics were barely passing, indicating that he had no inherent aptitude for science. This made him wary of new scientific advancements but paradoxically; the possibilities of technology did not escape him. It was quite common for Hitler to take an interest in pet projects such as the Volkswagen car, new tanks like the Tiger, or his beloved V-weapons and to require regular updates on their progress. His overconfidence in the outcome of the war and a misperception that his scientists would be able to work miracles at the drop of a hat eventually placed Germany well behind the Allies on the technological war front.

So this was the situation as the world approached the Second World War. Once the government got involved in science and technology, it was a short time until the military stepped in with pet projects and bulging budgets. But the approaching war was to be far different from any in the past. Germany had already made the commitment to field the newest weapons that her factories could produce. Britain, a long-standing opponent of the German empire, was soon working on countermeasures such as radar and competitive fighter plane designs. Japan was using weapons bought from several European countries to copy from and leapfrog ahead.

In the midst of this frenzy of rearmament, America was quietly recovering from the devastating economic collapse of 1929, which forced thousands of factories to close and millions to face unemployment. But the administration of Franklin Roosevelt pushed legislation through that financed a massive recovery program and put thousands back to work. Foreign observers from Italy, Japan, and Germany all agreed in their respective intelligence reports that American industry was once again becoming strong enough to make America a formidable enemy. Despite such estimates of American industrial prowess, most of the foreign leaders who were privy to the information were reluctant to accept that America would ever, as Adolph Hitler put it, "be able to manufacture anything except razor blades and refrigerators." [4]

Hitler's gross underestimation of American industrial potential was only one of the faults of the German system of scientific research. The foremost weakness lay in the Führer who preferred to maintain close control over his scientific organizations. Consider that late in 1941, it appeared that the war was over save the actual capitulation of the Russians. Overjoyed, Hitler ordered that all scientific projects estimated to last more than a year be halted immediately. This was primarily intended to save money and to set the German economy back on a peacetime footing. But the Russians did not fold and, instead, counterattacked with horrific precision and force. Within weeks, the Germans were pushed back from the brink of Moscow more than two hundred kilometers. Losses of men and equipment were heavy. Although it was a turning point in his war, Hitler refused to restart the numerous research programs, confident that the Russian offensive was the dying gasp of the Soviet army. Because of his obstinacy, the introduction of operational jet fighters, radio- and television-guided anti-shipping missiles, and advanced airborne radar systems were delayed just long enough to be ineffective against the massed might of the combined Allied forces. Had any of these been available a year earlier, there is the likelihood that the war would have lasted far longer than it did, with the outcome in doubt.

By the end of the war, German fuel supplies were virtually non-existent. Their advanced fighters such as this Me-262 had to be hidden in the forest. Hitler's interference in the development of this and other projects were as much responsible for the loss of the war as any of the bad strategic decisions he made. (U.S. Army)

Another fault of the German system was that there was no central agency coordinating research efforts. In America, Roosevelt, the wartime leader least suspicious of scientists, had specifically set up the Office of Scientific Research and Development (OSRD) under the guidance of the highly respected MIT professor Vannevar Bush. The OSRD organized the mobilization of America's scientific resources and acted as a brokerage house for the military's technological needs. During the war, the OSRD contracted out work of at least 500 million dollars for weapons and general scientific development.[5]

Germany had no OSRD. When the Allies began to take stock of the German research programs after the war, they were shocked to find an incomprehensible duplication of effort. For example, there were no less than twenty-two separate and independent development programs for proximity fuses in Germany during the war. Each was following the same basic principle and each competed for the same materials. No less wasteful was the German missile program, responsible for the V-1 and V-2s. This program, which did successfully field working weapons, was split between the Army (Wehrmacht), the Luftwaffe and the SS, also known by the name Shutzstaffel (the SS was the elite quasi-military unit under Heinrich Himmler that operated the extermination and concentration camps along with a vast industrial empire to take advantage of the slave labor.) Luckily for the Allies, there was just enough tension between the three services that the operational use of the missiles was delayed until after the Allied landings on Normandy. Had the V-2s been unleashed even twelve weeks sooner, the devastation to the landing troops might have been enough to disrupt or even cancel the invasion. And there was no countermeasure against the V-2, which was the first, if crude, ballistic missile.

One of the reasons why there were so many World War Two inventions was the appearance of counter-inventions. Consider this scenario: the British invent radar to "see" enemy bombers approaching and to vector their fighters into attack position. The enemy, reeling from loses to the fighters, switches to nighttime bombing using a precision radio beam to guide them to target. The British in turn devise a phony signal to misdirect the bombers. Germany retaliates with a new signal system that uses more than one signal, renewing their ability to precisely bomb from the dark. Britain responds with fighters mounting their own radar sets. Germany has a counter to this anticipated advance, strips of aluminum foil called chaff that clouds the radar screen, but the Germans are fearful that the British will use the chaff against German radar. Ironically, the British have had chaff for some time but do not want Germany to copy it until Allied scientists devise radar immune to chaff. In the end, Germany is awash in aluminum chaff strips raining

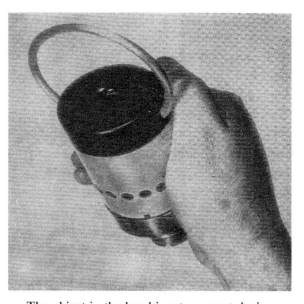

The object in the hand is a top-secret device that required thousands of factory workers, dozens of scientists and millions of dollars. The arched metal is its antenna, the body hiding an amazing assembly of circuit components and a battery that only activates when subjected to thousands of multiple G forces. The War Department called it a Variable Time (VT) fuze. In reality, it is the proximity fuze. Fired at an aircraft overhead, it only needed to get close to explode, the parts becoming lethal particles. The greatest achievement was the miniaturization of the electronics, forming a tiny radar set inside. (U.S. Army)

down from fleets of Allied bombers and the Allies win the war. The lesson from this is that the side that invented the most of the best first was probably going to win.

Choices

When one considers World War Two inventions, the Big Three—radar, the practical application of atomic power, and jet engines—are at the top of the list.[6] These are followed in significance by weapons such as the bazooka, guided missiles, the

Mid-war saw the American Army's Signal Corps field a number of air intercept radars. Conditions were supposed to determine which units used, but materials shortages and damage in shipping meant that what was available was used. This is an SCR-268, a popular unit, but heavy and difficult to land from a ship. (U.S. Army Signal Corps)

proximity fuse and landing craft, and so many others that this book, begun as a college paper grew rapidly to a manuscript of nearly a quarter million words. So I had to set some limitations. I have outlined my selection criteria here.

The first requirement for a subject's inclusion was the non-military, post-war use of an idea or invention. For example, the aforementioned Big Three were all military inventions, but they retain crucial peaceful functions.

Just as important is the date of popular usage or significant scientific achievement. When World War Two began largely depended on who you were and where you were living. For German Jews, the war began in 1933 after Hitler came to power. However, a man living in Mexico City was not overly concerned about the war until Mexico declared war on the Axis in June 1942, and there was the possibility that he might be drafted into military service. By 1933, however, all the major World War Two political players were taking their places on the world stage. Hitler came to power, the Japanese were flexing their military muscle in China and Italy was doing likewise in North Africa. In the spring of that year, newly elected President Franklin Roosevelt expressed "grave concern" about the ominous invective emanating from the new German Reich.[7] Therefore, for the purposes of this book, 1933 has been set as the first twilight year of the war.

Because of delays in returning to peacetime production, 1947 has been established as the cutoff year for selection purposes. This is not as arbitrary as it may appear. Military production needs, having dominated American industry for more than four years, needed time to retool for civilian products. Inventions from war research were being evaluated for conversion to civilian markets, which were more than ready for new consumer goods. The war-devastated economies of Japan, Germany, Italy, England, and France were all expected to be on the mend by this time with the help of the forthcoming Marshall Plan. The former colonies of France and England, having been abandoned by necessity during the war and now threatened with re-oppression by their returning masters, were beginning to agitate for independence. And the Jews, having been arguably the one group suffering the worst the Nazis could dish out, were vociferously demanding their own territory in the Middle East. And to satisfy the purists, we record here the little-known fact that President Harry Truman signed the legislation passed by Congress officially ending the Second World War on December 31, 1947.

The next criterion is the least clear-cut. The selection had either to have

Of all the items lost to the ration system during the war, tires ranked number one. Now that the war was over, tires slowly became available as rubber companies ramped up production. One challenge was to repair the damage to the rubber plantations done during combat operations or just from spite as the Japanese abandoned their hard-won territories. (USRCo)

The War Production Board produced posters such as this to reinforce the idea that any job contributes to the overall war effort. Making a measurable claim, in this case the number of bombers created per day, was thought to affect morale. (WPB/NARA)

played a role in the outcome of the war or have been a product of war-era advancements. For example, electric power distribution was included because of the policy promoted by President Roosevelt to electrify the rural areas of the United States beginning in the Thirties. Had this not occurred, America would very possibly have remained a weak, inefficient agrarian country, growing barely enough to feed her own population. Britain, so reliant on food imports, would have been faced with the poor alternatives of surrendering to the German submarine blockade or starving.

Popular usage had to have played a role in a selection as well. There were literally millions of ideas that came out of the World War Two years. Many of them had to do with specific manufacturing processes that are related only to those individuals involved, not to the general public. Even though they may still be in use at the present—occasionally even using the original machinery—their inclusion would make this volume impossibly long and ever so boring.

Popular usage also played a part in the general acceptance of a product, innovation, or idea. For example, the Diesel-electric locomotive was under development for several years before the war. Its introduction was slow due to the economic deprivations of the Depression and reluctance on the part of the railroads to abandon the reliable steam engines. World War Two transportation needs provided the driving force to demonstrate that the Diesel was far superior to steam, bringing that romantic era to an end. Just as important to popular usage is longevity. This is the true mark of a product's success. One-hundred plus years-old Coor's Beer is vastly more successful than Billy Beer.[8]

The final cut came with the question: Does the selection exist today with much of its original form and function? The last sixty years have been a wellspring of advances in the sciences and technology, and consequently, many of the "cutting edge" inventions from the war have faded into obscurity. The massively powerful radial engines that were used to propel the best of the Allied air forces for instance have become valuable museum pieces, having been replaced by jet or fuel-injected engines. Also, other innovations have subsequently been shown to be more harmful than good, precipitating their withdrawal from general usage, the insecticide DDT as an example.

Inevitably, most of the subjects in the entries have been updated or improved over the course of time. It would be nearly impossible for an

ARRIVING YEARS AHEAD OF TIME!

Here is an ad that reveals the rivals, American Locomotive and GM subsidiary, Electro-motive Division (EMD), combined their efforts to deliver the radical new Diesel-electric locomotive. This post-war ad touts the "many important new developments born of wartime research." (ALCo)

idea to avoid the evolutionary process completely. Probably the best illustration of this involves modern computers. The computers of World War Two were physically gigantic, power-consuming monsters that contained a tiny fraction of the memory found in today's machines. However, the architectural structure of computers first proposed in 1945 is functionally identical to a brand new laptop. Now that we have gotten this far together, let's take a look at just we owe to the Inventor's War.

Notes/Selected References

1   C. Lester Walker. *Secrets by the Thousands*. Aug. 1946. Harper's Magazine. Pp.329-336.
2   Asbell. Bernard. *The Pill: An Autobiography of the Drug That Changed the World*. 1995. P. 121.
3   Halle, Kay. *Irrepressible Churchill*. 1966. Pp. 175-76.
4   Weinberg, Gerhard, "Hitler's Image of the United States" *American Historical Review* #69. July 1964. Pp. 1006-1021.
5   Compton, Carl, et al. *Organizing Scientific Research for War*. 1948. Pp. 67-76.
6   Survey results: Siena College's Research Institute; Ten Most Significant Inventions of the Twentieth Century; Published in the Tucson Citizen; November 28, 1997 P. 9A.
7   Davis, Kenneth S. *F.D.R. The New Deal Years*. 1986. Pp. 123-125.
8   Billy beer was a brand of beer named after the then President Carter's earthy brother Billy. Its popularity barely lasted the term of Jimmy Carter's Presidency. Coor's is a registered trademark of Adolph Coors and Co.

1

Power to the People: Energy for the Twentieth Century

One of the most important inventions of the nineteenth century was the ability to generate, distribute, and utilize electric power. It was not only electric power that was harnessed but also a whole realm of energy sources that put the "industry" in to the industrial revolution. By tapping into the power of lightning and fossil fuels, mankind was able to work less for more, while enjoying the fruits of his labors longer.

For the first thirty years of the twentieth century, a great many Americans only dreamed of having access to their share of the new energy bounty. Although the electric lightbulb had been invented in 1879 and, more importantly, the alternating current electric distribution system in 1882, electric power was limited to very small areas of the United States. Even as late as 1935, great swaths of the country were still without electricity, primarily in the Deep South and the central northern states of Wyoming,

Haskell County KS. This typical of central American farms that would benefit from electrification. (NARA)

27

Montana and the Dakotas, where huge pockets of darkness dotted the land.

Two other energy sources, coal and oil, were still in widespread use throughout much of the country. Oil had been accidentally discovered in Pennsylvania in 1859, causing the birth of oil-fired lights and threatening the livelihoods of hundreds of whaling ship crews. In the following years, Pennsylvania crude would be central to a growing dependence on oil to fuel the American factories and machinery as she entered into her own industrial revolution.

But as fuel sources go, coal was still king. Coal has been used since the dawn of time as a means to keep warm and, later, to fire the kilns of the blacksmith's shop. Londoners experienced the modern-day problem of smog pollution in 1285 from the great quantities of coal being burned for heat and cooking. The growing iron and steel industries needed tons of coal a day to heat the furnaces and to process coke, a vital ingredient of steel. The railroads took tons more to heat the boilers of their locomotives. By the early twentieth century, chemists were beginning to break down the structure of coal and render its constituent materials into lubricants, kerosene, dyes, and later in the twentieth century, medicines and plastics.

Even though these three basic energy sources were already established to some extent, their very existence was to play a major role during the Second World War. Likewise, the war itself provided an impetus for vast improvements in the utilization of all three. Aside from using power, there are a number of more trivial but just as remarkable inventions and innovations that occurred just prior to or during World War Two that ensured their general proliferation. In addition, the war itself inspired the growth of a fourth energy source, atomic power.

Electric Power

Consider for a moment what the outcome of the Second World War would have been if America had been incapable of turning on her industrial might as one would a wall switch. The combined industrial and agricultural structure of the Axis far outweighed that of their British Commonwealth opponents. With the fall of France, Allied efforts were further stymied by the loss of several major production areas, which were converted to make German war products. When Germany overran the vast breadbasket territories of Russia, German grain silos became packed to capacity with confiscated food. In the East too, were factories and mines taken to meet German production needs. Even more plants were built all across the new Third Reich to take advantage of indigenous labor pools, usually in the form of slavery.

To protect their industry from the advancing invaders, the Russians shipped whole factories beyond the Ural Mountains, over a million rail cars of machinery and equipment in all. In spite of this massive movement, the Soviets would still need the infusion of material supplies under the Lend-Lease program. The total amount of materials the United States sent to the Soviet Union during the war culminated in the grand sum of 19.6 million tons.[1] Every one of these items required some form of energy expenditure to produce. Had the United States not been blessed with a wealth of quickly accessible power, the story might have ended in a far different way.

American Power and the Rural Electrification Administration (REA)

Between 1875 and 1905, America established herself as a technological dynamo. Americans invented the telephone, the electric lighting system and a multitude of electrical devices. Yet for all the greatness that this technological inspiration implies, the typical American citizen was living everyday life as if it were still the post-Civil War Reconstruction era. Travelling meant riding on horseback or walking. Washing clothes was an all-day affair, heating the water on a wood burning stove and using a washboard in a tub out-of-doors. Reading at night was by candle or lantern, much in the fabled manner of young Abraham Lincoln. Even many industrial concerns ran their machinery by means of an antiquated steam- or water-powered overhead jackshaft system that operated constantly.

By 1930, the first year of the Depression, 85% of urban American homes had electricity, a remarkable improvement from just twenty years before, when only 14% were electrified.[2] However, most of these homes were located in or near urban settings, where the delivery of electricity was much more cost-effective. Of the six million American farms surveyed in the 1920 census, only 452,620 had any electric power.[3] Fifteen years later, that number had barely grown to just a bit over 600,000, a vast portion obtaining

The best way to tell the farm is successful; the wires. This Haskell KS farm is one of hundreds monthly to get affordable electric power under FDR's program to electrify America. (NARA)

their electric power from small wind- or gasoline-powered generators located right on the farm.[4] This put the American farmer at a severe disadvantage when compared to his foreign counterparts. By this time, nearly all the western European countries had electrified more than 85% of their farms, making them more productive per acre than the Americans. Even the tiny island of Tasmania and the somewhat larger territory of New Zealand had provided electricity for the entirety of their agricultural community.

The biggest culprit was space. American farms were situated farther apart than their foreign counterparts. This presented a far larger task of building the generating stations, sub-stations, and power lines to the furthest reaches of the countryside. This also meant that someone would have to shoulder the expenses of construction. Privately-owned power companies would install the necessary equipment if the customer were willing to foot the bill of $2,000 or more a mile. Once the power was to the property line, there were the added expenses of wiring to the house, installing the necessary conductors throughout the home, and only then buying the appliances. For the farmer living five miles from the nearest line termination, getting electricity was an investment comparable to almost twelve years of his annual average income of $854.[5] There were options in what amounted to life-long servitude to the local electric company. Many utilities offered to extend service to distant farms if deposits of $500 to $1,000 were paid up front and the balance paid in higher utility charges, but there were few takers. The economic crisis was just too deep and prolonged for even this idea to be feasible.

Several areas in America formed electric cooperatives, groups of land-owners organized to share the costs and responsibilities of erecting and maintaining lines and equipment to their farms. However, the co-ops were at the mercy of the power companies providing the electric power. Unwilling to turn away the opportunity to turn a healthy profit, most urban electric generators charged their rural cousins up to 12 cents per kilo-watt hour, a rate twenty-five percent higher than that paid by residents in the towns.[6]

Newberry County, South Carolina. Electric co-op pole-setters at work. Every pole hole had to be dug by hand, a tough task in some of the thick clay soils of the region. (Bureau of Agricultural Economics/NARA)

In 1935, the Federal government stepped in to push forward the electrification of America's farmlands. President Franklin D. Roosevelt declared, "Electricity is no longer a luxury, it is a definite necessity."[7] Since his election in 1933, it had been the President's solemn duty to stump for one of his favored programs, the Tennessee Valley Authority (TVA). Another program, the Rural Electrification Act (REA), met with far less zeal by Roosevelt. FDR was originally against the REA, as he doubted that the expansive plan could be pulled off in any reasonable timeframe, but he changed his mind due in a large part to the perpetual nagging of his advisor Morris Cooke.[8]

Finally, with Roosevelt's grudging endorsement, the legislature acted. In 1934, Congress allocated 100 million dollars (of almost 5 billion that had been set aside for public works projects for Depression relief) so that the REA could begin electrifying rural America. The TVA, having been a favored Roosevelt program from the Hundred Days period of his administration in 1933, was further along in its development by this time.

From the beginning, both programs faced stiff opposition by the electric industry's lobbying organizations. There was much debate as to the true purpose of the electrification plans as well as charges of being Roosevelt's brand of Socialism. Critics also decried the government's involvement with what they claimed was clearly a job for private industry. Supporters countered that the industry was only focusing on the areas that could return the investment of transmission equipment in the shortest period of time

REA underwrote the job of installing this transformer by Newberry County, South Carolina co-op linesmen. Although there was a chronic shortage of critical metals, there was a constant effort to continue the electrification of rural America. (Bureau of Agricultural Economics/ NARA)

and overcharging those areas willing to pay the exorbitant prices demanded. Furthermore, the defenders of Roosevelt's plans could predict that, based on the present rate of growth, America's farmlands would not be wholly electrified for another 100 years.

Although the REA made substantial contributions to the war effort, the conflict actually slowed down electrification. This was mostly due to the restrictions placed on wood and metals—namely copper—and a shortage of labor. Nevertheless, even during the war, the REA was able to maintain the expansion of power delivery at fifty percent of what had occurred prior to 1942. In real numbers, 1,216,798 farms had electric power by 1944, more than double the 1935 figure.[9]

Hydroelectricity and "Power Pooling"

The Tennessee Valley Authority (TVA), was an ambitious plan "…for the proper use, conservation, and development of the natural resources of the Tennessee Valley drainage basin."[10] Flood control would depend on a series of dams to regulate the run-off from the 41,000 square miles that extended across seven Southern states (Georgia, North Carolina, Virginia, Kentucky, Tennessee, Alabama, and Mississippi.) Hydroelectric generating stations at each dam site would supply cheap power to an area where over 98 percent of the farms had no electricity and even towns had minimal service.[11]

During the First World War, the federal government had built a hydroelectric station on the Tennessee River to produce power for nearby

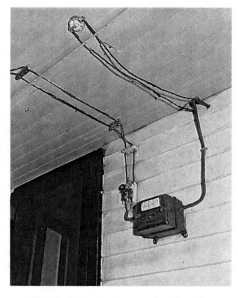

This is the typical meter hookup for a NEA-sponsored installation. The fifty-year-old home, belonging to James Robert Howard of Gilliam, McDowell County, WV, has a refrigerator, washing machine, iron, and a radio. Wiring outside of the walls was a matter of expediency and the dangers of overload and bare wires not well recognized yet. (Records of the Solid Fuels Administration for War/NARA)

nitrate production plants. Nitrates are the primary ingredients of explosives. The Alabama plant was abandoned after the war and subsequently attracted the attention of Henry Ford, who proposed re-opening the plant as a social experiment in electrifying agriculture. Congress showed little interest in getting into the power business and Ford's project languished, despite a widespread call for the facility and interest by such notables as Thomas Edison and the American Federation of Labor (AFL).

The Tennessee River was notorious for its bank-sweeping floods. Nearly every year, the river would send a torrent of muddy water into shore-side towns, washing out bridges, roads, and homes. Further upstream, the cities of Decatur, Chattanooga, Memphis, and Knoxville would find themselves sitting high and dry, the river having been drained of its runoff. When this occurred, commerce came to a virtual standstill, the bales of cotton and other farm goods left to the elements on wharves and stranded river barges.

The enormous Tennessee River project was intended to remedy such problems. In the mountainous canyons of the Appalachian range, the government built twenty-five high dams—each taller than two hundred feet—capable of generating electricity. Ten valley dams, which were wider but shallower, provided flood control and regulated the river level for commercial traffic. Even the lower dams took advantage of the river's energy, as power plants were built at each one. A totally new design for the generators had to be implemented, as the lower water level provided for less pressure—called "head" in industry parlance—to turn the heavy cast steel turbines. Thousands of unemployed men went to work on the construction gangs putting up the dams as well as building the hundreds of miles of

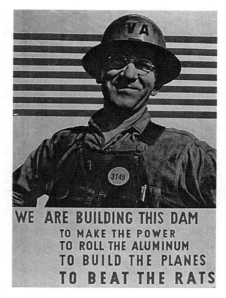

WE ARE BUILDING THIS DAM
TO MAKE THE POWER
TO ROLL THE ALUMINUM
TO BUILD THE PLANES
TO BEAT THE RATS

The TVA encompassed a great swath of the Deep South all the way into Virginia and parts of Pennsylvania. As such, the TVA was a huge impact to the American industrial component of the war effort. (TVA/WPB/NARA)

new roadways, rail lines, workshops, and other facilities that are necessary for such a mammoth project. Partly as a publicity stunt, whole towns were built to house the labor force, each town showcasing the benefits of electrically driven appliances.

Aside from the TVA, hydroelectric power was the subject of several other construction projects that were to be instrumental in the coming war. While the South was underdeveloped due to the lack of convenient energy sources, the American Southwest was largely devoid of a population demanding development. There were towns and occasional cities with their own power plants, but there were vast stretches of inhospitable desert and mountain often with densities of less than one person per square mile.

It was through this wasteland that the great westward migration beginning in the mid-nineteenth century had passed. Out on the Pacific coast of California, broad valleys of immensely fertile soil nestled between the sea and the mountains. Settlements had grown into towns, and what had once been sleepy towns had bloomed into cities. Water, not energy was originally in demand and the farmers looked to nearby rivers for relief. As the valleys became more populated, hopeful farmers attempted to settle the valleys to the east of the coastal mountains.

The Colorado River promised to be a potential source of water if it could be tapped. Draining the snowmelt of 242,000 square miles of the Rocky Mountains, the Colorado wound its way through portions of six states to the Gulf of California. In the late 1800's, an attempt to divert some of the water into the nearby Imperial Valley of California turned into a disaster when seasonal flooding washed away the canal's control gates in 1905. The valley, which had been far more bountiful than expected, was inundated by the rushing waters, forming the Salton Sea. Only through swift action by private businesses with an economic interest in saving the valley was the river turned back into its original channel.

The success of agriculture in the Imperial Valley inspired the government to consider a dam to control the Colorado. The Bureau of Reclamation, working through the Department of the Interior, was charged with designing and building such a structure. Beginning in 1920, exploration for a suitable site was undertaken. Even after a site had been chosen and plans drawn up, endless political wrangling over water rights and financing held the project in limbo. Massive unemployment during the Depression provided the final impetus to the construction of the dam, which started in 1930.

Boulder Dam—the name was officially changed to Hoover Dam in 1947—is a monolithic concrete structure over 726 feet high and 1,282 feet from canyon wall to canyon wall. Behind the dam, a lake 110 miles long captures two years of runoff. Within the flanking solid rock cliffs, tunnels provide passageway for tens of thousands of gallons of water to turn the turbines of the power plant.

The dam was dedicated on September 30, 1935. A year later, the generating station went into opera-

Hoover Dam from downstream. The power houses are on both canyon walls at the water line. Electricity from here powered the whole West coast plus any number of agricultural, mining, manufacturing and military facilities that dotted the desert. (Bureau of Reclamation)

tion with nine operating turbines cranking out 700,000 kilowatts (kW), making it the world's largest hydroelectric facility at the time. Despite material shortages, four more turbines went into the facility during the war. Eventually, seventeen generators would be installed, producing over two million watts of electricity.[12] Most of this energy was transmitted to southern California where factories were quickly displacing agriculture as the leading employer.

The transmission lines themselves represented a quantum leap in technology. Between the dam and the receiving station outside of Los Angeles, 287,000 volts traveled three hundred miles.[13] Never before had so much electrical energy been pushed over such a long distance. Attracted by a warm, sunny climate that offered virtually unlimited flying opportunities and emboldened by the influx of electrical power, aviation industrialists doubled their efforts to establish the California coast as a Mecca for their craft. Besides the growth of aviation factories, Southern California was to play host to a number of plants processing aluminum, steel, and plastics.

Power from the dam was also available for Nevada's growth. The new wealth of water and energy were instrumental in the decision to build a magnesium refining plant near the sleepy desert town of Las Vegas. Nearly one half the magnesium used during the war would come from this single facility. The availability of water and power was important in the decision to place several military bases in the southern Nevada desert.

South of Hoover Dam at Parker, Arizona, electric energy pumped water over the mountains to Southern California taps by way of the Colorado River Aqueduct, finished in 1941. Ninety miles downstream, the All-American Canal, completed a year earlier, replaced the ill-fated canals that had almost doomed the once lush Imperial Valley. The reclaimed land would prove a vital source of fresh fruit and vegetables not only for the booming civilian population boom but for the dozens of military camps being built in the American Southwest as well.

Far northwest of the Hoover Dam lay another area that would benefit greatly from the growth of Depression-era hydroelectric power. Conceived about the same time as Hoover Dam, construction on the Grand Coulee Dam lagged slightly behind for want of funding. At first, the need for regional electric power was more than covered by the newly-built Bonneville dam on the western end of the Columbia River between Oregon and Washington. Three hundred and fifty meandering miles upstream, the Grand Coulee was at first intended for flood control and as a water reservoir for the arid stretches of eastern Washington State. Almost as an afterthought two generating stations were added to the dam's design. Critics decried the hydroelectric aspect of the dam and dismissed the whole project as an enormous white elephant.

Fortunately, the advocates of the Grand Coulee dam carried the day and construction began on July 16, 1933.[14] The work was divided between moving the millions of tons of loose rock and soil overburden, building the base of the dam, and finishing it out to the final height. Secondary operations on the power plants continued until well after the end of the Second World War.

The dam itself was completed in mid-1940 with the cry of boondoggle still ringing in the air. However, the cry had lost most of its sting since Germany had invaded Poland only six months before completion, and the electricity was sorely needed for the multitude of factories already under construction in the Puget Sound region. By October 1941, the first main turbine went on-line and began delivering power.

The war silenced the dam's opponents because all available energy was now needed; yet the power plant was largely incomplete. By the time the manufacturers of the turbines and associated electrical hardware got orders to begin production—Congress was dragging its feet with funding—most of the necessary materials had been restricted. Consequently, the Grand Coulee went to war with only three of a total of nine generators running and three others nearly installed. Authorization for construction of the next three was issued, but the order for the final trio was quickly rescinded when an alternative was found at California's Shasta Dam.

When the war began, all work at Shasta was halted for the duration. In what has to be one of the war's most imaginative moments of impromptu recycling, two finished turbines from this dam were "borrowed." They had been built far in advance of the dam's completion and were sitting in storage on the west coast. The transfer presented a problem for the engineers at Grand Coulee, though. The Shasta turbines were designed to run counter-clockwise while the turbines and the immense concrete works at Grand Coulee had been built for a clockwise rotation. To make the Shasta generators fit properly, workers tunneled their way through more than eight feet of reinforced concrete and built the proper diversion appurtenances. Once installed, the Shasta generators worked quite well until they were removed and shipped back to their original home in the summer of 1945.

Energy from the Grand Coulee dam was routed to the seacoast factories of Washington and Oregon. With the six turbines and the two purloined units running at full tilt, the Grand Coulee was capable of producing 818,000 kW.[15] The lines from Grand Coulee were tied into the output of the Bonneville dam, forming an enormous circle of high-tension wires from the Canadian border to well south of Portland, Oregon. Each dam was capable of independently generating enough energy to meet either industrial or domestic demands during peak periods, but not both. However, the combined current was enough to meet demands with an added buffer of safety. This allowed for maintenance and repairs to be done on the turbines or associated electrical gear without creating shortages.

This mutual linking of generating stations provided the biggest long-term benefit of the war in the utility industry. Prior to the introduction of power from the gigantic hydroelectric generating plants of the west, electric power was limited by generating capacity. Each region had its own generators—coal-fired steam or hydroelectric—which were independent of neighboring systems. When there were unscheduled breakdowns or shortages of fuel—or dammed water—the customers of that particular system had to suffer the consequences.

This situation was largely the making of the privatized electrical generators. They jealously protected their territories, and there was no sharing of the lines. Despite public need, the companies steadfastly refused to break with tradition. The war, however, brought about rapid changes in this philosophy. The successes of the TVA working hand-in-hand with the REA would serve as a model for this change, but there was a technical challenge to overcome first.

One of the problems of an interconnected system, or network, is that the current has to be synchronized. American electrical equipment runs at sixty cycles per second (expressed as kilocycles: Kc.). Any slower and lights dim and motors slow down, creating damaging heat. Coordinating power from two differing sources to the same frequency was considered to be too big of a task, and the problem was compounded since hydroelectric dams generate at much lower frequencies—50Kc in the west and 25Kc on the TVA. The problem was like having deaf drummers miles apart try to match one another's tempo, possible but not likely.

New frequency-changing transformers were invented to synchronize frequencies. Earlier transformers, based on the mercury-arc light principle, were replaced by selenium rectifier sets. Capable of handling higher voltages with fewer failures, the selenium units were first installed at Hoover Dam in 1936. With some coercion from the government, which relaxed materials restrictions in the interests of homogeneity during the war, other power companies began purchasing their own converters and placing them online. Finally, with the new rectifiers and attitudes of cooperation in place, electrical pooling could begin.

Across the country, the "power pool," as the industry then referred to the nation-wide network, served admirably during the war. Where it was applied, there were no serious or chronic power shortages that affected war production. However, the central and northeastern states lagged behind in adopting the network and in the winter of

1944-45 widespread brownouts were the rule.

There, schools were closed and business hours severely restricted. Neon lights were banned, as were late-night happenings at bars and nightclubs. James F. Byrnes, Roosevelt's ubiquitous "assistant President" in charge of domestic wartime policies including materials consumption, attempted to take those restrictions on fuel countrywide. His order was openly ignored where there was a wealth of electric power, especially hydroelectric energy.

In the Northwest, the few shortages that did occur were of minor consequence, which was fortunate as there were several industries that were totally intolerant of any blackout at all. For example, the operators of Grand Coulee dam were to give nearby aluminum plants a three days' notice when there was to be a power outage because the molten aluminum would cool and solidify in the giant refractory chambers, necessitating the use of dynamite to break it apart.

As far as the war effort itself, the availability of power was often the deciding factor in locating a particular factory. With limited hydroelectric dams in the east, the great shipyards of Virginia, for instance, had to draw power from the distant TVA. So it was no coincidence that more than thirty percent of America's aluminum and fifty percent of her aircraft were built on the Pacific coast. Nor was it happenstance that the government later chose to locate two vital and extremely secret factories within scant miles of the great hydroelectric dams of Washington and Tennessee to manufacture the materials for the atomic bomb.[16]

Coal Mining Machinery

Even though there were a number of hydroelectric dams under construction across America when the shooting war broke out, the great majority of electric power was still produced by coal-fired steam. In addition, the steel industry, just recovering from the Depression, was rapidly restarting dozens of mills to fill orders for Lend-Lease contracts. They would need coal, in the form of coke, to feed the hungry furnaces.

The coal for those furnaces was typically loaded onto narrow-gauge railcars by hand. This hot, dirty job was the work of the miner, who was paid a pittance for every ton of coal loaded. The process was so antiquated that most mines were still using draft animals to pull the loaded hoppers from the mine.[17]

Underground Machinery

Immediately after the Market Crash of 1929, coal production took a serious downturn to a thirty year low.[18] Since the beginning of the century, the industry had been attempting to mechanize with automatic tunneling and loading machinery. Electrification was slowly coming to the mines, and the dangerous oil lamps and acetylene-fired miners' lights were being abandoned. A few mine operators had even begun to use custom-built electric locomotives. The Depression interrupted this evolutionary process temporarily until around 1935 when coal mining began to show signs of recovery. With the renewed interest in mining mechanization, mine management was after any machine that eliminated or minimized the mining cycle of drilling, blasting, loading, and advancing.

The Jeffery L400 movable loader, introduced in 1936, did just that. Having a low profile, the Jeffery machine was able to work in the tight confines of the smaller coal veins. It featured a relatively new technology, oil-based hydraulic controls and it operated on a caterpillar track rather than on rails. Three years later, the L400 was modified with a more powerful electric drive and offered as the L600. In an industry where selling a dozen of one particular model is considered to be successful, the L400 sold more than 150 in a five year period between 1936-41. Its bigger brother, the L600 was deemed vital to the war effort and the company regularly received their allocations of materials. Of the thirty to thirty-five machines built annually, every one was sold.[19]

One mine, Consolidated Coal and Coke, built their own version of a "continuous miner" with the help of an independent engineer around 1940. Throughout the war, it worked fairly well in the company's Denver mine. In 1946, the Joy Manufacturing Company, a direct competitor to the Jeffery company since the 1920s, discovered Consolidated's machine and bought the patent. At first, Joy engineers were appalled at the machine's design, as it looked frighteningly similar to several of their unsuccessful machines. Under testing, however, the continuous miner not only worked but also broke the coal into the size that brought the highest price. Over the next several years, Joy made 25 copies of the Consolidated machine with various modifications. Despite some design flaws that required rectification, by 1950, the Joy continuous miner was cutting coal faster than it could be transported away.

Mine Roof Supports

Underground mining of any material was (and still is) extremely dangerous. In the twenty-five year period ending in 1948, 30,450 coal miners were killed in work-related accidents. Of the fatalities, 16,702 came about as a direct consequence of the roof collapsing.[20] To stop this tragic roll call, two different devices were invented.

The first, roof bolts, are long metal rods driven into holes drilled into the ceiling. A wedge on the blind, or embedded, end of the bolt spread out the tip, effectively locking the bolt into the surrounding rock. Over the free end exposed to the miners, a perforated plate was placed and drawn up tight against the ceiling. The bolt—sometimes called a pin— compressed the layers of rock together, creating a nearly homogeneous overhead beam. Roof bolting also removed the motley assortment of timbers and wedges holding up the ceiling. This obviated the associated menace of accidentally ramming into a wooden column, precipitating a fatal collapse.

Roof bolt. The threaded bolt goes up the center hole and engages threads at the far (upper left) end. As the thread tightens, the sides of the bolt spread outwards, crushing against the walls of the rock hole. This puts direct pressure in the roof structure, locking the shattered pieces into one another.

In Germany, a totally different system was put into place. Two stout metal plates, one for the floor and one for the roof, were mounted horizontally between a set of vertical struts, forming a large, squared-off letter C. Special sliding joints allowed the supports to "walk" forward as the face of the mine advanced. The relatively empty space at the forward area of the support gave ample room for the miner to work and for the machinery to pass. The prototypes were tested in Germany's Hansa colliery in 1943, but the design proved unstable because the vertical "props" were too weak.[21]

Nevertheless, the idea made its way to Britain and America, where the defective props

A view of a modern long wall coal mining operation. The hydraulic roof supports are on the right with the overheads above. The continuous miner is at left with the recently cut coal piled in front. When this is done, the miner will return to the far end of the wall and the supports will advance one by one. (Taylor Mining)

were replaced with large hydraulic cylinders. Placed in long rows facing the coal seam, each roof support could secure up to 250 tons. Modern supports, still using the basic German overhead plate design, have anywhere from two to six cylinders with a capacity of over five hundred tons and are able to advance under their own hydraulic power.

Draglines and Strip Mining

Underground coal mining was not the only way to retrieve the precious fossil fuel. Open pit mining—strip mining in the modern parlance—was a method that had been used with more regularity on other minerals. The open pit was more amenable to mechanization as there were fewer restrictions on equipment size and maneuverability. However, an open pit mine was more expensive when moving the mass of overlaying rock and soil was taken into consideration. Laborers were cheaper than machinery, which was frequently poorly designed and broke down often.

In spite of these shortcomings, the machinery for removing great masses of materials was in the offing, inspired not by the mining industry but by the construction trades. The first steam powered mechanical digging machine was built in 1840 America. Although several were shipped to Europe where they saw little service, they gained wide acceptance in their land of invention. The machines continued to be improved and were instrumental in building the Panama Canal. As civil engineering projects grew in size, so did the "steam shovel." In 1934, one excavator weighing 650 tons was specifically built to dig a trench from the Colorado River to the man-made lake in the Imperial Valley eighty miles away.[22]

Machines of this magnitude were far from economical for coal mining, since the financial investment was too great and the payback too far in the future. The technology was considered immature, and powering a brute of such immense proportions required the combined output of several large Diesel engines. Consequently, in 1929, only 2.9 percent of all the coal mined in the United States was strip-mined.[23] Even that was with machines with a two yard or less capacity.

In subsequent years, the technology improved rapidly. More compact and more powerful Diesel engines evolved. Oil hydraulics became more commonplace. New manufacturing processes such as arc welding was used more often. Mining company managers began to see the benefits of large machinery—the experience of the Imperial Valley aqueduct was an eye opener—and more machines began to show up in the hills of Pennsylvania. By 1939, the percentage of coal being dug by large shovel in open pits had jumped to almost eleven percent.[24]

The war lent even more reason to the adoption of ever-larger shovels. Typically, a single miner hand-loading coal underground was able to move about twenty tons a day, give or take a few tons depending on the conditions. The Jeffery L400/L600 automatic machines were able to move that amount in a little over two hours.[25] By 1945, large open pit shovels moved that much in a minute. Mine owners saw that for every twenty tons loaded mechanically; one less miner would be needed in the mine. In the labor-tight war period, mechanization was tantamount to increasing the labor force.[26] What it meant after the war was greater profits.

Small Electric Motors

Operating machinery with electricity obviously requires motors. The first fractional horsepower D.C. electric motor was invented in 1880, followed by the alternating current (A.C.) motor perfected by Nicola Tesla in 1892. From this time on, motors slowly became more available for driving a multitude of machines.

This cast iron body motor dates from 1915. As a standard machine motor, it probably weighs close to thirty pounds. The paint chips indicate that it has gotten hot enough to blister the paint where it then captured some moisture and rusted. Just the savings in lighter copper windings in wartime motor designs garnered enough economy to make at least half the winding in a second motor. That was important to the war effort.

From the time motors were first introduced, however, they were subject to severe limitations of size and weight. The technology was just not mature enough to allow for small motors. This shortcoming forced manufacturers to over-build their products. To be fair, it was not entirely the manufacturers' fault. Some of the problem lay with the electric power that was available. The manner of controlling the phase and frequency of the current was still crude. Early motors were built with a great deal of additional mass to compensate for higher operating temperatures and operational events such as stalling.

Throughout the 1920's and 30s, the whole electric industry worked tirelessly, gradually improving their equipment. One major advancement came about with the introduction of oxygen-free high conductivity copper by the American Smelting and Refining Company (ASARCO) in the late 1930s. Copper smelted by prior methods contained too much oxygen. Under prolonged use, the oxygen combined with molecular hydrogen and caused the wire to deteriorate, eventually failing due to fracture.

The wires constituting the windings also had to be insulated from short-circuits. During the manufacturing process, the windings were dipped into a bath of varnish made from shellac, derived from the lac beetle of India. Once dried, the thick layer of shellac provided a hard, electrically isolating cover for the wires from water, dust, and other foreign objects that inadvertently got into the motors.

As the war in the East escalated, shellac became harder to obtain and the engineers resorted to a corn-based protein called zein. It was first discovered in 1821 but remained an oddity until the Depression when it was used as a decorative and protective facing for shelf paper. Zein became the focus of research in 1939 and was the primary ingredient of Zinlac, the wartime substitute for shellac. Not only was Zinlac more available than shellac; it was harder, more abrasion-resistant, and better at shedding moisture than shellac. Additionally, Zinlac was di-electrically stronger (offering superior insulation on a molecular level.) As a result, thinner concentrations could be applied to the windings, making the motor much less bulky.[27]

Another advance was the widespread adoption of plastics as insulators. Using the newly developed Bakelite for the plastic case, the Schick Company produced the first 120V A.C. motor, which was much more powerful and compact than the relatively safe battery-type D.C. voltage. First introduced in the early 1930s, the diminutive motor ran at an impres-

This is a larger, full horsepower motor that has obviously seen better days. The large opening on the end is typical of older motors. It is needed to provide enough airflow to cool the windings. Because large objects can also fall into the motor, the copper winding are made heavier and have a thicker varnish to resist damage. That makes the motor harder to cool, necessitating thicker varnish on heavier windings with larger ventilation openings, which then allow bigger heavier objects to fall into the motor. (Author's collection)

sive 7,200 R.P.M. to drive the stainless steel blades. Other manufacturers soon followed Schick's lead, producing a large variety of gadgets that ran off the newly installed electric outlets at home.

External conditions forced innovation as well. In the first example, a 1/8 hp motor to operate an air pump was required to operate in twenty feet of water. Engineers manufactured a whole new case and a system of shaft seals that revolutionized sealed motor technology. In another example, the challenge was to ameliorate the corrosive effects of salt spray inside the motor. Engineers mounted a ring inside the casing that intercepted the water and flung it off through centrifugal action into a catchment trap where it drained away.[28]

As warplanes used more radar, gun-control systems, radios and such, there developed a pressing need to improve the generating capacity of on-board electrical equipment. Shortly before Pearl Harbor, the U.S. Army Air Forces began design on long-range bombers that could transit the Pacific and attack the Japanese home islands. Part of the design included a radical new idea; alternating-current generators—alternators in present day parlance—instead of the ubiquitous D.C. generator. It was hoped that alternators would be a significant weight savings while producing far more power.

The Lima Plant of Westinghouse was given the highly classified contract to develop this alternator and its ancillary equipment. These units were to become instrumental in the operation of the B-29 bombers with all their complex electronics. Not only bombers, but other classes of aircraft could use the lighter, more compact, and more powerful alternators. In response, Lima came up with the P-1. Weighing only 42 pounds, the P-1 had thirty-five times the output of an equivalent weight D.C. generator. Lima engineers also made great strides in perfecting miniature voltage regulators and introduced such innovations such as glass fiber insulation and special brazing techniques that surpassed the strength of soldered joints.[29]

This poster for electric motors underscores the industrial nature of the Second World War.

All these improvements paid dividends when America was rearming. Small electric motors appeared everywhere, powering the complex machinery of war. Advancements in machining technology led to higher cutting speeds, which required water- or oil-based coolants. Electric motors were used to traverse turrets on American tanks and gun blisters on aircraft. A typical heavy bomber used no less than fourteen motors to pump fuel, extend the landing gear, retract the flaps, and operate instruments. As the planes became more sophisticated, even more motors were added. The new B-29, the prototype being built in mid-1942, featured 152 electric motors operating its many sophisticated systems. The electric current demand was even too much for six engine-mounted generators. Boeing was forced to in-

The B-29 was an advanced design when it was proposed in 1939. It had a pressurized fuselage, innovative electronic gun and engine controls, the most powerful engines of their weight class and totally new construction methods. Only the advent of the jet fighter made the B-29 obsolete. (U.S. Army Air Forces)

stall a special generator driven from a gasoline engine in the aft section.[30] Small motors were used on the heating and ventilation equipment in thousands of vehicles and planes, and even on electrical devices such as a massive computer built at MIT in 1945.

Motors played an important part in the Battle of the Atlantic as well. America entered the war against Germany while at a disadvantage in torpedo technology. Basically, the Germans were firing electric torpedoes that did not leave a wake while American "fish" were easily spotted by sharp-eyed lookouts. Then, in the winter of 1942, a German electric torpedo beached itself and was soon being dissected at the U.S. Navy's Torpedo Station at Newport R.I. With an original in hand, it fell to Westinghouse to copy it. General Electric was already struggling with an electric torpedo drive, but they were finding it nearly impossible to cram the contemporary and bulky motor components into a standard torpedo case and smaller motors were not powerful enough to produce the necessary speed or range. The captured German motor was to change all of that.

Although the U.S. Navy technicians jealously guarded the secret of their possessing a German torpedo (the fear of spies was ever present), they finally allowed engineers from Westinghouse an opportunity to examine the motor but nothing else. That was enough, and the engineers soon had a paper design that appeared to work. By March 1942, Westinghouse had not only won the contract for motors but had seized the entire project from their rival G.E. By war's end, Westinghouse had built 10,000+ electric torpedoes with more than 300 sinkings to their credit.[31]

Due, in part to the large influx of women into the factories, hand-held motorized tools had to be miniaturized. In 1942, the Milwaukee Tool Company introduced an electric drill weighing a mere 2.5 pounds. By incorporating numerous design changes including extensive use of plastics and innovative thin-wall aluminum castings, the new drill motor was half the weight of its predecessors.[32]

Miniature motors typical of today. Ten years ago a prototype motor was built where the entire mechanism was on a wafer of silicon no bigger than the period on this sentence.

Fluorescent Lights

Factories of pre-World War Two were, for the most part, operated eight hours a day, five days a week. They were typically loud, smoky, and gloomy. The high ceilings of the larger plants did not lend themselves to artificial lighting and most had huge banks of windows to catch any available sunlight to augment the anemic incandescent lighting. This situation had to change when the Lend-Lease contracts began to demand production levels on a twenty-four hour a day basis. Fortunately, the low-voltage fluorescent light had recently made its debut on the American scene.

The first fluorescent light made its debut in Paris in 1920, a distant cousin of the neon tube first invented in 1895 by George Claude of France. The glowing glass tube was coated on the inside surface with a naturally fluorescent element such as Willemite. A reactive gas such as neon or mercury vapor then charges the evacuated tube. Finally, a high-energy spark begins the photo-chemical reaction which is then maintained by a low voltage electrical current, creating a brilliant but diffused light.

Engineers from General Electric and Westinghouse traveled to Europe to witness the new lighting device but did not actively pursue the idea until 1934. Manufacturing the first tubes required painstaking hand processing. Willemite ore, chosen for its fluorescing properties, was crushed into a powder and then examined under an ultraviolet light. Each glowing particle was then collected with tweezers. All of this hand labor was expensive.

As interest in fluorescent lamps grew, the advancements came in rapid succession. Newer powders such as selenium or beryllium were discovered and safer mechanisms for starting the lights were developed. By 1938, General Electric had a commercially viable tube available for market. They were followed closely by Sylvania and several smaller regional manufacturers. At first, the tubes were marketed only as a means of making tinted lighting displays. Varying the composition of the gases and the phos-phorescent powders created a pallet of colors to choose from, and designers for the 1939 World's Fair adopted the fluorescent light to light the grounds in soft pastels. However, the lights were proving to be much more efficient than ever foreseen. Besides giving better overall illumination, fluorescent tubes offered substantial savings on electricity. Because of the nature of the resulting light and the physics behind the way the light was produced, a 15-watt fluorescent tube created the same amount of light as a 40 or even 60-watt incandescent bulb, this excess current being converted into waste heat in an incandescent bulb.[33]

In an English chalk mine, an electrician installs fluorescent lights for a new aircraft parts factory. Just as the Germans would do in a few months, the British went underground to deter destruction of their vital industries by heavy bombing.

Power companies tried to get the sale of fluorescent tubes restricted, or even banned. They contended that incandescent lamps gave off more useful energy—in the form of light—than they used in electricity. In their estimation, it was an unfair situation. When that nonsensical claim did not gain any sympathy, the power company spokespeople attacked the fluorescent manufacturers for falsely claiming the extent of their lamps' efficiency. This too had little effect on the sales of fluorescent lights. Fixture manufacturers added their voice in support of the tube makers. As fluorescent and incandescent fixtures were not interchangeable, they saw this as an opportunity to sell thousands of new fixtures. Seeing the writing on the wall, the power companies gave up their fight in late 1940 when all parties came to a formal agreement on the design and use of fluorescent lighting.

In December 1942, the Department of Justice attempted to break the agreement up under the anti-trust statutes. By this time, however, the ubiquitous tubes were illuminating thousands of factories and other facilities. The War Department successfully appealed the Justice Department's complaint on the grounds that any interference with the manufacture of fluorescent lighting would harm the war effort.

During the war, older plants installed fluorescent lighting to brighten work areas and to extend limited electrical supplies. As new plants were designed, fluorescent fixtures were specified wherever possible. The technology of fluorescing chemicals was "borrowed" by other industries which soon used fluorescent lighting on the dozens of gauges and instruments on combat aircraft, the ghostly green glow preserving the night vision of the aircrews. As the war progressed, new formulations for fluorescent compounds kept coming from the research laboratories. The new fixtures lasted longer and had better coloration. Improvements during and immediately after the war raised the life span of fluorescent tube lights to 7500 hours, more than three times that of a tube made in 1940 and an incredible 30 times that of a standard light bulb.[34]

Mercury Vapor Lamps

Although fluorescent lighting made huge gains in factories across America, there were a number of cases where even these new lamps showed themselves to be dim failures. What was needed was a whole new bulb of dazzling intensity. That is exactly what Westinghouse delivered. Mercury lamps had been in use for years but their light output was severely limited, and they used large amounts of power in comparison to their illuminating ability. The largest available prior to the war was an anemic 400-Watt lamp.

The concept of mercury vapor lighting was simple. Place argon gas in a sealed tube and add a drop of mercury. When the power is applied, the argon conducts current that begins to vaporize the mercury. In a gaseous state, the excited mercury molecules violently bump into one another, causing their electrons to vibrate and release radiant energy: light.

W. H. Kahler, an engineer at the Westinghouse Bloomfield Plant, set out to make bigger and better mercury vapor lamps, with his first goal a 3,000-watt light. When completed it measured four-and one-half feet long and needed special airflow cooling and high-temperature materials to handle the hellish temperatures that it produced. Special circuitry was devised to protect workmen servicing the light from being electrocuted. Such lamps were not for use just anywhere. They refused to start in cold weather, precluding their use outdoors in areas such as airports, mines and rail yards. Their light was so intense that looking directly at one from up close could blind, sometimes permanently. Their glare was far too intense to use around shops with shiny metal surfaces since the reflected light was nearly as blinding as the direct light.

Despite its many shortcomings, Kahler's light was a breakthrough. The glare problems were overcome by restricting their mounting to no less than forty feet from the floor. This restriction still meant that there were plenty of applications for mercury vapor lamps. Steel mills adopted thousands for their shipping areas, finishing rooms, and inspection rooms. In foundries and heavy welding shops, notorious for their smoky atmospheres, mercury lamp light cut through the haze with ease.

The Navy subsequently installed mercury vapor lamps in dozens of their massive blimp hangars. Originally, the designers of these huge buildings—1000 feet long, 300 feet wide and 175 feet high—called for 150 lamp clusters to provide enough illumination to see safely. Westinghouse's lamps reduced the number of light fixtures to just 42. Not only did this save on light fixtures, it spared untold amounts of copper, at this time more precious than gold, and other materials needed for the war effort. Two rows of light could be serviced from catwalks by one electrician, a great savings from the planned spider-web of lights liberally placed throughout the open wooden beam ceiling. The energy savings was just as impressive. On an average, the mercury lamps required only 133 kilowatts as compared to 225 kilowatts for the incandescent lights.

A-20 medium bomber at the Douglas Aircraft plant in Long Beach, CA. Note the bright work areas provided by the mercury vapor lamps in the ceiling. (FDRLPDC/NARA)

Later in the war, mercury vapor lamps did go into the aircraft plants with a reworked reflector system. Rather than allow the glare to be directed towards the floor, reflectors directed it against the ceiling that had been painted white. This created a diffuse glow that resisted shadows and eliminated the reflected glare from the finished aluminum skin.

Westinghouse continued to develop mercury vapor lamps throughout the war. Efficiency skyrocketed with special refining of the mercury droplet. A 1,000 watt circular tube was introduced that measured only four inches across and was the diameter of a pencil. When compared to its monstrous 3,000-watt kin, the smaller one was fifty percent more efficient. This single 1,000-watt tube equaled the light production of 125 40-watt incandescent bulbs or three 1,000-watt incandescent bulbs. Moreover, the 1,000-watt mercury tube could cool itself from natural convection, eliminating the need for special shields and thermal protection.[35]

Atomic Power

Early in the war, a 335-ton graphite ellipsoid located in an unused squash court at the University of Chicago became the focus of attention of America's preeminent physicists. Embedded within the twenty-five feet wide flattened sphere lay 92,990 pounds of radioactive uranium, the greatest source of power ever assembled until that time. America had been at war for nearly a year, and the energy within that sphere, when released, would end that war in another forty months.[36]

The development of atomic power is perhaps the greatest scientific achievement of the twentieth century. Its nativity was a drawn-out series of experiments and break-throughs by scientists from a number of countries. Every major power involved in the war had some sort of atomic research in motion well before the shooting war began. However, the task was so enormous that there was little chance that any country besides America, which had the industrial potential to bring to bear on the challenge, could turn the theory to reality.

The driving force behind the American atomic bomb project was the fear that Germany was actively pursuing its own weapon. On December 18, 1938, two German physicists, Otto Hahn and Fritz Strassmann, successfully split the atomic structure of a uranium molecule releasing not only energy but more fragments that were in turn capable of splitting other uranium atoms. The process, called fission, proved that a mass of uranium could be made to split in a series of steps, each one releasing massive amounts of energy in exponentially larger bursts.[37]

Non-German scientists, many of them having fled the European continent for Britain because they were Jewish or related to Jews, were stunned by this news. There was the immediate fear that Hitler's scientists would create a bomb that tapped into the power of uranium. Such a weapon would make the Germans all the more likely to attack their neighboring nations and, as was all too evident, would also make them a nearly unstoppable military power.

As the European war wound down, Allied scientists spread out in a desperate search to corner any Nazi technology for their respective countries. The Americans found this aluminum vessel that was supposed to be a German nuclear device. Twenty-four inches in diameter, it had layers of paraffin wax and uranium and was found in the pictured tank of water. (OWI/OSRD)

Despite calls to finance bomb research, the American government remained blissfully unaware of the true scope of the atomic threat. Several of the displaced European physicists wrote letters warning of German nuclear breakthroughs. Their entreaties were largely ignored while Germany attacked Poland and the world was thrust back into war.

Nuclear physics is both complex and simple. Each element in the natural world is made up atoms comprised of electrons, protons and neutrons. At the center of every atom lies the nucleus, which is made up of a number of protons and neutrons. The number of protons and neutrons determines the stability and characteristics of a particular atom. For example, hydrogen has only one proton whereas radioactive uranium can have 237 protons and neutrons. As the nucleus becomes larger, the physical element that the atom comprises becomes correspondingly heavier. Lightly structured hydrogen floats in air. Lead, with a nuclear population of 207, sinks to the bottom of the fishpond. More commonly, this number is referred to as the atomic weight.

As electrons orbit the nucleus, an electrical field is generated that maintains a balance, keeping the atom from either flying apart or collapsing in on itself. This balance assures that most elements remain naturally stable. However, certain elements such as radium and uranium are in a state of atomic degradation, making them unstable. Their heavy nuclei are constantly spinning off neutrons in an attempt to gain nuclear stability. Under natural conditions this process is called decay, which eventually transforms the once radio-active element into a stable, non-emitting mineral.

Decay can be accelerated when the atomic molecule is struck with a stray neutron. Just as a cue ball breaks a rack in billiards, the incoming neutron cracks the assembled mass of one atom. Depending on the momentum of the collision, one or more neutrons are released along with enormous amounts of energy. If the impact releases very few neutrons, just enough to sustain the process, slow fission is taking place. But if the impact is of sufficient force to shatter its neighbors, the resulting shower of neutrons builds exponentially. This is the fast fission of a nuclear bomb. One of the factors preventing a naturally occurring nuclear blast is that the elements, which make such an event possible, are extremely rare.

Uranium as mined has an atomic weight of 238, expressed as U_{238}. Although U_{238} is slightly radioactive, it contains a minute portion (1/140th) of the much more fissionable U_{235}. Eventually, the amount of enriched U_{235} that would be needed for a working atom bomb—Little Boy intended for Hiroshima—was about 92 pounds.[38] Little Boy—a misnomer as the ten-foot long bomb weighed 9,700 pounds—was extremely wasteful of its potential nuclear energy. The American scientists who built it purposely over-compensated the critical mass by nearly three times to ensure that the bomb would function.[39] This extravagance would later be avoided by the use of plutonium, a synthesized transuranic element.

Transuranic elements like plutonium do not occur naturally in measurable quantities. Rather, plutonium is found associated with refined uranium, but even then requires neutron bombardment to become chemically differentiated from uranium. When an atom of U_{238} captures a neutron, it becomes U_{239}. This makes the atom

Less than a mile from the Nagasaki epicenter, the ground is covered with masonry debris and ash. Fire consumed everything that could burn. For scale, note the two people above the cleared path and the bicycle on the path. (USSBS/NARA)

unstable, and it begins to spin off excess mass. The resulting "wobble" not only throws off the extra neutron but a second neutron as well. This discovery in the spring of 1940 by two American physicists, Edwin M. McMillan and Philip Abelson, took the scientific community by surprise. Previously it was surmised that there was no way new elements could be synthesized based on the basic uranium atom. Nevertheless, they had done it and to honor their success, they coined a phrase to describe the results of their new process: transuranics.

What McMillan and Abelson discovered was neptunium (NP_{239}, number 93 on the periodic chart). Once a way was found to create transuranics, others were soon to come. By August 1940, several other physics labs had produced samples of neptunium for research purposes. The goal was not to just unravel the secrets of Np_{239}, but to be the first to discover element 94, a predicted but as yet unknown element. In the intervening autumn months, it had become clear that element 94 existed. All that had to be done was to isolate it, purify it, and give it a name.

Near San Francisco, California, Berkeley University physicists Glen Seaborg and Emilio Segré simultaneously worked on element 94. They bombarded a miniscule sample (10 mg. or about half of the size of an aspirin tablet) for six hours. Tests performed on the specimen confirmed that element 94 was present. From this experiment, Seaborg calculated that 1 kilogram (2.21 pounds) of irradiated uranium would yield 0.6 micrograms (a microgram is 1/1 millionth of a gram or 1 billionth of a kilogram) of element 94.[40] However, element 94 was locked away within the structure of Np_{239}. The neptunium would have to give up some of its excess neutrons. As the unstable parent neptunium decayed, the mysterious element 94 emerged. Now that the process was understood, at least partially, the next step was to speed up the process of chemically separating the element 94 out of the neptunium. But the challenge was as great as the quantities were tiny.

When working with such small volumes, special techniques had to be established. Through 1941 and into 1942, Louis Werner and Burris Cunningham, specialists in ultramicrochemistry, were tasked by Seaborg with the isolation of element 94. They were familiar with the relatively new art of working with infinitesimally small amounts of chemicals using incredibly tiny tools. For example, the scale that they measured portions of chemicals on consisted of a single quartz fiber rigidly fixed at one end. The free end supported a minute pan of platinum, no larger than the period at the end of this sentence. The whole assembly had to be contained in a glass case to prevent the slightest breath of air from disturbing the measurement, which was determined by the deflection of the quartz strand.

Working with their Lilliputian laboratory equipment, Werner and Cunningham labored throughout the late summer of 1942. Through a tortured series of chemical recombination and precipitation, the two scientists finally wrested a minute metallic sample of element 94 from fifteen milliliters of uranium on August 20, 1942. Once exposed to air, the microscopic dot of metal, now tagged as plutonium (Pu_{239}), turned a delicate pink, belying its potential destructive energy.

By the time plutonium was actually in hand, the American government had gotten its wake-up call. One letter from Enrico Fermi had found disbelieving ears in the

U.S. Navy. It had taken the combined efforts of American and British scientists to do it. While the German war machine was crushing Polish resistance, Alexander Sachs approached President Roosevelt. Sachs, a trusted confidant and good friend to the President, had been asked call upon FDR with a letter outlining yet again the dangers of a German Bomb. In mid-August 1939, the communiqué, composed by Hungarian refugees Leo Szilard and Edward Teller in Sach's office, was signed by Nobel laureate Albert Einstein. It was felt that his signature lent credence to the seriousness of the situation. Delays brought on by the European situation prevented Roosevelt from getting the letter until October 11, 1939.

Although the President clearly saw the catastrophic potential of such a bomb in Axis hands, the government acted with agonizing moderation. Committees were formed and funding, a mere pittance of $6,000 considering the challenge and scope of the menace, was grudgingly provided. As all of Europe fell to the German might, atomic research moved forward at a snail's pace.

American scientists working in conjunction with several British physicists, some of who had escaped the continent with the Germans hard on their heels, mathematically proved that the likelihood of a bomb. Despite the growing surety of an Axis bomb, there were doubters. Nobel-laureate Niels Bohr, the Danish physicist who had determined the structure of the atom in 1913, saw what the Americans were trying to do and predicted that it would be possible only if "they [the Americans] turned the whole country into a vast nuclear bomb factory."[41]

The original grant of six thousand dollars went into a modest set of experiments that the Chicago pile would eventually be modeled upon. Atomic research got a boost in the summer of 1940 with the creation of the National Defense Research Committee (NDRC) headed by Vannevar Bush, a professor of electrical engineering and past dean of the Massachusetts Institute of Technology. Under Bush, science and engineering became a priority, especially where it could be applied to defense. In September 1940, Bush pressed for more money for the atomic program, and this was duly granted. He received a credit for $40,000, an amount that is barely impressive compared to what would eventually be spent.

The spring of 1940 saw British nuclear physics receive undivided attention from their government. The island nation had become a haven for most of Europe's scientific minds after Nazi policies emptied out the universities of "undesirable elements" such as Jews. Two of these minds, belonging to Otto Frisch and Rudolf Peierls, came directly from Germany. Both were theoreticians who followed the advances in nuclear physics emanating from their former homeland with great interest. The idea of putting together enough uranium to create a bomb was intriguing.

During the previous winter months, Frisch and Peierls had begun working out the abstract calculations to determine how much natural uranium would be needed for such a device. The resulting answer was in the tons, far too much to serve as a weapon. However, they determined, once the ore was refined and separated into its two isotopes, the critical mass (or the amount of nuclear material that spontaneously detonates upon assembly) was just a pound or two. Further calculations showed that the exponential progression of the neutrons splitting uranium atoms was fast enough to reach eighty generations before the explosion separated the mass and stopped the chain reaction. To their horror, they realized that an atomic bomb was more than feasible; it might even be possible within the next few years. To make matters worse, Germany was apparently at the forefront of atomic energy research.

With their calculations in hand, Frisch and Peierls documented their research in a two-part memorandum. They predicted that 5 kg of enriched uranium (around 11 pounds, having a mass about the size of a golf ball) would have the explosive power of several tons of dynamite. Frisch and Peierls even worked out a way to bring together the critical mass at the appropriate moment.

They proposed an explosive charge to drive together two half spheres, each less than the critical mass, into contact. Just how close they were with their speculations is chilling. Little Boy, the uranium bomb dropped on Hiroshima contained design features that were remarkably similar. Their memo also forecast expectations that such a bomb would create massive amounts of lingering radiation, enough to kill long after the blast. Furthermore, there was, in their opinion, no defense against an atomic bomb or its effects.[42] The Frisch-Peierls report made its way quickly up the chain of British government. Its implications were clear. Either the Allies would have to get the Bomb or be faced with nuclear annihilation.

In the short term, the memorandum inspired typical governmental response. They formed a committee. Operating under the code-name MAUD[1], it was convened in April 1940 to study the atomic threat and advise on appropriate actions to be taken. Its constituent members formed a who's who of British nuclear physicists.

Their goal was to determine the physics for such a bomb and to devise methods

---

1 From MAUD RAY KENT, thought to have been an anagram for 'radium taken' devised by Lise Meitner, a physicist trapped in Nazi Germany. The phrase allegedly confirmed English fears that Germany was actively gathering all of the radioactive isotopes in the conquered countries in an effort to build a bomb. Actually, the name belonged to a real person living in England who had tutored Neil Bohr's son. Nevertheless, the name was deemed suitable enough to disguise the group's activities from German spies.

of separating U_{235} from U_{238}. Since both isotopes[2] are chemically identical, it would be impossible to separate them through simple chemical manipulation. There was only one differentiating feature, that one isotope is slightly heavier than the other. This opened the door to probable separation by three techniques: gaseous diffusion, thermal separation or electromagnetic separation. A fourth process, centrifugal separation, was suggested but had to be discarded when insurmountable technical problems arose.

Each process had its benefits and pitfalls. Uranium ore could be converted into a gas, which was then pumped against a porous barrier. The larger isotopes would remain behind to be disposed of while the desirable U_{235} was collected. This gas, uranium hexafluoride (UF_6), is one of the most corrosive chemicals ever conceived. Hex, as it became known, quickly erodes all known metals with the exception of nickel. Additionally, hex reacts explosively whenever it comes into contact with oils or grease.

Despite these shortcomings, hex was chosen for two reasons. Hex is workable in gas or liquid forms at reasonable temperatures and pressures, reducing the number of engineering considerations when it comes time to convert the processes to industrial-scale production. Also, fluorine does not isotope well, a feature that becomes important when the enriched uranium has to be converted from its gaseous state.

Thermal separation worked on the curious scientific principle that heavy atoms move towards cold surfaces while lighter atoms are attracted to heat. A liquefied solution of uranium hexafluoride is pumped into a narrow passage formed by two pipes, one inserted into the other. As the inner pipe is heated and the outer one chilled, the uranium isotopes predictably separate. By placing the pipes vertically, the heavy atoms fall to the bottom and inversely; the lighter atoms rise to the top where they can be collected.

The third procedure, electromagnetic separation, relies on Newtonian principles to work. Gaseous uranium is first ionized (given an electrical charge) and then accelerated through an electric coil. The ionized particles pass through a series of slots, which direct the stream into a magnetic field. Just as a lighter automobile can corner better than a heavier vehicle, the lighter U_{235} isotopes separate away from the heavier, less-maneuverable U_{238}, which falls by the wayside. The U_{235} successfully makes the turn, striking a collector where, atom by atom, where they form flakes of metal.

All three separation methods were taken under consideration by the MAUD Committee. They favored gaseous diffusion and work actually began on a limited scale under the *nom de guerre* of the Tube Alloys project. The work of the MAUD Committee, particularly in the summer and fall of 1941, was regularly shared with their American

2 Atoms with the same number of protons but different number of neutrons is called an isotope.

counterparts. This influx of information lent an air of immediacy to the American effort. Within six months of entering the war, America had not only caught up with the progress that had occurred under the Tube Alloys project, but had surpassed it.

Even before the theoretical physics had been proven out through experimentation, the American government began wholesale sponsorship of manufacturing an atomic bomb. No longer would paltry credits be stingingly handed out like pennies to street urchins. In the summer of 1942, the National Defense Research Committee (NDRC) approved contracts for $400,000.[43] This was just the next step in the eventual expenditure of more than $2 billion dollars that were gambled to make the bomb work. 1942 also saw the simultaneous and rapid development of nuclear research and an unparalleled industrial construction program.

That same year, Colonel Leslie R. Groves finished his assignment of directing the construction of the Pentagon in Washington, D.C., and was hoping for a combat assignment. Instead, he was given the high-priority, super-secret job of organizing the vast atomic bomb project. His authority extended to the highest levels and superseded any other priority for materials, personnel, or money. As a part of his taking the post, he received an immediate promotion to Brigadier General. For the sake of security, General Groves' office was ostensibly established in New York City under the title of the Manhattan Engineering District. The name, particularly for insiders, became shortened to the Manhattan Project.

Suddenly, support for the bomb project moved relentlessly forward under the direction of General Groves. One of his first acts was to approve the purchase of 1,250 tons of raw uranium ore that had found its way into the United States from the Belgian Congo. That deal alone committed $4 million dollars of War Department funds to a device that no one was sure would work. The very next day, September 19, 1942, he signed the requisition order condemning 52,000 acres of land in Tennessee bordering on the Clinch River near a rural site known to the locals as Oak Ridge.

Enriched uranium production at Oak Ridge was not going to create enough to manufacture more than one bomb. It was decided that the far more powerful plutonium might be used instead of uranium. Enriched uranium was to be run through a nuclear reactor, thereby transmuting it into plutonium. The ultramicrochemistry work of Werner and Cunningham had to be magnified several million-fold to industrial-scale production.

The great danger in working with plutonium is that much less is required to achieve critical mass. No one had ever entered this realm of nuclear physics and there were grave concerns of an accidental explosion. Besides the obvious damage such a blast would cause, an accident would spread plutonium for miles. Although the isotope is only mildly radioactive, it is highly toxic to humans. After considering sites in Nevada, Tennessee, and Washington, the latter proved to meet all of the requirements including adequate electric power and a nearly limitless supply of water to cool the reactor piles. In late January 1943, General Groves purchased more than 500,000 acres of Washington farm and scrubland straddling the Columbia River for about $5.1 million.[44]

One more important appropriation for the Manhattan Engineer District took place in the mountains of New Mexico. It had been decided in September 1942 that the atomic bomb scientists would need a separate laboratory facility to finish their theoretical work and to assemble all the component parts for the actual device. Secrecy was paramount, yet it was obvious that there were going to be countless experiments requiring large tracts of open space. J. Robert Oppenheimer, the brilliant physicist from the California Institute of Technology and chosen leader of the laboratory, pressed for a desert location. One of Groves' deputies, Major John H. Dudley, suggested Oak City, Utah, but the site was largely made up of valuable farmland. The second choice centered on a canyon forty miles from Santa Fe, New Mexico.

Oppenheimer and Dudley argued over the choice. Dudley complained that the canyon was too confining and did not allow for growth. Instead, Oppenheimer took a liking to a mesa not far away whose sole resident was the Los Alamos Ranch boy's school. At Oppenheimer's insistence, General Groves begrudgingly acquiesced to the location, paying $440,000 for the ranch property, buildings, and a huge supply of riding tack.

So it became standard procedure for one of Groves' representatives to breeze through the door, hand over a signed document and a factory or plot of land was suddenly diverted to a mysterious purpose. Despite this heavy-handed practice, it also meant that boom times were coming. The government spared no expense when it came to building a bomb-related factory or associated contracts. In 1942, the number of local residences at Oak Ridge was expected to be approximately 13,000. By 1944, 42,000 lived there and, by the next year, the population swelled to 75,000. The Hanford, Washington site, where the plutonium would be created and separated from the parent uranium, would employ 45,000, while Los Alamos held a mere 7,000 residents.[45]

Back at the Tennessee enrichment site, Groves was faced with a dilemma. Research still did not indicate which method of separation would work best, if at all. Unwilling to waste time pursuing the traditional sequence of research followed by industrialization, Groves ordered the construction to proceed for every method proposed. Should time, he reasoned, prove one process a failure, then the infrastructure to proceed with the other processes would be readily available.

This redundancy was typical of the Manhattan project. For example, uncertainties about power requirements at the Oak Ridge plant led to the construction of no less than five separate electrical systems, one for each voltage and load conceivable. Similarly, the reactors at Hanford were built with a huge excess of capacity. This proved fortunate, for when plutonium production began, the reactors inexplicably refused to stay operating. The nuclear reaction was creating an unexpected isotope that temporarily interrupted the process. However, the problem was overcome by adding 25 percent more uranium slugs to the reactor's expansive channels. Had the extra capacity not been available, the Hanford reactors would have been a $300 million monument to shortsightedness.

The scale of the Manhattan Project's production sites was befitting the immensity of the threat should the Axis obtain the bomb first. For secrecy's sake, each facility was assigned a specific code name. Oak Ridge (Site X) was home to the gaseous barrier separation, thermal separating plants and the electromagnetic "racetracks" as well as the main administrative offices of the Manhattan Engineer District.

Building K-25 housed the gaseous separation machinery. Four stories tall, the half-mile long, U-shaped structure encompassed 42.6 acres under one roof. The gaseous barriers consisted of a series of pumps and pressure tanks through which the UF_6 flowed against a porous membrane made out of sheet metal. Each separation stage gleaned out such a miniscule amount of the desirable U_{235} that the uranium had to be repeatedly run through thousands of stages until the desired level of enrichment had been reached.

Down the valley from K-25 was the Y-12 electromagnetic separation plant. Costing $427 million to build, the complex consisted of 268 buildings, constructed by a workforce of 24,000 people. Y-12 was dominated by two monstrous structures, the Alpha and Beta buildings. The Alpha plant held five, and later, ten particle accelerators adapted from cyclotron designs that had been used in physics laboratories for years. Each accelerator, called a racetrack for its oval-shape, was made up of 96 colossal, twelve-foot wide magnetic coils. Inside the Beta building were modified particle accelerators of an improved, but half-sized design. Combined, the two two-story buildings covered the equivalent of more than twenty football fields.[46]

Liquid thermal diffusion had begun as an effort to produce enriched uranium for an experimental U.S. Navy propulsion system, not for weapons-grade uranium. Once the process had proven itself, President Roosevelt specifically ordered Vannevar Bush to exclude the Navy from the bomb project. Despite the official decree, the Navy sponsored construction of a 100-tube test plant at the Philadelphia Navy Yard's Boiler and Turbine Laboratory, in November 1943, with production scheduled to begin the following summer.

Roosevelt's dictum effectively moved the thermal program into the Manhattan Project's realm, but General Groves and the scientists of the Manhattan project at first considered liquid thermal diffusion a lost cause. To operate efficiently, the process required far greater quantities of steam than were possible at Oak Ridge. When problems arose with the K-25 process, however, the atomic bomb scientists reconsidered their view of thermal diffusion. Although the thermal process did not enrich the UF_6, it more than made up this shortcoming by producing massive quantities of low-level product, which cut the amount of time the subsequent refining processes would require. Thermal diffusion was quickly adopted. Spare Oak Ridge power capacity at was eventually found and diverted to make steam, and by September 1944, the first tube racks were in place inside a 500-foot long sheet metal barn (S-50) just around the corner from K-25.

The Hanford complex was equally immense. Three atomic reactors, placed six miles apart on the Columbia River, irradiated uranium slugs encased in aluminum tubes. From the reactors, the uranium was transported to one of two chemical separation plants. Eight stories tall, 800 feet long by forty wide, the separation plants were individually dubbed "Queen Mary," due to their size and resemblance to the luxury liner. Inside, the machinery to separate the plutonium was mounted in individual cells with walls up to seven feet thick to shield the operators from intense radiation of the slugs. Once production began, workers were unable to enter the cells. All maintenance duties were performed by remote control using closed circuit television monitors. As the plutonium became more concentrated, each successive stage processed smaller quantities to avoid assembling a critical mass, which could lead to a disastrous detonation.

Although the Manhattan project was receiving the highest priorities for rationed materials, shortages still presented difficulties. As construction progressed at Y-12, it became painfully obvious that nearly all the copper in the United States would be consumed by the manufacture of the coils. Rather than divert critical copper from war production, Lt. Colonel Kenneth D. Nichols, deputy director of the Manhattan Engineer District made a unique request to the United States Treasury for a preliminary loan of five to ten thousand tons of silver. Although the Treasury was willing to release the metal, the request was met with some pause since the Treasury dealt in terms of Troy ounces. Over time, 13,540 tons—395 million ounces valued at $300 million—were "borrowed."[47]

Working with the corrosive uranium hexafluoride meant that any surface it came into contact with had to be treated with impervious nickel. Early estimates predicted that the available stocks of nickel were far short of war requirements, and the Manhattan project's needs would further exaggerate the shortage. Further, nickel plating the insides of pipes had never been done before. The challenge was even greater since even one microscopic pinhole would allow corrosion to set in. One leak would contaminate the entire facility, rendering it permanently unusable. The answer eventually was to pump the plating solution through the pipes, saving nearly 95% of the nickel. This last example is illustrative of the elegant problem-solving skills involved in making the atomic bomb a reality.

With all the work going on, it was inevitable that there would be problems. The coils for the electromagnetic separation process became thoroughly contaminated with dirt and rusty particles, leading to short-circuits, and the entire plant was shut down for months of repairs. Other problems arose when the tanks surrounding the silver windings leaked coolant oil incessantly. When the big magnets were energized, neighboring components weighing up to fourteen tons were literally displaced as much as three inches by the powerful magnetic fields. At K-25, the porous membranes simply refused to stand up under the brutal onslaught of UF_6. One membrane design was found to be of an inferior material, necessitating the complete reconditioning of the factory built for the manufacture of the membranes. Pipes and fittings of the thermal diffusion plant leaked like sieves, as did those of the gaseous diffusion plant. Vacuum leaks were rampant as well. One supervisor reported that he searched for the best part of a month to find just one leak. At Hanford, canning the uranium slugs had become almost insurmountable. Unless the slugs were absolutely sealed, water and air would quickly oxidize the uranium, creating corrosion. Only after two years of trial and failure was a satisfactory submerged tinning process developed.

1944 was the climax year for major problems. Technical obstacles were met and slowly overcome. By January 1945, the scientists at Los Alamos were finally getting fissible materials so that they could begin to apply hard data to their theoretical work. As more engineers and scientists arrived at the New Mexico site, a battle of major proportions was brewing. General Groves had insisted on total compartmentalization for security purposes. The scientists chafed at the idea, claiming that such isolation would severely hinder progress and take away the vital tool of freely shared ideas. To his benefit, Groves yielded the point, although it continually tormented him that security would be breached. As it turned out, his fears were well founded. A member of the British contingent, Klaus Fuchs, one of the German refugee scientist and Soviet sympathizer was feeding the latest Los Alamos breakthroughs to a local contact later determined to be a Russian agent.

People-problems were also a constant source of aggravation for officials of the Manhattan Engineer District. When the magnetic separation lines were shutdown for rebuilding, thousands of trained personnel were idled. Not willing to lose their staff, administrators treated employees to movies, training classes, and other diversions such as chess and checkers. Out at Hanford, meat rationing was suspended as a lure for construction hands. The men who were available and willing to tolerate the dry, dusty environ were often less than exemplary citizens. One employment flier for Hanford suggested that the most important possession to bring was a padlock. The saloons in the Washington construction towns were built with windows conveniently hinged for easy tear-gas insertion.

The scientific achievements of the Manhattan project were finally to end the war. Moreover, the technologies required to control and manipulate the atom moved forward at a highly acceler-ated pace. Besides the obvious advancements in nuclear energy, the Manhattan project also created progress in electronics, materials, chemistry, fluid dynamics, computers, and medicine.

The other iconic photo of World War Two. (The first is of the Iwo Jima flag raising.) This is the atomic cloud over Hiroshima as the B-29 Enola Gay circles at 35,000 feet. Over a hundred thousand died from the immediate effects or injuries sustained in the blast and ensuing radiation pulse. (U.S. Army Air Forces/OWI/NARA)

The Alaskan Oil Fields

Throughout the Second World War, teams of geologists were dispatched to various locations about the country in a search for oil reserves. The fields of Texas, Pennsyl-vania, and California were capable of supplying the peacetime needs of the country but the mechanized war was going to draw heavily upon the proven supply.

In the summer of 1944, three regions of Alaska received special attention from petroleum geologists. The first, the Gulf of Alaska, was known to contain oil and was the site of the only operating well in the territory until its associated refinery burned down in 1933. Another suspected region of oil-bearing strata lay far to the west on the Alaskan Peninsula. Both these potential fields faced southern waters and were easily accessible for much of the year.

The third region, the northern coastline of Alaska around Point Barrow, was well within the Arctic Circle and the sea approaches were iced-in for months on end. The 70,000 square miles of wind-scoured tundra were protected from southern entry by the massive Brooks Range. These mountains stretch across the northern fifth of Alaska and rise up to 16,000 feet. Frigid temperatures, down to -71°F, and the rugged mountains protect the crescent of land from collecting precipitation, which amounts to no more than that received in Yuma, Arizona, or Las Vegas, Nevada.

The U.S. Navy established their Naval Petroleum Reserve No. 4 here in 1941. The region contained natural oil seepages, and early explorations confirmed the existence of rock formations compatible with oil. Despite the indications of oil and their claim on the area, the Navy was still unsure of how much oil was there or if it was recoverable. War priorities limited new explorations until the summer of 1944 when teams moved in to chart the geology and collect surface rock samples. The geologists brought along newly developed seismic sensor equipment and the military provided an amphibious airplane mounting a brand-new magnetic anomaly detector (MAD). The MAD unit could sense the presence of large concentrations of iron whether the submerged hull of a submarine or a subterranean ore body (see Large-area Metal Detectors in Chapter 3.) Using the MAD-equipped airplane, more than 13,000 square miles of desolate Alaskan terrain was surveyed in five mile wide swaths during the summer of 1944.[48]

One year later, the Navy stepped up their survey work. Contractors were retained to provide services such as air transport and engineering consultations. The U.S. Geological Survey was paid by the military for the transportation and operation of a complete portable drilling rig into the region where it was used to drill a test hole 2,000 feet deep. Another bore, penetrating 6,005 feet, came up dry but the sand samples brought up unmistakable traces of crude oil.

Exploration on the Alaskan North Shore continued on a seasonal basis for years after the war. Gas was struck in 1946, giving the men at the drilling camp a steady supply of fuel. That same summer, a shallow well near Simpson Point on the Arctic Ocean began producing 25-30 barrels a day. A larger drill rig was brought in 1948, capable of reaching 11,000 feet. Ironically, even with all the exploration, it took another twenty years before the big strike was made in 1968, prompting an unprecedented Alaskan building boom and the highly controversial Alaskan pipeline.[49]

Sea-borne Oil Drilling Platforms

Off the southeastern coast of Britain, there still stand a series of forts, seeming to rise out of the waters like strange sea-creatures marching out of the depths. Despite their awkward appearance, these gangly platforms were a vital link to the defense of the British Isles during World War Two.

Individual towers were grouped together to create Maunsell forts, named after their inventor, Guy A. Maunsell, who had been involved in a similar project during the First World War. The first tower was not completed before the end of that war, however, due to technical difficulties, including an ac-

Summer in cold country was no picnic. American G.I.s huddle for warmth out of the wind on a 1945 summer day on the North Slope of Alaska's Brookes Range. The U.S. Navy had investigated reports of spontaneous oil seepage from 1939 on by sending in small teams of prospectors and geologists. It was the last year of the war that serious drilling by military personnel took place. Twenty years will pass before the big strike is made near Prudhoe Bay (U.S. Navy)

cidental capsizing as the tower was towed from its construction port.

When the offshore tower idea was revived during the Second World War, the platforms were made of relatively inexpensive and plentiful concrete, reinforced with steel. The bottom halves of the fort's two vertical columns, measuring nearly 90 feet in length, were formed into hollow pontoons that could be flooded once the structure had been towed into place. Maunsell forts were designed to be sunk into water up to 80 feet deep, which meant that they could be placed well out into the open channel, in this case as far as eleven miles from shore.

The forts had several decks, five of them inside the pontoons, well above the flooded portion, to support the 36 crewmen who serviced the antiaircraft guns, searchlights, and radar equipment. Tanks of fresh drinking water were placed within the columns, as were the magazines for the shells, and auxiliary machinery such as pumps and the electric generators.[50]

Even before the war was over, petroleum engineers saw the potential of Maunsell platforms to open offshore drilling. Drilling offshore dates back to 1896, when oil had been found just a few hundred yards off the coast of California. To tap these reserves, wooden piers were built to reach over the water. Wood continued to be the material of choice for drilling piers, but wood restricted the size, capacity, and life span of the well. Wood also limited the depth of water that could be spanned, the deepest being a mere twenty feet. Just before America's entry into the Second World War, several wells were drilled into the bed of a fresh water lake in Louisiana. In this case, deeper water over the reserves was tapped by angle-drilling the well. But it was clear that angle drilling from wooden piers was only a temporary solution as near-off-shore reserves were depleted. The technology learned from the Maunsell

Off the southeast coast of England, the Maunsell forts rose out of the shallows of Channel. Their purpose was to act as a forward warning radar base and anti-aircraft battery. After the war, American engineers looked at the construction and placing methods of the forts to adapt them to off-shore oil platforms. (IWM)

forts came to the rescue. Even before the war with Japan had concluded, plans were underway to adopt Maunsell's sinkable pontoons.

The first offshore oil platforms, erected of the coast of Louisiana, were constructed totally of steel tubing and were built on the intended site. Building underwater towers was still in the experimental phase and the depth of the water was no deeper than that of the wooden platforms. With the success of these first platforms, however, deeper waters were gradually overcome. By the 1950s, 100 feet was considered to be the maximum attainable depth. Every decade that passed represented a doubling of the depth that the oil platforms were capable of being set. By 1978, Shell Oil Company had sunk their *Cognac* platform in 1,025 feet of water in the Gulf of Mexico.

When platforms began to reach these incredible depths, on-site construction was no longer an option. Like Maunsell's forts, structures of these proportions required the services of a shipyard. Borrowing on ideas first worked out by the British builders of the tower technology, larger oil and gas complexes are now built on shore and towed into place, although the modern versions avoid the use of concrete.[51]

Notes/Selected References

1   Rigge, Simon. *The War in the Outposts*. 1980. P. 87.
2   Nye, David. E. *Electrifying America*. 1991. Pp. 260-261.
3   Brown, D. Clayton. *Electricity for Rural America*. 1980. P. xv.
4   Nye, David. E. P. 299
5   The average income for a farmer in 1935 was a mere $854 a year. 5 X $2,000 = $10,000 +$100 for wiring the home itself equals $10,100/ 854= 11.827 years to pay of the debt, and that left no cash available for any other expenses.
6   Brown, D. Clayton. Pp. 10-11.
7   Nye, David. E. P. 304.
8   Brown, D. Clayton. Pp.34-35.
9   ibid. Pp. 96-97.
10 Davis, Kenneth S. *F.D.R. The New Deal Years 1933-1937*.1986. Pp.90-92.
11 ibid. Pp. 90-92.
12 Stevens, Joseph E. *Hoover Dam*. 1988. Pp. 27-28.
13 Kurtz, Edwin B. The Lineman's and Cableman's Handbook 4th Edition. 1964. Pp. 8-2 - 8-3.
14 Pitzer, Paul. *Grand Coulee*. 1994. P. 83.
15 ibid. P. 252.
16 ibid. Pp. 246-252.
17 Dix, Keith. *What's a Coal Miner to Do?* 1988. Pp. 79, 81.
18. ibid. P. 126.
19 ibid. Pp. 58-59.
20 ibid. P. 101.
21 Stack, Barbara. *Handbook of Mining and Tunneling Machinery*. 1982. P. 460.
22 Stevens, Joseph E. 1988. P. 258.
23 Barger, Harold, and Sam H. Schurr. *The Mining Industries, 1899-1939*. 1972. P. 187.
24 ibid. P. 187.
25 Dix. Keith. P. 59.
26 U.S. Bureau of Mines Informational Circular #7417: *Annual Report of Research and Technologic Work on Coal*. 1946.
27 Simonds, Herbert R., et al. *The New Plastics*. 1945. Pp. 90-97.
28 Woodbury, David O. *Battlefronts of Industry: Westinghouse in World War II*. 1948. Pp.124-126.
29 ibid. Pp. 84-91.
30 Collison, Thomas. *The Superfortress Is Born*. 1945. P. 91.
31 Woodbury, David O. Pp. 111-113.

32 Williams, Trevor I. *A History of Technology. Vol. VI parts 1&2*. 1978. P. 1089.

33 Bijker, Weibe E. *Of Bicycles, Bakelite and Bulbs*. 1995. Pp. 218-225.

34 Stokely, James. *Science Remakes Our World*. 1946. Pp. 211-221.

35 Woodbury, David O. Pp. 222-225.

36 Rhodes, Richard. *The Making of the Atomic Bomb*. 1988. Pp. 434-436.

37 ibid. Pp. 250-254.

38 ibid. P. 601.

39 ibid. P. 701.

40 ibid. Pp. 353.

41 "You see, I told you it couldn't be done without turning the whole country into a factory. You have done just that." Niels Bohr to Edward Teller. Teller, Edward, The Legacy of Hiroshima. 1962. P. 211.

42 Rhodes, Richard. Pp.321-324.

43 Jones, Vincent. *Manhattan: The Army and the Atomic Bomb*. 1985. P. 30.

44 Rhodes, Richard. Pp. 496-497.

45 Fermi, Rachel and Esther Samra. *Picturing the Bomb*. 1995. Pp. 32-33.

46 Rhodes, Richard. P. 490.

47 ibid. P. 490.

48 Weeks, L.G. Highlights on 1947 Developments in Foreign Petroleum Fields. *Bulletin of the American Association of Petroleum Geologists*. Vol. 32, No.6. June 1948. Pp. 1095-1097.

49 Reed, John C. Petroleum Possibilities in Alaska. *Bulletin of the American Association of Petroleum Geologists*. Vol. 30, No. 9, September 1946. Pp. 1433-1443.

50 McCaul, Ed. The Ingenious Maunsell Forts Defended the British Coastline Against Marauding German Aircraft and E-boats. *World War II magazine*. March 1996. Pp. 52-62.

51 McClelland, Bramlette, and Michael D. Reifel. *Planning and Design of Fixed OffshorePlatforms*. 1986. Pp. 4-6.

2

A Flight of Fancy: Airplanes, Helicopters and More

World War Two offered a number of exciting aircraft that far surpassed the aircraft of previous years in speed, maneuverability, and raw power. The craft from this period became a technological bridge between the fragile wood and cloth biplane of the First World War and the metal airplanes of the jet age. Despite the advantages of metal, many World War Two aircraft continued to be built with wood. Shortages of aluminum, magnesium, and specialty steels forced designers and manufacturers to rely on wood for trainers and even for combat aircraft.

To future airplane enthusiasts, the combination of old and new made for unique and strange airplanes. Probably the more extreme cases of this happened late in the war, when Ger-

American Navy frontline fighter made by Boeing Aircraft in the 1920's and on into the mid-30's. Aging designs such as this were soon to be replaced with single-winged aircraft that would introduce advanced features such as retractable landing gear, reliable supercharging, high-octane radial engines and pressurized cockpits. (U.S. Navy/NARA)

many combined two radically different technologies together in their Heinkel He-162 Salamander. Intended as a last-ditch effort to stop the Allied bombing, this single-seat fighter featured a wooden airframe with wood and cloth-covered wings, and sporting a jet engine! World War Two was the point in history when wood and metal aviation construction techniques finally diverged forever, but it also marked the beginning of widespread airline travel, particularly intercontinental travel.

Just prior to the war the airlines had built a fleet of transoceanic transports, effectively turning the world's oceans into extremely large lakes. However, having aircraft capable of flying the distance was not enough. The airlines also perfected the techniques and equipment to navigate long stretches of featureless water, often in inclement weather. When the war came to America, the military, faced with a two-ocean war, turned to these same airlines to supply the personnel, planes, and expertise that made global airlift a reality.

The Pressurized Cabin

On an early August morning in 1945, a single B-29 bomber released a single bomb from approximately 33,000 feet. Fifty-one seconds later, a flash of light marked the first time that an atomic weapon was used in combat. Two shock waves, one directly from the explosion and another reflected from the ground, battered the American plane, which had made a diving turn to gain the most distance from the blast. Had the bomber been any lower, its crew probably would not have survived. The B-29 was capable of flying at such a great altitude because the cabin was pressurized against the rarified, frigid air found at great altitude. The remarkable invention of the "shirt sleeve cockpit" was available for only a very short time before the war, and it necessarily followed the introduction of powerful new engines capable of attaining such high altitudes.

The engines that powered the new airliners of the 1930s were of reciprocal piston design. Effective and proven safe, they were capable of flying altitudes of fifteen thousand feet or more, if provided with a turbocharger (see more about turbochargers later in this chapter.) The combination of the turbo and brand new engines increased overall performance, allowing the pilot to gain altitude quickly and remain there at cruise for the duration of the flight. Even at higher cruising speeds, fuel consumption was reduced, saving the airlines money. At these higher altitudes, aircraft above the winds created by ground effects, providing a less turbulent ride for the passengers.

Extreme buffeting, especially over mountainous terrain, would toss an airplane about like a pea in a whistle. The ensuing stresses on the airframe caused metal fatigue and cracks leading to catastrophic failures. Because there was little understanding of metal fatigue, many an airplane that had taken hard turbulence stress crashed. Aircraft designers and mechanics recognized the direct relationship between sudden wind loading and spontaneous wing failures. Planes thus exposed were occasionally taken out of service for maintenance checks, especially at the bigger airline companies. Again, this cost the airlines money, so flying at higher altitudes to avoid adverse wind loading also reduced maintenance costs. Going higher definitely had a payback.

At high altitudes, however, passengers could become unconscious from low oxygen levels or freeze from the cold. With these conditions in mind, Boeing engineers set about to design an aircraft that could be sealed to contain an atmosphere. The task was substantial since a new way of constructing the airframe had to be developed as well as methods to seal the windows and doors. Without reinforcing the frame, decompression in flight at altitude could be devastating. Should the pressurized fuselage be punctured, the rapid changes in pressure would rip the plane apart, much like blowing up a balloon and popping it with a pin.[1]

Boeing designers went to work building an airplane that could fly higher without knocking the occupants senseless. They produced the Boeing 307 Stratoliner, the first totally pressurized aircraft, in 1940. The war interrupted the plane's mass-production plans. Boeing engineers put their experience to work building the pressurized B-29 bomber. For decades after the war and up to the present the same design principles were to go into the entire fleet of the world's airlines, one of the most popular being that of the Boeing 700 series passenger jets, allowing the contemporary traveler to cruise at 30,000+ feet in total comfort.[2]

Across the Oceans

Although Lindbergh made history by crossing the Atlantic solo and non-stop, regular passenger travel across the oceans remained at sea level, aboard passenger ships. There had been service by air to and from Europe, but it exploded in a massive fireball in May 1937, in New Jersey. The destruction of the airship Hindenburg created a travel vacuum that the airlines longed to fill. However, building a land-based aircraft capable of flying non-stop for 3,000 miles was not quite possible given 1930s aviation technology. Until then, flying boats were considered the only way to provide passenger air service across the oceans.

There was nothing novel in the idea, as nearly every nation in Europe and the

United States had been probing for the best transatlantic routes. The primary goal was to avoid the sudden and violent storms so common on the Atlantic. In order to make such long flights, the airlines had to concentrate on improving equipment, particularly radios, direction finders, and general navigation techniques. Then there were issues of traffic control and safety such as emergency equipment that would be necessary in case of a ditching at sea. Even the concept of emergency exits, unique in its time, was a point that would have to be addressed.

Germany entered the Trans-Atlantic competition early on with the Do-X. The largest plane in the world in 1928, it had a capacity of 60. Powered by 12 engines, it regularly commuted to America, using a flying boat relay system that relied on ships stationed at intervals in the mid-Atlantic. Beginning in 1931, the ships provided re-fueling and repair services, as well as safe haven in bad weather. These floating way stations served routes to South and Central America until the beginning of the shooting war in 1939. During the war, Germany introduced the advanced Blohm and Voss BV 222 Viking, designed to replace its smaller sister ships. Planned for introduction in 1940, the BV 222 was the world's largest production flying boat, with a maximum take-off weight of 108,000 pounds. Its first mission was to fly supplies into occupied Norway in June 1941. The BV 222 flying boats, thirteen in all, flew throughout the war, acting as cargo transports and maritime reconnaissance aircraft.[3]

On the other side of the Atlantic, the development of the Sikorsky S-42 flying boat in the early 1930s brought the continents closer together. Simultaneous experimental flights in 1937, one heading east and the other west, between Newfoundland and Foynes Island, Ireland, concluded successfully after twelve hours. Takeoff weight limitations and civil aviation rules concerning wing loads, as well as British intransigence about landing rights, doomed an immediate start of service, but another American plane was about to change that.

Based on the success of the S-42 and Do-X, the Boeing Company began building the 314, more commonly called the "Clipper." This ocean-straddling monster weighed an impressive eighty-two thousand pounds at take-off and had a range of well over three thousand miles.[4] To guide the ship, pilots relied on several new innovations, including a Sperry gyrocompass and artificial horizon instrument packages, allowing flight through fog and darkness. Regular passenger service commenced in 1939 and continued with limitations throughout the war.

The Pacific Ocean offered a similar challenge to commercial flights. After numerous attempts to provide passenger service, the Boeing 314 made transpacific travel feasible. A number of island stations were established with such amenities as rooms, hot and cold running water, hot meals, and cold beer. The war with Japan would soon interrupt travel, with a handful of stations, such as Wake Island and Midway becoming front-line locations.

When the military began requisitioning planes from the airlines, the highest priority was given to the Sikorsky and Boeing flying boats. No other aircraft except the four-engine Boeing 307 Stratoliners, of which there were only seven in service, had the capacity or the range to span the oceans nonstop. Even so, the shortage of commercial flying boats and long-range land planes was made up for by the adaptation of military bombers into transports, such as the B-24/C-87 variant. In 1943, Lockheed began production of their new four-engine Constellation, which not only matched the amenities of the Boeing and Douglas craft—it was pressurized as well—but flew faster and farther than either. In the summer of 1947, the

A B-29 (lower left) flies in formation with a C-97 cargo aircraft. The C-97 is a direct variant of the B-29 strategic bomber, using the wings, tail, engines and cockpit. The fuselage is bigger and easier to load large items, the new requirement for cargo craft. It was also large aircraft like these that had the range and size to make intercontinental commercial traffic truly possible. (U.S. Air Force/ NARA)

British airline BOAC[3] initiated transatlantic service using the three-tailed Lockheed. To publicize the event, one Constellation circumnavigated the world, flying 22,219 miles in a little more than one hundred and one hours, setting a new world's record.

Although the new airplanes made it possible to transit the oceans, the American military was lost without the experience of the airline pilots. General H.H. "Hap" Arnold, commander over all of the Army Air Corps, openly admitted to President Roosevelt that the Air Corps lacked the skilled manpower to fly the airline's routes. On December 13, 1941, F.D.R. issued a presidential order for the Army Air Corps to "assume possession, or any part thereof" of the airlines. Under an existing agreement

3   British Overseas Airline Corporation

between the airlines that constituted the Air Transport Association (ATA), the airline companies had already committed themselves to surrendering any or all of their fleet and staff to the government in the instance of an emergency.

Backed by the influential General Arnold, ATA representative Edgar Gorrell reminded FDR of the ATA treaty and pointed out that aircraft were already being taken over by the military. He reminded President Roosevelt that the railroads, taken over during the last war, were nearly destroyed by a government top-heavy with red tape and inefficiencies. FDR remembered the debacle and tore up the order.

With the airlines free of the onerous presidential order, they were better able to provide support to the war effort. Scores of civilian pilots and other aircrew went to work with the Army's Air Transport Command (ATC) and the naval version, the Naval Air Transport Service (NATS). Schools were set up to train thousands of novices and veterans alike the intricacies of flying across an ocean and living to tell about it. The RAF earned a place in the ATA-sponsored schools as well. Hundreds of Brits, already in uniform, attended the American schools and, upon graduation, went onto assignment in the RAF Ferrying Command.[5]

The post-war benefits of this massive cooperative training program were the growth of the transoceanic airline industry. Combined with the technology developed for the war, civilians and military personnel could be whizzed to any place on the globe in a matter of hours. [6]

Wind Patterns

As the newly founded airlines were discovering, flying through turbulent weather could be dangerous, and as flying became commonplace, pilots began to encounter unexpected wind patterns. Thunderstorms were the first intermittent natural phenomenon to challenge aviators. The internal circulation of winds in the typical storm includes violent vertical drafts that can easily tear an airplane apart. In one notable incident over Germany in 1938, fourteen paratroopers on maneuvers became caught in a vicious thunder and hailstorm. As their plane began to disintegrate, they bailed out, only to find themselves trapped by strong alternating drafts. Some deployed their parachutes, some did not. It did not matter. The men were repeatedly lifted and then, suddenly, dropped through the clouds. At lower altitudes, rain would soak them. When they were then carried back aloft their wet uniforms froze. This continued until the storm abated and the bodies, frozen solid, fell to the ground.

Rotors and Wave Cloud Formations

Like the winds, which caused the tragic paratrooper incident in Germany, drafts over mountainous terrain, with columns of air rocketing in both vertical directions caused numerous crashes. The connection between these winds and nearby cloud formations began to receive an elementary understanding only in the late 1930s. One important discovery was the wave cloud.

As a prevailing wind blows across a mountain range, the rising terrain forces the moving air upwards. When the air rises high enough it cools and begins to condense into clouds. This heavier, moister air, is pulled back down towards the ground on the lee, or protected, side of the range. Valleys, hills and other terrain features cause this rapidly descending air to rotate horizontally, like a log rolling downhill. This swirl of wind, called a rotor, creates more eddies, which then proliferate over a wide expanse of the range. The rotor itself becomes trapped in place over the foothills as faster moving winds flow over the top of it. The whirling rotor in turn traps the cloud formations, which often appear as rows of ribbons running parallel to the mountain crest. Except for the clouds, the entire maelstrom is totally invisible to the naked eye, waiting to ensnare any passing airplane and slap it into the ground like a fly. In January 1942, actress Carole Lombard, wife of movie idol Clark Gable, died along with twenty-two others when their plane crashed into the side of Table Mountain southwest of Las Vegas Nevada. She had been touring the country on a War Bond sales drive. At the time, the crash was a mystery, but it is now thought that the doomed airliner was caught in a rotor.

Although the phenomenon has been known since the war, meteorologists, using special laser visualization techniques, have seen the rotor in action only since the mid-1980s. Since then, the phenomenon has been measured to exceed thirty thousand feet altitude. [7]

Thermals

Thermals are less severe but no less insidious than rotors. Air currents rising over flat or undulating ground form them. As the sun heats the surface of the Earth, the surrounding air warms, too. The heated air ascends, creating these invisible air currents. In addition, the rotation of the Earth imparts a spin to the vertical column, creating a tornado-like effect. Unlike the common tornado, though, thermals create no visible clouds or threatening storms, though the twisters occasionally suck up loose dust that provides a measure of warning for pilots. These zephyrs can reach as high as several thousand feet, depending on upper-level wind conditions.

The vast deserts of the Southwest United States, with their intense heat and rocky terrain reflecting heat back into the air, tend to have the biggest and strongest thermals. During the war, military pilots trained in the desert and early on, even their instructors were ignorant of the dangerous twisters. As a result, chance encounters with these "dust-devils" resulted in a number of crashes, mostly of light trainers.

The Jet Stream

The third and perhaps most startling wind effect came to American notice in late November 1944[8]. A high-altitude bombing mission out of Saipan to Tokyo by B-29s encountered unusually high tailwinds that caused a bit of excitement. The Superfortresses normally cruised around two hundred miles per hour at thirty thousand feet. However, in this instance, the attacking bombers became caught in the grip of the tailwind. Astonished navigators could not believe it when their instruments measured the ground speed in excess of 445 miles per hour. Three days later, another raid caught a wind that hurtled the big bombers along at more than five hundred miles an hour. The 20th Air Force had discovered the "jet stream." Bombing from this speed was practically impossible, as the precision bombsights were not calibrated to such velocity. Despite the wind, both attacks were carried through, although less than fifty of the thousand bombs on the second raid hit anywhere close to the targets.[9] The bombing campaign over the Japanese Islands became effective only when General Curtis LeMay, new commander of the bomber forces, ordered the planes to fly at lower altitudes. [10]

The Japanese, who knew of the jet stream since the late 1920s, attempted to use this easterly wind

Japan was nothing if not ambitious on prosecuting their war against America. Made of mulberry paper, assemble with glue and transported on a wind pattern the West was just beginning to know about. Its amazing these balloons, which thousands were launched, made it across the Pacific Ocean. (OWI)

to their benefit. Building large balloons out of paper, they attached a simple explosive device and set the balloons to drift eastward. Intended to land in the American Northwest, many of these contraptions did actually survive the journey.

Now, the jet stream has been studied and mapped, its seasonal shifts charted. Aircraft regularly slip into the jet stream to take advantage of the time and fuel savings, whereas planes heading against the flow can avoid it. The understanding of other localized weather conditions has enabled better planning of flights, and the implementation of new technologies, such as wind shear warning radar, has reduced many of the dangers of flying.

The Civil Air Patrol

After the bombing of Pearl Harbor, Americans generally expressed widespread anxiety while civilians on the West Coast drifted into what could only be called a general panic. The military and public alike feared that the Japanese were going to invade the West Coast while the Germans, according to the most reliable rumors, were undoubtedly going to fly over three thousand miles to rain fiery death down on New York City, Milwaukee and Kansas City. As the first months of war passed without these dire predictions coming about, cooler thinking began to prevail.

As outrageous as some the fears were, there was a real threat. In the summer of 1942, the Japanese had briefly but ineffectively shelled and bombed the Pacific coast. German submarines cruised the Eastern seaboard, looking for targets of opportunity. The Germans represented the greater danger, as merchant shipping was being torpedoed within sight of the American coast ranging from New Orleans to Newfoundland. The severe shortage of destroyer escorts and other craft capable of battling the U-boats led the government to turn to civilian pilots for help. In late summer 1944 a long-range, four engine Ju-390 flew within twelve miles of New York City, turned around and returned to Germany. All this was done on its normal fuel load and carried a simulated bomb load.

Organized under the Office of Civil Defense, the Civil Air Patrol was conceived on December 1, 1941. The government provided 200 hours of special training, costs for plane rental, per diem allowances for room and board, and crash liability insurance reimbursements. Fuel, strictly rationed for the duration, was usually issued from military supplies, but sometimes the pilots bore the fuel costs. One estimate says that more than a million dollars was donated in this manner. One CAP pilot calculated that he received an average of $10 a month in six months of service. It was hardly enough to cover his meals.

The CAP took on many roles. They served as couriers, delivering top priority cargos, search and rescue, fire watch over distant forests, and towed targets for rookie gunners. The big job, though, was submarine patrol.

At first, they were not allowed to fly armed. But after CAP pilots helplessly circled a grounded U-Boat for nearly an hour, until it managed to wriggle free and slip away unharmed. Furious, U.S. Army Air Forces General Hap Arnold authorized the carrying of ordnance. The light civilian craft carried one hundred pound bombs, enough to cause disabling damage, while larger planes received 325-pound depth charges. Over the course of the war, CAP planes attacked 57 enemy submarines out of 173 sighted, damaged 17 and are known to have sunk one. The CAP was not casualty-free. Twenty-six fliers died in water-related crashes and another 33 dead from other causes. Flying on shoestring budget and little maintenance, water landings were not uncommon. Ninety planes ended up in the ocean, where the crews were safely rescued and inducted into the "Duck Club."

The CAP made itself known for their aggressiveness towards German subs. In 1943, the Germans changed tactics. This undoubtedly was due in part to the abundance of radar-guided long-range military aircraft, more escort ships and new Allied tactics with anti-submarine ordnance (Hedgehogs and launched depth charges), but the head of the U-boats, Admiral Doenitz, is reputed to have blamed "those damned little red and yellow airplanes."

Aside from making life miserable for the Germans, and impromptu swimming parties, the CAP's 8,000 men and women (20% of CAP were women) CAP pilots were also used to aid in search-and-rescue missions of downed military pilot trainees and patrol the southern border with Mexico. Another 20,000 CAP cadets, boys and girls in the age group between 15 and 18, served as spotters while learning to maintain the planes and eventually to fly on their own. The success of the CAP made it attractive to the Army Air Force, which absorbed the group as an auxiliary in 1943. In 1946, Congress passed legislation (Public Law #476) legitimizing the CAP as an "instrumentality of the United States," ranking equivalent to the American Red Cross. When the Army Air Forces became a separate branch of the military one year later, the newly named United States Air Force made the CAP an official branch of that service.

Their legal mandate is threefold, though Search and Rescue still constitutes their major mission. Anytime a distress call or missing aircraft report goes out, the CAP responds. These rescue operations provide an opportunity for the training of cadets and for aerospace education, the other two missions of the CAP. Under the Air Force's husbandry, The CAP now supports more than 53,000 members flying 535 light aircraft organized into 1,700 units, with unit organization, rank and discipline following military protocols.[11]

Air Ambulances

The Air Transport Command (ATC) and the Naval Air Transport Service (NATS) were not only involved with transporting men and materials into the war, they were also responsible for removing the casualties of war. Since 1931, the U.S. Army had a policy of equipping regular transport aircraft with litter-holding brackets in the extreme case where an injured man needed to be moved. But under no circumstances were aircraft reserved exclusively as air ambulances. By 1938, that restriction was somewhat lifted under pressure from the U.S. Army Surgeon General. He wanted seven planes dedicated to patient transport, but the funds were not available. Instead, flight training centers were given permission to convert a limited number of small airplanes to crash-rescue missions. Even so, the intent was to allow only for the rapid removal of victims to the home station hospital. There was, in effect, an almost inflexible moratorium on transporting patients over long distances.

This backwards attitude was abandoned in the summer of 1940, when an article appeared in the *Army Medical Bulletin* detailing German casualty air evacuation in the Polish campaign.[12] This article, along with the growing opinion in the American military that the country would soon be entering the war, served to crystallize the call for air ambulances. By the following September, the Chief of the Army Air Corps had grudgingly authorized plans for large commercial craft and smaller single-engine craft to be adopted for the role.

His decision was fortunate in its timing. No sooner were the first of the ambulance kits being delivered to the C-46 and C-47 transport squadrons than the Japanese struck Pearl Harbor. The kits included all the metal hardware necessary to brace and clamp litters to the walls of the cabin. Later on, the metal frames were substituted with webbing straps in an effort to minimize the consumption of metal and reduce the overall weight of the plane. Aside from the litter brackets, there were limited materials for the care of the patients, especially in the early part of the war. This usually consisted of the contents of a typical rucksack of a single medical corpsman. Doctors occasionally went along in the case of a critically ill patient, but they were generally too valuable to risk and in too short supply to release from their assigned stations. Almost from its inception, the air ambulances were to have registered nurses onboard, which it took some months to recruit and train. As the war progressed, these specially trained nurses were assigned to assist the medics on ambulance flights, and they had at their disposal a far greater supply of medical supplies and oxygen delivery systems fitted to offset the physiological effects of altitude on the patients. Another added feature of the latter kits were restraints and sedatives to confine the panicked or neuropsychiatry patient. [13]

Home is the next stop for some of these men. They will have to move through the chain of evacuation at a rear hospital or two, but there trek will be expedited by the wonder of their transport: C-54 Douglas Provider. It was capable to get all the way to Hawaii from Okinawa where they got their Purple Hearts. (U.S. Army/NARA)

But casualties from the Pacific were not the first to see the inside of the new air transports. That honor was for a large number of sick and injured soldiers constructing the Alcan Highway. Beginning in January 1942, C-47s made several dozen "life-flights" from strips as far north as Fairbanks to hospitals in Anchorage, Juneau, or even, weather permitting, the foot of the Alcan at Dawson Creek, Canada. From there, urgent cases could be loaded onto trains bound for United States hospitals.

On February 27, 1945 General of the Air Forces H. H. Arnold submitted a report to the Secretary of the Army Henry Stimson quoting an impressive string of statistics. In 1942 alone, the Air Transport Command had evacuated 12,000 stretcher cases. Two years later, an additional 525,000 casualties were flown away for treatment. The report, deservedly glowing, stated that the fatality rate had been held to an infinitesimally small seven deaths per hundred thousand man trips, thanks in no small part of the role the aerial nurses, medical technicians, and brave crews of the flying ambulances. [14]

Parachutes

Parachutes have been around for centuries, although no one knows who tried to fly with the first one. There are legends that as far back as 2,000 years, Asians were demonstrating the soft descent accorded by large umbrellas or sheets of fabric. With the advent of ballooning in the eighteenth century, parachutes were used sporadically, but only for experimental purposes. Serendipitously, at least three separate balloonists had the good fortune to survive accidents when fire or material failures turned their large linen bags into impromptu canopies. One of the most famous incidents occurred when Jordaki Kuparinto's envelope caught fire high over Warsaw, Poland, in 1804. Remnants of the fabric were trapped in the netting of the balloon and provided enough canopy for him to drop safely, albeit quite rapidly, to the ground.

Parachutes continued to improve and became a form of dare-deviltry in the latter half of the nineteenth century, with exhibitions being staged from balloons for the audience's benefit. But not until aircraft became common, around the time of the First World War, did parachutes gain the attention of the military. However, most pilots spurned the parachute as a negative statement about their flying abilities or their confidence in their aircraft. Many commanders agreed with the pilots, referring to parachutes as "circus stuff." In spite of the criticism, and resistance to their use, parachutes became a necessary component for the fliers of First World War and they saved many a life. However, there were a few incidences where parachutes failed and the war ended soon after the mandate, so parachutes still had a stigma about them for fliers. It would take another twenty years for parachutes to gain widespread acceptance.

Nylon Canopies

Americans were particularly interested in parachutes, and much work had gone into developing new equipment and techniques by the mid-1930s. This included the introduction of rayon and, as it became available later, nylon for canopy material to eliminate the reliance on Japanese silk. Such was the need for parachutes as the war progressed that the U.S. Army quickly overburdened the existing approved suppliers with orders. To accommodate the increased demand, Army procurement officers turned to the only other American industry with experience sewing the new nylon fabric, the ladies' undergarment industry. No less than sixteen of these companies accepted government contracts during the war. This created a marginal shortage of new underwear, as well as a total scarcity of nylon stockings.

The Quick-release Harness

Two Britons, Frank S. Wigley and Leonard F. Austing, first invented this device in

The man above is demonstrating the Irving device. In his right hand is the safety clip, an important part that keeps the harness secured to the body of the wearer. Otherwise, that fall could be long and painful. (U.S. Army/NARA)

1929. Known as the Irving device for the company that held the patent, it featured a metal box that contained four spring-loaded pins. When the four strap ends, two at the chest and two around the thighs, were inserted into slots in the box, the pins engaged in a manner similar to the snap on the modern-day automotive seat belt. This arrangement held the parachute rigging firmly to the wearer. At touch down, a simple twist of the cover plate and a slap to the mechanism worn on the chest unbuckled the straps.

There were, however, some problems with the original Irving design. The springs were too stiff for use in water and some aircrew drowned when they could not get out of their harnesses. Installing weaker springs seemed to work, although that opinion changed after half a score of premature harness releases sent test mannequins hurtling to the ground. As engineers on the project were fumbling around for another path to a solution, an answer came from Germany. The Germans had incorporated a hitch-pin that secured the depression plate from accidental release. This made the Irving device slightly harder to disengage, as a horseshoe-shaped pin had to be removed first, but the parachutist could rest assured that the harness would remain buckled. The Irving device has special post-war significance as it would go on to be adapted for use not only in parachuting but in automobile racing as the latching mechanism for the driver's safety harness.

Cargo Parachutes

Nearly everyone who lived through the 1960s remembers the excitement and the pride of watching the returning Gemini and Apollo spacecraft floating to splashdown under the voluminous domes of white and orange parachutes. The enormous canopies, each measuring nearly sixty feet in diameter, were direct descendants of aerial delivery parachutes developed during World War Two. Dropping materials from the air had been sporadically attempted during First World War but was quickly discontinued when the war ended. Another series of tests took place in the United States beginning in 1932, using materials from discarded man-sized canopies. Because of the condition of the materials available, the chutes were trimmed to a smaller diameter canopy, which reduced their efficiency. This meant that the cargo container could be no larger than a five-gallon milk can, severely restricting the type and amount of supplies for delivery. The project was abandoned after several loads crashed down with a resounding thump as the canopy disappeared in the ensuing dust cloud. In Germany, the cargo parachute was getting much more serious attention.

July 1969 was an exciting time. America's three astronauts return from their trip to walk on the moon. Here, the Apollo command module floats the last several hundred feet to the ocean, supported by the German-inspired ribbon parachutes. One has collapsed but here was enough redundancy to cover the need. (NASA)

A ribbon parachute in action. This one is easy to see the gaps between the concentric rings of parachute fabric.

With the full support of the Nazi government, Dr. Helmut G. Heinrich and Theodore Knack scientifically tackled the problems of parachuted cargo delivery, eventually perfecting several canopy designs that allowed for large amounts of supplies to be lowered safely.

One of their more remarkable discoveries was that a parachute did not have to be made into a solid sheet. They took strips of material approximately three inches wide (100 mm.) and wound them in a spiral that, when deployed, formed the rough shape of the standard parachute, but that was about as far as their new parachute resembled the older models. Instead of allowing the air to escape from the top vent—a necessary feature to stop the wild oscillations as air leaked out from around the edges—their ribbon chute allowed the air to pass through gaps between the strips. The gaps reduced the amount of wind drift affecting the accuracy of the drop because the canopy acted less like a sail; the ribbons letting the wind pass though. The major drawback to the ribbon chute was that it fell ten to twenty percent faster, an important consideration that precluded it from being used for live cargo. Packed properly, the higher fall rate had little influence on a load of ammunition, fuel, or food.

One of the most memorable instances of air dropped resupply took place in the bitter fall and winter of 1942 at Stalingrad when a massive Russian counter-attack cut off more than 300,000 German soldiers of the Sixth Army. Under constant fire, the encircled German units pleaded for withdrawal but Hitler refused. Instead, he arranged for relief through airlifts of supplies into the enclave. Bad weather, aircraft losses and a shortage of ribbon parachutes created a fateful delay that became a decisive victory for the Russians.[15]

Besides being used for logistical drops, the ribbon parachutes went on to become a standard for slowing jet aircraft after landing. Another canopy of a similar design, the cross-type, is a familiar sight for drag-race fans today. So advanced were the Germans that both Dr. Heinrich and Theodore Knack were among the group of scientists invited to come to America at the end of the war to continue their work.

Smoke Jumpers

The great forests of the Western United States became a target for the Japanese early in the war since the thousands of acres of tall pines represented an important natural resource for America. Besides the obvious wood and paper products, the trees were also processed into chemicals, cloth, paint, fuel, and even food products. In addition to the forests, Oregon and Washington war plants produced aircraft, ships, aluminum, and, unknown to the enemy, vital radioactive isotopes for a revolutionary new bomb.

The West Coast did in fact experience several attacks in 1942 and 1943. The most nerve-wracking came from Japanese aircraft flying from specially designed submarines to drop incendiary bombs on the dry forests on the forests of Washington, Oregon, and California. The attack was intended to ignite an inferno that would spread on the prevailing winds, inspiring panic and sapping vital manpower to fight the fires.

A similar attack was tried again in 1944 with the indirect delivery of a fleet of balloon bombs. Made of paper and carrying a collection of incendiary and high explosive projectiles, they were set to drift from the east coast of Japan across the Pacific on the trade winds. Although no one knows for sure how many made the trip—sources vary widely, estimating between three hundred to almost a thousand—many successfully landed on the North American continent. They were found scattered from Canada to Mexico and as far as Michigan. Fortunately, the bombs did little physical damage but six members of a Bly, Oregon church group out on a picnic were killed when they stumbled across one in 1945.

Unknown to the Japanese, America had already prepared for enemy attacks on the forests. Around 1935, the Forest Service began to look at using aircraft to airdrop water and other chemicals on remote fires. The previous year, a proposal to parachute firefighters had been forwarded but it drew little interest until 1939, when the Forest Service resurrected the idea of airdropped firefighters. Experts from the Eagle Parachute Company were brought in as advisors to nine volunteer jumpers at their base at Winthrop, Washington. Throughout the summer, nearly 60 experimental jumps were made into the forests of northern Washington.

The next year, the Forest Service expanded the program, now officially entitled the Smokejumper Project. Two teams of parachutists, one based at Winthrop and the other at Idaho's Moose Creek Ranger Station, stood by for action. The first operational jump took place on July 12 into the Nez Perce National Forest of Idaho. Before the season ended, a total of nine jumps had been made.

In their spare time, the jumpers worked on developing the equipment and tactics of the dangerous business. Protection for the jumpers as they descended through the heavy foliage was particularly needed. Helmets were acquired and thick metal screens added for face shields. Landing techniques were improved as well, including the now familiar "tuck-and-roll" maneuver.

All this activity drew the interest of U.S. Army Major William Lee, "father of the airborne troops." He spent some of the summer observing the smoke jumpers in training at their new camp in Montana. Obviously impressed with what he saw, Major Lee took what he had learned and adopted it for the Army's airborne forces.

As America drew closer to war, the smokejumpers' ranks grew to 26. The Missoula, Montana, camp was enlarged to accommodate the entire force. It had been decided that training and housing all in one place would be more cost effective. By this time, the government was contracting with an air carrier, Johnson's Flying Service, for planes and pilots, all based out of Missoula as well. The war attracted away the core personnel of the smoke jumpers. In 1943, there were all of five members left, including the lone instructor. Seventy volunteers, all of them enrolled in the Civilian Public Service (CPS) program, which was made up draftees who avoided military service by declaring themselves as conscientious objectors. For the rest of the war, the Forest Service relied on CPS to supply smoke jumpers.

When the balloon bomb attacks began in November 1944, there was little chance of fire erupting in the snow-covered Northwest. However, there were fears that if the attacks should continue into the following summer, there could be scores of forest fires, far more than the limited numbers of firefighters could handle.

In anticipation of this event, the Department of Agriculture, (USDA) in cooperation with the U.S. Army, organized a systematic fire-fighting plan, code named Operation Firefly. At the forefront of the operation was the first all-black paratroopers unit, the 555th Parachute Infantry Company. As their training intensified and their ranks grew to battalion size, about 400 men, they became convinced that they would soon be going to the European war. Instead, the 555th was shipped west to Pendleton Air Field, Oregon.

There, the 555th underwent an intensive three-week course on fire fighting, tree climbing, special techniques on landing in rough terrain, and survival. Because many of the Japanese bombs failed to explode when they dropped to the ground, bomb disposal methods were included in the curriculum. Fears that the balloon bombs would ignite uncontrollable forest fires were not realized. However, the summer of 1945 was especially dry, and there were a number of natural fires that kept the smoke jumpers and the men of the 555th busy. 1945 also marked the first year that the smoke jumpers held official organizational status with the Forest Service. With the success of the experiment, the Forest Service established two more bases at McCall, Idaho, and Cave Junction, Oregon. As the war wound down, the CPS crews were disbanded and, in September 1945, the 555th was released back to the Army.[16]

Helicopters

In 1944, off the coast of the Mariana Islands, a large, oddly outfitted freighter sat at anchor. Onboard, over a hundred skilled metal-smiths operated industrial machinery rarely found outside a major land-based factory. The ship, assigned to the Second Aircraft Repair Unit (2nd ARU) manufactured parts for the fleet of B-29s that were pummeling Japan. Japanese resistance was proving to be tenacious and between battle damage and the complex new bomber's teething pains, new parts were a constant necessity. To avoid long delays in the engineering and shipping cycle, it had become more expeditious to carry the factory to the war. To make the work of transporting the finished parts to shore easier, the 2nd ARU possessed another oddity, the first two operational helicopters in the Allied inventory.[17]

The helicopter has had a long and difficult genesis. Leonardo Da Vinci described the first one but the reality of the technology remained out of reach. Other inventors tried their hands at building a vertical lift machine but they were stymied by the complexities of the machine. They had no conception that each component of this awkward-looking machine, formally known as a rotary wing aircraft, serves a specific function. It first required development of the autogiro, or gyroplane, in the 1920s to bring about the contemporary helicopter.

Invented by Juan de la Cierva in 1923, the autogiro featured a hinged rotor. Now seen as a museum piece, an autogiro looks like a wingless airplane with a set of helicopter blades attached above the cockpit. Forward motion produced by the craft's front-mounted engine and propeller caused the rotor blades to spin. Set at a slightly pitched angle, the blades created lift just as a wing would. It was thought at the time that the autogiro was safer than an airplane as the autogiro wouldn't fall like a brick when the engine died but floated down more like a leaf. Moreover, the free-spinning blades were highly efficient airfoils and the autogiro needed far less room to take off than an airplane. Proponents of autogiros saw the strange aircraft as an answer to commuting in the larger cities, where rooftops could be used as runways, as well as a tool for traffic control or Coast Guard rescue work. There was even talk that the autogiro would displace the airplane in intra-city commuting. Unfortunately, the autogiro was too slow to command the sky but its benefits were not ignored.

The first problem was that of controllable lift. Any time either an autogiro or early helicopter got off the ground, the craft listed to one side because the wooden blades were simply bolted to the rotor hub, creating a stiff, inflexible assembly that often swung dangerously close to the ground. It was soon discovered that the rotor blades—simply very narrow, long wings, having a cross section similar to the main wings of an airplane—were losing lift as they retreated. Viewed from above, the turning rotor describes a circle with the fuselage below. As the blades swing toward the front of the fuselage, the entire load is carried on them. This is the lift portion of the cycle. As the blade crosses the front centerline of the nose, it enters into an area of reduced lift because the blades are moving away from the direction of forward flight. As the speed of forward motion increases, the speed of the air moving over the airfoil-shaped blade increases lift. On stiff-mounted blades, this increased lift was enough to upset the precarious balance between approaching and retreating blades, up- turning the craft and causing some breath-taking crashes.

Cierva's hinged blades prevented this from happening. The approaching blade, under load, wants to bow vertically upwards. The retreating blade, under less aerodynamic stress, tended to bow less. The answer to the mystery of the flipping autogiros was to mount the blades to the hub on joints that allowed flexibility in the vertical plane. If viewed at slow motion, the blades would be flapping up and down as the blades entered and left the zones of high lift. This is why modern helicopter main rotor blades always appear to droop.

Early helicopter builders also discovered that the engine driving the rotor imparts torque into the body of the craft, causing the body to spin in the opposite direction of the rotor. The German Focke-Achgelis experimental craft of 1936 used two sets of rotors turning in opposition, effectively canceling out the torque effect. The Focke-Achgelis helicopter proved that it had gotten beyond the experimental stage when, in 1938, it was flown inside the cavernous Duetschlandehalle in Berlin. Allied bombing hampered production of the six-seat FA 223 *Drache*, however, so few were ever made.

Heinrich Focke's local rival, Anton Flettner, took the twin rotor idea and incorporated it into the first intermeshing blade helicopter in 1938. The design proved to be so successful that the German navy bought several copies for testing. Two years later, Flettner began manufacturing his FL-282 *Kolibri* for Germany, beating out Focke-Achgelis by mere weeks to claim credit for fielding the first operational military helicopter.

In the United States, Igor Sikorsky tackled the torque problem with a tail rotor that spun ten times faster than the main rotor. Even though this proved to be a simple solution, damage to this small rotor set would have immediate and dire consequences, as the craft would corkscrew out of control into the ground.

Early attempts at helicopter flight also required an engine/transmission combination that could take the entire load of the craft in addition to the dynamic forces of flight. Add to that the torque, plus the unpredictable shocks from weather conditions, and pilot errors. The materials and manufacturing techniques of the 1930s were just beginning to achieve the level of competence necessary to produce the rugged drive train. Several test craft

A Sikorsky R-4 helicopter heading back to the front in the Philippines to pick-up more wounded. This is believed to be the first time that a helicopter was used for air evacuation. (U.S. Army)

had spectacular mechanical failures before the design was perfected.

The next difficulty encountered was directional control. As described earlier, the Germans used multiple rotors to compensate for torque, and by controlling the speed of the individual blade sets the pilot could change direction. On a single-rotor helicopter, this is a bit more complicated. Sikorsky used a system of linkages that changed the angle, or pitch, of the rotating blades. This made the rotor blades twist to "bite" into the air so that the aerodynamic forces could provide lift. By installing a similar system to the tail rotor, the pilot could adjust the blades and use the torque to swing the tail around, giving the helicopter its now famous maneuverability.

The Sikorsky helicopter, the VS-300, first flew on May 13, 1940. Within a year, it had set an airborne endurance record of one hour and thirty-two minutes. Sikorsky made more modifications to simplify the controls, and the new model, the Sikorsky R-4B, became America's first production helicopter and the standard by which all others would be measured. Over the next two years, the United States Army ordered scores of helicopters, but they saw limited service during the war due to restrictions on materials that slowed production and low priorities on training pilots. It was mid-1944 before the first squadrons were being released for duty in the war theaters. Besides the two that were assigned to provide ferry services between the factory ship and shore bases in the Marianas in the Central Pacific, several saw action in Burma and the Philippine Islands as emergency evacuation aircraft where the first tests of winch rescues were attempted.[18]

Hydraulic Systems for Aircraft

It is an old pilot's adage that the difference between flying and falling is landing in one piece. To expedite landing, some means of setting aircraft on the ground and slowing to a stop had to be devised. With the exception of the Wright Flyer, gliders and seaplanes, the common answer was landing gear and wheels. The planes of the First World War and after had landing gear assemblies simply bolted onto the bottom of the airframe. As the understanding of aerodynamics expanded, however, the need to move the gear out of the air stream became paramount. As air flows past a flying airplane, a certain amount of resistance to forward movement called drag is realized. This hindrance has to be overcome by the engine at the cost of airspeed. Lose too much airspeed and the plane will stall in the air, quickly revealing the distinguishing characteristic between flying or not. With that in mind, designers began to build planes dispensing with unnecessary features that created drag, improving the speed and performance of their craft. But the landing gear assembly with its struts, wires and wheels continued to impose an enormous penalty in drag.

The best place to stow the gear away is within the fuselage. Already, in 1920, the Dayton-Wright RB racing plane had the first fully retractable landing gear. However, the weight and complexity of a folding landing gear outweighed the benefits and the idea was rarely incorporated for the next fifteen years. The few planes that used similar concepts used a variety of methods to operate the gear. One or two examples took advantage of the small electric motors just coming to market. Far more common was the hand winch operated by the pilot. Even during the Second World War, this feature was used on some of America's front-line fighters. This is evident In Second World War-era films showing F4F Wildcat fighters taking off from aircraft carrier decks. As the plane lifts off from the deck, the wings noticeably wobble. This is due to the pilot frenetically winding up his gear by hand and inadvertently jiggling the control stick, which was usually held between the pilot's knees. Hydraulic systems promised to eliminate these situations.

Formally, hydraulics refers to the science of fluid displacement. Hydraulic force, utilizing water, has been used for centuries for everything from dealing with sewage in medieval Germany to operating gristmills in colonial America. Fluid displacement operates on the principle that a fluid cannot be compressed like a gas. If a column of liquid is placed under compression, the resulting fluid pressure is transferred to the walls of the column. This pressure generates a vast store of energy that can be channeled through plumbed passages and directed to do useful work.

These passages form the hydraulic circuit. The vital elements to the circuit are the reservoir/pump, the control valve, and the actuator. The pump draws fluid from the reservoir, compressing the liquid. Leaving the pump through attached plumbing, the fluid then encounters the valve. When the valve opens, the fluid goes to the actuator through more plumbing.

The actuator is often a simple cylinder made of steel tubing, polished internally and sealed at one end. On the other end is a sealed cap that has an opening to allow a shaft to pass through. The shaft, extending into the tube, has a piston attached. When the fluid enters the cylinder by way of ports located on the side of the tube, the fluid moves the piston/shaft assembly as a unit. Because the sealed end is fixed so that it cannot move, the movement of the shaft imparts mechanical force to shift a load.[19] A load can be anything, whether it is the blade of a bulldozer, the elevator at the shopping mall, or the landing gear of a 747. The elegance in hydraulic power comes from its simplicity and strength. A typical four-inch cylinder operating at 2,500 pounds of pressure can exert a force in excess of 15 tons. Two cylinders working in tandem would double that amount.[20]

The science of hydraulics came into maturity during the 1930s. Up until that time, most machines that featured hydraulic systems used either water or mineral oils. Water had the detrimental effect of corrosion that eventually made the components leak. Mineral oils worked far better but the selection of materials to seal the system from leaks and moisture was very limited. The problem of materials also limited the operating pressures of oil-based hydraulics. The material that held the most promise was rubber. Natural rubber is made from latex, which rapidly deteriorates in contact with petroleum-based oil. It was only with the German invention of the synthetic rubber named Buna that modern hydraulics could be possible. (More on Buna in Chap. 9)[21]

Oil hydraulics had been introduced in aircraft for shock-absorbing oleo struts in 1912. Having two tubes, one sliding into the other in a crude arrangement like a typical hydraulic cylinder, the oleo strut was a great advancement. Although the oleo strut was more of a shock absorber, it marks as one of the finest examples of early hydraulics. Despite the advantages of oleo struts, hydraulic systems saw very few applications over the next twenty years.

One of the first production aircraft to have hydraulically powered landing gear was the Brewster Buffalo in 1936. Considered to be obsolescent at the start of the war, these planes saw service in Finland and the Pacific with the Allies.[22] However, there were some bugs to be worked out of hydraulic system engineering first.

One memorable problem was with the hydraulically powered folding wings of the Chance-Vought F4U-1 Corsair—the airplane featured in the 1980s television show *Black Sheep Squadron*. If the pilot became careless or distracted, the selector switch that controlled the jacks operating the wing-folding feature would remain open to the unified hydraulic system. In this case, operating the hydraulics to pull in his landing gear would also cause the wings to fold up, a happenstance that is hardly conducive to flying. Only on later models were the wing cylinders separated from the landing gear system by automatic valves. In spite of the early problems, hydraulics eventually became an integral part of most military aircraft and would play a bigger role after the war.[23]

As aircraft got larger and faster, they also became more complex and more difficult to handle. The flight control surfaces that enable a pilot to change course and altitude are mounted at the back edges of the wings and tail. The ailerons (on the main wings), the elevators (located on the horizontal area of the tail) and the rudder (on the vertical aspect of the tail) are connected to their respective wings by hinges. As the pilot moves the control stick or pedals, a relative movement occurs at the respective control surface via cables running through the frame of the plane. In flight, air flowing over the displaced panel will cause a change in the plane's course, up or down, left or right.

On the big planes, post-war military and civilian, the control surfaces were correspondingly large. To move this abundant area under the pressure of airflow requires more energy than a man can physically generate. The power of hydraulics is the answer. The confined spaces inside the wing are large enough for the diminutive cylinders operating at pressures up to ten thousand pounds per square inch. The best and first true example of this effect was in the H-4 "Spruce Goose".

The Nose Wheel

Another development that came after the First World War was the invention of hydraulic wheel brakes. As aircraft performance improved, landing speeds increased correspondingly. Originally designed for automobiles, early hydraulic drum brakes relied on mineral oil to expand a flexible bag that would force the shoes against the drum, bringing the vehicle to a stop. This method proved to be effective on the ground, but for airplanes there was a drawback.

The airplanes of this era almost universally had resorted to the tail wheel or skid to provide ground space for the spinning propeller. Furthermore, the wings had to be set at a slight upward angle to get an additional lift from ground effects at takeoff.[24] In this nose-up attitude, the main wheels tended to be placed slightly in front of the center of gravity, the balance point where the weight was equal front and back. As a result, pilots using the brakes had to observe caution when braking. If applied too harshly, the forward momentum could very well tip the craft nose-down, digging great holes in the runway with the propeller and not doing much good to the prop either.

This situation lasted well into the

A C-54 landing at a forward airstrip, a Douglas C-47 in the background. One can clearly see the difference of the stance, or how the two sit on the ground. The C-54, also built by Douglas Aircraft, was able to go three times a far with almost two times the cargo. Post-war, the civilian version of the C-54 was the DC-4. (NARA)

1930s when National Advisory Committee on Aeronautics (NACA, the forerunner of NASA) researchers fitted a nose wheel and suspension assembly on an experimental craft. Tests showed that landing was faster and better controlled. Aircraft using a tail wheel had to be steered by means of aerodynamic forces acting on the rudder. As the plane slowed, steering responsiveness rapidly fell away, making last second maneuvers a chancy proposition. With a nose wheel, however, steering at any speed applied through the front wheel was more like that of a car and not dependent on ground speed. Thus, brakes could be applied with more vigor, the resulting weight shift forward being compensated by the nose wheel suspension.[25]

Nose wheels were incorporated into several famous American warplanes, notably the P-38 Lightning, B-24 Liberator, B-25 Mitchell, and the B-29 Superfortress, as well as several foreign designs such as Germany's Messerschmitt Me-262 Schwalbe jet fighter. In this case, the nose wheel solved the tail being in the aerodynamic shadow of the wings. The tail dragging Me-262 was too dangerous to take off or land. Nowadays, only rare examples of modern aircraft use the tail wheel, all being light civilian or crop-dusting varieties. The advent of the jet engine has permanently secured a place for the nose wheel in the future.

The Multi-Wheel Landing Gear

As the loads airplanes were expected to carry increased over the years, the capacity of the mechanism designed to support those loads had to become more complex. This meant that the weight of the suspension and wheels also had to be carried aloft, imposing a penalty on cargo capacity. The weight penalty extended to the tires themselves, exposed as they were to the brutal impact of landing.

The rubber tires of the time could tolerate the slow speeds of landing on grass or dirt fields, even when the aircraft gross weight extended into the seven-to-ten thousand-pound range. The advent of paved landing strips at first seemed to spell doom to the tires, but manufacturers responded with multi-ply tires. These new tires also meant that aircraft designers could add weight to the airframe or payload, negating the improved performance of the tires. Caught in this vicious circle, airplanes kept getting bigger and heavier, requiring subsequent tire improvements.

Considered a large bomber when it was designed in 1935, the B-17, as designed, can carry two thousand pounds of ordnance. By 1942 standards, this did not constitute a heavy payload. Single engine fighters were soon to come into combat that could do that feat. The B-29, designed five years after the B-17, carried the more substantial burden of ten tons of bombs. To support this load during taxi and the take-off run, the landing gears had to be considerably stronger and the tires comparably robust. Unfortunately, tire science had come to the limit of its technology. To get around this dilemma, engineers came up with multiple tires.

The bogie, or multi-wheeled landing gear as it has become known, was first tried on the bombers of the First World War. However, these craft saw limited service and the idea was discarded after the war as being unsatisfactory because the wheels affected performance too much. World War Two designers returned to the bogie to handle increasing weight. By that time, planes were also landing two to three times faster on pre-pared runways and be-ing exposed to several hundred degrees of heat generated by the brakes. The 100,000 pounds of a landing B-29 could, and routinely did, blow out one main tire. This would normally cause a single-wheeled airplane to ground loop (similar to a car spinning out) and crash, but with the multiple tire arrangement, ground loops in the big bombers rarely happened.

The landing gear of a modern passenger jet. It is easy to see how the weight of the plane is distributed through all of the wheels. An added margin of safety is imbedded within this design as it limits loss of control should a tire or two blow out.

Another reason for using the bogie was the landing surface itself. One tire focuses the entire weight that it supports directly onto the area of contact on the ground. Engineers know this as the "footprint." The parking areas at the Boeing factories producing the B-29 had to be specially reinforced, as the massive plane would crack the concrete parking areas. The benefit of having more than one wheel per side on the ground sharing the load spreads the weight out over a larger area. The larger the footprint, the less load per square inch applied to the ground, obviating the need to install massively thick concrete runways and parking ramps.[26]

An even more radical example is that of the gigantic B-36 Peacekeeper bomber. The original main gear consisted of one tire on each side ten feet tall and more than two feet wide. This would have been fine for a 100,000 pound airframe but the B-36A weighed 278,000 pounds. Not surprisingly, few air field concrete aprons could support such an immense load. Only with the introduction of the B model did the aircraft have a four wheel bogie main gear.

Post-war commercial aircraft adopted this design, the redundancy offering a measure of added safety. Aside from the gear itself, aircraft tire technology has been necessarily under constant development, having to sustain the abuse of ever-larger aircraft landing at even higher speeds. With today's three hundred and fifty ton airliners landing at 150 miles an hour, it is doubtful that landing gear will revert to the single wheel design.

Cargo Carriers

One driving force that caused the airplane to grow in weight and girth was the need to haul cargo. The military in particular used aircraft to carry its machines of war as well as troops. The successful German parachute attacks on the Low Countries in 1940 gave this requirement great urgency. The Allies realized that they were lagging in modern warfare technology.

The workhorse of the American military air transport system was the venerable C-47.
A converted airliner popularly known as the

A C-46 cargo plane swallows a light air ambulance with ease. A second fits in easily, a visual demonstration of the evolution of aircraft in just a few years. Ten years before, the smaller plane was considered to be, if not large, a medium weight, multi-passenger craft. Now, comparing planes like the 747 or Airbus 380, the C-46 is of the same class as the little ambulance plane once was. (U.S. Navy)

DC-3, it featured a large door on the left side of the fuselage that allowed for entry of troops and cargo. Later in the war, modified light vehicles could be maneuvered in, although in many cases, larger vehicles such as light trucks had to be partly disassembled. In some circumstances, specialized trucks were air freighted into remote landing areas in two loads.[27] All the other Allied cargo aircraft followed the same basic layout as the C-47. For the European invasion, features of cargo gliders copied from German examples were built with the cockpit mounted on hinges. Upon landing, the troops could fold away the front segment, revealing a cavernous cargo bay that could accommodate anything from a Jeep and a light artillery piece from the CG-4 Waco to a light Tetrarch tank out of the British-built Hamilcar glider.

As the joint German-Italian campaign in North Africa began to run into trouble from losses in shipping, German engineers produced a glider capable of carrying 48,000 pounds of material within it vast fuselage. The Me-321 *Gigant* (Giant) had a wingspan of one hundred and eighty feet and required three twin-engine Me-110s to tow it. Roaming Allied fighters found the lumbering giants to be easy prey and a significant number were lost.

Messerschmitt 323 Gigant (Giant) cargo aircraft is clearly loaded to the maximum. This is the motorized version of the German airplane with six radial engines. The unmotorized Me-321 used to require 3 two-engine bombers with tow cables to get airborne. That assembly of four was easy picking for Allied fighters. The 323 is not much more of a challenge, although it has gun positions that can present a threat to an unwary pilot. The multiple wheel landing gear is clearly visible.(IWM)

An armed version soon appeared, the Me-323, having been modified by fitting six engines to its wings, dispensing with the tow planes. The air-supply bridge across the Mediterranean soon met its inevitable end, but the idea was not lost on the Allies, who copied aspects of the German design for their gliders.[28]

Several designs for large drive-off cargo carriers were created, only a few of which were actually built. The "Spruce Goose" seaplane designed by Howard Hughes is one such example. Known to its builders as the H-4, it was built to transport men and equipment over the submarine-filled Atlantic. Weighing in at about 400,000 pounds unloaded, its size became the biggest hindrance to its development. The weight of such a plane severely restricted its landing sites to large bodies of water, a geographical feature that is absent in many parts of the world.

The gigantic B-36, successor to the B-29, had a cargo variant that actually flew in service. Known by its military designator C-99, it was capable of hauling more than forty-five tons for ten thousand miles and more. The statistics, as impressive as they are, go to show the inherent problem with gross aircraft weight. The B-36/C-99, tipping the scales at 205 tons, could land only at the three airfields on the North American continent that had massively reinforced twenty-four-inch-thick runways. This plane is an extreme example of immediate post-war capacity that illustrates the tremendous size of Second World War airplanes.

Superchargers, Turbochargers, and Turbo-Superchargers

An aircraft engine has to be lightweight but rugged enough to withstand grueling service. The first engines ran on gasoline, as did the planes that flew during the Second World War, but the latter had the advantage of higher octane ratings. (See more on high-octane fuels in chapter 9.) As altitude increases, the available oxygen level decreases, causing a corresponding loss of power. Generally, the more air, containing its constituent oxygen, that can be moved through an engine's combustion cycle, the greater the horsepower produced by the engine. This rule has limitations, of course, based on the total displacement of the engine and the efficiency at which it operates. One way to get more air through the engine is to compress the incoming air and force it into the combustion chamber. This is the function of the supercharger, which is simply a fan mounted in a case that bolts onto the engine block. The fan spins at very high speeds, drawing in air and sending it through ducts into the engine under pressure. To drive the fan, the common practice at first was to assemble a gear drive from the engine crankshaft. This drove the fan but at the loss of a disproportionate amount of power due to friction and airflow resistance. Both the German and British fliers attempted to improve their fighters' performance using the supercharger during the First World War. Neither country had any outstanding successes, the war ending before the technical problems could be solved.

In the inter-war period, a variation of supercharging—running the fan from escaping exhaust gases—gained favor. Close to being white-hot, these gases were mostly wasted energy. Called a turbocharger,[4] it took the exhaust into a turbine that drove the fresh air blower and overcame most of the troubles of power penalties. Trials of these turbochargers mounted on motor vehicles were wildly successful and had great results on production European cars such as Mercedes-Benz and BMW. But under certain circumstances encountered in flight, the hot gases would erode the fan and any other nearby metal, such as the turbine case, in a brief time. Metallurgical research in the 1930s led to new high-nickel stainless steel alloys that had far superior heat tolerance and abrasion resistance than their older counterparts. Even though the new alloys were

---

4 Superchargers obtain their drive from the engine mechanically. Turbochargers are driven from exhaust gases. Turbo-superchargers combine the best of both.

tougher, there were circumstances where brutal heat of the gases was just too much.

Aircraft fitted with turbochargers carried tanks of oil to lubricate the turbine bearings, but if the tank was damaged in combat, there was little to be done. If the turbine itself did not burn away, the bearings supporting the fan shaft would seize once the lubricant burned off, turning the driving gear to shards of metal that, in turn, could easily destroy the engine.

As the war progressed, engineers began to address the problems one by one. Automatic controls reduced the atmospheric and altitude conditions that caused melt-down. New bearing science reduced the lubrication issues. Engineers built two-stage, multispeed superchargers and turbochargers. As their name implies, turbo-superchargers combine the exhaust drive element, forcing air into the engine. Add to that an intake blower being directly connected to the crankshaft through a gear train and electric clutch assembly. Well before the end of the war, all manner of combinations of one-speed, two-speed, variable-speed and electrically regulated systems were in widespread use. [29]

The Fuel Injected System

Rudolf Diesel introduced fuel injection in 1892. His unique engine operated on the theory that an inferior fuel would spontaneously combust when sprayed into a chamber that contained extremely high-pressurized air. The fuel would first have to be aerosolized in such a manner that would immediately and thoroughly mix with air. To atomize the kerosene that he preferred, Diesel invented a nozzle that forced the oil through tiny passages, creating the necessary mist. His engine gained international favor and has been a staple power source ever since.[30] Diesel's engine was too heavy to work in aircraft. From the Wright brothers on, carburetion was preferred. The basic function of the carburetor is to mix the fuel and air before it enters the combustion chamber. As the engine crankshaft turns, the pistons reciprocate within their respective bores. The action of the piston drawing away from the sealed end of the bore creates a vacuum. This vacuum draws air through a valve that opens during a brief time in the engine cycle. The in-rushing air, as it is pulled through the venturi in the carburetor, will suck a portion of gasoline out of a small reservoir mounted in the carburetor.[31] The turbulence of the restrictive venturi and the journey to the combustion chamber mix the two into a volatile blend, which is then ignited by the spark plug. In theory, the fuel and air mixture should be thoroughly combined to give the best performance possible. Unfortunately, discrepancies in the quality of the fuel and other factors greatly affect this occurrence, creating an imbalance in fuel delivery and inferior performance.

The gyrations of the typical fighter precluded the use of the automotive carburetor, as the reservoir had to be kept in a nearly level state to perform well. Numerous complex designs to overcome this problem were tried with varying success. Elaborately constructed, these devices really never worked properly and were a maintenance headache. Instead, engineers incorporated tried and true carburetor design that gave the pilot a short period where they could fly inverted under power. This period, no more than a minute or so, would end with the engine stopping for fuel starvation. There was usually no challenge restarting the engine, but if the pilot was taking severe enough maneuvers to gas-starve the engine, odds were that an enemy aircraft was in close proximity. Not the optimum time to fly dead-stick.

The venturi came to be the weakest point in the aircraft carburetor. As air flows into the narrowing bore, the air pressure change causes a dramatic temperature drop that can easily fall below freezing. When flying among clouds, the presence of moisture is unavoidable and this sudden pressure and temperature change will lead to ice forming, plugging off the intake to the carburetor. Thousands of airplanes over the years have suffered engine failures as a result of carburetor icing, many of them fatally. The innovation of warming the choke was an improvement, but it did nothing to rectify the imbalance of fuel delivery.[32]

The idea of delivering the fuel in a misted form directly to the cylinders seemed to be the answer to all of the preceding problems. By adopting the pressurized fuel injection system with injector nozzles adapted for gasoline and state-of-the-art timing controls to charge the cylinder with fuel at the exact moment needed, the flyer of such a craft could out-perform any opponent.[33] Beginning in the early 1930s, the Germans began to develop a line of high-performance aircraft engines with the Diesel-type fuel injection but using aviation-grade fuel. By 1939, Luftwaffe was flying a number of engine types that used fuel injection.

Not surprisingly, Allied aircraft designers were reluctant to follow suit. They regarded fuel injection with suspicion and preferred to go with ever larger and more complex carburetors. They preferred to focus on improving performance by turbo-supercharging technology.

During the war, only one American combat aircraft, the B-29-B, specifically developed to deliver the atomic bomb, used fuel injection in the highly advanced Wright Cyclone 3350 engine. Postwar applications were much more extensive with the introduction of Pratt & Whitney's enormous R-4360 engine. Several large military cargo aircraft and sport racing planes used it and the latter still do.

American auto companies, not aircraft builders, eventually embraced fuel injection in the quest for horsepower in the muscle cars of the 1950s and 60s. As in the finer German cars in the pre-war years, fuel injection remained virtually the sole possession of the German auto industry in the post-war era and rebuilding was the first priority. It would be into the post-war decades before companies such as Bosch and Daimler-Benz would produce systems that would go into mass-produced export vehicles.[34]

The Jet Engine

No other method of propulsion has defined the second half of the twentieth century as has the jet, which makes it possible to travel around the world in hours, shrinking the globe to one calendar day.

Historically, the jet was anticipated for centuries. Steam-powered reciprocating engines built by James Watt led to the idea that steam might be used to power direct rotary motion, and already in 1784, the British patent office granted a patent for the steam turbine. Other inventors quickly began to introduce their own versions of the steam turbine engine and by the 1880s a turbine spinning at 10,000 RPM was operating a milk separator.

The efficiency of the steam turbine could hardly be ignored by the blossoming aircraft industry of the 1920s and 1930s. Inventors from Britain, Germany, America, France, and Switzerland were all attempting to adapt the steam turbine to propel the airplane. An officer with the Royal Air Force unwittingly led the pack. In his senior thesis at the RAF officers' college, Frank Whittle proposed a new power plant that would create a blast of hot, concentrated gases from the rear of an aircraft. The exhaust would potentially push the plane upwards to five-hundred-miles-per-hour, doubling the speed of anything flying at the time. Working from theories put forward by Newton, Watt, and Laval, Whittle proposed to compress the incoming air with a device based on an early turbocharger design and then injecting a mist of fuel into the compressed air, the latter idea borrowed from Diesel. Contained by the tubular wall surrounding the mixture, a spark would fire. The resulting explosion would create immensely hot gases, which would be ejected at tremendous velocity out the rear of the tube. He even reasoned that as the forward speed increased, the air flowing into the front of his engine would begin to compress itself, foreseeing the ramjet effect. This would in turn increase the efficiency of the jet, creating even more thrust. Whittle realized that there did not seem to be an upper limit to the potential velocity his engine could produce. The only shortcoming that he could foresee was that the materials of the time lacked thermal resistance to withstand the abusive white-hot gases.

Whittle's thesis, although successful in gaining his graduation, attracted little attention, so he undertook to develop the idea on his own. He patented the concept in January 1930, but was unable to finance further work. For six years, he slowly convinced a number of his friends and relatives to invest in the project. Whittle finally built the first turbojet to run successfully on April 12, 1937. Impressive as it was, the British government seemed to barely take notice. Small sums to finance testing were forthcoming, usually correlating to the increasing amount of threatening rhetoric from Germany.

The turbine section of a Jumo 004 turbojet from a Me262 fighter. It is easy to see the vanes of the rotor (the part that spins) and how they interface with the stator blades. (Towards the bottom of the section where the rotor vanes are visible.) The two sets of blades fit together like the fingers of two hands interlocked. The spacing between is miniscule, maybe just a few thousandths of an inch. In addition, the rotor spins at an incredible speed, sometimes ten thousand RPM or more. (NARA)

The Germans, on the other hand, were greatly interested in jet technology. Independently of Whittle's work, German engineers had begun to develop a similar engine in the mid-1930s. Their first trial run in September 1937 more than made up for their late start. Just four days before German troops crossed the Polish frontier on September 1, 1939, the purpose-built Heinkel He-178 began jet-powered flight tests.

This plane proved the concept but the airframe was deemed to be too fragile for combat. Over a number of months, Junkers, Messerschmitt and Heinkel competed for development contracts for the German government. One model, the Me-262, proposed to mount two jets on the wings leaving the nose open to mount a deadly nest of heavy machine guns. Thanks, in part to Hitler's insisting it should be dive-bomber; the Me-262 became stalled in the design and test stages until 1943. Further problems with the Jumo 004 engines delayed introduction even further. It would be in the summer of 1944 that the Me-262 took to the air for combat. A closely held secret, the Me-262 came as a stunning surprise to the Allies in the late summer of 1944. The Me-262 was, at first, devastating to the bombers. The premier Allied fighter, the P-51 Mustang was one hundred-miles-per-hour slower.

The only advantage the Allies had was when the jet was landing; the fighters would ambush the slow, easy target. This tactic, plus Hitler's resistance to producing the Me-262 as a fighter, vanishing German fuel supplies, and pilot shortages doomed the jet's otherwise shining career. That was fortunate for the Allies.

Lockheed's P-80 jet fighters over Italy, early summer 1945. General Electric copied the Whittle engine in the interest of getting a jet fighter in the air to face off to the German's growing fleet of jets. It was unnecessary; Germany was drained of fuel supplies. (USAAF)

The Germans had a number of other jet-powered craft under development at the end of the war. They even supplied samples and drawings to their Axis partners, the Japanese, who had fighters on paper or in development that resembled both the Me-262 and a manned V-1 cruise missile.

Allied reactions to Germany's aggression into Poland and Norway was to rush the Whittle jet to testing and a British jet, the Meteor, flew on May 15, 1941. To augment the successful production of the new technology, England entered into negotiations with the Americans. The British were naturally apprehensive at allowing this radical new device to leave the security of English control. However, the pressures of German air assault, lingering fears of German invasion as well as their industrial resources stretched to the end made the jet engine a valuable commodity to gain the favor of the Americans. Britain had spent practically their last pound buying American aircraft and other equipment to bolster their defenses. American isolationist laws in place restricted sales of arms only on a "cash and carry" basis. The passage of the Lend-Lease Act went far to remove the concerns of America's intentions but Britain had already opted to trade the secret for assistance.

This is the General Electric copy of the Whittle engine. The British fitted the same engine in their Meteor fighter and had it flying by 1944. It saw very little service across the Channel. Instead, they used it to chase down and take out the V-1 cruise missiles. (USAAF)

General Electric, the primary jet engine contractor, received blueprints and sample engines. The engines they produced went into a testing program that gave the United States its first jet fighter, the XP-59. Although it never saw service, it was the starting point for newer designs.

Post-war, the jet engine would become the exclusive property of the Allied military. Progress with jets was limited. Until the end of 1947, the Americans pushed the envelope for performance past the supersonic barrier. Britain fielded a second-generation fighter, the de Havilland Vampire, which more than 2,000 were built. The Soviet Union attempted to keep up with the western powers, now seen with renewed suspicion, by developing the MiG-9 using surplus Jumo 004 engine. Commercial jet aircraft would not be available until the early 1950s, which is beyond the scope of this book.

Turbo-Prop Engines

The turbo-prop is an amalgamation of the jet (the turbo) attached to a reduction gearbox that turns a propeller. Surprisingly, turbo-prop aircraft flew just a few months after the end of the war and the general opinion at the time was that the turbo-prop should be the engine of choice for future airliners. Having been handed the gift of the Whittle engine by Britain during the war, American airplane manufacturers doubted that the jet was relevant to commercial travel with its short life span and enormous fuel consumption. One airline executive reported to NACA in 1947 that, in his opinion, "the jet had no future in commercial aviation." Even the British aerospace industry considered the jet to be useful only to power the propeller. The official United States government stand was that future airliners should use either the turbo-prop or an unusual compound Diesel engine—which never was very popular—devised during the war.

Happily, perceptions and opinions have changed. Although the jet—with all its permutations—far outnumbers the turbo-prop, the propeller-driven liner has not been exiled to museum display. The great majority of private multi-engine airplanes sport baby-sized turbo-props, as do many of the smaller, regional commuter airliners. The military still relies on the turbo-prop for cargo transport (C-130 and Navy C-1 & 2), submarine hunting (P-3), and reconnaissance (Navy E-1 & 2, S-2).

Aircraft Design Technology and Testing Equipment

Like any other complex device, the airplane required a significant amount of engineering, development, and testing. Developed countries around the world all had their own aircraft industries during the 1920s and 1930s, with varying degrees of sophistication. Arrogantly, Americans assumed that they held the lead with their own domestic aircraft programs. Among the numerous rationalizations was the reasoning that: America gave the world the airplane, the Wright brothers, Curtis and Lindbergh were American and American companies such as Boeing and Douglas were building and exporting new models every year? Unfortunately, the Germans had secretly surpassed American design technology as early as 1934. This fact startled the American aircraft industry into reality when German and Japanese fighters were shooting down the cream of America's aircraft. The issue became more than painfully clear in the closing days of World War Two, when Allied troops began to overrun German aircraft laboratories.

Volkenröde, Germany, had been home to the Herman Göering Aeronautical Institute since 1935. A large complex of shops, labs, and wind tunnels, the facility was at the center of German aerospace research. Volkenröde housed special tunnels to test fire ordnance (machine guns, cannon, and missiles) against a 500-MPH crosswind created with specialized blowers. An engine test chamber discovered at Volkenröde had the ability to recreate altitude conditions of up to 50,000 feet, as did a similar facility near Oberweisenfeld. More research stations at Göttingen, Traüen, and Köchel, outside of Munich, replicated much of the equipment found elsewhere.

Despite their similar functions, not all these facilities shared their progress, particularly after 1941. After that time, Hitler began to show his unbalanced psyche. Reflecting his distrust of scientists, Hitler made policies that created fierce antagonism between the personnel of similar programs. He also promoted numerous projects that duplicated effort, an unnecessary waste that would cost Germany dearly. Prior to 1941, however, a spirit of cooperation existed, leading to numerous early developments. Leading scientists could travel about the Reich, presenting technical lectures on topics such as the aerodynamics of the swept wing. (More on this subject later in this chapter.)

The discovery of the research centers surprised the Allies. Even though there had been a few intelligence reports about the existence of the facilities, they were largely unconfirmed, hence, dismissed as rumor. The scope of the discovery was stunning. For example, there was a large selection of low-speed, sub-sonic, trans-sonic, and hypersonic tunnels that technologically outpaced the Americans by ten years or more. To take advantage of the treasure, a flood of American aviation engineers and scientists travelled to Germany, spreading across the land in teams. Tens of thousands of reports, drawings, and physical samples became part of the massive treasure haul taken back to America.

The quantities stagger the imagination. Nordhausen yielded parts to build one hundred V-2s and a thousand technicians.[35] An elaborate BMW plant near Munich, capable of creating the frigid atmospheric conditions of 40,000 feet, was torn down and transported to America along with its staff. This included the gifted designer of the Jumo 004 engine, Dr. Hans von Ohain. His capture led to the discovery of a number of secret jet technology caches in Austria. Interviews of German scientists compelled a trip to Salzburg. There, they found two remarkable jet-powered helicopters, the Flettner Fl-282. Its inventor, Dr. Anton Flettner, and two engineers were invited to come to America along with both of their unique aircraft.[36]

Not all of the discoveries concerned just aircraft. A team of American investigators found a remarkable fuel injector mechanism that surpassed anything American industry had managed to fabricate. At a Daimler-Benz plant, another team found a two-speed supercharger that attained an unprecedented efficiency. Part of the enhancement came from a revolutionary fluid coupling that allowed for better control over its range of function. Hardware was only half the story. In the city of Halle, Germany, an office revealed a document describing a secret plastic welding process. The resulting bond seam proved to be stronger than the base material, a measure of a successful fixation.[37] There were new radar systems, missiles that achieved multiple Mach speeds, electrostatically fired fuses impossible to defeat, sound-guided missiles. These were all prizes that were to become the basis for a whole new generation of technology. This trove overwhelmed the Allies. In just three months, 111,000 tons of documents were shipped to England where they were categorized and divided up among the victors.[38]

Most of the original machinery and equipment imported from Germany is now gone, as are many of the processes. The march of time and advancing technology has supplanted them with third-, fourth-, and even fifth- generation ideas. However, these present-day methods are a result of logical progression of the advanced concepts captured from the Germans over fifty years ago.

The Swept Wing

As post-war aviation engineers tried to figure out what to do with the jet engine, other engineers were poring over captured enemy documents. The wealth of technical knowledge, especially from Germany, seemed to be endless in such sciences as rocketry, chemistry, and aerodynamics. The lat-

He-162 Salamander or "VolksJäger" (People's fighter) was a last ditch weapon system. It was supposed to be simple to build, using mostly wood for the frame and airfoils. (OWI/NARA)

ter was especially rewarding, not only because of the jet engine, but also because of the general shape of their planes. Many of the newest German aircraft had an unusual swept wing. From an engineering point of view, this is harder to design and build. The engines, wing mounting points to the fuselage, landing gear, and any ordnance hung on the wings all needed to be aligned to the direction of forward flight. With the wing slanting off at an angle, this becomes more difficult to manufacture. As aircraft had typically performed satisfactorily without it; there seemed to be no point, or so the Allied experts said.

To understand the reasoning, it's necessary first to understand one point of aerodynamics; air behaves as if it were a fluid. As a wing cuts through the air, disturbances can arise within the flow, destroying lift. A wing requires a smooth, cross-section at the leading edge with a gradually receding tapered cross-section. This shape is best for creating lift with a minimum of air distortion. If the leading edge of a wing is too blunt, the air will dam up at the front, creating drag. The speed of the wing slicing through the air plays a role in this action as well. The wings of a biplane cruising at sixty miles an hour can afford to be less accurate in shape than a 300-MPH World War Two fighter. At higher speeds, these disturbances begin to graduate from eddies to roils and, at the extreme, shock waves.

The Germans' extensive experimentation with the jet airplane led them to discover that at jet speed these shock waves become strong enough to peel the wing surface like a banana. Wind tunnel testing showed that the leading edge of the main wing was creating an immense air dam that blocked smooth airflow. The jet engines, with their tremendous thrust, could push through the air dam with brute force. At this breakthrough point, the shock wave would begin near the wing root and travel diagonally across the wing's surface. Stresses from the wave would damage the bonding mechanism—rivet, glue, spot weld—of the skin to the underlying ribs. The change in air density created a momentary low-pressure area that would literally suck the skin off the wing.

After considerable study and testing, German aerodynamicists discovered that the shock waves became negligible on a wing that sharply angled backwards from the fuselage. As the speed increased, the air dams continuously shifted to a point farther out towards the wing tip. Unexpectedly, the buffeting experienced during high-speed flight tended to be reduced, an inadvertent benefit from the swept-wing modification.

Post-war engineers began to understand German interpretation and incorporated the feature into military and civilian aircraft. The balance between high-speed stability and low-speed dexterity is best seen in the swing-wing military planes like the F-14 Tomcat. At low speeds where maneuverability is required, the pilot will extend the wings nearly straight. During flights near or at supersonic velocities, the wings are folded rearward to minimize the shock waves. It is rare that a contemporary plane will have a wing leading edge at right angles to the fuselage, and the ones that do are all slower-speed craft.[39]

The Autopilot

The first autopilot was nothing more than a servo—a simple device that converted electrical impulses into mechanical motion—connected to a mechanical level. Should the wings tip out of the horizontal attitude, the servo would automatically restore the correct position. This allowed the pilot's hands to be free to navigate and maybe enjoy a moment or two of relaxation. In inclement conditions, it kept the pilot from becoming disoriented with vertigo and beginning a downward spiral, a fatal mistake that happens all too often.

The Sperry Corporation introduced a two-axis autopilot in the late 1930s. Operated on the gyroscopic principle, the early models of this device went into the Boeing 307 Stratoliner. Advanced for its time, the Sperry unit would keep the wings and tail level. Corrections could be input to the unit by means of rotating a sensitivity dial. Although the Boeing airliner saw service for only a very short time, the Sperry autopilot would become an extremely popular and important addition to the bombers' cockpit instrumentation package during the war. Installed in nearly every heavy bomber made in America, autopilots gave the Eighth Air Force the unswerving control they needed to maintain the now famous box bombing formations over Germany. Mounted in B-29s, autopilot controls gave the crew the chance to grab a nap on the long trip home. In one memorable instance, the pilot of a Superfortress awoke with a start to find the plane cruising along on autopilot with the entire crew fast asleep.

During the 1950s, the radio-directed autopilot system enjoyed a period of popularity. However, inertial navigation, an offshoot of the technology developed for the Navy's atomic submarine fleet, soon replaced it. Presently, the satellite-supported global positioning system (GPS) has replaced ground-based radio navigation aids. Airliners and military planes alike have linked GPS data and autopilot features through sophisticated computers. So accurate is this system that many of the newer airliners can, with program input from the pilot, take off, cruise, and land at the destination without assistance from the flight crew.

Radar-Guided Landing Systems

One of the greatest dangers of flying is landing. This is particularly true if the field is enveloped with clouds. As previously stated, the majority of prewar flying took place during daylight hours and in mild weather. The airlines of the 1920s and even as late as the 1930s scheduled their flights so as to avoid having to land at night or in poor conditions. Pilots had to keep in mind an alternative airport should inclement weather break over the intended destination.

To the military, however, this was an intolerable option. The training program for the hundreds of new pilots had to continue throughout the year, regardless of the weather. In fog-bound England, landing fields had to be available around the clock for returning bombers, which were quite often short on fuel, battle-damaged, and carrying wounded crew members.

In the first three years of the war, the RAF resorted to a plan that took advantage of the fact that there was a large surplus of gasoline in Britain. To disperse the English mist, rows of burners were placed at the fringes of the runways. Burning up to one thousand gallons of gasoline a minute, the pots would heat the air enough to raise the cloud ceiling to nearly 500 feet. As an added benefit, the glowing fires could be seen, depending on the conditions, for two to three miles, giving the aircrew an unmistakable beacon for home. The fire-pot plan worked and seven major airfields had the equipment installed. By the time American Army Air Forces bomber units began to arrive in large numbers, the fire pot system was phased out.

The Americans struggled through their first winter where the fog claimed many planes through collisions. In the fall of 1943, radar had developed into a cutting-edge technology. Scientists at MIT began to work on the landing problem. They developed a radar system that not only showed the range and

Modern aircraft can land without the assistance of the pilot, which is a bit of an evolutionary jump from this rig. Started in 1943, the radar in this van and an accompanying trailer was designed to guide the bomber fleet into their home runways without visual references. This was a bonus for the Eighth Air Force who had to deal with the famous English fog. (USAAF)

azimuth of the plane in relation to the runway, but gave enough detail that the operator could talk the pilot into the correct glide slope. The latter is important so that flying blind, the plane would touch down on solid ground instead of clipping nearby trees or buildings that often rimmed the fringes of the Brittish airfields.

To work as intended, an ingenious arrangement of radar antennas was needed to perform the job. The first rotating antenna would "see" approaching aircraft about thirty miles away. Contacting the pilot by radio, the radar operator would direct the craft into approximate alignment with the runway. At ten miles out, another pair of radar sets would come into use. A flat panel housed twin radar beam emitters in a cruciform shape, linked to two separate scopes. One set plotted elevation and rate of descent, while the second showed direction and distance. At such short range, the two radar sets could detect the slightest deviation from the flight path, allowing the pilot time to correct any error.

The radar and radio equipment were crammed into a trailer, along with the five operators, and parked alongside the runway. Several dozen of the finished units, called ground-controlled approach (GCA) were sent overseas and performed wonderfully. They proved to be pivotal in January 1945, during the last days of the Battle of the Bulge.

In a last gasp of defiance, German troops stormed the American lines through the Ardennes. Covered by a massive weather front, they tried to drive a wedge between the American and British armies. Grounded for weeks in England because of dense fog, heavy bombers could not fly to the support of the ground forces. Yet the fighters and ground-attack planes based on the continent could still fly to land with the help of GCA. Unfortunately, flight restrictions still applied as visibility over the battlefield was severely limited. Only when the Belgian skies cleared did the full might of Allied air power fall onto the German offensive.

In the post-war years, the United States Civil Aviation Authority (CAA) began testing the GCA. With a number of improvements, mainly the simplification and reduction of the bulky electronic gear, it would come to take its place in air travel. The trailer-borne radar displays would move into permanent buildings, while the multiple antennas would be consolidated into one array. It took twenty years of progress for the GCA to be adopted at all the larger airports, but nowadays, radar based on the GCA principle is used even to direct aircraft taxiing on the ground.[40]

Notes/Selected References

1 The metal-fatigue problem would come back to haunt post-war designers when two de Havilland Comets, the first jet-powered airliner, mysteriously crashed. In an amazing display of engineering insight and imagination, the problem was traced to the repeated stress of pressurizing the plane. The framework, constantly expanding and contracting, weakened and eventually failed. New methods of manufacturing were instituted and now similar fatigue problems are recognized and rectified.

2 Taylor, John R. Editor. *The Lore of Flight*. 1978. Pp. 132 -136. D'Alto, Nick. "Above It All." *Air & Space*." September, 2009. Pp. 12-17.

3 Bishop, Chris. *Encyclopedia of The Weapons of World War II*. 1998. Pp. 366.

4 Scammell, Henry. "Across the Atlantic." *Air and Space* April/May 1996. Pp. 32-40.

5 Serling, Robert J. *When the Airlines Went to War*. 1997. Pp. 18-32.

6 Taylor, John R. Pp. 136-138.

7 Posey, Carl A. "In the Grip of a Whirlwind." *Air and Space* magazine June/July 1996. Pp.49-55.

8 Wasaburo Ooishi made the first documented observations of the jet stream. Using balloons, set aloft to between three to nine mile high, he made over 1,200 tests between March, 1923 to February 1925. Ooishi's discovery gained little attention because current technology was incapable of attaining that altitude.

9 Wheeler, Keith. *Bombers over Japan*. 1982. Pp.101-103.

10 Marshall, Chester W. and Warren Thompson. *Final Assault on the Rising Sun*. 1995. Pp. 35-37, 69-71.

11 Materials derived from CAP website; www:caphistory.org/museum.

12 *Army Medical Bulletin, #53*, July 1940. Pp. 1-10·

13 "Flying Nurses." *Popular Mechanics*. October, 1940. Pp.494-495.

14 Palmer, Katherine Bell. "Flying Our Wounded Veterans Home." *National Geographic* Vol. 88, Num. 3. September 1945. Pp. 383-384. and Smith, Clarence McKittrick. *The Medical Department: Hospitalization and Evacuation, Zone of the Interior."*. 1956. Pp.426-446.

15 Sweeting, C.G. *Combat Flying Equipment*. 1989. Pp.73-117.

16 Breuer, William. *Geronimo! American Paratroopers in World War II*. 1989. Pp. 365-371. and Huntington, Tim and Dennis Golik. History of the Smoke Jumpers at: http://www.fs.fed.us/fire/operations/jumpers/redding/history.html and Sweeting, C.G. Pp. 73-119.

17 Marshall, Chester W. and Warren Thompson. *Final Assault on the Rising Sun*. 1995. P.52.

18 O'Connor, Roger. "Medevac From Luzon." *Air & Space*. June/July 2010. Pp.62-67.

19 Frankenfield,Tom. *Using Industrial Hydraulics*. 1986. Pp. 1-4 — 1-10.

20 ibid. Pp. 1-3.

21 Stokely, James. *Science Remakes Our World*. 1946. Pp.68-69.

22 Ford, Daniel. "The Sorry Saga of the Brewster Buffalo." *Air & Space* June/ July 1996: Pp.73-77.

23 Poolman, Kenneth. *The Winning Edge*. 1997. P. 176.

24 Four notable exceptions: the Voisin LA5 of France (1914), the Italian Caproni Ca.42 (1918), the British Vickers Vimy (1916), and the Zeppelin RV.1from Germany (1918). All of these bombers had nose wheels but could not be steered. The gear was intended to support the large payload of bombs while the airplane was on the ground.

25 Taylor, John R. Pp. 106-107.

26 ibid. P. 107.

27 Church, John. *Military Vehicles of World War II*. 1982. Pp. 49-51.

28 Weal, Elke C. and John A. Weal. *Combat Aircraft of World War II*. 1977. Pp. 126-127.

29 Taylor, John R. Pp. 186-225.

30

Strandh, Sigvard. *A History of the Machine*. 1979. Pp. 145-149. And Green, Constance McLaughlin, et a.l *The Ordnance Department: Planning Munitions for War*. 1955. Pp. 291-292.

31 The venturi is a tapered tube that is placed so that the small end is downstream of the airflow. As the air traverses the length of the tube, the restrictive taper forces the air to accelerate. This creates a partial vacuum that siphons liquid gas and vapors into the airstream. The operation is based on the principle first described by G. B. Venturi (1746 -1822), Isaacs, Allen. *Dictionary of Physics*, 3rd ed. 1996. Pp. 452-453.

32 *Manual of Flight, Cessna Integrated Flight Training System*. 1976. Pp. 3-12 to 3-15.

33 Burton, Jerry, Zora Arkus-Duntov. 2002. Pp.162-167. and White, Graham. *4360: Pratt&Whitney's Major Miracle*. 2006. Pp.292-309

34 Burton, Jerry, *Zora Arkus-Duntov*. 2002. Pp.162-167.

35 Samuel, Wolfgang W.E., *Watson's Whizzers*. 2010. P. 68

36 ibid. P. 72

37 ibid. P.72

38 ibid. Pp. 74-75

39 Pappalardo, Joe. "Swing Wings." *Air & Space*. August/September 2006: Pp. 34-35 Garrison, Peter. "Model Behavior." *Air & Space*. February/March 2007: Pp.32-37

40 Anonymous. "New Landing System Ok"d." *Impact: The Army Air Forces "Confidential" Picture History of World War II."* July 1944. Book 4, Pp. 30-31. Reprinted 1980.

3

Gizmos and Doodads: Television, Radar, Computers, and a Medley of Electronic Devices

Perhaps no technology has affected the life of so many people as electronics. Only the most primitive tribes in the farthest jungles have not been exposed to these devices that speak, buzz, beep, cook, clean, entertain, and guard each and every one of us today.

The founding of the electronics age can be placed squarely in the twentieth century. Some earlier breakthroughs such as Bell's telephone and Marconi's radio can be called electronics, which they were, in a sense. An early definition called electronics the use and study of or the movement of free electrons. This definition, could apply to lightning, something none of us want to have strike our computers. A more practical definition of electronics is the science dealing with the development and applications of devices and systems involving the flow of electrons in a vacuum, a gaseous medium, or semiconductors.

A Quick Lesson in Physics

An electron is a negatively charged particle that is a constituent part of the atom, as are protons and neutrons. Positively charged protons combine with an equal number of neutrons to form the nucleus. Orbiting the nucleus is a number of electrons. The relative numbers of these three components determine the substance, whether it is iron or a bird's feather. Normally stable except for the radioactive elements described in Chapter 1, this atomic structure can be unbalanced by the removal or addition of one electron.

Electric current works in the same way. The flow of negative electrons in a wire displaces neighboring electrons as the current moves toward a positively charged ground. Removing the ground, or common wire, interrupts the current, and the electrical device ceases to function. This flow of electrons creates a magnetic field. The higher the current, or amperage, the stronger the field and the larger its influence. For this reason a television screen, with its high-voltage power supply driving the luminescent picture tube, attracts dust—much to the dismay of the fastidious homemaker.

The simplified dynamics of electromagnetism here outlined evolved from almost fifty years of research. German scientist Heinrich Hertz finally coerced electromagnetism to produce radio waves in 1887. He demonstrated that the waves behaved exactly like light. They could be reflected, refracted (as light in a prism), diffracted (focused and manipulated to turn corners) and polarized (simply put, tuned to specific bandwidths much in the same way tinting on a window does to sunlight). In addition, Hertz revealed that electromagnetic waves traveled 186,283 miles per second, which has become known as the speed of light. This groundbreaking discovery stunned the scientific community and opened potential new frontiers.

The actual discovery of the electron came in 1897 when Englishman Joseph J. Thomson used evacuated and sealed glass tubes to research electric discharge phenomena. With a pair of metal pins separated by a gap and placed within the tube, he could create an arc. As the pressure in the tubes was reduced, electron flow from the negatively charged pin, the cathode, began to glow from blue to pink, and finally the glass itself gave off a faint green shimmer. Tiny particles, now known as electrons, were being stripped from the cathode material and drawn towards the positively charged anode pin. The electrons caused the tube to glow as they interacted with trace elements in the glass and excited their atomic structure to ionize, or become electrically charged. This was an important practical step towards the invention of television.

The invention of the Fleming valve in 1906 and the DeForest triode in 1907 were the next major breakthroughs for modern electronics. Basically a vacuum tube, the Fleming valve was the first of the breed of tubes that could switch, focus, or act as a one-way gate for electrons. Placing energized metal screens in the gap between the anode and cathode, amplified the triode's electron stream; a miniscule amount of power could thus control a proportionally greater amount of power. Tube performance was further enhanced with the addition of mercury vapor or argon gas instead of a vacuum.

Radar

Guglielmo Marconi developed the radio in 1896 England and was soon broadcasting signals across the Atlantic. Marconi's practical application of electromagnetic radiation was the first step in the development of radar.

Radio works by assembling a set of electrical circuits designed to take verbal or keyed communication and converting that into an electrical signal. Once the signal is amplified, it can be transmitted by way of electromagnetic radiation to any receiver so wired as to convert the signal back into a legible voice or Morse signal. There are a number of reasons why the signal could be interrupted between transmitter and receiver. Storms and other natural atmospheric disturbances commonly disturb the radiation as does geological formations such as mountains or even the curvature of the Earth. In the early days of radio, stations were carefully sited to avoid such interference. Hence, it was a surprise when station operators discovered the signal was not only being blocked, but something was causing to turn back on itself and return to the transmitting station's antenna as echoic interference. Despite the repeated opportunities for twenty-plus years, no one made the connection between cause and effect of the phenomenon. Or if there was a connection seen, no one took it seriously. Take the instance of the anti-collision device for ships based on radio beams patented in 1904 in Germany and Britain. The system was never produced beyond the prototype and it soon faded into obscurity.

In the 1920s, officials with the Royal Mail service, who oversaw the operation of Britain's radio stations, noted that when an airplane passed close to transmitting antenna, there was an immediate increase in interference. Rather than investigate, the airspace within a mile of the tower was declared off-limits.

A few years later, an experimental radio station, operated by the U.S. Navy and the Department of Commerce on the banks of the Potomac River, experienced interference when ships passed between the transmitter and a receiver placed on the opposite shore. This inspired two employees to suggest to American naval authorities that similar stations could be used as "gatekeepers" for harbor entrances. The idea was summarily judged as being worthless, and dismissed. However, the idea intrigued the two Navy officers, Albert H. Taylor and Leo C. Young, who went on to build a makeshift system for Navy consideration in 1934. Their layout proved to be faulty because the sending station transmitted a pulsed signal directly to the receiver, drowning the latter in an electromagnetic "noise." In spite of this early failure, the situation was put right and the test continued using the reflective qualities of radio waves. The test proved conclusive enough that the Navy became interested in further research, which proceeded at a snail's pace due to budget constraints. Money may not have been an issue if it had been widely known that, during this same period, the Germans, Italians, Russians, and Japanese were also developing their own radar technologies. This simultaneous development was purely by chance, since each country was working in closely held secrecy.

Far from the hush-hush secrecy, the radio had become a mainstay of civilian life during the Depression. By 1934, the radio was the major communication medium throughout the world, bringing entertainment and news into the home. One item that was increasingly in the news both in England and America was the German Chancellor, Adolph Hitler. The inflammatory rhetoric from the German leader was making some members of both countries nervous, but the British were far more sensitive to the threat.

Under the direction of Robert Watson-Watt, Superintendent of the Radio Department at the National Physical Laboratory, powerful radio signals were broadcast straight up and the reflected signals recorded. Watt had trained as an engineer and had worked diligently studying thunderstorms and their effects on radio signals. He had gone on to work in general problems of radio static and was at that time researching the ionosphere with radio beams.

Still remembering the bombing raids from the First World War, former Prime Minister Stanley Baldwin predicted in 1932 that "...there was no power on earth that can protect [the man on the street] from being bombed."[1] A number of politicians and private individuals joined in the cry for action, if not directly at Hitler, then at least improving their own country's defenses. One intra-agency memo within Whitehall had gone as far as to predict that, lacking improvements in present technologies, the next war would almost certainly be lost.

Air Ministry Headquarters rose to the criticism and, at the behest of Henry Wimperis, the Ministry's director of scientific research; a committee was formed to look into how technology could be used to alleviate the Nazi threat. The situation was grim indeed. Other than a haphazard attempt to improve their aircraft, the British government had devoted little attention to the air menace. The plans that were in place, for the most part, were left over from the last war when they had been barely capable of combating the German raids.

In that war, the British employed barrage balloons in the faint hope of snagging enemy aircraft in the tethering cables. Another idea relied on utilizing the detection of sound from hostile engines by means of a unique sound reflector dug into a seaside cliff. Blind citizens, having a natural enhancement of their hearing, manned immense ear trumpets. Fighter pilots, lacking radios, were vectored towards the invaders by following directions indicated by large white arrows, mounted on pivots on the ground.

Some of the ideas in the months and years leading to World War Two were mired in the same archaic thinking. The Royal Navy worked on anti-aircraft defense devices to blind enemy pilots with a high-intensity strobe light called a "dazzle gun." Ships were rigged with acoustic gear that was intended to hear approaching planes. Much work went into improving shipboard sound equipment when the wind became a nuisance. After numerous tests with all manner of materials, common bathroom sponges, made into baffles, proved to work the best.[2]

1934 was the era of the Buck Rogers science fantasy craze when the British Air Ministry offered a prize of one thousand British pounds to anyone who could devise a "death ray " that "could kill a sheep at one hundred yards." Robert Watson-Watt was consulted in 1936 about the possibility of such a death ray. To conceal the intention of the line of inquiry, Watt was asked to determine how much radio energy was required to heat eight pints of water seven degrees "at a distance of five kilometers and at a height of one kilometer."[3]

Watt saw right through the question. It was obvious to him that those specifications could only be the pilot of an airborne craft approaching the British coast. Nevertheless intrigued, he put the query to his staff. After some calculation, they decided that it was impossible to create that much radio energy given present knowledge, but they did offer an alternative solution. They recalled that short-wave radio communications, suffered from interference whenever aircraft passed near. This could, NPL engineers speculated, be an answer to the Air Ministry problem. Watson fashioned a message to the Air Ministry that would change history forever. It laid the foundation of radar.[4]

Watson-Watt's final memo outlined the operating principles of his scheme. Using contemporary technology, he suggested transmitting a pulse of radio waves towards the target area. The waves, travelling at light speed, would reach out and reflect, like light from a bright surface, back towards the radio station. The interval time from transmission and return could be calculated and from the resulting difference, the range of the target could be determined. Using the familiar cathode-tube display—not unlike the small television picture tube of the 1950s—the signal was represented by a travelling line on the screen. Overlaid with a calibrated scale, the returning wave would be seen as a "blip" on the otherwise flat trace line. Much of this technique with the cathode-tube had already been used at the NPL for Watson-Watt's ionospheric studies.

Watson-Watt proposed a series of radio detection stations as an early line of defense. This radar "fence" would include a means of determining not only range but also height and direction, giving advance warning of probable target intentions and an interception vector for the fighters. But the presence of these friendly aircraft would confuse the reflecting wave, so a method of determining the difference between enemy and defender would have to be devised. (See Identification, Friend or Foe later in this chapter.)

Radio waves, as shown by Hertz, travel in an undulating pattern. (An example of sine wave is on page 130.) The highs and lows of the wave mark the points at which the wave is measured over a one second period of time. The interval between the two points determines the wavelength, or cycle (also named Hertz.). A wave with a measurement of 7,500 thousand Hertz—7500 kHz—will have approximately two hundred meters between the peaks of the wave pattern. The closer these peaks are to each other, the larger the Hertz number. Watson-Watt knew that radio technology in the 1930s best detected aircraft in the fifty-meter range, but this relatively long wave had a limited broadcast area since the longer the wave, the faster it dispersed—attenuated—in the atmosphere. If the waves could be compressed using the same amount of power, Watson-Watt hypothesized, the range of detection could be extended to nearly two hundred miles.

Work progressed rapidly with of the Air Ministry providing funds. The Hertz problem was well in hand, as were other issues outlined in the Watson-Watt's memo. In 1935, the same year that Germany repudiated the military-limiting Versailles Treaty, two test transmitters were erected and the preliminary work completed. But the transmitters installed in the first ground station weighed several tons and threatened to divert the entire capacity of the power grid to the exclusive use of the station. Besides the ground units, the researchers pushed for the development of an airborne detector and in 1937, they field-tested airborne radar set, in which, unintentionally located several ships at sea in the process.

In spite of this success, the Air Ministry threatened to cancel all work on the latter two. Ministry officials were concerned that these were a distraction. They insisted that the coast-side radar stations were of a higher priority, and that Watson-Watt and his team, now working for the Air Ministry, were to complete them first. Faced with this ultimatum, work resumed on the ground stations. By late 1938, a series of ground stations, called Chain-Home, looked out over the east and south coasts of the English Channel with electromagnetic pulses. Although Chain-Home represented a significant advantage over any approaching aircraft, it was often blinded by its own shortcomings. Unable to generate a signal of less than one meter (300 megahertz), the moisture-laden air over the Channel caused the signal to deteriorate far too soon to provide effective coverage.

Germany's invasion of Poland in 1939 lent new immediacy to the need for radar development. Stronger transmitters and more sensitive receivers were needed, as was the ability to see lower on the horizon. A number of new ways of creating the miniaturized wave patterns, in the multi-centimeter range and less, was needed. The eventual key to the successful evolution of radar lay in a pair of devices that had been invented several years earlier.

One, the klystron, was originally designed to be the source of microwaves in a primitive aircraft navigation aid. Narrowing a stream of electrons into pulses produced high-frequency power. The shortcoming of the klystron was that the pulses were limited strictly to a high hertz output, while much less than was needed to serve as a true centimeter radar source.

The other device had been invented in the 1920s to replace the triode. Called a magnetron, it was a vacuum tube surrounded by a magnetic coil. It could produce centimeter wavelength radio signals, but only at about forty watts of power, which was much too low to reach out to the two-hundred-mile range. However, by combining the best features of both designs, the British researchers reasoned, the problem should be overcome. Unfortunately, the two designs seemed to have divergent features that would resist integration.

The klystron had doughnut-shaped cavities that bunched the electrons together, whereas the magnetron had a large cathode/anode assembly that produced centimeter wavelengths. The solution to the integration conflict was to build a cylinder about one-half an inch in diameter, with the center hollowed out to receive a negatively charged cathode capable of being mechanically rotated. A series of cavities would surround the center hole, running parallel to it and connected by slots. The remaining material of the cylinder formed the positive anode

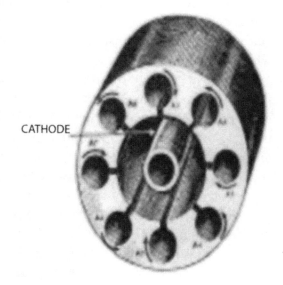

A line drawing of a cavity magnetron. The cathode is clearly marked in the center, the cavities are clearly marked with the direction of their respective electron flow. The diameter of the anode is about one-half-inch (13 mm).

portion of the device. As power was applied to the rotating cathode, electrons would be attracted to the stationary anode. The magnetic field produced by the electron flow would start a rotating cloud of electrons past the slots. Some of the electrons would fall into the cavity and create bursts of microwave-length radio signals.

The signal could be modulated—tuned—by controlling the diameter of the cavities and rotational speed. From the cavity, the radio wave could be transferred to an antenna by conventional antenna wires. During the test phases, this design produced radio waves measured at 9.5 centimeters with a power output of an impressive 400 watts. Later, production models would generate fifteen kilowatts, an improvement of nearly 4,000%.[5]

By the beginning of 1942, cavity magnetron-generated radar had advanced enough for orders to be placed for thousands of gun-laying, searchlight-guiding, and ship-detection radar sets. The older, energy-gobbling radar sets that were installed in large capital ships, the only ones capable of generating the necessary current and offered enough space for the bulky electronic gear, were replaced with more compact, efficient sets. As radar became smaller, the more modest vessels in the fleet such as destroyers and escort ships were fitted with radar to search out and fire at targets. Submarines had miniaturized sets installed in their periscopes so that they could use their radar while still submerged.

The cavity magnetron proved to be the breakthrough event that shaped radar development for the next fifty-plus years. The radar that turned the tide for England went on to provide the means to defend the West against an expected Soviet attack during the height of the Cold War. Radar has also been adapted to look down from aircraft and satellites to map the Earth, search for mineral deposits, locate buried archeological sites, discern potential underground targets for the military and fathom the depths of the oceans. Other radar units have traveled the cosmos to map our moon and distant planets. The weather has been watched for years on radar, helping us to plan our weekends and holidays. Much to the driving public's chagrin, radar in the hands of the police has made speed laws easier to enforce. The airways are controlled by radar, and onboard sets peer ahead of aircraft for terrain, weather, and other obstacles. An American vehicle manufacturer has been testing radar set to warn drivers of school buses when a wayward child is in danger of being struck.

The Microwave Oven

Microwave energy from the cavity magnetron has found uses outside radar, most familiarly the microwave oven. Excessive heat problem was one of the obstacles that researchers at M.I.T. had to overcome. One unsubstantiated report stated that a Chain-Home station had an accidental power surge that burned out its transmitter; within minutes, a number of sea birds were found near the antennas, cooked to a turn.[6] The first documented case of microwaves cooking something came from a scientist at Litton Industries. Working with an experimental cavity magnetron, Dr. Percy Spencer reached into his pocket for a candy bar. Finding the confection had turned into a sticky, gooey mess, he postulated that the magnetron had excited the water molecules within it. A quick test with popcorn and eggs confirmed his theory, and a new industry was born. It took several years to work out the problems of shielding, but it is the rare house or business today that does not have the fast, convenient appliance.[7]

Microwave Communications

Another application for microwave is the transmission of communications signals. Until the advent of fiber optics, fully 85% of all long-distance phone service in America was transmitted by microwave. Towers were set up at intervals, usually by line of sight, across the nation to carry millions of calls daily. The microwave system proved to be so reliably fast that it was chosen to provide the link for the emergency 911 system.

Identification, Friend or Foe (IFF)

With the advent of radar, a way to identify aircraft was badly needed. No longer would it be possible visually identify high-speed airplanes flying at great altitudes. Only two days after England declared war on Germany, in 1939, the first two aircraft shot down by radar-guided British fighters were themselves British. This incident underscored the need for an IFF system.

The method of IFF identification is deceptively simple. A radio signal is simultaneously broadcast along with the radar signal. A special transceiver on Allied aircraft would sense the radio beacon and respond with a short, coded message in reply. This reply was decoded by the radar station, and with the proper identification made, would highlight the friendly aircraft on the radar screen. The code could be changed daily to obviate the chance of an enemy craft sporting a captured IFF unit sneaking through the screen.

IFF systems are still very much in use. Military and commercial planes all fly with their IFF transponders active, and thanks to better electronics, more information is relayed back to the ground now. Besides simple identifiers, the signal can also be programmed to tell of aircraft system failures, fuel status, and destination. It can also warn of in-flight emergencies such as hijacking.

Sonar

Like radio waves, sound can be broadcast in a multitude of frequencies. Musical instruments are good illustrations of this principle. The deep rumble of the bass gives us the lower frequency waves while the high notes of a flute demonstrate the other end of the scale. There are sounds outside this range that are impossible for humans to hear. Sonar, in its infancy, used a lower frequency that, like radio, lost signal cohesiveness at medium ranges. The higher the tone, the farther the sound wave will travel and return with a usable echo.

One way to create sound waves is by piezoelectricity, from the Greek meaning "pressure electricity." Discovered in the nineteenth century, piezoelectricity is a crystal-based technology in which certain crystals give off a burst of energy when subjected to electricity or pressure. This phenomenon was an important step in the invention of phonograph cartridges, microphones, and earphones, all components of two of the greatest inventions of the 1800s, the telephone and Edison's phonograph.

The idea of using sound waves for search purposes came after the Titanic disaster in 1912. Large boxes were fitted to the bows of ships venturing into the foggy North Atlantic, where collisions were common. This rudimentary sonar plied the seas well into the 1920s with little change, although the range of detection was poor and it failed completely when the ship's speed exceeded five knots.

Sonar received a momentary boost from the scientists of the First World War, when they tried to adapt the shipboard sound devices to locate enemy submarines. The U-boat menace was nearly strangling England, and some countermeasures were desperately needed. The British formed a commission to develop the equipment under the name of Asdic, an acronym for Anti-Submarine Detection Investigation Committee, but the war ended before they had made any significant headway. Sonar saw no further work, at least in the West, as military spending generally took a backseat to legislated social programs. The politicians were confident that their newly formed international treaties and the League of Nations would prevent further wars.

Russian engineers, however, developed a means of using ultrasound to detect flaws in metal parts in the late 1920s. Several other countries adopted the method for quality control in manufacturing. Intrigued by the obvious possibilities, two Austrian brothers,

Karl and Friedreich Dussik, worked at adapting the industrial tool to do something X-ray machines could not do, see into the skull. Their trials met with failure, as their machine was unable to generate enough energy to pierce the massive bone structure. However, their 1937 tests are notable for introducing the means of attenuating sound waves.

World War Two brought renewed life to sonar. Electronics and the work of the Dussik brothers had matured to the point that sonar was a fully functional, reliable tool for warfare. Technology advanced enough to build hardy microphones and transmitters, packaged in unitized, watertight cases. Called a transponder, this device could be lowered into the ocean for days on end without flooding or corrosion, either which can damage the circuitry.

In a twist of logic, American submarine commanders were ordered to forsake the use of the sound-generating portion of their sonar sets, as the loud pinging would give away their position. Instead, they were to use the sensitive underwater microphones, used for active sonar, to listen for ship traffic. On the other hand, the Atlantic convoys used the pinging as a "warning bell" to scare off any lurking U-boats. When the Germans adopted their multi-boat "wolf-pack" tactics, the pinging became a homing signal from the convoys, setting them up for coordinated attacks.

In late 1943, airdropped sono-buoys were developed by the Americans to counter the wolf packs. As the name implies, the sono-buoy contained a miniature transponder and a separate radio to relay the microphone signal to a nearby ship or plane. This allowed sonar signals, acting as decoys, to be placed far from the convoy. Specially trained anti-submarine forces reversed the tactic on the Germans, drawing the prowling U-boats near. As they approached, passive listening on both aircraft and idling escort ships would hear the sub's arrival. An unknown number of German submarines fell into the trap. It was just one more step to win the Battle of the Atlantic for the Allies.

After the war, piezoelectric-generated sound waves would be seriously studied for adaptation to the civilian market. Prenatal and pediatric health care applications received enormous interest. Sonar, in particular, was able to view the fetus without exposing it, or the mother, to the dangerous emissions of X-rays. From that sonography would grow into a specialty all its own, enabling doctors to view many of the soft tissues of the body.

Other sonar equipment was developed for non-medical applications, too. Miners and geologists could determine the presence of subterranean structures that were known to contain certain minerals, such as oil. A shock wave from a small explosive device was sent through the ground. Sensitive gauges would read the reflected shock patterns and mathematically graph the underground features. Later, with the aid of computers, actual images could be produced to visualize the topography instantly. This new technology, introduced in the late1970s, proved to be a boon to archeologists, and paleontologists.

Another adaptation of sonar went back to the water as sports fishing became more popular in the late 1960s. Using equipment nearly identical to the wartime gear, fishfinders gave fishermen a new edge in their search for the big ones that would not get away.

Sound-range Recorders

Once a submarine had been located on sonar, the escort ship had to maneuver and set an interception course that sonar had indicated. A series of 500-pound depth charge bombs were then rolled off, or later, shot off the fantail of the ship, where they sank to a predetermined depth. The ensuing explosion disturbed the water so badly as to make sonar ineffective, sometimes for several minutes. This often gave the unharmed U-boat plenty of time to creep away, recover, and setup for another attack. In this manner, it was only with extreme luck that depth charges were successful.

To overcome the problems with depth charges, the British developed the "Hedgehog." Twenty-four 7.2-inch bombs could be launched over the bow of a ship, throwing a circular screen of explosive charges that was smaller than the length of a submarine. The bombs had a special fuse that only operated if the bomb hit a solid object such as the hull of a U-boat. If they happened to miss, the water remained calm enough for the sonar to get a new bearing on the sub.

To make the Hedgehog more effective, the British introduced the sound-range recorder to create a visible plot of the return signals picked up by the sonar gear. Signals from the sonar were recorded on a chemically treated paper drum by means of an automatic stylus. This record gave a visual indication of the submarine's position in relationship to the sonar transponder. Used in conjunction with the Hedgehogs, Allied anti-submarine forces had their prey constantly targeted.

After the war, automatic recorders based on the sound-range recorder were disseminated throughout industry for use in automatic processes and quality control. Automakers use recorders for assuring the temperature of the ovens use for heat-treating metals and baking the paint finish. Bakeries use recorders to measure the volume of flour that goes into the breads and rolls. There are literally thousands of other examples, all adapted from the British device used to hunt submarines.

Infrared Sensors

Fog represented one of the greatest challenges to both sides during the war. Soup-thick haze often blocked out viewing any distant objects with clarity. In the European theater, fog-bound airfields would be closed for weeks at a time, disabling the Allied air offensive. In the northern Pacific, entire islands would disappear in blankets of miasmic vapor in a matter of a few minutes, blinding naval gunners and bomber pilots alike. But for the pilot of a disabled aircraft, fog and clouds served as a sanctuary from marauding enemy planes. All the problems presented by this natural weather phenom-enon could be rendered moot if a way were to be found that allowed for unimpeded sight regardless of the prevailing weather conditions.

In the spectrum of emitted electromagnetic energy, infrared radiation is the bridge between radio signals and visible light. Like its energetic brethren, infrared radiation is the result of vibrations and rotations of molecular excitation. There are two ways infrared may be used: passively and actively. Passive instruments detect the heat from a body or object that is warmer than the surrounding atmosphere. Hot objects such as the exhaust pipes of an aircraft or the warmer surfaces of a fog-shrouded island surrounded by a colder ocean are readily visible. Active infrared instruments take ad-vantage of the fact that some materials attract and retain infrared energy much better than others. A light that is tuned to project only infrared-wavelength energy is shined onto an area. Buildings, especially masonry, become visible when viewed through a set of infrared glasses. Dirt, such as that exposed on a road, glows brilliant green against a darker contrast of the grassy verge. Metals also gain a relative contrast to the darker background, showing vehicle parks, service areas, and collection points.

Infrared equipment was just becoming available in the late 1930s. Infra-red energy would strike individual molecules of fluorescent chemicals coating the surface of special glasses. The variations of temperature could be seen in a ghostly green image. Throughout the war, newer chemical combinations were evaluated to give ever clearer infrared imaging. Radar, which could "see" farther and give a better indication of the speed, heading, and number of aircraft, had usurped infrared's potential as an early-warning anti-aircraft device. However, other uses for infrared were found.

In the central Pacific, Marines carried experimental sniper scopes, both active and passive, that were used to locate and target nighttime Japanese infiltrators. Drivers had active infrared light systems mounted on their vehicles. Using infrared glasses, they could drive in total darkness with no headlights to give away their location. Passive infrared films, developed by Kodak just before the war, were available for photoreconnaissance missions, although they were seldom used.

The Germans fielded a number of combat units equipped with armor, which relied on infrared spotlights both small and as large as 1-meter flak battery lights. These units saw action in the last months on both the East and Western fronts. Despite clearly on the losing side, these units were very effective night fighters, being able to move and fight in the dark. Limited fuel supplies were their ultimate downfall.

An American company came out with a passive smoke detector that used an infrared light emitter to monitor large rooms for the presence of smoke. Placed near the ceiling, it sent out a constant beam of infrared that struck a reflector, which then triggered a light-sensitive pick up. Should smoke begin to collect; the beam's intensity would be diminished. This would set the alarm off, automatically alerting firefighters. During the war, several dozen of these alarms became standard on every ship in the American fleet.

American troops tasked with the defense of the Rhine River bridge at Remagen used an infrared light called a Canal Defense Light (CDL) in March 1945. Several German sappers were spotted swimming downstream at night in an attempt to destroy the bridge. Highlighted with the CDL, the Germans were picked off one by one.

Presently, infrared devices surround us. The remote control for the family television and stereo operates on infrared signals. In the home or business, infrared detectors are widely used for security alarm systems. Police and military agencies use advanced infrared equipment for search and target viewing. Fire departments and maintenance service personnel use infrared viewers to locate heat sources in buildings, electrical equipment and machinery, any place where heat can be an early indicator of potential problems.

Metal Detectors

In the vast Saharan desert of North Africa, Allied troops faced a new hazard to life and limb: land mines. The Germans sowed these deadly explosive packages by the millions wherever they went to guard against enemy incursions into their rear areas. There were several types of mines available, not only to the Germans but to the Allies as well.

The first general type of mine was the anti-tank mine. This was a large metal canister containing several pounds of high explosives, enough to disable the largest vehicles. Anti-personnel mines were much more insidious and common, though not always killing the unlucky victim outright. This meant that others would have to traverse the minefield to render aid. Later in the war, the Germans introduced the "Bouncing Betty," which, when triggered, popped into the air to waist height by means of a small propellant charge, then exploded. The second blast was designed to spew dozens of small steel pellets horizontally in a radial pattern for about forty feet, hitting all standing objects within reach.

Aside from the time-consuming method of searching with bayonets, which tended to set off a mine if care was not taken, there was no precedent or known way to safely locate and clear a minefield. Allied scientists responded with the development of the mine detector.

Consisting of a pole-mounted antenna, an electronics package and headset, it works on the radio principle. A tuned radio signal is sent out the antenna as it is held a few inches above the ground. Metal in the ground causes a disturbance in the signal that the electronics package relates as a tone in the headset.

Large Area Metal Detection

Mines were not the only weapons of war that scientists were detailed to locate. A joint effort by Columbia University, Bell Laboratories, and the Naval Ordnance Laboratory created the first airborne metal detector in 1943. Called the "aerial doodle bug," this torpedo-shaped container flew beneath and behind the towing airplane. It had to be separated by at least one hundred feet to avoid detecting the metallic fuselage of the plane in error. Stubby wings provided stability to the doodlebug, which was flown exclusively over the water. Instrumentation packages inside responded to large masses of iron, which meant in all probability, submarines.

The doodle bugs were perfected too late in the war to be of much use in combat, but mining companies found sufficient uses for them, searching for mineral deposits. Later, as the Cold War heated up and the Soviets began to place more submarines into fleet service, the doodle bugs were resurrected. Mounted on the extended tails of U.S. Navy submarine-hunting aircraft, they performed excellent service as magnetic anomaly detectors (MAD).

The Transistor[5] and Component Miniaturization

---

5 Even though the transistor was revealed to the public one year after the scope of this book, 1948, much of the work took place during the war, was a direct result of war technology, and the importance of its nature was enough to create an exception and add it to the story.

During the war, the need to mount ever more complicated electronic circuitry in ever smaller spaces, particularly in aircraft, led engineers to look at shrinking the vital components. In the infancy of electrical knowledge, materials were considered either conductive—able to transmit electric current—or not. As the technology matured and voltage requirements dropped, a series of metals that behaved oddly came to the fore. As the name suggests, semiconductors exist in a nether world, acting like an insulator at times and at other times allowing the free passage of electrons. This unique feature provided the opportunity to control the action of electrons without the difficulties created by mechanical devices or glass vacuum tubes. Another benefit of semiconductor components was that they were potentially much smaller.

Semiconductor rectification—a sort of one-way gate for electrons—had been demonstrated in 1874 by Karl Ferdinand Braun, the same engineer who invented the cathode ray tube. At the turn of the century, the cat's whisker rectifier was the most common method of detecting radio waves. A fine tungsten wire—the whisker—was placed in contact with a crystalline sample of lead sulfide, an early crude semiconductor. Electromagnetic energy in the form of broadcast radio signals would strike the whisker, and the energy would convert from radio waves into direct current through the crystal. The truly magical aspect of the crystal radio was that it did not need a battery or other source of power to work. Therein lay the drawback. The crystal did not possess amplifying qualities, so when a signal was weak or variable, the crystal radio would become unstable and practically useless.

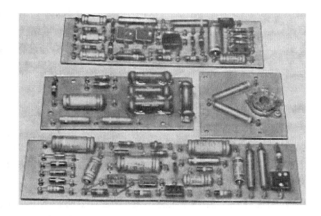

Circuit boards, a word that did not even exist in 1941, are collected here for display. The bottom one is shown at about 2X scale. It was an important aspiration to continue striving for the smallest, most powerful, and most functions possible. This meant radios, radar, television, or any other electronic device, became smaller, more powerful and more functional. (OWI/WPB)

Bell Laboratory engineers formed a team of top-notch scientists led by Mervin Kelly to explore the physics of semiconductors. This proved an arduous task, as there are hundreds of materials that qualify as semiconductors. Beginning in about 1936, the work progressed at a leisurely pace until the European war began.

The first big breakthrough in understanding the physics of semiconductors came from radar research undertaken for the United States Navy at Bell Labs. As a result of an effort to improve signal reception, the glass-encased rectifying diode tube created problems. Operating at a higher temperature, the tube's heat was generating "noise"— an inherent anomaly found in all circuits that become worse as it heats up—that was interfering with reception. Furthermore, electronic circuit designs of the time promoted the production of heat through resistance.

Electricity moving through wires, tube sockets, cathodes, and so on encounters resistance at every step along its path. As the heat builds, so too does resistance. Higher resistance, in turn, creates more heat. This vicious circle builds upon itself until the point of fatal breakdown is reached and components begin to fail. Semiconductors not only run at cooler temperatures, but their design eliminates a number of the points of resistance, thereby lessening heat. The reduction of resistance also had an unsuspected benefit. The shorter path resulting from the improved design allowed for slightly faster signal processing.[8]

After studying numerous possibilities, Bell researchers settled on silicon as the material of choice. Silicon proved to be problematic, as laboratory samples behaved inconsistently. Rectification, the ability to allow electric current to flow in only one direction, would occur randomly or not at all. The answer lay in the material itself. Raw silicon stock was produced in a special vacuum oven, formed in large blocks similar to loaves of bread, called ingots. Once solidified, the ingots would be allowed to cool. During this process, minute amounts of impurities would crystallize in the coal-black silicon. Scientists recognized that the puzzling variances of the test samples were caused by the contaminating elements.

As the chemistry of silicon was slowly mastered, the contaminants boron and phosphorus were identified. Bell Laboratories invented an industrial process to cast silicon from a single crystal, in which the unwanted contaminating elements were reduced to 1/1000th of one percent. The addition of controlled amounts of boron was found to be beneficial in that it enhanced conductivity and reduced the incidence of component failure. Added to pure silicon during crystallization, this process became known as doping. With additional research, the performance of the crystal was further manipulated with trace amounts of aluminum, antimony, arsenic and beryllium.

In addition to those elements, germanium showed promise. As common as silicon, germanium had the added benefit of greater conductivity. The electrical charge required for electrons to move to subsequent elemental atoms is substantially less.

In fact, a component made from germanium could do the same amount of work as a comparable silicon structure with less than half the energy. This also meant that the germanium crystal had roughly twice the life of silicon.

Silicon rectifiers were developed to go into radar sets for aircraft, submarines, and artillery shells, and for electronic applications such as miniaturized radios. Once these units were perfected enough to be standardized production items, there was a sense of relief. Now, with a little more time to work with semiconductors, scientists began to think about new applications of the new materials. One device that could likely be improved upon was the triode. Similar to the diode, the triode had an extra-energized "grid"—it looked very much like a piece of window screen, smaller than a postage stamp—that allowed for significant amplification of electrical signals. However, solid-state devices such as the silicon diode allowed little room to copy the designs of vacuum tubes like the triode. A whole new method of manufacture had to be invented.

The challenge was accepted at Bell Laboratories in Murray Hill, New Jersey. Several months before the end of the war, Bell Laboratory scientists William Shockley, John Bardeen, and Russell Ohl teamed up to tackle the solid-state devices project. Reviewing the basic concept and the work done to date, they soon had designed a crude solid-state device that, on paper, appeared to modulate the electron flow, just as a triode did. In practice, though, their gizmo obstinately refused to operate. The addition of Walter Brattain to the team in October 1945 lent new perspective to the problems, and the team returned to studying the basic principles of semiconductors. This meant looking hard at the research done on silicon and germanium. The group spent the next two years refining their semiconductor-based triode. On June 30, 1948, Brattain and Bardeen were presented to the press along with the first public demonstration of their device, the point-contact germanium transistor.

Unreliable and difficult to manufacture, the transistor nevertheless was a boon to modern electronics. Hundreds of the tiny metal cans with three wires protruding could fit in the same area that one glass tube triode would occupy. Other transistors were to come. The junction transistor, necessary for the modern computer, was released in 1949. Soon after, Texas Instruments introduced the silicon transistor, cheaper to manufacture and better suited for portable use. Miniature appliances such as radios, not much larger than a pack of cigarettes, began to show up on the market.

In 1958, Brattain, Bardeen, and Shockley shared the Nobel Prize for physics. Little could they know that within forty years, the idea of modern life would revolve around the electron speeding through wafers made of silicon originally proposed by the trio. Although silicon is still widely used, other semiconductor metals have been successfully used as well. Exotics such as indium, gallium, cadmium, and tellurium are alloyed with other, similar, elements to increase processing speeds of computer chips.

Electronic assemblies have made quantum advances since the days when transistors were built by hand. Super-miniaturization, made possible with the advent of chemical etching, vapor deposition, and multi-layer substrate construction have been joined with surface mount technology to produce transistors smaller than the period at the end of this sentence. Without a doubt, electronics, born from the need to see bombers before they were overhead, has transformed our society.

Computers

Conceived and constructed as a mechanical way to perform mathematical calculations, the first true machine to operate semi-automatically was the adding machine built by Pascal in the seventeenth century. Although able to carry tens forward in addition or subtraction, the gear-driven box was a far cry from the computer.

Nearly two hundred years passed before the next computer predecessor made its appearance. With support from the British Admiralty, Charles Babbage designed a "differential engine" to solve navigation problems in the mid-18th century. No more than an advanced calculator, the machine featured programming language devised by Lady Lovelace, daughter of Lord Byron. It could, like Pascal's machine, do mathematical functions, and it had a memory for collating data. A system to input data was adopted using stiff paper sheets with holes punched through at specific points that relayed the information. This idea had been successfully employed twenty years earlier when a loom was built in France that used similar punch cards to change the weave pattern and would last well into the twentieth century as punch cards. Escalating costs and difficulties encountered with available technology killed the differential engine project before it got built.

Built to count the 1890 American census forms, Herman Hollerith based his "computer" on the weaving loom and the differential engine. Using the punch cards proposed seventy years prior, the responses to census questions were represented by holes in the cards. Fed into the electromechanical "tabulator," the holes would align with pins that fell through, striking an electrical contact. The various connections would record the results of the data gathered, and from this the census was completed in six weeks rather than the six years that was the previous average. The machine was a remarkable step. It revolutionized the business community, which used variations upon the theme for accounting and record keeping. The Hollerith Tabulator Company would eventually become the business giant International Business Machines (IBM).

There was a profusion of electro-mechanical computers in a handful of countries in the 1930s, with no less than ten machines under construction by private companies and governments. A proliferation of technology led to a great need for mathematical calculations for everything from astronomy and artillery ballistics to the infant specialty of quantum physics. One of the more memorable early computers forecast the war. IBM soon claimed the lion's share of the office business machinery and looked to the computer as a logical extension of their company.

Representing a giant step forward, the Harvard Mark I computer was finished in 1943, after seven years of planning and building. Still reliant on mechanical action, the five-ton monster had over 750,000 parts and could do three functions in a second. The programming was dependent on gear drive and a paper strip that contained the now familiar punched holes. The impressive aspect of the Harvard machine was that it could run automatically. Set to work on naval architecture tables, it worked for the next fifteen years.

Of a similar design, the British secretly constructed a computer for breaking the German "Enigma" code. This code, which was thought by its creators to be absolutely unbreakable, was used for nearly all the military radio traffic emanating from the German Reich. Before the war, in 1929, Polish intelligence stole a copy of an Enigma machine from the Germans. This complex machine used a series of thumb-wheels that set the code. The setting of the wheels is determined by a "key" of five letters issued in a code book. A German spy had given some of the early keys up, for a price, and other keys were captured later in the war. Through these two avenues, enough messages had been decoded, providing a pattern that a computer could use as a model.

Named for its stately rural home, the electromechanical Bletchley Park computer was used to decode the mass of radio signals sent out daily. Even without knowing the exact keys, the Bletchley Park computer could take a coded message and, in a matter of minutes, have the complete, clear language text available for the translators. The project was of the highest classification and disguised under the code name "Ultra."

Another computer of note developed during the war was the Electronic Numerical Integrator and Computer (ENIAC). This machine was developed from a series of special-purpose machines in high demand for war work. With the onset of hostilities, the U.S. Army found itself having to accelerate development of artillery shells and the corresponding ballistics tables.

Prior to the war, women worked at a leisurely pace producing sheets of numbers that artillery gunners used to set their weapons to fire at distant targets and be reasonably sure that the rounds were hitting the mark. Seven different variables could affect the trajectory of any given shell, and each variable had to be accounted for in the tables. Each table anticipated approximately three thousand different gun settings and ranges, each with its own unique value.

To create the table, the women, who were actually called "computers," would be issued a tabletop mechanical adding machine and a series of known values for the particular shell. Through formulas devised for the specific variables, a set of forms constituting the firing tables was filled out. The typical table could employ a hundred of the human computers for a month, as each calculated entry took one to two days. This enormous amount of time delayed the fielding of the new arms coming from the factories at an ever-increasing pace.

To remedy the bottleneck, John Mauchly, assistant professor at the Moore School of Electrical Engineering at the University of Pennsylvania, suggested the design and construction of ENIAC. Having design elements of its predecessors, ENIAC would feature 1,500 relays, 6,000 switches, 10,000 capacitors, 70,000 resistors and 18,000 vacuum tubes. Intended to perform 5,000 calculations per second, ENIAC would quickly outrun the punched-paper programming. Instead, the programming was done with interconnecting wire sets that could be plugged into different receptacles, much like an old-fashioned telephone switchboard. This method was to prove tedious and time consuming, but the totally electronic ENIAC could run calculating circles around the electromechanical machines, even the Bletchley Park monster.

ENIAC was completed in November of 1945, far too late to be of service in the war. Working two shifts a day, workers had taken two and a half years to build the fifty-ton giant, using up 15,000 square feet of space. One rumor has it that the lights of Philadelphia dimmed when ENIAC was first energized. With its thousands of inefficient electrical components, ENIAC produced one hundred and fifty kilowatts of waste heat. This hourly consumption is equivalent to what a normal, present-day home

Two operaters of the gigantic ENIAC computer. The machine occupied thje space of a small contemporary house. The cables are part of the process of programing it. (NARA)

consumes in roughly four days.

Even before ENIAC was finished, the engineers of Moore, now joined by John Von Neumann from the atomic bomb project, proposed a better version of the computer. ENIAC had several shortcomings that rendered it nearly useless for the higher mathematics that were beginning to be used in the rapidly expanding physics research taking place in New Mexico. ENIAC's biggest problem lay in its relatively tiny data storage and the mass of hardware needed to control it. Ten thousand of the 18,000 tubes involved in ENIAC inner workings were solely devoted to storing one thousand single-digit numbers—125 bytes in modern computer language.

Purely a paper project, the new machine, Electronic Discrete Variable Automatic Computer (EDVAC), offered many of the characteristics that would shape the modern computer. The first to use binary numbers, its memory—the term was coined during EDVAC's design phase to visualize an anthropomorphic comparison—would be eight times that of ENIAC. The logical layout of EDVAC foreshadowed that of future computers. The memory would serve as the heart of the machine, while all information, input and output, was routed through this central core. A separate arithmetic unit would function as a calculator, similar to the modern math coprocessor. A control unit would be able to interpret instructions from the memory, not unlike the way the processor functions in performing instructions from the disk operating system. This style of computer construction has become known as "the Von Neumann architecture," and the term has entered in to the lexicon of computerese.

Computers have obviously become far more sophisticated and so commonplace that it is practically impossible not to own a computer. Most appliances have elements of computer technology, as do many toys, TVs, stereos and clocks. Not a single American automobile built since the mid-1970s has appeared without an onboard computer to monitor and regulate engine functions to control emissions. The uses and application of computer technology could fill volumes, many in arcane and surprising places, and far too many to be included here.[9]

Television

Electronics has brought another appliance into the home that, although not vital to our lives, has shaped our tastes in entertainment and our views of the world and has educated us all. The glow of the picture tube really had its beginnings in the 1800s with the discovery of photosensitive elements. Selenium was the first of these, but a number of others were found to be more efficient as the years went by.

The success of the telegraph led inventors to want to transmit pictures over wire. A series of contraptions to "see by telegraphy" were designed using selenium, but the material just did not lend itself to the rapid electrical changes needed to duplicate a moving image. Many of these contraptions faded into obscurity, while a notable few offered ideas that would prove to be stepping-stones to the development of television.

One of these was the method of creating the image called scanning. Basically, the image was illuminated through a rotating disc perforated with a spiral of holes. Each hole would pass over a portion of the image, the light and dark areas in that portion creating a change in voltage of the selenium pickup. As each successive hole passed over the image, another section would be viewed by the pickup. This process would systematically cover a whole image, as one would read a written page. The Nipkow disk, as this German invention was called, had serious defects but was still rushed into use as a propaganda tool in 1935, so that the Nazis could lay claim to having the first television service. The principle of scanning is still in use today, although it is done electronically. By controlling the electron stream with magnetic coils placed in the throat of the picture tube, the electron beam moves line by horizontal line, across the picture screen. This is analogous to how our eyes move across the printed page, reading each line before moving onto the next one. However, television scanning moves much faster, up to one line every .0001 seconds.

The failure of selenium did little to dampen enthusiasm, as advances in technology began to fill in the voids. The discoveries of the cathode-induced rays and the working cathode ray tube between the years 1876 and 1897 formed the next step for the television. The electron stream could be steered inside its vacuum tube by magnetic coils. Coating the inside end-face of the tube with a luminescent powder, the electrons would create a phosphorescent glow as they struck this surface.

A crude form of this system was displayed for limited audiences by at least three inventors in the 1920s. Primarily to gain financial support for their projects, the hopeful television pioneers emphasized the amount of work that was still required. The exhibitions went off as planned, but the picture quality was poor. Lacking a sense of achievement, the prospective investors left unimpressed. Undaunted, the inventors returned to work, but mostly abandoned the electronic approach in favor of the mechanical disc. The electronic method was not to die so easily, though.

Throughout the 1920s, new entrants into television produced their own versions of the electronic marvel. Their work, however, was overshadowed by the apparent success of the mechanical machines. Forced into marketing by public demand and entrepreneurial desires to recoup some of the huge investment, the smart business people were going with what worked.

In what would become a race to develop television in the United States, Philo Farnsworth found himself pitted against the Radio Corporation of America (RCA) in the persona of Russian immigrant Vladimir Zworykin. Farnsworth had precociously read and studied physics, electronics and chemistry while still a freshman in high school. As a teenage boy living on an Idaho farm, he had visualized television while doing his chores. He managed to gain sponsorship money from a number of individuals and set up a threadbare shop in San Francisco. It was here that he and his team of hired technicians developed television into reality. Over the next five years, he quietly invented a majority of the components that would eventually make television a household fixture.

For instance, the large, slightly convex television screen face is an innovation that came from the Farnsworth labs. He also devised the original electron multiplier, then called a multipactor tube, that increased the strength of the electron beam by ricocheting the electron stream off a series of plates. The resulting impact gave off more electrons than merely striking it did, a kind of chain reaction that built on itself. Electron multipliers are commonly found in large outdoor television sets even today.

Zworykin, on the other hand, built the Kinescope in August of 1929. This glass tube would be the premier picture tube design for the next sixty years. Shaped like a bell, the electron source is located in the narrow neck of the tube. At the base of the tube is a cathode, simply a tiny heater placed within a cup and coated with a chemical compound that releases electrons as the temperature increases. The electrons rocket away from the cathode and pass through a series of apertures in focusing grids connected to control circuitry. This control circuitry carefully tunes the polarity and voltage at the different grids, causing the electron stream to condense to a fine shaft. As the neck of the picture tube begins to widen, a large electromagnet placed on the outside of the glass imparts a field that

This is a nine inch Bush Model TV12 television from 1948. The cabinet was made from Bakelite. Television stations were few at this time, but that did not matter to the viewers of this set. It only got one channel.

136

steers the electron beam horizontally or vertically to collide with the front coating of the tube face, causing it to glow. The previously mentioned scanning process is replicated electronically, the picture being reproduced on the screen one line at a time. Thus, the basic television receiver was finished.

The television camera worked in much the same way, although the image to be transmitted had to be converted into an electric signal. To allow this, the subject had to be brightly lit and the reflected light waves "seen" by a plate coated with light-sensitive potassium hydride. The darker shades created less voltage and the lighter ones more. An analog value was placed upon that particular segment of the plate. Since each spot on the plate had a discrete location, the scanning pattern could copy the image and send the resulting electrical signal to the receiver.

Developing television from the first working laboratory models still required another five years of hard work and trials. By combining the best of Farnsworth's and Zworykin's ideas, RCA prepared to begin TV broadcasts in 1940. The first all-electronic commercial sets were offered for sale in July of 1941 when the Federal Communications Commission (FCC) finalized the standard frequencies and relevant technical details. In just a few short months, America was at war with Japan and television took a backseat to war production priorities. A few sets were used at the Hanford, Washington processing site of the Manhattan Project. Once the plant was operational, producing highly poisonous plutonium, maintenance crews were required to perform their duties by means of remote control, and TV sets allowed them to see the otherwise unapproachable work spaces. Allied and Axis engineers alike experimented with television mounted in the noses of unmanned missiles.

One project featured rocket-pro-

Its not a flat screen but this view of a bridge and gasoline storage tank is more remarkable in that it is from the nose of an American bomber flying up the Potomac River. By 1945, electronics had achieved impressive advancements that were gong to change the post-war world. (U.S. Navy/Radio Corporation of America)

pelled bombs. Travelling at 550 miles-an-hour, the "Gorgon" carried an RCA television camera and transmitter capable of sending the signal nearly 200 miles. Old, worn-out B-17 bombers were also converted into gigantic, TV-guided missiles, a program that was wisely dropped. In 1946, television cameras recorded the nuclear bomb tests at Bikini Atoll.

Color Television

In 1940, at about the same time that the government was holding hearings on whether to allow commercial monochromatic television broadcasts, an engineer from Columbia Broadcasting System (CBS) announced that his company had successfully tested a color TV. Not truly electronic, this device used a rotating disc with the three basic color filters spinning at a synchronized pace with the pattern scanning. By reversing the process at the set, the color picture was achieved.

Like black-and-white TV, the war interrupted the introduction of the color TV set, but after World War Two had ended, another war would begin over which company would have its system adopted by the government as standard. CBS and RCA, both competing for the lucrative color market, tried to get support for their respective color processes. CBS was actually allowed to test theirs briefly before the war, but the FCC tossed out RCA's suggestion to develop electronic color. On October 10, 1950, CBS was permitted to begin color television broadcasts.

The post-war period became the Golden Age for television. Depression-era studio equipment was dusted off and civilians, their pockets bulging with cash from war work, rushed out to buy the newest sets. A whole culture formed around the glow of the tiny picture tube, as the new medium of entertainment entered the home. Owning one became a symbol of affluence, only to be overshadowed when color sets become available. New variations on the same theme were offered: portables, giant screens, special sound systems and miniaturized sets that fit in the palm of the hand. The computer offered new markets for set manufacturers. Now, after sixty-plus years of use, television is beginning the new century with the advent of digital signal and flat-panel screens. In a few years, the Farnsworth picture tube will be a relic, as will all of the other technology that made it work.

The Oscilloscope

Part of the performance increase in World War Two aircraft came from the high intensity ignition systems that were developed just prior to the war. But on the downside, these systems also required far more maintenance when they went "poof." Hence, the oscilloscope left the laboratory and became a diagnostic tool for the mechanic.

Basically, an oscilloscope is a television set that can get picture signals from the actions of electron fluctuations in electrical devices. The first application of an oscilloscope occurred in 1942 with the P-47 Thunderbolt. The massive Pratt & Whitney engines ran erratically, and everyone was certain that the problem was the ignition system. Westinghouse engineers adapted an oscilloscope to read and record the activities of the complex spark patterns and their changing voltages. After careful analysis, it was recognized that the spark wires had miniscule bubbles in the insulation, which allowed the current to leak. Production problems were soon fixed at the wire plants and the "Jugs" were on their way to war.

With this victory, the oscilloscope gained huge recognition. Oscilloscope technology abounded, and specially trained technicians were in great demand. This was particularly true with the introduction of the B-29. Its four engines were notorious for their sensitivity to fires as many of the parts were made from flammable magnesium alloys. A late or early ignition spark could create overheating that would turn the bomber into a flying inferno. Each and every B-29 had a single "scope" in the flight engineers

The research that achieved radar, VT fuses, dozens of radio devices, even the atomic bomb all required special diagnostic equipment such as this oscilloscope variation, a synchroscope, was vital to the technician or engineer. Electrical signals were wired into the unit and formed a trace on the small cathode ray tube. Based on what the trace did, trouble, or lack of it, could be deciphered. (WPB)

position that could be tuned to any or all engines. By reading the scope data, the flight engineer could manipulate the controls back to optimum performance.

This was especially critical for the long flights over open ocean where the big bombers flew near the limit of their range. With a scope onboard, the engineer could stretch the fuel supply to new extremes, balancing the engines on the razor's edge between overheating and wasting precious fuel, bringing home airplanes and crew that would have otherwise been lost.

Frequency Modulated (FM) Radio

As previously stated, radio created a revolution in communications. Crystal radios were built by children in the 1920s to enable them to not only learn about the new science but to possibly catch their favorite radio shows featuring Little Orphan Annie or The Shadow. By 1928, radio technology had progressed to the point where regenerative feedback circuits had been invented. Feedback is a phenomenon that amplifies the incoming signal by cycling a portion of the radio wave through an amplifier. From there, the signal immediately travels back into the receiver to begin the process over again, constantly and continuously building upon itself. An example of modern feedback amplification is the bothersome screech from an improperly tuned microphone.

The radios of the day, broadcasting from fairly weak transmitters, were enslaved by the vagaries of atmospheric and meteorological conditions. Regenerative circuitry did little to eliminate interference. Even the use of one of the newly introduced household appliances could turn radio reception into a cacophony of ear jarring static.

RCA engineers determined to eliminate static altogether, and asked the independent inventor of the feedback circuit, Major Edwin H. Armstrong, to come up with a solution. By 1933, Armstrong had built a "little magic box" that exceeded all expectations. Displaying the device to an RCA executive, Armstrong showed that not only did the invention work, but the overall quality of the sound was greatly enhanced. Instead of working within the limitations of the contemporary radio, he had created a new way to broadcast the signal.

All radio, from Marconi on, has transmitted an electromagnetic wave that carries out to any tuned-in receiving antennas within range. Acting as a carrier for the broadcast voices and music, the wave undulates at a specific intensity. Devoid of any messages, the wave's intensity does not change until a supplementary signal is added in the form of an actor's voice or music.

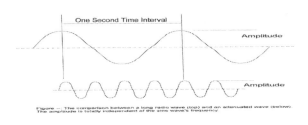

The comparison between a long wave radio wave (top) and an attenuated—short—wave (below). The amplitude is totally independent of the sine wave's frequency. (Author)

140

Then, the wave's intensity will increase in relationship to the tone and strength of the added signal. Known as amplitude modulation (AM), this change of signal is mimicked in nature by lightning and the magnetic fields produced by household appliances, hence static. Armstrong's radio changed the distance between the high points of the radio wave, the frequency, to remove the static. By modulating the frequency, he confronted popular belief that such a system was impossible. The frequency modulated (FM) wave would gradually change frequency as the sound source changed volume. The receiver, wired to look for this frequency variation, would reliably translate the waves back to sound without the interference experienced on AM signals.[10]

RCA provided Armstrong with facilities to begin testing the system in a studio in the Empire State Building where, for barely a year, the work progressed. Abruptly, in 1939, RCA dropped FM radio in favor of another broadcast medium, television. Armstrong continued developing FM on his own, and stations began operation in early 1940. The war interrupted the wholesale proliferation of commercial stations, but the military adopted FM for some of their communications systems. For Armstrong, the popularity of FM was a hollow victory because he was in a perpetual dispute with RCA over patent rights. Finally, after nineteen years of legal and business squabbles and nearly penniless, he committed suicide.[11]

Presently, FM and AM stations live together harmoniously, sometimes one or both broadcasting mediums being operated in a market area by the same company. AM still can reach farther than FM because the frequency tends to get a "bounce" off the ionosphere. FM, on the other hand, provides a better sound and is preferred for music, especially in heavily industrialized countries where the proliferation of electric interference is substantially larger.

This is rare shot of the inside of an American M-4 half-track with both tactical radios. The one on the right (the large grey, two box unit) is an AM SCR-193 and a FM SCR-510 (the black one on the left). It is easy to see the difference in size. Yet the FM radio could be used further with voice transmission and was immune to weather and electrical interference. (U.S. Army Signal Corps)

The Electron Microscope

Zacharias Janssen is credited with having invented the compound microscope in about 1590, and Leeuwenhoek invented the first practical, high-resolution microscope in the seventeenth century. Leeuwenhoek studied spermatozoa, blood, and muscle tissue, among other items, revolutionizing science. For the next two hundred years, few changes to the basic lens system invented by the Dutch cloth merchant occurred. Then, in 1935, the first commercial electron microscopes were built, inspired by French physicist Louis de Broglie. In 1924, he suggested that electron beams might behave in a manner similar to light. He also reasoned that the actual wavelength of such a beam would be much shorter than that of a beam of light.

The electron microscope illuminates with a beam of electrons rather than light. Electrons are generated using a hot tungsten filament in an electron gun mounted at the top of the microscope cylinder. The cylinder, housing the lenses, the specimen chamber, and the image-recording system, holds a vacuum, as the electron beam cannot be concentrated and the filament will burn out in an atmosphere.

Two types of electron lenses are used, electrostatic and electromagnetic. They create electric and electromagnetic fields both to concentrate and to move the beam. The magnification in magnetic electron microscopes is determined by the strength of the current passing through the lens coils

Changing the current through the objective lens coil focuses the image. In the optical microscope the image is determined by absorption of light by the specimen; in the electron microscope the image results from a scattering of electrons by atoms of the specimen. Since an atom with a high atomic number scatters electrons more than does a lighter atom, the former appears darker. As the beam passes against a specimen, each tiny variation in the structure of the specimen causes a variation in the electron stream. The image produced is then projected onto a fluorescent screen or recorded on film. The electron microscope, with its tremendous resolving power, can magnify specimens over 50,000 times.

During the war, electron microscopes were widely used in the medical and physical sciences. As interest grew in biological studies such as that associated with antibiotics, the electron microscope became a valuable tool. In Germany, the only electron microscope was used to study everything from metal samples for experimental aircraft to nuclear energy research.

The invention of the electron microscope revolutionized microbiology. For the first time, researchers could see virus cells in detail, providing important clues to possible ways to defeat them. Other uses of the electron microscope include research into genetics, parasitology, and pathology, to name a few. The improvements in the scanning electron microscope have resolution and coloration, but the contemporary design is still based on the 1935 machine.

Magnetic Recording Tape

Originally, possession of a telephone was a sign of high status. Naturally, a person important enough to own such a device should not be required to stand guard over it, waiting calls from other important people. Such was the reasoning of Valdemar Poulsen, the Danish inventor of the telephone answering machine.

Patented in 1900, the Poulsen machine featured a steel wire that could be magnetized. The variances in the magnetic field on the wire directly corresponded to the amplitude of the signal. In addition to the wire, Poulsen used the same principle for recording to a disc and steel tape. Although the idea had merit, there was no demand for it.

Slowly, businesses in 1920s Europe adopted Poulsen's recorder for dictation and telephone messages. Still relying on wire, the newer machines incorporated newly developed electronic amplifier circuitry. This greatly improved the sound and reproduction quality. However, the wire tended to get brittle and break, usually at the most inopportune times.

In 1933, AEG and BASF, the latter then a division of the German mega-corporation I.G. Farben joined forces to create an alternative to the wire recorder. They began with the idea of applying a coat of iron oxide powder lacquered to paper tape as suggested by Austrian Fritz Pfleumer in 1928. AEG engineers built the first machine, called the K1, to use this tape in 1935. A later version, the Magnetophon, built by German electronics firm Telefunken gained the attention of the Nazi's Propaganda Ministry. They saw the potential of the high fidelity recorders and bought several for use in German radio stations to rebroadcast speeches, news reports and music.

During the war, the recorders were responsible for some serious puzzlement on the part of Allied intelligence specialists. Radio monitors regularly tuned into German broadcasts for a broad range of information. Who was where, who was doing whatever, and it all went to build an intelligence picture that might give the Allies an edge. Monitors began to notice that senior Nazis appeared to be in three or more places at the same time give the same speech. Short of developing time travel, intelligence officers determined that the Germans had perfected some sort of recorder that paralleled the quality of live broadcast.

After the war, several hundred technically trained men were tasked with searching out the secrets of German technology. One of these was an Army Signal Corps soldier named John T. (Jack) Mullin. He thought he was on a hot trail of a rumored German device that was supposed to fire an electromagnetic pulse at aircraft to interfere with its ignition system. In a radio studio near Frankfurt, he saw his first Magnetophon. As an audio engineer back in civilian life, he recognized what he had and managed to get two machines and fifty roles of recording tape. Once home, he worked non-stop for two years perfecting and tinkering with the machine. His dream was to get Hollywood studios to adopt the new technology, which he would just happen to own. But events had already transpired to undermine that dream.

As already stated, radio stations across Europe were equipped with Magnetophons. One of these stations was Radio Luxembourg, which had been seized by the German army in its drive westward in 1940. The station was notable because it had one of the most powerful transmitters in Europe. German propagandists used the facility to broadcast the width and breadth of the conquered continent. Much of the material, by necessity, had been pre-recorded on magnetic tape.

In the fall of 1944, American soldiers captured the station intact. One of the officers assigned to oversee the operation of the station was John Herbert Orr. A self-educated electrical engineer, Orr was part of the Psychological Operations department of Eisenhower's Headquarters. Orr was impressed with the fidelity and simplicity of the Magnetophon. His natural interest in electronics inspired him to search out the scientists behind the technology and he eventually tracked down Fritz Pfleumer. Pfleumer was happy to supply all of the documentation and research material to Orr who then transferred this treasure trove of knowledge home. Not knowing about Jack Mullin, Orr setup a factory in Opelika, Alabama to make magnetic tape. It would not be long though, before Orr found out about him.

In California, Jack Mullin was making rounds to several studios demonstrating his Magnetophon to executives. At the second studio, Murdo Mackenzie, the technical director for Bing Crosby was in the audience. Bing, probably the most successful singer/actor in Hollywood at this time, was not happy with his present situation. His contract with NBC called for his live radio performance 39 weeks a year. Besides the onerous schedule, the work of a live show was very stressful. Bing had been asking to incorporate several new types of recording technology but nothing delivered the same crispness that live broadcasting did. Mackenzie arranged for Mullin to give Bing a personal demonstration, who then presented the Magnetophon to his studio bosses.

They agreed on a trial. On October 1, 1947, Bing Crosby sang his season premier and the Magnetophon got its American debut. Soon, the advantages of tape became obvious. Splice editing allowed for the removal of bloopers, technical glitches and permitted pacing the show better. It also created the ability to employ "canned" laughter. But Orr and Mullins were not alone.

Alexander Poniatoff, a Russian émigré and electrical engineer who had spent the war developing airborne radar for the U.S. Navy, came home and founded his own company, AMPEX, in 1944. The company built generators, motors for the Navy and commercial heater fan motors, but real interest lay in audio equipment.

Not long after the end of the war, work began on audio tape recording machines based on the same Telefunken machines that Orr discovered in Europe. Poniatoff was instrumental in developing a professional quality magnetic tape recorder using the latest advancements in electronics manufacturing. Not surprisingly, singer Bing Crosby, who desired the best equipment possible, supported Poniatoff with a $50,000 investment and an order for 60 machines. In later years, AMPEX would be instrumental in developing video recording. As early as 1948, television broadcasters began to experiment with magnetic tape to store video data. The early videotapes were specially made two-inch-wide tapes that had been subjected to elaborate quality specifications. This tape, in a much narrower form would go on into the 1980s as the Betamax and Video Home System (VHS) recorders.[12]

With the growing popularity of magnetic tape recording, wire recorders died a slow, agonizing death. Various alloys and coatings were tried with limited success. As fine as a human hair, the wire tended to tangle and kink, leading to more breakage. Like open spools of recalcitrant thread, the wire routinely unwound itself to fall around the drive capstans while loading. This problem was addressed by the introduction of the cassette case. Now enclosed, the wire could be easily handled without direct hand contact. However, there were never any real long-term solutions to the fragility of wire and magnetic tape continued to gain popularity.

Bing Crosby's support went a long way to dooming wire recorders within the professional recording industry. Multi-track magnetic recorders, a development devised by AMPEX, allowed for a revolution in music recording. Each track reproduced the input from an individual microphone. This permitted the recording engineers to adjust the tonal qualities of a single instrument without disturbing the other tracks.

The closely linked movie industry embraced plastic recording media not just for its fidelity but because it made synchronizing the sound track with the film easier. Since the photographic film was made of essentially the same material as the recording tape, it was simple to manufacture raw film stock with a few minor changes in production methods.

Borrowing the technology of the recording industry, the eight-track tape would carry the quality of high fidelity sound into an easily carried package. In the early 1970s, the eight-track soon gave way to the diminutive cassette tape that would eventually lose dominance to the Compact Disc (CD).

By the late 1940s, the blossoming computer industry needed a means of storing data in an easily handled medium. Magnetic tape made by 3M and other companies proved to be the perfect choice. Large reels of tape weighing several pounds held thousands of bits of information for years until the flat 5¼-inch disc replaced it. As the iron oxide chemistry and production improved, more data could be compressed into a smaller space. The successor to the "floppy" discs, now 3½ inches and mounted in a hard plastic case, is still called by the misleading name. The days of the magnetic computer disc are now numbered as recordable CDs have become the exclusive media.

Most modern shoppers carry samples of the German tape in wallet or purse. On the back of every credit card is a strip of tape that is magnetically loaded with information about the owner. The ease and convenience of debit and credit cards are such that cash purchases are predicted eventually to disappear.[13]

Notes/Selected References

1   Buderi, Robert. *The Invention That Changed The World*. 1996. P. 53.
2   Pawle, Gerald. Secret Weapons of World War II. 1957. Pp.70-75.
3   Buderi, Robert. P. 55
4   An acronym for **RA**dio **D**etection **A**nd **R**anging, first contrived in 1940 by the U.S. Navy.
5   Buderi, Robert. Pp.56-89.
6   Pawle, Gerald. P. 123.
7   Panati, Charles. *Extraordinary Origins of Everyday Things*. 1987. Pp. 125-126.
8   Veatch, Henry C. *Transistor Circuit Action*. 1968. Pp.1-10.
9   Campbell-Kelly, Martin and Aspray, William. *Computer: A History of the Information Machine*. 1996. Riordan, Michael and Lillian Hoddeson. *Crystal Fire, The Birth of the Information Age*. 1997.
10 Riordan, Michael. Pp. 6-7.
11 ibid. P. 243.

12 Ampex Corporation: www.fundinguniverse.com/company-histories/Ampex-Corporation-company-history.ht.

13 Katz, Ephriam. *The Film Encyclopedia.* 1994. P. 1271. Morton, David. John Herbert Orr, tape recording pioneer, and founder of Orradio Industries, Inc.: www.rci.rutgers.edu/~dmorton/orradio. and Morton, David. *The Chronology of Recording Tape.* and www.rci.rutgers.edu/~dmorton/minifon. and www.rci.rutgers.edu/~dmorton/wire.

4

From the New Deal to the United Nations: Social Changes

The Depression of the 1930s and the war less than a decade later brought about more than technological change. The entire social fabric that was torn apart by the failed economy had barely begun to mend when the Second World War erupted. Just prior to the war, America was enjoying a second industrial revolution and the cities were beginning to expand while the agrarian sections of the country were benefiting from the proliferation of new machinery and practices. As America was drawn into the war, parents saw their sons and daughters going off to fight in yet another foreign war, and young husbands reluctantly separated from their wives. Families, having just settled into new communities and lives, were uprooted again to pursue high wages in the defense industry plants that were sprouting up across the country.

New laws sponsored by Franklin Roosevelt to stabilize the financial crises became a standard for the next fifty plus years of legislation. New Deal programs touched upon every facet of American life, affecting the way business was conducted, making comfortable retirement possible, controlling crop production, and lighting the remotest farms. The arts got a boost from Roosevelt who created programs supporting writers, photographers, and artists.

The shortages of manpower, food, and fuel, and the breakdown of the family organization during the war led to further alterations of the way society viewed itself and behaved. Absent parents, having gone to war in the foxhole or the factory left a whole generation to fend for itself. This set a precedent for later generations to drift

BOOKS ARE WEAPONS IN THE WAR OF IDEAS

"... where books are burnt, human-beings will be burnt in the end." Heinrich Heine, German poet, 1820.

further away from the familial bond, often with lamentable consequences. Only recently has the family unit begun to regain importance and priority in America.

Women in the Workplace

Probably the greatest single social gain from the war years was the foothold that women achieved in employment. Whether it was on the factory floor, behind the manager's desk, in uniform, or at the controls of an airliner, women were accepted, sometimes grudgingly, at work and for the most part they have remained there. Prior to this time, the common notion that the woman's place was in the home was universally accepted in all industrialized nations.

Past wars had always allowed for women to do their part, usually taking over the operations of the family farm. During the American Civil War, the creation of the American Red Cross opened the door to women who served as nurses to the innumerable sick and wounded of both sides, and this practice continued during the wars to follow. The women of frontier America got the opportunity to take on man's work, such as riding the range, working with the livestock and serving on

Mrs. Virginia Young (in hat) confers with fellow war widow Ethel Mann. Both women have found a certain amount of personal vengeance for their husbands in taking jobs where they could have a direct effect in the war effort at the Assembly and Repairs Department of the Corpus Christie Naval Air Station in Texas. Mrs. Young was one of the first war-widows of the war, her husband dying in the attack on Pearl Harbor. (FDRLPDC/NARA)

cattle drives, but these examples are out of the ordinary.

There were other ways that women could enter the workforce. Thousands of young women were accepted into certain businesses such as the textile industry. As the food industry grew, women were hired on as sorters and cleaners. But working beyond the age of 23 was considered to be socially limiting and nearly guaranteed a life of labor and spinsterhood. Women were expected to marry and have families.

The family at the turn of the century revolved around the home. Children, parents, and often grandparents all lived within the same community, if not in the same house. This arrangement gave the children a sense of group identity, security and having the mother at home stabilized the family even more. The desperate times of the Depression began to erode this idyllic picture as fathers moved on to find work, hoping to send for their families if times got better. During the Dust Bowl days of the mid-1930s, whole families moved from the Midwest to new states north and west. This upheaval put great pressure on the family as a whole, which had to make do or do without.

Class also played a part in this social structure. Judged in a large part on income, the lower the class, the more likely the women would be expected to take whatever employment was available. It was not unusual for an exploitive factory manager to place women in heavy, dangerous conditions that would be considered typically man's work. This is even more certain in that the boss is able to pay half (or less) of the male's pay rate.

Women had already gained a small toehold in the factories, although most often through the previously described method. That was about to change. The newly formed electronics industry, producing such items as radios, had quickly recognized that women could manipulate the small, delicate parts better than men could. Female caution and attention to detail had been a prized asset before the

SUBJECT: MACHINE SHOP WAGE AND HOUR SURVEY

DATE: March 1, 1943

NUMBER OF FIRMS PARTICIPATING: 44

NUMBER OF EMPLOYEES REPRESENTED: 18,729

TOTAL WEEKLY MAN HOURS REPRESENTED: 938,156

• • • • • •

NUMBER OF HOURS WORKED PER WEEK ALL CLASSIFICATIONS:

MALE:-	High: 79½	Low: 34½	*Average:	50.1
FEMALE:-	High: 58	Low: 40	*Average:	49.4
COMBINED:-	High: 79½	Low: 34½	*Average:	49.9

BASIC HOURLY RATES ALL CLASSIFICATIONS:

MALE:-	High: 1.73	Low: .40	*Average:	1.001
FEMALE:-	High: 1.80	Low: .40	*Average:	.743
COMBINED:-	High: 1.73	Low: .40	*Average:	.989

* All averages shown are weighted averages.

• • • • • •

—CONFIDENTIAL—

This document contains information affecting the national defense of the United States within the meaning of the Espionage Act, 50 U.S.C., 31 and 32. Its transmission or the revelation of its contents in any manner to an unauthorized person is prohibited by law.

• • • • • •

This survey conducted and compiled by A. Bertram Locke, Associated Industries of Minneapolis, under direct authorization of the United States War Department.

Women may have gotten their foot in the door for the better paying jobs but they still were second place when payday came. It was a step forward that the bottom scale was the same. (NARA) war in the few jobs available in the munitions industry. This certainly was an advancement, for until then, women were generally limited to office work, domestic help, food services, nursing, teaching, sales, and cosmetic services, all having little potential for advancement.

With some foresight, Roosevelt's policy of re-arming the military opened new opportunities to the men and set the basis for work-force requirements. The first jobs went to men, as even late-Depression-era unemployment was still quite high. When this group had occupied the best available occupations, the unemployed women, those who needed to work, began to fill whatever open positions that might be left. This category of women employees would also be able to fulfill the newly available job as more war industry plants opened. That was the basic employment practice until the United States entered the war.

After the Japanese attack on Pearl Harbor, the men patriotically swarmed to enlist, leaving vacancies in industry. This exodus, as well as newly created positions, drained the last remaining labor pool that desired to work. The only large group left was the full-time housewife who resisted or didn't need to work outside the home.

Thousands of young women sought jobs in the aircraft industry. The pay was adequate for them while their men were at war. Their clothing caused quite a stir in the early days of the war, but gained acceptance over time. The two are Ruby Reed (left rear) and Merle Judd of Grumman Aircraft. (OWI/NARA)

Mobilizing these women became a minor industry of its own. Appeals on the radio, in magazines, and by volunteer recruiters became commonplace. The federal government, operating through the U.S. Employment Service, urged, wheedled, challenged, and cajoled the resistant women to enroll in work programs. Primarily based on patriotic rhetoric, the ads lent an air of fear of the consequences of not joining in the production battle lines. Posters showing the multitude of ways that women could do their part also addressed issues such as retained femininity, overcoming loneliness, joining an elite group, and the emotional tag of supporting the son, brother, or husband away at war. This mass appeal was extremely successful. By 1945, the United States had some nineteen million women at work, up by sixty-three percent in five years.[1]

Louisville Ordnance plant. Women liked working in industry. They likened it to skills they used at home. Do not drop the baby; do not drop the shell. Nothing to it. (NARA)

Factory work was not the sole destination of these women. Many became police officers and firefighters, as well as pilots, truck drivers, miners, mechanics, loggers, and railroad equipment attendants. Heavy industries such as steel and shipbuilding, traditionally male-dominated bastions, began to have women on the job welding, cutting, riveting, and pouring molten steel into castings for tanks. The women proved that they could perform right alongside the men, often doing a better job than previously done by their stronger peers.

Another male bastion that fell during the war was in the field of sports. Philip Wrigley, the chewing gum magnate and owner of the Chicago Cubs, created the All-American Girls Professional Baseball League for the 1943 season. Women had actively participated in minor league softball for some years, but this was the first time that they would be seen playing hard-ball.

The women were required to play like the men but behave like ladies. Wrigley enlisted the assistance of Helen Rubenstein's finishing school to provide "social polish" to the ladies. Impeccable manners and feminine grace were stressed. Fines were established for infractions of the strict rules and codes of conduct. At least on one occasion, a player was called back to the dugout for not having her lipstick on.

At the height of their popularity, the eight teams—double that of the previous year's offering—attracted over a million fans. Wrigley tried to dump the women's teams at the end of the war but he was persuaded to turn the league over to his assistant who ran the league until 1954.

Domestic chores trained women to do many of industry's tasks. Mixing chemicals to be used for explosive ordnance was referred to as "no harder than putting the ingredients together to bake a cake."[2] Women who compared it to the patterns they had used to sew family garments cut intricate patterns out of metal sheet in record time. The same sharp eyes that located slivers in children's fingers could also spot minute defects at the inspection bench. One plant that needed extremely close filing on production parts resorted to hiring ex-manicurists for the job.

Men, even as cooks, salespeople, and office clerks had dominated the business world. Women replaced men in these jobs described as "essential civilian employment." Not nearly as glamorous or publicized as industrial work, this category accounted for the largest number of women who entered the work force, a five-fold increase. They tackled the necessary but mundane chores such as clerk/typists, cooks, and cab drivers.

Immediately after the war, many of these women became displaced by men returning home, although a large portion was glad to be finished so that they could resume their lives. Women who enjoyed the opportunities of working and the associated benefits were unceremoniously pushed out so that returning men could be employed.

Two women working on rework for a P-51 fighter. A lot of aircraft plants had large outdoor work areas that lacked sufficient illumination as above. Note that both are wearing plastic half-face shields, a recent addition to the new wealth of safety gear offered for workers. (NAA/ NARA)

The men tried to closet their women back at home, but the women would hardly remain there for long. For the duration of the 1950s saw a return to domestic roles for women. This trend lasted until the feminist movement began in the 1960s. With renewed desire for independence, women would completely integrate the workplace, forever changing the face of society. This did not occur overnight, nor without trials and tribulation. Sexual harassment, unequal pay, and familial responsibilities are still points of contention to be resolved, but women are at work to stay.[3]

Women in Uniform

Going to work in the factories was not the only destination for women. During the First World War, the U.S.Navy discovered that, although there was no precedent, regulations did not restrict women entering the armed forces. Accepted late in this war, approximately thirteen thousand women entered the Navy and the Marines Corps. Enlisting to do their part, most wound up doing laundry and typing.

The opening days of the Second World War brought women out to volunteer again. This time they were welcomed with open arms after only a minor struggle. The years between wars had seen a number of military reports praising females for their sense of duty and requesting that, in the future, women be accorded equal "rights, privileges and benefits as militarized men."[4] But these reports frequently could be found in the bottom of filing cabinets and rubbish cans. The military and Congress paid little heed to these official recommendations until they were forced to introduce legislation in the spring of 1941. Even then, despite popular support, the creation of the Women's Army Auxiliary Corps (WAACs) took a full year to pass, being signed by President Roosevelt on May 15, 1942. Hard on the WAAC's heels was the Navy version, the WAVES, and the Coast Guard's SPARS.[5] The Marines, avoiding any theatrical acronyms, simply called their female counterparts Marines. Vetran female marines sometimes use wams to describe themselves. The acronym translates to wide-ass marines.

This is a photo not seen often. Reserve Women Marines in what can be described as their take on Golden Gloves on board a Coast Guard-operated troop transport in the South Pacific. The lady Marines were expected to complete a combat training course that was similar to the obstacle course the men faced. (U.S. Navy)

When the recruiting stations opened on May 16, the recruiters were overwhelmed with women wanting to join. That one day's enlistment of thirteen thousand women nearly matched the total number of women who had participated in the First World War. Within three months, 110,000 women had requested entry into the WAACs and by the beginning of the new year, the WAACs were looking for another half million.

The multitude of women went to work at military jobs as diverse as in the civilian sector. They formed the core unit that perfected Air Traffic

Control, a method so new that when newspapers printed the story, three paragraphs were spent describing the job to readers. Many of the women took over jobs that had been filled by men, just as in the factories. Other positions were uniquely military in nature. Cryptographers, ordnance storekeepers, radar operators, and reconnaissance photo interpreters are just some roles that required skills not normally found in civilian life. Like industry, the military discovered that women had a knack for detailed tasks. At radio schools attended by both sexes, females routinely outscored men in reading code and repairing radios.

Enlistment was not limited to the lower ranks. Professional women were sought out at colleges and universities for a variety of jobs: psychologists to treat battle fatigue and wounded soldiers' mental states; civil engineers and architects to design new camps; physicians; engineers—the list goes on and on. Some of these WAAC officers so impressed their superiors that sixteen of them were sent to the Army's exclusive Command and General Staff College at Fort Leavenworth, Kansas, where they achieved staff rank of major or better.[6]

Women also played a part in flying aircraft for the military. Military aviation involving women began

WOMAN'S PLACE IN WAR
The Army of the United States has 239 kinds of jobs for women
THE WOMEN'S ARMY CORPS

The Woman's Army Corps (WACs) was proud of their ability to take over for the men in the rear areas and the Zone of the Interior (Army-speak for the Continental U.S.). This poster depicts a WAC repairing a radio with a soldering iron. (Records of the Office of Government Reports/NARA)

in Britain with the Air Transport Auxiliary (ATA). Its primary mission was to deliver finished airplanes from the factory to the destination units. Approximately twenty-five American female pilots went to England soon after hostilities commenced with Germany. The British begrudgingly accepted their help and slowly, women pilots, American and English, became entrusted with larger front-line aircraft, including the enormous Lancaster bombers.

American War Department officials had similar qualms about female pilots. An underground movement of women pilots began the Women's Auxiliary Ferry Squadron (WAFS), with no small help from the husband of one of the organizers, the Deputy Commander of the Army's Air Transport Command. Performing an identical service to that of the ATA, women operated under strict training requirements as an experimental group. Although not officially a part of the service, these women trained to be pilots at their own expense and based themselves at an Army airfield in Delaware.

Texas became the focal point of another group of women who would not take no from the military. The Women's Air Forces Service Pilots (WASPs) started operations about the same time as the WAFS. The major difference between the two was that the WASP pilots had less flight time and experience than members of their sister organization. As the two groups began to duplicate duties, the Army Air Forces combined them under the WASP name, though they remained civilians.

The impact that women made on the commanders during the war had a lasting effect, and women have become an indispensable component of the military, performing their duties with honor and integrity. All branches of the service now offer opportunities for females and in recent years, women have begun to take their place in front-line units. Women are flying Navy combat jets assigned to aircraft carriers, while others are piloting reconnaissance and tanker aircraft. These advancements have not been without controversy and heated debate. Women are still not allowed to participate in armored positions, nor are they permitted to serve aboard submarines. They are now acting as drivers in convoys in active areas and as medics with infantry. Someday soon, they may win the privilege to participate in these groups, given the way they have persistently made headway against all opposition in the past.

Maternity Leave

The entry of millions of women into the work force inevitably forced industry to address concerns about pregnancy. In the less enlightened days of the late 1930s, women were still regarded with some chauvinistic patronization as the "fairer" sex. Female problems intimidated men, particularly on the subject of reproduction. Part of this attitude was left over from the Victorian era. Contemporary medical opinion proposed that pregnant women should not be standing or walking for long periods nor should any heavy labor be undertaken for fear of inducing a miscarriage.

Industrial managers naturally believed this and for the most part responded unfavorably when a female employee reported her pregnancy. Fearing lawsuit if the fetus should miscarry, the general practice was to immediately fire the employee. Research by the Department of Labor showed that there had not been a single instance of spontaneous work-related abortion or miscarriage, but companies continued to remove expectant female employees from the factories.

Paradoxically, these same businesses complained about the costs of recruiting and training new employees. In response to this contradictory practice, the Federal government set forth a policy to protect women working in war industries. The 1944 plan set out limits for pre- and post-natal leave; common-sense injunctions on overtime, night shifts, and it prescribed light-duty assignments. Seniority, usually the gauge that sets the wage level, became protected, making return to work desirable for working mothers.

Day Care Centers

The number of women going to work meant that many left some other occupation behind. For married women, this often included being mothers. The oncoming war saw the explosion of marriages and little "reminders" of the new husband began to arrive within months. This was actually the beginning of the "Baby Boom" that would see the birth rate skyrocket for the next twenty years. With the father off to war and government pressure on the mother to take on war work, many of these children had to be left in the care of surrogate mothers. Add to this formula the fact that many of these young parents had left the family farm or town to search for jobs during the Depression or for the defense industry boom, and the result was that the new mother was most often surrounded by strangers.

The war inspired a lot of change, sometimes faster than it ought. Helping out with the family shopping was a good opportunity for this young man to learn the food ration coupon system. Of all the combatant countries, America had generous food rations thanks to early government influence and general cooperation of the people. (NARA)

Such newly employed mothers discovered that there were only a limited number of options for someone to look after their children. Because many of these women were entering established companies, they tended to be at the lower end of the seniority scale, so the only shifts available to them were during evenings or the midnight stretch. A number of incidents of children who were left unattended at home were well publicized. The care centers that were available were designed either for upper-class families, with equivalent price tags or Works Progress Administration facilities intended for extremely low income families where the mother absolutely had to work. Even with these two types of centers, the expected one-and-a-half million children left alone by working mothers could hardly be accommodated.[6]

To address this problem, Congress passed the Lanham Act of 1942 to provide funds to create safe havens for children. The Act focused its assistance on localities that were the worst effected by population shifts due to war industries. This precluded those towns that had rapid growth from military bases or large sub-contracting manu-facturers. One Illinois survey found 178 preschool children without care in just a few blocks. A similar study in Alabama found that 167 preschoolers had no facilities while their mothers were at work. Even where the law ap-plied, communities were expected to kick in their share of funding.[7]

The War Manpower Commission (WMC), the federal agency charged with finding and providing industry with workers issued a policy in 1942 that seemed to discourage the hiring of women with young children. Among the list of irrational and contradic-tory guidelines was the gem; "If any such woman are unable to arrange for the satisfactory care of their chil-dren … adequate facilities should be provided…Such facilities should be developed as community projects and not under the auspices of individual employers or employer groups." The employers were essentially getting a pass on any responsibilities.[8]

In spite of the WMC recommenda-tions, a few companies such as Doug-las Aircraft and Kaiser Shipbuilding had excellent facilities that were

This poster features what appears to be a war wife (a ring on the third left-hand finger) doing her part. The implied promise at the top was a real incentive; who would not want a war to end soon? (OWI/WPB)

praised for their progressiveness. Nannies were hired to staff modern centers that could offer play areas, hot meals, beds and even medical care. These facilities were the exception to the rule. Several cities began to develop their own shelters but the results were haphazard. Some privately run nurseries did little more than warehouse their charges. In one horrific example in California, witnesses testified, "…the odor was so bad that I couldn't stand it. In the backyard (we) found children in individual kennels. The children looked at me through the bars and cried."[9]

In spite of government indifference and the limited options open to parents, the idea of organized child-care centers caught on and survived through the next thirty years, though the government program for underprivileged children languished to the point of extinction until its revival in the 1960s as the Head Start Program. While the number of women working has fluctuated over the years, the day-care industry has nonetheless slowly grown. It experienced a boom beginning in the 1980s as mothers placed increasing importance on their careers, and the cost of living rapidly outpaced the single income family. Now, a reverse trend is beginning to occur as home-based employment is becoming more common and at least one parent is at home to be with the children.[10]

The Child as a Separate Entity

During the war, children found a growing advocacy in a number of psychiatrists and psychologists. Two books in particular were influential. *The Infant and Child in the Culture of Today,* published in 1943 by Yale University psycho-clinician Arnold L. Gesell and his assistant Frances Ilg, proposed that the infant should not be subjected to totalitarian rule but rather given autonomy. This philosophy of behavioral standards got even more publicity in 1946 when pediatrician Dr. Benjamin Spock issued his timeless classic, *The Common Sense Book of Baby and Child Care*. Later editions would be retitled *Baby and Child Care* and would become one of the biggest selling books of all time.

Teenagers

Teenagers were not invented during World War Two, although the phrase was. One story of dubious authenticity claims that the phrase was coined by a frustrated Los Angeles police officer describing the alleged perpetrators of a street fight that had turned into a bloody riot in 1943. Groups of slum youths, called Zoot Suits for the outlandish baggy clothes they wore, provoked and attacked servicemen on leave. In retaliation, a mob of approximately 2,500 soldiers and sailors beat up a contingent of local Zoot Suiters, many of them of Mexican descent. This violent episode led the Los Angeles City Council to outlaw the wearing of Zoot Suits and to tighten up enforcement of the curfew laws.[11]

The overall incidence of delinquency among young people was up nationwide. Several theories were postulated for this. The first and most

Roosevelt High School, Oakland CA. Youth of this age had a new name: teenagers. This student was pursuing education in automotive repair. Others like him could get out early with parental permission to join the military or go to work on half day at some defense plant jobs. (NARA)

A Mexican youth dressed in the baggy clothes associated with the "Zoot-suit". This movement began in the hispanic neighborhoods of Southern California and spread from there to encompass areas north of Los Angeles.

probable was that the youngsters, having the typical high energy of teenagers and reduced parental controls—with father off to war or working long hours at the war plant with mother—would spend their time out on the street. This inevitably led to some form of trouble from the law or the neighbors.

This problem was worsened with the relaxation of the child labor laws. To accomplish war production quotas and to train young people for industry in the event that the war might last several more years, the government instituted a plan in 1943 in which minors were hired to work in factories. The boys and girls, age 15 and up, were

Its remarkable how ad copywriters jump on new language. In this case it is "teenagers", a phrase so new that the spelling and punctuation is in doubt. There was no doubt about whom the target audience was and what they longed for; beauty; glamour; acceptance. This is a good example of applying psychology to selling, a novel strategy that would be seen more in the coming decades. Caveat Emptor.

paid the standard wage, and the day was supposed to be split equally between school and work. Unfortunately, many of the adolescents chose to stay on the job, forfeiting their education. The wages of an adult in the pockets of a child led to adult appetites. Arrests of drunkenness among minors hit an all-time high.

Another appetite that youngsters, especially the girls, acquired was for sex. Called "khaki wacky" or "Victory girls", these young women staked out places where GIs gathered with the intention of giving themselves in a misguided display of patriotism. The problem became so pervasive that prostitutes plying their trade became angered with the competition, inspiring several memorable catfights. Victory girls were also cited as the source for more than sixty percent of all venereal diseases treated by the military. In some locales, the incidence of VD was as high as eighty percent.[12]

Another attempt to place blame for misbehavior was set directly at the feet of the popular new singer to

Police and personal friends see that their charge, a young Frank Sinatra is not trampled or otherwise overwhelmed by female fans. Some of his concerts required the deployment of dozens of law enforcement because of excited fans, who went as far as to tear his clothes and rip out his hair.

come out of New Jersey, Frank Sinatra. The hysteria at Sinatra's concerts was a phenomenon unheard of in the entertainment business up to that time. Teenaged girls screamed, cried, fainted at "Old Blue Eyes'" concerts and afterwards swarmed him to the point of endangering his life. One performance in New York had an attendance in excess of thirty thousand and, when a riot seemed certain, several hundred police were dispatched to restore quiet. Not until the Beatles made their American debut in 1964 did anything similar to the Sinatra phenomenon occur.[13]

Immigrant Farm Workers

The shortage of farm labor in 1942 created a vacuum that was eagerly filled by another labor pool from south of the border. The love affair between the United States and Mexico was notoriously fickle over the previous fifty years. American farmers actively recruited Mexican laborers in the 1880s, and mining companies offered free transportation to volunteer workers interested in earning good wages. There were numerous other examples of individuals and businesses engaging Mexican labor to cross the border. This practice continued with a wink from Uncle Sam even after the Immigration Act of 1907 was passed prohibiting the entry of destitute aliens.

The business boom caused by America's entry into the First World War attracted more than seventy thousand legal immigrants, all after jobs in mines, railroads, and construction. Many of these workers were returned to Mexico in 1921 just to find themselves the target of inducements to come back again. This time, the foreign laborers' presence was desirable until the market crash and ensuing Depression. Then the newly formed Border Patrol began to gather the immigrants together and send them home. This time, the closed-door policy lasted until the Americans got involved, although staying on the sidelines, in another war.

In 1941, the Farm Bureau Federation of Arizona petitioned the U.S. Employment Service (USES) to allow the importation of 18,000 Mexican laborers. Not long after this request was denied, Texas and New Mexico placed similar demands with the USES for additional foreign labor, which was again summarily refused. Critics of the farm organizations suggested that there would be fewer labor shortages if the farmers would pay decent wages. The farmers, on the other hand, decried the idea arguing that they would have to continue paying inflated wages after the war was over, undermining their long-term efforts at keeping wages low as possible.

The labor crisis came to a head when Japan attacked Pearl Harbor. Mexico resisted renewal of any labor contracts with America as they still harbored bad feelings about the mass deportations thirteen years previously. Despite misgivings, several factors, all financially oriented, served to sway the Mexican government. But any agreement would have to include guarantees of fair treatment and non-discrimination. Clearly, the Mexicans held the initiative.[14]

On July 23, 1942, the United States and Mexico successfully concluded negotiations and the "Bracero" program was under way. Simultaneously, Congress passed Public Law 45 in 1942 allowing thousands of agricultural laborers under contract to stay anywhere in the United States from 45 to 180 days. This time, recruiters went to the smaller villages that had

Cortaro Farms, Pinal County, Arizona. Break time for this Mexican laborer from the cotton crop harvest. Many Mexican men got legal employment in the U.S. through the Bracero Program. (Bureau of Agricultural Economics/ NARA)

Mexican women trimming and packing broccoli near Eloy AZ. The men who did heavier labor often brought their spouses, but not always the rest of the children unless they were old enough to help too. (NARA)

been ignored by earlier drafts. The bracero program did not end with the war, though. It continued unabated until 1964. This virtually guaranteed that there would be a continuous flow of traffic across the border. The lure of good wages just across the largely deserted border was too great an incentive to the destitute laborers. It became almost a tradition to enter the United States, work for six months, and return with wages that could last for the rest of the year or more.

The importation of American dollars into Mexico had a destabilizing effect on the Mexican economy as well. During and after the war, many American agri-businesses went south to take advantage of low-cost labor and cheap land. They set up their processing plants near the flatland farms, which were operated by wealthy landowners who had held their vast plots for generations. In the surrounding mountains, the typical poor dirt farmers were practically ignored. Unable to compete with the partnerships and banned from selling to American firms, many farmers sought to survive by joining the labor force after selling their plots and migrating to America, legally or not.[15]

America's Black Citizens

World War Two effectively ended the Depression and began the end of the shameful treatment of black American citizens. The war that freed the slaves had ended more than seven decades previously and the practices of racism had hardly been changed since then. Blacks were still excluded from participating in most professions, being relegated to menial jobs, sharecropping, and heavy, dangerous labor. The military provided few opportunities different from those found in civilian life. For example, the U.S.Navy only accepted black recruits for the position of wardroom stewards (the Navy way of describing waiters for NCOs and officers.). A few colleges were established to provide for higher education after the turn of the century, but admission was spotty and segregated. The war of 1917 saw a great migration to the north as jobs opened up for all comers, regardless of race. The U.S.Army began to accept more black recruits, but only as stevedores and laborers. Frederick Douglass spelled out this attitude in 1865: "The Negro had been a citizen three times in the history of the government, in 1776, 1812 and 1865. In the time of trouble the Negro was a citizen and in times of peace he was an alien."[16]

The Depression struck the black populace the hardest. Already at the bottom of the socio-economic ladder, Negroes were further tried by the same farm failures and unemployment that beset the whites. The resurgence of the Ku Klux Klan in the 1920s reached epic proportions during the misery of the Depression. With the tacit approval of local courts and law enforcement, blacks were nearly helpless to combat the violence. An Arkansas tenants' uprising in 1935 was a typical example.

Evicted from their rented land, twenty-seven black sharecroppers sought relief from the courts to force the owner to allow them to return. In their suit, they claimed their contract had been violated. The black farmers then formed a union with assistance from the Agriculture Adjustment Administration (AAA), the federal agriculture agency that oversaw the readjustment of agricultural issues during the Depression. Their complaint was dismissed in court and an appeal directly to the AAA resulted in vague promises.

For their temerity in going to the government, the union and its organizers became targets of a reign of terror. Meetings were disrupted, often violently. The members were arrested on trumped-up charges, or just plain kidnapped, subjected to whippings, beatings, and, in a few cases, murdered. Federal officials got a taste of the savagery when one of their own officials was beaten and taken to the county line. Left there with the warning of much worse if he dared to return, he reported the incident directly to President Roosevelt. This incident and other brutal mob hangings led to the creation of a federal anti-lynching bill. Unfortunately, the President decided that, due to important matters before the politically strong Southern

"They also serve!" The Office of War Information produced posters as this one to underscore the need for all Americans to join together to fight their common enemies. The war became a platform to bring marginalized citizens, colored women are targeted here, into the mainstream where they could become accepted based on the weight of their participation. (OWI/NARA)

members of Congress, his endorsement of such matters would be the death of his recovery plan. This did not stop members of his Cabinet from taking independent action. This exception also extended to his willful wife, Eleanor, with the understanding that F.D.R. would disavow her activities at the moment it became politically expedient.[17]

Mrs. Roosevelt, sometimes perceived as being overly vocal in matters of national importance, undertook a crusade to improve the lot of blacks. Having the ear of the President and his powerful staff, she instigated small reforms were intended to change the attitudes of the populace. This combination of Presidential aloofness and First Lady activism paid great rewards in the perception of the voting public. F.D.R. was thought to be on the side of the white landowners by his silence, while Eleanor was the champion of the blacks and by association, so was Franklin. This bit of political illusion was partly responsible for the continued re-election of F.D.R., as one of his largest voting blocs, where allowed, was the Negro. This was a recent shift since the election of 1932, when most blacks registered and voted Republican. Now, they were casting ballots for Democrat Roosevelt, in spite of his apparent lack of an official stand against racist violence.[18]

The war brought a new migration of blacks to industrial centers in the hope that work could be found. As in the past, jobs available for blacks were limited to the most detestable, dangerous work shunned by the whites, or menial labor that was no more than window dressing for cynical, socially conscious companies. The abandonment of jobs by men going into the military provided opportunities for blacks, like those enjoyed by women, which illustrates where the black man registered on the social class scale. The challenge that the Negro faced in northern cities was not different from the intolerant attitudes that Southerners had shown for the past two hundred years. Many of these attitudes came north with poor white Southerners who had come to find jobs too. The Negro, hoping to find a new start and economic freedom, discovered that the hateful people they hoped had been left back home surrounded him, or her.

As the influx of Southerners continued, the original residents moved into newer sections of town. Wages in the war plants far exceeded peacetime wages, and they left their broken-down houses to the immigrants. These hand-me-down homes, being the only shelter available, became grossly overcrowded as migration increased. This led to a downward spiral of poor sanitation, pervasive emotional depression, and the inevitable alcohol and drug problems that bigots could point to as being a sign of the blacks' inferiority.[19]

The situation came to a head when Negroes found discrimination within government defense plants and even federally sponsored training programs. Calls for the abolishment of Jim Crow policies in every federal agency were followed by the threat of a march on Washington D.C. by the predominantly black Pullman Car Porters' Union. The government responded with an appeasement program that did little to solve the problem. Not impressed

World War Two became the great experiment with blending of the races. America was faced with two evils; the foreign enemy that wanted to destroy our way of life, and the domestic one that wanted to keep it as it was. The problem was they did not differ much. (FDRLPDC/NARA)

with the meager proposal, union leaders, now joined by similar black organizations, continued to push for a presidential order that had some teeth.

Seeing the intransigence of the unions, Roosevelt finally relented. To stop the march and lessen the likelihood of other minorities vocalizing similar threats, the President issued Executive Order Number 8802 on June 25, 1941. It called for the "full and equitable participation of all workers in defense industries, without discrimination because of race, creed, color, or national origin."[20]

Now regarded as a landmark step, the Order affected all federal programs and became a standard addition to the thousands of Federal contracts that were being implemented in the defense industry. To administer the plan, the Committee on Fair Employment Practices (CFEP) was established and worked to end discrimination. Having baby teeth at best, the CFEP was nonetheless destined to become a component forming the basis of the Civil Rights Act of 1964.

The Black Soldier

America's first enemy, the Germans, were engaged in a racial war against the "sub-humans"— Jews, Gypsies, Bolsheviks, people of color and whites of poor "genetic stock." Japanese racist policy was more limited to the white man. Japan's expansionist policy was based on the premise of "Asia for the Asians," justifying the invasion of countries as "... throwing off the yoke of the imperialistic white race."[21] At home, many blacks observed the coming war skeptically, denouncing their involvement with comments such as: "Just carve on my tombstone ' Here lies a black man killed fighting a yellow man for the protection of a white man.'"[22]

The American Negro, despite atrocious treatment at the hands of the

Black troops of the 93rd Infantry Division train at Arizona's Ft. Huachuca. Although this photo was taken in the spring of 1942, it is clear that certain minds within the War Department were still reliving the tactical errors of the First World War. These brave men are preparing to, once again, to go "over the top" in a casualty-rich frontal attack. (U.S. Army/NARA)

whites, still desired to show his patriotism by entering the military. He would not be alone but he was still a minority. There were less than five thousand black enlisted men and five black officers in the entire American military. Jim Crow was prevalent in the service even though the U.S. Army had had a number of black units in years past. The U.S. Navy strictly limited blacks from serving, except at the mess table, and a few hundred blacks were given the dubious honor of loading cargo, namely explosive ordnance, onto ships.[23]

The Army offered little better and only under intense pressure from Washington D.C., patronizingly agreed to form combat units. These units were placed in out-of-the-way locations at several camps in the south and west, usually on marshy ground or near sewage ponds. Off-duty diversions were limited as the typical camp had no movie or Post Exchange (PX)—the military general store that carried simple necessities and refreshments—for blacks. Segregation of the troops was strictly observed with the Army providing separate train coaches, trucks, and equipment for black units. The bias of the time was so pervasive that the Red Cross segregated the blood supply by the color of the donor. The earliest Army units formed were slated to specialize in the Engineer Corps (doing heavy labor and menial chores) or Quartermasters (driving trucks or handling war materials). These units were sent to the North African and British theaters of war where, to the racists' dismay, blacks were accepted without bias. Die-hard bigots attempted to undermine this by spreading outrageous lies about the Negroes as having tails and being murderous brutes.

Hap Arnold, the head of the Army Air Forces was solidly against the idea of the black pilots. He said," Negro pilots cannot be used in our present air force, since this would result in having Negro officers over white enlisted men."[24] However, Arnold was a pragmatist. He realized that the political climate and civil rights organizations would soon overwhelm white resistance and attitudes. Congress had already passed legislation, in 1939, that forced the Civil Aviation Authority to open its training programs. Arnold was sure there would more.

Faced with the inevitable, he authorized the formation of the 66th Air Force Flying School at the Tuskegee Institute in Alabama. These men would go on to claim fame as the Tuskegee pilots, but not before they had endured a gauntlet of passive official racism. The recruits were rigorously tested for their I.Q. and health and underwent numerous board reviews. At any of these steps, the recruit could be disqualified for minimal, if not purely fantastic reasons. The pilots trained under white officers and a few black pilots who had managed to become certified as instructors before the war, although the latter had not been trained in the United States. (Most of the black flight instructors had volunteered for the RAF by going to Canada, where they became involved in the Battle of Britain.) An unofficial quota system eliminated a majority of the men in the cynical belief that the Negro could not manage sophisticated machinery such as an airplane. The Army did not seem to want to commit the Tuskegee pilots to battle so they just flew training sorties, adding hours of experience that white pilots did not normally get.

In April 1943, the Tuskegee airmen were sent overseas to North Africa as the 99th Pursuit Squadron. For the first months, they were restricted on combat assignments, being given those that were of dubious value or were based on unsound intelligence reports. The squadron was placed so far from the front that they rarely saw enemy aircraft. These impediments created an apparent lack of aggressiveness, and negative reports began to emanate from the area commanders. The detractors, some in positions of Congressional power, viewed the squadron experiment as a failure. Conniving to remove the 99th squadron from service, these Congressmen went as far as commissioning pseudo-scientific reports that "proved" that the Negro was physically incapable of being in the cockpit. The squadron was salvaged only with the quiet support of Mrs. Roosevelt and several advocates in Congress.

The 99th continued to fly and gain notoriety incrementally. By the time the war moved to Italy, they had gained a reputation of reliability regardless of the mission. In addition, the squadron received the hottest new fighter, the P-51. Their old planes, P-40 Warhawks were war-weary and obsolete.

First thing they did was to have every vertical tail of the planes painted bright red as a means of identification. The new fighters and bold paint job seemed to invigorate the unit. There was little that the military could do to stop them or the formation of more all-black fighter squadrons. Eventually four squadrons of fighter pilots, joined under the common unit designation of the 332nd Fighter Group racked up an impressive score. Flying out of Italy, the "Red Tails" provided escort for bombers. In two hundred missions, not a single bomber was lost due to enemy fighter action, a record that no other Fighter Group can claim. The 450 Tuskegee airmen are also credited with sinking a destroyer and the downing of the first three German jet fighters, the Me 262, among many other targets such as 409 damaged and destroyed enemy aircraft, 124 steam locomotives, 40 barges and boats, and 564 railcars. They received a Presidential Unit Citation as a group as well as 1,727 individual medals and decorations.[25]

Despite the successes of the 332nd F.G., tying the hands of the Negro with obstacles continued throughout the war. Petty discriminations and major attempts to bait the blacks occurred wherever they served. The successes or failures of the units, in retrospect, were directly linked to the attitudes of the officers and ultimately to the commanders. Attached to the 5th Army in Italy under Lt. General Mark Clark, the 92nd Infantry Division had its performance judged "less favorable than any of the white divisions." Yet, the commander of this division, Major General Edward M. Almond, would later be severely criticized for incompetence in the Korean War.[26] General Clark was involved in the debacle at Anzio and thoroughly castigated for not exploiting the initial surprise. Of this, Sir Winston Churchill bitterly complained, "I had hoped that we were hurling a wildcat onto the shore, but all we got was a stranded whale."[27]

Black soldiers had begun to prove their worth to the narrow-minded

These truck drivers have something to smile about. They have driven more than 20,000 miles without an accident, a remarkable feat. African-Americans typically were consigned to the labor or rear-area units because of perceived inability to understand complex duties. A component of the 82nd Airborne division, the 666th Quartermaster Truck Company. The 82nd was in combat in every major action of Northwest Europe. (OWI/NARA)

American military. Interestingly, as the black units engaged in battle, the whites' biased attitudes usually disappeared. Generally speaking, the Negro soldier served with valor and honor in World War Two. President Truman officially desegregated the United States military in 1948 with Executive Order Number 8891. It took another six years to accomplish acceptable integration due to resistance from all the military branches.

Employment of the Handicapped

World War Two labor shortages had a way of eliminating some of the biases that had previously restricted opportunities. One group that enjoyed relatively no joblessness was the physically handicapped. American industry made widespread, imaginative occupations for the handicapped.

In heavy industries that used extremely loud machinery, deaf people were enthusiastically sought. They replaced employees who had to be rotated often—the damage could be cumulative when exposure was chronic—and wear bulky, uncomfortable hearing protection.

The aircraft industry made use of blind workers to salvage nuts, rivets, and other hardware that had been dropped on the floors. Once swept up, the valuable materials were sorted by feel alone. And, although their stature is not a handicap by modern standards, midgets and dwarfs found ample employment assembling aircraft.[28] Their small size fitted them perfectly for getting into the tight confines of fuselage and wing spaces and positioning internal components that would have been nearly impossible to place any other way. According to the War Manpower Commission, almost 200,000 handicapped workers were hired in 1943, about eight times as many as were put to work two years earlier.[29]

Much of the incentive for employing the handicapped came from the White House itself, occupied by another disabled person; Franklin Roosevelt. His paralysis, caused by polio contracted in 1926, rarely interfered with his capabilities as the chief executive, although some accommodations had to be made. For example, the President was issued a series of specially built aircraft that took his need for a wheelchair into consideration. One plane, a militarized Douglas DC-4 (C-54), featured the first elevator ever installed in an aircraft.[30]

The 79th Congress (1944-46), cognizant of the contribution that the handicapped were making to the war effort, passed a proclamation with Roosevelt's support observing a "National Employ the Physically Handicapped Week" beginning in 1944. Public interest quickly waned until the next year's event, but the steady influx of veterans with war-related disabilities lent more incentive to promote the program.

When Roosevelt died, the handicapped issue very nearly died with him. Harry Truman was beset with major concerns about rebuilding a peacetime American economy, negotiating with the Russians, whom he did not trust, and facing down recalcitrant unions who were threatening to cause rampant labor walkouts. Despite these

Daddy's home! That he is disabled probably did not mean one bit to his son. After a while, this soldier will be looking for work and hopefully, he will find prospective employers having the same attitude. The war had a great influence in the acceptance of the handicapped, as many were found indispensible when there were more jobs than applicants. (NARA)

concerns, Truman revived interest in handicapped employment at the behest of Dr. Meyer Wiener, a fellow Missourian and ex-Navy physician.[31]

In an April 1947 letter to Truman, Dr. Wiener proposed that the President form a committee to "observe and promote the National Employment of the Handicapped Week...." As a credential, Wiener cited the formation of a national association for the purposes of handicapped employment in Washington D.C. the previous December including among its ranks 351 separate organizations. Wiener suggested that the Presidential committee use the association as an advisory body and urged the appointment of Vice Admiral Ross McIntire as chairman.[32]

Through the offices of the Department of Labor, the Committee on the Employment of the Physically Handicapped was formed with Admiral McIntire at its head. Its first meeting, held on November 4th, 1947, was attended by a who's who of American industry, union, press, and social and government agencies. On the agenda, one of the first items made perfectly clear was that this was Truman's committee and he would be providing the staff for its functioning until Congress could be persuaded to appropriate funds at the next session.

The committee aired complaints that the use of the word "week" would undermine year-around interest in the program and that there would be difficulties adopting physically disabled workers with respect to workers compensation laws as they stood. Besides these lesser concerns, the committee sought to develop local sub-committees to promote interest and work with businesses to improve employment opportunities. One of the biggest obstacles facing the committee was that businesses feared that the disabled would be less productive, have higher absenteeism, and generally be a burden. The committee saw that education could destroy these preconceived notions. Working with state employment agencies, potential workers could be placed into jobs using war-inspired aptitude tests (see Multiple Battery Aptitude Tests later in this chapter) and establishing community rehabilitation centers.

Most of the committee's proposals were accepted with few changes. The Federal program has since taken a backseat to the state's rehabilitation programs, although the states receive funding and guidance for much of their work through the Department of Labor.

As an added incentive for getting business leaders involved, the committee suggested an award system. Both individuals and organizations were eligible for consideration after certain standards were met. This incentive program led to the creation of the prestigious Presidential Award for the Employment of the Handicapped, which has been given out every year since 1948.

Psychologists

First World War brought the discipline of psychology out of the academic setting and placed it firmly in an active war role. Psychologists were given the task of administering the military's newly adopted intelligence tests. Over the next twenty years, psychologists were seen more often away from the campus environment, testing one theory or another. As Clifford T. Morgan observed at the 1947 conference on "Current Trends in Psychology"; " (The) biggest of them all is that in the past thirty years psychology has shortened its hair, left its alleged ivory tower, and gone to work."[33] As the First World War got psychologists noticed, World War Two opened the door for psychologists to take an even larger part in their country's war efforts. Besides being available for treating psychological disturbances, they were put to work developing aptitude battery tests.

Additionally, psychologists were going into the factories, jointly sponsored by management and the government, trying to get more production out of the workforce. Because the war-plants suffered an intolerable level of absenteeism and turnover, psychologists, as part of interdisciplinary teams made up of engineers, business managers, and social scientists, were tasked with discovering solutions to the problem. This was the first example of an organized, widespread application of scientific methodology to the American worker, in essence, the birth of human resource management.

The American Psychological Association (APA)

Between World Wars One and Two, psychologists as a group had been split between two ideology camps. Behaviorists stressed the need for techniques of control over one's self or others, psychoanalysts emphasized the use of punishment and reinforcement.[34] One mild example of this widely held belief was outlined in J.B. Watson's 1928 best-selling book *Psychological Care of Infant and Child:*

"There is a sensible way of treating children. Dress them and clothe them with care and circumspection. Never hug or kiss them, never let them sit in your lap. If you must, kiss them once on the forehead when they say goodnight. Shake hands with them in the morning. Nest habits, which come from coddling, are really pernicious evils."[35]

Watson proposed in another work that words should be used as whips and that talents could only be brought to their fullest by "some kind of shock or punishment."[36] Another behavioral psychologist of some renown was Ivan P. Pavlov. His work with dogs and conditioned responses illustrate the best and the worst of behavioral modification techniques.[37]

The other camp, psychoanalysis, sought to delve into the deep-rooted personality deviations everyone without exception, it was believed, had hidden away. Out from this group sprang such authorities such as Jung—whose work was partly based on Sigmund Freud's philosophies—and Abraham Maslow. Maslow in later years formulated his pyramid-shaped "hierarchy of needs" that became a key element in human resource management in the latter half of the century.

These two diametrically opposed ideas frequently gained mention in the popular press of the time, providing for much confusion among the public. Adding to this bewilderment was the off-beat and obscure ideas that occasionally received brief publicity such as those postulated by Dr. Benjamin Spock and Joseph Justrow, who braved to speak out against the principles of Watson, clearly going against the tide of popular assumptions.

This clearly defined separation of beliefs endured through the Depression years. Behaviorism was favored. Corporal punishment was harsh and swift. Employers turned a blind eye to unsafe conditions and became violently retributive to provocative employees. But the most obvious adaptation of behaviorist philosophy was undertaken in Germany, where undesirables were subjected to an escalating series of punitive actions to drive them from that country.

With America's entry into the war, steps were taken to end this rift. In 1943, the leaders of the various factions—which had been formed into their own professional associations in the 1920s and '30s—convened a series of meetings to organize into one unified body. Under the banner of the American Psychological Association (APA), originally founded under that name in 1892, the convention adopted a set of bylaws that allowed for autonomous divisions between the groups. However, those same bylaws outlined the united position that the body would constantly pursue the growth of psychology as a science and a profession "promoting human welfare."[38]

The Legitimization of Psychotherapy

As early as 1942, troops suffering from a medley of psychological disturbances began returning to the continental United States, where they required the services of clinical psychiatrists—medical doctors trained in the treatment of mental disease and disorders. Even this workload, smaller than expected by some if the war should be prolonged, proved to be far beyond the abilities of the available force of psychiatrists, as there were only ten of them in all of the War Department's staff as of December

1941. Because of the shortfall, the federal government declared psychologists to be a critical profession, the only such classification of any social scientific occupation. Thousands of psychologists, some with only the rudimentary training they needed to deal with the difficulties of battle-induce psychological trauma, were inducted to work in military hospitals.

By the end of the war, 44,000 of the 74,000 cases in Veteran's Administration (VA) hospitals were classified as being psychologically disordered or mentally ill. Of the 16.3 million American men and women who had entered into the military, almost 80% indicated that they would take advantage of some form of counseling to overcome the hardships experienced during the war.[39] Responding to this enormous responsibility, the Veterans Administration began training psychologists not only to work in the hospitals, but also to be stationed at universities and colleges, giving advice and aid to the students, many of them enrolled in the military's "V" education programs. Although they were still using some methods from the prewar days, the psychologists were modifying and perfecting their treatments on the ever-increasing number

Mental health treatment got a new perspective in the Second World War. In the previous war, mental patients were institutionalized with little real treatment. Now it was a combined effort of all manner of specialists. Here, a nurse is getting a visual aid in learning the "wheel of cooperation". Interestingly, the term "psychologist" is not called as such. Instead, they are referred to as "social worker's". (U. S. Army Medical Corps)

of eligible veterans. Much of this on-the-job experience would serve as the basis for modern psychotherapeutic techniques used today.

The APA responded to the rapid and welcome growth of the profession by redefining the tasks and training of their membership. This applied mainly to the thousands of new psychologists, trained under the auspices of the VA in highly accelerated programs, who began graduating in 1947-48. Over the years, these practices and standards changed as psychological thinking evolved. However, there is no doubt that the community of professional psychotherapists saw its greatest expansion during the Second World War.[40]

Multiple Battery Aptitude Tests

With the large influx of men and women into the American armed services after Pearl Harbor, the military had to classify aptitudes so that new recruits could be placed into jobs best fitting their abilities, skills, and personalities. The military had testing with the tens of thousands of inductees during the First World War. This program had proved so successful that it became standard for all enlistees and laid the groundwork for dozens of new tests in the 1920s.

However, the next war was to provide a new challenge for the War Department. Technology had made great strides in the intervening years and the recruits were needed to fill positions that were far more complex than those their fathers had experienced.

To this end, psychologists with the United States military devised a number of tests that determined not only the participant's mental stability but their strengths under stress as well. As the war continued, more tests were used developed to isolate traits required for essential occupations. Typically, very high aptitude scores could land a recruit in an officer's training school. In an accelerated program typically taking three months, these men and women were supposedly taught all that they would ever need to know about leading men into battle. The troops, however, regarded these junior officers—unkindly called "ninety day wonders"—as a greater threat to their individual survival than the enemy ever could be. It was a common but unanswered question whether O.T.S. high test scores indicated intelligence or idiocy.

By 1945, testing had become so pervasive that, for example, the Army Air Force alone had 9 of 19 volumes of psychology manuals dedicated to describing the great quantity of tests available for use. Many of these tests have been discarded over the years. However, many others have been adapted for use in civilian educational and industrial settings.[41]

The Minnesota Multiphasic Personality Inventory (MMPI)

This test was developed by research psychologists S.R. Hathaway and J.C. McKinley in 1940. To qualify their test, they gave it to a group of approximately 1,500 people judged to be "normal" psychologically over the following two years. Other groups diagnosed with specific mental illnesses were used to establish the "abnormal" parameters for each of the ten clinical scales that the MMPI measures.[42]

Released in 1943, it became the standard test for civilian and military purposes. Mental health professionals widely acclaimed the usefulness of the MMPI and readily accepted it as the most precise of psychological tests. Over the years, the test itself has undergone very little change. However, several versions of the MMPI scoring atlas have been released for special groups including high school and college students, and with the massive adoption of computers, the MMPI was converted to a computer-graded test in the late 1970s.

The MMPI has inspired no less than 8,000 references in professional research papers. All of this scrutiny naturally led to a whole plethora of variations on the grading and interpretations of the scores, making the MMPI the most sophisticated of the psychological tests to have come out of the war.[43]

Standardized College Entrance Exams

Beginning in the 1930s, colleges began depending less on essay questions to sift through their admission applicants. The responses took too long to grade and there were problems of objectivity. However, each school had its own entrance exam. A student applying to several schools did not know what to study for or to expect. It's undoubtedly true that many excellent students were rejected merely because they didn't know how to prepare.

Twenty years earlier, the College Entrance Examination Board (CEEB) had attempted to overcome this discrepancy. Their placement procedures enjoyed regional popularity but were far from universally used. When the efficacy of the military's battery testing program had been demonstrated during World War Two, the CEEB joined with testing services provided by the Carnegie Corporation and the American Council on Education to form Educational Testing Services (ETS). This organization began to take responsibility for the entrance exams of the rapidly growing number of college and government educational programs in 1947, developing the now familiar Standardized Aptitude Test (SAT) that nearly all college-bound students take.

The SATs are not without competition though. In 1959, the American College Testing Program began offering their version of a standardized exam called the ACT. At present, the two tests dominate the field of scholastic examination, and both are logical products of the of the post-war college boom.[44]

American Education

After the First World War, education in America slowly gained importance in national life. Children were expected to go onto secondary schools such as high school or trade school after their elementary school years, and from 1918 to 1940, there was a steady increase of enrolled students in American public secondary schools. Two years later, there was a sudden decrease in enrollment that reflected the withdrawal of the first students who chose to enter the wartime workforce. High schools reported a similar drop in graduates in 1944-46, mirroring the earlier losses in enrollment.[45]

The 1930s saw a shift in American education. In 1930, more schools began providing students with free textbooks. More communities formed junior high schools to prepare grades seven through nine for high school. High school curriculums were comprehensively re-engineered to prepare students for college. Colleges, in turn, attempted to standardize their curriculums. More emphasis was placed on technical or scientific knowledge and gradually, subjects such as Latin and Greek were dropped from the requirements. (This did not set well with some of the more conservative European universities, which felt that classical education created a well-rounded student.)

Scientific Education and the War

As the Second World War reached American shores, there was a period of frantic scrambling to place all scientists and engineers in defense related work. Their ranks were augmented when the class of 1942 was given an early out. The military naturally consumed the majority of these graduates as technical officers, but many were given draft deferments to finish their education.

It had become painfully clear that the Axis, specifically Germany, was technologically far ahead of the Allied nations. In America, a college education had been for out of reach for the average person due to the high cost and the inherent elitism of the scholastic system. This created a large gap between the Axis and Allied countries in the sheer numbers of educated scientists and engineers. Some of the shortfall was made up by the American system of free enterprise, where men and women with natural-born talent, who had taken on the responsibility of their own self-education, went into business and became "bootstrap" successes. An excellent example of this is the career of Henry Ford.

However, America could not rely on the self-motivation of a few gifted citizens to fill the shortages in the laboratories and factories. Immediately after the Pearl Harbor attack, thousands of undergraduates spontaneously left school to join the military. Presidential scientific advisor Vannevar Bush estimated that, between 1942 and 1943, 150,000 baccalaureate graduates and an additional 17,000 post-graduate candidates had been lost to the military.[46] America's schools of higher learning became virtual ghost towns.

President Roosevelt, appalled by the apparent abandonment of education at a time when science was a critical commodity, initiated a short-term solution of rapid education. The campuses of more than five hundred colleges were literally taken over for war-related classes. Approximately 300,000 men and women, already enlisted in the service, were placed into such programs as the Army's Specialized Training Program and the Navy's V-12 program.

The military, on the other hand, saw their ranks being simultaneously decimated by battle casualties and the training programs. In a letter to Roosevelt in late 1943, Army Chief of Staff George C. Marshall criticized the training plan as wasteful and begged for the return of his recruits. This shortsighted attitude was intended to win the war, setting all else aside and science be damned. After some deliberation, the two education programs were severely cut back and the students released in time to participate in the invasion of France.

The training programs had proven a point, though. The modern military was tied to technology and vice versa. Once the war in Europe was essentially won, consideration was again given to the education programs. No longer under the "V" symbol, the military allocated an enormous amount of their budget to form the Reserve Officer Training Corps (ROTC) program. Students under this plan went to school with the understanding that the government would subsidize their education and they in turn would fulfill their military commitment upon graduation.

The National Science Foundation

Incidental to the war requirements, industry and the sciences had developed a harmonious relationship, which was a significant change in itself. As the two diametrically opposed institutions melded into a cooperative relationship, Roosevelt foresaw a continuing need for such an organization after the war. In November 1944, he proposed the formation of a federal program that would not only subsidize but oversee the continuing development of science. This program, in 1950, became the National Science Foundation.

The GI Bill

In November 1942, Franklin Roosevelt was already concerned with post-war education programs for the country, especially for returning veterans. One of the motivating forces behind his seemingly premature worry was the memory of the last world war when American vets were peremptorily dismissed with some vague promises of a war service bonus to be paid at some vague time in the future. Other than that, vets were left to their own devices. Most had returned to their farms and villages largely uneducated except to the horrors of war.

The commission on education that Roosevelt established broke all speed records finishing their report and had it on his desk in less than a year. It suggested that the government subsidize one year of advanced schooling for the majority of the veterans, and for the select few who had shown particular aptitude, an extension of two to three years. Evidently Congress remembered the injustice done to the First World War vets, because long standing objections to federalized education plans, not just for veterans but also for anyone, quickly evaporated.

The previous January, a similar plan had been proposed by the American Legion, acting as the voice of American war veterans. The Legion's plan differed in that it proposed the creation of a centralized government agency to run the veteran's program and suggested government guarantees of up to half the value of home, farm, or business loans for ex-service personnel. The two plans were joined under the general heading of the GI Bill of Rights. Roosevelt made a big show of signing the Serviceman's Readjustment Act of 1944 on June 22, 1944.

As written, the GI Bill offered one year of education, regardless of level, for every year of military service plus one more year, up to four years, all at government expense. Additionally, it featured low interest, low down payment loan guarantees for homes, farms, and businesses. Many servicemen found that their old jobs were no longer available. The Veterans Administration made specialists in job searching available. During this period of unemployment, the government paid a special weekly stipend of twenty

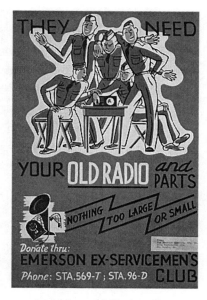

As early as 1942, American servicemen were getting discharged for their combat injuries. Often they would seek to organize their own club as the one above. Money must have been short or, more likely, unable to get a tightly rationed radio; they resorted to their military technical training to make their own. Later on, the G.I. Bill would offer financing for homes, businesses and college. As a result, ex-servicemen's clubs would be less common. (War Production Board/NARA)

dollars for no more than fifty-two weeks—called the 52-20 Club—to help pay the rent and other living expenses.

From 1945 to 1947, more than a million GIs took advantage of some form of educational benefits. By 1955, the government had spent $14.5 billion in tuition and related costs for the veterans. Between 1947 and 1955, approximately 7 million veterans attended college. This included more than 250,000 black veterans.[47]

But the numbers do not do justice to how the GI Bill altered the American education system. The returning veterans were products of the Depression. They knew firsthand how being uneducated limited opportunities. For the first time in American history, large masses of people were being given the chance to make something of themselves and they enthusiastically grasped it. Moreover, they passed on their attitude for higher education on to their children, who also embraced the ideal of going to college. In the sixty-some years since the war, the annual total of all college degrees—baccalaureate and higher—conferred in the United States has more than quadrupled from those handed out in just 1940.[48]

Unfortunately, there were a number of veterans who resisted or even feared going to colleges. However, a new type of experimental college was started in the 1930s called a junior college. Like a junior high school, junior college was intended to prepare the student for further education at the next level. Many veterans found the confidence that they needed to get their degrees by attending the smattering of junior colleges around the country. As the demand grew, more were opened in communities, offering basic classes at less cost.

Recycling

Recycling has been practiced for thousands of years. Neolithic tribes of Western Europe picked up and hurled back the stick and rocks thrown by their enemies. Later warriors prized their foe's bronze and iron weapons. Temples and other structures were commonly torn down to render materials for new buildings. In all regions, clothing of the deceased was reused, often promoting the furtherance of communicable diseases. During the First World War, peach pits were collected for processing into charcoal for gas mask filters. What makes the Second World War different are the wide range of items recycled and the near unanimous participation of the public.

Even before the Japanese attacked Pearl Harbor, the government began to call for a nationwide recycling program to bolster the military's supply of strategic metals. Aluminum and steel were first on the "hit list." The National Defense Aluminum Col-

Parade to raise participation in the local metal recycling programs. Any metal imaginable was collected, regardless of its historical or sentimental value. (FDRLPD/NARA)

lection, held from July 21-29, 1941, saw several dozen American cities collect great piles of discarded and donated aluminum kitchen utensils. Even with the whole-hearted support of the citizens taking part, America was dramatically short of the basic materials needed to field a modern military force.

The American military never comprehended the possibility that the Japanese juggernaut would encompass so much territory so fast. By seizing most of the islands of the Central Pacific, Japan cut off supplies of tin, manganese, rubber, kapok, sugar, and other essential foods and medicines. The German U-boat menace made shipping even the barest necessities from South and Central America a risky venture. Shipments from the African continent and from European factories and mines were similarly endangered.

Additionally, the government began to seize and ration all of vital materials already available in the country for the war effort. The United States had grown fat on consumption and it was time to go on an immediate diet. Rationing was the diet, recycling was the fodder. Everything conceivable was gathered up into enormous piles, to be converted into war goods.

If America proved to be an aggressive recycling nation, Germany and Japan were absolutely militant about it. Japanese housewives were pressured into donating all their aluminum cookware, save one pan. This token container was saved only at the behest of the Emperor himself, who interceded in the military's call for aluminum scrap. Thousands of bronze bells, some several centuries old, were removed from Shinto shrines and recycled into Japanese war materials. Germany took great pains to gather up every tidbit of metal in the occupied countries for recycling. Valuable manpower was used to salvage crashed aircraft, whether Allied or Axis, whenever opportunity presented itself.

Steel

World War Two equipment relied on steel as the metal of choice for nearly every activity. One aircraft carrier used about thirty thousand tons, while even a Sherman tank required fifteen tons. One rifle, of the 17,000,000 manufactured in America alone, consumed six and a half pounds of steel. As a result, millions of pounds of steel scrap went into furnaces and foundries across the country. Precious relics and antiquities, some of them priceless, were thoughtfully donated, their historic significance being lost forever. Hundreds of automobiles, many considered to be antique even in the early 1940s, were melted down, creating a valuable post-war market for the few remaining examples. Even moon-shiners got into the spirit of recycling. In 1942 alone, at least two illegal stills were voluntarily, and anonymously, set out for collection.

The patriotic fervor did not strike everyone. Frank Schumak of Valparasio, Indiana, had to be forcibly removed from protecting his scrap heap. Estimated to weigh over 200,000 pounds, he refused to sell it at the government's price of $18.75 a ton, preferring to hold out for a better deal to fund his retirement.[49]

Aluminum

Aluminum was also desperately needed for aircraft production. America has large reserves of aluminum ore, or bauxite, but recycling the metal takes a mere five percent of the electric power needed to convert the ore into metal. By war's end, eighteen billion tons of aluminum was produced in the United States alone.

Parties of Boy Scouts scoured their neighborhoods, begging for aluminum cookware, toys, and any other usable scrap. Bonuses and medals were offered to the boys and girls who collected the largest amount of scrap aluminum in a given time. Ironically, the medals were unable to be cast, for

Aluminum cookware was the focus of the second wartime recycling drive. Until new bauxite (the ultimate source of aluminum) mines could be opened and smelters built, the existing supply would have to do. Electricity demand for aluminum from bauxite is nineteen times that for recycled. This underscores the importance of the TVA and the western U.S. hydroelectric dams. (OWI/WPB)

a shortage of tin existed until near the end of the war.

Other Non-ferrous Metals

The government set out to secure tin, brass, lead, chromium, nickel, and zinc, all strategic materials in short supply. Even before the war, an all-out effort to locate new, domestic sources was undertaken, but until the new mines could come into full production, every conceivable trinket that contained even the minutest amount was called for. Padlocks gave up chrome and nickel. So much costume jewelry was donated that the Federal government ended up with a years' supply of zinc. Convicts at several state prisons were put to work raking shooting ranges, gleaning the empty brass cases for recycling.

To assure compliance with the recycling efforts, trade-ins were required for some products. Fats, animal and vegetable, were needed for their glycerin content, a vital component of high explosives. Homemakers were encouraged to salvage their waste fats by storing them in empty tin cans. Each pound of fat was redeemable for one extra meat ration point, not a small reward. The tin was then salvaged from the can after the fat had been removed, essentially recycling two birds with one stone. Toothpaste, sold in tubes made of pure tin, could be bought only if an empty tube were traded-in, no exceptions allowed. The same held true for car batteries (lead and copper), shaving creme cans (steel and tin), and flashlight batteries (carbon, lead, and tin).

Wherever the Germans faced the Americans, their prisoners always revealed that they hated the incredible shelling the Americans inflicted. Every shell casing was made from brass, (later some were steel), a valuable metal. The landing craft above is setting out to a homebound ship which will be loaded with this and other materials of war that would eventually re-enter the supply pipeline. (U.S. Army/NARA)

Paper

It's hard to comprehend how much paper was used during the Second World War relied on a great deal of recycled paper. It was used as a replacement for all sorts of containers and cartons. Foods that had previously enjoyed the security of tin, aluminum, or glass now came paper-wrapped. The entire rationing system relied on redeemable coupons, all made of paper. The millions of war bonds, which financed the war, were printed on precious paper. As the war became more mechanized, thousands of instruction manuals were printed to train the soldiers, sailors, and airmen going into battle. Millions more pages of reports, surveys, plans, maps, designs, and assessments poured from government offices and printing presses. The military even had specialized vehicles, designed to travel along with the fighting troops, to print everything from the latest military intelligence updates to free-passage surrender slips, the latter being dropped behind enemy lines by airplane and artillery shell—all of which were shipped overseas wrapped in waterproofed paper.

All this paper usage meant that there was a shortage of paper for more conventional uses. Newspapers and magazines were reduced in size and volume. Potential new subscribers were discouraged from sending money. Instead, the publishers recommended that a used copy be shared amongst the readers, but only until the war was over. The paper-recycling program had one unexpected result. So much paper came in that there was a temporary shortage of chlorine to bleach the paper. Newspapers, in particular, took on a sickly gray hue that was stoically accepted by a news-starved public.

Paper started to show up in even more unlikely places. Building products were made from paper, using new waterproof glues developed on the eve of the war. Suitcases were made from fiberboard, another paper product. The

PAPER IS STILL A NO. I
WAR MATERIAL SHORTAGE

The Pacific War is calling for thousands of tons of paper packaging to protect vital supplies against the long sea journey, heat, cold, moisture, contamination and storage hazards. Won't you help by sharing this magazine with others—then turning it in for salvage?

This notice was a different from the pre-war philosophy where the magazine buyer was expected not allow any other from reading the magazine, thus increasing circulation. This ad, too, shows the depths that business realized the importance of cooperating with war restrictions and limits. (WPB/OWI)

Japanese made use of rice-paper balloons to attack the American northwest. In Britain, paper use for publishing purposes began strict and continued to face greater constraints as the war progressed. Rare shipments of pulp from the Commonwealth and, wonder of wonders, paper made from trees reached the docks of London. In 1941, Norfolk swamps provided reeds in a trial of pulp source, although no word on the results has been issued. One cause for the paper shortage was blamed on the wholesale fire-bombing of southern population centers, where individual properties held relatively large stocks of paper in books and other printed materials.

Rubber

The rubber shortage, which has been dealt with in other chapters of this book, was profound. After Pearl Harbor, America had less than a years' supply, based on typical peacetime usage. Government assessments predicted that the supply would be exhausted in less than six months with increased wartime military needs.

Millions of pounds of rubber were traded in, sacrificed at the altar of winning the war. Further economies of rubber were realized by reducing the national speed limit to 35 miles-per-hour and strictly rationing gasoline. All other rubber products were limited as well. Shoes, garden hoses, and sports equipment such as golf and baseballs were in short supply. The list is even more extensive than one might

This is another example of the depths America would go to recycle. On the right is a pair of combat boots that has seen better days and probably came off a casualty. The pair on the left are reconditioned boots that looked like the others at one time. Within weeks of securing France, the Americans setup a facility with French civilians reworking similar boots. (OWI/NARA)

imagine, as plastic substitutes were not nearly as prevalent as they are now. Synthetics, especially for tires, would eventually become available, but on a limited basis and only at the end of the war.

Consumer Goods

Guns and binoculars were collected for shipment to England to augment their domestic defense forces in the early days of the war. Clothing was sent to Britain to replace what was lost during the bombing campaign of London in 1940-41. Fifty out-of-date destroyers, slated for the salvager's torch, were made ready for sailing to England to reinforce the Royal Navy forces and for convoy escort duties. Women voluntarily gave up their precious nylons and silk hose. Attics and garages were scoured in a search for old wooden toys, long out of fashion, replacing the metal ones that had been donated to the war effort. It became a source of pride among the neighborhood children to compare the age of their particular plaything, older being better. This led to a resurgence of wood toys that still lingers today. One recycling project even led to the direct destruction of Japan as a sea power.

The remnants of the U.S. Navy Pacific Fleet consisted of a few aircraft carriers, some smaller warships and a large contingent of submarines. Hoping to use the subs in a bid to regain the Pacific, Navy command sent out the subs to sink Japanese ships with a newly developed torpedo trigger mechanism.

For the next eighteen months, sub skippers kept reporting that their torpedoes were failing to explode. Unwilling to admit that their new weapon might be faulty; the Bureau of Ordnance (BurOrd) blamed the men at sea for the failures. BurOrd steadfastly refused even to test the torpedoes, disavowing any responsibility. In the meantime, the submarines on patrol with defective ordnance were missing opportunities to sink major Japanese warships and unintentionally prolonging the war.

Matters came to a head when the submarine squadron commander at Pearl Harbor ordered an investigation. A mock-up of a torpedo and the trigger mechanism were dropped on a steel plate, simulating the side of a ship. A small pin in the trigger was found to be crumpling under the impact. At a local machine shop, new pins were quickly manufactured and successfully tested. The torpedo failure rate immediately went from 18 out of 19 to 1 out of 9. From that time on, American submarines cut a swath through the Japanese fleets, decimating their ranks in little more than two years. It is no small irony that the material for the new firing pins came from steel salvaged from wrecked Japanese fighters, shot down over Pearl Harbor on December 7, 1941.

The Worst Form of Recycling

In what is probably the most macabre example of recycling, the Germans instituted a policy of salvaging any and all of the possessions of concentration camp inmates. Obvious items such as clothes, shoes, luggage, furs, jewels, and silver were just a few of the thousands of reusable castaways that accumulated with every train. Special units of Jewish craftsmen sorted and, when necessary, repaired the goods for use. Some went directly to the military, while other goods were made available to the populace to replace items that had been lost in the bombings of German cities.

For example, the concentration camp at Oranienburg placed 3,000 alarm clocks back into the supply system in the summer of 1944. 500 were taken for the camp's guards and the balance shipped to Berlin for distribution.[50] The recycling operation was not limited to personal effects or valuables though. German efficiency dictated that bodies of the inmates held value of themselves.

Upon entering the camps, women selected for slave labor, had their hair shaved off. Men's hair was also taken, but only longer than 20 mm (about 7/8"). The shorn locks were then collected, baled, and sent away for processing. Three separate factories specialized in turning the hair into a variety of goods such as rope, mattress stuffing, and sheets of felt for socks used by German submarine crews. In a turn of fate, most of the railroad workers who operated the transports carrying the Jews to their death wore boots made from human hair likely harvested from their recent passengers. It was discovered that strands of hair made an ideal material for the fusing mechanism of bombs. Cleaned and baled, the hair was worth about one-half a mark per kilogram, around $1.09.[51]

However, the Germans also utilized their captives in more gruesome ways. 1943, Dr. August Hirt, Director of the Strasbourg Anatomical Institute, required a number of specific racial types to fill out the Institute's skeleton collection. The authorization came down from the highest level of

Riches that boggle the imagination; and so did their source. In a mine complex near Merkers, Germany, Allied officials discovered a mass of Nazi wealth stashed away in bags. Currency from a dozen different nations, gold in every form including teeth removed from concentration camp dead, and other valuables from Nazi victims. The loot totaled up to an excess of hundreds of millions of dollars. (OWI/War Department)

Nazi power to arrange for the "salvage" of 109 Jewish, two Polish and four "Asiatic" skeletons. Appropriate bodies were found in the combined concentration camp population, shipped to Natzweiler-Struthof concentration camp where they were gassed and forwarded on to Strasbourg for final preparation.[52]

Early on in the war, the bones and ashes of exterminated prisoners were taken for processing into animal feed and fertilizer. Human fat was converted into soap[6]. When the supply of raw stock outpaced demand, the program was dropped as being too expensive.

Germany did continue with another practice that was far more profitable, taking dental gold from the victims of the gas chambers. From the camps the gold was shipped to the Reich bank in Berlin where it was smelted down into bars and stored. Several thousand bars valued at $2 billion were sent to Switzerland for storage or to be sold to pay for Germany's war debt. At the end of the war, American troops discovered about 285 tons of gold bullion in an abandoned salt mine near Merkers, Germany. Besides this treasure, they also made the macabre find of several hundred boxes of gold dental fillings, most forcibly removed from concentration camp dead.[53]

The United Nations

Even while the shells were still falling, the Allied powers were contemplating the post-war world. Politicians wanted an organization made up of member countries to act as a forum for disputes and a court of opinion for enforcement of international treaties.

The First World War had given birth to a similar concept, the League of Nations, formed in 1919. Unfortunately, the high principles of the League were undermined by the high-handedness of two of its primary nations, France and Britain. With the League of Nations acting as an enforcement body, Germany was virtually imprisoned by the restrictions of the Versailles Treaty. Later, the League would tie the hands of Ethiopia by an arms embargo when the rampaging Italians invaded that country. Italy had to

---

6 There have been great disagreements about this subject. Respected historians have come down on both sides of this allegation. In 1983, this author has actually held and examined a sample of "soap" liberated from Buchenwald by a friend of the author. The veteran, who assured that the item was human fat soap, is dead now and the artifact gone. It was loaf-sized oval cake about 6" X 3", pale cream in color and waxy. There was a faint odor, not unpleasant but unremarkable. On one end, there was the eagle/swastika and a five digit number stamped into the surface. The owner allowed a small shaving taken and used to lather, which it did. Unfortunately, he refused an offer to have the item lab tested or to return it a Holocaust organization. C.S.

face the Leagues' sanction of an embargo against importing nitrocellulose, which was mainly used for the manufacture of Italian Ping-Pong balls.

America refused to join the League when opponents pointed out that the wording of Article X virtually guaranteed that American troops would be involved in every European border war and territorial squabble. The loss of the United States as a member weakened the League immensely. Infighting among its members undermined the League further. Unable to provide any meaningful intervention, the League withered away. Sixteen of sixty-four countries pulled out before 1939, leaving an organizational shell as hollow as its ability to intercede with conflicting nations. The coming war would assure its collapse.

Despite its shortcomings, the League served a purpose as a court of international mediation. Its replacement, the Atlantic Charter, began humbly enough as a private agreement between President Roosevelt and Prime Minister Churchill on August 11, 1941. Although Roosevelt had serious reservations about endorsing an "international organization," the Charter would serve as the basic framework for the United Nations. In eight points, the Atlantic Charter outlined the "common principles on which they based their hopes for a better future for the world."[54] Furthermore, the Atlantic Charter aimed to "eliminate the use of force" as a means of political coercion and initiate a "permanent system of general security" worldwide.

Interestingly, the phrase "United Nations" was to come into the popular vernacular less than four months later. On January 1, 1942, twenty-six nations issued a formal declaration subscribing to the Atlantic Charter, which used the phrase "United Nations." The name had come almost simultaneously to Roosevelt and Churchill at the last moment. From this time on, the term was used synonymously with the term "Allies" to indicate the forces at war with Germany and the other Axis powers.

It was the will power and the political savvy of the two leaders, along with the legitimacy of the Atlantic Charter that brought the nations of the world together under the United Nations flag. By late 1943, plans were well under way for the formalization of the United Nations. Congress was struggling with issues concerning the Big Four Powers veto (China, Russia, Britain, and the United States), questions about who would supply the world security forces, and the establishment of a permanent body, all sensitive points that had helped to destroy the League of Nations.

Representatives of all four countries met in the summer of 1944 at Dumbarton Oaks, a stately mansion near Washington, D.C., to iron out the procedures to create a formal charter for the United Nations. The conference broke up in the early fall, with the structure intact, but the recalcitrant Russians were holding out for a larger share of votes. The following February, the Allies again met, this time at Yalta, a resort city on the Black Sea, when Germany was mere weeks away from total collapse. The Russians reiterated their voting demands and, just as suddenly, accepted a compromise offered by President Roosevelt. This action paved the way for a full charter conference to take place in San Francisco, California.

On April 25, 1945, less than a week before Germany fell, delegates from 50 countries met to consider the Dumbarton agreement. With some modifications, the United Nations Charter was completed and signed on June 26, 1945. Thirty-two days later, the United States Senate overwhelmingly passed the charter with only two "no" votes cast. It would be another three months before the required number of nations ratified the charter, but by October 24, 1945, the United Nations officially existed.

The charter provided for a Security Council of five permanent members and an additional ten elected from the body of the member nations. Russia, England, France, China, and the United States would hold the five permanent positions. Any one might conceivably veto an action by the Security Council, whose task would be to oversee the general peace and security of the world. Rules to override a veto were enacted in 1950 after Russia very nearly impeded the West's reaction to Socialist North Korea's invasion of their southern pro-Western neighbor. The General Assembly, made up of all member nations can and will overrule the Security Council's inaction by a two-thirds majority vote.

Over the years, the United Nations has essentially performed as designed. By providing a forum for complaints, the General Assembly acts as a court of world opinion, often pressuring malefactors back into line. There is more to the United Nations, though.[55]

The International Court of Justice

An International Court of Justice acts the official seat of jurisprudence for the United Nations. Fifteen judges, elected by the General Assembly and the Security Council, listen to disputes from any nation, even non-member countries, Similar to the American Supreme Court; they provide non-partisan legal advice to the United Nations and member nations.

The Economic and Social Council

Under the auspices of the General Assembly, this organization works to improve the economic and social conditions of member countries. In addition, the council oversees the activities of several different United Nations agencies that are charged with specific tasks such as health, education, welfare, and human rights.

Although some of these agencies have been created over the years as a reaction to changing technology or world events, there is a core group that has its origins in the tumultuous days immediately following World War Two. These particular organizations are as follows.

Food and Agriculture Organization of the United Nations (FAO)

Founded in 1945, the FAO abides by the age-old axiom that if a man is given a fish, he eats for a day. If he is taught to fish, he can eat everyday. Headquartered in Rome, Italy, FAO experts teach new methods of planting, nurturing, and harvesting the farms, forests, and waters of member countries. The FAO is largely responsible for the resurrection of the European farms after the war, staving off mass famine.

International Civil Aviation Organization (ICAO)

This is another charter agency of the United Nations. The ICAO had its beginnings as a provisional office in 1945 to organize, standardize, and regulate airline traffic and procedures between member countries. The great influx of technical advancements after the war was disseminated by this agency. Such was the volume of work; the ICAO lost its provisional status in 1947.

International Bank for Reconstruction and Development (IBRD)

This agency has the more recognizable name of the World Bank. The IBRD works in conjunction with the International Monetary Fund, which together form a base of financial security for countries. America initiated the IBRD as a war-recovery agency in 1945. It was meant to provide loans and technical advice to further the rebuilding of Europe. In 1947, the United Nations adopted the IBRD as its own entity.

International Monetary Fund (IMF)

Like the IBRD, the IMF was founded in 1945 as a Federal program. The IMF loans money to nations facing devastating economic crises and recovering from natural disasters. Additionally, the IMF brokers deals between countries for financial bailouts and currency exchanges.

United Nations Educational, Scientific, and Cultural Organization (UNESCO)

Since 1946, UNESCO acts as the general brokerage house of up-to-date information for members of the United Nations. Their goal is to spread knowledge and educate the world about science, industry and encourage the exchange of cultural understanding. Based in Paris, France, UNESCO serves to bring about peaceful interactions between countries by eliminating misperceptions, biases, and misunderstandings.

World Health Organization (WHO)

The World Health Organization, based in Geneva, Switzerland, is the medical arm of the United Nations since 1948. Through WHO, countries get advice, technical assistance, and supplies to deal with specific medical problems such as the AIDS epidemic. WHO also documents statistical data on epidemiological events, which is then shared with member nations. Much of the world's drug supply is overseen by WHO inspectors to assure that standards are being held and that testing follows WHO guidelines.

United Nations Children's Fund (UNICEF)

World War Two affected the lives of millions of European civilians. This included a large population of displaced, emaciated orphans wandering the countryside when peace broke out. UNICEF was set up in 1945 to assist with these children, housing, clothing and finding relatives to take them in. Once the work in Europe was done, UNICEF went on to aid similar children in other, developing countries.

Notes/Selected References

1   Weatherford, Doris. *American Women and World War II*. 1990. P. 124.
2   "If you've followed recipes exactly in making cakes, you can learn to load shells." Bailey, Ronald H. *The Home Front: USA*. 1977. P. 90.
3   Skolnick, Jerome H. and Elliott Currie. Editors. *Crisis in American Institutions*.1979. Pp. 169-172.

4   Weatherford, Doris. P. 29.

5   Waves = Women Accepted for Volunteer Emergency Service. SPARS was derived from the Coast Guard motto "Semper Paratus"—Always Ready.

6   Weatherford, Doris. P. 99.

7   ibid. P. 170.

8   ibid. P. 170. and

9   Yellin, Emily. Our Mother's War. 2004. P. 60.

10 Weatherford, Doris. P. 171.

11 The phrase "teenagers" was first used in an article in *Popular Science* monthly magazine. April 1941.

12 Lingeman, Richard R. *Don't You Know There's a War On?* 1970. Pp. 88-89.

13 Bailey, Ronald H. Pp. 146-149

14 Garcia, Juan Ramon. *Operation Wetback*. 1980. Pp. 18-29.

15 Skolnick, Jerome H. and Elliott Currie. Pp. 136-140

16 Motley, Mary Penick. *The Invisible Soldier, The Experience of the Black Soldier in World War II*. 1987. P. 23.

17 Davis, Kenneth S. F.D.R.:The New Deal Years:1933-1937. 1986. Pp. 481-485.

18 ibid. Pp. 629-630.

19 Burns, James MacGregor. *Roosevelt: The Soldier of Freedom*. 1970. P. 462.

20 ibid. Pp. 123-124.

21 Myrdal, Gunnar. *An American Dilemma, The Negro Problem and Modern Democracy*. 1972. P. 1006.

22 ibid. P. 1006.

23 Port Chicago in the San Francisco Bay area was the scene of the greatest Navy disaster on the Continental US when an explosion totally destroyed the port, sinking two ships and killed the entire contingent of ship's company and the black loaders. Fearing another disaster, several dozen loaders refused to resume work after the port had been reconstructed.

24 Parrish, Thomas. Editor. The Simon *and Schuster Encyclopedia* of *World War II*. 1978. P. 639.

25 Motley, Mary Penick. Pp. 195-209.

26 ibid. P. 258. Quote attributed to General Mark Clark.

27 As a result, the landing forces stalled on the beach without any enemy resistance. By the time they got moving, elite German armored units moved into place and the landing forces were nearly pushed back into the sea. This situation lasted for nearly six months and cost thousands of needless casualties. Sulzberger, C.L. *American Heritage Picture History of World War II*. 1966. P. 373. and Churchill Quote: Benford, Timothy B. *The World War II Quiz and Fact Book*, 1984. P.71.

28 Busy Little Men Do Big Job In Close Quarters. *Popular Mechanics* magazine. April 1942. P.26.

29 Lingeman, Richard R. P.166

30 Serling, Robert J. *When the Airlines Went to War.* 1997. Pp. 200-211.

31 Wiener, Meyer in a letter to Dr. John R. Steelman, April 17, 1947. NARA Document 443-B. Harry S. Truman Library.

32 Official Report of Proceedings: Meeting of President's Committee on National Employ the Physically Handicapped Week. November 4, 1947. NARA Document 443-B, Harry S. Truman Library. P. 5.

33 Morgan C.T. *Human Engineering.* Essay: Reprinted in Leahey, Thomas Hardy. *A History of Psychology.* 1980. P. 370. First published in: *Current Trends in Psychology.* Wayne Dennis, editor. 1947. Reprinted in Leahey, Thomas Hardy. *A History of Psychology* 1980. p.370.

34 Benjamin, Ludy T. *A History of Psychology in Letters.* 1993. P. 190.

35 Watson, J.B. *Psychological Care of Infant and Child.* 1928. Pp. 81-87. Reprinted in Leahey, Thomas Hardy. P. 361.

36 Watson, J.B. The Behaviorist Looks at the Instincts. *Harper's* 1926, Vol.155. Pp. 345-352; Reprinted in Leahey. *A History of Psychology* 1980. P. 362.

37 Russian physiologist Pavlov conducted a series of experiments in canine digestive systems for which he received a Nobel Prize in 1904. During the course of the medical experiments, he noticed that there was an incidental increase in reactions to expected actions, the conditioned response." He spent the next thirty-two years researching condition responses in dogs, the theories of which were then applied to human psychological behavior. Although his experiments were hardly cruel (he was strict about asepsis and minimized the amount of trauma that the animals were subjected to) his methods would most likely be construed today as extremely inhumane.

38 Leahey, Thomas Hardy. P. 365.

39 ibid. P. 363.

40 ibid. Pp.356-367. and Glasser, Ronald J. *365 Days.* 1996. Pp.149-178.

41 Anastasi, Anne. *Psychological Testing.* 1988. Pp.12-15.

42 The ten scales are; hypochondria, depression, hysteria, psychopathic deviate, masculinity- femininity issues, paranoia, psychasthenia (phobias and compulsions), schizophrenia and social isolation traits. ibid. P. 527.

43 Freeman, Frank S. *Theory and Practice of Psychological Testing.* 1957. Pp. 472-474. and Anastasi, Anne. Pp. 523-534.

44 ibid. Pp. 16-17.

45 Kurian, George Thomas. *Datapedia of the United States.* 1994. Pp.136 ,141, 144

46 Davis, Kenneth S. P. 464.

47 Parrish, Thomas. Editor. The Simon *and Schuster Encyclopedia* of *World War II.* 1978. Pp.231-232.

48 U.S. Bureau of Census. *Historical Statistics of the United States, Colonial Times to 1970.* 1975. P. 385.

49 Bailey, Ronald H. P. 85.

50 Distel, Ruth, and Ruth Jakusch, Editors. *Concentration Camp Dachau, 1933-1945.* 1978. P.138.

51 Berenbaum, Michael. *The World Must Know.* 1993. P. 149.

52 Walters, Guy. *Hunting Evil.* 2010. Pp. 112-112

53 Bower, Tom. *Nazi Gold.* 1997. P. 91.

54 Davis, Kenneth S. Pp. 129-132.

55 ibid. Pp. 125-138.

5

A Trip to the Doctor: Drugs, Treatments, and Health Care

It is an unfortunate coincidence that medical science and war go hand in hand. It's also true that wars have a tendency to push medical practices to new heights. In merely the past century and a half, each war has brought about changes in techniques, procedures, and medical thinking. Through the work of Florence Nightingale during the Crimean War, nursing standards and the wholesale acceptance of trained women nurses for the wounded became standard practice. Bloody European conflicts also gave inspiration for the founding of the International Red Cross (IRC) in 1859 that sanctified the persons and equipment of battlefield medical providers. At about the same time, the American Civil War became the setting where organized ambulance services manned by specially trained litter-bearers applied rudimentary first-aid and retrieved the wounded from the battlefield, essentially becoming the first paramedics. After the United

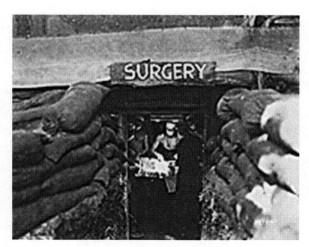

New Guinea field hospital surgery. Forward facilities were dug in and extensively sand-bagged due to the problems of shelling, deliberate or not.(US Army Medical Corps)

States occupied Cuba during the Spanish-American War, the American War Department dispatched a team of physicians led by Dr. Walter Reed to quell a Yellow Fever epidemic there. From their work, an inoculation was developed that protected against the disease. Further advances came from eradication efforts control the mosquitoes responsible for the spread of the disease. Within a year, Yellow Fever was just a bad memory in and around Havana. The First World War, as we shall see, offered up its own share of medical marvels.

The Second World War was no different. Although most of the "modern" surgical procedures—with the exception of thoracic surgery—had already been developed, the great challenges to medicine lay in the ultimate defeat of infection, the further development of therapies using electricity, and the adoption of and refinements to professional medical practices. In the earliest years of the war, being a medical practitioner was simultaneously thrilling, in that new breakthroughs were clearly on the horizon, and exasperating in that there were illnesses and diseases that required those treatments now.

Amphetamines

In 1930s Germany, medical researchers actively worked to uncover the mysteries of hormones. The center of their attention was on the human sex hormones, but they also explored other glandular organs such as the adrenal glands located on the kidneys. The adrenal glands secrete several important hormonal substances from their layered structure. The outer layer, called the cortex, produces hormones that regulate blood chemistry, sexual characteristics, and energy consumption within the muscles. The medulla generates the hormone adrenaline that governs blood flow by constricting the arteries and veins during stress or rest. Adrenaline gets released into the blood supply on command from the nervous system to help the body deal with stressors such as fright or shock.

German medical science pioneered the formation of biochemists, a title that made the members of a new specialty others of that community considered aberrant. Despite their contemporaries' disrespect, they learned to synthesize hormones and attempted to replicate adrenaline. Its practical uses included treating low blood pressure, heart problems, gastric complaints, and opening the constricted airways of asthmatics. As close as they came to making adrenaline, they missed their goal. What they discovered instead was a white crystalline powder that mimicked the stimulant charge of adrenaline. This new compound, generically called amphetamine, acted upon the central nervous system to heighten the senses, increase energy, and stimulate mental alertness. The downside was that the effects were short-lived and were followed by depression and, in some cases, heart failure.

Highly addictive, this entire class of drugs became useful during the Second World War for troops who were required to stay alert for extended periods of time. Amphetamines were airdropped among the tons of medical supplies to the French Resistance. Crews of B-29 bombers, struggling to stay awake for the long round trip to Japan, fortified themselves with coffee and Benzedrine (a brand-name form of amphetamine) tablets. Benzedrine sulfate tablets were also included in survival packs that all crewmembers carried in case they were marooned. Medical officers handed out the little white pills on request in volumes that, by today's standards, crossed the border into gross medical malpractice.

It was only in the pop culture of the 1960s that physicians came to realize the true nature of amphetamine use. Illicitly available from street dealers, amphetamine abusers often display rash and unpredictable behavior. What is now known to be amphetamine psychosis, which imitates paranoid schizophrenia, caused scores of deaths nationwide. Amphetamines are now strictly regulated and controlled by law, although methamphetamine is one of the most popular and dangerous illicit drugs on the market today.

Methadone

Despite Hitler's confidence as to the brevity of any forthcoming war, cooler heads within the Wehrmacht medical department pressed for a domestic source of opiate-based anesthetics. Morphine, which is derived from opium poppies indigenous to the Middle East, could become scarce if the war should last longer than anticipated. Queries to fulfill this need went out to all the major German pharmaceutical companies.

Bayer AG was already noteworthy for their research into a number of innovative products such as the popular aspirin tablet, and Bayer scientists were confident of quick results. Work began in mid-summer of 1939 and within a year the first production lots of methadone were ready for shipment. The pressure for the drug had been so intense that drawn-out clinical trials had been generally dispensed with. Instead, hospitalized German casualties were given either morphine or methadone in a semi-organized double blind trial. As methadone usage became more common, doctors reported that the drug had fewer negative side effects than its natural counterpart. Specifically, methadone appeared to be less addicting for long-term users, yet its painkilling abilities were longer lasting for a given dosage.

At the close of the war, methadone was just another war prize. Based on German wartime experience, the formulation for methadone was added into the pharmaco-poeia of the Allied nations where it was used almost interchangeably with other opiate medications. As it was inexpensive to manufacture, Veterans Administration hospitals relied on methadone as a way to break the physical morphine addictions of recovering soldiers who had received the drugs during the course of treatment for their war wounds. Although there were relatively few cases of profound physical and psychological morphine addiction, American doctors were well aware of the dangers of addicting their patients and severely restricted the usage of opiates, obviating the effects of chronic exposure. As the ranks of addicted GIs shrank, so too did the usage of methadone. It appeared that the synthetic drug was going to be just another inter-esting German invention that had had its day.

That is, until Dr. Marie Nysander began using it on heroin addicts in a study at the Rockefeller University in New York City. She and Dr. Vincent Dole, an expert in metabolic disorders had been doing research on treating the addictions of longtime hard-core illicit drug users throughout the early to mid-1960s. The idea was not to cure them—repeated studies in the past had shown that the great majority of opiate addicts were hopelessly stuck using drugs for their lifetime with ever-increasing dosages as their bodies developed a tolerance for the drugs—but to find a drug that allowed them to maintain dosages and possibly even function in society. When the experiments had clearly failed, the two doctors turned to methadone to detoxify the addicts prior to their release from the hospital.

Incredibly, the subjects' behavior changed radically within days of receiving methadone. No longer did they subsist in a drug-induced haze or suffer the painful effects of withdrawal. Instead, they were taking an active interest in life again. One patient wanted to begin painting while another expressed a desire to resume his college education. Dr. Nysander concluded that the methadone satisfied the body's chemical craving for opiates but did not suppress the higher brain functions like other opiates did.

Other investigators reached the same general conclusion and as a result, metha-done, the drug that was meant to ensure that war casualties were comfortable was to become the gateway to new life and hope for hundreds of thousands of drug users.

Anti-Malarial Drugs

Malaria ravaged the European continent for centuries. Italy was especially hard hit because of the large tracts of swampy land and the seasonably warm weather; hence the illness was given its name from the Italian for "bad air." Spread by mosquitoes, malaria is endemic in tropical and temperate regions worldwide and takes a disproportionate number of victims every year.

Until the 1920s, there was only one known treatment for malaria, quinine, which is derived from the bark of the cinchona plant, which was brought home to Spain around 1633 by explorers returning from the New World. While its reputation as an anti-malarial drug grew, so did demand. The Spanish government closely controlled the sale of quinine to approved buyers. One hundred-and-twenty years later, the Dutch undermined the Spanish quinine monopoly when they established cinchona plantations on their Pacific islands. Over the score of intervening decades, the Dutch constantly raised the price of the quinine they sold to their British neighbors. Not willing to abide by any monopolistic activities that affected their own business interests, the British sought out a substitute. They found William Perkins. Although he failed in his task to synthesize quinine, he succeeded instead in making a name for himself with artificial dyes. (We'll meet him again later in this chapter.)

Young cinchona plant being shown to War Department representatives. Cinchona is the plant source for quinine, which was available only from the Philippines, now under control of the Japanese. These plants came from a bag of seeds smuggled out at the minute when Manila fell. The drug is derived from the bark of adult plants. These would be adult about the time the fires of Nagasaki burned out. (OWI/NARA)

By the 1930s, the Dutch and the Spanish had lost their quinine monopolies. Most of the world's supply of quinine now came from the Philippine Islands. It was cheap and plentiful and America maintained a strong military presence there. No one saw any reason to grow it elsewhere. Germany's I.G. Farben synthesized quinine (called Atropine) in 1920 but it proved to be too expensive to compete with the naturally derived substance.

That all changed in December 1941. The Japanese invaded the Philippines and within a few months controlled the Allie's sole supply of quinine. But when it became obvious that the islands were going to fall, an American planter escaped with two bags of cinchona seeds. The bags journeyed to Central America where they were planted, but it would take several years for the plantation to produce even a fraction of the Allies' requirements.

Meanwhile, British forces in North Africa were capturing Italian troops who were carrying small packets of yellow pills. Under questioning, the Italians revealed that the tablets were supposed to prevent malaria. Samples of the tablets were rushed back to the United States, where they were analyzed and found to be ersatz copies of the Farben drug. Soon, American pharmaceutical factories were turning out thousands of the tiny yellow pills. As the first shipments reached the South Pacific in late 1942, the troops were expected to take one each day. They openly detested the ritual as the drug is extremely bitter tasting and has an unpleasant tendency to turn the skin a ghastly, albeit temporary, orange. Furthermore, the drug occasionally caused head- aches, nausea, vomiting, and, rarely, a temporary psychosis that terminated just as fast as it appeared, if the drug were withheld from the victim. One side effect that caused much resistance to its acceptance was that it caused impotency.[1]

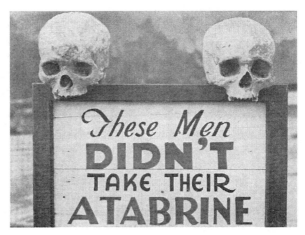

This grim reminder was brought to us by means of the Army Medical Corps. Atabrine was synthetic anti-malarial. After Japan seized the world's supply of quinine, Atabrine became the replacement. It was far better than the I.G. Farben drug, atropine. It was bitter and turned the skin orange. (U.S. Army Medical Corps)

As the war progressed, scientists in America succeeded in improving Farben's drug. Some areas, North Af- rica, certain Pacific islands, and Italy for example, have quinine-resistant malaria strains. In 1944, two young scientists, Robert Woodward and Wil- liam Doering, succeeded in synthesiz- ing quinacrine (trade named Atabrine) which was effective in preventing onset of the disease.[2]

Meperidine (Demerol)

As German scientists were attempting to synthesize opiates and anti-malarial drugs such as atropine, their work naturally resulted in some surprises. The meperidine class of drugs was one such surprise.

The constitutional structure of meperidine is quite similar to atropine, which the Germans substituted for quinine. During the clinical research phase, it became evident that meperidine shared many of the qualities of an opiate; it had analgesic effects like that of morphine, it depressed the central nervous system, and it repressed spasms of smooth muscle tissue—an important side effect for the treatment of injuries. But meperidine was far from being a replacement for morphine. It appeared that meperidine was a halfway drug, falling squarely between cocaine and morphine as an analgesic.

In some respects, meperidine was better than morphine. It was not nearly as addictive and dissipated rapidly, reducing the cumulative effects of opiate toxicity. Demerol, the proprietary name for meperidine, is a highly effective short-term painkiller with the added benefit of being a mild sedative. Injected, Demerol came to be useful as a pre-surgical anesthetic that increased the effects of gaseous anesthesia and reduced the amount of gas required for analgesia. In addition, it helped to control patients in the depths of psychological panic attacks. It was documented that a large dose of Demerol by mouth put the patient into an easily aroused slumber without too great a risk of respiratory failure, an ever-present risk with opiates.

Introduced in 1939 by German chemists Eisleb and Schaumann in a German pharmaceutical journal, Demerol soon was under production in America. When the United States went to war in 1941, Demerol was still undergoing trials and just becoming available to the medical community. Throughout the war, Demerol gained favor and proponents as more about the drug became known. Numerous studies during and after the war refined its uses and defined the precautions that had to be observed.[3]

Antibiotics

Infections have posed the greatest danger to mankind in previous centuries. A simple scratch could turn septic and lead to blood poisoning in a matter of days, causing an inevitable and unpleasant death. Until an agent could be found to destroy the infection without harming the patient, infections would continue to be the leading cause of death. The development of antibiotics, the name given to the whole class of infection fighters, came in a series of serendipitous discoveries that began in Victorian England.

For centuries, cloth was dyed in a limited selection of colors available from animal or vegetable sources. William Perkins of England discovered in 1856 that a coal tar derivative had stained his laboratory smock purple. The by-product that he had been working on was intended to be a type of artificial quinine. Instead, he had accidentally created the first artificial dye. Within months, Perkins' formula had made its way to

205

Germany. There, chemists began looking at coal for other colored dyes, and it was not long before German chemical firms were manufacturing a whole rainbow of colors from coal tar. One group of these, azodyes, proved to be interesting to the medical and biological sciences. (The "azo" prefix refers to the nitrogen molecules that this particular compound contains.)

During the last decade of the nineteenth century, microscopic examination of various substances became quite popular. To view the minute objects, numerous dyes and stains—the azodyes in particular—were tested. As a result, the responses of different compounds on the test organisms began to suggest that there were germicidal properties within some of the stains. From this experimentation, three solutions—acriflavine, mercurochrome, and gentian violet—all had periods of widespread use as local and general antiseptics. These are not truly antibiotics, as they do not kill the microbes; rather, they compete with the metabolic functions of the bacteria, effectively starving them. Each solution eventually lost its glamour as reports of toxic reactions accumulated when the common effective ingredient, arsenic, accumulated in the tissues. The cure had become worse than the disease. But there was hope in the near future.

Sulfa Drugs

One synthetic azo dye called Prontosil, formulated in 1905, was found to be effective on skin infections caused by streptococci. Workers in the German chemical plant where it was produced showed a marked decrease in the number of infected injuries and suffered from fewer upper respiratory tract infections than normal. This raised curiosity. Researchers found that Prontosil acted to eliminate staphylococci and trypanosomes—the parasitic microbes that cause such diseases such as sleeping sickness—in mice. When Prontosil was introduced as a treatment for skin injuries, incidents of blood poisoning, typically fatal, quickly dropped. But the big breakthrough for Prontosil was in the treatment of syphilis. Like the other azo-dye solutions, Prontosil contained significant amounts of arsenic, which is obviously poisonous. Research into arsenical compounds continued and, although less toxic arsenic substances were introduced, the toxicity problem was never fully solved. Common wisdom among medical researchers was that there was no way to surmount infections without risking the patient.

However, hope springs eternal. In 1927, chemist Gerhard Domagk, working for the German firm of I. G. Farben, began a systematic search for any chemical substance that affected bacteria. Five exhausting years later, his search had come full circle back to azodyes. One in particular, a red dye used in leatherwork, showed a remarkable tendency to control streptococcal infections, but the arsenic remained a problem. In Paris, Swiss physiologist Daniel Bovet received a sample of Domagk's Prontosil Red for further study. Bovet discovered that the ingested drug metabolized into two separate components. One of these parts, sulfanilamide, interfered with the bacteria's ability to reproduce. This news spurred Domagk to rush sulfanilamide into production and distribution.

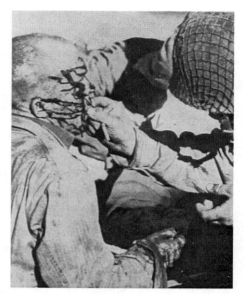

Medic gives injured American soldier a sulfa tablet. Sulfa had only a few years of practical applications but it was successful in treating a host of infectious problems. Even so, the introduction of penicillin would earn the drug the title "miracle drug." (U.S. Army)

Although it was effective against a number of common ailments, sulfanilamide could not cure one of the greatest killers of the period, pneumonia. Research was taken up to find similar drugs. In 1938, Briton A.J. Ewins discovered sulfadiazine while an American, Walter Fosbinder, simultaneously and independently introduced sulfathiazole.

The timing of the introduction of a wide variety of sulfa drugs, as they became commonly grouped, could not have been better. Sulfa drugs were a major reason for the dramatically reduced mortality rates among military casualties during the Second World War. Every Allied soldier was issued a small packet of sulfa powder that was to be sprinkled directly upon any open wound as soon as possible. This act alone reduced the incidence of infection, often eliminating the need for a protracted convalescence. Aside from trauma injuries, sulfa drugs also ended an infection that threatened the very outcome of the war. Busy with the multitude of war concerns, Winston Churchill became weakened and eventually contracted pneumonia. His swift and uneventful recovery was precipitated by a course of Ewins' sulfadiazine.[4]

Penicillin

In 1928 in England, a laboratory dish of culturing bacteria was discovered growing an unidentified mold. A very few spores, drifting into the small laboratory in London's

St. Mary's Hospital on a fortuitous breeze, had contaminated the staphylococcus culture. As it grew, the blue mold excreted a chemical that destroyed nearby staph and changed the course of medical history.

The director of the laboratory, Dr. Alexander Fleming, reported on the antibacterial actions of the mold, *Penicillium Notatum,* in a report published in a 1929 edition of the *British Journal of Experimental Pathology.* In his paper, he speculated on the possibilities that the mold would be effective in obstructing the growth of bacteria. In February of that same year, Fleming gave a lecture on his discovery to an assemblage of pathologists. Naturally a quiet and modest man, Fleming's nearly inaudible presentation lacked the enthusiasm to match his discovery's import. The conference attendees missed out on an opportunity to make history while the report and presentation faded into near-oblivion.

Dr. Alexander Fleming, the original discoverer of penicillin, gives a young serviceman a narrative of the drug he isolated. The contents of a similar vial saved the life of this soldier, just as did thousands of others. (U.S. Army Medical Corps)

Penicillin was not without its troubles. It tended to be easily contaminated with toxins and was difficult to grow in quantity. Despite repeated attempts to separate the active component from the mold excretion, obtaining a pure sample seemed beyond possibility. Nevertheless, Fleming offered samples of penicillin-laced ointment around the hospital where it had a number of modest successes. When Domagk's sulfa drugs became available, interest in penicillin waned. It appeared that penicillin would continue to be a laboratory curiosity.[5]

The unrelenting economic woes of the Depression played a part in its resurrection. Two researchers, Australian Howard Florey and Ernst B. Chain, a German refugee, started studies on the mold at the Sir William Dunn School of Pathology, part of England's prestigious Oxford University. The school had been teetering on the edge of financial collapse and, in desperation, turned to the Americans for help in 1939. With an annual grant of $5000 from the Rockefeller Foundation and Merck Laboratories, the Dunn School was to pursue purely basic research on potential antimicrobial agents.

Florey wanted to pursue his line of research based on a naturally occurring agent found in human tears. He looked up and read every one of almost two hundred scientific papers on the subject. It was during this stage of research that Florey chanced upon Fleming's paper. Penicillin appeared to have far more potential, even though it had been virtually ignored for nearly ten years. At Florey's insistence, penicillin was added to the Merck research project.

Within a year, penicillin had been chemically charted and analyzed and samples were ready for testing on animals. They injected a group of eight mice with streptococcus-tainted serum. Half the infected mice then received injections of penicillin 45 minutes later and again at three hours. By the wee hours of the next morning, all of the penicillin-treated rodents showed no signs of infection, while those that had not been treated were dead. Certain of their success, the Oxford team turned their attention to producing more of their drug so that human clinical tests could begin at once. There was one catch; the mouse experiment had completely depleted the supply of penicillin.

Almost all of 1940 passed before more penicillin was available. Much of that time was spent recreating files and records for shipment to America. The Blitz was at its worst and the future of Britain looked grim. Nevertheless, Florey and Chain pressed forward at home. The laboratory was turned into a makeshift penicillin factory, with every available container put to work fermenting the drug. Stacks of cookie sheets, pie pans, and milk bottles competed for space with Petri dishes and conventional laboratory equipment. It was found that the most efficient receptacles were bedpans from the nearby Radcliffe Infirmary.

Armed with more of the drug, the research team began to look towards limited clinical trials on humans. In the early days of 1941, Florey approached the director of the Radcliffe Infirmary for help to find a likely candidate for the drug's initial trials, which represented a considerable risk for the participant. A patient who was already dying was preferred.

Their first patient, Albert Alexander, was a forty-three-year-old constable who had been scratched on the face by a thorn, and the wound had turned septic. He had multiple infections about the head, face, eyes—one eye had already been surgically removed—and the lungs. Soon after the intravenous injection of penicillin, his fever dropped. But the available amount of the drug, by the physicians' calculations, was not enough to provide for a full recovery. To acquire more, the doctors collected Alexander's urine and refined the unabsorbed penicillin back into a deliverable form. Unfortunately, this method of recycling fell short of requirements. After Alexander rallied to nearly full recovery, the drug supply ran out and he died. Other patients with a variety of infections received the new antibiotic as part of the clinical test—mostly children, as the required dosages were lower than for adults. Of six cases treated, four showed marvelous recoveries; one died from conditions that penicillin could not treat—a ruptured vessel in the brain—and the other was the unfortunate constable, Albert Alexander.

The American side of the research program got high priority. With financing from the Rockefeller Foundation and with laboratories provided by the United States Department of Agriculture's Northern Regional Research Laboratory (NRRL) in Peoria, Illinois, the investigation continued. The NRRL developed a culture medium that would favor production of the greatest amounts of penicillin. In addition, they worked to create the most productive strains. Working with the NRRL, Merck Laboratories began limited production in its plant in New Jersey. In the beginning, only minuscule amounts of the drug could be cultured as the formula for the growth culture became perfected.[6]

Even as the multitude of government agencies and pharmaceutical companies worked to make penicillin, the clinical trials continued. A number of minor cures, remarkable in their own right, took place, but none as spectacular as the case of Ann Miller, in 1942.

A wife and mother of three young children from New Haven, Connecticut, Ann had contracted a streptococcus infection from her son. Pregnant, she soon miscarried, as the bacteria spread throughout her body. Taken to the hospital, she received blood transfusions and sulfa drugs and had surgery to tie off inflamed blood vessels. In desperation, doctors even gave the woman rattlesnake venom and scarlet fever serum in the vain hope of beating the infection.

By strange coincidence, a friend of a member of the Oxford research team was in the same hospital as Mrs. Miller. Ill himself, he learned about the Miller woman and related the experiences of penicillin as he had heard them from his associate. Contacts at Merck agreed to supply the new drug and promptly sent along a supply that amounted to approximately one teaspoon. After twelve days of one-hundred-and-four-degree fever, and only hours after receiving the penicillin, Ann Miller's fever broke. By that same afternoon, the recently semiconscious woman ate her first meal in four weeks.[7]

The remarkable recovery of Mrs. Miller added steel to the determination of the research program. The potential of saving thousands of troops from infected war wounds provided the impetus to begin mass production. So thorough was the search for new strains of likely molds that the two most prolific ones were found on a rotting cantaloupe in an alley garbage can in Peoria, Illinois and an aging orange in the refrigera-

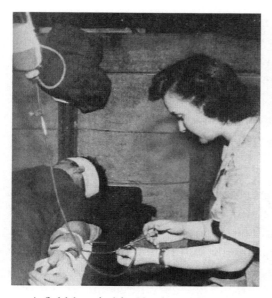

A field hospital in Northwest Europe. The soldier is receiving blood plasma from the bottle, a breakthrough in treatment. In addition, the nurse is injecting him with a phenomenal new drug, penicillin. It was isolated in the days before the war and remained unknown to the Axis, although prisoners were given the drug when enough was available to give everybody. Untold thousands were saved by the therapy. (U.S. Army/NARA)

tor in neighboring Urbana. Dozens of plants were built and hundreds of personnel hired to tend the giant stainless steel vats. Trials to find the best fermentation media resulted in a corn "liquor" solution. X-rays and ultraviolet radiation mutated other strains. The results of the work were impressive. Before January 1943, commercial penicillin production was so insignificant that its volume was virtually unrecorded. In May, 1943, 400 million units became available. Even this amount could treat only about four hundred hospitalized patients, however. Within a month, another 425 million units came out of the gigantic fermentation tanks. Production of the precious liquid continued to rise until the end of the war, when the monthly output of penicillin was measured in billions of units.[8]

The importance of the rapid development of the various strains of penicillin and the massive production cannot be overemphasized. Although there is no way to measure the numbers of lives saved from the use of penicillin, it is a safe bet to say that the number of Allied dead would be far higher than 2.19 million.[9] Furthermore, there were scores of thousands of Allied POWs who were disabled with a large variety of exotic diseases and chronic infections that would have been largely incurable except for the new antibiotics.

Standardized Penicillin Units

By war's end there were over one thousand known strains of penicillin, each with its own level of effectiveness, making it essential to establish a standardized unit. In October 1944, an international dosage was declared by treaty. The Oxford University team had determined an arbitrary standard that measured the amount of the drug that inhibited culture growth in a 24mm circle, or about an inch. As the newer strains were many times stronger than those first experimented with in 1940, a common strain under culture in both the United States and Britain was chosen to become the standard instead. Thereafter, strain G was selected as the one that all others were measured by. One milligram of dissolved strain G penicillin contains 1,667 units. By exhaustive testing, all other strains could then be graded and their individual dosages determined.[10]

Streptomycin

While Florey's penicillin studies were beginning in England, Selman Waksman in America was noting that soil had the curious ability to cleanse itself of the pathogenic agents that cause diseases such as leprosy, influenza, and the plague, to name a very few. With the exceptions of tetanus, botulism, gangrene, and anthrax, the soil was rarely found to be the source of disease despite repeated contamination. Numerous studies since the days of Louis Pasteur had failed to turn up any specific agent responsible for this quality, although several theories abounded.

Waksman, a Russian immigrant and noted soil biologist working for the U.S. Department of Agriculture, was attempting to isolate the mechanism that cleaned the dirt. He discovered that under certain conditions of moisture and aeration, the soil harbored microorganisms that produced chemicals toxic to pathogens. Waksman systematically gleaned samples of these organisms from a variety of unlikely places such as a freshly manured field, swamp mud, and from the throat of a chicken. In 1940, Waksman had isolated actinomycin. Extremely lethal to bacteria, it proved to be too toxic even for animal trials. Despite this minor setback, Waksman continued his research. Three years later, he discovered a mold, *Streptomyces griseus* that produced a drug he called Streptomycin.

Laboratory tests indicated that Streptomycin differed greatly from penicillin, which, by now was being acclaimed as a "wonder drug." In particular, Streptomycin selectively attacked cholera and typhoid. Both diseases thrived wherever overcrowding occurred and hygiene services, such as fresh water delivery and sewage removal, had broken down. These conditions were all too prevalent on the Eastern Front where hygiene was already poor and the extraordinary brutality of the German occupation exacerbated the conditions. Although Streptomycin was not available early in the war, mass production of the drug had accumulated enough to be used in the post-war treatment of victims of the prison and concentration camps as well as spot outbreaks worldwide.[11]

Other mold-based organisms became the sources of new drugs. As fewer natural compounds were found, post-war laboratories poured forth a wealth of synthetic antibiotics originally derived from natural materials, such as tetracycline, Erythromycin, and Terramycin. Presently, the list continues to expand and new drugs are constantly being sought. The unfortunate result of the antibiotic miracle is that the targeted germs eventually become immune to the actions of the drugs. The new threat is MRSA (Methicillin-Resistant *Staphylococcus Aureus*), a nasty bug that has shown resistant to the latest and best of the synthetic antibiotics.

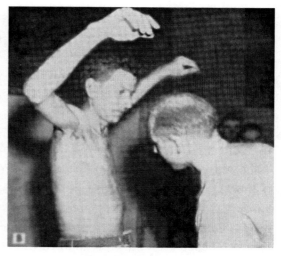

The prisoners of the Japanese all came back in some degree emaciated. Some, because they had been held in cooler climates, had very little parasitic burden. This poor fellow however has three different parasites and tuberculosis, a disease that he acquired compliments of his hosts. The medical issues these men lived with for the rest of their lives makes one wonder how they managed to survive the Japanese. (US Army Medical Corps)

Anesthesia

Surgery before anesthesia was discovered was not an experience undertaken lightly. Whenever a procedure involving deliberate cutting of flesh was performed, a number of strong assistants would be employed to restrain the patient. Even then, cries of anguish would rend the air. Surgeons adopted techniques that minimized the actual time spent wielding the knife. Surgery within body cavities was unheard of and remedial limb surgery consisted of removal. With some pride, physicians would advertise their superior amputation techniques as being the fastest and therefore the least painful.

Beginning in 1844, with the introduction of nitrous oxide, invasive medical procedures were looked upon with less reluctance by both patients and surgeons. An impressive array of anesthetics soon followed, although many of the early anesthetics had destructive side effects that went unnoticed for years.

First discovered in 1830, chloroform did not become popular until just prior to the American Civil War. Touted as a wonder anesthetic, it was widely used for nearly eighty years, until it was blamed for a delayed onset of liver damage. Cocaine enjoyed a period of widespread use for its analgesic effects but eventually lost favor because of its terrible addictiveness. Ether and ethyl chloride were somewhat safer, but an overdose was all too easy to administer in light of the crude delivery systems of the time.[12]

Injectable drugs became quite popular with the introduction of Novocaine and Procaine. This whole class of local anesthetics, derived from coal tar, came into use at the turn of the century. Looking for faster-acting intravenous drugs, German researchers produced the barbiturate-based hexobarbital and sodium pentothal. The latter gained notoriety as a so-called truth serum because it lowered blood pressure to the brain, making its victim light-headed and more likely to talk freely.

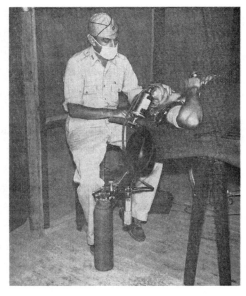

Oxygen/ether anesthesia was the preferred method for field surgery. The equipment was minimal, the effects sure, and relatively safe. (US Army Medical Corps)

Cyclopropane

When the negative side effects of contemporary anesthesia such as chloroform began to appear, experts recommended gases as the best means of putting someone to sleep. Cyclopropane was the first of the important gaseous anesthesia, developed in Canada beginning in the mid-1930s. It is rendered from propylene, the base chemical compound that also forms a major plastic, polypropylene. When used with oxygen, this gas apparently has no negative effects on the liver, kidneys, brain, or heart, and it dissipates from the body rapidly. Even better, the amount of gas needed for deep anesthesia is minuscule. The real danger of cyclopropane lies in its potency. Unless the anesthetist closely monitors the patient, overdose can occur, causing breathing to stop. Then it is up to the physician to apply artificial respiration to save the patient. It was decided that the answer to this dilemma was to insert an airway before surgery. To do that the patient needed to stop breathing. It was another dilemma leading to another solution.

Curare and the Endotracheal Tube

In 1935, naturalist Richard C. Gill, recently returned to America from the wilds of the Amazon River basin, told of indigenous tribes that used an ingenious hunting technique. The hunter would dip the tip of his arrow into a sticky brown paste that he carried in a gourd. When the arrow struck the target, the poison in the paste would paralyze the prey, eventually causing death from asphyxiation. The poison could be eaten and touched with impunity as long as there were no open sores in the skin or the mouth. Hearing of this, researchers set out to find the mysterious toxin. What they eventually found, in 1938, became the perfect anesthesia adjunct. Curare affects primarily the nervous system to interfere with muscle control, in particular, the muscles of the diaphragm. It does not cause liver or kidney damage, is controllable in that its effects are temporary, and it allows the introduction of an airway.

The idea of the endotracheal airway, which had been only occasionally used since its inception in the late 1800s, began to gain widespread favor. The curare paralyzed the patient's gag reflex momentarily, allowing the passage of the tube into the throat. Once in, the tube permitted the introduction of the new gaseous anesthesia and oxygen, both closely monitored by the anesthetist.[13] During the course of the war, thousands of surgical cases used endotracheal tubes with curare, forming a base of valuable experience for post-war medical applications. Much

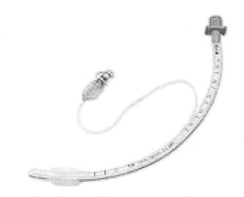

An endotracheal tube. The large one went into the trachea, the small one inflated to hold the tube in place.

later, the active agent of curare was synthesized into a drug called succinycholine and it remains an important part of modern surgical medicine.[14]

Trilene (Trichlorethylene)

Trichlorethylene is another chemical that got its big break with the growing plastics industry. Beginning in 1935, the search for the ultimate gaseous anesthesia led to a small-scale trial using Trilene, a highly purified trichlorethylene. Although the results were promising, financial considerations of the time led to the study's abandonment.

In the midst of the London Blitz of 1940, British physician C.L. Hewer reintroduced the use of Trilene as a non-explosive anesthesia agent. Under Hewer, Trilene's safety and efficacy were proven beyond a doubt, ensuring its addition into modern pharmacopoeia.

The Oximeter

Developments of military aviation in the inter-war period were limited by the human requirement of oxygen for survival. Generally, most people are incapable of staying for long above 12,000 feet above sea level without succumbing to unconsciousness. As far back as the First World War, a number of schemes were devised to deliver oxygen to aircrew, either carried on their persons or as an integral part of the aircraft. The technology lagged, however, as a large number of challenges complicated the problem.

The equipment needed to be extremely light and yet robust as well as immune from freezing and icing in a sub-zero climate year-around. It needed to allow for unimpeded speech while the delivery mask completely sealed the nose and mouth. Despite this full facial coverage, the vision was not to be restricted in any way as being able to see the cockpit instruments was just as important as being able to see an attacking enemy plane. Furthermore, there were differing conditions in which crewmembers required oxygen, at work or at rest, under stress or quite relaxed. Either way, the physiological demands for oxygen were widely different and a large man would need even more volume than one with a small frame. The challenge was so great and the hurdle so daunting that the American authority on aircraft oxygen systems and director of the U.S. Army Air Corps School of Aviation Medicine, Maj. Harry G. Armstrong M.D., stated in his 1939 treatise that, "up to the present time no method of oxygen administration has completely fulfilled this ideal and there appears to be little chance that such will ever be attained."[15]

Despite this influential proclamation, the Allied forces in 1942 were well on the way to developing several reliable oxygen delivery systems, thanks, in part, to the Luftwaffe. Captured samples of German aircraft revealed that their scientists had made some leaps in the technology. These examples were soon dissected and American versions installed in a number of research facilities around the country.

Volunteers, mostly Army Air Forces enlisted men and a few college students were recruited and subjected to a variety of tasks wearing the oxygen masks while being enclosed in specially built altitude chambers. Some walked or ran on treadmills while other test subjects moved heavy boxes to replicate handling ammunition cases at altitude. Others attempted to perform mathematical problems without the benefit of oxygen while a control group repeated the experiment with oxygen. The latter experiment would hardly be considered ethical now, as it is too dangerous to expose members of an investigation to such a hypoxic state. However, it is not as if the scientists had no way of closely monitoring the oxygen content of the test subject's blood.

Early in the experimental period, around 1940, the photoelectric oximeter was developed for the express purpose of measuring this vital function. The device depended on the opacity of the fully flushed ear, where the actual measurement was taken. A light-emitting diode was caused to shine through the ear lobe into a light-sensitive pickup. The resulting light at the pickup generated a tiny voltage that was directly correlated to the percentage of oxygenation within the blood. Direct contact with the blood was not required. Remarkably, the accuracy was constant at any temperature or pressure, ensuring that later trials in actual aircraft would replicate what had been observed in the laboratory.

Throughout the war, Allied air cadets also wore the oximeter during their first few flights to ensure that they had no undiagnosed respiratory or blood diseases that would cause them to lose consciousness and die from hypoxia, an event that happened all too often.[16] The oximeter is rarely clipped on the ear anymore, as the finger is much more convenient.

Blood Plasma Products

The component materials of human blood became apparent with the invention of the mechanical centrifuge in 1889. By placing fresh whole blood in a glass tube and rapidly spinning the tube, bottom out, the heavier cells separated from the liquid, or plasma. This procedure became quite important in later years in performing the important diagnostic procedure called a blood count.[17]

In 1901, Dr. Karl Landsteiner discovered blood typing, clarifying the need to match the donor with the recipient. This milestone has been regarded as the first true human organ transplant.[18] It also became a basis for understanding cellular rejection. The blood types A, B, 0 and later, AB, refer to the antibodies within the whole blood. For example, type A blood contains antibodies that react unfavorably with other blood types, causing the cells to clump together. This clotting, known as agglutination, can lead to kidney damage or even death for the recipient. The same holds true for the other types, although 0 can be given to A, B, and AB type recipients.[19]

Blood plasma storage: CBI Theater. World War II has been occasionally referred to as a racist war. In this situation the critics are right. The blood plasma on the left is Chinese, reserved for their exclusive use. On the right are blood products only for treating Anglos. This should not be such a surprise. Until the 1950's—later in some places—American blood supply was segregated between Black and White. (US Army Medical Corps)

The transfusion of fresh blood became more common as the new century progressed, although typically between family members since blood types are passed on genetically. The first wholesale use of stored blood came during the Battle of Cambrai in 1917. It had been discovered that whole blood could be kept fresh for up to a month if chilled and slightly diluted with sodium citrate. The treatment was used as a last resort though.[20]

Finding willing donors was a problem in obtaining enough blood for emergencies. The Russians tackled the problem in their own unique way in about 1932. They began to siphon off blood from fresh cadavers and to establish storage facilities for it. This was the first example of the modern blood bank. The idea made its way into Western Europe and America, where live donors were preferred.[21]

At about the same time, Cook County Hospital in Chicago adopted a plan for storing donated blood. This program, begun by the American Red Cross, was to prove important during the coming war. It had been realized, though, that the thirty-day period suggested in 1917 was too long. Ten, or at best, fifteen days, was the maximum that blood could be stored and remain fresh. This was impractical for troops on the front lines, as quantity shipments could take longer than time allowed. Clearly, a new way had to be found.

Just before the attack on Pearl Harbor, Harvard University researchers, at the request of the American military, started to study the problems of storing and shipping blood. New technology from Sweden for freeze-drying food was adapted to the plasma component of blood. Bottled as powder, the plasma would last indefinitely at room temperature. On the battlefield, the medic would have only to add distilled water to reconstitute the life-saving fluid. Wounded GIs by the tens of thousands received transfusions either directly on the battlefield or soon after being evacuated. There is no way to document the scores of otherwise doomed soldiers who were saved from death due to blood loss and shock.[22]

Further studies during the war revealed that there were more blood constituents to be found, such as different blood-borne enzymes that perform various functions. Albumin, for example, controls the balance of fluids retained in all the cells. The body's natural protection from uncontrolled bleeding relies on fibrinogen and thrombin, two enzymes that work together to begin the blood-clotting process at an injury site. Gamma globulin, an important part of the immune system, is manufactured in the lymphatic system. All antibodies are gamma globulin molecules. When the body detects an infective agent, the specific protein molecules react chemically to the foreign substance to destroy it. These enzymes were removed from the whole blood, preserved, and made available to physicians and combat medics to support their patients.[23]

Even more advancements came from blood studies immediately after the war. Packed red cells were used to treat anemia, which causes poor oxygen-carrying capacity. Leukocytes, or white cells, became available for replacement therapy in patients being treated for leukemia. When certain chemotherapies destroy the body's platelet supply, another component of the blood attaches to damaged tissues and forms the bulk of the clot, bound together with fibrinogen to stop bleeding. Diseases such as hemophilia can be treated with massive transfusions of platelets.

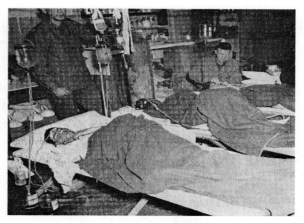

Shock ward in France, 1944. Shock was a problem for the doctors during the war. They had observed it during World War I, but they thought it was due to volumetric blood loss. Now they could replace the blood volume, but shock still occurred. Wards like this, analogous to intensive care today, helped but the problem remained for another ten years. (US Army Medical Corps)

The Tetanus Vaccine

Over the centuries, lockjaw, to use the ancient and descriptive name for tetanus, has befuddled military doctors. Although the tetanus bacillus is quite common, it takes an open wound contaminated with spores of the dirt-borne agent to become dangerous. Even with those favorable conditions, tetanus does not necessarily begin to grow. It favors deep, dirty wounds, left untreated for hours or even days at a time. It likes a host who lives outdoors, getting little proper rest and food, wearing down natural resistance. Unfortunately, those are the conditions that perfectly describe the soldier.

During the First World War, a rough antitoxin was developed that was somewhat effective on the wounded if the treatment were given in a timely manner. Doctors in that war saw the tetanus death rate drop from ninety percent to fifty percent. That statistic also depended on the injured soldiers' home country. German soldiers never had better than a seventy-five percent chance of recovering while the Americans, benefiting from their allies' past experiences lost only one man in nine.[24]

The antitoxin was a wonder for the men in the trenches but they were instructed that they had to receive a dose every time they got even the slightest scratch. Even though the men had seen friends and comrades die horribly of unchecked tetanus, it just would not work for them to stop in the middle of battle to seek out treatment for incidental injuries. Even when they did get the injection of antitoxin, more often than not they had severe serum sickness—marked by aching joints and muscles, fever, and general malaise—that took them out of the fight for up to two weeks, and there were even a few fatalities. It became a choice between dying at the hands of the enemy from without or from toxin created by the enemy within. Morale on all sides plummeted over this rational fear.

There were the usual promises of research, but the war to end all wars came to an end. There was little incentive to push government-funded research into high gear, and private funds were limited in the post-war era. With an effective antitoxin, the death rate of tetanus would return to its normal rate incidence among farmers and such, or so went the reasoning.

At the end of the war, Georges Ramon of the Pasteur Institute in Paris, began what would become a ten year research project on a diphtheria vac-

American servicewomen getting their periodic inoculations. The advent of a truly effective tetanus vaccine was well timed. (US Army)

cine. Prior to this, the diphtheria vaccine was basically a weakened version of the live virus, still capable of delivering a fatal illness if the patient weren't in tip-top health. Ramon sought to detoxify the vaccine and eliminate the side effects of the purported cure. Finally, he and his team created a vaccine that provided lasting immunity.

Being pragmatic, Ramon then turned his attention to "piggybacking" vaccines. Patients didn't want injection after injection for some disease that might not strike in the first place. Although there seemed few similarities between diphtheria and tetanus, Ramon well understood how tetanus worked and realized that the tetanus antitoxin acted remarkably like the old diphtheria vaccine, with the same reactions, the same serum sickness, and the same need to treat the illness in the early stages.

From 1926 on, Ramon worked on tetanus. His first experimental cases were horses from the French Army. His work was soon rewarded with a marked decrease in tetanus infections of the entire stable, but there was little notice taken. In the mind of the public, there was a vast difference between diseases of a horse and those of humans. For lack of a large body of two-legged volunteers predisposed toward tetanus infection, Ramon's vaccine would be just an interesting article in some obscure professional journal. Such was the way of science, at least until 1934.

That is when the U.S. Navy decided to try Ramon's vaccine aboard the hospital ship *Relief* under the direction of Commander W.W. Hall. Fifty volunteers received injections at various intervals. The idea was to determine the levels of immunity for a given number of injections and the efficacy of the general vaccine. Midway through the test, a newer version of the tetanus vaccine became available, and the experiment took on a whole new aspect, comparing the new with the old as well as determining the values of protection for both inoculations. Spread over three years, the Navy's test was enough of a success, especially with the new vaccine, to warrant a larger body of recipients.

A whole new batch of the new vaccine was acquired, and the football team of the U.S. Naval Academy enlisted in the cause. Blood tests confirmed that the serum was instilling immunity but there numerous problems with serum illness and allergic reactions that took players out of the game. Another puzzling change was the fact that immunity inexplicably wore off after two weeks, a far cry from lifetime immunity.

Believing that the limit number of participants skewed the test, Hall induced the entire Academy class of about twenty three hundred to take the vaccine. Soon, nearly two dozen midshipmen were reporting to sickbay suffering from chills, fever, aches, and pains, and one very nasty case of hives. Eight weeks later, the "Mids" were subjected to a second round of injections to boost the body's reaction to the tetanus toxin. This time more than fifty volunteers had reactions, one so severe that he nearly died. And there were still five hundred of the original two thousand three hundred who had not received their shots. Hall was appalled. Clearly the football team was not to blame.

Back in the lab it was determined that the vaccine had been contaminated during manufacture. Hall developed a series of tests to check for the purity of the serum and modified the manufacturing process to improve the vaccine slightly. Bucking up his courage, Hall approached the final—and understandably skeptical—five hundred and gave them their shots. One can only imagine Hall's trepidation at having more men succumb to the ravages of serum sickness and the long wait for the hammer to fall on his career. But it was not to happen. There was not one single case of reaction, no fever, no chills, no systematic shock.

This last victory and a thorough explanation for the debacle to the academy's senior officers gave reason enough for one more mass test. The incoming classes of 1939, all seven hundred and ninety three, were to be inoculated. One by one, they received the needle and after three days, not one had become ill. There was not even a single complaint of sore arm. Based on the evidence in hand, naval medical officials made tetanus vaccination compulsory. And just in time too.

In a few short months, the British and French forces had been encircled at Dunkirk on the French coast. Under constant fire for nine days, the British made an astonishing withdrawal of over 338,000 troops. Conditions on the beaches were quite similar to those experienced in the First World War. Rations were short, medical attention spotty. The men were demoralized, tired, dirty, and exhausted from weeks of fighting and running and hiding from the Germans. Conditions were perfect for a huge influx of tetanus infection. Of the 16,000 inoculated casualties to make it back across the Channel, not one came down with tetanus. But the British Army had been sanguine about the vaccination and had not made it compulsory. As a result, there were eight cases of tetanus out of the eighteen hundred men who did not get their shots.

When the reports of the outcome of the Dunkirk evacuation came to America, the outstanding fact of the tetanus vaccine's efficacy spurred the Surgeon General to order that all service people be inoculated immediately and that they receive annual boosters. Due to this action, there were fewer than twenty incidents of acute tetanus infection for all services throughout the war.[25]

The Pernkopf Medical Atlas

Of all the medical references produced throughout the ages, the Pernkopf Anatomy Atlas—its proper name being *Atlas of Topographical and Applied Human Anatomy*—is "the standard by which all other illustrated anatomical works are measured," opines David Williams.[26] Used more in European medical schools than in America, the atlas features large, full-color paintings of the human anatomy.

A highly regarded anatomist in his day, Eduard Pernkopf contracted with the University of Vienna to produce the book in 1930. His team of artists had their work well under way when the war erupted. Since Pernkopf was sympathetic to the National Socialist (Nazi) movement, many of the paintings from this early period were signed with swastikas or other runic symbols used by the Nazis.

A malignant anti-Semite and ardent Nazi, Pernkopf was instrumental in removing 153 Jews and other "non-Aryans" from the staff of the university. Within days of Hitler's annexation of Austria, in 1938, the Nazis named Pernkopf as the Medical Faculty Dean. Five years later, in a further gesture of gratitude, the Nazis promoted him to the office of President of the University.[27] It was that same year that the first volumes of his anatomy books were published. He remained at the head of the University until he was captured at the end of the war. For crimes real or imaginary, Pernkopf was to spend three years in a Russian prison camp at hard labor. In his absence, work on the atlas continued. Upon returning to Vienna, Pernkopf resumed his work with his loyal artists, most of them having survived the war, and subsequently finished the texts. Having made his professional mark on medical literature, Eduard Pernkopf faded into obscurity.

The seven-volume set was updated in early 1963 with new materials. Medical progress had developed a need for lung, heart, and brain anatomy, which the German publishers of the book were ready to meet. Reduced to two volumes, the atlas used a quantity of the early art work in addition to drawings done in the late 1950s and X-ray plates. The decorative Nazi symbols were removed—not surprising as the post-war German government had outlawed the display of any Nazi symbol in 1948—as were the extensive textual descriptions that made the early books so voluminous.

As the text states, Pernkopf's anatomy book was corrupted with Nazi-sponsored runic symbols, that were relics left in the art. This author has a two-volume set and looked for it. At first glance, the above (pg.259) was soon evident. F. Bratke is obviously the artist's name. Following is what appears to be the double lightening symbols of the notorious SS. (below) A blow-up of the above picture is immediately below, which reinforces the contentions.

As the Pernkopf story goes, this project took over ten years to complete. The artists signed and dated their work, as it should be. A few pages away, the artist signed his name again. But this time it was in 1949. Looking close, F. Btatke drops the first two numbers from the date. His four, though, still looks like one runic S. It is pretty conclusive that the much maligned Pernkopf books; not that they did not deserve some, is not promoting the SS, but is the victim of an artist with careless printing of his numeral fours. Further investigation in volume 1 shows that the artist F. Bratke butchers his fours on several dates, including 54(pg.39), 42(pg.242), 44(pgs.244-245), 49(pg.253), 44(pg.254),and 49(pg.270).

Then, in 1986, David J. Williams, professor and director of medical illustration at Purdue University, presented a professional paper on the atlas. Questions arose as to the source of the cadavers used in the early volumes. The ensuing firestorm of indignation over the possibility that concentration camp victims may have been used as models created a debate that rages still. Williams believes that the models were victims of political terror, mostly Communist sympathizers and criminals executed by the Gestapo in Vienna, Munich and Prague.[28]

A complete investigation is underway to discover if the bodies actually came from the camps. A suggestion to include a commemoration in each newly published edition honoring the victims of the Nazis is being considered.

The Physiology of Transplanted Tissue

The effects of war damage more than bone. Explosions, fire and ripping of flesh by projectiles all cause enormous amounts of harm. Repairing the skin, the body's first defense from infection and fluid loss, is always a priority. Physicians tried for years to graft new skin from animal and human donors over damaged areas, but in vain. The graft would begin to adhere and seem to grow to the host site, yet the transplant would die within a few days.

As the German Blitz over London intensified, Peter B. Medawar, a young Syrian zookeeper/biologist, joined a team of prominent British scientists to study tissue rejections. Medawar reviewed all the work on grafts up till then and made his report. In his opinion, a skin graft could not come from another human or an animal if it were meant to be permanent. He explained that the same antibodies that caused reactions in blood transfusions were inducing the graft failure.[29]

By 1942, he started clinical experiments with rabbits. Taking a round sample of skin from the donor and affixing the "button" to the recipient animal, he conclusively proved that a reaction from the immune system was defeating the graft. He further showed that identical twins could exchange tissue without fear of rejection. His work eventually led to a Nobel Prize in 1960 and has been praised as the cornerstone of modern transplant successes. The first successful, permanent kidney transplant, in 1954, from one twin to another can be directly linked to Medawar's wartime work.[30]

Reconstructive Surgery

During the First World War, thousands of horribly mutilated British soldiers were essentially rebuilt, and one man, Dr. Harold Gillies, made most of the advances. When the next war broke out, Gillies founded a plastic surgery unit at Queen Victoria Hospital in East Sussex with his cousin, Dr. Archibald McIndoe. There, Gillies and McIndoe began treating a whole new class of war injuries, massive and deep burns caused by high-octane aviation fuel. Dr. McIndoe, well acquainted with war injuries that included bone and other structural damage, found burns to be far different. Recovery for these unfortunate men would require years of surgery. To differentiate the techniques that Gillies and McIndoe were using as compared to the older ones, McIndoe coined the phrase reconstructive surgery.[31]

Nylon Sutures

Prior to the era of plastic, closing wounds, whether traumatic or from surgical procedure, was accomplished by the use natural materials. There were two major types, absorbable and non-absorbable. The most common of the non-absorbable sutures was made from silk, dyed to be more visible and sometimes waxed to prevent wicking in bacteria deeper into the wound. Silk had to be carefully handled as the strands were subject to weakening in storage or during the sterilization process.

The most popular of absorbable suture materials was catgut, actually made from the lining of sheep's small intestine. The gut is meticulously washed and scraped of all extraneous materials and, once inspected, twisted into strands. As the chemical makeup is nearly pure collagen—the same basic organic structure that forms everything from the soft tissues to fingernails—the gut will slowly be absorbed in the normal course of biologic renewal.

Physicians were not limited to the two materials though. There were a number of animal sources of suture. The hairs from a horse's mane and tail were quite useful for the fine stitching in reconstructive surgery. Kangaroo and wallaby tendon was the thread of choice for hernia repairs, while the lining of the abdominal wall of the ox rendered a massively strong suture for repairing smooth muscle tissues.[32]

Obviously, there were risks associated with use of animal-derived suture materials. First and foremost, steps had to be taken to ensure the absolute cleanliness of the raw material, especially in a time when there were no comprehensive antibiotics to fend off infections. Secondly, despite the close monitoring of quality, there were instances when small imperfections caused the thread to break. It was the fortunate surgeon who had this happen while the operation was still underway. However, that was not always the case. There is no way to record the numbers of patients rushed back into surgery to replace defective sutures, which spontaneously separated. All sutures also held other risks as well. As the foreign materials were basically made up of proteins, there was no small risk that the host body would react negatively to them. Once this allergic reaction began, there was nothing to do but to remove the stitches and replace them with another type that, hopefully, did not instigate another unfavorable reaction.

Nylon obviated all the shortcomings of animal-derived sutures. In 1938, the DuPont Company presented, with much fanfare, their synthetic substitute for silk. (More on Nylon in Chap. 9) While American women saw Nylon as a way of stretching their hosiery budget, the medical community saw an opportunity to avoid the nagging problems of septic and suppurating wounds caused by animal sutures.[33]

Between 1938 and 1939, several American companies introduced their versions of Nylon suture material. There were of course, extended trials and papers published in the medical journals, but all of that was short-lived with the outbreak of war in Europe. England had a pressing need for medical supplies and was willing to try the sutures virtually sight unseen. Glowing reports of recovery and a remarkable lack of infections stressed the importance of Nylon's contribution to the war effort.

Medical Specialties

In the 1930s, specialization became a catchword for medical professionals. As medical science grew in scope, specialization gradually became almost compulsory. Technology and contemporary knowledge were advancing too rapidly for any one physician to keep up with all the changes. The medical community as a whole looked at specialization as a way to measure its advancements. Typically, specialties were created within medical schools, often with the collaboration of the American Medical Association (AMA). Under this organization, education standards and training curriculums were established and board certification tests written. By 1941, fifteen specialty boards had been created and the specialty of internal medicine was divided further into sub-specialties such as cardiovascular disease and gastroenterology. General practitioners could declare themselves as specialists without serious repercussions. According to AMA estimates, about 36,000 doctors became specialists, forty percent of them board certified.[34]

It was during this atmosphere of change that the American medical community went to war. The war further promoted the trend toward specialization since the specialists were the first to get higher ranks, higher pay, and choice stateside assignments. When the GI Bill became law in 1944, it applied to military doctors as well. Many took the opportunity to go back to school for post-doctorate degrees and specialty training. Veterans Administration hospitals pushed the trend even further when all doctors on staff were required to become certified in their chosen fields. Even if no formal AMA board existed, ad hoc committees from the VA conducted certification tests. The formation of the National Institute of Health (NIH) in 1944 sealed the fate of the uncertified general practitioner by channeling millions of federal dollars into medical research, fanning the fires that forged the necessity of the specialist.

Anesthesiologists

In the years before the war, anyone could be an anesthetist. In fact, rural doctors often trained local lay-people or family members to act as surgical assistants whose duties included administering anesthesia. Communities with hospitals often had formally trained anesthetists, usually nurses who had taken on the added responsibilities and were experienced in administering chloroform and ether. As newer drugs became available, however, their training became obsolete. With the rapid changes they now had to learn to insert endotracheal tubes, to control gaseous flows, to administer curare, and so on. The gases required the operation of complex anesthesia equipment that needed constant attention. In the late 1930s, anesthesiology had grown to the point that medical doctors were going through a two-to-four-year training course in that specialty. It was claimed, with some obvious sexist bias, that the nurse-anesthetists could not understand the elaborate science, given their limited training. Even the word "anesthesiology" was coined during this period with the AMA's creation of an Anesthesiology Board in 1941.[35]

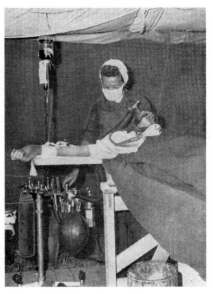

France 1944. Whole blood hanging in the bag, oxygen/ether anesthesia flowing, surgery is imminent. This nurse has obviously had training to operate this equipment and, more importantly, monitor the patient for signs of impending trouble. (US Army Medical Corps)

Internal Medicine

Already a specialty by 1936, internal medicine was undergoing a massive division at the beginning of the war. A large number of medical disciplines reflected the growth of wartime medical knowledge and specialties in general. Medical school residency programs in 1940 offered only 700 internist positions, but ten years later, the number of available slots had grown to 3700.

Besides the cardiovascular and gastroenterology subspecialties, there were endocrinologists who dealt with the new hormonal therapies being intensely researched. As an outgrowth of endocrinology, allergists, with their own board created in 1943, pursued new treatments in immunology and treatments for maladies such as hay fever, asthma, and similar conditions. It was no accident that an allergy specialist recommended to the American War Department that beds in military barracks be arranged so that the occupants slept head to foot, minimizing the chances that a cold could be transmitted during the nighttime.[36]

Dermatology

This specialty got its beginnings with the industrial revolution of the latter half of the eighteenth century, when toxic chemical compounds became more commonplace. Most general practitioners attempted to treat skin complaints as they arose, but the treatments were haphazard and results often unsatisfactory. This trend continued unchanged well into the late 1930s when the military began to expand their bases into tropical regions. In 1939, the Medical Department of the United States War Department established a separate Dermatological Services specifically for research, training, and treating skin diseases. This set the stage for the creation of the American Board of Dermatology in 1955.[37]

Plastic and Reconstructive Surgery

Based on the reports of Gillies and McIndoe, the American Society of Plastic and Reconstructive Surgery in 1941 foresaw the great changes that were to come from the European war. Although plastic surgery was a direct result of the First World War, the Second World War was to provide a wealth of opportunities for further advancements. According to the *Oxford Companion to Medicine*, "By the end of the Second World War, the scope of plastic surgery had been defined."[38] New materials such as silicon and nylon went a long way toward improving treatments, as did the works of Peter

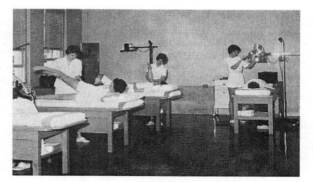

In June 1942, the influx of troops in need of physical therapy in the Zone of the Interior (military for the continental United States or the ZI) was just a trickle. This gave the first cadre of physical therapists a chance, as above, to practice on one another their techniques and hone their skills. (US Army Medical Corps)

Medawar and Joseph E. Murray, who made important contributions to skin grafting. Plastic surgery took on a special cachet in America, where the Army's Valley Forge General Hospital, providing space for more than 2,500 cases, was designated as the preeminent facility for reconstructive therapy.[39]

Physical Therapy

Although physical rehabilitation requiring special expertise began in the First World War, very little attention had been given to rehabilitating the lame and the halt in the interim years, though some work had been done with polio patients. In 1942, the U.S. Army and Army Air Forces adopted the goal of complete rehabilitation. They turned to Howard Rusk, who is credited with the almost single-handed development of modern physical therapy. Working at an Army Air Force hospital, Rusk promoted "the profitable use of convalescent time" and emphasized total rehabilitation of the chronically disabled patient. By 1944, the specialty had become so sophisticated that discussions were begun to establish a separate board, which came into being in 1947.[40]

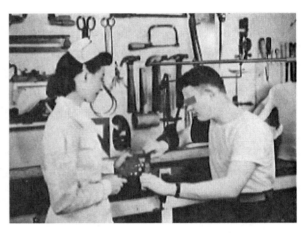

Physical rehabilitation got a new facet with the Veterans Administration's adoption of occupational therapy. As the name implies, this was designed to provide a chance for the patient to recovery from their injuries using either familiar or new work-oriented physical labor. The woman is not a nurse, despite her uniform, but a specially trained rehabilitation specialist. (U.S. Army Medical Corps)

The Family Physician

Ironically, as specialists formed their own professional organizations, the general practitioner also got into the act. The family doctor having been the mainstay of medical assistance for centuries, it was decided that general practice would now become a specialty. Formed in 1947, the American Academy of General Practice was founded to promote and maintain high-quality standards for family doctors. In 1971, the name was changed to the American Academy of Family Physicians, reflecting the shifting nature of primary health care.[41]

Licensed Practical Nurses

Although female nurses were fixtures in military settings since the Revolutionary War, tradition dictated that they be regarded with deference, existing somewhere between the social extremes of the lowly "camp follower" and the exalted "healing angel." Needless to say, the former view was much more prevalent. Even after they gained official sanction as the Army Nurse Corps during the Spanish-American War, nurses were definitely second-class citizens, particularly in the military medical community.

By the 1930's, both military and civilian registered nurses had exerted enough influence that they now occupied an occupational niche providing them with what could be ostensibly be called fair pay and, more importantly, professional respect. These women worked closely with doctors, who occupied the top level of the medical provider pecking order. Beneath the nurse were nurse trainees and, at the very bottom of the social ladder, the volunteer nurse's aides, better known as "candy stripers."

However, there was a growing faction of medical professionals that were pushing for a new category of nurses with less training than registered nurses but with many of the responsibilities. This threatened the position of the registered nurses who had gone through several years of formal training and had withstood the abuses of their superiors and, while nurse trainees, suffered the humiliations of doing less than glamorous chores, such as bedpan duty. Many registered nurses saw this new level of nursing as usurping their positions without the training—and adversity—they had all achieved. Due to the collective intransigence, programs for training licensed practical nurses failed to coalesce,

A Red Cross Volunteer hands out treats to American women soldiers apparently being deployed to the front or near to it. Already armed with the ever-present cup of coffee and doughnuts, these nurses (officer's insignia on front left woman's collar and woman with B61 on helmet) would be responsible for saving the lives and morale of hundreds of our men. (OWI/NARA)

remaining short nursing courses sponsored by individual hospitals.

In the days immediately following the Pearl Harbor attack, there was a public call for 50,000 nurses immediately. This was an enormous build-up of staffing, as there had been only 672 nurses in the Army in 1939. America as a whole had only approximately 200,000 nurses in practice at the time. This included the aged semi-retired and those who worked part-time due to health issues and a very few of what could be labeled as LPNs, the latter being unlicensed home-grown nurses trained by Md. relatives.

Clearly, a four-year training program could not deliver the number of nurses needed. The Army Medical Corps undertook a number of conservation changes. Nurses were removed from administrative positions and male enlisted personnel were trained as clerks, medics, and ward aides. The military's requirements fluctuated as the months passed. Often there were huge surpluses of nurses while civilian hospitals struggled with severe shortages. By 1943, Congress stepped in and, through the U.S. Public Health Service, established the U.S. Nurse Cadet Corps. The government supplied all funds for tuition, books, room and board, and uniforms as long as the graduate nurse worked for at least three years as a nurse, either civilian or military.

The course work, though, more resembled that of the present day Licensed Practical Nurse. The training lasted one year — later, ten months in a compressed format — and, at best, skimmed over esoteric subjects such as surgery, psychiatry, psychology, and essentially all of the medical specialties. It covered only the minimal education in pharmaceuticals. As the title suggests, the practical side of nursing was stressed. The course work focused on the daily care of the patient and addressed the immediate care by LPNs of "the subacute, convalescent, and chronic patients in their own homes or institutions, under the direction of a licensed physician or registered nurse." It also included "household assistance when necessary."[42] The student LPN was expected to become adept at changing dressings and rolling and moving the patient without inflicting further injury. One historian of nursing stated that the nurse in training impressed their instructors, "by the efficient manner in which they took hold of simple nursing tasks for which housewifely experience provided a valuable background."[43] As a result of the great success of the training programs and subsequent performance of the nurses, the LPN became a legitimate and generally accepted member of the medical community.

The Emergency Room

One other specialty had its beginning during the Second World War. Though not exactly a treatment, it encompassed a realm of techniques that are now called emergency medicine, a specialty all its own. With experience gained from the early war years, the British Orthopedic Association recommended that hospitals create "clinics" where accident and war-related casualties could be brought for primary triage and treatment of acute injuries. Doctors assigned to these clinics trained the nurses in the latest resuscitation methods and special techniques for stabilizing traumatic injuries. Although the contemporary emergency room has evolved several generations over, this is regarded as the first civilian example of the emergency room.[44]

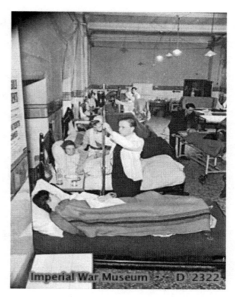

The receiving hall of Guy's hospital in 1941. The Blitz and subsequent attacks had shown it was better to create a central receiving station for the medical personnel, facilities and materials to be available instead of running from collapse to blast zone, never sure there were live patients or dead victims. (IWM)

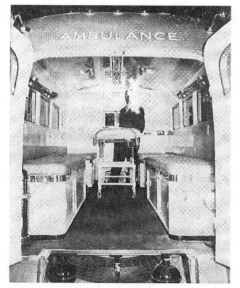

Fear of aerial attack after Pearl Harbor inspired Chicago officials to sponsor the construction of this advanced ambulance. Taking civilian field emergency medical services to a new level, this vehicle carried the necessary supplies for more than a hundred minor injuries and four major. This marks a turning of emergency medicine philosophy where the treatment begins at the scene. (OWI/NARA)

Ambulance Service

Moving the hurt or sick patient is hardly a new idea. Horse-drawn ambulances stood by at strategic locations during the American Civil War to clear the battlefield of the barely living. Loaded wagons transported their gruesome cargo to nearby field hospitals where treatment would commence. With the introduction of the automobile, ambulance service remained merely a means of getting the injured to medical help. Often, there was no ambulance at all in the community. In these cases, local mortuaries hired out their hearse as a means of emergency medical transport.

American officials, seeing the devastation and injuries wrought by roaming Axis bombers began to take a look at their own capabilities should similar attacks take place at home. One of the improvements suggested was the creation of mobile emergency medical treatment vehicles. Provident Hospital in Chicago commissioned such a van based on a truck chassis in 1941. Designed to carry as many as five doctors and six nurses, the "catastrophe hospital" accommodated up to one hundred minor injury cases. Equipped with a rudimentary surgical suite, it could even deal with a limited number of serious operations. This was one of the first examples of the critical-care ambulance that now are commonplace.[45]

Chemotherapy

Until the Second World War, doctors were nearly helpless to treat cancer. What limited drugs they had were meant to comfort, not cure, the patient. In the late 1920s, treatments were developed using radioactive radium although the burns and other side effects left the patient with a multitude of new medical complaints. Naturally, surgery to remove the tumor, or at least the largest part, often had to be performed. Both radium and surgical treatments did have their occasional miracle cures, but, for the most part, a diagnosis of cancer meant almost certain death.

Then a bizarre accident of fate occurred. Concerned that the Germans would initiate chemical warfare in retaliation for the Allied landings in southern Italy, the Allied Supreme Command ordered the stockpiling of mustard gas aerial bombs. The weapons, loaded with liquefied chemical agent but not fused to explode, were secretly shipped to Italy. The sole munitions ship arrived at Bari Harbor on December 1,

A rather narrow veiw of the future for cancer therapy. This is clearly prior to the Bari Harbor attack and subsequent discovery of chemotherapy.(Nat'l Cancer Soc.)

1943 to find the harbor completely choked with other ships landing cargo. Forced to wait at anchor, the vessel, and its deadly cargo, was a fat target just asking to get hit.

The Luftwaffe could not resist such a tempting target. More than one hundred medium Heinkel bombers attacked and made hits on twenty-three ships. Seventeen sank, including the one with its load of chemical ordnance. As the raid progressed and ships burned, many sailors were forced into the water, now contaminated with mustard poison. The conflagration created enormous amounts of billowing smoke, spreading toxic fumes far across the town and the surrounding countryside.

After the bombers had left, men pulled from the bay were summarily sent to local hospitals for treatment. During such attacks, it was not unusual for the casualties to be immersed in fuel oil from ships' leaking oil bunkers, to have flash burns, shock, exposure or other traumatic injuries. It was unusual that survivors with seemingly routine injuries begin to exhibit strange symptoms such as eye irritation, blisters, skin lesions and respiratory distress. The first victims died within eighteen hours.

Local Allied military hospitals began to run out of beds for the wounded, a final tally of military injured that eventually exceeded one thousand. Of these, more than six hundred were critically ill with the puzzling symptoms. Having been exposed to the smoke-borne gas, hundreds of Italian civilians also became ill, inspiring a general panic. Those not already sick fled to the countryside.

The situation was compounded by the secrecy of the shipment. No manifests or bills of lading existed that detailed the cargo. The bombs had been escorted to Bari by a team of chemical warfare specialists, all whom had died in the attack. Doctors, suspecting that a chemical contaminant was responsible for the mysterious illness, requested the assistance of a chemical warfare specialist. Allied headquarters dispatched Lt. Col. Stewart Alexander, an acknowledged expert on the medical effects of chemical agents, particularly nitrogen and sulfurous mustard poisons. Examining the stricken men, Col. Alexander determined that the suspicions were correct and confirmation of chemical poisoning was forthcoming in the discovery of bomb cases retrieved from the bottom of the harbor.

By the end of the month, eighty-four men had died. Autopsies revealed that their lungs had been damaged from an "inhaled toxic agent." Furthermore, "were it not for other factors, the individuals would have recovered from the (injuries) to their lungs."[46] Microscopic studies concluded that exposure to the gas had a deleterious effect on the white blood cells. The absence of these important infection fighters had resulted in the ensuing deaths. The mustard had apparently destroyed the tissue that forms the white blood cells. Other organic damage occurred in the lining of the digestive tract, the lymphatic system and, to a lesser extent, the liver and kidneys.

Col. Alexander submitted a report on his preliminary findings as of December 17, 1943, predicting that further study of records and pathology reports would "…permit accurate appraisal and evaluation."[47] Research facilities and military units involved with chemical warfare received copies of the report.

Cornelius P. Rhoads, chief medical officer of the Chemical Warfare Service, U.S. Army, naturally received one. "Dusty" Rhoads, as he preferred, had a passionate desire to eradicate cancer in his other job as head of Memorial Hospital in New York City. The report, citing the systemic effects, struck a note for Dusty as he was fully aware of previous, albeit small, victories with cancer using drugs. For example, Dr. Charles Huggins, a urologist from Chicago, had injected the female hormone estrogen into a patient dying of prostate cancer in 1937. He theorized that the presence of male hormone could be accelerating the cancer's growth. The treatment included the removal of the testes, the source of the naturally occurring testosterone. The estrogen, acting to counter the growth, might arrest the process. The idea worked, allowing the patient to live in relatively good health for fifteen more years.

Other chemicals were tried on cancer after this. One notable program in 1942 used nitrous mustard. A close chemical cousin to sulfur mustard, HN3, as it was known to its military developers, differed only by having a nitrogen atom in place of the sulfur. The study, involving seven patients with cancer, was to determine the effects of intravenously injecting HN3. With limited success, the study was expanded to more patients, using another form of nitrogen mustard. Again, the test met with inconclusive results.

It took the final report from Dr. Alexander to stir up new interest. He suggested that mustard compounds might be used "... for the possible treatment of neoplastic disorders of the tissues that form white blood cells."[48] The new research led Dr. Sidney Farber, a pathologist at Boston Children's Hospital, to initiate trials on his new drug, aminopterin. This compound, derived from the essential vitamin folic acid (the B group), was found to be effective in arresting leukemia. Like mustard gas aminopterin halted white blood cell reproduction at its earliest stages. The chemical did not cure the cancer, but by obstructing the growth of malignant cells, normal white cells had the opportunity to grow. In the group of sixteen patients that Dr. Farber initially injected, ten showed signs of total remission.

One of these children went on to be the poster child for cancer research. Given the pseudonym "Jimmy," he appeared on radio and lent his pseudonym to a charity that collected more than $150 million. Years later, "Jimmy" was to reveal his identity in an article in *People Magazine*[49] to be Carl Emar Gustafson, a sixty-two-year-old trucker from New England.

The drugs used today reflect their indebtedness to these first therapies. Although the original mustard compounds are occasionally used, different sources of chemical agents derived from plant and microbial material are more common. The new drugs now react to different stages of cellular development, giving doctors the ability to modify treatments as conditions dictate. The major limiting factor to these newer drugs is still the amount of toxicity that the human body can tolerate.

After the war, Dr. Rhoads continued his personal vendetta against cancer. Convinced that the Bari disaster held a key, he began to attract other like-minded physicians to Memorial Hospital. Realizing that the facilities could not support the kind of research that he envisioned, "Dusty" started to elicit financial assistance. He attracted the attention of the founders of General Motors, Alfred Sloan and Charles Kettering, who provided the funds to establish New York City's Sloan-Kettering Institute, now regarded as one of the foremost cancer research centers in the United States.

Nuclear Medicine

An extraordinary influence on medicine was the invention of the X-ray machine in 1895. The ability to see internal structures painlessly made it the radical tool of the age. Improvements soon followed that increased the image intensity, making details easier to view. Using compounds such as barium and bismuth, it was possible to reveal the features of internal organs such as the gall bladder, digestive tract, kidneys and urinary system. Tuberculosis lesions and cancerous tumors could be seen at early stages, improving the chances of survival.

Wilhelm Roentgen, the inventor of the device, had serendipitously discovered the energy while working in his physics laboratory at the University of Wurzburg, Germany. Like many others, the new cathode ray tube fascinated him. An associate of Roentgen discovered that an unusual fluorescent effect seemed to be caused by emissions from the cathode tube. The effect, previously shown to occur at very short distances, was appearing at unprecedented distances. Intrigued, Roentgen pursued the research and discovered a phenomenon that is now known to be as deadly as any poison.

The case of Clarence Daily is a good example of the deleterious effects of X-rays. An assistant to Thomas Edison, Dally repeatedly exposed his hand to the invisible rays to ascertain that the machine was actually operating. In addition, he had inadvertently exposed parts of his own body to the ray, as its habit of ricocheting off a variety of surfaces was not understood. At still other times, he would place fresh films and samples in the path of the continuously running machine, not realizing the dangers associated with radiation. He soon developed lesions on his skin, particularly his hands, and began to lose his body hair.

Suffering a multitude of burns, swelling, reddened skin and pain, Dally began to lose fingers from enormous ulcers that had erupted on his hands. No amount of medical attention could heal the damage, and the doctors agreed that the only recourse was to amputate the limb. Malignant ulcers continued to appear on his arms, and eventually he had both arms removed. Still in constant pain, Dally lingered for another two years until his death. Described as "an especially horrible end," Dally's experience permanently put Edison off ever having X-rays taken for medical reasons.[50]

The death of Dally, and many others, from cancerous lesions led some doctors to realize that the radiation from X-rays simulated the behavior of certain cancers. Cancer is cellular growth gone wild. Normal cells are constantly dying as new cells grow to maturity guided by our own unique genetic coding. For reasons still not fully understood, the cancer cells deviate from the pattern. They grow larger and faster and in some cases are aggressive to other nearby cells. If X-rays can mutate cells to become cancerous, researchers pondered, could X-rays kill cancer or change it into something less harmful?

The research into this hypothesis became even more intriguing with the Curies' discovery of radioactive elements. A limited number of chemicals that were radioactive were tried experimentally with equally limited results. Only after the emergency atomic development programs undertaken by the United States and Britain during the Second World War were new developments forthcoming.

Scientists discovered that new radioactive elements of greater power could be made by artificial means. Bombarding selected elements with high-energy radiation would transmute the element into an isotope. In theory, malignant tissue, sensitive to the emissions of a particular isotope, could then be made inactive. Many of these isotopes found their way into clinical cancer studies with surprising results. The flooding effect of early X-ray emissions is no longer necessary, as newer isotopes can be injected or aerosol sprayed with greater precision and selectivity.

The treatment of malignancies is not the only use of nuclear medicine. The ability to track the emission of radioactive particles from outside the body can be used as a diagnostic tool. As the actions of various biological processes occur, changes in chemical composition related to the processes simultaneously take place. For example, the thyroid gland traps iodine—an important nutritional supplement—from the bloodstream and utilizes it as needed. With the new nuclear compounds, iodine can be made radioactive, enabling doctors to visualize the activity of the thyroid gland. Should the glands deviate from the expected behavior; proper steps can then be taken to treat the disease. Other organs that can be so examined include the liver, spleen, lungs, kidneys, bone, brain, and the adrenal glands, to name a few.

Now, radiation can be introduced directly into a tumor by combining a radioactive molecule with different antibodies that have an affinity with the targeted growth. The radiation can be focused on the malignancy, avoiding damage to nearby healthy cells. Doctors developed a surgical procedure to deposit radioactive pellets directly into prostate cancer for long-term exposure. As the technique proved it efficacy, other target organs now get the treatment.

It is virtually impossible for the lay person to keep up with the advancements in cancer research but is safe to say that the history is clear; the necessity of wartime research has opened many doors for medical cures today.[51]

John Lawrence, the father of nuclear medicine, used radioactive phosphorus to treat blood cancers. (NARA)

Modern Aviation Medicine

Aviation medicine as a science began in 1912 Berlin, Germany, by Nathan Zuntz who studied pilot endurance and the effects of altitude. After the war, German interest in aviation medicine hardly wavered, although the common wisdom at the time was that the airplane was never going to advance beyond its then-current state. Throughout the 1920s and 1930s, whenever funds were available, slow but steady progress was made on flight safety. Using centrifuges, pressure chambers, and actual flights, German investigators determined the proper mixtures of oxygen and the reasons for pilot blackouts. They also probed the sources of carbon monoxide poisoning and ways of preventing them, and they proposed new equipment such as fleece-lined clothing and parachutes.

Hitler ordered that the research proceed with maximum effort. The military began to fund enormous projects with the stipulation that the scientists were to get results and keep them secret. The scientists did not fail.

They provided information that led to the adoption of the first successful ejection seat and refined oxygen-delivery systems. With many valuable aircrews lost in the frigid waters of the English Channel and Baltic Sea, German medical doctors also pursued treatments for water-induced hypothermia. This research was located, in part, at the Dachau concentration camp, where prisoner subjects were immersed in iced water for hours. The anguish they suffered was heard throughout the camp in the form of agonized screams. Another avenue of interest, high-altitude sickness and air embolism, led to another series of infamous experiments at the same facility. After the war, Allied officials found photographs that graphically depicted the pain they felt as their brain's ruptured from the pressure differential. Witnesses told of the dozens of inmates and Russian POWs that were subjected to excruciating deaths in the name of science.

At the end of the war, the Allies discovered, to their dismay, that the Germans managed to be years ahead of them in aviation medicine. This led to a frantic rush to discover and seize or copy as many of their innovations as possible. A detailed search was initiated to gather the best and the brightest of German scientists. American, French, British and Russian agents scurried about Europe, confiscating any device, document or expert they could lay their hands on. There was no more "Allied" war effort and anything went as far as stealing, kidnapping or wheedling the prize out of some other agency's possession or country's region. To protect their precious scientists, these same Allied agents, with the cooperation of their governments, attempted to cover up facts of Nazi Party involvement and their prizes' participation in war crimes. Much of the German research was publicly declared as being worthless, which it may have been. However, the debunked Nazi researchers and their work became the most sought-after treasure for post-war exploitation. The renunciations, mostly window dressing for public consumption, appear to have been applied to only the worst of the excesses perpetrated in the camps.

When captured by the Allies, the German medical doctors involved in flight medicine research were, for the most part, absolved of any wrongdoing. With few options left—either stay in desolated Germany and possibly starve or probably be arrested for war crimes by vindictive Russians—they were offered positions in America to work on military medical projects. Thirty-four of the German doctors involved in Nazi aviation medicine were brought to the United States under contract with the Army Air Force. Relocated to San Antonio's Randolph Air Force Base, they worked at the School of Aviation Medicine. Not long after this, part of the group was requested to begin working on another project to anticipate problems of travel in a zero gravity environment—space. So in 1949, the emergence of space medicine makes it clear that the view to the future was directed at the stars.[52]

The Nuremberg Codes

The revelations of the German extermination camps at the end of Second World War were the best known of a long litany of horrors perpetrated by all the participants of the war including the Allies. The Japanese had done unspeakable medical and biological experiments on Chinese civilians and dozens of Allied POWs. The Americans were still withholding treatment for acute syphilis from a large group of Negroes in an experiment that dated to 1932 and would continue for another forty plus years. During and after the war, tens of thousands of unwitting American citizens were knowingly exposed to nuclear by-products to determine their effects on a population. Across the Atlantic in 1942, the British had begun researching anthrax as a biological weapon in a full-scale test on the Scottish island of Gruinard. Smaller scale anthrax experiments were taking place at Porton Down in Dorset. But the German medical experiments became the driving force behind a post-war drive to reinforce the ethical canons of Hippocrates.

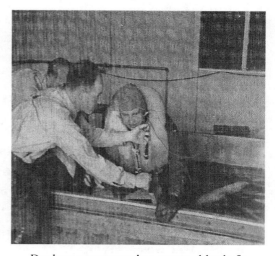

Dachau concentration camp, block 5; the medical experiment block. The first man on the left is Sigmund Rascher, a Luftwaffe doctor and researcher. The person in the flier's clothing is not a volunteer, nor is he happy about this. He is helping them learn how long a person can stay in ice water and the best way to revive them when they go unconscious. Many died, some were damaged physically. They were put out of their misery; after all, to the Germans, they were just üntermensch: Russian POWs. Millions had already died. (USHMM)

After the first wave of the war crimes trials, the Nuremberg Code was drawn up by Allied powers to clarify the standards of behavior for medical researchers and the rights of participants. Within its ten points, the code called for voluntary, well-informed participation in experiments with the right to quit at any time for any reason; it reiterated the physicians' code of doing no harm; it established minimum levels of researcher education and required that experiments be terminated if the likelihood of injury or death should arise.

The Declaration of Helsinki further modified the Nuremberg Codes in 1964 with the differentiation between therapeutic experiments and non-therapeutic research. Beginning in the 1970s, several new guidelines were issued by various government and professional agencies basing themselves on the principles of the Nuremberg Codes. Not long after this, the story about the Tuskegee syphilis studies broke and the ensuing public outrage forced the United States Congress to pass The National Research Act on July12, 1974.[53]

The National Health Service (NHS)

English medical care before the war was primarily organized along class lines. There was excellent care for those fortunate enough to have the money to pay. The working class had some insurance, although it was fairly limited in benefits. The poor had to make do with charity hospitals and, most often, second-rate physicians who lacked the skills or connections to make a successful practice in the big cities.

To the charity hospitals that had barely managed to survive the lean Depression years, the war was a saving grace. The British government, faced with the prospect of thousands of wounded, militarized more than 1,500 charity and low-income public hospitals under the Emergency Medical Service late in 1939. Hundreds of English doctors patriotically volunteered for military service and found themselves stationed at these outlying facilities, whose administrators could only have dreamed of having such talent on their staff before the war.

While all of this medical reorganization was taking place, British economist Sir William Beveridge was drafting a report on health care and other social ills. Entitled *The Beveridge Report on Social Insurance and Allied Services*, it cited five basic threats to the masses: Want, Ignorance, Disease, Squalor, and Idleness. Beveridge singled out each one in turn and recommended solutions. For Disease, he called for a total revamping of the British medical system so that all would receive care regardless of economic or social standing. Insurance would, Beveridge stipulated, become superfluous. Published in 1942 when the country was still on the verge of starvation, the Beveridge report created only a few waves of comment.

After the war was over, the British government held its first elections in July 1945. The liberal Labour Party soundly defeated Winston Churchill and his Conservative Party. To wide support, the Beveridge report was dusted off and given a prominent position in the incoming government's priority list. While the war raged, most of the country's hospitals had come under government control and were well ensconced in the steady flow of taxpayer money. It was foreseen that if the hospitals were to go back to relying on patient payments and contributions, most would fold. Furthermore, the hospitals' administrators had already grown used to doing business with the government, which simplified adoption of the Beveridge plan.

Nine months after the elections, Parliament began considering a National Health Service. Minister of Health Aneurin Bevan proposed to nationalize all the hospitals, beginning with the charity and public facilities. The country was divided into regions, each with a number of hospitals and at least one medical school attached to a teaching hospital. Regional boards were responsible for overseeing their realm. The teaching hospitals, historically attracting the best and the brightest of England's physicians, became the flagships of Bevan's empire and were accorded near-autonomy. This was in no small part a reward for the schools' support of the NHS plan in its early days. By November 1946, the NHS received the requisite royal nod and implementation was slated to be complete on July 5 1948. The intervening twenty months were going to be needed to get all involved parties up to speed, and it would be no small task. In all, 2,698 hospitals containing 480,000 beds were slated to join the NHS.

Getting the doctors to accept the NHS was another matter. Most looked forward to having the latest in equipment and therapies, but they also resented that they would beholden to the government for a paycheck. The specialists, enjoying an elitist position, were enticed into signing on with sweeping promises of independence and the right to keep private practice patients at the NHS hospitals. General practitioners, however, were not in position to demand such bonuses, at least not until they banded together in a united front. A February, 1948 survey concluded that 88% of the British Medical Association was unwilling to accept NHS service. Bevan responded with promises of general practitioner autonomy similar to that of the specialists. This promise and Bevan's assurance that there were no plans for salaried practitioners within the NHS overcame the opposition and the inauguration day came as scheduled.

Although the NHS was far more expensive than Bevan foresaw, it proved a major improvement for the British citizen. Infant and maternity mortality rates plummeted.

Due to the wide availability of affordable medical assistance, deaths from diseases such as tuberculosis, influenza, and pneumonia fell below comparable deaths in America. Although the NHS represented an enormous cost to the financially strapped government, it was an unmitigated success. The British style of socialized medicine has become the model for several other systems, most notably those in other Commonwealth countries such as Canada.[54]

Prenatal Care

With the rise of Nazi Germany came the legitimization of their main goal, establishing themselves as the "master race." Of the many different programs they instituted to further that cause, the proper care of mothers-to-be and their unborn children proved to have lasting influence.

As early as 1931, Hitler's elite bodyguard unit, the SS, instituted a set of regulations governing marriage as a condition of membership. To belong to this elite group, one had to meet standards for physical build, athletic prowess, education, and most importantly, racial purity. Lower ranks—sergeants and less—had to have documents that assured Aryan ancestry going back two generations, while officers' ancestry had to date back to 1750. The SS member, upon application for permission to wed, had to provide a family history proving his intended bride's Aryan heritage. Additionally, she needed to submit to a physical examination and be photographed in a bathing suit in an attempt to detect signs of racial impurity. The bride was further trained in official schools to care for the future children and home. The benefits of the woman's health were stressed repeatedly, as she was "...a link in the clan's endless chain."[55] With permission forthcoming, the couple was expected by their Nazi sponsors to produce a minimum of four children.

The Nazis went to great lengths to reward prodigious reproduction during the heady days before the war when the German economy was booming. The SS presented its members with a silver candlestick and spoon on the birth of the first child. Newlyweds could apply for a state loan to purchase a house and furnish it. The loan would be forgiven when the fourth child was born. The Germans even created a prestigious award for women called Der Mutter Creuz—The Mother's Cross—for bearing children. The medal had several levels of importance and value, beginning with the birth of the fourth child. The crosses were awarded annually, on August 12, the birthday of Hitler's own mother.

To further the child propagation plan, the SS established special facilities in 1935 to house married and unmarried mothers of SS children. Operated under the poetic

German mothers with their newborns. The Third Reich put heavy emphasis on the value of family and progeny. Each child put the mother in higher esteem with the government and was recognized publicly for their patriotic act of procreation. Even young women were induced to mate with members of the SS, whom were determined to be superior samples of humanity, without the benefit of marriage.

name of "Lebensborn" (The Well [or Fountain] of Life Foundation), these homes provided medical care, instruction in proper nutrition, and general health practices, all at no charge. Presaging a common wisdom that would not be widely accepted in the West for another fifty years, the young expectant women were discouraged from smoking and consuming alcohol. The German doctors adopted standards for weight gain and diet, and they prescribed periodic examinations, not unlike present-day prenatal management. Even during the birth, specialists would be in attendance to ensure the safety of the child and mother.[56]

In the Western countries, the understanding of the health relationship between mother and child, although acknowledged, was not emphasized until after the war. In 1937, approximately half of all deliveries were hospital born; by 1950, this figure was ninety-five percent.[57] To prevent unapproved switches of infants in the hospital, newly born children had their footprint inked to their birth certificates and to their hospital records. Paper tags containing vital information about the parents were affixed to the wrist and ankle of the infant. Some hospitals even tagged the child's back and blankets.[58]

The birth process came under scrutiny during this period as well. British gynecologist Grantly Dick-Read felt that physicians were causing much of the pain associated with childbirth. He propounded natural methods in his first book *Read Method of Natural Childbirth* (1933) that attracted little attention. In 1942, he released *Childbirth Without Fear*, essentially outlining the same methods as in his first book, but in the era of the child, this later one became a bestseller. Read's methods were widely disseminated after the war just in time for the Baby Boom.[59]

Sonography

The development of ultrasound imaging which appeared in hospitals in the late 1940s was a direct result of antisubmarine warfare detection programs. To locate submerged U-boats, pulsating sound waves would be transmitted through the water. Any obstacle that interfered with the spreading pulse could be tracked with sensitive microphones picking up on the reflected sound. Referred to as Asdic (Anti-Submarine Detection Investigation Committee), and promoted primarily by the British, this device enabled the Allies to break Hitler's blockade of the Atlantic. (See Chap. 3)

After the war, the desire to see the fetus became the catalyst for soft tissue ultra-sonography in the late 1940s and early '50s. Medical personnel used ultra-sonography to monitor fetal growth and fetal skull width in relation to the mother's pelvic dimensions, ensuring that proper nutrition and a safe delivery were in order. On the parents' part, the ability to visualize the fetus tended to alter attitudes toward the fetus. Seeing fingers, toes, facial expressions and determining the gender, the parents considered the fetus more of a person. With this information available, many unborn children are now named months before birth.

As part of the government's interest in health, which was generated by the need for less absenteeism, grew this chart of the basic seven. It was this type of information, derived from the latest science in nutrition that also aided in establishing the ration amount and regional supply quotas. (OWI/NARA)

Synthesized Vitamins

Among the important discoveries concerning health and nutrition during the 1930s is the class of chemicals called vitamins. Found naturally in most foods, vitamins became the focus of study during the chemistry revolution beginning at the turn of the century. Just prior to the Second World War, the newly discovered vitamins formed the basis of nutrition, which became a catchword to improve the general health of the populace. Homemakers received pamphlets to teach the best ways to cook so as to preserve the precious vitamins. Servicemen in all theaters including the POWs in Axis detention camps got specially prepared tablets of multiple vitamins. These pills survived the war to become;

Special Formulation Multi-vitamins

Modern health gurus have built a cult around vitamins. A billion dollar-a-year industry has been established hawking the benefits of the various combinations. Special formulations for bodybuilders, women, children, and the elderly are sold. Numerous books are written each year offering new insights to one therapy over the others. Our animals even get nutritional supplements formulated to meet their special needs.

Once-A-Day Multi-Vitamins and the R.D.A.

One of the scourges of the Depression era that carried over into the Second World War was the inadequate diet of most of the population. Medical science had shown that vitamins, readily available in a balanced diet, were essential for good health. However, medical experts were still debating the necessity of supplemental vitamins, even though few could afford to eat proper diets. In spite of the controversy, several pharmaceutical companies began to develop packaged vitamin tablets. The first of them were put on sale in 1934, containing only vitamin A and available only by prescription. The accompanying media blitz touted vitamins as a cure-all, and patent remedies began to appear on the market under a variety of names that implied inclusion of the nutritional supplement.

In October 1940, Miles Laboratories of Elkhart, Indiana, joined the vitamin revolution with their product One-A-Day® vitamin tablets. The soft gelatin pills contained not one but two vitamins—A and D. People were going back to work and could afford better nutrition. Despite the Miles-supported advertising campaign on radio and in print, pill sales languished. Bucking the trend, Miles offered a separate pill, still bearing the One-A-Day® brand, but now containing B vitamins in January 1942. A year later, Miles combined the formula into the true multi-vitamin tablet. The timing could not have been better. Sales skyrocketed and the One-A-Day® brand became an urban icon.

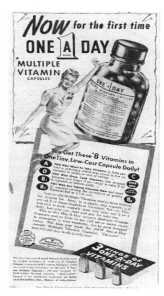

Nutrition and vitamins were becoming big business even before the war. During the war, the government got into promoting the health benefits and how good health was patriotic. In addition, the Red Cross delivered vitamins in the food packages supplied to Allied prisoners of war. (Miles Laboratories)

The very same year, the National Research Council (NRC) released a study sponsored by the federal government establishing the Recommended Dietary Allowances, (R.D.A.) The reasoning behind the study was to ascertain what foods to release for civilian consumption and at what levels rationing should be maintained. The ensuing publicity from the study broke open the market for vitamins. This led to an all-out media campaign to educate civilian cooks—meaning homemakers—on the value of nutrition and healthy eating.

Vitamin B[1]

When Commodore Perry forced Japan into a trade agreement with the West in 1854, he sparked the beginnings of Japan's rise as a sea power. As the Japanese navy grew in size, it became evident that the traditional diet of rice was far from perfect for life at sea; for the next twenty-five years the Japanese navy tolerated the scourge of beriberi. Appalled at the mounting loses of men, the director-general of the Imperial Navy Medical Service changed the sailor's diet to include more vegetables, fish, and beef and replaced the ubiquitous polished rice with barley rations. Following this change in 1888, beriberi virtually disappeared from the Imperial Navy in just a few months. The Japanese had discovered that certain foods contained elements necessary to the well being of the human body. It was this experience that inspired researchers to begin to look for those elements.

Vitamin B[1] was isolated in 1928. The first of the B group, its structure was analyzed and a number of plants were tested to obtain quantity amounts. Derived from rice husks, which polished rice does not have, the mineral became commonly known as thiamin. Subsequent studies showed that it was also effective for appetite control and several types of neuritis, an inflammation of the nervous system.

With some difficulty, chemists synthesized thiamin in 1933. The process involved many complex chemical reactions and did not lend itself to immediate industrial-scale production. One of the unforeseen consequences of the manufacture of thiamin was that the workers began to emit an odor that smelled strongly of burnt rubber. Synthesized thiamin at first sold for three hundred dollars a gram but only nine years later, 1942, the price had dropped to fifty-three cents a gram. In the interest of public health, the USDA introduced a program to sell only flour enriched with nearly two milligrams of thiamin per pound. Jewish religious leaders expressed concerns about the additive until they had been reassured that it was kosher. [60] Enriched flour is now a staple item all over the world. Laws require its use in bakeries and loose flour. Its inclusion has all but wiped out beriberi in countries where the flour is used.

Vitamin B^2

Derived from the same sources as B^1, B^2 is a heat-resistant counterpart. Also known as riboflavin, it treats keratitis—a blinding eye disorder—as well as mouth ulcers and is also good for strengthening poultry eggs. Added to flour, synthetic B^2 was placed into mass production in 1941.[61]

Vitamin B^6

B^6 was accidentally found while work was continuing on riboflavin. Discovered in 1935, it took another four years to refine a synthetic form. It is important in preventing anemia and convulsions in infants.[62]

This addendum is due to a factual error made during the editing process. We apologize for it.

Vitamin C

Nineteenth century sailors understood that consuming lemon or lime juice significantly stayed the effects of scurvy. Prior to this, the nutritional deficiency killed mariners on long ocean voyages with little regard for rank or status. In fact, scurvy had so devastated the ranks of conscripted sailors that the Royal Navy was on the verge of losing its command of the seas. Not knowing the specific nature of the cure, it was nonetheless known that the juice stopped and even reversed the symptoms.

Since the mid-1800s, Italian peasant farmers produced the world's finest ascorbic acid. Soil and weather conditions conspired to give Italy perfect lemon-growing regions. Used to flavor candy, beverages, tanning leather and for a number of industrial processes, the acid also became the primary source of Vitamin C. Created by a simple method of distillation, crystalline acid was being sold on the world market for the admirable price to the seller of $213 dollars an ounce. This enviable price went a long way to improve the lot of the impoverished Italian economy, especially after the bankrupting devastation of the First World War.

Then, in 1932, two researchers in America revealed the chemistry of ascorbic acid. A year later several scientists synthesized the chemical from a variety of sources. Then in 1934, ascorbic acid was produced from a massive field of gladiolus leaves in New Jersey. In 1937, American sources of ascorbic acid, mostly using refined synthesis, caused the price to drop to $57.00 an ounce. Due to continuing mass production methods, the price continued to plummet. In August 1940, when the market price was $2.00 an ounce, seventeen tons of vitamin C was produced in the United States alone. A year later, production shot up to more than one hundred tons.[63]

Italian farmers, now facing utter ruination at the prospect of losing nearly twenty percent of their irreplaceable export sales, set up a hue and cry to their leader, Benito Mussolini. Unable to do more than make loud speeches about it, the delusional dictator happily declared war on the United States in 1941. It is only left to speculation that the development of synthetic ascorbic acid, and America's apparent act of economic warfare, was not too far from his memory.

Nicotinic Acid

Despite its deceptive name, this member of the B complex vitamin has no connection to tobacco. Also called niacin, its sources eventually included thirty-five different crops including buckwheat, peanuts, yeast, and wheat germ. USDA research during the Second World War discovered many of these latter sources. Niacin is vital for skin health, digestive function, and nervous system vitality.[64]

Vitamin K

Bacteria in the digestive tract normally produce this essential element. It is an important building block that the

Benito Mussolini in his official regalia as the commander of the Fascist Militia. A former teacher and newspaperman, he founded the extremist anti-Communist Fascist movement in the 1920's. His secret desire was to resurrect the greatness of the Roman Empire and to become its Twentieth Century Caesar. (NARA)

liver uses to produce the compounds needed to clot the blood. However, newborns do not always have these microbes and are at risk of bleeding to death. But this breakthrough discovery did not result from human doctors; researchers did it from the U.S. Department of Agriculture.

Farmers occasionally suffered episodes of an unusual disease that caused their chicken hatchlings to bleed to death. However, chickens that were fed meal that was processed close to the ocean never bled. The feed was being supplemented with waste fish products from nearby fisheries and this provided the clue that the scientists needed. Alfalfa was found to contain concentrated amounts of vitamin K, hence its value to farm animals as feed.[65]

Having been identified in 1934, two variations of the vitamin, K^1 and K^2 were isolated and synthesized by 1939. The importance of the vitamin was immediately evident with the need to have soldiers, facing injury in the coming war, be well protected with the blood-clotting agent. In addition, Vitamin K injections became a standard treatment for all newly born infants in 1941 to fortify them from infantile hemophilia.

Vitamin E

An oily substance derived from wheat germ, vitamin E was first noted as a dietary supplement required for lab rats to reproduce. Vitamin E had been discovered in 1922, but its complex formula required almost twenty years to synthesize. It is responsible for metabolizing amino acids for muscle strength. In recent years, it has been promoted as a conditioner for the cardiovascular system and as an antioxidant in cosmetics and capsule forms to retard aging.[66]

Notes/Selected References

1   Cowdrey, Albert E. *Fighting For Life: American Military Medicine in World War II.* 1994. P.63.
2   Reynolds A. K. and Lowell O. Randall. *Morphine and Allied Drugs.* 1957. Pp. 273-295. and ibid. Pp. 453 and 472.
3   ibid. Pp. 453 and 472.
4   Porter, Roy. Pp. 453-454.
5   Keister, Edwin. A Curiosity Turned into the First Silver Bullet Against Death. *Smithsonian magazine.* November, 1990. Pp. 173-187.
6   Raper, Kenneth B. Penicillin. *The Yearbook of Agriculture. 1942-1947.* 1947. Pp. 699-710.
7   Keister, Edwin. Pp. 173 – 187.
8   Raper, Kenneth B. Pp. 707-708.
9   Haskew,Michael E. Editor, *World War II Desk Reference.* 2008. P.433. This number excludes all civilian casualties and the entirety of the Soviet Union's casualties.
10 ibid. Pp. 704-706.
11 Porter, Roy. Pp. 457-458. and Cartwright, Frederick F. *The Development of Modern Surgery.* 1967. P. 233. and Waksman, Selman A. Soil Organisms and Disease. *Yearbook of Agriculture 1943-1947.* 1947. Pp. 511-517.

12 Lyons, Albert S. and R. Joseph Petrucelli. *Medicine: An Illustrated History*. 1987. Pp. 518, 528.

13 Keane, Miller. *Encyclopedia and Dictionary of Medicine and Nursing*. and Berkow, Robert F. Editor-in–Chief. *The Merck Manual of Diagnosis and Therapy. 16ᵗʰ Ed*. 1992.

14 Angel, Jack E., Publisher. *Physicians' Desk Reference 37ᵗʰ Edition*. 1983. Pp. 773.

15 Armstrong, Maj. Harry G. M.D. F.A.C.S. MC, USA. *Principles and Practices of Aviation Medicine*. 1939. Pp. 305-306.

16 Andrus, E.C., D.W.Bronk, et al. *Advances in Military Medicine, Vol. 1*. 1948. Pp. 296-317.

17 Reiser, Stanley Joel. *Medicine and the Reign of Technology*. 1979. P. 133.

18 Warshofsky, Fred. *The Rebuilt Man: The Story of Spare Parts Surgery*. 1965. P. 140. All components of the human body can be broken down into two categories, either cellular or organ system. Cellular components make up the bulk of the organs, whether they be the heart, intestines or the brain. However, there are a number of organs that are not typically viewed as such. The skin, hair and blood are all components of organ systems, and therefore are susceptible to transplant. Blood is not often thought of as being an organ, but it is, by definition.

19 Keane, Miller, *Encyclopedia and Dictionary of Medicine and Nursing*. and Berkow, Robert F. P. 151.

20 Starr, Douglas. *Blood: An Epic History of Medicine and Commerce*. 1998. Pp. 48-49.

21 ibid. P. 65-71. and Warshofsky, Fred. P. 139.

22 Kendrick, Douglas B., Brigadier General MC, USA. *Blood Program in World War II*. 1989. P. 24.

23 Thomson, James, Editor. *Lectures on Peace and War, Orthopedic Surgery*. 1943. Pp. 282-284.

24 Maisel, Albert Q. *Miracles of Military Medicine*. 1943. Pp. 142-143.

25 ibid. P. 162.

26 Op. Cited. Minneapolis *Star Tribune* August 4, 1997, Metro Edition: News P. 5A.

27 Israel, H. and Seidelman, W. *Nazi Origins of an Anatomy Text: The Pernkopf Atlas*. JAMA letters; November 27, 1996.

28 Minneapolis *Star Tribune* August 4, 1997, Metro Edition: News. P. 5A .

29 ibid. P. 43.

30 ibid. Pp. 45-48.

31 Porter, Roy. Pp. 618-619.

32 Zeigler, Paul F. *Textbook on Sutures*. 1936.

33 Melick, Dermont Wilson, M.D. *Nylon Sutures*. Unpublished thesis manuscript, 1941.

34 Eiler, Mary Ann. *Specialty Profiles*. 1988. P. xi.

35 ibid. P. 504.

36 Eiler, Mary Ann. Pp. 41 and 96.

37 ibid. P. 40.

38 Beeson , Walter J. and R.B. Scott. *The Oxford Companion to Medicine.* 1986.

39 Eiler, Mary Ann. P. 433.

40 ibid. P. 628.

41 ibid. P. 5.

42 Jamieson, Elizabeth M. and Mary F. Sewall. *Trends in Nursing History.* 1949. P. 499.

43 ibid. Pp. 515-516.

44 Cartwright, Frederick F. P. 159.

45 Mobile Catastrophe Hospital Handles Major Operations. *Popular Mechanics magazine.* April 1942. P. 38.

46 Infield, Glenn B. *Disaster at Bari.* 1971. P. 191.

47 ibid. P. 241.

48 ibid. P. 246.

49 Foege, Alec and Duffy, Tom. Jimmy Found. *People magazine.* June 8, 1998.

50 Kevles, Bettyann Holtzmann. *Naked to the Bone.* 1997. Pp .47-48.

51 Cartwright, Frederick F. Pp. 91-99. and Reiser, Stanley Joel. Pp. 58-60.

52 Bower, Tom. *The Paperclip Conspiracy.* 1987 Pp. 231, 245, 254-56.

53 Maloney, Dennis M. *The Protection of Human Research Subjects.* 1984 Pp. 31-33. and Porter, Roy. Pp. 650-651.

54 ibid. Pp. 652-655.

55 Mollo, Andrew. *A Pictorial History of The SS.* 1976. Pp. 84-85.

56 Mayer, S.L., Editor. *Signal: Years of Triumph, 1940-42.* and Hillel, Marc and Clarissa Henry. *Of Pure Blood.* 1976. Pp. 64-67. and Lucas, James. *World War II Through German Eyes.* 1987. Pp. 53 - 59

57 Warshofsky, Fred. P. 73.

58 Baby's Tags and Footprints Prevent Hospital Mix-ups. *Popular Science magazine.* October 1940. P. 518.

59 Porter, Roy. Pp. 696-698.

60 Major, Randolph T. Industrial Development of Synthetic Vitamins. *Annual Report of the Smithsonian Institution, 1942.* Pp. 277-278, and 281-282.

61 ibid. Pp. 277-278.

62 ibid. Pp. 276-277.

63 ibid. Pp. 273-274.

64 ibid. Pp. 276-277.

65 Bird, H.R. Feeding Poultry. *Yearbook of Agriculture, 1943-47.* 1947. Pp. 235-237.

66 Reuben, Carolyn. *Antioxidants, Your Complete Guide.* 1995. Pp. 40-46 and 142-145.

6

Going to Work: Ideas That Affected the Workplace

World War Two was a unique experience for business in that this was the first time that labor, management, and, the normally aloof scientific community joined forces. Faced with the challenges of fighting a two-front war, which could still be lost, the three entities set aside old prejudices in a patriotic fervor. Managers listened to employees, who offered a virtually untapped well of experience and know-how. Scientists left their theoretical worlds and entered into the alien landscape of factories to offer up their own suggestions.

Workplace Safety

During the Second World War, the call for increased industrial production rang throughout the land. Along with that call was an underlying message to be safe. It would hardly do to recruit, train, and, equip employees to have them get seriously hurt a short time later. Equipment, accessories, and, practices for the safety of the work force were just as important to the war effort as production itself.

Protecting the worker from harm had been only randomly practiced for centuries. With the attitude of profits before people, most businesses regarded their employees as commodities that could be easily replaced. Naturally, skilled workers such as metalsmiths enjoyed a higher regard, as their skills were harder to replace. But for the average laborer, there was little protection against injury or death at work. Steelworkers had an adage: for every load of steel to leave the mill, one employee went to the undertaker.

Beginning about the time of the First World War, a very few companies realized that a significant expense could be eliminated by investing in safety. One of these pioneer industries, of necessity, was the railroad. The government implemented a series of laws that required rail companies to make changes to reduce the appalling death and injury rates of rail workers. Mining, another occupation that suffered an atrocious fatality record, fell under the authority of state and federal legislation. State inspectors were empowered to inspect mines for mandated safety equipment and practices, which were crude by today's standards. Punitive fines could be levied against companies that refused to follow the law, but, at best, enforcement was lax.

One of the best

One would think that industrial safety was small potatoes when contrasted with the massive caulties of the war. The truth is that industrial deaths and disabling injuries often surpassed those of the combined military branches on a month-by-month basis. This poster goes right to the point the former losses could be avoided. (OWI/NARA)

Gremlins were to blame for a lot during the war, so it is not surprising that they would get starring roles in safety posters. A lot of people who had never set foot anywhere near a factory were now appearing for work forty-plus hours a week. It could be overwhelming. (OWI)

examples of safety laws being winked at was the construction site of Hoover Dam. This giant, federally funded project, employing thousands of men in the early 1930s, was to build an enormous dam across a steep-sided canyon on the border between Nevada and Arizona. The rampaging Colorado River had to be diverted into four huge tunnels bored through solid rock. Facing restrictive deadlines and seasonal weather conditions, the men had to complete the tunnels in

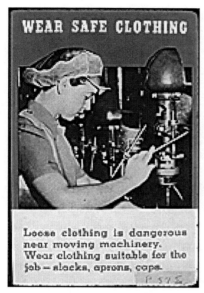

WEAR SAFE CLOTHING

Loose clothing is dangerous near moving machinery. Wear clothing suitable for the job – slacks, aprons, caps.

It took a number of injuries to begin to get this message across. It is interesting that safety glasses are still not evident. Part of the reason was that safety tempered-glass was critically rationed and polycarbonate plastics still too crude to make optically clear. (NARA)

on-the-job hazards. Technology to guard against poisonous fumes was developed. The importance of ventilation had become all too clear with the Hoover Dam "gas cases." Testing equipment for carbon monoxide soon became quite common and nearly every workstation, vehicle, and mine was tested

record time. To expedite the work, the crews worked with gasoline-powered dump trucks, a procedure that was known to be dangerous in an underground project and the results predictable. Several hundred men succumbed to carbon monoxide poisoning, although the number is unclear due to poor record keeping. This was a clear violation of state mining laws, which Nevada attempted to enforce. The company appealed the citation with the aid and encouragement of Federal attorneys. The case was finally closed four years later, not in civil court, but through an out-of-court settlement with 54 plaintiffs.[1]

The adverse publicity had lingering ramifications for the safety movement. Companies began to pay more attention to the costs of protecting workers from

Fuel oil fire in a training class for employees of a defense plant. The thin pipe the man on the right has a fog head, where the water comes out in a fine mist to cool the air and rob the fire of the heat it needs to progress. It is hard to see but the fire on the ground is nearly out and the tank will be next. (OWI/WPB/NARA)

for the insidious gas. By the late 1930s, other gases such as methane, ammonia, mercury, cyanide, and, carbon dioxide, to name a few, all had special detectors.

Although the following examples mostly took place during the years 1933-1936, they represent the times where safety appliances were first used. These devices and products became the standard for other companies to adopt just before the war when the defense industries were getting started.

Steel-Toed Safety Shoes

Steel-toed shoes were devised to protect the feet of factory and mine employees. One automobile company saw the costs of foot injuries drop 5,800% when the shoes were introduced. One memorable accident occurred at the machine shop of a steel mill when a thousand-pound solid steel roll fell off a machine directly onto the foot of a machinist. The steel toe saved the man's foot from a potentially crippling accident; instead, he walked away without even a limp.[2]

Safety Glasses and Goggles

Factory workers were losing their eyes at a terrible rate as industry mechanized. In one tractor factory, an eye was sacrificed at the altar of higher profits on an average of every eight calendar days. Before the safety-conscious age, the only workers who wore glasses were those who needed them to read or to correct their vision. As the costs of injury spiraled out of control, however, companies began to mandate the wearing of tempered-glass spectacles. Operators of grinding machines had full enclosure goggles, as a grinding wheel explodes with the power of a half stick of dynamite. High-impact polycarbonate lenses would replace the glass during the war, to remain the material of choice to this day.[3]

Respirators and Air Filtration

In 1933, silicosis attracted widespread public attention. The problem had been known for years, by names such as stonecutter's cough, potter's asthma, cabinetmaker's cough, and, grinder's mold. This disease develops when miners and others who work in dusty conditions inhale microscopic particles of dust, primarily silica, which is an abundantly common mineral. In the lungs, the razor-sharp edges of the particles scratch the linings of the small air sacs within the lungs. This damage, occurring over a number of years, creates thick, inelastic scar tissue that causes the victim to experience shortness of breath, weakness, and, eventually, emphysema and leads to a slow, lingering death. When the disease and its causes were identified, thousands of claims poured in for compensation.

To avoid the continuation of lung-related claims, industrial researchers introduced the respirator. Filter packs carried on the back scrubbed the particulate material from the breathing air. While this was an answer to the problem, the packs were expensive to buy and maintain and the employees objected to wearing the cumbersome equipment all day long.

Borrowing from the relatively new technology of air conditioning, ventilation equipment mounted on the building was devised to carry the bulk of the dust away from the work areas. Added benefits soon became apparent as dust levels fell. Machinery became more reliable and maintenance costs fell since the dust had been just as abrasive to the metal as to the workers' lungs. By capturing the dust created by work going on in the factory, valuable products were also recovered. The chemical, cement, and, stonecutting industries found a significant portion of their product had been floating out the door in the form of dust. More than one company recovered the cost of the ventilation and filtration machinery merely by salvaging the debris from the filters.[4]

Hard Hats

Workers at the Hoover Dam project faced a whole plethora of dangers to life and limb. One of the most dangerous tasks was the removal of loose or excess rock from the canyon faces. Called high scaling, the men would dangle from the high cliff faces, manhandling heavy jack-hammers, suspended by only bosun's chairs that were tied off by ropes to anchors at the top of the cliff. Not only were they themselves exposed to dropping several hundred feet into the gorge, but they also constantly ran the risk of getting hit from objects and rock falling down on top of them. Lacking any redundant safety belts, the victim of a dropped object impact might tumble from his precarious perch to his death.

In response, the cliff-scalers devised their own homemade hard hats that would go on to become standard items of safety equipment. They dipped soft cloth hats, already used on the site as protection from the blazing desert sun, into buckets of tar. Once hardened, the hat could fend off a sizable tool or rock. More than one worker was struck hard enough to break his jaw but avoided further serious injury by wearing the hard hat. Impressed by the effectiveness of the headgear, construction company management commissioned the manufacture of thousands of them, which were then issued to employees in exposed areas. According to most accounts, this is one of the first instances where hardhats were widely accepted on a construction site.[5]

Industrial Safety Training

When liquid ammonia became available as a household cleanser in 1911, homemakers rushed out to buy the cleaning agent. Contemporary reasoning held that anything that smelled so strong had to kill germs. Following this misguided logic, countless housewives and domestic servants added chlorine bleach—a much older, established cleaner—to the ammonia with disastrous results. Combined, the two chemicals make phosgene gas, which would

Fire is always a danger. During the war, hundreds of thousand of green troops were finding out for the first time the dangers of explosives, incendiary munitions, and high-octane gasoline. In addition, they were being housed in barracks with dozens of other men and trained inside and out under conditions that could be ripe for disaster with one careless match. (OWI)

soon earn a dastardly reputation as a highly toxic gas that killed thousands of soldiers during First World War. Dozens of domestics, homemakers and, their unwitting families were hurt or killed outright by the gas, which resulted from plain ignorance and poor education as to the dangers of home chemicals. The industrial setting offered even more creative means of mayhem.

In a Mid-western machine shop, a newly hired machinist was tending three machines at once, all of them producing aircraft parts. Distracted by a problem with one machine, he never noticed that the coolant on the lathe—

Safety practices in action in the machine shop. This machinist is cleaning up the magnesium chips from his milling machine. Magnesium is explosively combustible under certain circumstances. In addition, it is very difficult to extinguish and burns so hot the damages are worse than from a typical fire. (WPB/NARA)

cutting a magnesium engine part—had stopped flowing. Excessive metal chips in the coolant tank had plugged up the pump. By the time the hapless machinist reacted to the growing disaster on the lathe, the fire had grown hot enough to permanently warp the frame of the valuable, hard-to-replace machine tool.

By the 1930s, technological knowledge was coming together at a rapidly increased pace. Scientists had unlocked more of the mysteries of chemistry and physics and the two sciences were being applied in industry in more creative ways. Unfortunately, the ordinary man or woman was terribly unversed in the new ways of science and industry. When the defense factories began hiring as many workers they could find—regardless of their experience—the stage was set for tragedies that would far outclass the ammonia-chlorine debacles. The new methods and materials led to costly and even horrific accidents on an industrial scale.

Magnesium, a substance that formerly had limited uses, became a vital element in incendiary bombs, rockets, and, other missiles. New aircraft designs called for magnesium—stronger than steel but lighter than aluminum—to be used as a replacement metal in engines and other components. It had to be handled with care, especially when it was being machined. If the metal were allowed to overheat, it would erupt into a fire so hot that it would melt cast iron, which is what most machine tools are made of. Conventional fire fighting methods do not work on a magnesium fire. Originally, sand was used to fight magnesium fires, but that was supplanted by a special graphite-based powder with additives that, once exposed to the heat of the flame, formed a hard shell over the fire, effectively smothering it.

Raw chemicals were another hazard the uninitiated workers faced. As with the lethal ammonia/bleach combination, a whole new range of chemicals for painting, cleaning, degreasing, sealing, etching, and, finishing became available to mix together, sometimes with startling results. In an unnamed aircraft factory, a new employee used a seemingly empty bucket to retrieve acetone, a chemical used as paint thinner. As soon as the liquid acetone touched the bottom of the bucket, flames burst forth into the unlucky man's face, severely burning him. Unwittingly, he had grabbed a container that had formerly held chromic acid. The acid had dried, but the residue was still as volatile to acetone as a match is to gasoline.

These examples are just a few of the thousands of accidents that occurred during the war due to ignorance and carelessness. Clearly, the entire war industry effort was at risk of exploding, burning, or melting at the hands of inexperienced employees. A number of crash programs were undertaken to train the new employees in general safety, basic chemistry, shop, and, lab safety. Rules were set into place to clean machinery and workspaces regularly, removing any collected materials that could potentially cause a disaster. Posters were strategically placed around factories, reminding employees that the war effort was dependent on their safety.

To further the cause of workplace safety, a number of technical and shop practices had to change. Containers meant for specific chemicals received special markings to exclude them from general use. Paints, solvents, and, other dangerous chemicals had special explosion-proof storage cabinets. Paint rooms, the air thick with fumes of volatile solvents, were a virtual bomb waiting for a spark. To eliminate the dangers, special wet-walls were built, now called water-curtains. The water would be allowed to flow in a thin sheet down a wall. Particles of paint and larger droplets of solvent, carrying a strong static charge, were attracted to the water, which then washed the bulk of these materials away to be circulated through a filter system. The fumes that could not be removed by the water-curtain were removed from the air by ventilation. These are just a very few examples of the great lengths that industry, working with the government, underwent to secure the factories, mills and, mines from the devastating effects of accidents.

The Gremlins are back to cause some more mayhem. Many posters from this time were mostly directed to the workplace. These Gremlin posters cover a more generic safety concerns. (OWI)

Training programs in industry and in the military instructed personnel on the steps to be taken to prevent further accidents such as the chromic acid incident. Periods of time were reserved for all employees to clean their machines. More maintenance people were hired and preventative maintenance programs developed. Fire and medical training were given to selected employees, assuring that there was a minimum of trained personnel on hand at all times in the event of an emergency.[6]

Most of the training plans fell apart after the war. Safety again took a backseat to profits for a short time until the unions, along with the government, pressured industry into mandated plans. With the passage of legislation and the formation of agencies such as the Occupational Safety and Health Administration (OSHA), workplace safety practices were finally formalized.

Income Withholding Tax

War is always an expensive endeavor, and the Second World War was more so than all previous wars. One of the major reasons for this is that the United States was supplying most of the Allied side with arms, food, equipment, and, even cash loans in addition to supporting her own war expenses. Financing the war became the burden of the American public, which it accepted with patriotic fervor.

War bonds were the first method of raising the necessary capital. They were available in denominations from $25 to $10,000. This had the effect of absorbing the excess of cash—$70 billion—that resided in the private sector in checking and savings accounts. This much loose money available to the marketplace raised concerns over inflation. As more consumer goods became restricted, the excess cash could very well go towards purchases on the "black market," which would siphon products out of the normal delivery chain. The two concurrent events would inevitably cause shortages and prices to rise dramatically.

Eight bond drives were held in all, garnering a whopping $252.7 billion in Federal debt. With an expected cost of $100 billion a year in war costs, the government was predicting a major shortfall of income. However, much of this deficit was vanishing into pay envelopes, $135 billion just in 1943.

To tap this resource, the Federal government decreed that beginning January 1, 1943; employers were required to withhold payroll taxes from every paycheck. The amount would be amortized based on the previous year's individual income taxes. With the new plan, the government could expect a continuous flow of cash. The withholding scheme was supposed to last only for the duration of the war, but there was always some reason to maintain it, whether it was for the Marshall Plan, or the Korean conflict, or the Cold War, or the space race, or foreign aid, or welfare, or Desert Storm, or 9-11, or. ...[7]

Company-Provided Healthcare Benefits

Far out in the barren wastelands of the California desert of the Depression era, a young physician, Sidney A. Garfield, M.D., was struggling to maintain his twelve-bed hospital near where construction crews were digging the Los Angeles aqueduct. Garfield had borrowed the money to open Contractors General Hospital to serve the thousands of men who had sought out the project in desperate times. Poorly paid, they were unable to pay for his services. A few of the men had medical insurance, but the companies were slow to pay. However, Dr. Garfield was unwilling to turn anyone away. On the verge of bankruptcy, the good doctor became inspired. He suggested that the insurance companies pay a fixed amount to his facility, a pittance of a nickel for every covered worker per day. This pre-payment would entitle the insured men to receive medical care for work-related injuries and illness. Another five cents a day bought total coverage, whether the need for treatment was related to their work or not. This amount, ten cents a day, was a considerable sum in the cash-strapped Depression. Nevertheless, thousands of the workers signed up for Dr. Garfield's plan, making his hospital an instant financial success.

With the completion of the waterway, the hospital closed and Dr. Garfield moved his operation to the next largest construction project in the West, the Grand Coulee Dam in Washington State. The 6,500-man workforce had had the services of a hospital, but it was run down and provided only the bare essentials for medical care. The owner of the construction company in charge of the dam project, Henry Kaiser, had heard about Contractors General Hospital and the innovative prepayment plan. Kaiser engaged Dr. Garfield to update the medical facilities. Dr. Garfield persuaded several other doctors to join him and founded the first "prepaid group practice."

In 1940, the Federal government was fairly certain that America's involvement in the European war was inevitable. To stave off a repeat of the inflationary effects that had gripped the American economy in the First World War, a series of price controls, overseen by the Office of Price Administration (OPA), went into effect in 1941. This capped the pay scales that companies, now flush with lucrative government contracts, could pay their employees. The demand for employees was fast outpacing the available supply, especially for skilled trades-people. To attract the best ones, the companies had to resort to unconventional compensation packages, which were not restricted by the OPA.

Henry Kaiser had made a name for himself as a bold entrepreneur before the war. His company had been essential to construction of the Grand Coulee and, to a lesser extent, Hoover dams, both of which had been completed ahead of schedule and under budget. Based on this success, Kaiser talked the government into letting him have the first contract to build the Liberty ships, transports designed in Britain. He had proposed building the badly needed ships in record time by using techniques that he and his construction managers had perfected on their many large construction projects. The outcome of the venture—which is a whole other story— is even more remarkable in that neither Kaiser nor his top men had ever seen a shipyard before.

At the Kaiser Shipbuilding plants, the employees were held in the highest regard.

One of Kaiser's shipyards. In the foreground center, foredeck plates are being assembled without the benefit of a hull. That the assemblies fit together so well is remarkable, given the sizes of the sub-assemblies. All large capital ships are now made in this modular process. (Kaiser/NARA)

Kaiser managers had a ready ear for suggestions, which were often implemented immediately. Off the job, the company maintained an interest in the employee's welfare as well, sponsoring child-care centers, schools, and hot-meal cafeterias. When housing became a problem, the company built more homes on company-purchased land.

Faced with the same restrictions on pay that Kaiser was, other companies, especially on the West Coast, adopted similar plans. Government officials visited the medical offices and investigated the procedures at length. Satisfied that there was no violation of the wage laws, the same bureaucrats spread word of the insurance plan nationwide.

Kaiser again brought in his favorite doctor to establish a medical care system. Employees could see company-provided doctors at will, having a small deduction taken out of their pay for the privilege. Hospitals were built to accommodate the serious cases, again paid for from the cooperative Kaiser Foundation Health Plan. Other companies followed

the Kaiser example, forming their own health-care facilities. At the end of the war, a large majority of these plans fell by the wayside, as mass layoffs and other cost-cutting measures were undertaken. Dr. Garfield's staff shrank from 75 to just a dozen in a matter of months. But, Kaiser, looking towards the future, assured Dr. Garfield there was a need for the prepaid plan. With the assistance of the Kaiser organiza-

Permanente Foundation's first hospital. It opened in 1942 when the demand of the shipyard's hospital forced Dr. Stanley Garfield to ask for bigger facilities. (Kaiser-Permanente Healthcare)

tion, but not officially part of the Kaiser company, the Kaiser Foundation Health Plan opened to the public, on October 1, 1945.

Patients flocked to the company. Within ten years, 300,000 northern Californians had signed on. Cashing in on the Kaiser name, which was widely hailed for Kaiser's entrepreneurial skills, the company in 1952 adopted the name Kaiser-Permanente—the latter was the name of the wash where Henry Kaiser had built his first cement plant in Santa Cruz, California. Over the years other plans sprouted up nationwide. Thus, from the deserts of California came the first "prepaid group practice," what is now called a Health Maintenance Organization, the HMO.[8]

Quality-Enhancing Management and Statistical Control

During the industrial revolution of the late eighteenth century, demand for consumer goods far outpaced supply. Labor and raw materials were generally inexpensive and quality was less planned than accidental. This is not to say that manufacturers desired to sell shoddy products, as many companies strove to build the finest products possible. Nevertheless, there were enough companies and individuals willing to sell poor quality goods in the desire for a quick profit. Unfortunately, the buying public was willing to tolerate the occasional inferior commodity as a matter of "buyers beware." This situation continued well into the 1920s although there were some improvements in quality as manufacturing techniques modernized.

By the 1930s, a new consumerism began to sprout. Money was tight and the few buyers there were began to demand more for their limited cash. Japanese products were especially susceptible to this initiative because they had a reputation for shabbiness and, in the American public's mind, a habit of making cheap copies of someone else's products. The Japanese response was a bit of underhanded chicanery. They renamed one of their industrial cities "Usa." All products made there then got labeled "Made in USA."

Even before the new consumerism had really begun, corporations were looking to improve their profits. Starting in 1924, testing a theory that there was a link between productivity and employee satisfaction, studies was undertaken to prove or disprove it. One major investigation—conducted at the Hawthorne Works of the Western Electric Company plant in Cicero, Illinois— would continue for the next nine years.

Aware that there were too many variables to track at once, the organizers committed themselves to following scientific methodology, changing one variable at a time. Early on, the researchers came to the realization that the employees in the study performed better merely for being involved in the test, a reaction now called the "Hawthorne effect." It became evident that the workers wanted to have an input into their work process. Now known as the Hawthorne studies, these findings were important factors in understanding what motivates employees, and brought about many changes in the workplace.

One of the employees working summers at the Hawthorne plant was William Edwards Deming. Although he was not directly involved in the tests, he was certainly aware of them and this knowledge would play a part in Deming's future, as he was to promote the next great revolution in business—quality management.

After obtaining his doctorate in physics, Deming pursued a career at the U.S. Department of Agriculture. While there, he met statistician Walter A. Shewhart, who had devised a method of "statistical control."

Basically, statistical control is the final step in a multistage process where a problem is identified, affecting variables quantified, and the results analyzed to gain some improvement—or control. The entire process is a combination of scientific methodology, engineering disciplines such as math, and, a good measure of common sense. America was first to apply statistical analysis to everyday life with the introduction of the workplace satisfaction surveys in an effort to acquire more productivity out of a given workforce.

Certainly not the originator of the idea, but one of the most noteworthy of statisticians was George Gallup, a modest academic from Chicago. He moved to New York in 1934 to take a job with a high-caliber advertising agency. There, Gallup applied statistical analysis to random person surveys that revolutionized business-marketing planning. He silenced most of his critics with his remarkably accurate prediction that not only would President Roosevelt be re-elected in 1936 but predicted the percentage of popular votes to within a fraction of a percentage point.

But statistical analysis has greater potential than predicting an election or determining who is going to buy laundry soap. In the coming war, it meant who would live or die. Consider the following two examples.

Early in the war, the RAF was looking for ways to reduce their losses of combat aircraft. Adding armor would do wonders to the survivability of the planes but would also degrade performance. The trick might be to add armor exclusively to the most vulnerable areas. To determine what was at risk, hundreds of battle damaged planes were examined and a statistical model developed. Then common sense kicked in. Investigators realized that the planes being surveyed had survived the gauntlet, and that there was no way to look at the destruction that knocked down aircraft either in the English Channel or in occupied Europe. Therefore, it was reasonable to assume that the undamaged areas were actually the most likely to be the most vulnerable. Gallup's surveying tactics were applied in determining from the aircrews which battle damage gave the crews the most trouble. From the data, hypothetical armor locations were determined. A few aircraft were fitted with new armor and results were not long in coming back. After just a few combat sorties, planes in the experiment were sporting impressive dents in their armored belts where heavy flak had struck without a single loss. With minimum delay, the rest of the British air armada was fitted with armor and losses quickly shrank to a tolerable level.

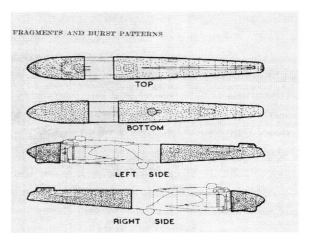

The U.S. Eighth A.F. surveyed nearly three thousand B-17s and detailed every puncture for anti-aircraft fire. Casualty numbers were figured into the formula and a revelation occurred. B-17s were prone to loss when shrapnel came through the bottom and caused casualties. Based on this, changes were made to protect the belly and surfaces the crew stood on. (US Army Air Force)

Faced with overwhelming shipping losses, the Allies also applied statistical methods to winning the Battle of the Atlantic. Reports from survivors of sinkings, from other witnesses and, from battle reports were meticulously reviewed. It became evident that the retreating U-boats could only be moving away in a limited number of directions. This obvious solution could easily be reduced to a mathematical problem. Factors such as convoy location and the number of warships available to pursue the subs had to be figured in, but within months, the fleet of escorts was given a series of patterns that they could use to intercept the submerged U-boat.

As anti-submarine force commanders became more experienced with the new patterns, U-boat losses skyrocketed, much to the consternation of the German Navy. But it was not just the mathematical application of predetermined attack courses that made the difference against the U-boats.

There were hundreds of applications of statistical mathematics. These led to the development of a new anti-submarine bomb called the Hedgehog, the atomic bomb, and, new artillery shells. Air force experts used statistical math in planning raids and

A U-boat is strafed when the crew is surprised on the surface. Radar was an operational leap forward by "seeing" the marauders from long distances and through cloud and night. .50 caliber slugs usually did not penetrate the pressure hull but they injured the men in the tower to where they delayed the submergence process. (U.S. Navy)

assessing bomb damage, although their formulas were far from accurate until 1944. Gallup-type surveys were put to use for the first time in military history when Allied troops were asked to rate everything from the quality of the food to the effectiveness of their officers.

Statistics were collected about every imaginable subject. Garbage was weighed to determine how to reduce food waste. Casualties were examined to find out what weapons were killing and maiming our soldiers and why. Accidental trauma from non-combat circumstances was recorded to help control the losses of men. Miles driven were tabulated to improve maintenance and quality of replacement parts for every type vehicle in the inventory. There was even an investigation on why the grass on the grounds of Army bases was failing to grow properly and how expected growth could be achieved.

As a result, the American military knew they could save "$20,000,000 a year by roasting meats at proper temperature."[9] They discovered that the standard Japanese 6.5 mm rifle bullet was "inferior" and "not designed for chamber pressures common in more modern weapons."[10] They realized a reduction of 2.6 days per patient of hospitalization for non-fatal, non-battle injuries.[11] Statistics also revealed that officials of the Ordnance Department favored Ford Motor Company model GAA engines over General Motors' engines due to endurance qualities that "were unpredictable and reliability the lowest of all engines tested."[12] And after thorough review they found that the maintenance and operation of Army bases was done in a haphazard manner and recommended, "introducing up-to-date management techniques."[13]

Statistical Quality Control (SQC)

Deming soon became an acknowledged expert on statistical analysis. During the war, government and private corporations desperately looked to him for ways to improve productivity and reduce employee turnover. Over the next four years, Deming taught his quality management practices and ideas to over 31,000 engineers, inspectors, and, military officers. As a result, Statistical Quality Control (SQC) became integral to the overall war effort.

SQC gave employees a say in how they did their jobs. Less restricted employees meant they were happier which in turn resulted in increased total production and record-setting profits. Government procurement officers liked SQC as it reduced both delivery delays and wasted time in rejecting below-standard components. As production and quality increased through employee-inspired suggestions, production costs plummeted.

Despite the overwhelming success in SQC and statistical analysis, post-war America abandoned it. Industry re-adopted the older Taylor method, which dictated strict rules and regulations to control employee performance. This autocratic domination was the basis for the production line, with mind-numbing routine that allowed no room for change. The worker was relegated back to being a virtual slave to methodical movements without any deviation. Much to Dr. Deming's dismay, his program of SQC had virtually disappeared from the American workplace by 1949.

However, Japan was ripe for Deming's ideas. The economy had been devastated and industrial capacity bombed into ruination. Only one major city, Kyoto, remained generally untouched. Farm production was down to sixty percent of pre-war levels and dropping further. The populace had lost all confidence in themselves and their government. Despite the war-related loss of more than 668,000 civilian lives, the Japanese were eager to rebuild.

Dr. Deming traveled to Japan in 1947 at the request of the Allied military government. While there, he found the Japanese people to be friendly and industrious, but their plight shocked him. Dr. Deming befriended a number of Japanese and, with their guidance, studied the language, history, and, customs. This new friendship developed to great lengths; he won their respect and was invited to address the post-war generation of industrialists and government officials who were determined to regain Japan's place as

Japan would have to join the world economy if they wanted to recover their war damages. This is just one example of the war industry turning out product for peace. Deming had a lot of influence in this process. (American Mach.)

an industrial nation. As it turned out, Japanese culture and the quality control philosophies of Deming and Shewhart fit perfectly together.

He offered up the examples of Britain and Switzerland as examples of countries that produce quality products to purchase food and other staple items. Mindful of the critical needs of Japan, he proposed that his new friends could do the same.

The rest of the story is one of the best-known illustrations of industrial reorganization in his century. Japanese products rapidly became accepted on the world market. No longer viewed as junk, cameras, electronics, machinery, and, vehicles poured out of Japan. As the years went by, Japanese goods even began to outpace their foreign counterparts in sales. Less costly, delivering better performance, and of a higher overall quality, their cars displaced the behemoth American cars when the oil crisis hit the West in 1972. Americans flocked to purchase Hondas, Toyotas, and, Nissans and be rid of their Detroit-made gas-guzzlers. Between the new environmental laws and the Arabs, Japanese carmakers got their chance to leverage the American market.

American auto engineers insisted that the only way to reduce emissions and subsequent pollution was to use a catalytic converter. This expensive device consisted of a canister with platinum-coated plates that scrubbed the noxious gases into harmless elements. On the other hand, Japanese engineers met the new standards by less expensive, more conventional means. This was just one of a number of practices that led to the decline of American dominance in many manufacturing fields. Throughout the 1970s and '80s, American-made electronics, cars, shoes, clothes, appliances, hardware, hand tools, and, machine tools became non-competitive. Heavy industries such as steel almost died as cheaper Japanese and Korean steel flooded the market. Children's toys and games from Taiwan dominated the shelves.

It has been only in the mid-1990s that the American

Inspection of a jet engine fixture. A fixture is a production tool that holds a part or parts in position for machining. Inspection of tooling has to be as near absolute as possible, but production parts rely on the statistical methods proposed by Shewart and Deming. Sample lots of every operation and every operator are checked. If all the tested parts meet standards, statistically, all parts will meet them. (Pratt & Whitney) economy has recovered. Japan took the American idea, which had been instrumental in an Allied victory, and turned it around on to its inventors. American companies realized that they were on the verge of defeat and rediscovered the Deming quality methods, now named Total Quality Management (TQM). Presently, quality is a key word in industry. Workers have regained their input into work methods and managers are being constantly reeducated on the principles of Shewhart and Deming.[14]

The Ballpoint Pen

In 1884, the Waterman fountain pen became the first pen with a reservoir ever marketed. Considered a major improvement at the time, these new fountain pens could not only carry their own ink supply, but the ink flow could be adjusted to compensate for differing paper absorbencies and textures. For the next fifty-nine years, fountain pens dominated the writing world, only to be toppled in 1943 by two Hungarian brothers, Laszlo and George Biro, and, their writing instrument, the humble Biro ballpoint pen. For such a simple item, the underlying story is more complicated than is generally realized.

Ballpoint pen construction consists of four main components: the reservoir, the ball and its housing, the body, and, the ink. Each item was separately invented during the Second World War, although not necessarily for the ballpoint pen. The beauty of this pen is in its simplicity. To make the pen work successfully, an extremely tiny metal ball is housed in a socket within the writing tip. Constantly fed from the ink reservoir by capillary flow, the ball rotates freely and applies quick-drying ink onto the paper.

The ballpoint pen overcame many of the flaws in the popular fountain pens. For example, the fountain pen's nib, usually made of gold, would often clog up with partially dried ink. Because the golden nib was soft, iridium plating was used to provide better wear-resistance. This made buying and maintaining a pen a significant investment, and, losing a pen could be a considerable financial setback. For the traveling businessperson, altitude played havoc with the fountain pen as well. The ink reservoir, basically a sac of flexible material, would break or otherwise leak, dribbling its contents out in an ever-growing stain, usually on one's best shirt. For the resourceful inventor, there was obviously a market for a non-leaking, inexpensive pen.

The first patent for the Biro ballpoint pen was submitted in 1938 while Laszlo and George were still living in Budapest. From there, Laszlo traveled to Paris, reporting on the heightening tensions over German threats of war. When the Germans invaded France in 1940, the Biro brothers fled to Argentina. There, they arranged for a new source of capital to revive their work on the ballpoint pen. They got financial backing from British financier Henry Martin, who would eventually set up a factory in England, working in conjunction with Frederick Miles, to produce pens for use by the Royal Air Force. However, that gets us ahead of the story.

In Argentina, the Biro pen still faced a dearth of problems. Steel balls for the pen were difficult to obtain, as most ball bearings were either too big for the capillary tube or needed for the war, which was siphoning every available bearing off the market. Then, one of the Biro brothers obtained a sample of a new ball bearing from Sweden.

Before the war, Swedish roller bearing manufacturer SKF was getting its necessary nickel, tungsten, chromium and other alloying metals from Germany. When the shooting war began in 1939, these elements were declared vital to German industry. Cut off from their supplies of alloying materials, Swedish metallurgists searched for an acceptable replacement. They found it in the form of silicon. Not only was silicon adequate, but also the resulting steel proved to be superior in certain ways. The balls could be ground smaller and to closer tolerances. One drawback, though, was that they did not have the life span that the harder balls containing the conventional alloys had exhibited. For Biro, this was not a problem, as the ball would certainly outlast the ink supply.

Inks of the early twentieth century left a lot to be desired. The prevalent ink was India ink, made from lampblack—a carbonaceous residue left on the insides of kerosene lanterns—and air-drying solvents. India ink was slow to dry and, depending on its quality, often smudged. Improvements on the solvents were abundant, but they seldom worked on a universal basis.

In Argentina, Laszlo happened to be at a printing plant that was using a new ink from Germany. He noted that the ink dried quickly and resisted smearing. George analyzed the ink and found that it contained an unfamiliar solvent. George turned to Austrian-American chemist Franz Seech, a Jewish refugee living in California, to identify the secret solvent. He recognized it as a chemical that had been formulated in Germany right before the war.

When Dr. Gerhard Schrader discovered the organo-phosphates that went on to become Tabun nerve gas, Hitler's scientists went to work on planning mass production. For greater efficiency of disbursement, the gas was diluted with an isopropanal ester—a modification of the alcohol molecule. This became an important step in the manufacturing process, aiding in stabilizing the poison's chemistry. Once the gas began to disperse, the alcohol agent had to evaporate immediately, which it did with unprecedented efficiency. This same isopropanal ester had been added to the printer's ink used in Germany, which then found its way to Germany's South American trading partner. This is the ink that Biro adopted for his new pen.

Commercially, the Eterpen Company sold ballpoint pens first in Buenos Aires in 1945. However, Biro had forgotten to get a United States patent, so he lost any monopoly on the giant North American market. In the United States, copies of Biro's pen were sold as "the first pen to write underwater." This must have met an unsatisfied longing as some 10,000 were sold at Gimbel's Department store in New York on October 29, 1945. Britain was not far behind America with their first pens, made by the Miles-Martin Pen Company, which had been manufac-

The Biro brothers' new pen was just getting its start on the civilian market. They did not realize it yet, but the fountain pen industry was on the way out. (Time/Life)

turing the ball-point pens for the British military, the RAF in particular, since 1944. Having satisfied their lucrative contracts, Mile-Martin pens became available to the general public at Christmas, 1945.

Ballpoint pens have grown into a major, worldwide industry. There are no less than 400 companies plying their version of the Biro invention. France's Bic Company bought out Miles-Martin soon after the war and developed their ultimately successful line of Bic disposable pens. Such is the volume that one pen alone, the Bic Crystal, has daily sales of 14 million units.

Forklifts

World War Two is the first war in which moving materials became a priority. Never before had such energy and facility been committed to getting men, weapons, and myriad supplies to the battle lines. The emergency program to build the fleets of Victory ships, cargo aircraft, and, trucks were unprecedented. Because shipping space was at a premium, vehicles and planes were packed partially assembled in crates. Likewise for weapons, ammunition, food, clothing, spare parts, and, the thousands of other items that a modern army needs to live and fight. Industrial machinery for Russia, Britain, India and the British Commonwealth countries received the boxed treatment as well.

Prior to the war, nearly all cargo was loaded onto ships either by crane or conveyor. Large items such as motorcars or trucks could be driven directly to the wharf and lifted aboard. Small boxes and barrels were manhandled using carts or dollies, or just bodily carried up the gangplank. Another method of loading was to pile cases, cartons or boxes in a cargo net that was then hoisted onboard via the ship's derrick. In the hold, the net was then hand unloaded and stacked. To unload, the process was reversed. Labor intensive as it was, these methods were perfectly satisfactory at the time. Other than the ship's owners, who had an economic incentive to get underway, there was no real rush to load the cargo. In fact, the longshoremen, whose job it was to manhandle the cargo, preferred it this way. In addition their union had been shown to be particularly resistant when it came to changes regarding new machinery or any change that risked losing potential man-hours, which equalled a fuller pay envelope.

However, war requirements increased pressure to get ships loaded and out of port. To handle the rapidly increasing volume of cargo, a relatively new machine called the "forklift" was tested. Its development began in the last days of the First World War and proceeded slowly. By 1939, the more familiar form had transpired with rear steering, twin forks and lift mast. Powered by a small gasoline engine, the machine could lift and carry substantial loads. Directly in front of the front wheels was a telescopic mast that used an oil-based hydraulic cylinder to raise and lower the forks. Attached to the mast, protruding to the front, these forks could easily slip under the crates and move them about with ease. The mast allowed for stacking, a storage technique that had been done previously by hand, an arduous and dangerous job. Logistically, the forklift could do

Guam, 1945. This is better than carrying it by hand for S1/c M.D. Shore. Given the stacks of materials, the forklift and wooden pallet has been a blessing for the men who have to organize it. By this time, nearly all the islands that have been captured have been turned into recreation facilities or, like Guam, enormous supply and repair depots. This was all part of the build-up for the anticipated invasion of Japan. (U.S. Navy)

the work of ten or more men. Except for servicing and refueling, it was inexhaustible.

The Wooden Pallet

To handle the smaller boxes with forklift-type machinery, the pallet was devised. Cheap to make, the pallet could provide a surface for any number of coils, cartons, tins, or bales. The first pallets were of random sizes, often exclusive to fit one particular dimensioned container. It was only with some effort was the American military able to enforce a standard size of either 42-inch or 48-inch square semi-hardwood frame with planks on top and bottom to serve as a platform and vertical planks supporting the middle. However, by 1943, the modern pallet had achieved its final form.

The pallet gave inspiration for other uses of the forklift. The first and most logical was to use the pallet as a work platform. This was found to be hugely unsafe with men riding atop were thrown off while driving. The man-baskets, with rails and safety chains provided a place for workmen to stand when the forklifts were used to lift them off the ground. Maintenance mechanics availed themselves of forklifts with jib hooks placed on the forks to lift heavy machinery components for repair. By removing the forks, accessories such as clamps and poles could handle giant rolls of paper or canvas.

The modern forklift is little changed from its ancestors. Larger models have been built, handling loads of 20 tons and more. All-terrain tires and suspension, plus four-wheel drive, have placed the forklift on construction sites. There are even portable forklifts that can be attached to delivery trucks to speed the unloading process.[15]

Fasteners

There were literally thousands of new fasteners invented during the Second World War for the myriad tasks at hand. As new designs for vehicles, planes, machinery, and equipment quickly evolved through their infancy, they required better, cheaper, and easier means of production expending less time, energy, and materials than ever before. No idea was too crazy nor was any material not considered.

The aircraft industry led the way with innovative ideas. To further reduce drag and increase performance, flush head rivets, previously used sparingly because of more difficult assembly processes, became more common. Production needs inspired a whole range of quickly installed "pop" rivets that could be installed by one worker using an automatically fed air tool. The DuPont Company came out with a unique rivet that was placed into the mating holes and heated with a tool that looked similar to a soldering iron. Within the blind side of the rivet was a cavity filled with a small explosive charge that, once heated, exploded, deforming the end and permanently fastening the sheet-metal panels together. One man—or woman—working alone could set 20 to 25 of these rivets in a minute.

There was often a need to know how much strain a bolt had been subjected to so that corrective repairs could be made before there was a catastrophic failure. Special bolts were made that had either mechanical or electrical sensors to monitor the condition of the bolts. Another use for strain-sensing bolts was to prevent over-tightening, which could lead to premature metal fatigue of either the bolt itself or the casting that it was fitted into.

Another class of screw that became prevalent during the war was the socket head. This fastener has a six-sided internal pocket that takes a special wrench—called a hex wrench—instead of a screwdriver blade or external tool fitting the flats found on most bolts. Dozens of different styles of socket head

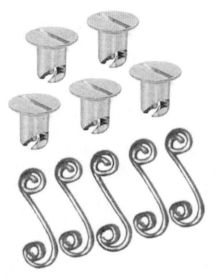

It's not art, its Dzuses. Dzus are quick release; quick attach devices first invented for sheet metal panels on aircraft. Often mechanics need to access a compartment for a rapid adjustment. Rather than tear half the airplane apart, the manufacturer thoughtfully put an access panel on the outside. To secure for flight but to make easy to get to, they used this device. One twist counterclockwise releases the catch (top) from the retainer (bottom) which can be attached to the airframe with either rivets, screws, or welded in place. This just one of the many fasteners the war inspired. (American Fastener)

Three different types of socket-head screws. The one on the far left is the hex-style made famous during the war. (American Fastener)

277

screws were made for specific needs, mostly in aircraft engines and for tooling in the factories. It is within the latter that socket head screws have found a permanent home, being used to assemble machinery and other production equipment.

The war inspired the fashioning of thousands of special clips, retainers, clamps, and other fasteners, many of which were to become adopted by other industries after the war was over. Most of today's appliances, cars, airplanes, furniture, homes, and offices are held together with these fasteners, all from World War Two.[16]

Thread Inserts

Aluminum was quickly becoming the material of choice for building aircraft in the 1930s, although one of the drawbacks to the soft metal was that it did not nearly approach the shear strength of steel. This meant that threads cut into aluminum had the nasty habit of tearing, often under a dynamic load such as during takeoff or a banking turn at altitude. For this same reason aluminum was discarded, albeit temporarily, as a metal for automotive uses.

To overcome the thread problem, the thread insert was invented. The most popular type was the *Aero-Thread*. Made from a hard phosphor-bronze, the spring-shaped insert would be threaded into the softer parent material. The patented form was designed to spread the load of a torqued fastener throughout the sides of the hole, while a standard, high-strength bolt was used internally. The *Aero-Thread* was also intended to protect against wear for frequently removed bolts.

Late in the war, *Helicoil* inserts were invented. These new thread inserts were made of stainless steel—phosphor bronze was a valuable and scarce commodity—and abandoned the *Aero-Thread*'s semi-circular exterior thread form. Engineers favored a sharp, 60°

This Heli-coil insert is actually upside-down. The tang across the inner diameter is used to drive the insert into place. Once there, the tang is broken off with a small punch and removed from the hole. Spring tension and surface friction hold the insert in place.

Keensert thread inserts do not require special tools like the Heli-coil tap, but this insert needs more wall thickness between the hole and edge of the part.Once in place, the small stakes have to be driven into the insert where they lock the thread in place.

diamond shape that proved to be far superior. Making the new thread angle was much faster in the parent material as well, as the tooling was no different in shape from any other threading tap. Other competing inserts were developed as well. *Keenserts* were introduced late in the war, not as an alternative to *Helicoils*, but to be used in specific applications where *Helicoils* were considered inappropriate. *Keenserts* are made from solid stock, threaded internally and externally. Once installed, two small wedge pins are driven into the mating external threads, permanently locking the insert from backing out.

Even before the war was over, production machinery had been adapted to install threaded inserts automatically. The thread inserts found their way into other industrial settings and, naturally, into the automotive industry. For the shade tree mechanic, threaded inserts—especially *Helicoils*—were life-savers when engine-block bolts, seized by rust, had to be drilled out. Rather than discarding the damaged engine block, the appropriate *Helicoils* could be installed in a matter of minutes. Now, the inserts are available in a variety of sizes for standard American and metric sizes as well as all the common spark plug threads, in a corporate nod to all homebound mechanics.[17]

Industrial Machinery

World War Two was a conflict whose outcome rested on the factory floor as well as on the battlefield. Unlike the case in any previous war, rising to the technological challenges to out-produce the enemy was tantamount to victory. The thousands of trucks, tanks, guns, airplanes, munitions, and, sundry items that were necessary to win the war all required some level of industrial processing, usually by machine tools. Historically, the manufacture of arms drove the development of new machines to cut, form, and, shape metal components, so that by the 1930s, a good selection of machines was already in existence. However, there were a few machine tools invented during the war period that continue to play important roles in present-day industry.

Industrial Band Saws

The industrial, metal-cutting band saw is one of the last of the basic, modern machining processes to have been perfected. First introduced by Leighton A. Wilkie in 1933, the band saw uses a thin, flexible metal blade that has teeth along one edge. One of the two basic types, the horizontal sawing machine is meant for straight cutting of bulk metal stock into specific lengths as a preliminary stage of the mass-manufacturing process. The vertical band saw (Pictured) features a table to support the work while the blade passes downwards through it. The vertical machine makes it possible to cut blocks of metal into complex shapes, a process called contouring.

The vertical band saw is the work-saver of the machine shop. Variations on the machine can be found in lumber mills, wood and cabinet shops, butcher shops, and the hobbyist. (Do-All)

Contouring was a big step in the rapid manufacture of most of the production machinery and tools used in America during the war. No longer would complex shapes have to be painstakingly cut by acetylene torch—which leaves ragged, uneven edges that may be impossible to cut—or machined from the solid block, a time consuming and materially expensive process. Even though it had seven years to mature, band sawing was largely ignored by the great mass of American industry until 1939. Even the authoritative *Machinery's Handbook,* long referred to as the machinists' bible, contained no information on band saws until the 1943 issue.

In spite of the apparent indifference, band sawing has come to be a specialty in its own right. A multitude of blades can be selected for cutting materials from the softest aluminum alloys to the hardest tool steels. Plain knife-edged blades are used to cut cardboard and plastics. Stainless steel blades slice up tomorrow's roasts and steaks at the packing plants or the butcher's shop. Diamond coated blades can trim glass and ceramics, leaving behind a nearly polished edge.

The Bridgeport Mill

This machine represents the backbone of the whole body of machine tool trades and indispensible addition to American industry. Also called a knee mill, it features a table that can be adjusted in three dimensions. With a multi-purpose head driven by a small but powerful motor, general milling, drilling, and, shaping can be done easily and rapidly. Although the parts that are made on it are usually small in size—a stock Bridgeport mill weighs only about 2,000 pounds and has a table travel of about 12" X 30"—the Bridgeport mill's versatility and accuracy make it virtually indispensable to any shop or factory, regardless of the nature of the product. (Pictured)

The first model, comprised of only the motor and high-speed speed shaft assembly, was made in 1932. Over the next six years, the partners Rudolph Bannow and Magnus Wahlstrom added features as customer's requested. In 1936, the Bridgeport Model C head was a popular tool but many complained that the milling head really needed its own mounting platform. On the back of a scrap paper bag, Bannow sketched his original ideas. It took another three years for the partners to present the finished product.

Remarkably, the Bridgeport mill has undergone few changes. One major modification was to do away with the cylindrical ram supporting the head. Instead, a more rigid knuckle device allowed the head to be tilted in two axis. Over the years, improved motors, variable-speed belt drives, and attachments have been added to the armory of tooling for the mill. Electronic positioning scales and even computerized retrofit packages are available to get the most performance out of the ubiquitous Bridgeport mill.[18]

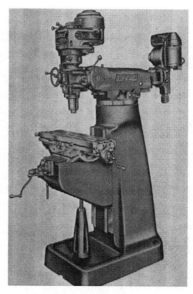

This is a Bridgeport milling machine, also known as a knee mill. The large object at the top far right is a shaper head. Across the turret (where the logo is) is the mill head. It is mounted on a unique knuckle device that allows the head to be tipped in two axis. Below the mill head is the table, which can be accurately moved in three directions: up/down, in/out, and side to side. The flexibility of this machine made it a required tool for every machine shop. (Textron)

The Moore Jig Grinder

Over the course of years, industrial technology has endeavored to improve on the dimensional quality of component parts, a vital element of interchangeability. The origins of interchangeability lay with the development of military arms. As late as the American Civil War, guns were handmade, each one unique. Should a part such as the hammer or trigger break, it required the skill and tools of a gunsmith to fashion a new piece. Interchangeability meant that any number of guns could be torn apart, the components mixed together and successfully reconstructed in working order. To enable this, each piece has to be made to exacting specifications, with little variation. After the gun-makers, the automotive industry and the watch-making trades were quick to adopt the principles of interchangeability for mass-production purposes. As decades passed, the standard inch had been divided and re-divided into ever smaller portions until the difference between a good part and bad was measured in units of one ten-thousandths of an inch. In relative terms, this is splitting the human hair by as much as ten times.

Repeatedly holding these types of tolerances requires a great deal of skill and experience, two traits that are not likely to be found in the large number of people in a Second World War factory, even those who had some experience with mass production. But with properly made tools, gages, and assembly jigs— devices for holding parts while they are being put together—semi-skilled workers could produce a finished product that was dimensionally identical to the next one. New machines like the jig grinder were necessary to make these tools. (Pictured)

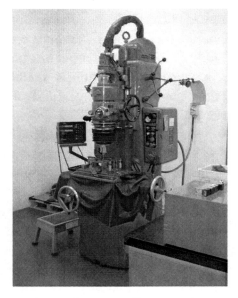

In 1940, American Richard F. Moore invented the jig grinder. Resembling the construction of the knee mill, the jig grinder table could move in only two directions. Special bearings and locks allowed the operator to make table movements as small as fifty millionths of an inch. (That is $1/3,125^{th}$ of the period at the end of this sentence.) This incredibly tiny movement was displayed on crude—by today's standards—digital readout screen that used vacuum tubes to show the numerical values of position.

One of Moore's greatest accomplishments was the development of the orbiting head. At the center of the orbiting head was a high-speed spindle that mounted a variety of grinder points. This spindle could be adjusted to form precision holes and other shapes while the orbiting head could create

A must for a manufacturer using or making interchangable parts, mass production, or production aids like jigs and fixtures. The Moore jig grinder is capable, with a skilled machinist, working down to millionths of an inch. That kind of accuracy is absolutely necessary for any of the above manufacturing processes. (Moore) its own radial path, and could be adjusted to the same microscopic proportions as the table. With an experienced machinist at the controls, the Moore jig grinder could cut and grind hardened tool steels to unprecedented tolerances, often within .000002". As a result of the jig grinder, the millions of tools and production aids needed for war production could be made in a relatively short time. Even better, identical assembly and inspection tooling for a second or third distant factory could be made so that more than one plant producing the same product could get the soldier or sailor what he needed faster. Most importantly, those parts would be undistinguishable and universally interchangeable.

Surface Roughness Measurement

As a tool such as a lathe or mill cutter passes across the surface of a metal part, it leaves tiny grooves or marks behind. Not only are these aesthetically displeasing, they can lead to an eventual waste of the metals and all the labor that has gone into them. If, during the cutting process, the metal is not finished to a fine enough surface, then there is no way to gage its size with any certainty, especially when the dimensions are plus or minus .0001". Furthermore, when parts that mated together to form a seal or press fit is of unacceptable finish, they can be damaged upon assembly.

By 1937, William Taylor of England had worked out a system of standards for surface texture and roughness based on mathematical calculations. To accompany his standards, he developed his patented *Taylorsurf* machine. Like the grooves in a record, the tool marks can be measured with a stylus similar to a phonograph needle. Through the machine's electric amplification, the surface texture can then be tested and recorded. Variations indicate problems with the machine, the cutters, or the material itself, all easily rectified with a minimum of lost time and materials. Parts with a poor finish can be quickly weeded out, saving the time and trouble of inadvertently scrapping good components and the enormous costs of rework.

Electric Discharge Machinery (EDM)

A number of new and exotic materials were just beginning to become common in American factories during the war. Ceramics, carbides, tungsten tool steels, and, a whole range of steel alloys presented challenges to machinists and engineers. Many of these materials were just too tough or hard to cut by conventional methods. Etching metals with acids had been around since 1865, but the process was extremely slow

A small toolroom electric discharge machine (EDM). EDM machines are useful for removing broken hardened steel tools such as threading taps and drills. Complex shapes are easier to machine with an EDM. (Author's collection)

and did not work at all on acid-resistant nickel and stainless steels.

But, in a moment of inspiration, electric power was tried. Like a short-lived electrolytic machining process developed in 1930, electric discharge machining (EDM) used a low-voltage, high-ampere electric current through a shaped carbon electrode to abrade the surface metal away. Immersed in a tank of dielectric fluid that flushed waste away from the work area, the relatively soft electrode could be machined to any contour, shape, or size that would then be burnt into the work piece. Also known as spark erosion, this 1943 invention could sear its way through the hardest materials within a matter of minutes.

Still in use, EDM has garnered a niche in the

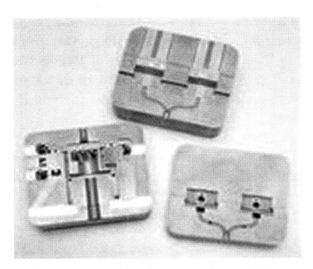

These are mold halves made with an EDM. The detail and intricacies are far too difficult to machine with conventional methods. Even if could be done, it would cost much more in time. The EDM is a specialty machine that should be carefully apporpriated work that would be uneconomical in any other way.

machine shop. The growth of injection molding has secured the continuous use of EDM as cavities, corners, and, hollows that are impossible to fabricate any other way can readily be machined with EDM. Another EDM process that is an outgrowth of the war version is wire EDM. Using a long, continuous strand of very thin wire and computerized controls, intricate shapes can be cut with surprising accuracy and minimal waste.

Welding Processes

There are literally hundreds of methods for joining metals permanently together. The craft dates back well into Roman times when bronze statues were regularly repaired. Blacksmiths fused steel together in forges fired with forced air and either hardwood or coal. By the nineteenth century, acetylene and oxygen had been isolated and, when combined, produced a flame that burned in excess of 3,000°F, well above the melting point of steel.

Electric power provided a new source of heat for welding. Beginning in 1886, bare rod arc welding—also named for its inventor Elihu Thomson—would be revolutionary, but there were more developments to come.

Submerged Arc Welding

Before the popularization of electric arc welding in the 1930s, a great many assemblies were simply riveted or bolted together. Thomson welding methods consisted mainly of spot welding—the same process that fuses the frames of the present-day automobile together—or butt-welding thin sheets end-to-end. Metallurgical science of the time was too inexact to accurately predict weld strengths, and inspection methods were crude at best. Furthermore, electric power for welding required an enormous amount of current from a reliable source, a commodity that was not always available without causing brownouts elsewhere. Before 1940, the great percentage of welding was done with DC current derived from engine- or AC motor-generator sets that were not necessarily dependent on external electric suppliers. With expanding electric service and better inspection techniques such as ultra-sound and X-ray, arc welding became more common.[19]

Submerged arc welding used a powder

This is a mock-up of a submerged arc welding set-up. The tube at the left delivers the stream of powder flux, the center places the overlay powder and the last (at right) being the wire guide electrode. The welding speeds attainable with this process are truly amazing.

flux to protect the freshly molten steel from oxidation and chemical embrittlement, two serious flaws that led to cracking. The flux also allowed for automatic welding of ship's hulls, a process separately developed by the Russians and American in 1936. Although the process received considerable attention at the time, it came into more widespread usage during the dark early days of the war when Henry Kaiser promoted it to assemble his Victory ship fleet.

The idea of welding the hull together did not sit well with the troops and merchant seamen, though. In heavy seas, the sides of the ship popped and boomed like a gigantic beer can flexing. Several of the Victory ships actually developed major cracks on their first Atlantic crossings, and at least two were lost with heavy casualties when the ships broke apart. The welding process was modified and the cracking problem soon became a bad memory.

Automatic welding processes went on to become a major factor in the success of the army's armored forces as well. Previously, the steel plates of tanks and armored cars had been riveted, a manufacturing policy that dated back to the First World War. With the advent of high-powered machine-gun and automatic cannon rounds, rivets became too hazardous. Even if the enemy-fired projectiles did not penetrate the steel, enough lucky bullets drove the rivets through with equally horrifying effects on the vehicle's occupants. By early 1943, nearly all the manufacturers of Allied armored vehicles had abandoned the rivet in favor of welded bodies.[20]

Tungsten Inert Gas (TIG) and Heliarc Welding

Atmospheric-gas contamination had prevented the development of welding processes on non-ferrous metals for decades. While the base metal was still in a liquid state, molecular hydrogen atoms would corrupt the base metals, creating an unstable and weak crystalline structure. Welding aluminum, magnesium or stainless steel seemed to be a futile endeavor until 1940, when the Russell Meredith[21] at Northrop Aircraft tried his hand at it.[22]

Starting with a thin stainless steel sheet, he gradually developed a fusion method using a welding handle with an electrically charged tungsten electrode as a heat source. Around the electrode, he flooded helium gas, which created an impervious barrier between the air and the vulnerable joint. The resulting arc plasma—a highly ionized gas—melted the field in a neutral gas environment in which the electrode added no material. Fill metal came from a hand-held wire that was slowly added as the weld progressed. The new process was called "Heliarc" welding.

Emboldened by this success, the aircraft industry quickly began a concerted effort to expand upon the technology. Other gases were tried in place of the valuable helium. Argon, carbon dioxide, and, a variety of mixtures were all found to have specific uses and positive benefits. As a result, aluminum, nickel steels, and, a variety of exotic metals were being welded by the end of 1943. Although the machines that produce the electric current have grown smaller and the controls refined, most of the TIG welding processes have remained virtually unchanged.

One rule has always held true: aluminum and some steels cannot be welded. That rule ended with the introduction of Tungsten Inert Gas (TIG) welding. Here the welder is striking the arc with the electrode in his left hand while holding the fill rod in his right. This was an important step in manufacturing aircraft because the higher speeds and introduction of jet power meant that more exotic metals will be included in the construction. (Northrop)

Weldments as a Substitute for Casting

Even before America entered the war, there was a great increase in the production of all sorts of arms and products needed to fight aggressor armies. Production of heavy steel goods such as tanks and ships required what little foundry facilities there were in existence. This led to a massive shortage of cast components for ship drive gears just when the need for replacements was reaching critical levels.

Westinghouse engineers developed a whole new method of manufacturing gears from plate steel. The sheets were cut out to form the sides and periphery of the gear and, once the outer ring was rolled into the proper diameter, welded together. The finished surfaces, such as gear teeth, seal surfaces and finished bore dimensions would be machined in using conventional methods. In the early days, there were problems with the weldment's finished dimensions changing when the welds suddenly released built-up stresses, causing the assembly to "sproing[7]." If bad enough, the weldment would need to be remachined, but techniques of sequential welding and stress-relief

7 Sproing is not an ill-conceived word formation. When a large weldment is poorly assembled and welded, there is a series of noises, crackles, snaps, and literal groans as the stress builds. This process culminates with loud metallic noises similar to those of a dropped steel plate bouncing and reverberating. Sproing fits best.

shot-peening reduced the problem. Further development of weldment technology was adapted to replace the forgings and castings of the turbine casings themselves. Special care in re-enforcing the high-pressure chambers had to be observed, but as time went on, fewer of the hard-to-get cast components were being used in favor of the factory-built welded ones. Not only did this method take a lot of the burden off the foundries, but also it saved enormous amounts of precious steel for other requirements and reduced the weight of the drive train. The less weight carried in the engine room directly translated into more cargo or troops the ship could load without reducing the efficiency of the hull, a determining factor in calculating a ship's fuel range.[23]

There is a lot of machining to finish these gear blanks. Rather than cast, the weldment process can save a huge amount of steel. The bores are already close to finish and the outer surface will finish when the gear teeth are cut. (Westinghouse)

Situations such as that described above happened thousands of times a year in American industry during the war. Weldments could be created in nearly the same time. A casting required enormous ovens to melt the large quantities of steel and mammoth forms to pour the cast. This type of facility was a limited quantity in the U.S. and there were some parts, such as armored tank turrets, that could not be fabricated any other way. Engineers and craftsmen were given full authority to think creatively and to come up with solutions to problems never before encountered. Postwar, the science and art of designing weldments was greatly responsible for the growth of large industrial mining and construction machinery.

Metal Spraying

Until the Thomson welding process grew into a production process, welding had been the exclusive territory of the maintenance mechanic. One of the most frequent uses for welding was to "build up" worn shafts. When a spinning axle of a machine rubs against another part of a machine, such as a shield or a bearing, the shaft will eventually begin to wear. If allowed to continue, the shaft will break, often dramatically.

To repair worn shafts, arc welding was the answer for some years. It was relatively quick and it took little skill to do. However, as new steel alloys began to become more prevalent, welding presented a new challenge. The high heat of the arc could easily damage the base material, leading to cracks or irreversible stresses that created warping. From the development of TIG welding came metal spraying.

First, the worn shaft would be placed in the rotating chuck of a lathe and preheated with a torch. Then a tungsten rod created an arc that melted powdered metal as it sprayed onto the slowly turning shaft. The heat was not nearly high enough to warp the shaft or crystallize the metallic deposit during the arc process. Because of the relatively lower heat, the shaft could be machined and returned to the

Metal spraying on a lathe. Off the spools (on the left), the wire go through the head (the operator's right hand) where the flame liquefies it. Because the shaft is turning as this happens, the amount applied is equal on all sides. Once this process is finished, the shaft will cool and then be machined to size. Metal spraying is frequently faster than fabricating a new part. During the war, metal was often in so short supply, that even replacing a shaft of this size was unlikely. (OWI/NARA)

mechanics in less time to return the production equipment back into use. During the war, downtime was unpatriotic.

The Bathythermograph

The end of the war and a return to "normalcy" meant that scientific research would either pick up where it had been abandoned four years previously or totally new avenues would be explored, having been opened by the war. Research in the world's oceans was to get a big boost from war technology.

The development of SCUBA gear went a long way toward freeing researchers from the confines of attached air hoses. (More on this in Chap.8) Advances in physiology had led to the invention of the decompression chamber, a vital, lifesaving machine that could reverse the bends, the effect of nitrogen bubbles forming in the body of a distressed diver. Miniature submarines had come along nicely since the Japanese,

Italians and the British had all developed small, submersible craft for wartime attacks. And the bathythermograph was invented.

Scientists and submariners had known that the ocean is made up of layers of water, some significantly colder than others. Because the warmer strata are quite a bit saltier, hence denser, it was discovered that sonar reflections would behave differently against the colder waters than in warmer surface waters. The bathythermograph measured and recorded those constantly changing conditions outside the submerged boat. The permanent record would serve as a guide to the nearest thermal layer, should the submarine come under sudden attack.[24]

After the war, bathythermographs became a necessary tool for oceanographers as they charted the undersea currents in an attempt to understand their relationship to the weather. Bathythermographs are also used by professional fishermen to isolate cold-water fish. Oil tanker captains use the information about warmer water to improve their ships' profitability. Warm oil pumps more easily—and more quickly—than cold oil. The smart tanker crew steers into the warmer waters to gain the extra few degrees of heat to thin their cargo, especially a day or two from port. On the large supertankers, this course change alone is credited with the savings of 15 hours of port time per trip.

Notes/Selected References

1   Steven, Joseph. *Hoover Dam, An American Adventure*. 1988. Pp. 206-214.
2   Life Saving Inventions Pay Dividends. *Popular Mechanics* magazine. May, 1938. Pp. 699-701.
3   ibid. Pp. 699-701.
4   ibid. Pp. 698-701. and 152A.
5   Steven, Joseph. P. 104.
6   New Disguises of the Demon Fire. *Popular Mechanics* magazine. June, 1942. Pp. 50-54.
7   Cohen, Stan. *V for Victory*. 1991. Pp. 60-61.
8   Data and information derived from Kaiser-Permenante website: http://www. kaiserpermanente.org/about/50years.html
9   Risch, Erna and Chester L. Kieffer. The Quartermaster Corps: Organization, Supply and Services. 1955. P. 70.
10 Beyers, Maj. James C. *Wound Ballistics*. 1962. P. 96.

11 Cook, Edgar L. Maj. and John E. Gordon. *Preventative Medicine in World War II: Personal Health and Immunization: Accidental Trauma.* 1955. P. 267.

12 Green, Constance McLaughlin, Harry C. Thomson and Peter C. Roots. *The Ordnance Department: Planning Munitions For War.* 1955. P. 300.

13 Fine, Lenore and Jesse A. Remington. *The Corps of Engineers: Construction in The United States.* 1989. Pp. 304-308.

14 Walton, Mary. *The Deming Management Method* 1986. Pp. 6-19.

15 Gateway to the World. *Popular Mechanics* magazine, April, 1942. Pp. 42 and 162.

16 Soled, Julius. *Fasteners Handbook.* 1957.

17 Oberg, Erik and F.D. Jones. *Machinery's Handbook 11th ed.* 1941. P. 1311 and R.D. Simonson. *The History of Welding.* 1969. Pp. 135-147. and Soled, Julius. *Fasteners Handbook.* 1957. Pp. 48-51.

18 Bridgeport data: Fundinguniverse.com/company-histories/Bridgeport-Machines-Inc-Company-History

19 R.D. Simonson. Pp. 135-147.

20 Green, Constance McLaughlin, et al. Pp. 378-379.

21 In *American Secret Pusher Fighters of World War II*, Gerald H. Balzer states that Vladimir Pavlecka spearheaded the magnesium welding research that culminated in TIG welding. P. 111

22 R.D. Simonson. Pp. 150-152.

23 WoodBury, David O. *Battlefronts of Industry: Westinghouse in World War II.* 1948. Pp.48-61.

24 Wheeler, Keith. War Under the Pacific 1981. P.70

7

Around the House: Conveniences for a Brave New World

Near the end of the Depression, the American home underwent a major revolution with the introduction of cheap, reliable electricity, new plastics, and a whole new philosophy towards the homemaker. Manufacturers and advertisers aimed at improving homemaking with products to minimize the daily chores. At least for advertising purposes women were promoted to "queens of the house." The Second World War interrupted this transformation.

In a sense, some good came out of the abrupt suspension of consumer goods production. Typically, a new product undergoes growing pains as the public discovers faults and weaknesses that the manufacturer never foresaw. Quite often, a product, no matter how good, can fail during this consumer "shake-down" period. During the war, the military often accepted less than perfect products, with the understanding that improvements would be instituted on the next production run. In this way, faults were identified and remedied, usually at government expense and without any negative publicity.[8]

In the spring of 1942, the government curtailed or diverted production of nearly all consumer goods for the duration of the war. After four lean years, the American public was starved for new consumer goods. When consumer production resumed, household appliances, cars, and other goods were snapped up with abandon, regardless

---

8 At this time in history, there were axioms for successful businesses: A happy customer will tell two friends, and unhappy one tells ten. Another was: The customer is always right.

of their quality. The most popular items were those that had been introduced immediately before the war and then adopted for military uses, such as the television and the automatic transmission. As a rule, these items had been perfected under wartime conditions to commercial quality.

The changing attitudes toward the homemaker were an ironic twist to the pre-war attitudes. Even long before the Depression, men were expected to work while women tended the home. During the war, women were asked, albeit with some patriotic arm-twisting, to work outside the home. Children, husbands, and the home were expected to take a backseat to winning the war. This led to a new-found independence among the women. They also had money, they were driving the family car, and they had simultaneous responsibility for job and home, challenges to which they rose admirably.

Throughout the war years, and even after, Madison Avenue advertisers promoted the American homemaker as a model of patriotic sacrifice and a perfect housewife. Wartime commercialism hawked "instant" prepared foods after a long day at work, cosmetics for looking beautiful for the shift at the aircraft plant, and elixirs for getting the best night's sleep for the next day's work. Women who stayed home during the war found themselves doing domestic work, even those fortunate women who had used hired help in the past. With the wages available at the war factories, the maids abandoned their employers. This left the ladies of the house to wash, clean, and cook.

The Hydra-Matic automatic transmission was a marvelous bit of engineering, having been tried to the ultimate in American combat tanks. After the war, it was the ladies who got the opportunity to try out the new device. This too was a carrot to get the women out of factory, or at least that is what they were willing to make the men believe. (Chevrolet Division of General Motors)

This period led to a whole range of quickly prepared foods; many that survived the intervening years with surprising durability.

As the men returned from the front, the women were expected quietly to return to their traditional places. However, four years of war had proven that women could handle a life of independence and they wanted to keep it. The men, confounded by this unaccustomed resistance at home, resorted to underhanded bribes. The new consumer products—saving labor and time and attractive as well—were used to lure the women back home.

Promotions for a wealth of products for the home flooded the airwaves and pages of women's magazines. No longer was going to work glamorized. The home was the new frontier for the "modern" housewife. Kitchens featured pressed-steel cabinets painted with hard enamel paints that cleaned in minutes. Countertops made of innovative water-proof glue. Dishwashers automatically cleaned the cookware and table settings after a meal cooked in an oven with revolutionary heating elements derived from war technology. Frozen foods and prepared foods reduced the effort that went into cooking. Plastic aprons protected clothes from spills, allowing the lady to retain her feminine dignity for guests. Many women wanted to return home anyway. With the treasure trove of new goods facing them, who could blame them?

Every company saw the post-war time as new opportunities to branch out into new product lines. Their big sales pitch was the hope of an amazing new period of prosperity filled with the wonders of the scientific breakthroughs from the war. (Kalamazoo Steel Products)

Structures

The great migration to do war work meant that there was an immediate and severe shortage of housing. Overcrowding led to a myriad of problems. Outhouses were placed near water supplies; food stores were swamped with unwanted customers, and the permanent residents, fearing that their bucolic hometowns would never be the same, vandalized construction projects. Towns-people were induced to open their homes to renters. Some enterprising souls resorted to "hot bunking" their tenants, renting out the room for eight- to twelve-hour stretches, two or three shifts a day. Near the larger plants, dormitories were erected. However, three new forms of housing were just becoming available.

House Trailers

Thousands of Americans lost their homes during the Depression. The fortunate among them went to live with relatives. Many others, forced into destitution, managed the best they could, living in their cars, on the road or in camps, following what work there was to be had. The gravy years of the 1920s had seen the start of the camping trailer fad. Equipped with a Spartan kitchen and some space to sleep, such trailers became homes for the few that had them.

During the late 1930s, manufacturers such as Airstream began to factory-build travel trailers. Sheathed in polished aluminum, they offered amenities such as gas stoves, space heaters, and padded beds. Quite a few factory models were sold, but the majority of Americans still could not afford such luxury. A contemporary magazine reported that there were 160,000 travel trailers in the United States, but only 35,000 factory-built. Plans for do-it-yourself trailers were available through mail order and in craft magazines. Using the metal parts scrounged from junked automobiles, the homebuilder was expected to use some ingenuity to complete the project.[1]

Modular and Mobile Homes

At least one far-sighted architect offered up a solution for the shortage of low-cost Depression-era housing. By applying the techniques of assembly line production, he proposed building houses from lightweight materials inside a factory. Wiring, plumbing, appliances, and lights would all be installed at the same time and designed to fit within the limited space of the home. The components would be interchangeable to allow the consumer the privilege of customizing the home. Naturally, the basement and the foundation could be eliminated, as the home could just sit on the ground. With the prediction that the cost of the first unit would exceed one million dollars, including factory

This older Airstream trailer has seen better days. This large one would probably have housed six or more, not an unusual number then. Hundreds of these trailers, built beginning in 1935, became home for thousands of war workers. (Author's Collection)

start-up expenses, the plan appears to have gone nowhere.[2]

New materials such as pressboard, chipboard and melamine enabled production of realistically priced mobile homes. Thinner and lighter than plywood, these new materials could be used for floors, walls, and ceilings without sacrificing space. Fractional size lumber, a previously unheard-of concept, was now coming onto the market. Instead of getting a board that truly measured two by four inches, mills were cutting the boards a quarter to a half- inch thinner. This again saved precious floor space and increased the number of boards available from the same-sized tree.

Finally, the public was ready to accept pre-built housing[9]. As the architect had predicted, the homes could be built for about sixty percent of the normal cost. An experimental program was underwritten by the new Federal Housing Administration (FHA) to manufacture and test several prototypes, incorporating most of the features found in today's mobile homes. These early experimental homes leaked terribly and lacked any insulation. Glues binding the pressboards together would dissolve if allowed to get damp. Even with all the shortcomings, however, they proved that the concept was workable. In 1939, limited production was begun.

The war inspired the growth of modular housing. Industrialists such as Henry Kaiser established large tracts of land for his employees to live on in trailers. Consolidated-Vultee, one of the many defense contractors needing employee housing, offered similar accommodations with community shower rooms and laundries, predicting the look of the now common organized trailer camps.

Making the Home: Building Materials

The vast number of rationed and scarce materials due to the war created a huge challenge to those who made it their business to build private homes or furniture. Once again, imagination had to be combined with science to create new materials.

Laminated Wood Product Adhesives (Modern Plywood)

Plywood has been around in some form since 1840, when it was used primarily for the construction of furniture. Placing thinly sliced layers of wood together with their grains at right angles to each other makes plywood. The laminate is bonded together with glue, which was the weak point for the original plywood. Protein glues, as fish

9 This is not prefabricated housing where the home is made in the factory and assembled on the home site. That method has been offered for years through retailers such as Sears & Roebucks.

and animal adhesives in the form of resins, are exceptionally intolerant to moisture and readily grew molds and bacteria, even if kept dry. These glues did not impart much strength into the finished product either.

Synthetic resins developed during the Second World War were responsible for the rapid acceptance of plywood as a general building material. Removing the non-protein organic nutrients from milk derived the most common prewar adhesive, casein. The remaining material was referred to as precipitate. Its central fault was that its nature too closely resembled the other

A laminated wooden beam. Well over one hundred feet long and not one piece over six inches wide or one inch thick. The secret; a mixture of phenol and formaldehyde glues. To get a good idea of the scale, there is a man sitting at far right waving. The real impressive feature is the pallets hanging from the beam loaded with heavy bags. Even if one could get a solid piece of wood this big, the loads applied by the pallets would certainly fail. This beam would work as a rafter for a large aircraft hangar. (Century Wood Products)

biological glues. Without an additional plasticizer, precipitate swells and shrinks in damp or wet conditions.[3] But there were new synthetics to use.

Urea is the root chemical of Bakelite, invented in 1909. (More on Bakelite in Chap 9) In the late 1930s, DuPont chemists combined formaldehyde to react with urea in proper proportions and conditions that rendered methylolurea (DMU). More important as an impregnating preservative, DMU is an important adhesive resin.[4]

Another compound of interest is synthetic phenol resin. Phenol is made from coal tar and by itself is a relatively poor adhesive. However, with the addition of formaldehyde or furfural, it makes adhesive that has been called "spectacular."[5] As a plastic, phenol resin is best worked hot. A process familiar to plastic manufacturers, using a steam press to apply heat and pressure to the sheets of plywood, was used. This method gave a finished product unparalleled wet protection and is dimensionally stable in any degree of humidity. Mold and bacteria, the traditional enemy of wood, was nearly nonexistent, even when the product was soaked.[6]

The final adhesive developed was melamine[10]. It was first synthesized in the early 1800s when made from calcium cyanamid but its use was limited and was more of a curious substance for years. Over time, research showed it to be reactive to humidity, mixable with water or water/alcohol, and tolerant of a wide range of ph. It was in the

10 To avoid confusion, there is a modern countertop material called Melamine that does contain the glue of the same name. However, melamine in the context of this book refers to the glue alone.

late 1930s that it was discovered when melamine was mixed with formaldehyde, it creates a new resin. In this state, melamine gives extraordinary performance. When added to urea instead, a glue of high quality is created. An addition of just 7% melamine to urea eliminates joint failure completely; the base wood fails first.[7]

Adding phenol to melamine produced higher fungal resistance and structural toughness. One prewar use of phenolic melamine was for aircraft construction plywood. Melamine bonded ply tested far superior in tensile and shear strength than any other wood-based material.

The wide range of chemicals melamine reacted to make it unsurpassed for the wide variety of manufacturing conditions in which it could be worked. Because there are a number of mineral or cellulose-based fillers that are compatible, melamine was favorable for a large selection of molded and laminated products. Having a high dielectric strength, (resisted electric conduction) melamine was extensively used for electric cabinet and panels. Its apparent unlimited uses made it a favorite for use in general construction panels as chipboard, pressboard, and paper-laminated countertops.[8]

Sheetrock

Also known as plasterboard, sheetrock was first introduced shortly after the First World War, when there was a shortage of experienced plasterers. Composed of a mixture of gypsum and plaster of Paris laid in sheet form between two layers of heavy paper, it enjoyed a very short commercial life and disappeared from the market by 1922. For the next fifteen years, the older, wet plaster reigned supreme.

Post-World War Two housing shortages inspired the manufacturers of gypsum products to bring sheetrock back. This time, the product was vastly improved over its predecessor. Aluminum foil backing gave an added element of thermal insulation and wet joint compounds were now available to seal and hide the seams. Best of all, the rock could be installed by minimally trained workers in far less time than plaster.

Aluminum Siding

Many of the homes built during the Second World War were designed as temporary shelters. No one expected that these homes would remain standing, much less still be in use, when the war was over. However, returning servicemen began to compete for the limited housing along with the thousands of recently laid-off war-workers returning to their hometowns. This led to a furtherance of the war-induced nationwide housing

Migrant farmworkers' homes. This is a good example of wartime home construction. Not a lot of effort went into making the building permanent. Bare wood, tar paper roofs, wood-to-Earth contact ensured termite infestation. However, the end of the war saw homes like this command a premium because one could walk upright inside. This is where aluminum siding had its moment. (NARA)

shortage. One of the answers to this was to renovate the wartime homes.

The great majority of them were of 2x4 frame construction with clapboard exteriors. This method was fast and cheap. Developments in paint chemistry had improved protection against the weathering effects on wood products such as clapboard, but most of the homes had received only a cursory coat of paint when built and none since. This left the boards to rot and split, sometimes barely hanging in place by the wedging effect from warp. Lumber for replacement boards was in short supply, most of it being commandeered for new military or industrial construction. A way to protect the exterior was suggested by an unlikely source, the faltering aluminum industry.

Like many businesses that had gone into war production, the aluminum industry had gone all out. Dozens of plants were built to manufacture sheet, billet, and cast aluminum, all vital to the highly mechanized war effort. When the fighting was over, many plants went silent, while others severely reduced their output. As a matter of economic survival, engineers began to look for civilian uses for aluminum. With some ingenuity, they introduced a process that rolled, formed, and cut sheets of aluminum sheet into precisely the shape needed to cocoon the clapboards in a weatherproof, non-degrading material. Using electrolytic plating methods developed during the war, the aluminum could be colored in a limited rainbow of shades, mostly variations of white at first.

Aluminum siding became a major industry in its own right, saving many homes from eventual weather-induced destruction. The siding could not refurbish the worst of the boards, which had to be replaced, but it did stop the further loss of valuable and scarce lumber. As an added benefit, the siding weathered so well that it never needed painting, a chore most homeowners happily avoided.

U-Haul©©

The new home is ready. Now you have to get your furniture and belongings there. What are you going to do? If it's after 1947, you would probably say, "I'll get a U-Haul©."

During the war, L.S. Shoen was in the Navy, where he was fortunate enough to stay stateside. Able to have his family with him, they moved from base to base, toting their belongings in borrowed trailers. It was during this time that L.S. envisioned his idea of people renting small trailers for one-way moves.

With the end of the war, L.S., his wife Anna Carty Shoen, and their son moved to the Carty family ranch outside of Ridgefield, Washington. With her family's help and $5,000 he had saved from his military pay, he began building small light trailers of his own design. The post-war era was shaping up to be one of mobility and his idea was for people to rent the trailer, hitch it on their own car, and return the bright orange trailer to another local dealer. He got those dealers by offering an incentive for the renter to find a service station that would agree to become a dealership. Once a dealership was established, L.S. would give a commission for every rental and the station would get sales for additional services such as installing hitches, and from selling sundry items such as fuel and pre-trip services. Later, there were conveniences such as temporary hitches, moving blankets, dollies, and boxes.

By 1949, there were dealerships in virtually every community in America. U-Haul© has come to be the largest renter of trucks in the world, with well over 12,000 independent service centers and another 1,000, plus company-owned offices.[9]

Paintbrushes, Toothbrushes, and Nylon Bristles

In the years before World War Two, every toothbrush in the United States included hog bristles. China was America's main source of hog bristles, exporting an average of more than 3,500,000 pounds annually. Toothbrushes accounted for a lot of that figure. But more than half went into paintbrushes, as that was how everything was painted outside of a factory then.

With the Japanese advancing into China, the ability to ship that amount of material was greatly hampered. Any cargo aircraft that was return-flying the Hump, the air route between India and China over the Himalayan Mountains, was loaded with tin, tungsten, or returning servicemen. Occasionally, there would be room enough to get a crate or two of hog bristles aboard, but that was unreliable. Certainly it was not enough to make a difference, and yet the aircrew managed to find room for the vital, if unusual, cargo. General Joe Stilwell, commander of Allied forces in China, is reputed to have said, "Will someone please tell me what the hell we're doing carrying a #&*@!#$% load of pig bristles? Don't those silly *∂◊◊#@"%~'s in Washington know there's a war on?"[10]

Dental hygiene ran a sad third when it came to matters of personal cleanliness. Often, toothbrushes were so hard to obtain that they were used to clean their guns. It was more important to have an operable gun than to treat halitosis. Later in the war, nylon bristle brushes for the firearms became available while toothbrushes were still rare for front-line troops. (U.S. Army)

Unknown to General Stillwell or almost anyone else in the CBI Theater, brushes were a big deal and a strategic asset. There were thousands of industrial uses for brushes and almost every one was derived from animal fibers. A great deal of science went into choosing the right brush and bristle for the job. Stiffness, taper, length, color, size, provenance, and "flag" (the split on the end of the hair) were all factors in selection. The entirety of American industry was depending on these fibers. American sources were not acceptable, especially for pig bristles. American slaughterhouses had become too mechanized and the process for skinning the animals destroyed the hairs. Too, domestic hogs were not allowed to age as were Chinese hogs, which meant the hairs did not grow as long as on the latter.

Fortunately, DuPont Company chemists had formulated a material they called Nylon quite by accident in 1931; they began to make commercial quantities available in 1937. In an ongoing attempt to gauge the utility of Nylon, DuPont began to make Nylon fibers for a wide range of products on a trial basis. The first commercial production of Nylon toothbrush bristles was in Arlington, New Jersey, in 1938.

Paintbrushes were another matter. The primary fiber for the typical paintbrush was 55% hog bristle, 45% dressed horse mane fiber. Some horsehair was domestic and an equal part came from South America, but two thirds of the American supply came from China. As with toothbrushes, there were qualifications for the "right" hair. The taper was important, as was the cuticular scales, which were thought to provide capillary flow to the paint. Flag was another desirable feature. It was believed that it gave a nice, even flow from the tip to render a streak-free finish.

War Production Board officials (WPB, the Federal agency empowered to control the supplies of materials and determine the priorities of what needed to be made) saw the supply of Nylon as limited and refused its use in paintbrushes. Only after the military realized they had just a few weeks supply left, did the WPB relent. It was well after Pearl Harbor that the brushes went to war. It took some months for engineers from at least four companies to achieve production methods to produce Nylon bristles that matched those (fiber, flag, texture, and taper) of the natural bristle.[11]

Now that the war was over, companies like DuPont looked to cash in on their technology. Some, like Nylon, dated back to the Depression, others such as the Lucite, was war-technology. No matter, the companies did not want to resurrect one thing; the terrible economy of the Depression. (DuPont)

Twisted Wire (Bottle) Brush

A surprising number of procedures were still in use twenty years after the First World War. The Massachusetts State Armory (equivalent of the Army National Guard) approached the Fuller Brush Company to "refill their wooden cores" in 1936. The core is a wood slug that has wire or fiber bristles attached in such a way as to use it for cleaning the bores of their French-built, World War I artillery pieces. At that time, it was common for companies to try to entice customers to upgrade their equipment to a more modern style. Their recommendation, along with samples, was to use a new manufacturing process in which two heavy wires were set side by side and bristles were placed so when the wires were twisted together, the bristles, now locked in place, could scour inside any cylindrical object.

Naturally, this had to be approved by the War Department. Tests and evaluations followed, and in 1938, Steelgript© brushes got their first big break. In January 1939, the U.S. Army formally adopted the new brushes for the services. The following October, 3000 brushes for 37mm guns were ordered. Variations of the bristle material changed from a fiber/wire mix to bronze wire in brass twist wire. Another change desired was to mount the brush on a threaded stem so that just the stem and the worn-out bristles could be disposed of. The Fuller Brush Company was asked to provide similar brushes in every caliber that the Army had, from .22 all the way to .50 calibers. More than 25 million small-arms barrel brushes were delivered by the end of the war. But that was not all.

The simplicity of the design attracted other uses. Labs used them for cleaning glassware, particularly test tubes. Ammunition factories used the twisted wire brushes to smooth out the inside edges of shell cases. Police departments requested them for use in their own firearms. Variations on the theme became brushes for toilets and urinals, typewriters, field kitchens, radiators, optical repair, boilers, Venetian blinds, and so on. The list was endless. And, of course, after the war, the baby boom virtually demanded the brushes for cleaning formula bottles.[12]

Epoxy Glue

Today, any homeowner knows that when some knickknack gets broken it's time to reach for a tube of two-part epoxy glue. It's relatively fast-drying, strong, and it resists degrading in the atmosphere. However, epoxy was first formulated to bond panels on the wings of World War Two fighter aircraft without the use of rivets.

In 1943, a lab technician at the Chrysler Corporation concocted a paste that did exactly what he was looking for, make paint stick to aluminum. But he got more than he bargained for when, by experimentation, he discovered his resin created a bond that was stronger than most surfaces it was applied to. Almost simultaneously, Dan Bradley and W.R. McConnell of the Shell Chemical Laboratories in Detroit developed a similar formula that had almost identical properties. It was inevitable that the two separate research groups joined together and produced "Cycleweld," a resin adhesive that required heat and pressure to render its strongest bond. Despite this added step in manufacturing, Cycleweld found many uses. It glued aluminum nose caps onto antitank shells. It successfully joined panels on production planes. It bonded brass information plates on aircraft and vehicles.

With the advent of jet aircraft, which saw service even before the end of the war, an even stronger bonding agent was necessary. Using Cycleweld as a starting point, true epoxy resins were soon formulated and became the basis for today's adhesives.[13]

Aluminum Foil

One of the lesser-known uses of aluminum foil during the war was as chaff.

Dropped by airplane, these thin strips of foil would float through the air, jamming enemy radar. Code-named "Window," the tactic is still used today to jam radar-guided missiles. Thousands of pounds of it were used during the war, giving the European continent a misleading Christmastime appearance with tinsel-like chaff hanging everywhere. Ironically, on more than one occasion electric power was interrupted when entire bales of chaff, failing to disperse properly, dropped into transmission lines or transformer installations, temporarily shorting out sections of the German electric grid.

Aluminum foil was slowly developed after the First World War. Tin foil, much easier to roll into thin sheets, had been used as a protective wrap for tobacco products, namely cigarettes. Additionally, tin foils wrapped ice cream treats, candies, and chewing gum, and were used as Christmas tinsel decoration. By the early 1930s, Reynolds Metals Company was experimenting with aluminum as a replacement for tin. While aluminum foil was still in its infancy, the depths of the Depression limited the company's chances to sell the innovative foil. This did not stop the company from testing aluminum foil, sometimes in a rather disorganized way.

Thanksgiving, 1932, saw one notable test. Richard Reynolds, president of Reynolds Metals, brought home a sheet of the foil to cover the turkey. When the bird was served, he was amazed to find that the meat had retained its moisture. The foil had protected the bird from the drying action of the oven. Even though the impromptu experiment had proven successful, aluminum foil was still too expensive to produce for general use.

When the war came to America, aluminum became a vital war metal. Aluminum Company of America (Alcoa) had a virtual monopoly on the aluminum market, controlling the lion's share of the raw material—bauxite—and the process to convert it

Piles of Window to drop at Jerry. This young English lass has her hands full of aluminum foil strips and more coming off the machine. A pile such as this is unusual that the strips were bundled in length as they were cut. Window came in a variety of widths, lengths and thicknesses as different radar systems came into use. On longer bunches, it happened that the paper banding did not always come off and the aluminum fouled electrical equipment on the ground. (IWM) into a metal. The Federal government, taking a dim view of monopolies, built their own aluminum plants. Operated under contract to entrepreneurs like Henry Kaiser or Richard Reynolds, the plants turned out the billions of tons of aluminum stock needed for the war. This massive production organization, instrumental in winning the war, fell silent when the war ended. Some of the plants were sold to Kaiser and Reynolds along with the patented Alcoa process. This effectively and finally broke the Alcoa monopoly, which had been summarily declared illegal in a letter to Alcoa from the Department of Justice on August 30, 1945.

Facing the enormous task of utilizing their windfall, Reynolds went to work developing consumer products for a peacetime market. Using technology developed from before and during the war, Reynolds began to produce a foil of unprecedented thinness. Sheets of foil less than one thousandth of an inch thick were sold to wrap all sorts of consumer products. Laminated to wax-coated paper, the foil was used in wrapping frozen foods, packaging perishable goods, and as a holiday decoration. When Reynolds introduced aluminum rolls in 1947, it was immediately welcomed. Home-makers liked the non-rusting, odor-proof metal that could be shaped to any form and retain its protective seal. Millions of turkeys would be roasted under the foil, enjoying the same juice-protecting effect that had been discovered fifteen years previously.[14]

Duct Tape

At the beginning of the war, most of the American military's ammunition was still being packaged into wooded crates. The prospect of fighting in the humid South Pacific raised fears that some shipments would be damaged beyond use from moisture. In response, Army officials put out a call for a waterproof tape that could be torn by hand. Johnson and Johnson offered up their entry based on a medical tape that had been on the market for years. They created a three-layered, plasticized tape faced with tenacious rubber glue that

This 75 mm field gun has one feature that got its inclusion in this book. The muzzle is covered with what appears to be piece of tarp to keep dirt and moisture out. Holding the cloth in place is undoubtedly the contemporary version of duct tape. (U.S. Army/NARA)

Loading a P-40 for a fighter-bomber sortie. The English weather for most of the year was mild, but there was always the famous fog and rain, which was hard on finished metal such as gun barrels. That is why there are small patches of duct tape sealing off the machine guns. If they were fired, the bullets would pass harmlessly through the tape. (U.S. Army/NARA)

passed all trials with ease. Despite this packaging advance, by the time the United States joined the war, wooden ammunition cases were rapidly being replaced with the more familiar steel ammo cans, but there was still a future for the tape.

Japanese advances into the Aleutian Islands presented a whole new threat to the American continent. Bases and roads into the wilds of Alaska were quickly being built and year-around occupation contemplated. American vehicles were sorely lacking in winterized comforts such as cabin heaters. Automotive engineers adopted the tape as a rough and ready means of sealing off flexible heater ducts—hence the name—and to seal insulation leaks.

By 1944, duct tape had taken on the role of a general use fix-it tape, a position it would enjoy into contemporary times. Air force mechanics used the tape in combat theaters to repair everything from torn heater ducts in B-29s to torn uniforms. Fighter aircraft went into battle with tape covering their forward-facing gun ports in an attempt to keep out moisture and debris and to reduce drag. Similarly, artillerymen discarded the manufactured metal muzzle covers in favor of the tape that could be shot through if, in the heat of battle, the cover was forgotten. Even in the New Mexico desert at the Trinity site, scene of the 1945 atomic bomb test, duct tape was lavishly used to exclude dust from the inner workings of the unassembled bomb.

The Wind Chill Factor

In early 1941, American Army and Navy units were sent to Iceland and Greenland to establish military bases for transports and to provide air cover for convoys traveling to and from embattled British shores. Almost immediately, American GIs discovered to their dismay that their winter uniforms were sorely deficient in cold weather protection, particularly against the frigid Arctic winds that relentlessly scoured the landscape.

In response to the demand, heavier coats, over-pants, boots, and gloves were soon to become the focus of an intensive research program under the auspices of the Quartermaster Corps working with the Army Medical Department. It soon became clear that the development of cold weather gear would require a full understanding of the climatic conditions that the military could expect. Furthermore, even the understanding of the nature of cold on human physiology needed clarification and some means needed to be found of objectively measuring cold climatic conditions.

Fortunately, there was one man who had just done the latter. Paul A. Siple, well known to his contemporaries as the youngest member on Admiral Byrd's Antarctic expeditions of 1928 and again in 1934-35, was to become immortal for his work in cold weather science. Although he had obtained a Bachelor of Science degree in biology and published two books, all in the years between his expeditions, the young Siple had a desire to travel. Siple indulged himself to a backpack journey to Africa and the Near East Asia where he met an American geographer who inspired the young scientist to focus his interest in the ways geography, particularly in harsh environments, affected humans. Before he could formulate an education path for this dream, Siple was called back to America to join Byrd on the 1934 expedition.

After nearly two years of travel at the bottom of the world, Siple returned home, determined that he would obtain "honest work" for a regular salary so he could support his new wife and family. He enrolled in Clark University and, using his vast experience and expeditionary contacts, traveled once more to Antarctica in 1939. This trip was solely devoted to research on his chosen doctoral thesis, "Adaptations of the Explorer to the Climate of Antarctica."

As part of the research, Siple and a close associate from past expeditions, Charles Passel, placed a 250 cc cylinder of water outside in the elements. Siple correctly forecast that the process by which water in the plastic container froze was largely dependent on the wind speed and outside air temperature. This "chilling" effect of the wind became a major component of the American military's research in developing cold weather gear well before the end of the war. Furthermore, the wind chill factor, the term coined by Siple, would eventually affect the development of all manner of commercial products from cold weather clothing and camping equipment to insulation materials for the construction and transportation industries, not to mention the advisories issued by local weathermen during the winter months.[15]

As for Dr. Siple, he found work as a civilian employee of the Army Quartermaster

Corps, contributing his vast knowledge and experience in cold weather conditions to develop military clothing, housing, and dozens of other items that were necessary to fight the war in frigid surroundings.

Layered Clothing

It could hardly be less obvious—unless you are the United States Army Quartermaster General, that is— that the key to keeping warm during inclement weather is to wear more layers. Until 1940, the Quartermaster Corps resisted making any changes to the standard uniform, whose design dated back to the First World War. Field exercises in Louisiana showed a number of shortcomings with the standard uniforms, while armored and paratroop uniforms underwent extensive innovations. This was by and large due to the fact that both these specialized services, being relatively new, had very little tradition with which the uniforms were burdened. Hence, the Quartermaster Corps was working on a clean slate and could do just about anything they wanted without some General officer coming back to say, "That's not how it was done and will not be done now!"

Thus, when American forces saw combat in North Africa, they soon discovered that the new tank crew uniforms—wind-resistant, water-resistant, wool-lined and smooth on the outside to avoid catching on the many protrusions one finds in and around armored fighting vehicles— were quite popular, not only with American troops but with Germans as well. Hundreds of captured Axis soldiers in the course of the North African campaign were found to be wearing these uniforms, "mute testimony that enemy soldiers also considered them to be a highly desirable piece of equipment."[16]

The secret to the tanker uniforms great acceptance was that it allowed for layering of clothing depending on the weather. It was roomy enough to wear with woolen underwear, wool trousers and shirt, or even herringbone twill. Likewise, warm weather demanded cotton under the tanker clothing. The Quartermaster Corps took the pattern of the tanker uniform and adapted it to the standardized infantry uniform. From this time on, cotton clothing was tightly woven to be more wind-resistant while woolens were less tightly woven to allow the material to breath. Field trousers and jackets used water-resistant sateen that had a 'semi-glazed" outer surface to repel mud and dirt and to resist snagging.

In May 1943, a representative of the Quartermaster Corps was sent to the Mediterranean Theater to teach the men about the new clothes and layering. Unfortunately, the immense task of producing hundreds of thousands of individual items for this new ensemble made it impossible to outfit the troops very quickly. It was not until the early fall of 1944 that quartermasters could issue the new uniforms. Nevertheless, despite its common sense origins, layering was by then an established fact, or so said the United States Army Quartermaster General.[17]

The Electric Blanket

The miracle of electricity brought inventors out in force to create a wealth of new conveniences. The first electric blanket, no more than a pad about twelve square inches housed in a choice fleece, was devised for heating the chests of tuberculosis patients. This medical appliance was prohibitively expensive, selling for $150 in 1912.[11] Larger models were soon to follow, but they flopped commercially. Safety was of considerable concern, as was cost. There were problems with wires breaking and shorting out, sometimes causing devastating fires. This led to an understandable lack of faith in electric heating blankets.

The United States military began to experiment with electrically heated flying suits late in the First World War. The designs proved to be unworkable as the electrical supply was inadequate to operate the suits for long, and the wires would frequently break. When America became involved in the Second World War, they were still flying unpressurized bombers, but now at altitudes in which the air temperature got down well below zero.

In this rarified altitude, unprotected fingers froze in a matter of minutes and the chill drained the body's strength within an hour. Metal control handles and machine gun triggers actually stuck to the flesh on contact. The bomber crews were issued electrically heated suits, socks, and gloves that had to survive the rigors of combat. As the war progressed, the old deficiencies were gradually rectified.

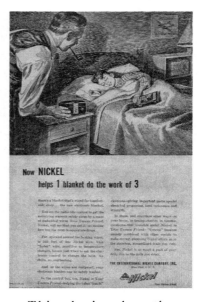

This device has the American 8th Air Force to thank for the technology of the electric blanket. Interestingly, this ad was not from the blanket company, but the metal processor. Just like all other businesses, there was great pressure in keeping the wartime economic boom continuing during the peace. (INCo)

---

11 To compare, the lowest level first class ticket for the Titanic, which sunk in 1912, was $125.

Finally, by May 1944, a wire was developed that could be flexed up to 250,000 times without breaking. Composed of silver, Beralloy—a beryllium-nickel-copper blend—and bronze, the wires would successfully complete the war and were incorporated into full-sized electric blankets for sale on the commercial market beginning in 1946.[18]

The Automatic Clothes Washing Machine

The first known washing machine dates back to 1848 in Chicago, but it wasn't until the turn of the century that mechanical, hand-cranked laundry washing machines began to replace the not-so-popular washboard.

Over the next thirty years, manufacturers made their products more attractive to consumers by creating labor-saving add-ons. Such devices as the wringer to squeeze excess water from the clothes and an agitator to generate the scrubbing action were helpful improvements. In that pre-electric age, the machines had to be equipped with power take-off drives for gasoline, kerosene, or steam engines, and there was even one that used a dog on a treadmill. To create flexibility, Maytag advertised a combination butter churn ice-cream freezer that worked in place of the agitator. One machine made by the Thor Company was designed to do double duty as the "Dish and Clothes Washer."

Then, in 1939, the Bendix Company introduced the first automatic clothes washing machine. The Bendix Model S required only two dial settings to complete the washing cycle. As advanced as the controls were, improvements were sorely needed to the machine itself. The greatest drawback to the Bendix machine was that it had to be bolted to the floor. If not, vibrations from the clothes being out of balance would send the machine waltzing across the room. Bendix's machine found very few individual takers but the U.S. Navy adopted the Bendix automatic washer for shipboard use. Imaginative naval technicians well versed in fixing machinery, eventually solved the vibration defects.[19]

The post-war years saw civilian versions come to market, where they were quickly snatched up. A number of improvements were soon added. The wringer gave way to the spin dry cycle in 1953. New fabrics and treatments for clothes led to necessary changes in machine features. Throughout the 1940s and 1950s, adjustable speeds and fabric softeners dispensers were introduced.

Clothing and Fashion

Slacks for Women

World War Two changed the world. It changed fashion as well. War work could be heavy, hot and dirty. As more women entered factories, they began to wear trousers. This was not a new phenomenon by any means. Frontier settlers, women disguising themselves as men during the Civil War, and female teamsters all wore pants at some time, even though men might express surprise or revolt at the audacious display. According to some men, pants were too masculine. In spite of this popular male wisdom, pants slowly became grudgingly "acceptable" but only under "proper" circumstances. Ladies had to wear dresses in public places and refrain from being seen in trousers. This laughable attitude carried on until the Second World War.

Then safety necessities and fabric shortages made pants not only accepted but required. Companies hired famous clothing designers to develop stylish work uniforms to attract much-needed workers, and pants became commonplace. In the wintry north and northeast United States, dresses were abandoned for warmer slacks. By 1943, clothing manufacturers were offering lines of ladies' pants cut especially for the woman's figure. Trendy and feminine colors were added to the selections, as were softer blends of cotton, rayon, and, late in the war, nylon.

Field nurses also had problems with slacks—the problem was that they didn't have them. When they arrived in North Africa in November 1942, they had the same service uniforms they had trained in back in the states. They were expected to climb down rope cargo nets hanging over the sides of the transports into bobbing landing crafts and wade ashore in dresses, hose, and Oxford shoes, not the most auspicious, or modest, entry into military duty.[20]

Instead, all of the nurses had somehow gotten

Our model sports the new fashion of 1942, where excess fabric is frowned upon and utility is in. Innumerable matrons gasped at the audacity of the form fitting pants and risky blouse. To them, morals were one step closer to extinction. (Time/Life)

their own sets of G.I. pants, shirts, wool socks, and/or overalls. Many, unable to secure proper government-issue shoes, spent their own money on workable shoes in the hectic last days of embarkation. This gave the nurses the look of a ragtag lot but they had no choice. Too late was it discovered a man had written up the Table of Equipment (TEs) for the hospital units where the nurses were assigned. There was no precedent for women entering into a combat area, and previous guidelines called for "skirts and Cuban heels."[21] Some officers found the jumble of uniforms and multitudinous mismatched shoes appalling and totally devoid of military discipline. Higher command, however, was happy to overlook sloppy uniforms because of the great work the women were doing for our wounded men. It would be another year before the Quartermaster Corps would issue a special order for correct sized and fitted clothing and shoes appropriate for combat areas.[22]

The Bikini

A deep rift between fashion trendsetters marked the post-war period. Many women abandoned slacks look for more conventional dresses with more than a hint of Victorian stuffiness. At the other extreme, slacks were just the start for a more daring future. French designer Jacques Heim introduced his new bathing suit on the French Riviera. Consisting of two small triangles of cloth covering the bottom and a skimpy brassiere, it was held in place by the thinnest of fabric straps.

Inspired by the recent revelations about nuclear technology and the diminutiveness of the particles that made it work, Heim called his creation the *atome* and actively advertised it as the world's smallest bathing suit. As the a*tome* gained popularity in 1946, nuclear tests on the Pacific atoll of Bikini caused rumormongers to speculate that the entire world would be consumed in an atomic fireball. Fatalistically, believers of the gossip began to party as if there were no tomorrow—they literally believed that to be the case—and all inhibitions were cast aside. The *atome*

The introduction of the Bikini in France caused quite a stir, especially in the U.S. Even presently, many can tell where and when the swim suit was created. Not many, however, can remember the model filling it. It is Micheline Bernardini.

became the unofficial badge of the rebels, who soon gave their attire the name Bikini.

American troops, having never seen such decadent exposure of flesh in public before, bought the daring bathing suits and brought them home for wives and girlfriends. Unfortunately, authorities at beaches in the United States were not as open-minded, and the bikini was banned. It took another twenty years for the American public generally to accept the bikini as legitimate in polite company.

Bikini! Need we say more?

Fireproof Treatment of Fabrics

Fire became a significant cause of casualties during the First World War, especially for aviators. Post-war research on cottons resulted in the introduction of fire-retardant chemicals such as ammonium phosphate and a mixture of borax and boric acid. Although the treatment was fairly effective, both washed out in laundry water.

It was only during World War Two that permanent treatments were discovered. The main formula, tetrakis hydroxymethyl phosphonium chloride (THPC) could be applied to cotton and rayon fabrics. Uniforms that were most likely to be exposed to flame were treated first. This included flight uniforms, fuel handling men, firefighters and rescue personnel, and tank crewmen. The war ended before the use of THPC could be utilized throughout the Allied forces.

After the war, THPC saw widespread usage, eventually being mandated for use in clothing for children.

Tupperware

For all of material shortages and rationing during the war, there was always some scrap lying about that no one knew what to do with. Such was the case of polyethylene and Earl Tupper.

Having worked at DuPont as an engineer, Tupper struck out on his own. In 1942, he declared that his company would produce "tomorrow's designs with tomorrow's

314

materials."[23] He managed to inveigle several tons of waste plastic from DuPont and spent the next months perfecting his formulation. Polyethylene was quite tough, resistant to abrasion and extreme heat, but it cracked easily. Tupper's self-assigned mission was to render the waxy material into a higher level of flexibility.

He was successful, albeit modestly, with his improved plastic going into gas masks and signal lamps before the end of the war. Even though he managed to cash in on the war production bonanza, his heart was still set on housewares. By 1947, his plastic was being sold in medium to large sized lots, formed into bowls, cups, tumblers, and cigarette cases. One insane asylum (as it was then termed) preferred Tupperware plates and table service to the previously used aluminum dinnerware because it could be destroyed, as a contemporary Time Magazine article put it, only "by persistent chewing."[24]

Always the engineer, Tupper began to introduce new designs that reflected his flamboyant style mixed with his Yankee practicality. His butter dishes were shaped to fit a stick of butter. Cakes could easily be set inside his cake canister without any wasted space. Tupper offered his wares in a rainbow of colors. Tupperware was hailed by the media as "Fine art." So sure was he of the plastic's indestructibility, Tupper guaranteed to replace any piece if it chipped, peeled, cracked, or fractured.

The feature that truly distinguished Tupperware from the competition was his unique seal. Containers from the war era had been made from steel, ceramic, or glass. Not only did the latter two break with alarming frequency, but none of them could be securely sealed. Tupper's air- and liquid-proof lid not only sealed, with the famous "burp," but, once closed tight, could not be reopened by accident. Even dropping a full container to the floor would not usually pop the top.

By 1950, Earl Tupper became frustrated with declining sales. He suspected that the retailers, typically men, were not showing potential customers how to close the tight-fitting lids properly. The buying public, always wary of new ideas that required dexterity, avoided Tupperware. In a novel marketing move, Tupper established the now popular "Tupperware ladies." Trained as salespeople, women would organize neighborhood Tupperware parties to show, sell, and teach potential customers how everything worked. Sales immediately improved. Homemakers appreciated the personal, feminine sales approach as well as the simple tutorial that did not focus on a man's brute strength, but on a lady's delicate touch.

Tupperware is now an American icon. There is hardly a home or business refrigerator that does not have some leftover meal sealed in a Tupperware container waiting to be eaten. Tupperware toys give hours of entertainment to infants and toddlers, while

Dad sneaks the Tupperware funnel out of the kitchen to change the oil in the car.

The Paper Milk Carton

Prior to World War Two, milk was generally delivered to the home or the store in a glass bottle. Late in the 1930s, a German invention called kraft paper made its way to America. Several layers of paper were coated in paraffin and tightly compressed; the resulting paper stock could then be shaped or folded as necessary, creating a homogenous, moisture-proof container. Kraft paper was used briefly in its native country to make food containers during World War Two until shortages of wax precluded its use.

In America, the public regarded paper containers with suspicion, especially for foods with a substantial amount of moisture, so when kraft paper milk cartons first appeared in markets in 1938, they were spurned. The buying public doubted the durability of paper for liquids. But the manufacturers of kraft paper refused to relent in their quest to gain acceptance. They undertook a marketing campaign to stress the advantages of paper cartons.

Some points of benefits were: paper cartons were less susceptible to breakage, especially around the rims where glass containers often chipped. This defect caused a constant problem with glass getting into the milk. The square paper carton could be packed into a refrigerator with less wasted space, an important point because the refrigerator of the late 1930s did not offer an excess of shelf space. Paper was lighter than glass, a feature that shoppers at the newly formed supermarkets would appreciate as they carried their own groceries home. Bottles had to be placed outside for pickup, where, in the summer, they would begin to smell if not promptly retrieved. By contrast, the paper carton was disposable, obviating the worry that the container had not been properly washed and sterilized, as was the case with reusable glass. By 1940,

A new use for paper. The British devised a way to press-form a paper-fiber mix that was light enough to be used on aircraft as drop tanks. One benefit was that the Allies would stop making the gift of aluminum to the German war effort. In the Pacific, the introduction of gelled gasoline, also known as napalm, took advantage of the bursting properties of the paper tanks to make airdrops of the incendiary. (U.S. Army/NARA)

these advantages had begun to show results, as more milk buyers were using paper.

The war secured the future for paper since glass was sorely needed for war products. In addition, beer, which had begun to be sold in cans in 1935, reverted back to the bottle because of the shortages of tin. Other containers of waxed, pressed paper also came out during the war. Motor oil, previously packed in glass or tin, was sold in round cans of kraft paper, the same style that lasted well into the 1980s. License plates went from metal to kraft paper for the duration. The plates were made from a variety of composites, soybean and paper pulp being the most weather-resistant. These plates proved to be very popular with farm animals, who were documented numerous times feasting on the mobile treat. Plastic has now replaced kraft paper as the material of choice for milk containers, although many millions of kraft cartons are still sold in sizes of less than one gallon.[25]

Shopping Carts

One of the first and probably best known chain markets was the Atlantic & Pacific Tea Company, otherwise called the "A&P." As chain supermarkets grew, so did the number and variety of products available for purchase. The housewife who did the shopping for the 1930s family could make do with a small basket hanging from one arm, but this was no longer true. The weight of the filled basket was becoming too burdensome.

Sylvan Goldman, owner of the Standard and Humpty Dumpty grocery stores in Oklahoma City, put the first shopping carts into service during the summer of 1938. This original cart was no more than a folding metal frame with wheels and a handle. It was based on the design of the folding metal chair, and shoppers were expected to place their own hand baskets onto the cart and stroll the aisles. The loaded basket would then be placed on the checkout counter where it was unloaded, inventoried, paid for, and packaged.

Mr. Goldman's idea was a stroke of marketing genius. He reasoned that shoppers would stay longer if they did not have to carry a heavy basket. Assuming that the cart would ease the chore of shopping, his repeat business would increase. Unfortunately, he failed to account for his customers' attitudes and the carts stood unused. Male shoppers spurned them for fear of appearing weak and unmanly. Wheeling a cart around the store was too reminiscent of using a walker, a device that made the older folks appear helpless. The largest shopping group, the young female housewives, saw the shopping cart as unfashionable.

To gain acceptance, Goldman hired a number of models, young and old of both sexes, to push the carts around, pretending to be customers. He also instituted the policy of stationing a "greeter" at the front door to welcome shoppers and offer them a cart. Slowly, the carts became an accepted accessory for getting the groceries, even though they remained a local phenomenon.

Other stores offered similar alternatives to carrying a heavy basket. One of these, the military commissary at Carlisle Barracks in Pennsylvania, had a series of roller tracks that carried the basket. Similar to a cafeteria serving line, the customer pushed the load along the waist-high shelves throughout the store. The obvious drawback to this idea was that it took up too much room and made shelf spaces difficult to reach.

Word of the Goldman carts spread, and a breakthrough point came with the rapid growth of military bases in 1940-41. Some major military installations were equipped with commissaries to supply food for families of servicemen living at the base. By 1942, the entire commissary system had adopted the wheeled shopping carts as standard.

After the war, with Goldman's idea having taken root, new designs were soon to come. Private grocery chains and stores had to wait for the war to end so they could get their own. No longer would the shopper have to provide his or her own basket. The simple wheeled frame, with a heavy wire basket attached to the front became a little more familiar. The baby

Grocery shopping in the New Mexico laboratory community of Los Alamos was no different from anywhere else, except many stores did not have these shopping carts yet. It was the U.S. Army that adopted the idea early in the war and used them in all of their base commissaries. (LANL/ NARA)

boom inspired the folding child seat, well within reach of the parents. With fleets of carts, the stores discovered there was a scarcity of parking space for them. The basket

318

was tapered and one side hinged and, by 1950, the modern interlocking shopping cart was accomplished.[26]

Cheerios®

Cold breakfast cereals were a major innovation at the turn of the century by Dr. John Kellogg, the brother of the inventor of corn flakes. He advocated consuming grains for general good health and optimal digestive tract function. So popular were his theories and associated products that, soon, there were many imitators. Different grains such as wheat, corn, rice, and oats gained and lost favor over the years with some cyclical predictability.

Nutrition was again an important subject by the end of the 1930s, especially when it concerned children. As for grains, the popular favorite was Quaker Oats, which had snared a major share of the competitive cereal market with their hot cereal. Prior to oats, the same company had introduced Puffed Wheat and Puffed Rice, which used a new cooking process that heated the grains and then shot them from a gun-like device. The ensuing explosion partially separated the cellular structure, creating a fluffier, lighter-textured cereal.

Quaker Oats' patent on the gun process expired in 1929, leaving the process wide open for anybody to use. At General Mills, the gun became the focus of their own in-house researchers, who produced a small scale, much-improved version for the laboratory as well as larger machines for the production lines. Alongside the scientific work, General Mills undertook a massive consumer testing campaign. Company scientists spent countless hours testing various shapes and sizes of cooked grain. They discovered that precooked oats, having been shot through the gun, had thousands of tiny air bubbles in them. When added to milk, the cereal floated. Hundreds of consumer tests revealed that shape mattered as well. The washer-shaped tidbits that are still one of the most popular cereals were the winner of popular choice. They were introduced in 1941 under the name of Cheerioats. Quaker Oats Company protested that they had a trademark on the word "oats" and threatened a suit in 1945. Hence, General Mills adopted the shortened name, Cheerios.

Converted Rice

For many Americans in the Depression years, rice was a dessert ingredient, an interesting side dish or something meant to be eaten with Oriental food. As a grain, all the essential nutrients exist primarily on the outside husk, the core being mostly empty starch. This in itself made rice unattractive in America for a long time. It also had to be stored carefully or it would spoil or get "buggy." But then the British devised a method to force vitamin B^1 into the body of the grain, or, in technical parlance, convert it. Using high-pressure steam, the vitamins travel from the bran into the starch, where it stays.

An American, Gordon Harwell, brought the British technology home and offered it to the U.S. War Department, then deeply involved in the Second World War. Converted rice was served on American chow lines almost exclusively from 1943 until well after the war. Harwell then took his rice and began planning its introduction on the open market. Stuck for a name, he and his partners chose a popular Negro Texas rice farmer affectionately known as Uncle Ben for his symbol. Unfortunately, Uncle Ben had died years previously, so no photos of him were available. A kindly Chicago maître d', Frank Brown, volunteered to pose for the box-front artwork, which has given him an immortality of sorts, his likeness appearing on the cover of every package of Uncle Ben's Converted rice.[27]

Minute Rice®

One day in 1941, a man identifying himself as the cousin of the king of Afghanistan walked into the executive offices at General Foods and, within minutes, cooked up a pan full of delicious rice. The inventor of this marvelous rice, Ataullah Durrani, had spent the previous eighteen years experimenting with ways to process rice so that it could be cooked quickly. His process involved precooking and then quick-drying the grains. Some problems of mass production had to be overcome first, though. Durrani's process required intense heat to dehydrate the rice and complications arose from spoilage.

Before solutions were found, America was at war and the government had begun to requisition the General Foods facilities for the production of military rations. The rice formulation, still not perfected, was added to the Army's menu as quick-cooking rice and as a staple dessert in the form of rice pudding. Two Minute rice plants were federalized and a third—located near Orange, Massachusetts—was close to being requisitioned when the war ended.

The war experience was a valuable asset for Minute Rice®. The government in effect supported the final research that perfected Minute Rice®. That in itself was fortunate. Before the war, preliminary market research had shown that rice would be a welcome addition to the American table, but rice was difficult to cook and the results often led to a sticky, unpalatable mess. Cost- and quality-conscious homemakers were loath even to try to serve such a disaster to their families. However, the new instant rice was an instant success with the troops, which brightened the prospects for General Foods.

In the early spring of 1946, General Foods began test marketing Minute Rice® in Atlanta and Philadelphia with an intense media campaign. Radio spot announcements and newspaper ads all promoted the product. General Food's salesmen set up displays in grocery stores. As plant capacity increased, more cities were added to the test market. In 1948, a second plant was built in the center of America's rice belt, Houston, Texas. By 1949, Minute Rice® was on sale nationwide, making rice a major staple of the American diet.[28]

Aerosolized Whipping Cream

Whipping cream was one of the multitudes of dairy products impossible to obtain during the war. Substitutes successfully imitated the taste and creamy richness of the real thing but tended to dry out and spoil in the refrigerator. One of these wartime concoctions, called "Sta-Whip," had real potential, or so thought a St. Louis salesman named Aaron "Bunny" Lapin.

Working through his brother-in-law's dairy, Lapin began to market the whipping cream substitute in 1941. Sales were initially brisk, but inexplicably dropped off as the summer commenced. Lapin responded by having a dispenser designed specifically for commercial soda fountains. The "dispensing gun" design proved to be so effective that Lapin moved to adapt it to a disposable, hand-sized can for home use. Drawing inspiration from the newly developed spray cans of insecticide that the military was using, Lapin created a can/nozzle combination that is still in use today. (More on the insecticide and cans in Chap.9) The secret of Lapin's fortune, though, was the nozzle, which whips the cream as it passes through under pressure. Shortly after the end of the war, cans of Reddi-Whip® were beginning to show up on refrigerator shelves nationwide. Through Lapin's efforts, consumption of whipped cream doubled and then doubled again.[29]

M&M® Chocolate Candies

"The milk chocolate melts in your mouth, not in your hand."™ This inspired slogan has endured for nearly sixty years and is eminently linked to the small, sugarcoated candies that are consumed by the millions every year.

M&Ms were originally developed by two chocolate-loving acquaintances, Forrest Mars and Bruce Murries, both of them born into chocolate industry families. Chocolate had been a popular treat for years, but its major drawback was that it melted too easily, especially in the pre-air conditioned summer of 1940. While Mars was living in Britain, he got the idea for M&Ms from a British product called "Smarties," with a protective hard sugar coating inspired from the pharmaceutical industry. Back in America, Mars teamed up with Murries and introduced M&Ms in 1940 with the now-familiar catch phrase. Available in only one color—violet— M&Ms were an instant hit. One of their biggest customers, surprisingly, was the military, which put the candies into ration packages for troops stationed overseas. Imitators soon appeared, so M&M borrowed from the drug industry again, using the same printing processes that are used to mark medicines to identify each and every M&M.[30]

Artificial Vanilla

Spanish explorer Cortés discovered this spice being used in a native beverage in Central America. Unable to pronounce the Aztec name, *tlixochitl,* for the bean pods that gave off a wonderful aroma, the Spaniards renamed it *vainilla.* In time its name anglicized to the now familiar "vanilla," and it became the most popular spice to be imported into the Old World for the next four hundred years. Not was only vanilla a key ingredient for *chocolatl,* a drink made from crushed cocoa beans and the source of hot chocolate beverages, but it was also used in perfumes, soap, and flavoring for confections such as ice cream.

When the Second World War broke out, the majority of the world's supply was virtually trapped on the Indian Ocean islands that grew the vanillin beans. Central and South America, two other sources, were somewhat easier to access, but transportation was a problem. Shipping was costly, and the voyage involved crossing oceans heavily patrolled by enemy naval forces. As with many of the other imported goods suddenly cut off from the American marketplace, artificial substitutes were hurriedly sought. The answer for vanilla came from an unlikely source; the pulpwood industry.

Masonite panels were just becoming popular at the start of the war. Made of compressed waste wood from the lumber mill, Masonite sheets were replacing glued-together wood planks in furniture, roof sheathing, and interior walls of homes. Since the production process included using steam and extreme pressures to bond the wood fibers together, there was little solid waste. There was, however, a by-product of the

Masonite process. Wood sugars, called hexosans and pentosans, washed out of the pulp before it was compressed into sheets. With thousands of gallons of dirty water, the first impulse was to dump it. Fortunately, a chemist analyzed the water and found a significant amount of these sugars in the form of carbonyls. This discovery became an important source of wood alcohol, ketone, acetone, acetic acid, formic acid, and glycerin, all vital chemicals in short supply for war industries. Along with the carbonyls was lignin, which constituted about a fifth of the volume of the washed-out wood pulp. Lignin contains the active chemical in vanilla. Through a simple distillation process, lignin is converted to vanillin, or artificial vanilla. Because distilling removes all the impurities encountered in natural vanilla extract, the end product is purer than the natural and quite a bit less expensive.[31]

Twinkie® Filling

This confection was the Continental Baking Company's Depression-era invention to weather the lean years. The first Twinkie snack cakes had a banana-creme filling, which proved to be quite popular. During the war, bananas became scarce due to reduced shipping capacity. Unwilling to forgo Twinkie production for the duration, company officials switched the flavoring to artificial vanilla. When bananas again became plentiful, the buying public rejected banana flavor in favor of the vanilla flavor, as it remains today.[32]

Chiquita® Bananas

By 1944, transport problems to and from Central and South America had been solved. There were more ships available and the German U-boat threat had been largely eliminated. Fearing that they had lost a significant following, the United Fruit Company, which had been the major importer of bananas into the U.S. since the turn of the century, decided to make bananas a brand name item.

At this stage of the war, Brazilian entertainer Carmen Miranda was at the peak of her popularity and the lands south of the border were being romanticized in movies and song. United Fruit Company officials, cashing in on the craze, hung the Spanish-sounding name on their new product line.[33]

Freeze-dried Food

When food freezes, movement of the water molecules inside every cell is suspended into ice crystals. The crystallization causes the volume in the cell to expand, rupturing the walls. If the temperature is raised ever so slightly, the ice crystals begin to melt, causing the fluids to leak out. Over a period of time, the food will dry out, becoming leathery and tasteless. Left behind after moisture is drawn off are empty cells, virtual skeletons of unbound organic matter. Without water, there is little for bacteria to grow on, as the greatest majority of bacteria need moisture as a growth medium. The absence of water also stops the chemical reactions that cause foods such as fruit to ripen—which is an aging process.

Incredibly, if hot water is added to the skeletal shell, it will reconstitute to its original form, taste and texture. However, the process requires that the cellular fluids be frozen rapidly and drawn off in a vacuum chamber. Not only is this difficult, it needs to be controlled with absolute accuracy, a daunting task for 1940s freezing technology.

A Swedish process first developed by native Laplanders made its way to the United States as a possible challenger to frozen foods. Unfortunately, the war interfered with the commercial development of the process for foods, but it became a lifesaver when it was applied to storing blood plasma. Late in the war, freeze-drying was again taken up in an experimental government program for processing foods into ration kits. Although the experiment was successful, the rations came too late to be fielded for general use. Unwilling to abandon all the expensive research, marketers introduced freeze-dried foods onto the commercial markets with mixed results. Eventually, freeze-dried foods became more accepted in food packets for survivalists, outdoors-people, and space voyagers.

Instant Coffee

In 1930, Brazilian coffee growers had the fortunate bad luck to have a series of bumper crops. There were so many coffee beans that they were using them to fill potholes in the roads. Facing ruination from the bean glut, the Brazilian government turned to the Swiss firm Nestlé to help find new products for their surplus. After eight years of experimentation, Nestlé introduced Nescafé.

Public reaction was lackadaisical after having been subjected to numbers of "instant coffees" that tasted nothing like coffee and were of dubious origin. However, the U.S. military was to change the perception of instant coffee forever.

Four years after Nescafé came out; Maxwell House began shipments of their instant product. Using a secret process developed by General Foods specifically for army K rations, the coffee became widely accepted as a beverage and for trading. After the war, Instant Maxwell House coffee was successfully offered to the public.[34]

Dehydrated Foods

Dehydrated foods are the oldest form of preserved food known, dating back to before Biblical times, when crushed or pitted fruits were wrapped in palm fronds and buried in the sand. This rapidly desiccated the pulp into leathery, bite-sized morsels that never spoiled. Nearly every culture on the Earth has developed some form of dehydration, many of which are still in use today. However, the Second World War provided the motivation to include formal science into the process and introduced a greater number of people to the final products. By 1944, America alone counted at least 139 processing plants where more than 400 million pounds of fruits, vegetables, meats, and milk had been processed. By U.S.D.A. accounting, vegetable production alone exceeded one billion pounds.[35]

One memory shared by people who served in the armed forces of the United States during World War Two is the horrible, tasteless glop that was euphemistically called dehydrated eggs. More than 300 million pounds of eggs were dried in a process that was developed by the Western Regional Laboratories of the Department of Agriculture.

The eggs were broken open by hand, individually inspected for spoilage and then sent to a liquefying tank, which was nothing more than a gigantic egg beater. Whipped, the liquid eggs were sprayed onto a moving conveyor that traveled through a drying oven. The desiccated eggs would then be powdered and packaged for shipment to the troops. Especially during the early years, much of the egg product turned rancid during shipment, leading to some of the bad experiences that are indelibly etched in memory. Variations in the feed and care of the production flocks led to a wide assortment of objectionable flavors and colors as well.

During this period, plant workers reported the presence of olive-colored and blue-tinted yokes while taste-testers found samples that had become "fishy," "sour," or "burnt." The discoloration and odd flavors were directly attributed to poor feeding routines, feed that lacked certain nutrients—the fishy taste was from a shortage of nutritional copper—or poor raw egg storage techniques.[36]

USDA scientists, working at the request of the Army Quartermaster Corps, refined the egg drying process. They found that controlling the acidity of the eggs would increase their shelf life by 400%.[37] Adding hydrochloric acid prior to whipping made the eggs nearly as stable as fresh ones. After drying, sodium bicarbonate was added to neutralize the acid. When being prepared for consumption, the addition of water activated the two chemicals, effectively canceling each other out with a residual taste of sodium chloride, normal table salt. Early batches of the acid-treated eggs were reportedly too salty, but it was unknown if there had been too much chemical added at the processing plant or the cooks in the field were unaware of the salt content and added more.[38]

Carrot Cake

Even though the disaster of the eggs was never fully rectified, the lessons learned had significant applications for other foods. Vegetables and fruits were dehydrated through similar processes. One modern-day confection that started as a dried vegetable is carrot cake.

Although the confection had been around in one form or other since the Middle Ages, it was known in the United States as a limited regional item handed down within families. George C. Page inadvertently instigated that familiarity. A purveyor of dehydrated foods in Los Angeles found himself in possession of several thousand pounds of canned dehydrated carrots at the end of the war.

On August 15, 1945, the Japanese government surrendered unexpectedly. This caught the U.S. military with tens of thousands contracts for war materials worth tens of millions of dollars that were no longer needed. Government inspectors, instructed to cancel as many contracts as possible so that payment could be withheld, were summarily rejecting entire batches of goods, thereby voiding any contractual obligations. Page's contract was among those nullified. Nonplused, Page gave some cans of carrots to an acquaintance, who happened to be a baker at a popular local hotel. Experimenting with the carrots, he developed carrot cake. It became so popular that, within months Page unloaded his entire warehouse of dehydrated carrots, showing a healthy profit in the end.[39]

Frozen Foods

It took the Japanese army fewer than six months to capture the Malaysian peninsula and the Dutch East Indies, which lie just to the south of the Asian mainland. Among the prizes claimed were more than two hundred tin mines, where nearly ninety percent of the world's tin was produced. The metal was so essential that only iron, lead, and copper exceeded it in production and use. Besides being a constituent material for bronze, one of its chief uses was for coating other metals against corrosion. As tin became scarcer in the United States, canned foods, long a staple for the average family, were strictly limited.

Fortunately, frozen foods were becoming commonplace and were available to replace many tinned foods. Introduced soon after the First World War, frozen products were looked upon at first as luxury items. Most homes did not yet have refrigerators and small, household-sized freezers had not been invented yet. Furthermore, the technology of freezing food had hardly been perfected. Unless the food had been handled carefully and protected from thawing even a few degrees, its taste and texture would be irretrievably lost.

Throughout the 1920s and '30s, research into improving frozen foods advanced considerably. During this time, machinery and processes were developed to flash-freeze fresh foods. Plastics such as cellophane and polystyrene made packaging simpler and less uncertain. Transportation problems were rectified with the innovation of refrigerated railcars and trucks. General Foods, makers of Birdseye® brand, and other companies had a vested interest in propagating the line. They installed freezer cabinets in stores for free and hired nutritionists to give public talks about the benefits of the food. With the invention of Freon in 1938, home freezers were just a step away, but war production needs interrupted mass introduction of the appliance. (More on Freon in chap. 9)

Frozen food proved to be a boon to harried families, especially where the adults were busy at war jobs. As demand grew, more stores stocked the

The advent of safe home refrigeration was so novel that copies of this flier appeared in popular magazines. Refrigeration made a significant impact on the problems from consuming food that had spoiled. In addition, the appliance introduced homemakers to the magic of frozen foods, a new product now widely available due to the war. (NARA)

icy meals. The Department of Agriculture published pamphlets on how to defrost and cook frozen foods to preserve the nutrients and avoid spoilage. Even without a freezer at home, the food would last for two or three days as it thawed in the refrigerator.[40]

The popularity of freezer foods is evident in the statistics. Between 1942 and 1945, consumption of frozen vegetables increased by 300 percent. Appalled by this statistic, the canning industry fought back. They collectively raised questions about nutrition, which were not totally baseless. Despite scoring one or two points against frozen foods, the canners' attacks backfired. The publicity inspired the American Medical Association to issue strong endorsements for frozen foods, especially for fruits and vegetables. Nutritionists lauded the convenience, selection, and off-season availability of frozen foods. This universal praise undermined the credibility of the canning industry and hastened the public's acceptance of frozen foods.

After the war, home freezers were high on the list of desirable appliances for many homeowners. The proliferation of the appliance guaranteed a bright future for the frozen food industry. In turn, they tirelessly developed a wide variety of new products. There are now more than 3,500 different items available at the grocer's freezer case.

Frozen Concentrate Orange Juice

During World War Two, the War Department often went shopping for what it wanted if a suitable product were not readily available. In 1942, one such product was inexpensive orange juice powder. A $750,000 contract was offered to the person or company that could create it.

The National Research Corporation seized upon the opportunity. They soon perfected methods to concentrate and freeze fresh orange juice, a landmark achievement in itself. The drying process proved to be considerably harder even though the technology for dehydrating food had been imported from Sweden and used with success on blood plasma during the war. The company had barely completed their self-imposed task when the war ended, along with the military's offer. Hoping to recoup the expensive research and development costs, company president John Fox began marketing the frozen concentrate. He chose the moniker "Minute Maid" as a play on words to describe the juice's quick preparation time. His product could not have come out at a worse time.

Wartime pressures on the farmers of America to increase production were just beginning to show results, and the crop of 1945 was a record breaker. The market was flooded with fresh goods at rock-bottom prices. Who would want to buy frozen? On top of this, a spate of poor-quality frozen goods had reached the marketplace and the ensuing bad publicity had virtually destroyed any goodwill the public had extended to frozen foods in general.

Now facing a financial disaster, John Fox enlisted the aid of a Boston advertising agency. Through them, "Minute Maid" sponsored a series of radio shows featuring singing legend Bing Crosby. He plugged the orange juice so often and convincingly that a majority of the public thought he owned the company. Crosby's ad campaign became so successful that by 1949, 30 other companies had fielded their own frozen orange juices.[41]

Notes/Selected References

1   Burkhart, Bryan, and David Hunt. *Airstream, The History of the Land Yacht*. 2000. P. 28.

2   Homes Assembled Like Autos Would Cost Two-Thirds Less. *Popular Mechanics* magazine. February 1937. P.192.

3   Simonds, Herbert R. and M. H. Bigelow. *The New Plastics*. 1946. Pp. 209-211. and Scholten John. A. Prefabrication on the Farm. *The Yearbook of Agriculture. 1943-1947.* 1947. Pp. 879-882.

4   Simonds, Herbert R. and M. H. Bigelow. Pp. 8-9.

5   Scholten John. A. Pp. 879-882.

6   Stam, Alfred J. and G.H. Chidester. New Goods From Wood. *The Yearbook of Agriculture 1943-1947.* 1947. Pp. 725-732. and Hartley, Carl. Fungi in Forest Products. *The Yearbook of Agriculture 1943-1947.* 1947. Pp. 883-887.

7   Simonds, Herbert R. and M. H. Bigelow. P. 53.

8   Hartley, Carl. Fungi in Forest Products. *The Yearbook of Agriculture 1943-1947.* 1947. Pp. 883-887. Stokely, James. *Science Remakes Our World.*1946. P. 41.

9   Material derived from the company website: www.u-haulinternational.com/history and www.fundinguniverse.com/company-histories/AMERCO-Company-History.html

10 Quote: Denison, Merrill, *Bristles and Brushes*. 1945. P. 15.

11 ibid. Pp. 92-107.

12 Simonds, Herbert R. and M. H. Bigelow. Pp. 140-144.

13 The Paste That Welds Anything. *Popular Mechanics* magazine. July 1959. Pp. 78-80, 232-234. and Stokely, James. Pp.151-154.

14 Panati, Charles. *Extraordinary Origins of Everyday Things*. 1987. Pp. 113-114. and *Hoover's Handbook*. 1991. P. 462. and Risch, Erna. *U.S. Army in WW II. Quartermaster Corps: Organization, Supply and Services. Vol. 1.* 1953. P. 203.

15 ibid. P. 81.

16 Ross, William F. and Charles F Romanus. *The Quartermaster Corps: Operations in The War Against Germany.* 1965. P. 175.

17 ibid. Pp. 171-178.

18 Sweeting, C.G. *Combat Flying Equipment* 1989. P. 18.

19 Interview with William "Bill" Davis October 18,1998.

20 Risch, Erna. Pp. 113-117.

21 Ross, William F. and Charles F. Romanus. P. 174.

22 Monohan, Evelyn and Rosemary Neidel-Greenlee. *And If I Perish.* 2003. P. 27.

23 Fenichell, Steven. *Plastic, The Making of a Synthetic Century.* 1996. P. 231.

24 ibid. P. 232.

25 Cohen, Stan. *V For Victory.* 1991. Pp. 88, 272.

26 *Carts Before Shoppers.* Southern Living magazine. May 1990. P. 22.

27 Wyman, Carolyn. *I'm a SPAM Fan.* 1993. Pp. 68-69.

28 Press Release from General Foods *The Extraordinary Mr. Durrani.* ca. 1951. and Launching a Bestseller. *GF Newsletter.* Vol. X, Number 9. September 1949.

29 Wyman, Carolyn. P.127.

30 ibid. P. 105. 1991.

31 Stokely, James. Pp. 77-80.

32 Wyman, Carolyn. P. 20.

33 Material from: fundinguniverse.com/company-histories/Chiquita-Brands-International-Inc- Company-History.html

34 Information derived at: fundinguniverse.com/company-histories/Kraft –Foods-Inc-Company –History.html and Hoover's Handbook. 1991. P. 399

35 Bell, Mary T. *Mary Bell's Complete Dehydrator Cookbook.* 1994. Pp. 3-6. and

36 Herrick, H.T. New Uses For Farm Crops. *Yearbook of Agriculture 1943-1947. 1947.* P. 696
Lightbody, Howard D., Harry L. Fevold. Biochemical Factors Influencing the Shelf Life of Dried Whole Eggs and Means for Their Control. Printed in *Advances In Food Research, Vol. 1.* E. M. Mrak and George F. Stewart, Eds. 1948. Pp.149-192.

37 ibid. P. 194

38 Herrick, H.T. New Uses for Farm Crops. *The Yearbook of Agriculture 1943-1947.* 1947. Pp. 696-697.

39 Terkel, Studs. *"The Good War"* 1984. P. 314.

40 Hooker, R. W. New Trends in Marketing. *The Yearbook of Agriculture 1943-1947.* 1947. Pp. 912 – 914.

41 Wyman, Carolyn. Pp. 33-34.

8

Playing Around: Diversions and Toys for all Ages

The legacy of World War Two is not limited to machines of war or tools for everyday life. The inventors of that war also gave us a number of ways to amuse ourselves in a free moment or to enjoy the time of an extended vacation. This was not deliberate by any means. The scientists and engineers exerted enormous energies getting the best that their country had to offer to the fighting front where it would do the most good. It was only through the imagination and inspiration of post-war business people and marketing experts that the tools of war could be converted into peacetime playthings.

The Slinky®

One of the few new children's toys to emerge from the war, invented by marine engineer Richard James who was working on a new suspension system to protect delicate ships' instruments from the rolling of heavy seas and the concussion of battle. The shortage of rubber precluded conventional cushions, so he turned his focus to the simple spring.

The spring, usually made of special steel that is tolerant of repeated flexing, is a simple mechanical device that stores energy in its coils when it is distorted or deflected. To get the recoil and flexibility that he desired, James had a variety of large-diameter, rather loosely coiled springs custom-made. One day, he accidentally knocked one of the larger springs off the shelf above his workbench. He watched in awe as the spring, casually "walked" under its own power to a lower level shelf, then proceeded to negotiate the bench itself and a stack of books, finally coming to a stop in the middle of the floor. Amused with his serendipitous discovery, he took the springs home to his children, where they spent hours playing with them. They quickly discovered, as their father could have told them, that the springs were proficient in descending stairs. Betty James, Richard's wife, saw the potential for a toy. The undulating action and the sound of the coils moving together caused her to suggest the name Slinky®.

Marketing began in 1946, and the company formed by the Jameses has sold millions of Slinky® toys to date. Oddly, the toy has found practical uses. During the Vietnam War, metal Slinky® coils thrown into overhead foliage served as rough-and-ready antenna extensions for radio operators in the jungle. A version of the Slinky® has been used in pecan pickers and in machinery to sort bolts.

Although Richard James' springs never amounted to much for the war effort, researchers discovered years later that the motion of earthquakes is very similar to the action that Richard James had originally intended for his springy invention to overcome. Much credit is due to both Richard James and the subsequent work of these scientists who took the Slinky® and used it as the inspiration for a super-heavy duty spring used to earthquake-proof buildings.

Silly Putty®

When the Japanese expanded into the western Pacific, they seized the majority of America's rubber source. Synthetic rubber compounds were frantically being sought by several American companies to make up the shortage. General Electric engineer James Wright, intending to create a cheaper synthetic, combined several formulations of silicone oil and boric acid. One combination resulted in a wad of material that outperformed rubber in bounce, stretch, and tolerance to temperature variations; it also had the unique habit of creating a mirror image on its surface when pressed down on a printed page. However, the putty-like substance resisted vulcanizing, a process which made it hard enough to hold a permanent shape.

Having no obvious value to the war effort, the putty was abandoned and James Wright went on to other work. The compound remained a company oddity, having been given the name "nutty-putty." For laughs, it would be shown to visitors, who were often invited to suggest a use for the material.

After the war, samples of "nutty-putty" were sent out to more than 100 engineers and scientists worldwide along with the challenge for them to find a practical use for it. Years went by and there were no responses. However, in 1949, Peter Hodgson, an unemployed copywriter, attended a party in Bridgeport, Connecticut, where samples of the putty were being passed around as a gag. He saw the potential for the goo and approached General Electric. Borrowing $147 from an acquaintance, Hodgson purchased the rights to manufacture "nutty- putty." He hired a group of students from Yale University to slice his batches up into one-ounce balls and packaged them in pink plastic eggs for Easter. The toys, originally intended for adults, flopped commercially, but Hodgson eventually prevailed. The following August (1950), Hodgson's unusual toy got mentioned in *The New Yorker* magazine. Within four days, he had orders for more than $250,000 of the goop. Over the next 17 years, Hodgson became quite wealthy. When he died in 1976, his estate was worth more than $180 million.

His putty, given its more common moniker in 1950, has been used in a variety of jobs. It went into outer space with the astronauts on Apollo 8 as a tension reliever and a way to paste tools down in the weightless environment. Because it lifts greasy stains—newsprint and comic book ink are particularly subject to this phenomenon— Silly Putty® can be used to clean typewriter keyboards without leaving any residue. Dust can be removed just as well from clothes and furniture, though when used a number of times as a blotter, the putty will begin to take on the texture of dried oatmeal.[1]

Model Making

Leonardo Da Vinci made models of his creations, as did engineers of ancient Egypt. Shipbuilders created models to sell their crafts to potential patrons and sailors made similar models whiling away the hours on long voyages. Glen Curtis and the Wright brothers used models built with extreme care and detail to prove their aircraft designs before they built the full-scale thing. As leisure time became more common, making models of airplanes, ships, and buildings grew into a favorite pastime of all ages.

The Second World War, with its wealth of new aircraft, opened a new era of model making, but for a new purpose. Gunners on the ground or in the air could get confused identifying the swift aircraft, and incidents of friendly fire occurred quite often. In fact, the first aircraft shot down by English interceptor aircraft over the Channel in September 1939, were, unfortunately, British. Unable to spare the extra planes being knocked down by their own guns, the RAF instituted a program of identification training that included the use of three-dimensional scale models.

Children, under adult supervision, were given blocks of balsa wood and detailed plans to build the scale-model airplanes. Templates, included on the printed plan sheets, were used to check the curves of wing and fuselage contours. Stiff competition and adult expectations of a high level of workmanship meant that having a model accepted was an extreme honor. The selected replicas were then issued to active squadrons and training units.

The model-making program found its way to America. Thousands of young people, many of them Boy Scouts, voluntarily spent hours cutting, sanding, and measuring their entries. More than one hundred thousand examples of Allied and enemy aircraft had been completed before the end of the war. This was only the beginning of the model airplanes' popularity.

As the documents in the picture say, these are recognition training aids. Manufactured by the relatively new plastic injection molding process, tools to train the men were important. On the left is a P-51 Mustang, the right a P-38 Lightning. (Author's Collection)

Wooden model airplanes had their place, but the modern injection-molded plastic plane also got its start during the war. Bill Topping, a salesman for Goodyear Aircraft, saw one of the wooden airplanes during a sales call. Wanting the plane for his son, Topping discovered that the plane was valued at $7.50. An experienced industrial production engineer, he knew that he could produce the plane for much less. Using plastic, a material still fairly new to industry, and pressure die-casting developed for making zinc-amalgam toys, he began a whole new industry.

In 1943, Topping Model Company began producing scale airplanes with unprecedented details. The military was a ready-made market for his planes. Aircraft manufacturers also loved the models for their detail and portability, and they were economical enough to serve as promotional giveaways in pursuit of new military contracts. Topping's models graced Pentagon desks and shelves by the hundreds. Topping developed an injection die method where the operator had only to pull and push a series of handles in the correct order. No other assembly was required, and except for painting, the model was ready to ship.

Topping's business lasted well into the 1960s. Other companies entered the model market shortly after the war, eventually forcing him out of business. Classic cars were first produced, and the demand for models just kept growing. Airplanes, ships, and later, spaceships and racecars practically flew off the retailers' shelves. Plastic models are now a tradition, a rite of passage and bonding handed down from father to son.[2]

Football Helmet Suspension

Among the hundreds of pieces of equipment that had to be evaluated during the Second World War, the old "Tommy" head covering of British design that had been used since the First World War was done away with by the American military. The M1917, as this style of helmet was formally known, had proven itself for its ballistic protection, but it hardly won any awards for comfort, especially with troops involved in special duties such as machine gunners, runners, and artillerymen. Complaints that the suspension—the system of straps and cushions designed to provide some measure of clearance between the hard steel and the wearer's scalp—allowed the helmet to bounce excessively and slip out of place during hard running or when the wearer was bending over showed that there was lots of room for improvement.

In the intervening years between 1918 and 1934, the U.S. Army Ordnance Department kept up a leisurely interest in helmet development. A limited number of improvements were made, and by 1935, the M1917A1 became standardized. This helmet featured an adjustable hair-filled pad liner, which supplanted the earlier suspension design.

Despite having spent seventeen years on that particular change, the looming threat of war in 1940 inspired a renewed effort to incorporate recent developments in metallurgy, plastics, and manufacturing. The Metropolitan Museum of Art in New York was brought in on the project along with a number of industrial firms to redesign American combat headgear.

A two-piece helmet was deemed more desirable because the ballistic steel outer shell would be more reliable if it were not pierced during the manufacturing process to accommodate rivets or other fasteners for the suspension system. Further, it was decided that it would be advantageous for troops in rear areas to wear some protective head cover, though they didn't need the higher impact strength of the steel outer shell. Hence, the proposed plastic impregnated fabric liner could serve both as light duty head protection and a foundation for the as yet undesigned suspension system. Interestingly, this helmet liner proved to have many similarities, such as weight, level of protection, surface finish, to the hard hat from the Hoover dam project.

However, some unknown person, undoubtedly a football fan, from the Army Ordnance Department came to the rescue. It was noted that the largest American manufacturer of football equipment, the Riddell Company, had introduced a wholly new style of suspension for football helmets in 1939. The design used plastic components which are lighter than steel. Another advantage was that the new helmet, more dome-like than the M1917 models, allowed for more room within the liner for ventilation and also provided an allowance for "crush," the term used for damage to the outer shell that transferred deformities to the inner liner if struck by a non-penetrating missile. Furthermore, the Riddell suspension provided more security from "rock," the tendency for the helmet to slip forwards or backwards during fast movements and provided more adjustments to get the perfect fit for each individual.

With all these benefits in mind, the Army approached John T. Riddell about his invention. Seeing the importance of their need, he allowed the government to use his design in the new M1 combat helmet, which became standardized for common use on June 9, 1941, sans hair cushion.

From that date until August 1945, 22,363,015 M1 helmets were produced. But before the war was over, the effectiveness of the Riddell suspension system was proven and, in 1943, both the National and American Football Leagues made the use of football helmets mandatory. The Riddell suspension was not so named, but it was implied and the common wisdom of the day dictated that the Riddell system was the most desirable.[3]

The inside view of an American M1 infantry helmet. The suspension is that of the then new Riddell football headgear. The seam between the outer steel shell is visible just outwards from where the chin straps attach (at 6 and 12 o'clock) (US Army Medical Corps)

Female Cheerleaders

From the beginning of the twentieth century, collegiate sports were widely popular. To inspire the teams on to victory, fans were led in ovation by groups of uniformed male students who recited a litany of prepared cheers and exhortations. The more creative cheer squads even instituted series of acrobatic stunts and maneuvers to attract higher levels of excitement and fan participation. Most cheer squads were exclusively male, as women's acrobatic displays were considered immodest and inappropriate. There were schools, such as Tulane University and Trinity College in San Antonio that permitted female cheerleaders as early as the mid-1920s but these were the exception to the rule. Other schools, such as state-sponsored Alabama and Tennessee allowed co-ed cheer squads. Nevertheless, even these schools generally restricted their female members to leading cheers and restricted their participation in tumbling and gymnastics.

Many of the male cheer squad positions were filled by tryouts, just as positions on other competitive teams were filled. But the schools that sponsored championship-grade teams also had the highest regarded cheer squads. These squads were filled by scholarship, and competition was keen.

An all-girl cheerleader team. In 1948, they are a rare bunch but not for long. Men gradually moved away from cheer and pep squads, quite possibly because the Kinsey sex study was recently released. The groundbreaking survey reported that a large number of men were secretly homosexual and this created an air of homophobia and abandonment of any activity that appeared less manly. (Tulsa Historical Society)

When American participation in the Second World War began to escalate, collegiate cheer squads suffered losses to the military just as other sports programs did, but there was a ready source of new cheerleaders: the female students. The change was gradual and there a few negative comments, but the general opinion among fans was positive. After the war, cheer squads remained coed for more than a decade, but slowly, the squads became almost the sole domain of women.[4]

35mm Color Film

World War Two was the first war to be brought to the home front in modern media. Millions of still photographs and billions of feet of movie film were shot to record the war. Although much of this work was done in black and white, new color images vividly portrayed the true horrors of war for all to witness.

The Second World War was really the first where enlisted soldiers on all sides were tasked with filming the war from its most forward point. Here is a member of the U.S. Army invests his Emo movie camera his total attention at the cost of dry socks. Such is war. (OWI/NARA)

The story of color film actually goes back into the 1800s. Numerous attempts to produce color images were tried with mixed results. One method, subtractive color, was suggested in 1869. Instead of using colored solutions to generate the color effects, dyes within the film would be used. The film could be coated with three very thin layers of emulsion, each sensitive to one of the primary colors. Exposed to light, the emulsions would record only the portion of the image that was visible to it. But chemistry had to catch up to the idea, an event that would have to wait another 65 years.

With the development of azo dyes for medical research and clothing, the next step towards color was achieved in 1934. From these stains came emulsions sensitive enough to be suitable commercially for amateur photography. Developed by Kodak, KodaChrome, was available only for 16mm movie cameras at first. However, Kodak's German subsidiary, Kodak A.G., had displayed Germany's technical prowess in lenses for spectacles and in instrument making by introducing the first 35 mm precision Kodak Retina camera in 1933. With the simple-to-use camera, a large demand for still color film ensued. Kodak quickly responded with color slide film in 1936. But not until 1942 did color negative film suitable for prints become available.

For the professional photographer, color was an interesting addition to the craft, but developing color film was tricky and needed to be carefully controlled. For this reason,

Agfa, the German company in competition with Kodak A.G. for this 35 mm film was a world leader for photographic films. It was only natural, given the vast experience of the parent organization I. G. Farben, the German super-conglomerate industry. (Signal)

the early war years saw very few color shots that were of high enough quality to print outside of Germany . Amateur shutterbugs used color film much more often, when it was available, to record the war. Even before the war was over, color emulsions had improved to the point that processing was no longer such a delicate task. Professionals, mostly in military service, began using Kodak's EktaChrome films and chemical kits direct from the Kodak labs to develop their own work. In 1946, EktaChrome became available on the civilian market.

Progress has continued since the war. Cartridge film simplified loading. High-speed cameras and special flash mechanisms have slowed down time, making visible action that is too fast to see ordinarily. High-speed films needing minimal light are available, making the flashbulb unnecessary. Infrared film can record heat signatures of people, animals, and objects. Photography has become an integral part of everyday life, as a tool, a teacher, and a communicator that knows no language barrier.[5]

The Polaroid Land Camera

During a 1943 family vacation, chemist and physicist Edwin H. Land took a picture of his three-year-old daughter. Like any typical young child, she was supremely impatient to see the finished product and became quite upset when it was explained that the film had to be processed. During this trip the inventor of light-polarizing lenses began working on the Polaroid camera in his head.

Land proposed using a film containing a packet of chemicals within each frame of film. The chemicals would act as a processing fluid to develop and fix the photographic image right to the film as it came out of the camera. However, the photographer had to peel away the negative portion of the sheet that overlaid the print. To protect the print from fading, a stick of special fixative wax had to be applied as well, making the original Polaroid film less than totally self-developing.

Land's first attempts at the instant film were far from perfect. Introduced in 1947, the resulting colors had a noticeable brownish coloration to them. Called a sepia tone, the discoloration was both welcomed for giving photographs a warm, antique look and spurned for the color's inaccuracy. Polaroid's popularity with amateur photographers grew during the 1950s as a way to retake shots that were badly done the first time. Professionals attached themselves to Polaroid films that gave them a chance to set up their studio equipment with test shots, sepia color notwithstanding. After they were satisfied with the lighting, setting, and composition, conventional film would be used.

It was not until 1972 that Polaroid introduced a film, the SX-70 that was entirely self-developing. New chemical compositions sped up the processing time to ten minutes and the sepia tones were gone. The advent of digital photography has almost made the Polaroid a dinosaur among cameras, but there is a small but dedicated group that clings to the Polaroid camera.[6]

Photojournalism

On November 23, 1936, *Life* began. The project, instigated by Henry R. Luce and his associates at Time, Inc., had been shrouded in secrecy. A few years previously, a revolutionary new 35 mm camera had been developed that allowed for unprecedented portability. With an ever-growing selection of lenses, filters, and attachments, the new camera far outperformed its predecessors. Up until that time, published photography had been stiff, posed and two-dimensional.

As much as the equipment contributed to the phenomenon of *Life*, the real success lay with the management's attitude. Deviating from the typical magazine of the day, *Life* endeavored to tell stories with pictures. Relying on the adage that a picture is worth a thousand words, *Life*'s pages were filled with dynamic shots of every conceivable subject, while the text was limited to short details describing the circumstances of the pictures. In this form, *Life* magazine's greatest innovation was letting the picture tell the story, creating the photo-essay. Getting the shot often meant being exposed to harm. Besides the thousands of military photographers that were required to go into battle, there were hundreds of civilians volunteering to go. Their names are familiar, Robert Capa, Joe Rosenthal, Margaret Bourke-White and Carl Mydans. *Life* magazine sent 21 photographers to war, five were wounded, another 12

Even in the deep jungle of the Pacific Islands, there was always time to take a break and catch up on the latest news from Yank. World War Two marked a new trend where the combatants were mostly literate and the demand for reading materials strong. Yank was directed at the enlisted personnel audience, being written by enlisted personnel. This edition is "Yank: Down Under", indicating it was produced in Australia. (Yank/U.S. Army)

sickened with malaria.

Innovation leads to duplication. Foreign publishers quickly embraced photojournalism, France's '*Paris-Match*,' for example. Because the new medium accommodated itself to propaganda, aggressor countries adopted photographic magazines for their own purposes. From Germany came '*Signal.*' Published fortnightly in twenty languages, its circulation encompassed all of the territories under the Nazi thumb and beyond. Before the United States entered the war, *Signal* was even available in America. This allowed a glimpse, however distorted, into an otherwise closed society. Like Germany, Japan offered a magazine that presented the slanted viewpoint of its publishers, the military-dominated government. Entitled '*The Weekly Photographic News,*' it focused on subjects that promoted the Japanese militarism and philosophy of "Asia for Asians."

Life magazine has had moments of controversy. Over the years, printed stories showing how to undress (both male and female), the birth of a baby, and the gory realities of war all brought cries of shock and dismay. The editors of *Life* stood by their decision to run these types of story, maintaining the objective outlined in their original mission statement:

"To see life; to see the world; to eyewitness great events; to watch the faces of the poor and the gestures of the proud; to see strange things—machines, armies, multitudes, shadows in the jungle and on the moon; to see man's work—his paintings, towers and discoveries; to see things thousands of miles away, things hidden behind walls and within rooms, things dangerous to come to; the women men love and many children; to see and to take pleasure in seeing; to see and be amazed; to see and be instructed..."[7]

Now there are numerous photo-essay magazines. Nearly every one has adopted and adapted the innovations of *Life*. The original weekly magazine survived until 1972. It was revived as a monthly issue in 1978, having spent the intervening years as a semi-annual special issue production.

Ebony Magazine

Another magazine of national importance came about as a direct result of the Second World War. In 1942, John Johnson began a periodical aimed at the growing black population in Chicago. He got a five-hundred-dollar loan on his mother's furniture to raise the capital to produce the magazine, but he met resistance from local news-vendors, who doubted that there was sufficient market. Johnson persuaded several hundred acquaintances to ask for the publication to give the impression that the sellers were wrong. His plan worked and *Black Digest* hit the streets on a trial basis.

The understandable deception continued, with all of Johnson's associates buying every copy. Convinced that they had a hit, the vendors welcomed full, citywide distribution. Within a few months, fifty thousand copies were moving off the racks. Johnson persuaded Eleanor Roosevelt to write a guest article, "If I Were a Negro," which attracted nationwide notoriety. As a result, an enlarged circulation soon approached two hundred thousand a month.

Even with a rapidly growing readership, Johnson found that very few businesses would pay for advertising. Johnson's shrewd mind went back to work. He wrote an article about the 1909 North Pole expedition that featured black explorer Matthew Henson. Johnson then approached Commander Eugene McDonald, the president of electronics giant Zenith Corporation, who was also a member of that same expedition. Obviously impressed with the article and probably a bit nostalgic, McDonald began to buy advertising space. This inspired other reluctant companies to support the magazine.

In 1945, Johnson saw that the large number of black troops returning from the war would be settling down and restarting their civilian lives. They were ripe for a periodical that would show a fresh view of the world and present success stories about other blacks. Named *Ebony*, the magazine was an instant hit. About one quarter of American adult blacks were reading *Ebony* and they wanted more. Next, Johnson introduced *Jet*, aimed at the single black male. With all three magazines combined, Johnson counted over 12 million readers comprising his circulation.

Now, John Johnson Publications has become a powerhouse. From that first risky venture, *Ebony* and *Jet* have become major influences in the black community. Another magazine, *Ebony South Africa* informs that country's enormous black population. In addition to publishing, the company has expanded into cosmetics and fashion. Shows organized by the Johnson family business have attracted sponsors that have raised millions of dollars for nearly two hundred charities.[8]

Seventeen Magazine

The war years were scarred by a pervasive problem with eroding family values and a severe increase in teen pregnancies and venereal disease. Psychologists disagreed as to why girls were running wild; some suggested that the girls were reflecting the unpredictability of the times while others blamed the disintegration of the core family. Whatever the true basis of the situation, everyone agreed that the problems with adolescents were getting worse.

Enter Walter Annenburg. His father, Moses, had made a fortune by publishing the daily *Racing Form,* required reading for horse race gamblers on the East coast since 1922. Aside from this publication, Moses had operated a number of other gambling services and was rumored to be an inveterate gambler. Walter took over the family business when his father was convicted of tax evasion in 1940.

Walter saw an opportunity to remove some of the tarnish from the family name and at the same time cash in on the newly-defined teenage market. The prevailing sentiments in those times were that teenaged girls were lost: lost to their identity, lost within society and, to the eyes of some observers, definitely lost to their hormones. Annenburg's new magazine told teenaged girls it aimed to "provide guidelines to your place in the home, in your schools and social life, and in this complex and confusing world."[9]

Seventeen magazine featured articles of interest to young women as well as entertaining readings of nonfiction and fiction. More importantly, there were regular columns dealing with sex, developing adolescent bodies, relationships, social, and family situations, and question and answer forums. The magazine offered to run stories written by teens to describe experiences and problems that they had overcome. *Seventeen* editors recognized that the girls were not "children, but growing ...young people."[10] To this end, fashion and makeup tips were featured, as well as articles that covered adult topics. Almost from its inception, *Seventeen*'s editors stressed the point that teen girls should begin to shoulder more responsibilities by being aware of contemporary issues and being politically involved.

In the years after the war, the magazine sponsored annual fashion shows just for teenaged girls. With all its features and timely advice, the magazine could hardly fail to be immensely successful. Within three years of its introduction, Walter Annenburg's magazine—called the "Acne and the Ecstasy" by industry pundits—was selling over a million copies a month. At present, *Seventeen* is on its fourth generation of teenaged girls and still going strong.[11]

Paperback Books

Before 1939, recreational reading was generally limited to newspapers or occasional magazines. Sales of books were unwittingly restricted to well-to-do customers. Of the some five hundred bookstores in America, most were concentrated around the twelve largest cities. Stationery shops sold a limited stock of books, mainly novels and Bibles. Public libraries were rare and poorly funded. However, when public facilities were available, they were generally well used by a broad cross-section of the community.

As a result of indifferent marketing efforts, publishers had remarkably small sales. A successful book was one that sold more than ten thousand copies, and a million-seller was the writer's Holy Grail. To be fair, all the blame should not be placed at the publishers' feet. The Depression left little money with which to buy books. Furthermore, the illiteracy rate during the 1930s was still around forty percent. Attitudes toward books were different then too. Books were looked upon as an investment. Hence the binding, paper, and printing were required to be of first-class materials and workmanship.

This is not to say that all books were hardcover. Since colonial times, paper- and cloth-backed texts had been printed. Religious tracts, sermons, political pamphlets, and schoolbooks all had soft covers. European publishers successfully used paper binding long before the colonists ever set foot in America, and paperback books were particularly popular in Germany. Millions of copies of English-language texts, Roman and Greek classics, and philosophy books were sold well into the 1930s. Despite their European popularity, paperbacked books remained an American rarity.

Then, in 1935, British publisher Allen Lane founded Penguin Books. His idea was to sell books to the average reader. For a few pence, he felt, anyone should be able to buy a quality book. Within three years, his belief had paid off handsomely. Penguin had sold more than 25 million copies of fiction, nonfiction and classical writings.

Barely one month before England went to war, Penguin Books established an office in the United States. Importing finished books into America, Penguin relied heavily on sales through college bookstores. The orange and white paperbacks featuring the company imprint of the penguin were to become a campus icon for devoted readers on a strict budget. But Penguin Books had competition.

John DeGraff, an experienced American publisher, had observed the phenomenon of Penguin's success in Britain. He proposed opening a publishing house based on the ideas of Allen Lane to two like-minded newcomers, Richard Simon and M. Lincoln Schuster. Industry detractors scoffed at the concept of cheap books, saying that what worked in Europe did not apply in America. They pointed out that books had been offered to the public before and they had been generally rejected. These critics seemed unmindful that their marketing practices had defined buying books to read as an elitist pastime. In spite of the pessimism, DeGraff began selling under the Pocket Books label in June of 1939.

He began modestly. Restricting his premiere to New York City, DeGraff used a relatively new marketing tool, the consumer survey, to determine what the public wanted. The results of the survey produced a list based heavily on past sellers. It became the first offering of ten books. DeGraff's first production run, 10,000 copies per title, reduced his risks should failure loom. Certain that cynical buyers would think that the smaller, inexpensive books would be lacking in content, he initiated a phrase now common to readers, "Complete and Unabridged."

There was little cause for DeGraff's caution. Pocket Books were nearly impossible to keep in stock. The covers, coated with new material called plastic, resisted stains and tearing. Their small size easily fit into the pocket—hence the name—for handy carrying. And the titles, chosen by the public, were favorites.

After the initial success, Pocket Books moved rapidly across the nation. Offsetting production costs through mass distribution and volume sales, stores were enticed to stock the books. In this manner, DeGraff offered the books through more than 100,000 outlets nationwide. Racks were placed in typical locations such as stationery shops and bookstores. DeGraff also extended his sales into food stores, cigar shops, nickel and dime stores, drug stores, and bus and train station kiosks. Magazine sellers and newspaper vendors, non-traditional outlets for bound books, all became salesmen for DeGraff.

Pocket Books also set standards of production that changed the industry. The bindings were glued, as opposed to the time-honored method of sewing. The paper stock, made from cheaper coarse fiber rather than the cotton/pulp mix favored for hardbound editions, reduced expenses. The smaller size also lowered production costs. However, the greatest savings came from the volume of production. Able to sell vast quantities of the same book, the printing runs were necessarily huge, reducing the cost per unit to one-tenth that of hardbound printings.

Business practices for obtaining the creative works were changed too. Publishers had commonly paid writers a portion of the cover price, typically ten percent, as a royalty. Should the book sell more than a predetermined amount, the royalties would increase. If the book became adapted to any other form—paperback, serialization, sales to book clubs, movie or stage plays—then royalties were split between the original publishers and the author. This is called subsidiary payment and often represents the largest profit from the book. Pocket Books cut this percentage to four percent. Again what they saved in costs was made up in volume.

DeGraff initiated the practice of commissioning books. Especially at the beginning, when hardcover publishers owned the rights to the only intellectual works available, Pocket Books had to buy the rights from those companies. It was far cheaper to direct that a specific book be written for a flat fee to the author. Any number of anthologies, collections and pocket dictionaries were created in this manner.

Together, Pocket Books and Penguin Books stormed America. Starved for knowledge and entertainment, the American public began to gobble up books in an intellectual feeding frenzy. Significantly, two of the best-selling books were of the self-help genre; *How to Win Friends and Influence People* by Dale Carnegie (1940) and *Baby and Child Care* by Dr. Benjamin M. Spock (1946). Separately, they sold about a million copies a year, their sales hardly diminishing in later years. The latter, still in print, has sold in excess of 35 million books—a 1985 statistic—and the publisher have since lost count.

Back in England, Penguin Books was suffering from war nerves. The government had taken control of paper stocks and the necessary materials for printing and binding the books were strictly rationed. Unable to ensure shipping, the company moved their production to the United States soon after the war began. With the war, paperback books had become even more popular. The restrictions on shipping, paper, inks, and labor made the diminutive volumes a value in the eyes of government overseers and still were available enough to be a perfect avenue of escape from the war, if only for a while. Troops, far from home, found reading to be one of the few diversions for their off-hours. And they demanded more books, many more.

Besides the thousands of paperback books the government acquires for the troops, programs such as this supplied substantial quantities. The Red Cross also acted as a conduit for organizations that gave books to the men in POW camps. Some camps had hundreds of books in established libraries. (NARA)

To this end, the American government became a publisher through the Council on Books in Wartime. Beginning in 1943, Armed Services Editions, Inc. produced a variety of books especially for the military. Selected fiction, non-fiction, war, mysteries, humor, and the classics were all distributed free of charge. The most popular of these genres, westerns became a commodity in their own right; a new edition was worth a fifth of Scotch. Forty titles of 155,000 copies each were released each month. Concerns that the editions would flood the civilian market were addressed by making the service books flimsy, giving them a limited life. They were printed in two sizes, both fitting into regulation military uniform pockets.

For the first time in history, the Allied armies found that the majority of their forces were literate. Schools were established for remedial education and paperbacked books became a vital component of the curriculum. Allied prisoners of war got a limited supply of books delivered through the American Red Cross. The larger POW camps in Europe began to collect enough books to create whole libraries. The less fortunate camps made do with the odd book or two brought in by soldiers or airmen who had them in their pockets when they were captured. In these situations, the books became camp property. Individual chapters were ripped from the bindings and passed around. The slower readers might miss out though, as the finished pages were often used as cigarette paper, another precious and rare commodity.

By the time the Editions for the Armed Services closed in 1947—the name changed in 1944—nearly 123 million books had been printed and released under 1,322 titles. Pocket Books were responsible for a vast proportion of this number. According to Wallace E. Howe, of Pocket Books, Inc., "16,000,000 Pocket Books were sold to the Army and the Navy between January 1942 and June 1946, approximately 90 percent going to the Army." Furthermore, Howe later estimated, "… that a total of 50,000,000 Pocket Books went to soldiers through one channel or another."[12] According to *Books for the Army*, the totals are even higher, 25 million hardback volumes, 200 million paperbacks, and 265 million periodicals between 1941 and the fall of 1946.[13]

An unprecedented achievement, the book program exposed innumerable men and women to the joys of reading. The sales figures proved beyond a doubt that the war experiences had lasting effect. In 1950, 200 million copies were sold for an estimated $46 million. Cover prices began to reflect the growing industry. Starting at a quarter in the 1930s, the consumer price held through the war until 1952 when seventy-five cents was the norm.

Over the years, paperback books have gained a reputation for lurid prose and trashy stories. Cover art featuring semi-nude women in suggestive poses, often with no relevance to the book itself, has not helped this image. Paperback books have changed somewhat from those garish times. The modern romance novel still reflects vestiges of the "trashy" novel, but it has gained respectability and is now aimed at and sold to women of all educational and social levels. Paperbacks still fill a niche as an educational tool, fulfilling the role of textbook at the lower production costs initiated by DeGraff.

The heady days of experimentation are all but gone. The hardcover book is back as the vehicle of choice for the serious reader. Lost is the ideal of quality at the cheapest price. Nevertheless, the paperback book will never die because it takes all of us on impossible and improbable trips into our imaginations.[14]

Radio-Controlled Machinery

With ever-smaller electronic components and the ability to transmit clear radio signals over longer distances, remote-controlled flight became a reality during the Second World War. The military was particularly interested in the technology, applying it to reconnaissance missions and flying targets. The first radio-controlled drones were tested as early as the spring of 1936. A three-horsepower gasoline engine pulled the eight-and-a-half-foot machine through the air at 45 MPH. A short-wave transmitter set controlled the three electric servomotors operating the plane's throttle and navigational surfaces. Work on radio-controlled aircraft continued sporadically throughout the rest of the 1930s as money permitted. In January 1941, a test-bed aircraft—a preproduction craft that is fitted with a variety of experimental hardware—was flown for the Army Air Corps and received tentative approval for production.

This new machine was much larger than its predecessor, almost 20 feet long, with a 30-foot wingspan. It was developed from the manufacturer's civilian aviation model and actually retained the cockpit and controls for a pilot to do maintenance checks and to ferry it across country. The United States Army and Navy procured more than 2,000 of these airplanes for target practice.

Besides being a training target for American gunners, radio-controlled aircraft were put to use as rough-and-ready guided missiles. Working under the code name of

On the beach with new technology. These Navy landing officers are taking some time to experiment with a German radio-controlled demolition vehicle. The idea was to drive the machine into massed vehicles or troops and explode it. The plan never worked as well as hoped and like this one captured on the Normandy beach, became a curious war prize. (U.S. Navy)

Operation Aphrodite, war-tired B-17s and B-24s were outfitted with radio receivers and appropriate servomechanisms to control the planes in flight. They were then packed with high explosives and flown with minimal crew—pilot and co-pilot—near heavily defended German facilities such as the U-boat pens on the coast of France. The two men bailed out at a predetermined spot and the plane continued under the control of a "mother ship" containing the radio transmitter. Under the operator's guidance, the sacrificial bomber was then steered into the target, while the crewmen were plucked from the sea by rescue surface craft.

It was on one of the early Aphrodite training missions that Joseph Kennedy, brother of the future President, was killed when his B-24 drone exploded shortly after takeoff. Although the investigation was inconclusive, it is thought that either an electrical short circuit or static electricity set the detonators off prematurely. One later mission was unsuccessful, the plane veering off course and missed the targeted port facilities.[15]

Germany fielded a few operational radio-controlled weapons. Best known of them is the Henschel Hs 293 air-launched guided missile. Its evolution dated back to 1939, being developed as an anti-shipping weapon. The body of the missile was a standard five-hundred-kilogram bomb. On the bomb's steel case, a pair of wings, a tail and propulsion package was added, the latter being liquid-fuel rocket attached underneath. The radio control unit consisted of an eighteen-channel system that controlled steering in two axes. Guidance was rather crude, achieved by the bombardier in the launching plane—the Focke-Wulf 200c *Condor* or the Dornier DO 217—visually tracking the Hs 293's red tail flare that ignited on launch. From there, the rocket was sent on a series of arcs that approximated a true path to the intended target. Because the range of the Hs293 was only about 5 kilometers (a little more than three miles) and the plane was required to fly straight and level for best guidance results, the attacking plane was usually well in the range of the naval anti-aircraft artillery, making the use of the Hs293 nearly as deadly to the attacking plane as it was to the target.[16]

At about the same time of the Henschel bomb, the German industrial firm of Ruhr Stahl offered up their creation; the Kramer X-1. To become known also as the Fritz 1, it is the first radio-guided glide bomb, differing from the present day "smart bomb" only in the guidance mode. As with the Hs 293, the Fritz 1 was watched by means of the bombsight and steered by means of a joystick-type of apparatus. Again, the aircraft needed to stay straight, level, and in this case, throttled back to stay above the bomb in flight.

The last notable radio-controlled weapons from Germany was the series of demolition carriers built by Borgward. Intended from the outset to be radio-controlled, they were built as cheaply as possible to be expendable. Development began in 1939 with a mine-clearing vehicle weighing 1.5 tons. These models—B-1 and B-2—never saw combat but imparted valuable knowledge, which was applicable to further models. These were much smaller, significantly less than one-half-ton. Their designed task was to create paths through mine fields and barbed wire. All models had a cargo compartment for explosives to destroy targets such as machine gun nests. Their fate was to be damaged or worse, their loss expected. One, the diminutive "Goliath," weighed a half ton or less, it was controlled by wires leading at most a half kilometer from a simple hand-held box. Thousands were made and saw service on every front.

Never ones to be satisfied, the Wehrmacht insisted that the German engineers at Borgward build larger vehicles. In 1942, experience on the Eastern Front showed there was a need to have a vehicle capable of delivering a larger demolition charge to destroy bunkers and fixed positions further forward. Borgward built an enlarged vehicle that could to carry a 500 Kg. (Approximately 1100 pounds) explosive package on its fore plate. Armored, it was capable of maneuvering over any terrain that any other tanks could cross. These machines were issued to panzer units because that was the only way the operator could get close enough to the front to observe its progress. The final variation, the B-IV, was the largest. It had more armor, a larger engine and weighed nearly 5 tons. It had a driver's position for operating behind the battlefront. The Tiger tank was selected to be the command tank, being equipped with the extra radios, controls and training for the crews. In battle, the operator would maneuver the B-IV into position; remotely unlock the charge where it would slide off the front of the machine as it backed away. As the explosive dropped off, a time fuse would begin so the B-IV was out of danger. Over 300 were made during the war.[17]

Operation Aphrodite's' demise did not stop American research with radio-controlled bombs. An OSRD designed attachment to the standard 1000 pound general-purpose bomb was fielded in mid-1944. Its flight path could only be steered about three-thousand-feet left or right, which is referred to as the azimuth. As a result, the bomb received the name Azon. Its use in the Mediterranean and Italian areas was disappointing. As the heavy bomber tactics dictated that large formations bomb a target en mass, it was impossible to tell where the Azon bombs hit. Tactics in CBI were different. Often, small groups of planes attacked targets in a line, one behind the next. This way, if the target is destroyed with the first or second bomb, aircraft still armed could search for other targets.

Azon bombs had fantastic results. In one instance, one bridge in Burma had managed to stay up even after two years of bombing attacks. Three B-24s, carrying a total of nine Azon-equipped bombs, blasted the center span and badly damaged a second one in just three passes.

Within months after this, the OSRD sponsored another guidance package that accommodated for the missing range capability of the Azon. Called the Razon, it was steerable via radio to shorten or lengthen its flight path (range) and from side to side (azimuth). Unfortunately, it arrived in the Pacific Theater in August 1945 and never had much chance for trial in combat.[18]

Radio-controlled machines are very much in use today. Aside from military uses, the commercial aspects of radio control are abundant. Much of the blasting for construction and mining is done by means of radio control. Cranes in large steel plants and factories and portable cranes are radio-controlled. This lets the operator the freedom to move about to see the load and potential problems, an important safety consideration. Police departments are beginning to field radio-controlled robots to search buildings and to deactivate potential bombs. And for the sheer pleasure of it, thousands of average folks are operating their own radio-controlled hobby aircraft, helicopters, boats, and cars. Although the best of these models can cost hundreds and even thousands of dollars, there is a growing supply of less expensive vehicles—less than a hundred dollars—for younger novice operators.[19]

Scuba Diving Gear

Scuba gear, or **S**elf-**C**ontained **U**nderwater **B**reathing **A**pparatus, was invented and perfected by none than other Jacques Cousteau, the famous French cinematographer/oceanographer. He received his first movie camera while still a young boy and became a proficient and avid moviemaker. He also found himself being attracted to water; either visiting the sea or reading about adventures at sea, so it was a natural that he would combine the two loves, photography and the sea, into a lifelong passion. As a French naval officer, Cousteau traveled extensively during the 1930s, photographing China, Japan, Russia, and America. In 1936, a car accident left his left arm temporarily disabled. On medical leave, he was transferred to the French Navy base at Toulon, on the Mediterranean Ocean. Given light duty, Cousteau took the opportunity to study the wonders of the nearby sea while swimming to strengthen his arm.

When France surrendered in 1940, Cousteau was still assigned to the Navy in the South of France. Mustered out of the navy with thousands of other French soldiers after the armistice, Cousteau pursued his passion for diving. He had longed for a reliable device that would allow him the freedom to dive and swim without attachments to the surface. Previously, what little diving equipment there was relied on cumbersome recirculation filters to cleanse the stale air. This closed-circuit system was not only bulky, but it was dangerous at depths below twenty-six feet. In 1926, the first high-pressure tank to use regular air was introduced by another Frenchman, Yves Le Prieur. Cousteau had experimented with Le Prieur's system, but it spent more time on the repair bench than in the water.

Through his brother, Cousteau connected with Émile Gagnon, an engineer from the French compressed gases firm Air Liquide. As an expert in pressurized gas, Gagnon had invented a regulator to run French automobiles on compressed natural gas. This device, in modified form, proved to be instrumental in perfecting Cousteau's desired diving tank. The first tests, in the winter of 1943, failed when a poorly positioned exhaust pipe retarded the airflow as the diver was in the inverted position. A quick fix resulted in a patented diving tank system that was called the Aqua-Lung.

All through the summer of 1943, Cousteau, Philippe Tailliez and Frédéric Dumas, friends from Cousteau's navy days, made more than five hundred Aqua-Lung dives off the Mediterranean coast. By the following fall, they had achieved the impressive depth of 210 feet. At this depth, Dumas made another discovery; nitrogen narcosis. Plagued by dizziness and profound confusion resembling drunkenness, the divers found themselves offering their air hose to passing fish and indulging in other unsafe silliness.

The Gagnon-Cousteau regulator was nearly an instant success for encumbrance-free diving. Before the war was over, navies from Britain and the United States were testing it to replace the hard-hat diving suits that were used for underwater salvage, exploration, and repairs. After the war, copycat regulators came onto the market to challenge the patented original. Some fell by the wayside, while others found their own niche. Scott Aviation Company of Lancaster, New York manufactured one of the latter. Sold as the Scott-Pack, it has proved to be an essential tool for firefighters and rescue personnel.

Cousteau made his fortune on the regulator, but he achieved immortality by the resulting explorations using the diving equipment he had been instrumental in developing. Photographs and films

Old and new. The suit on the right is a diving rig that the U.S. Navy used for years after the end of the war. Cousteau's diving apparatus (on the left) freed divers from the heavy bronze head shell and stiff canvas-like cloth. (U.S. Navy)

from the oceans have made a drastic impression on our perceptions of the planet. Never again would the mysteries of the sea be completely hidden away from sight.[20]

Suntan Lotion

During the 1920s, the pale skin look fell out of fashion among the affluent, which preferred a bronzed complexion. It bespoke of prosperity and leisure time to spend lounging in temperate regions. A number of patent ointments were available to advance the desired glow, some of which turned the sunbather's skin into a rainbow of colors. However, an effective solution to protect and enhance the skin's hue in the sun resisted discovery.

Beginning in 1940, the American military began to expand their bases in the Pacific in response to escalating Japanese threats. Working under the intense sun, the troops suffered from debilitating burns that often required hospitalization. The innovative United States Army Medical Corps adopted sloppy red goo called Red Veterinary Petrolatum as a stopgap measure. The ointment did provide burn protection, but it stained uniforms a sickly shade of gray and trapped insects to the skin, where they would often bite or sting repeatedly.

To improve on the makeshift petroleum jelly, a team of scientists was set to the task of devising an improved formula. From the Southwest United States, known for its intense sun, they obtained a cactus called aloe vera. The natives had used it for centuries as a burn ointment and skin moisturizer. To the aloe, they added zinc oxide, an ultraviolet insulator, and titanium dioxide, the same pigment as used in house paint. This solution gave good protection for sunburn and did not wash off in water, an important consideration for aircrew floating on a life raft under the roasting equatorial sun.

One of the team of researchers, pharmacist Benjamin Green, was not satisfied with the utilitarian cream. While the war was still raging, he opened a drug store in Coconut Grove, Florida. There, he worked on restructuring the formula not only to give protection against sunburn, but also to heighten the pigmenting effects of the sun. He added a number of different ingredients, which he tested on himself. One notable recipe included cocoa butter and jasmine. By war's end, he was selling the three-ounce jars of Coppertone Suntan Creme to visitors from the north. Coppertone would go on to become a major industry. The company has changed hands a number of times, as has the lotion. The original formula has fallen by the wayside, as new compounds have been synthesized that are far more effective. Now, sunscreens have a scale (SPF), European in origin that indicates protective power.[21]

Sunglasses

First popularized by the public's love affair with aviation, wearing sunglasses became a fashion statement during World War Two for the adventurous, devil-may-care crowd. Heroic figures like General Douglas MacArthur only furthered the glamour of sunglasses as his success against the Japanese in the Pacific increased. The dark-lensed spectacles had a rather different purpose at the moment of conception, however.

In the first few years after the First World War, the United States Army Air Corps was beginning to appreciate the fact that airplanes were becoming capable of far greater performance than they had recently experienced. Other than the fleece-lined flying suit and goggles, which were both late additions to the pilot's wardrobe in 1918, there was little thought given to protecting the pilot from the elements when flying. As the aircraft of the 1920s were pushing into new frontiers, the army decided that maybe something should be done about the bright sun glare encountered at what was then considered high altitude.

In 1926, the American optical company Bausch & Lomb was approached by the Army Air Corps to develop a glass that would shield a pilot's eyes from the harsh glare of the sun. Not only would this fixture provide the pilot with a measure of comfort, but there were safety considerations as well. Anyone who has flown a commercial jet will know the sudden and uncomfortable sensation of momentary blindness when the cloud cover is penetrated. This glare caused a number of close calls for the military when formations of aircraft narrowly avoided collision. It was discovered in the 1930's that the sun is 1.2 times brighter at 72'000 feet than it is at sea level.[22] For this reason, too, was the how the sun also played a well-known role in the tactics of attack during air combat where the opponent dives out of the sun.

After nine years of work, Bausch & Lomb perfected a green-tinted lens that filtered out the yellow band of the light spectrum. The glasses were issued free of charge to military pilots and aircrew but the company, looking to capitalize on the idea, introduced them publicly as Ray-Ban aviator sunglasses. For a day at the beach or a drive in the country, the new glasses became very popular and chic, especially when Hollywood stars began to use them.[23]

Polaroid Light Filters

Ray-Ban sunglasses used a tinting method to separate the portion of sunlight that created the worst of the glare encountered when flying. Effective as they were, scientists and engineers needed to be able selectively to filter other elements of light.

One of the most practical examples of light filtration is the visor for welders. When the electric arc is struck, the operator is bombarded with the entire spectrum of energetic light waves from infrared to ultraviolet. Unless he or she is sufficiently protected from them, these waves can cause serious damage to the human body in the form of incapacitating burns and blindness.

Light itself had largely remained a mystery up to this time. Essentially, light is a continuous flow of electromagnetically charged particles called photons. Depending on their specific charge, the photons travel in a variety of different paths, whether circular, elliptical, or linear. As light enters a prism, the photons arrange themselves by wavelength, revealing their presence as the various colors. Therefore, a leaf is seen as being green because the chemical composition of the leaf's tissues absorbs all the other colors. The activity of photon filtration is totally dependent upon the chemistry, the density of the substance, and the wavelengths of the light.

The Polaroid light filter, first introduced in 1938, replicated this absorption action. Relying on the new plastics chemistry that created long continuous chains of identical molecules, Edward H. Land devised a method by which individual wavelengths of light could be selectively filtered. To work successfully, the plastic molecules of the filter have to align themselves like the strings of a harp, but exceedingly close together. Land's first achievement lay with iodine molecules polymerized into a sheet of clear plastic. Measured at 50,000 lines per inch, the iodine absorbed the light's electromagnetic energy, which is the determining factor in its wavelength, hence its color. Higher and lower value photons pass through this molecular screen largely unaffected. But should a second, similar screen be placed over the first at right angles, then a larger amount of photon energy is intercepted and the filter becomes almost black from the lack of passing light.

This ad came from a 1946 magazine. Even though Polaroid has been producing their polarizing films for the war effort, it was evident in their ad that they were unable to supply all of the demand a year after the end. This reinforces the contention that it took time to convert from military to civilian product production. (Polaroid)

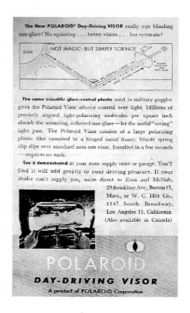

By carefully controlling the amount of iodine in the sheet, the filtration effects—called dichroic polarization—can be predicted to block out unwanted wavelengths. From these developments came a vast variety of filters for photography, infrared and ultraviolet sensors and emitters, glare-reducing coatings for automotive headlamps, welders' glasses and goggles, and tinting for home and car windows. The 3-D movie craze of the 1950s relied on cheap plastic lenses using the Polaroid effect. Although other styles of dichroic polarizers have since been introduced, the Polaroid method remained the primary one for mass manufactured products until recently.

The best modern example of dichroic light generation is the laser. Formerly the subject of science fiction and the speculation of military weaponry, the laser have come into the home and into businesses in computer disk devices and entertainment equipment for movies and music.[24]

Notes/Selected References

1   Lacy, John. Connecticut Crossroads website. www.courant.com/entertainment/xroads/pleasure/putty.stm

2   Harris, Jack C. *Plastic Model Kits*. 1993. Pp. 5-9. Slattery, Chad, The Model Man. *Air and Space* magazine. October/ November 1996. Pp. 77-83. and Cohen, Stan. *V For Victory*. Pp. 233, 186.

3   Beyer, James C. Maj. MC, USA., et al. *Wound Ballistics*. 1962. Pp. 641-647. and Tenner, Edward. "Hardheaded Logic". *Invention & Technology* magazine. Vol. 19, No. 1. Summer 2003. Pp. 38-39.

4   Watterson, John Sayle. *College Football: History, Spectacle, Controversy*. 2000. Pp. 201-202.

5   Kodak website: www.kodak.com/aboutKodak/kodakHistory/milestones33to79.shtml and The History of Photography website: www.kbnet.co.uk/rleggat/photo/history/colour.htm

6   Travers, Bridget, and Jeffrey Muhr, Editors. *World of Invention*. 1994. Pp. 334-335.

7   Mission statement from *Life Magazine*. Reprinted with permission. © 1998-2011. Time Inc. All Rights Reserved. Reproduction in whole or in part without permission is prohibited. "Of all the branches of the journalistic profession, none played a more central role in reporting the events of World War II to the American public than photography." and Opinion Cited. Voss, Frederick S. *Reporting The War: The Journalistic Coverage of World War II*. 1994. P. 41.

8   Panati. *Extraordinary Origins of Everyday Things*. 1987. P. 361. Johnson Publishing website: www.ebony.com/historya.html

9   Ivens, Bryna, editor. *The Seventeen Reader*. 1951. P. v

10   ibid. P. v

11   Schrum, Kelly. "Teena Means Business" Innes, Sherri, editor. *Delinquents and Debutantes*. 1978. Pp. 134-162. Shawcross, William. *Rupert Murdoch*. 1992. P. 401.

12   Jamieson, John. *Books for the Army: The Army Library Service in the Second World War*. 1950. Pp. 285-286.

13   ibid. Pp.1-3.

14   Davis, Kenneth C. Trends in Twentieth-Century Mass Market Publishing. In *The Dictionary of Literary Biography* Vol.46. Pp. 397- 406. and Wilkinson, Carol Ann. Armed Services Editions-Editions for the Armed Services. In *The Dictionary of Literary Biography* Vol.46. P. 16. and Ames, Gregory P. Penguin Books. Printed in *The Dictionary of Literary Biography* Vol.46. Pp. 281-282.

15   Blair, Clay. *Hitler's U-Boat War: The Hunted 1942-1945*. 1998. P. 620.

16   Bishop, Chris, Editor. *Encyclopedia of Weapons of World War II*. 1998. P. 417. and Spilling, Michael, Editor. *Luftwaffe Squadrons: 1939–1945*. 2006. Pp. 73, 126, 128.

17   Chamberlain, Peter and Hilary L. Doyle. *Encyclopedia of German Tanks of World War II*. 1978. Pp. 150-154.

18   Theismeyer, Lincoln R., John Burchard. *Combat Scientists*. 1947. Pp. 281.

19   *The Catalogue of the United States Air Force Museum*. 1982. P. 50. Radio-Driven Model Plane Is the Target for Guns. *Popular Mechanics* magazine. May 1935. P. 673.

20   Munson, Richard. *Cousteau, The Captain and His World*. 1989. Pp. 24-41.

21   Scully, Michael. A Look Back. *Your Company magazine*. Dec, 1998 - Jan.1999. P. 88.

22   Armstrong, Harry G. *Principles and Practice of Aviation Medicine*. 1939. P. 188.

23   Bausch &, Lomb material from: www.fundinguniverse.com/company-histories/ Bausch-amp;-Lomb-Inc-Company-history.html

24   Schurcliff, William A. *Polarized Light*. 1964. Pp. 7-141.

9

It's a Material World: Chemicals, Plastics, and Metals

Just as the mysterious grainy black dust called gunpowder changed the face of warfare when it was introduced in 1313, so too did the many material inventions of World War Two make irreversible changes. Most of these later inventions and discoveries would not have the earth-shaking consequences of gunpowder, although their contributions were not insignificant.

Metals and plastics all result from man's inquiring into the nature of chemistry. Even though chemistry as a science has been advancing since before the days of the alchemist, the first two World Wars were more reliant on the manipulation of the atomic structure of natural products than any previous conflict.

Optical Glass

Optical glass is unique in that it has no flaws to affect the way light passes through it. In a method first devised by the French in 1790, the glass is repeatedly melted to remove bubbles, specks, and other imperfections. During the melt, handheld iron rods stir the glass. Once cooled into blocks, the blocks are then sorted for clarity and inclusions. The rejected material, nearly ninety percent of the volume, is scrapped. The rest is recast, inspected once more and, if it passes quality standards, shipped out to go into spectacles, lenses for scientific equipment, cameras, and other optical devices.

The First World War completely cut off supplies of optical glass to the west, as Germany had largely monopolized glass production methods and formulas. An emergency production plan was launched to increase the manufacture of the specialized glass in America. Still using the antiquated French methods, barely enough was produced to fill the military's needs before the war ended.

After the First World War, Corning Glass Works researchers looked into the problems of manufacturing the specialized glass. There did not appear to be any great hurry or incentive to rush the work, as the French method did work just fine, and there was plenty of other glasswork available. Throughout the post-war years, Corning focused on manufacturing glass for construction and filling orders for the automotive industry. Corning weathered the Depression by providing the glass for the building boom, which saw the initiation of several large construction projects such as the Chrysler and the Empire State Buildings.

Then, in 1938, several major domestic users and the military approached Corning. Another war with Germany was looming and any conflict, even one not directly involving America, would mean restricted importation of lenses and bulk precision glass. The increased demand inspired the company finally to act with some haste, although there would be a large gap of time between the experimental phase and actual production.

One of the more promising areas of investigation seemed to be to melt the glass with electricity. A series of experiments begun in 1920 by Dr. S. Fulcher and revived in the late 1930s showed that better control of glass quality could be achieved in electrically heated furnaces. Meanwhile, other Corning scientists approached the problems of mass-producing optical glass on several fronts. They sought to cut down impurities instilled into the raw glass from the refractory materials of the melting kilns. On still another approach, a research team led by Dr. Charles F. DeVoe promoted a time-consuming series of developments to create and improve the performance of automatic stirring machines. In a flash of genius, Corning physicist Dr. John F. G. Hicks developed an automatic machine, which blended molten glass by pouring it from one container into another and back again. Platinum-clad melting chambers reduced the impurities absorbed from the refractory lining or inadvertently knocked into the molten glass by the iron stirring rods.

The experimentation was far from complete when the military let a contract to Corning for 125,000 optical lens blanks in 1943. By the French method, many months would pass until the order could be filled. Government procurement officers impatiently requested weekly progress reports, only to be told again and again there was no glass available yet.

Gradually, Corning engineers and scientists placed their new machinery into pro-

Solidified optical glass as it comes out of the refractory furnace. The yardstick the man is holding behind the sample is clearly visible, although the glass is about six inches thick. (Corning Glass Works)

duction. Every step in the process—stirring, mixing and blending—all became mechanized. The task was frustrating to both the military and the Corning staff. For example, Dr. De-Voe's team built more than twenty-five electric furnaces, all of which failed in one way or another. It was with more than a little relief that Dr. DeVoe finally reported that half the order was finished and the second half would be ready in a week.

Corning had finally perfected a furnace that was capable of making fifty pounds of glass, all meeting the high military standards, in an hour. With improvements to the rest of the process, glass production steadily increased. By war's end, more than 5,000,000 pounds of optical glass had been manufactured.

While Corning was beginning their struggles with optical glass production problems, the government also financed research in new formulations of optical glass. Typically, glass is a mixture of soda, lime and silica—derived from sand. This mixture still represents the great bulk of glass in use. When the ingredients of glass are melted, the molecules arrange themselves in a random pattern, which then solidifies as it cools. While this structure is fine for general use in windows and for glass containers, the randomness scatters light waves just enough to make it impractical for the ever-growing precision necessary with scientific instrumentation and high-resolution photography. To overcome the short-comings of silica glass, researchers invented a whole new breed of optical glass that totally eliminated the problematic silica. A joint effort by scientists at Kodak and the U.S. Geological Survey (USGS) announced their new formula, a combination of tungsten, tantalum, and lanthanum, on April 21, 1941. Initially, the project had been inspired by the USGS to improve the results of aerial photography, which was just beginning to be used in mapping large, uncharted areas of the world.

The development was fortuitous in that the Allies would be taking millions of photographs of enemy-held territory to plan for and assess damage from the bombing campaigns as well as for intelligence purposes.[1]

Fiberglass

As the plastics industry grew from infancy, researchers began to look for ways to reinforce the new materials. Leo Baekeland, the inventor of Bakelite, had used flour and ground walnut shells to stiffen his plastics. Later, old rags and cotton were used with fair results. Any material, though, would absorb water, thereby diminishing the dielectric strength that had been an important characteristic. In addition, organic fillers tended to decompose; leaving a myriad of voids that fatally weakened the structure of the plastic.

Throughout the 1930s, several companies pursued research into glass fibers, mostly as an additive for plastic electrical components. Without some such material, the practical evolution of electric distribution was at a standstill. As it happened, Corning Glass Works and Owens-Illinois Company discovered similar glass fibers almost simultaneously. Despite the keen competition between Owens and Corning, a mutual agreement was reached in 1938 whereby both companies marketed the material under the trademarked name of Fiberglas.

Through experimentation it was found that the spider web-thin filaments were nearly as strong under tension as comparable steel wire and could be woven into a soft, flexible fabric. As a replacement for asbestos, Fiberglas was capable of withstanding temperatures up to 900°F and therefore well suited for insulating electrical connections, steam and cold water delivery pipes, and home appliances such as refrigerators and water heaters. The Army Engineer Corps found that collapsible water and fuel bladders made of the heaviest weight of canvas available deteriorated rapidly in the fungus-laden Pacific. In 1944, the "new" glass fiber, combined with a core of canvas duck became the answer. The solution was so successful that 20,760 tanks of various sizes were delivered by the end of the war.

Mixed with synthetic resins such as urea or the infant forms of silicone and, later, towards the end of the war, with epoxy-like resins, Fiberglas could be formed into nearly any shape to create rigid, lightweight fuselage panels and body components for aircraft. Manufacturers looked to Fiberglas to replace parts of their products in order to save precious materials and pounds—all military goods had weight limitations to conserve shipping space and payload. Even the helmets that American troops wore into combat had liners made of glass fibers.

Immediately after the war, auto makers, still unable to get steel for car bodies, turned to a type of fiberglass—the trade-named product received its more popular spelling after the war—called glass fiber reinforced plastic (GFRP) as a replacement material. Although no immediate post-war models were sold that were totally built from GFRP, several prototypes were introduced as the latest idea to come out of Detroit. In 1953, Chevrolet fielded the first production car to have a fiberglass body with a historic moniker that would become classic, Corvette.[2]

Silicone

Silicon synthesis technology realized its full potential during the Second World War. A primary ingredient of glass, silicon is one of the most abundant elements in the world. Around 1932, Corning Glass Works scientists began to do research into the nature of organic silicon compounds. With the rapid growth of plastics, company managers felt that the days of glass, particularly as cookware, were numbered. However, they reasoned that if they could create a hybrid of glass and plastic, they might be able to postpone that fateful day indefinitely.

Beginning in 1932, Corning scientists sought to make a compound of carbon and silicon, eventually devising material that could be used in place of either. It took the next six years with many failures and minor successes to produce a practical silicone resin. They had started with silicon, a naturally occurring element and combined carbon, magnesium, chlorine, and bromine. The result was silicone, a polymer string based on a repeating chain of silicon and oxygen. Adding other elements determined whether a fluid, paste or solid would form and what characteristics it would display.

Even before Corning researchers had perfected a way to manufacture quantities larger than milligram samples, their first customer, the U.S. Navy, was pounding on the door. Hyman Rickover, the officer in charge of electrical devices in the Bureau of Ships, and the future father of the atomic navy, wanted an electrical insulating tape to upgrade the motors on submarines. A small batch of experimental tape that met his standards was made up at once. When he was shown the tape and its efficacy demonstrated, Rickover stated, "I want it tomorrow."[3]

Despite Rickover's demand, it was not until 1938 that Corning announced that they were able to produce the tape. Borrowing new technology from the Corning/Owens-Illinois partnership, the new tape featured glass fibers sealed within a cured-silicon resin. Known as 990A®, it featured unprecedented water-tightness and the highest dielectric strength—the ability to resist electric arc through a material—ever recorded from a flexible material.

Work continued at Corning on producing more silicon derivatives. The same year that 990A® came out, Corning Glass Works had joined forces with Pittsburgh's

Mellon Institute of Industrial Research to further silicone development. Much to this consortium's dismay, they learned that General Electric scientists had been working on silicones in their own labs. Now, the race was on to achieve primacy—the key to gaining a patent—to cash in on the expensive research.

Many new formulations were made and tested, often to the bitter disappointment of the scientists. In 1940, Corning scientists stumbled upon a silicone formula that had all the makings of synthetic motor oil. However, when they tested it in a small Briggs and Stratton engine—the type found on lawnmowers—the silicone reverted to its parent material, silicon. With a crankcase filled with slurry containing sand-like particles, the engine died a gallant death in the name of science.

Failures such as these led to small victories, though. In 1941, Corning lawyers began to file the multitude of patents that were beginning to come out of that company's laboratories. Within weeks of the primary patent filings, the government, citing defense needs, clamped a lid of secrecy on any patent or idea that might have a use with the military or provide a technical advantage to the enemy. Silicon fit that category, effectively ending the race between Corning and General Electric.

Production problems continued to bedevil Corning, and the Navy's orders kept slipping further behind schedule. Finally, in 1942, the U.S. Navy insisted that Corning Glass Works join with Dow Chemical Corporation, which would supply the expertise in chemical production while Corning would provide the basic science. It was through this "shotgun wedding" that Dow-Corning Chemical Corporation was born in 1943.

By starting out with chemically pure silicon, the chemistry was manipulated into a thick greasy paste, commercially known as Dow-Corning 4®. In this form, silicone was used as an ignition system sealant to overcome corona, which is a physical phenomenon where high-tension spark-plug wires leak electrical energy, causing a loss of power and, quite often, the downing of the aircraft. Dow-Corning 4® far surpassed the prior sealant, permitting the big American bombers to remain at 35,000 feet for up to eight or more hours. Additional silicones were developed for waterproofing electrical instruments and cloth. Additional silicone pastes, putties and seals were used in kits to waterproof the thousands of vehicles used in the D-Day invasion of France.

Dow-Corning, joining the rest of American chemical companies, vigorously sought a substitute for rubber. One of their early failures would eventually become a unique toy called Silly Putty. (See Chap. 8.) Although rubber—as used for tires and hoses—was slightly beyond the technological reach of silicone during the war, seals for engines, transmissions, and machinery of all sorts were to be made from silicone. Silicone was also formulated into a lubricant replacement that refused to freeze. The addition of certain chemical compounds made silicone cure into a resilient, putty-like gum that resisted water, oils, and paint.

Silicone fluids found use during the war as releasing agents for tire and other casting molds. Previously, waxes had been used, but wax build-up led to a large number of rejects and a substantial amount of lost time cleaning the molds. The tire industry rejected the original silicone agent, as the solution contained flammable additives. Within a short time, Dow-Corning scientists had reformulated the silicone to be water-soluble. With the new agent in hand, American tire companies virtually eliminated scrap on their production lines from wax-caused defects.

The success of the tire industry led to a request from the nation's commercial bakeries for a similar releasing agent. Instead of wax, the bakers used lard, spread by hand, to coat the baking pans. Excess lard burned off as the pans went through the automatic baking ovens, creating a smoky haze throughout the entire bakery. The charred grease often flaked off, spreading obnoxious black flakes over every loaf of bread. Even the unburned lard had to be cleaned off occasionally. Otherwise, it would leave a sticky, yellow scum on the sides and bottoms of the pans that would cause the bread to stick like glue. Harried bakers would violently beat the pans to get the loaves to release, necessitating constant replacement of dented pans.

Again, Dow-Corning applied their unified expertise to the problem and soon had a test chemical spray, Dow-Corning® 200, that could be sprayed on the pans. After the initial spray, the pans could be used for up to 150 baking cycles before needing a second treatment. Word spread quickly and by the end of 1947, Dow was shipping 10,000 gallons of Pan-Glaz® a month to America's commercial bakeries.

Dow-Corning also entered into the direct consumer market with another variation of their silicone products. In Corning, New York, Corning Glass Works researchers serendipitously discovered that Dow-Corning® 200 was a marvelous glass cleaner. In late 1945, local optometrists were given sample bottles of liquid silicone, to be given out free. Reports came back praising the wonderful new cleaner, but the consensus was that no one liked to carry the bottle around. Unfazed, Dow-Corning applied the fluid to a soft tissue paper, and reintroduced it as Sight-Savers®.

In the fifty-plus years after the war, silicone has had a long and glorious career. This book is far too short even to begin to enumerate all of the uses for silicone and its close chemical relations. The original industrial product, Dow-Corning 990A®, resulted in no less than 125 different products, protected by 19 patents. High-tension cables for automotive and electronic applications were coated with silicone-based plastics because of their inherent electrical resistance. Silicone pastes are used as a sealant where absolute, water-tight integrity is important. Where cold or extreme heat causes petroleum-based lubricants to fail, silicone substitutes have been devised. And who can forget the one black mark against silicone: it was used for years as filler material in breast implants.[4]

Plastics

In the years before the outbreak of the First World War, the chemical revolution was reaching its peak. Beginning in the mid-nineteenth century, coal and its by-products were finding manifold uses. From the mines of America, Britain, Germany, and France emanated wondrous new formulas for pitch: for coating the hulls of boats; for fuel; for light and heat; for pigments; for clothing and inks; and fertilizer for crops. New ways to derive gases such as acetylene and ammonia from coal were discovered and in the course of time became vital for industrial use. New drugs from coal were beginning to be found to treat men's and women's ills. Then the plastic age began.

Collodion was the first artificial substance to replace a natural product. Made by adding nitric acid to cotton fibers, giving us gun cotton to use instead of black powder, it was then dissolved in ether and alcohol. The resulting clear, viscous cream would be allowed to dry, forming a transparently smooth, hard shell. A number of ingenious uses for collodion were soon found. Spread over flesh injuries, it formed an airtight shell that remained clear enough for doctors to observe the healing process. Placed over photosensitive silver nitrate glass, it made possible wet-plate collodion photography. By casting and molding the goo, collodion knife handles, brushes, and combs were manufactured. Dyed to resemble ivory, collodion made its appearance as jewelry. What finally did in collodion was the great cost of the solvents. Quality control, having been set aside to reduce the price further, became a major issue with the buying public.

Collodion had a rebirth with the billiards industry. A forecast made in 1880 stated that 22,000 elephant tusks a year would be needed for all the ivory products then in use. A century before PETA or the Sierra Club, this news of a bleak future for the elephant population caused quite a public uproar. Coating spheres of wood pulp and bone dust with collodion made a proper substitute, except for one problem. The dynamic "click" of the balls, so important to the pool connoisseur, could become a "bang" if the mildly explosive coating was struck too hard.

By adding camphor, collodion became flexible celluloid. Molded under heat and pressure, celluloid could be shaped. Re-heating softened the material so that it could be worked into new forms. This cycle could be repeated endlessly, making celluloid the first thermoplastic. Celluloid, as flexibly thin, transparent ribbon, would become the material that would be the basis of the movie industry. Just as important as photographic film, celluloid-coated garments soon began to substitute for rubber slickers. Weighing substantially less than the traditional Macintosh, the celluloid-impregnated clothing also resisted oils, something that the everyday sailor was beginning to work with more often.

In 1909, Belgian immigrant Leo Baekeland mixed formaldehyde and phenol under pressure and high heat. The resulting lump of yellow material, called Bakelite, promised a bright future. Immune to all known chemicals, it also resisted burning. With a high dielectric strength, it proved to be the perfect insulator for the growing electrical industry. Baekeland himself proclaimed that Bakelite was the "material of a thousand uses." Within ten years, the inventor estimated that there were forty-three industries using Bakelite. Ten years after that, in 1929, Baekeland stated that he could not think of forty-three industries that did not use it. Unlike celluloid, Bakelite could be cast or molded only once, marking it as the first thermoset plastic.

An Army Jeep wades through the water off-shore in the South Pacific. It took many new materials to enable this to occur. Neoprene seals in the axles, drive shafts and gearboxes. Acrylic sealed the instruments in the dashboard. Silicone grease lubricated the steering. The seats provided a semblance of comfort with polyurethane covered with vinyl. (U.S. Army)

Two major commodities—ivory and rubber—were replaced by synthetic substitutes. Bakelite replaced celluloid as a plastic in products such as billiard balls. Common wisdom dictated that alternative compounds would replace other natural products. The race to discover them was on.

Polyethylene

Robert Watson-Watt had barely gotten the series of radar stations operational on the British coast when the Air Ministry interrupted his Chain Home Project work with a new task. Could he design an airborne model? In his free moments, he considered the request. One hurdle he foresaw was that the original equipment weighed several tons and required electricity on an industrial scale. To miniaturize the complex electrical machinery down to a manageable, aircraft-mountable scale, he speculated, would require an insulating material that would resist decay under enormous voltage. Called dielectric strength, this degeneration becomes significant when a current overcomes resistance and leaks to ground. Rubber and gutta percha, the only known natural flexible insulators, worked well, but they were heavy and broke down over time. Watson-Watt needed a lighter, longer-lasting substitute.

Polyethylene was the solution. It was first created accidentally during an experiment in 1933 at the British corporate giant Imperial Chemical Industries (ICI). Unfortunately for the chemists, unintentionally blowing up the high- pressure vessel that created their discovery also meant that polyethylene would have to be rediscovered surreptitiously. Working at night and without management's approval, ICI chemists R.O. Gibson, E.D. Manning, and Dr. Michael Perrin combined ethylene and benzaldehyde. Pressurizing the chamber to two thousand atmospheres and heating the chemical broth to 170° C, they ended up with a snowy white powder.

After two more years of trial and error, ICI developed a pressure system that could retain the dangerously high pressures needed to force polymerization. The new material matched the dielectric strength of rubber at one-third of the mass. For high-frequency applications, polyethylene was perfect, and radar used high-frequency electromagnetic waves. Watson-Watt's new slimmed-down version of radar could be—just barely—fitted inside a Blenheim light bomber. Other versions, sveltely trimmed from the original six hundred pounds, would continue to be introduced as the war continued.

It would be another eight years after Germany surrendered that Karl Ziegler of Max Planck Institute for Coal Research at Mülheim, West Germany would perfect an ambient atmospheric pressure catalytic process. Although this would be the breakthrough that made polyethylene an inexpensive household plastic, there would be nothing that could overcast the import to the war effort that the three ICI chemists and Watson-Watt made.

Polyethylene still serves as coating for wiring. The high-tension leads in the common television set are a good example of its versatility. Both low- and high-density polyethylene make a multitude of products. Rope, garbage cans, water tanks, garbage bags—the list is endless. Of all of the plastics, polyethylene is generally regarded as the most useful.

Nylon

If polyethylene is the most useful, then nylon may be considered the most desired, at least during the Second World War. Nylon is one of the polymers discovered from the search to find a replacement for silk. The natural fiber was expensive and not very durable. Silk became fashionable especially for women's hosiery as hemlines rose in the 1920s; it was desirable for its glistening luster and sheer elegance. By 1938, an estimated $700 million a year was being spent on silk products in America.

At DuPont Chemical Company, this represented a challenge. Germany had led the way during the First World War with synthesizing scarce materials for civilian consumption. Even though most of these products failed the test of time, they set a precedent that the management of DuPont wanted to emulate. In 1927, the DuPont board of directors allowed the astronomical sum of $25,000 a month to go into a basic research laboratory budget.

With that kind of money, DuPont was able to attract the best scientific talent available. One of their shining stars was Wallace Hume Carothers. He was a highly capable man, usually mastering any scholastic course that he set upon. Given a position at the newly expanded DuPont lab, he worked on a variety of projects that focused on the nature and structure of monomers and polymers. His life would doubtless have continued unfettered by corporate interference, but the Depression struck. Even a big company such as DuPont did not have deep enough pockets to survive such a financial calamity, and management was soon looking for results from their costly and unprofitable laboratory.

Fortuitously, the chemists had been working on a rubber substitute. Although it did not exactly match the characteristics of the rubber used for tires, it was suitable for a variety of products that used rubber as seals, hoses, and sheet goods. The new discovery, named Neoprene, saved the lab from closing, if only for the time being.

In the meantime, Wallace Carothers continued his work. He wanted to achieve his Holy Grail: create a plastic that exceeded a molecular weight of 6,000. To chemists, the molecular weight of a plastic is an indicator of its strength and flexibility. Natural rubber has a molecular weight measured in the tens of thousands and any synthetic plastic that approached this number would have many of the desirable properties of rubber. Carothers knew this enormous molecule would open the door to ever larger and more complex synthetics, earning for him a place in plastics history and permanently saving the DuPont labs.

While attending a professional lecture, one of Carothers' assistants was fortunate enough to be shown a new machine—a molecular still—that captured gaseous molecules and trapped them in the long monomer molecular chains that define plastics. With one of these stills working in their laboratory, the DuPont scientists soon had an unidentified white chunk of material residing in the reaction vessel of the still. Heated, the mass could be pulled like taffy into long streamers. When cooled, the filaments turned brittle, shattering at the slightest touch. Carothers found that if the strands were slowly stretched during the cooling stage, they became elastic, able to be pulled up to seven times their original length.

Further research indicated that the molecular structure of the new, unnamed plastic was a disorganized jumble when it was first heated. But as it was stretched, the molecules arranged themselves in long lines parallel to the direction of the tension. Compared to silk, the plastic was far more elastic and stronger as well. This shock-absorbing characteristic was an advantageous characteristic for towropes for tactical gliders, hawsers and docking ropes for the Navy, climbing ropes for Ranger-type assault teams, and nylon fishing line for life-raft survival kits.[5]

In spite of the excitement initiated by Carothers' announcement of his discovery on September 1, 1931, the new synthetic "silk" was to defy production applications. The ingredients were too expensive and the plastic strands cooled too rapidly to be mass-produced efficiently. Over the next four years, Carothers and his team of researchers worked on developing a workable formula. Finally, in 1935, DuPont introduced polymer 66. It took a further two years to get the production lines set up and operating relatively problem-free.

It was expected that Nylon®—it got its formal name in 1937, but the lower case version soon came into universal usage—would eventually be marketed as a replacement for an imported material, but when the call came for its debut, it was from a wholly unanticipated source. Until 1938, American toothbrushes exclusively used hog bristles imported from China. The Japanese invasion of Manchuria and the escalating war in China drastically cut down on the supply of the hairs. Facing a nationwide epidemic of halitosis, the oral hygiene companies approached DuPont to make nylon bristles. Within months, the first brushes featuring synthetic bristles went on the market. (More on this in Chap. 7)

The successful production of the thick filaments, however, was not the same as drawing the spider-web-thin strands of nylon used for stockings. Bedeviled by problems on the production line, DuPont delayed the plastic's entry into the lingerie department. But when it did go on sale, on September 1, 1939, it did so with great fanfare.

The media played up the grand opening at Wilmington, Delaware, and also broadcast some basic rules. No one could buy more than three pairs of stockings and all potential buyers had to show proof of being Wilmington residents. Only six stores were stocked with the hosiery, priced almost double the price of similar silk items.

Nevertheless, after three hours, all four thousand pairs had been sold. On May 15, 1940, national sales opened and the hosiery practically flew off the shelves.

The swift popularity of Nylon hosiery was unfortunate from one standpoint. So much Nylon was produced and sold that sales of silk products virtually ended. This rebuff amounted to a spontaneous boycott of the natural material and, coupled with widely held public sympathies for the plight of the Chinese—who were under brutal treatment by the Imperial Japanese Armies—imports of silk plummeted to around ten million dollars in 1940-41. To the attentive Japanese bureaucrats and politicians, those who monitored such things, it could hardly be seen as anything but an act of economic warfare by America.

Less than a year later, the war would necessitate the total recall of nylon hosiery, to be used in towropes and parachute lines and shrouds. Nylons became premiums, rewards to be used as a bonus for excellent

The soldier above is attaching the combination tow-line/ communication wires for a CG-4 Waco assault glider. The line will be connected to the C-47 behind which is the tow plane. The line is our focus, and the reason nylon hosiery is totally unavailable back home. Nylon was favored for its strength and light weight. (OWI/NARA)

work at factories or as an enticement for an intimate date with a lonely GI.

Nylons became such a desirable commodity and developed into such an instrument of influence that the American government reopened an abandoned weaving mill in New Jersey in the early summer of 1942. There, five hundred pairs of hosiery were manufactured with military-supplied nylon, to be used as bribes for French officers commanding Foreign Legion troops facing the Allied landing beaches in North Africa. Army planners hoped that the supply of nylons would convince the French, who were ostensibly the enemy at the time, to lay down their weapons. Several dozen pair were smuggled into Algerian cities to American agents, who then used the filmy undergarments as a reward for information clandestinely gathered by female friends of French military officers.

The silk trade never did really recover from the invention of nylon. During the war, silk was about the only product that Japan had an excess. Oddly, most Japanese spurned the wearing of silk garments, except for the traditional kimonos, as being decadent, frivolous, and unpatriotic.[6]

Polyurethane

The ultimate goal for industrial chemists during the Second World War was finding a reasonable substitute for rubber. Polyurethane was another near miss. Its internal structure is a combination of a rigid molecular group situated in a string pattern alternately with a soft, elastic molecular group. The production and research of polyurethane was held very closely during the war, but in 1947, the lead researcher, Adolf von Baeyer, wrote a paper on the subject. In it, he admitted that the original purpose for the project was to replicate nylon without violating the patent held by DuPont. It was only after the war began and the rubber crisis was at its peak the research changed.

Polyurethane was important to the war effort in its own right, though. It was discovered that during mass production, carbon dioxide was released as a by-product of the curing. This left millions of tiny bubbles in the material that weakened the rigid formations. What was left was a spongy mass that sprang back into shape, regardless of the weight applied atop it. For cushions of hundreds of thousands of vehicle and aircraft seats, there could be no better substitute than foam rubber. Wherever the requirement was for cushioning or protecting a hard surface or edge, this item was coated or otherwise protected with polyurethane foam. In addition, very flexible thin sheets were found to be perfect for backing wall-to-wall carpeting in homes during the post-war building boom. It was in those same homes that mats of urethane were used for insulating the walls and ceilings in the northeast United States

By changing the formulation slightly some years later, scientists discovered that very fine elastic threads could be drawn. This led to the super-lightweight, form-fitting material called Spandex.

Acrylic (Plexiglas)

World War Two aircraft were instantly recognizable by their sleek lines, massive reciprocating engines, transparent windows, canopies, and gun blisters. These tough, clear windscreens were the invention of a German chemist, Dr. Otto Rohm, who had made his first fortune in Germany synthesizing tanning solutions before the First World War. His chemical solutions were so popular that he established branch plants worldwide. With a secure income, Dr. Rohm returned to his passion, researching the mysteries of acrylic esters.

Acrylic compounds had been discovered and rediscovered in the late nineteenth century by at least two researchers. There are even unsubstantiated tales that an acrylic-like substance was presented to the Roman emperor Tiberius (42 BC–37 A.D.) Acrylics are the chance combination of carbon, hydrogen, and nitrogen molecules that link together to form a plastic chain at near normal pressures and temperatures. As scientists worked with celluloid, they began to find acrylic resins. One of the first commercial uses for the clear goo was to place it between two sheets of glass. If the glass was struck hard enough to break, the acrylic would hold the pieces together instead of letting them spray out, eliminating a hazard to occupants and bystanders. In 1928, the motoring public was introduced to automotive safety glass. This would be replaced eventually by vinyl acetate resin, an outgrowth of vinyl research during the Second World War. The acrylic would frost up in high humidity and bubbles, expanding in the hot sun, failed to hold glass shards when the glass was broken.

At that time, however, acrylic resins never set into a hard substance, which meant they were practically unusable as a true plastic. Otto Rohm changed that. In 1931, he introduced a crystal-clear, solid acrylic sheet that could be cut with standard tools and shaped into complex forms with the application of heat. Throughout the mid-1930s, Rohm made himself busy making and fitting his plastic panels into a variety of new functions. German industry began using Rohm's acrylic, now called Plexiglas, to make windshields for their bomber fleet.

Plexiglas found its way to America by way of a patent-sharing agreement that Rohm had with a former American business partner, Otto Haas. When samples of the plastic came to the United States, the military and Detroit automakers were approached with suggestions for its incorporation into a wealth of products. General Motors, through their subsidiary Fisher Body, used Plexiglas to build their classic Plexiglas Pontiac for the 1939 World's Fair. Plexiglas was used to fashion a whole room at the fair as well, including Plexiglas tables, chairs, dining utensils, and even the walls.

The war provided the impetus for the wholesale inclusion of Plexiglas in the war machine. New methods of forming the plastic were developed by means of molding and vacuum forming, processes that are still used today. As the Haas employees became more adept at manipulating the plastic, larger pieces were made. Entire sections of nose and side blisters were manufactured in one piece, giving the aircrews unprecedented and unobstructed views.

Plexiglas was not without its teething troubles, though. Boeing Aircraft faced unexpected problems with Plexiglas in their new long-range B-29 bomber. Featuring the first remote-controlled gun turrets ever placed on an airplane, the plane was intended to be pressurized at altitude. To operate the guns, crew members had to sit behind large, hemispherical domes of Plexiglas so they could aim and fire at the attacking enemy. In early tests, the Plexiglas worked just fine, but as the plastic was constantly exposed to the sun's ultraviolet rays, it became brittle and foggy. It was evident that there was a serious problem when even the slightest scratch could cause the whole bubble to shatter while under the increased pressurization of the fuselage. More than one gunner was literally sucked out of his seat and summarily tossed to his death. The resulting decompression was fatal to the plane itself on at least three occasions, in each case killing the entire crew of eleven highly trained men. In one memorable instance, a gunner was actually photographed as he perilously hung outside the B-29 at 29,000 feet, held in place by a safety strap that he had designed himself for just such an occasion. After ten hair-raising minutes of being repeatedly bounced against the side of the plane, he was safely pulled back inside by another crew member.[7]

The American maker of Plexiglas, Rohm & Haas, had to reformulate their plastic to weather the severe ultraviolet exposure. This problem would be multiplied by operations in the sunny Pacific tropics and long hours at high altitudes, which had the effect of lessening the atmospheric filtering of the damaging rays. It took nearly two years and several dozen formulas to get an acceptable solution.

Plexiglas windows provided another, unexpected effect for the pilots— magnification. Looking through the shaped plastic was similar to seeing through a lens. When the conditions were just right—sun, humidity, and pilot exhaustion—pilots reported that the plastic windscreen magnified the view. In one instance, a B-29 pilot coming in for a landing misjudged his

Putting the finish shine on the Plexiglas noses of A-20 medium bombers. The plastic was a tough, resilient material that was easy to work with hot or cold. (NARA)

height and literally slammed his 100,000-pound aircraft onto the runway from fifty feet up. Happily, the B-29 was a stout machine and no significant damage was done. Nevertheless, this incident served as a lesson to the other pilots of the disorienting effects of Plexiglas.[8]

The military still uses Plexiglas for windscreens and canopies. Industry has adopted the plastic for a myriad of products and components used in the manufacturing process. Almost all the automatic machinery used in factories today has Plexiglas shields and guards covering the operating areas. Consumers are enticed into buying products exhibited on light-weight Plexiglas display cases. Acrylics have also been used as a basis for woven threads in carpets and cloth. The uses for Plexiglas are limited only by the imagination.[9]

Teflon

This material, synonymous with slippery substances, was the result of a laboratory experiment gone awry. In 1938, DuPont chemists were studying Freon and closely related compounds when they prepared a batch of tetrafluoroethylene gas. They stored the gas in cylinders and placed them for the night in cold storage. In the morning, they found that the gas had converted to a waxy, opaque powder. Cutting the cylinder open, the scientists were amazed to find that the entire inner surface was coated with the white substance. The gas had spontaneously polymerized itself overnight.

Even more intriguing was that the material was nearly indestructible. Samples placed in extreme cold, even down to absolute zero, were unaffected. It would not char over a flame and began to melt only at 620 degrees F. Even then, instead of liquefying, it changed into diaphanous goo. Exposure to a number of chemical solutions, including boiling acids, solvents, and fuels, only washed off the surface, leaving it unmarred. With a seemingly impervious nature—it can be sanded only with great difficulty—the plastic was virtually friction-free. It surpassed the slickest object known—wet ice on wet ice—hands down.

Given the name Teflon, the substance remained a curiosity until the war was well under way. Scientists, trying to separate the minuscule amounts of mildly radioactive U235 from U238 by gaseous diffusion, began to use fluorine gas as a carrier. Exceedingly corrosive, the gas ate through the solid nickel pipes at the Oak Ridge, Tennessee, plant. General Groves, the Manhattan Project director, approached DuPont for any possible cure. In 1944, Teflon was used to coat the pumps, pipes, and fittings for the top secret atomic bomb project.

The military began to coat artillery shells with it to reduce wear on gun barrels. Teflon lined tanks of cryogenic rocket fuels, protecting the steel outer casing from fracturing from the bitter cold. Used to insulate wires for airborne radar, Teflon's superior abrasion resistance meant fewer short circuits, one of the primary causes of failure.

Of course, Teflon has made its mark on the post-war world as a non-stick coating for cookware and irons. Carpets, upholstery and clothes can be sprayed with an aerosol version of Teflon to resist stains. Tape and paste containing the plastic are an essential sealant for plumbers. Easy to machine, Teflon bearings support shafts, buildings, and bridges in hostile environments that would destroy any other material. And Teflon has gone into space in a variety of applications.

Vinyl

Anyone who has seen World War Two pictures of troops waiting to board ships bound for the beaches of Normandy may have noticed that their rifles were wrapped in sheet plastic. This protected the weapons from sand and water contamination, which could foul the working mechanisms at precisely the wrong moment. The material, a vinyl sheet called Saran Wrap, was a relative newcomer to the world of plastics.

Vinyl is a term loosely used to describe a whole family of thermoplastics—plastics that can be repeatedly heated and shaped into new forms—that had been under development for twenty years. The first true vinyl plastics were developed in 1924 at Carbide and Carbon Chemical Corporation, the forebearer of the Union Carbide Corporation. This company patented a combination of vinyl chloride and vinyl acetate. The compound was not commercially viable as it quickly degraded at high processing temperatures. Two years later, a chemist for B.F. Goodrich Rubber Company invented polyvinyl chloride (PVC). Challenged to find a practical use for PVC, the chemist, Waldo Semon, hit upon laminating it to

On board a LCI (Landing Craft, Infantry) headed for the Normandy beaches, the men appear calm and confident. One point of confidence is from their certainty their rifles would stay dry and sand-free wrapped in polyethylene sheet bags. The plastic was strong enough to take considerable abuse and easy enough to tear off by hand. The speed that all plastics found applications occurred at a head-spinning rate. (U.S. Army/NARA) fabrics to make them waterproof.

It took another five to seven years (there are conflicting stories about the dates) for vinyl chemistry to advance to the status of a stand-alone product. That happened when new types of vinyl such as cellophane, polyethylene, and Naugahyde were introduced. Of the three, cellophane was the quickest to come to the marketplace as a wrapping for cigarettes packages. Naugahyde was an experimental material meant to be a substitute for fine leather, which was widely used on furniture. Although the experiment was a success, the material found few buyers in the cash-tight times of the late Depression. Movie theater owners were the first real mass purchasers of Naugahyde for their theater seats, which sustained incredibly hard wear from the throngs of moviegoers.

In 1943, Naugahyde was accepted as the seat covering of choice for the United States military. This move was already moot. For nearly four years, the material had been widely used by manufacturers of military machinery for seat covering. On board ships, the vinyl had proven to be impervious to the harsh effects of salt water and constant humidity. As leather became scarce, jackets, gloves, aviator helmets, and other goods were made of Naugahyde. Post-war, Naugahyde was to play a part in the manufacture of fine home and office furnishings. One-quarter to one-half as expensive as leather, Naugahyde was used extensively to convey a sense of elegance and warmth as leather and wood paneling—long the ideal of wealth and influence—gave way to Naugahyde and to plastic-coated, artificially grained plywood.

During the 1930s, Henry Ford took a serious interest in plastics for his booming automotive industry. He sponsored the development of research that led to the discovery that soybeans, a crop that received little attention from American farmers, could be manipulated to give up a variety of chemical compounds for paints, fabrics, and plastics. In 1935, the equivalent of a bushel basket of soybeans was being used in every Ford car off the assembly line, and in 1940, old Henry himself introduced what would today be called a concept car that appeared to be a stock 1941-model sedan. This car, however, was made with a radical tubular frame covered in plastic panels made from soybeans. The paint was enamel that also came from the legumes, as were most of the plastic interior fittings and seat covers. With the grace of Paul Bunyan felling the North Woods, Henry took an axe and enthusiastically struck the trunk lid. To the massed reporters' surprise, the deck flexed under the mighty blow and promptly sprang back into shape without a mark on it. Even the paint, a glossy cream color, showed no sign of the abuse that had just been inflicted upon it.[10] The demonstration had been a publicity stratagem to promote Ford's research and development department's achievements.

One company, considering Ford's new plastic for the VT[12] fuse nose cones, tested samples by throwing them against a shop radiator. If the plastic held up to this abuse—trivial compared to the 20,000 G's[13] experienced at firing—the material was deemed good enough to be used.[11]

Henry Ford's vinyl car was not to be. Within months of his remarkable display, his factories would stop all auto production in favor of jeeps, airplanes, and engines. Plastic-bodied cars were not going to be mass-produced for the consumer market until the early 1980s, but even then, they would constantly have to fight the appearance of being dangerous death traps as they lacked the metal bodywork to protect the occupants from harm.

One safety feature on automobiles is that of safety glass. As described earlier in this chapter, two panels of tempered glass sandwich a sheet of vinyl acetate resin, which sticks to the glass with a tenacious, flexible bond. If an object should hit the glass, the vinyl acetate will absorb a large part of the momentum. The glass will crack, maybe even shatter, but the fragments will stay in place, more or less.[12]

The end of the war was just the beginning of the plastic revolution. Ever since, more plastic products and materials have appeared than were ever dreamed possible by the chemists of the 1930s and '40s. Now, carbon fibers have supplanted molecular carbon as a basis for featherweight synthetics. These newer materials can withstand temperatures far higher than even Bakelite, are lighter by volume than Henry Ford's soy plastics, and are stronger—measured in tensile strength—than steel.

Buna (Synthetic) Rubber

A World War Two P-47 fighter used nearly a ton of rubber, as did a M4 Sherman tank. A B-17 needed about three tons and the shipyard installed over ten tons in every destroyer. Obviously, rubber was vital for the war and Japan had seized all the Western Pacific plantations. Ironically, American businesses had given away the right to make an artificial rubber in a measure that was intended to protect the interests of one American company, the Standard Oil Company of New Jersey.

In 1930, Standard Oil wanted exclusive rights for the coal-to-gasoline formula devised by the German chemical firm I.G. Farben. After some negotiation, I.G. Farben

12 VT stood for Variable Time. This was misdirection for security purposes. The VT code-word referred to the proximity fuse, a remarkable breakthrough in electronics miniaturization.(See Chap. 3.)
13 One G equals the force of gravity on a mass. 2G is two times the force of gravity. A hundred-fifty pound person at 2G feels as if it weighed three hundred, 10G would feel like one thousand five-hundred pounds.

and Standard Oil struck a deal in which both companies would share patents, giving each party exclusive advantage on their respective sides of the Atlantic.[14] Standard Oil chemists had discovered a way to create butyl rubber from crude oil. Farben's staff likewise began to make Buna—synthetic—rubber from coal tar. Under the trade agreement, already in effect for eight years, the two discoveries–coal to gas for synthetic rubber–should have been swapped evenly. Like many such unions, this one fell apart abruptly after a lengthy period of increasing deceit.[13]

I.G. Farben financially supported the rise of Hitler. Hence, the company willingly came under the domination of the Nazis. Instead of a straight exchange, the Germans took Standard Oil's formula with the promise of getting government permission to release the Buna formula. German leaders knew the importance of rubber and, by controlling the formulas they held an important advantage. It comes as no great surprise that the Germans reneged on the pending deal and Standard Oil never got the reciprocal synthetic rubber recipe.

A cube of U. S. Rubber synthetic rubber as it came out of a process machine. It took some time for American rubber companies to recover from the loss of the synthetic rubber race but it was achieved. (U.S. Rubber)

The German industrialists, working in collusion with the Nazis to engineer the deceit, even went as far as setting up phony meetings with several American rubber companies to forestall work on independent development of synthetic rubber. They reasoned that the Americans, believing that the formula was in the offing, would not spend precious resources to experiment on an already invented product. The deception was revealed when Farben officials notified Standard Oil executives that the patent would be licensed in America without the vital technical details. Lacking the latter, the patent was essentially worthless paper. Having lost the synthetic rubber gambit to German chicanery, the United States was on the verge of going to war without a secure supply of rubber, real or not.

Overcoming the rubber shortage was one of the greatest domestic obstacles to winning the war. Within days after Congress ratified the Declaration of War on Japan,

---

14 This violated the Sherman Anti-Trust Act and was a betrayal of America's national security. Standard Oil's hand was slapped with a small fine and the company was essentially forgiven immediately. There was a war on after all.

December 9, 1941, the Office of Production Management banned the sale of tires and inner tubes to civilians. Administrative boards were set up to ration out the remaining tires, with certain occupations receiving priority allotments. The call went out for every nonessential rubber product to be turned in for reclamation. Within four weeks, 450,000 tons of scrap was donated. It came from every conceivable source. Floor mats, garden hoses, golf balls, raincoats, overshoes, bathing caps and, in a memorable event, the entire female cast of a Broadway musical wriggled out of their girdles in public to add to the pile. Although much of the rubber had already been reclaimed once, making it unusable for reprocessing, the drive alerted the public to the seriousness of the shortage.[14]

Industrial chemists worked hard to catch up. In a crash program, fifty plants, consuming a million tons of structural steel, were soon built across the nation. Forming an informal association to share information and talent, industry and universities set aside their mutual antagonisms. Formerly competing companies did likewise in a refreshing atmosphere of cooperation. With the billion dollar commitment, underwritten by the Federal Government, emanated the mandate that production of synthetic rubber would reach the 800,000-ton level by 1944. Remarkably, this goal was not only met by mid-year, but was surpassed.[15]

THESE BOYS NEED GOOD TIRES. YOU CAN HELP THEM GET THE BEST BY LOSING NO TIME IN TURNING OUT THE INSTRUMENTS NEEDED TO MAKE MORE SYNTHETIC RUBBER

Synthetic rubber production was one of the greatest challenges for the first three years of the war. Natural rubber was in such short supply that the government imposed a nationwide rationing quota for tires and gasoline. (U.S. Army Signal Corps/NARA)

Metals

Name any metal and it was sure to be on somebody's priority list during the war. Aluminum cooking pans ended up on the scrap pile next to the pile of costume jewelry rich in tin, copper and traces of silver. Padlocks containing steel and bronze were melted down in the same furnaces that converted Grandfather's Model T into armor plate.

Copper was in such short supply that steel became the metal of choice for pennies.

During the war, three metals—aside from the radioactive materials already described in Chapter 1—received unprecedented attention for their unique qualities, which would irretrievably change the course of history with their usage. A fourth material, aluminum was an old hand at warfare, but scientists were going to expend enormous energies changing its characteristics with innumerable alloys and heat treatments.

Aluminum Alloys

Ever since before the First World War, aluminum has been common in a variety of products. In 1903, German chemist Alfred Wilm discovered that by heating a sample of aluminum alloyed with copper, magnesium, and manganese and quickly cooling it in water, the aluminum took on tensile attributes similar to steel. This characteristic represents the maximum elongation that a material can deform until failure under tension. Materials that can be stretched like a rubber band also tend to crack less, meaning the entire assembly was less likely to fall apart under great stress.

Wilm called his material Duralumin, which gave Germany a significant edge during the First World War. Duralumin was to come to America in the 1920s, where it represented an incredible step forward in metallurgy. During the Second World War, Duralumin was used in thousands of aircraft, and dozens of experimental machines and devices. New processes to manufacture and alloy aluminum led to a growing inventory of the varieties of Duralumin. This expanded experience, derived from wartime aluminum technology, was to make possible unprecedented uses.

In 1946, a one-hundred-foot span bridge was constructed outside of Massena, New York. The massive beams, made from a war-developed grade of Duralumin, weighed 60% less than a comparably sized steel beam. Over that bridge traveled semi-trucks made with similar aluminum frames. The benefits of lighter aluminum alloys became all too obvious in the northeast areas of the United States, where salts used for deicing winter roads quickly deteriorated the steel of bridges, as it did the steel bodies and frames of the vehicles. Over the last fifty years, more than four thousand Duralumin and other aluminum alloys have been developed. Elements such as silicon, zinc, chromium, nickel, and titanium have joined the original three alloying elements to make aluminum one of the most versatile metals of the modern era.[16]

Magnesium

Aside from its role as an incendiary, magnesium played a crucial role during World War Two. The method of refining metallic magnesium was discovered in Germany in 1886. Nearly all the magnesium used in the world came from that European country until the First World War. With supplies abruptly interrupted, American industry developed processes to smelt the extremely light, silvery-white material.

Magnesium is most remarkable for its feather-like mass. One cubic inch of steel weighs more than four times that of an identical block of magnesium. Despite its misleading weight, which implies fragility, alloyed magnesium is less prone to stress fatigue than most steels. Fatigue comes about when a component is stressed repeatedly, but not enough to deform the original shape permanently. Under these stresses, the metallic structure—the lattice—becomes brittle and begins to crack. Eventually, the cracks extend far enough to join together, causing a traumatic fracture. Magnesium resists this stress, making it a good choice for parts that are subjected to severe punishment, such as landing gear for aircraft, connecting rods in reciprocating engines, and wheel rims. Magnesium is an important element for the processing of other metals as well. It is used to deoxidize nickel and nickel alloys, making them easier to work with. Electronic components that require an absolute vacuum do so because oxygen can severely restrict the components' longevity or effectiveness. To overcome the oxygen problem, electronic devices have a part called a "getter" installed. Made from pure magnesium, the getter attracts and holds onto stray oxygen molecules, improving the reliability of the components.

As World War Two approached, the American government foresaw that magnesium supplies were far short of expected needs. Chemists had determined that seawater held a significant proportion of vital war materials, including magnesium. A pilot project to extract the metal from the sea was initiated at Freeport, Texas. There, the Velasco Defense Plant Corporation's facility produced 72 million pounds of magnesium over a one-year period beginning in June 1942.

Experiments during the war showed that magnesium was just as susceptible to improvement as aluminum. Along with the more common alloying agents—manganese, zinc, silicon, tin, and aluminum—exotic elements such as silver, thorium, zirconium and rare earth elements were used. Heat treatments similar to those used for Duralumin improved the ductility—the ability to permanently deform without breaking—of magnesium by more than double.

Magnesium was, and still is, an essential metal for aircraft. In addition, magnesium is used for a myriad of tools and equipment where light weight is important. Magnesium getters are still installed in vacuum tubes, specifically the picture tubes on television sets. And magnesium, alloyed with aluminum, is a highly desirable option for the sports car enthusiast.[17]

Beryllium

This hard, silver-gray metal had very few uses before the Second World War. In the early 1920s, copper and beryllium were alloyed to make a harder copper for springs and contactor blades used in electrical hardware.

In the later 1930s beryllium powder was widely used in fluorescent light tubes. Only years afterward did physicians discover that the white powder caused a serious lung disease called berylliosis. But that would be at a much later time.

The 1930s were a great time of discovery. It was then that physicists discovered that the metal reacted to radiation exposure by giving off its own energetic emissions far in excess of any other material tested. It seemed that beryllium was generating its own radioactivity, but only when inspired to by another radioactive source. After a great amount of tireless experimentation, it was shown that beryllium was expelling a neutral particle, a neutron, from its atomic structure. The beryllium neutron was capable of piercing the nucleus of other atoms with less expended energy than either of the other basic known atomic particles—electrons and protons. This discovery alone was a major step in nuclear physics. However, beryllium as a metal continued to be a laboratory oddity until the Manhattan Project.

With the atomic bomb quickly becoming a reality, physicists needed a powerful neutron emitter to initiate the chain reaction that creates the release of energy in an atomic bomb. Beryllium sheets, thinner than cigarette paper, were wrapped around a core of polonium—a very active source of alpha-type nuclear particles. When the bomb's explosive outer shell squeezed the initiator with enormous implosive pressure, the beryllium would amplify the radioactive emissions and spark off the largest firecracker the world has ever seen up to that time.

Beryllium was not only one of the vital breakthroughs for the atomic bomb, but it was also a major component of another earth-shaking event, the space program. Beryllium has a remarkable tendency to dissipate heat. Electronic components, highly sensitive to any excess heat, are mounted on wafer-thin plates of beryllium oxide ceramic, called a heat sink. Thousands of heat sinks are used on such diverse products from the family car to satellites and electronic gear on board manned space vehicles.

Additionally, beryllium ceramics are used in the construction of high-wattage lasers used in industry, scientific research, and medicine. Because of the thermal properties of beryllium, nearly all the high-powered electronics of today operate faster, more reliably and longer.[18]

Titanium

Although metallic titanium was first produced in 1896, the white metal was too brittle to have any foreseeable uses. The problem with the smelting process was that nearly every gas in a free atmosphere, as well as carbon, and all known refractory materials easily contaminate titanium. By 1910, General Electric was producing minute amounts for experimental purposes in a improvised vacuum oven made from an old bomb casing. Work on creating a workable titanium formula continued for the next twenty-eight years, with only limited success.

One researcher, W.J. Kroll of Luxembourg, found that a solution of titanium tetra-chloride reduced with chemically pure calcium would realize a softer metal that lent itself to industrial methods. His discovery, in 1939, was hampered by the outrageous cost of the calcium and was also quickly overshadowed by the war. Kroll immigrated to America, where he took a job with the United State Bureau of Mines and pressed on with his titanium studies. There, he found that pure magnesium would serve better and was easier to work with than calcium. He built a furnace that reduced liquefied titanium tetrachloride into a bath of melted magnesium. Through the use of the furnace, Kroll was able to establish the melting point of titanium, a basic but important step in designing processes for specific metals.

Although the furnace that Kroll made in the 1940s is no longer in use, it opened the way for other, more efficient ovens. Now, large, consumable electrode furnaces can produce massive titanium ingots, some weighing several tons. It took another twenty years for industry to find a use for titanium, which is six times as strong as aluminum even though it is only half again as heavy. Its first widespread use was in aircraft wing and body panel stiffeners. Thin sheets of the metal are bent in to accordion-like folds called corrugate. Sandwiched between the outer skin of an aircraft member, a wing or an appendage, the corrugate makes the panel many times as rigid as solid aluminum at a fraction of the weight.

Ironically, Russian scientists brought titanium to the American marketplace in the late 1950s. They used the work of Kroll to produce the finest metallic titanium available in the world. When American military planners wanted to build a replacement for the

U-2 spy plane—made famous for its role in aerial espionage over Russia—the CIA purchased all the titanium needed for the prototype airframes for the SR-71 Blackbird supersonic spy-planes from Russia through a shell corporation. The Soviet Union also adopted titanium as a hull material for deep-submergence submarines beginning in the late 1950s. The strength-to-weight ratio of titanium made the "Alfa"-class attack submarine the fastest, deepest-diving war machine of the 1960s and '70s. The Alfas were eventually scrapped in favor of a later model—the Sierra-class—that were then cut up for salvage when the Soviet Union collapsed in 1990. In a case of modern swords to plowshares, much of the titanium taken from the Alfa submarines was exported, where it was turned into the head of a remarkable golf club.[19]

Powder Metallurgy

The relatively old process of powder metallurgy was redefined and perfected during Second World War to manufacture many of the bits and pieces needed in complex machinery. The process begins with any metal base of known purity. The material is ground into particles and screened for consistent size. Depending on the required results, the powder may be as fine as talc or as coarse as coffee grounds. Two or more metals may be blended together while still in powder form to obtain the desired finish characteristics. The powder is then poured into steel molds that are squeezed with tremendous pressure and heat that fuses the particles together. Sometimes, the heating process is controlled to bond, but not to fuse, the material into a cohesive shape for future, finish machining. Other products, such as bronze fuel filters, come out of the mold in their final, deliverable state.

Powder metallurgy was first used for production purposes in the purification and manufacture of platinum components used in the growing chemical industry of the early nineteenth century. Nearly one hundred years later, tungsten filaments for light bulbs were made in special vacuum arc furnaces, a process still in use today. About the same time that electric bulbs were being mass produced, the automotive industry adopted powder metallurgy to manufacture sintered bronze bearings.

Sintering is an extension of powder metallurgy that takes ingots of cast bronze that are then pulverized into a flour-like dust. Oil, thickened by paraffin wax, is mixed into the bronze and pressed into cylindrical shape. The wax is vaporized under the heat of the pressing process, leaving behind the oil. In use, the oil weeps out of microscopic pores left between the particles of bronze, lubricating the bearing and rotating shaft. Until the widespread adoption of anti-friction bearings—ball and roller bearing were first devised at the beginning of the twentieth century and required a number of years to become commercially practical—sintered bronze bearings were used in all manner of machinery.[20]

Powder metallurgy came into maturity during World War Two. Parts made with new alloys, virtually impossible to manufacture by any other means, were simply made by powdered metal. Quality control was vastly improved, as contaminants could be closely monitored. Parts that were made from basic metals, such as aluminum, zinc, or nickel, could be made in far less time and effort than by conventional means. Components with a specific use, such as the pure nickel porous barriers used to separate the heavier uranium isotopes from the less frequent but desirable U235 needed for the atomic bomb, could be designed with the exact task in mind.

Powder metallurgy is still an important part of manufacturing. Thousands of consumer and industrial products, far too many to name, are made with powdered materials. These products, though, are not limited to metals, as there were two other breakthrough technologies—sintered carbide cutting tools and high-efficiency magnets—that had a bearing on the outcome of the war and for industry forever after.[21]

Tungsten Carbide Cutting Tools

At the turn of the century, a new material possessing remarkable properties was introduced to manufacturers who previously had to only cut steel. Even with the softest steels, machinists had to slowly shave their parts with high-carbon steel tools. If the tooling was run too fast or the coolant flow interrupted, the cutter would quickly dull and burn up. This remained the biggest obstacle to increasing factory production during the industrial revolution. However, the new metal, called tungsten steel resisted intense heat. In experiments, cutting speeds could be safely doubled. At the higher speeds, the tool remained sharp, which also improved the surface finish of the part, an important step to maintaining close tolerances. (See

This is a Panzerbüsche 7.5cm PaK41 tapered barrel anti-tank gun. It used solid tungsten carbide core rounds, which the Germans could not spare from their industry. (U.S. Army)

Surface Roughness Measurement in Chap. 6)

Tungsten is a metal of various, although limited uses. Hard, brittle, and gray in its unalloyed form, tungsten can be used as the filaments of light bulbs, contacts in electrical equipment, and in paint pigments. The richest ore has only about one percent of the actual metal. In the new tools, 15 to 20 percent tungsten oxide was added to steel. It was this alloy that would support the factories during the First World War and the automotive boom in Detroit. Because of its incredible strength for resisting tension, it became invaluable as an alloy in armor plate.

Then, on April 5, 1938, Philip M. McKenna received a patent for his version of metal containing tungsten, which dispensed with the steel. In his process, he combined three powders: concentrated tungsten, aluminum, and calcium carbide. The resulting reaction, generating temperatures in excess of 4000° F, rendered a block of tungsten carbide. The charcoal-gray mass was then acid leached to remove any remaining impurities and ground back into a fine powder of equal sized-grains. The powder was then placed in a high-strength steel mold after cobalt and paraffin were added to act as a binder during the pressing stage.

The tungsten carbide mixture was subjected to enormous pressure in a hydraulic press. The resulting slug was still relatively soft or "green." Partial hardening took place in an oven at about 1,200°F. The paraffin would vaporize and the cobalt would begin to plasticize, forming a permanent bond around the particles of tungsten carbide. Now about the consistency of chalk, the semi-finished blank could be machine-worked to form a finished shape through grinding, turning, and drilling. After being inspected, a final hardening occurred in a vacuum oven between 2,500° to 2,800° F.

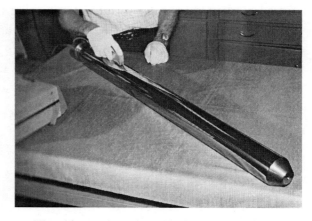

The shiny rod on the table is a solid tungsten carbide plunger. Due to the new science of powder metallurgy, custom mixtures could be produced capable of very selective qualities. The finish was ground by a diamond wheel. The device the man is holding is a surface finish tester like that described in chapter 6. With even as fine as finish that is obvious, under the types of pressures the plunger operates, the least surface defect could begin to crack, spall, or even shatter. The latter could easily kill the machine operator. Spall is a type of surface fracture that is analogous to a scab on the skin. (Kennametal)

The addition of titanium made tungsten carbide excellent for cutting all metals. Test cuts on standardized steel bars—used to maintain the integrity of the tests—showed that the tungsten-titanium carbide could make a cut four to six times faster than its nearest competitor.[22] The depth-of-cut test, a measurement that determines how much material can be removed in one pass, had similar results. With the newer steel alloys just appearing in industry, the timely innovation of tungsten-titanium carbide was remarkable. Tool steel that formerly took weeks to whittle down could now be pared off with impressive dispatch. On some machining operations, the waste chips of metal came off the base material so fast that a helper had to be assigned to shovel them into a scrap metal barrel.

At first, tungsten-alloy carbide tools were an expensive, exotic answer for exotic metals. But as carbide tools became more available, industry eagerly adopted them. Reports of remarkable performance were soon to follow. In Detroit, a machine ran out of coolant during a production cut. The tool had turned visibly red-hot—about 1,400°F—but, upon inspection, it had not been damaged and was returned to service. Managers complained that motors were being burnt out, as overzealous machinists raced to outdo each other's production output using carbide tools. Continuously boosting the machine's speed and feed rates, the motors would overheat from the load and be cooked to a crisp. However, the carbide tooling survived. Many machine tools had to have their coolant pumps up-graded to a higher output to keep the metal cool. There was no question about the carbide alloy tooling's ability to tolerate the friction heat; it could be run at a red-hot color without coolant. The coolant was to keep the base-metal chips from welding themselves into an unmanageable lump.

Besides turning the machine tool trade on its head, tungsten carbide had other uses too. Deep extrusions, like those used in manufacturing artillery shell casings, could be made more economically with solid tungsten carbide dies and drawing plungers. Because carbide has such a high resistance to abrasion—fully hardened, it can only be

Tungsten carbide inserts for turning on a lathe. They have a yellow tantalum coating meant to ease the passage of the metal chips over the top of the insert. There are thousands of shapes available plus variations of grade, composition and coatings. (Sandvik)

finish-ground with diamond-faced wheels—it proved to be an excellent material for parts that wear rapidly. Sand-blast nozzles, sleeves and bushings for slurry pumps, and rock excavators all began to have their wear parts replaced with carbide.

It was known immediately before the war that the immensely dense tungsten carbide readily pierced armor plate. Knowing this, German weapons engineers created a series of novel tapered-bore anti-tank guns that achieved an unprecedented shot velocity by applying the Gerlich principle[15]. Three gun models were produced; the 2.8-cm schwere Panzerbüsche[16] (2.8-cm sPzB 41), the 4.2-cm leichte Panzerabwehrkanone[17] 41(4.2-cm lePaK 41), and the 7.5-cm Pak41. The shells for these guns featured a unique solid tungsten-carbide core. The largest shell, combined with the high velocity, defeated the armor of any vehicle introduced, even the later super-tanks fielded by the Russians. The limiting factor for the shell, known as the AP40, was that tungsten was in very short supply and needed for manufacturing.[23]

Plant security pose for pictures in front of stacks of magnesium at a smelter south of Las Vegas. The plant's operation is only possible because of the substantial power supply from Hoover dam. (NARA)

Presently, it is estimated that if carbide, in its many grades and formulation, were to become unavailable, industrial production would immediately drop by more than half. This dense, hard, heat- and erosion-resistant metal has found itself in thousands of unlikely applications. Only three other materials surpass it in hardness: diamond, carbon boron nitride—a man-made diamond— and a few high-tech ceramics. But it cannot be denied that the invention of tungsten carbide went a long way in aiding the Allies to defeat the Axis in the production war.[24]

---

15 The Gerlich principle suggests that a projectile in a narrowing or tapered bore will be subject to exponentially increasing pressure that will translate into higher projectile velocity and range.
16 Translation; schwere Panzerbüsche: heavy tank projectile.
17 Translation; Panzerabwehrkanone: anti-tank cannon.

Magnets

Interest in magnets increased at the turn of the century with the fantastic growth of the electrical, automotive, and telecommunications industries. Magnets were going into all sorts of new products and the search was on to increase magnetic properties—technically, enlarging the coercive field—while reducing bulk. In 1926, Bell Laboratories developed a soft iron-nickel powder magnet, "Permalloy," that far out-functioned all previous magnets.

The 1930s saw a new proposal applying the well-established domain theory of magnetism. The domain theory set out those individual atoms of a metal will tend to align their fields with an external field, such as that developed by electric current. Materials containing atoms that react poorly to such stimulation are called paramagnetic substances. However, metals such as iron, nickel, or cobalt—ferromagnetic substances—respond energetically to an electrical influence. These metals radiate a magnetic field that can be assigned regions, or domains, that tend to line up in one direction, reinforcing its neighboring fields. But researchers believed that a material, to be used in permanent magnets, could be found that replicated the domain theory effects without the induction of any external force such as electricity.

With much experimentation, powdered alloys of aluminum, nickel, and cobalt were found to generate such a field. By abbreviating the names of the major components, the Bell engineers called their new magnets Alnico. Its lifting force was five to seven times that of a comparable iron magnet. By gradually changing the alloy combination, the magnetic force was increased to more than ten times that of the older iron. Smaller magnets could be made to do the same work, reducing the size of all sorts of electrical and electronic gear. Generators for vehicles and airplanes shrank in size and weight. Magnets were used in the scores of pumps, servos, solenoids, and small D.C. motors for dozens of applications on aircraft alone. Alnico magnets were placed in trash-bars, which were dragged around the thousands of war factories, picking up valuable hardware that had been inadvertently dropped. Because Alnico magnets took full advantage of powder metallurgy, thousands of them were cast as miniaturized components for speakers of headsets for radios and intercoms of fighting machines.[25]

Freon and Air Conditioning

Air conditioning was a much-sought-after dream for centuries, but to be cool and comfortable as the summer heat and humidity rises has been possible to the average person for only the last hundred years. Dr. John Gorrie developed an early version of air conditioning in Florida. He invented an ice-making machine in 1849 and, with fans blowing across the ice, used it to cool his small hospital. Further north, other buildings used similar systems, mainly getting the ice from winter lakes and storing it in icehouses. The idea worked in principle, but it did nothing to remove the moisture from the air.

Willis Carrier solved the problem of removing moisture at the turn of the century. His device, a modified boiler that used cold water and fan circulation, was not new. The true innovation of his system was the manner in which he customized the installation. He carefully measured and balanced the air flow and temperature throughout the building, getting the optimum cooling effect. Because his calculations were so exact, the air drafts that he created dried out the air even further, increasing the chill.

Carrier's successful "air conditioning" was sought out by businesses first. Among his early clients were printers and textile companies, who had long been beset by uncontrolled humidity, affecting the quality of their product. Soon, movie theaters demanded air conditioning, and by 1930, more than 300 had Carrier's machine cooling their audiences. Office buildings and stores were another early market. Managers discovered a comfortable workplace substantially increased employee efficiency and productivity. Workers came early and stayed late voluntarily just to be cool on sweltering days. Home was just too uncomfortable.

But this primitive air conditioning relied on cold water. The larger systems used a water chiller tower to reduce the water temperature through evaporation, but the cost and size of installing the equipment to support early air conditioners was enormous. With the synthesis of ammonia, a new form of compact and cheaper air conditioning was possible.

Ammonia is normally a gas that is atmospherically present in trace amounts. To form it into a liquid requires that the gas be subjected to high pressures. At these pressures, ammonia liquid is a frigid -28°F. A fan blows room temperature air over coils that contain the liquefied ammonia. As it releases the cold, the ammonia returns to gas as it travels back to the system compressor to start the cycle over again. This is the manner in which early refrigerators were transformed from mere iceboxes into modern kitchen appliances. As the ammonia system gained favor, trucks and rail companies began to adopt ammonia cooling to transport perishables. However, ammonia gas is a respiratory tract irritant—ammonia is the active ingredient in smelling salts—and when concentrated it is extremely poisonous and flammable.

In 1929, the Chicago area had at least twenty-nine fatalities due to ammonia refrigerant leaks. Two other chemicals, sulfur dioxide and methyl chloride, had lesser use as cooling agents but were just as toxic. Methyl chloridewas also explosively flammable. Due to the inherent dangers, owners of the new refrigerators began placing them outdoors.

In response to the growing danger, that same year the DuPont Company began a search for a safe replacement for ammonia. After a series of false starts, DuPont chemist Charles Midgley Jr. discovered the whole family of chemicals called chlorofluorocarbons (CFCs). The combination of chlorine and fluorine molecules, a process known as halogenation, created a refrigerant that transferred heat like its lethal predecessors. Because it had a higher boiling temperature than ammonia, it needed less pressure to convert back to a liquid, so the compressor could be smaller and work less, mak-

Fresh cauliflower getting its ice bath before the long train ride in Centerville, CA to an Eastern market. Before the adoption of chemical refrigeration with Freon, this was how fresh food stayed that way. Most ice for this is made in an industrial ice plant that uses ammonia, very dangerous for home use. (NARA)

ing the self-contained air conditioner, beginning in 1938, feasible for the homeowner.

During the coming war, Freon would play several important roles. Refrigerated ships and boxcars, previously cooled by ammonia, were refitted to handle Freon gas and served to transport fresh vegetables to market and processing plants. Foods could be safely and efficiently freeze-dried by the millions of pounds, while fresh meats were frozen and shipped in that state to American soldiers and our allies. Freon-charged air conditioners and food storage facilities were widely used in naval ships and at remote bases alike without the inherent dangers of a toxic chemical leak.

Freon had other practical applications. The nonflammable gas was used as a propellant in canned products such as paint and hair spray. Inhaled medications for asthma were sprayed by non-toxic CFCs. By adding hydrogen to the chemical mix, hydrochlorofluorocarbon (HCFC) solvents were created. This class of cleaner is very popular for washing oils and other contaminants from electronic equipment and precision bearings during the manufacturing process.[26]

Freon as an Impromptu Chilling Agent

Early in the war Dr. Lyle Goodhue of Westinghouse-Springfield initiated the use of Freon 12 to aerosolize insecticide chemicals. Large pressurized tanks were made available to the military but the tanks were cumbersome. After much effort went into developing a hand-sized spray can, an official from DuPont, the Freon manufacturer, suggested that Westinghouse be brought into the manufacture of the bug bombs. Westinghouse originally developed the refrigerator recharging cans for Freon and adapted the standard container.

Releasing one of the million-plus bug bombs the government provided. He must not have heard the news that it went better with beer. Maybe there is none available. (US Army/NARA)

The Army anticipated enormous production rates. Initial contract talks estimated 10,000 cans of insect spray a week during the production setup phase. Later, this volume would be accelerated to 10 million cans a year. Once production was underway, each can made in the nearly automatic line cost a $1.25 each. By war's end, more than 30,000,000 cans of bug spray were delivered to the military, far more than expected. Upon investigation, Westinghouse learned that our troops had made a startling discovery. A can of bug spray could be submerged inverted into a pail of water or outer helmet shell filled with bottles of beer. The Freon escaping in liquid form immediately chilled the water and refreshments alike. Undoubtedly, this makeshift beer cooler went just as far in restoring morale, as did living bug-free.[27]

Fire Extinguisher Chemicals

Even before the war began, fire suppression was to undergo a revolution of sorts with a renewed interest in the chemical nature of fire. The military in particular began to field more combustible materials such as magnesium and sodium—the latter being used in engine valves—and fuels that burned with intense heat. Fire itself became a weapon of war with the development of incendiary bombs, napalm, and fire throwers. Besides airfields, with their large arrays of fuel and bomb-laden aircraft and bulk fuel storage tanks, industrial plants and even cities were all potential targets of a much-feared fire-bombing campaign. With the proliferation of electricity, more electrical fires were to be expected as well. Plain water, the traditional choice for firefighting, was obviously not to be used on such a fire. Thus began the search for new extinguishing chemicals.

Mechanical Foam

This extinguisher is an outgrowth of soda/acid extinguishers developed in 1877, where the combination of the two chemicals resulted in a thick froth that smothered the fire. Although soda/acid was used almost universally after

Oil burning on the surface of Pearl Harbor after the Japanese launched their pre-emptive attack at American forces in the Pacific. This attack opened a forty-five month long conflict that would span the entire Pacific basin. (U.S. Navy/NARA)

1920, there were problems with it. It was inefficient for large fires, and the nozzle and hoses tended to clog. This led to the development of mechanical foam.

Foam, by its very nature, is essentially a mass of gas-filled bubbles. Being lighter than most oils, it floats on top of combustible liquids, preventing the mixture of oxygen, effectively smothering any flame or retarding the ignition of the fuel.

Differing from chemical foam, which was derived by the chemical reaction of an acid and a base, a pump was used to mix and aerate the foam solution, hence the "mechanical" term. A simple rotary pump would take in water and a foaming agent, similar to laundry soap, and discharge it through a hose. Some of the earliest agents, developed by the RAF in the mid-1930s, were derived from coconut oil.

Although the early foam proved to be inadequate, new agents were under continuous development. A whole litany of plant glycosides, called saponins, had their chance all during the 1930s in both Britain and Germany. Most were found to be of little use, as they were unstable or lacked the heat resistance of the chemical foam. In spite of the shortcomings of mechanical foam, special trucks were built to carry the necessary ingredients and pumps to deliver the foaming agents to the fire.

Protein Type Mechanical Foam

America watched the British development of foaming extinguishers from afar, apparently uninterested. However, the United States Naval Research Laboratory (NRL) was gearing up for its role in the war by quietly pursuing a slightly different approach. Realizing that saponins are just a type of plant protein, the Navy began to look to other, less soluble, materials of a similar nature.

Structurally, proteins are large molecules composed of one or more chains of amino acids. The foam was delivered in much the same way that straight mechanical foam was, by mixing water with foam concentrates. Derived from natural sources, these protein foam concentrates contained a combination of processed animal and vegetable fats and metallic salts, such as aluminum sulfate, to aid in the strengthening of the bubbles. An organic solvent helped the foam to spread evenly under any temperature. The new Navy foam was far superior to its British counterpart, having more heat resistance, stability, and resistance to burn-through.[28]

Fire was a constant danger whether working with aircraft or ordnance. In this case, an airplane has been destroyed by an enemy attack. Quick action by ground crew and the use of mechanical foam kept the damage from spreading to other machines. It is clear to see how the foam clings to surfaces, even vertically. (OWI/NARA)

Wetting Agents

In the 1930s, synthetic detergents arrived on the market, quickly displacing the traditional soaps of yesteryear. One of the most remarkable advantages to these detergents was their ability to simultaneously cling to and repel water. Because of this dual affinity, chemically modified detergents were added to mechanical foam as a wetting agent. With this additive, the expansion ratio of the foam was about 20 to 1, more than double the expansion rate of mechanical foam alone. Translated, three gallons of concentrate containing this "high expansion" additive would produce 1,000 gallons of foam, usually more than enough to extinguish a small aircraft fire.

In addition to the greater coverage provided by wetting agents, there was an immense reduction in the surface tension of the water. Even without the presence of foam concentrates, the lowered water tension improved penetration, flow, and diffusion, allowing the water to get into nooks and crannies with much less difficulty.[29]

Sub-surface Foam Applicators

The U.S. Navy relied heavily on enormous stores of fuel contained in large aboveground tanks. Although there were few deliberate attacks on these facilities—the Japanese attack on Pearl Harbor virtually ignored this Achilles' heel, leaving intact several hundred thousand gallons of practically irreplaceable fuel oil stored in plain sight at the Hawaiian base—the navy wanted to be prepared. Beginning in 1943, tests were carried out in Ohio to develop and perfect a way to extinguish a tank farm fire from within. A special foam—having low water content and only a 4% expansion ratio—was derived from standard mechanical foam. By the time the work had reached the stage of fielding the equipment to generate the special mixture, the war was nearly over and the project was dropped.

In 1965, the Mobil Oil Company revived the navy's foam system and applied it to their own tank farms. The only difference between the two systems was that they were now using an improved version of the World War Two extinguishing agent with fluorine as an added ingredient.[30]

Halogenated Fire Extinguishers

Halogenation is one of those miracles of chemistry that were coming out of the laboratory during the first thirty years of the twentieth century. The process takes a known flammable substance, a hydrocarbon in need of oxygen to burn, and combines it with a chemical that has an excess of oxygen—an oxidizer. The resulting gas, or liquid if held under pressure, makes an excellent fire-extinguishing agent.

The first of the halogenated suppressants, carbon tetrachloride, was introduced in 1907. It was in use only a few years when it was realized that the decomposed chemical was highly toxic and had killed and injured a number of its users. The replacement for carbon tetrachloride was just as toxic and, under limited circumstances, flammable itself. The latter compound, methyl bromide, was a near kin to carbon tetrachloride, the difference being the use of a bromine molecule in place of the chlorine molecules.

During the war, Germany adopted a composite of the two failed extinguishers, chlorobromomethane. It was primarily used on their naval and merchant fleets with good results. After the war, the formula was to find its way into aircraft of the Army Air Force. However, another, more efficient halogenated had already been invented, although no one knew it. With the development of Freon refrigerant gases, it was only a short step to add a couple of fluorine molecules. This finally occurred in 1947 and, for three years, it was extensively tested. In 1950, the American military slowly adopted "Halon" fire extinguishers for applications where the contaminating powders of dry chemicals or the wet messiness of foam would ruin valuable equipment such as computers, electronics, or machinery.

Shot onto a fire, Halon would interfere with the fuel/air chemical reaction needed to maintain the flames. It left no residue, so it could be used on the most delicate equipment without causing more damage. Sprayed on flammable liquids, such as gasoline, Halon had the added benefit that it resisted re-ignition. Heavier than air, Halon envelopes the fuel puddle, blocking the supply of oxygen just like its wet cousin, foam. In confined spaces, for example, on a submarine, Halon was an excellent fire retardant. Tests showed that it could replace up to 20% of the atmosphere without harmful effects on humans.[31]

Due to environmental concerns, chlorofluorocarbon- and hydro-chlorofluorocarbon-based refrigerant gases (CFCs and HCFCs) are now banned worldwide, with overuse has been cited as the reason for the depletion of the ozone layer. New refrigerant chemicals are now coming onto the market after some years of development.

Fueling the War Effort: High Octane Fuels

The hydrocarbon molecular chains can be categorized by their makeup. The simplest form of fossil fuels, methane, is created when one carbon atom unites with four hydrogen atoms. The linkage is so simple that it requires very little pressure or heat to form. As the atomic structures increase in complexity, more force is needed to cause the union. When the number of carbon molecules increases, so does the boiling point. Gases such as methane, ethane, and propane are all simple hydrocarbons. Heaviest compounds like asphalt, tar and paraffin wax are massive chemical structures, having dozens of carbon atoms.

Because of the consistent arrangement of fossil fuel chemistry, the molecular structure can be shaped and changed nearly at will. The larger chains can be "cracked," in much the same way that little rocks can be made from larger ones. Through a process of "cracking," a fossil fuel like oil can be broken down to form heating oil, kerosene, and gasoline. Cracking, which requires a great deal of pressure and heat, breaks the oil's constituent molecules apart. A 55-gallon barrel of crude oil that is cracked might render forty gallons of heating oil, ten of gasoline and fractional quantities of tar, paraffin, and asphalt. As in the rock metaphor, smaller chips of hydrocarbons are created in the formation of waste gases like ethane and propane, which are burned off at the refinery.

Besides cracking, oil can be processed into gasoline through another process called "polymerization." The exact opposite of cracking, polymerization takes small, gaseous particles of hydrocarbons and reconstructs larger molecules, much like gluing the broken pieces of rock back together again. The advantages of polymerization are that specific oil products can be obtained and that waste products like methane can be utilized. Polymerization is the process invented by Standard Oil of New Jersey, which was so naively given to I.G. Farben as a lure to get the synthetic rubber formulas in trade. During the war, the Germans successfully used polymerization to turn coal, with an enormous hydrocarbon chain, into usable fuels for their armed forces. Without any domestic sources of crude oil, Germany was forced to resort to polymerization. One hundred tons of dry coal could yield 62 tons of gasoline and 28 tons of gaseous fuel and ashy residue. The process was hardly economical, though. For every ton of coal that went into the high-pressure chambers at the refinery, another ton had to burn to run the plant.

As the Germans filled their fuel reservoirs with polymerized gasoline, the American oil firm, Humble Oil and Refining Company (now better known as Exxon) installed new process equipment for alkylation. First discovered three years earlier, in 1935, the process originator, Dr. S.F. Birch, combined isobutane and butylene with a catalyst of sulfuric acid. The resulting chemical was still 100-octane gasoline, but now with alkylation, production at Humble tripled. By 1943, fifty-five American refineries had cold acid alkylation, as it became know, facilities. In that year, industry estimates were that 15 million gallons a day of 100/130-octane aviation gas were produced. Within two years, that output would exceed 25 million gallons a day.[32]

High Octane Fuel

An alert goes out to RAF fighter fields that a flight of German bombers is approaching the English coast. Supermarine Spitfires and Hawker Hurricanes race off to meet the incoming threat. As they gain altitude, the twelve-cylinder, supercharged Merlin engines power the British fighters flawlessly through 20,000 feet. The pilots marvel at the fact that their planes do not begin to stagger and choke in the rarefied air. In the fuel tanks is a new fuel formula received from America a few days previously. What they were using for the first time was high-octane aviation gasoline.

Not all gasoline is created equal. In the cracked form, gasoline has seven or eight carbon molecules. One molecular structure called octane has eight carbon atoms. On each exposed side of the carbon atom string reside 18 hydrogen atoms. When this particular formulation burns in the standard internal combustion engine, it flashes so rapidly that the expanding gases pound the walls of the cylinder, causing an annoying and destructive pre-ignition phenomenon called knock. Over the years, no less than 33,000 additives were tried to eliminate ignition knock. Tetraethyl lead proved to be the answer to knocking but it fouled the engines' inner workings. Another additive, ethylene bromide, became available in 1933. With these two additives, ethyl gasoline became widely popular with the motoring public. However, tetraethyl lead was not only expensive, at $585 a pound, but it came from Germany. With the increased demand, a process to manufacture tetraethyl lead from lead and ethyl alcohol was soon set up in the United States. These added ingredients were perfectly acceptable for the largely peacetime period of the 1930s, but once the shooting war broke out, the manufacturing capacity was stretched to the limit and beyond.

Fortunately, since the late 1920s chemists had been at work trying to modify the basic formulation of the octane molecule. In a game of musical atoms, they had relocated three of the carbon atoms away from the original carbon chain. Eighteen hydrogen atoms remained, but their positions made the new fuel, called iso-octane, burn more slowly. At first, iso-octane cost more than $300 a gallon, but improvements to production procedures brought the price down to a more reasonable $9 a gallon. At this price, iso-octane is still too expensive to use regularly for general fuel, but it performs so well as a gasoline it became the standard by which all other formulas are measured.

A scale of knock, called the octane rating or octane number, was devised in which one hundred represented the total absence of knock. With the research and experience derived from iso-octane's development, other formulations could be tried. Improved performance came with the higher octane number fuels because they burned cooler. The lower temperature meant that less fuel was being turned into waste heat, which in turn went out the exhaust pipes, or into the engine block. A hotter running engine also tended to wear out sooner, requiring expensive and time-consuming replacement. Most importantly to the Allied air forces, the slower burning gas was less altitude sensitive.

100 octane fuels arrived in Britain in May of 1940 and were immediately distributed to the beleaguered RAF fighter squadrons. The effects were immediate and irrefutable. Top speed was boosted by an average of 20 knots, or about 35 miles an hour. Ceiling, the maximum of designed flight which is limited by engine performance, improved by 2000 feet or more. Rate of climb, the ability to get to the altitude where interception of bombers was possible, was enhanced from forty to sixty percent over the old fuel. Unable to replicate Allied gasoline, the German fighter forces lost the technical advantages they had enjoyed during the early days of the war. Generally considered to be better at speed and maneuverability until then, Luftwaffe pilots discovered that they could not outrun the RAF even at the high altitudes that had previously given them some protection.[33]

Methyl Methacrylate Ester

Besides being a tongue twister, this sinister-sounding chemical compound was a critical material in winning the Second World War on the Russian front. Methyl methacrylate ester is a close relative to the basic chemical formula for acrylic plastics including the tough, clear plastic called Plexiglas, which was invented in Germany in 1931. However, while the work on Plexiglas was underway in both Germany and America, one of the research chemists associated with the American project discovered that the associated alcohol-based ester had the remarkable ability to prevent oil from thickening, regardless of its temperature.

A patent was taken out on the ester compound, but it remained a curiosity despite its obvious uses. At the outbreak of the war, American government officials combed the files of the U.S. Patent Offices for lost or forgotten ideas that might have a use in the present emergency. There, duly filed away, was the formula and a description of the remarkable methyl methacrylate ester.

This time, the importance of the chemical compound's anti-freezing qualities was not ignored. With government sponsorship, tests proved that the entire patent claimed was true and barrels of the compound were soon on their way overseas. Sent to the frigid Eastern Front, methyl methacrylate ester was added to the many oils that were being used in all sorts of mechanisms. Artillery pieces need oil for the recuperator—the device needed to slow down the recoiling barrel after the weapon is fired. Aircraft have up to a dozen functions that are operated by hydraulic or lubricating oils. Ground vehicles use oils for lubrication, steering and suspension. In the winter of 1942, encircling Russian troops trapped the Germans at Stalingrad. The Russian's equipment, well saturated with methyl methacrylate ester, worked without a hitch. On the other hand, the Germans were had difficulties getting their machinery to start in the bitter Russian winter, which often dipped to -30°F at night. Added to the failure of the Luftwaffe to supply their comrades from the air, Stalingrad became the turning point of the Eastern Front.[34]

Notes/Selected References

1   Stokely James. *Science Remakes Our World*. 1946. Pp. 151-152.
2   ibid. Pp.145-147.
3   Warrick, Dr. Earl L. *Forty Years of Firsts*. *1990*. P. 21.
4   Rochow, Eugene. *Silicon and Silicone*. 1987. and Warrick, Dr. Earl L. *Forty Years of Firsts*. *1990*.
5   Denison, Merril. *Bristles and Brushes*. 1949. P.104.
6   Fenichell. Stephen. *Plastic, The Making of a Synthetic Century*. 1996. Pp. 134-174. and Simonds, Herbert R. Pp.117-130.
7   Wheeler, Keith. *Bombers Over Japan*. 1982. P. 111.
8   ibid. P. 37.
9   Fenichell, Stephen. Pp. 212-218. and Stokely James. Pp. 43-44.
10 ibid. Pp. 176-223, 253-254.
11 Boyce, Joseph . *New Weapons for Air Warfare*. 1947. P. 123.
12 Stokely James. Pp. 143-144. and *Industrial Engineering Chemistry*. May 1939. P. 563.
13 Bailey, Ronald H. *Home Front U.S.A*. Time-Life Books. 1977. P. 181.
14 ibid. P. 84.
15 Simonds, Herbert R. Pp. 229-245.
16 Sullivan, John W.W. *The Story of Metals*. 1951. Pp. 181-193. Oberg, Franklin D. Jones, and Holbrook L. Horton. *Machinery's Handbook* 23rd Edition. 1988. Pp. 590-604.
17 Sullivan, John W.W. Pp. 193-199. and Oberg, Erik. P. 605. and Stokely, James. Pp. 133-134.
18 Rhodes, Richard. *The Making of the Atomic Bomb*. 1988. Pp. 159-164 and 578-80.
19 Sullivan, John W.W. Pp. 217-219. McNeil, Ian. *An Encyclopedia of the History of Technology*. 1990. Pp. 141-144. Clancy, Tom. *Submarine*. 1993. P. 257.
20 Stokely, James. P. 123. and footnote P. 123.
21 Sullivan, John W.W. Pp. 128-135. Rhodes, Richard. *The Making of the Atomic Bomb*. 1988. Pp. 493-946.

22 McCarthy, Willard J. *Machine Tool Technology*. 1968. Pp. 557, 513-515.

23 Bishop, Chris, Editor. The Encyclopedia of the Weapons of World War II.1998. P.185

24 Bateman, Alan M. *Economic Mineral Deposits* 2nd ed. 1950. Pp. 598-599. Kennametal, Inc. *Properties and Proven Uses of Kennametal Hard Carbide Alloys*. Company flier. 1977. Pp. 3-38.

25 Stokely James. Pp.123-126.

26 Raymond, Leonard. Today's Fuels and Lubricants and How They Got That Way. Reprinted In *History of Aircraft Lubricants*. 1997. P. 67.

27 Woodbury, David O. *Battlefronts of Industry: Westinghouse in World War II*. 1948. Pp. 143-149.

28 Tuve, Richard L. *Principles of Fire Protection Chemistry*. 1976. P. 167. Bryan, John L. *Fire Suppression and Detection Systems*. 1993. P. 89.

29 ibid. Pp. 91-92, 331-332.

30 ibid. Pp. 147-148.

31 ibid. Pp. 192-199.

32 Ogston, Alexander R. *A Short History of Aviation Gasoline Development. 1903-1980.* Published in History of Aircraft Lubricants. Society of Automotive Engineers. 1997. Pp. 10-11.

33 Stokely, James. Pp. 24- 34.

34 Fenichell, Stephen. Pp. 217-218.

10

Down on the Farm: Agricultural Science and Machinery

Soon after the First World War ended in 1918, government price supports, intended to make sure the American farmer would survive, disappeared, as did the foreign sales of food. Thus, the agricultural economy was thrown into a depression—ten years before the 1929 Wall Street crash—that forecast the despair and gloom that would grip America and, eventually, the world. By the time the Wall Street meltdown came about, the American farm was dying from the agony of years of financial neglect. In 1920, 31 million farmers accounted for 27% of America's working population. Ten years later, the number had dropped to barely above twenty percent, or about 30 million. Although productivity was up, the glut of product forced prices to an all-time low. Market prices

El Cerrito, San Miguel County, NM. Using the irrigation practice of breaking down the berms. Looking at their farm in photos, it seems to be barely a subsistence operation. The acreage under plow is minimal and there is no mechanization. Most telling, all the labor, plowing, planting, weeding is done by hand. (NARA)

were a fraction of production costs. In response, the farmers staged a number of well-publicized protests in which they destroyed their crops rather than accept a pittance for them.[1]

By the mid-1930s, American farms were in bad condition. Farm practices over the years had depleted the ground of vital nutrients and moisture. Clear-cutting of fields and buffer zones had created a flat plain that the wind whipped across relentlessly. Plowing furrows without regard to the natural drainage lessened the ground's ability to slow the flow and retain the runoff.

Worse, Mother Nature refused to cooperate. The 1930s saw some of the worst weather in memory or recorded fact. Alternating floods and drought pounded much of the heartland. In the South, the relentless sun broiled the tired soil to a light, powdery dust. Winds picked it up, transporting it east. On May 11, 1934, one terrible wind-storm blew topsoil from the central states of Oklahoma and Texas all the way to the East Coast. Airplanes attempted to fly above the dust cloud but were limited by the crafts' ceiling. In New York and Washington D.C., dust blotted out the sun at mid-day. Two hundred miles out in the Atlantic Ocean, ships' masters reported dirt falling onto their decks. It was estimated that this one storm had removed 300 million tons of irreplaceable soil, enough to cover the entire state of Rhode Island with almost three inches of additional dirt.[2]

In the Northern and the Gulf Coast states, flooding was the rule. Hills under cultivation eroded away as runoff from the rains dug great trenches into the slope. Unchecked rivers, running red with sediment, washed out lowland farms, towns and roads. In Georgia, a chasm was cut where a schoolhouse had once stood on the side of a hill. If the building had remained where it was originally, it would be suspended two hundred feet over the center of the newly formed canyon.[3]

President Roosevelt understood the importance of a stable and strong agricultural base. He initiated a num-

Georgia, 1940. A farmer plowing the field behind a draft horse. For a Depression-era farmer, having two animals is fairly wealthy. Tractors are soon to come into use, not from the desire to retire the animal but to improve the production of all farm acreage. (NARA)

ber of policies to assist the farmers and protect the American farm. In the first hundred days of the new administration, the majority of federal legislation directly concerned itself with agricultural issues. These laws and policies would bolster the farmers, allowing them to go on to feed much of the world during the next war.

Beginning with the Depression, food production and agriculture in general became an important component to a foreseeable domino effect. Without the intervention of the Federal government during the Depression, it is doubtful that the United States could have supplied a fraction of the food needed by the Allied nations. In a replay of the submarine tactics used in the First World War, Germany would have succeeded in defeating Britain. Without a free and defensible Britain, the Allied forces would not have had a base from which to launch attacks into northern Europe. Under this scenario, Hitler's dream of a "thousand-year Reich" was all too possible.

Soil Conservation

Even though it was a Depression-era program designed to rehabilitate the American farm, the government's Soil Conservation Service was even more important during the war to increase harvest yields. The Soil Conservation Service was set up to teach farmers how to work the land and protect it. During the war years alone, more than 1.2 billion acres of land were rehabilitated from neglect dating back to the Depression. It is incalculable as to how much food came from this acreage in support of the Allied war effort.

Erosion is taking the edge of this field. Erosion is a natural and necessary process. Erosion on the scale of the Depression era devastated thousands of square miles.

Contoured Plowing

Plowing involves turning and shaping the ground to form a corduroy pattern of high dirt—the berm—and valleys called furrows. The most efficient way of plowing was to form the furrows in a straight line, regardless of the slope or three-dimensional shape of the land. These created natural ruts that rain water could follow, washing away the soil. By contrast, contouring slows water as it runs off the slope. The shape of the terrain is taken into account when the plowing is planned. Furrows are cut at approximately right angles to the slope. The berms then become a series of small dams, each capable of retaining a portion of the runoff, which never gains enough velocity to wash away significant amounts of soil.

Government engineers and survey teams scattered across America, plotting out their suggested changes. Plans in hand, farmers began to plow the now-familiar sinuous patterns across the land. On the steeper slopes, the land was abandoned to grass, and trees were planted. In some instances, flat steps were cut into the hillsides, creating terraces. Terracing, however, was the exception to the rule, as the costs of moving the excess soil usually outweighed the benefits. As very few farms were on perfectly flat ground, most farmers adopted contour planning, which was entirely voluntary.

Again, as with soil conservation efforts, the benefit of contour plowing to the war effort was vast but there could be no way to subjectively place a value on the results.

Crop Rotation

Crop rotation is another innovation carried forward from the Depression. Farmers consistently planted the same fields year after year with the same crops. This tended to deplete the soil of nutrients. With crop rotation, fields were planted in alternate seasons with high-value crops such as corn, tobacco or cotton, and then allowed to rest with other, less stressful plants such as herbal vetch, rye, and Lespedeza, an annual legume native to the South. It was found that crop rotation with edible legumes — peanuts, peas, beans, and so on — returned considerable quantities of nitrogen to the soil, restoring its fertility.

The rotation method not only restored the ground to usefulness, it helped to lessen erosion. Nutrient-packed dirt has a greater amount of decomposing organic material — stems, leaves, bits of wood, weeds — that absorbs and holds water. With the moisture, fertile soil clings together, making it harder to wash away. Low-growing legumes provide further protection from hard rains by their canopy-like leaves and tight root systems that stabilize the soil.

Grasses and other ground cover were studied for these same characteristics. Research scientists also looked for drought and disease resistance. Species of grass were systematically bred with the desired properties; quite a few of the modern turf grasses were developed during this time.[4] The gullies, if not diverted and filled in, were planted with kudzu, an insidious, fast-growing vine from Asia which has virtually taken over sections of the South, clogging ditches and invading fields where it fouls up the farm machinery.

Waterways and Flood Control

1946 Dakota sugar beet fields. Mommy is in the field helping bring in the crop. All hands were needed for times such as this; although Junior is a bit small to be operating a tractor. The simple harvester behind scoops up the beets and drops them on the conveyor where they then drop into a trailer. No doubt that it had to be emptied, allowing time for this break. (NARA)

Through the Soil Conservation Service and the federal Department of Reclamation, rivers, particularly those with older, poorly maintained dams, were dredged out. The soil was salvaged and returned to nearby fields that suffered the worst damage from erosion. A number of new masonry dams were built to halt the free flow of water and to act as reservoirs during dry years. One system of twenty-five dams in the Tennessee River Valley, the TVA, served not only for water storage but also provided electric power and regulated the river level to provide predictable commercial barge transportation.

At the turn of the century, a number of dams were planned for the western United States, but construction was constantly delayed for political and financial reasons. The Depression provided the impetus to build them at Federal expense. No less than eleven dams, all of them more than two hundred feet high, were built between 1930 and 1948 in five states. Hoover Dam, straddling the Nevada–Arizona border, provided water, energy, and flood protection for southern California and six other states. In Washington, the Grand Coulee dam supplied power to the great aircraft factories and shipyards around Puget Sound. A series of dams on the Missouri river stretched from Montana to South Dakota. Fort Peck dam, an earth and rock-filled structure finished in 1940, held the record for fill volume — 125,825 million cubic yards[5] — until 1973.

All this water opened up previously untenable farmland. By the eve of America's entry into the war, crop yields were, on the average, up more than one hundred percent. For some grains such as corn, the increase might be as much as five-fold. In light of the production needs for the world war, the soil conservation plan was very timely. Had the program not gone into effect, the number of dead from starvation, especially in the famine-threatened post-war years when America was feeding the not only Allies but the defeated countries as well, probably would have been counted in the millions.[6]

Multi-Stage Submersible Well Pumps

The dust bowl effect created by the droughts of the 1930s wreaked havoc on the central United States. The farming practices of the time caused the loss of thousands of acres of productive farmland. One hindrance to effective crop management was the inability to draw water efficiently from well sources during drought.

The hardware necessary to irrigate the fields was beginning to make its way onto the farm with the introduction of the centrifugal pump in 1930. This submersible pump worked better than the reciprocating pump first used in the 1870s. One drawback to the centrifugal, besides its cost, was that it was limited in size relative to volumetric capacity. For the farmer to pump a greater volume of water, the pump's overall size would have to be appreciably increased. This required that a larger well be dug, which could be cost-prohibitive.

The advent of the jet well pump in 1938 solved this problem. This submersible pump had a series of fins (impellers) mounted on a common shaft. Each impeller set was housed in a bell-shaped casing threaded onto the next casing. As the impeller rotated, water was drawn into the lower-most casing. Pressurized by the spinning blades, the water was forced upward into the next casing, a process continuously repeated for every casing/impeller set. The simple modular design allowed the farmer to increase the pump's capacity with the addition of casings and corresponding impeller sets. Since the diameter of the pump never changed, the same well could be used for any volume pump, the well capacity being limited only by the volume of the existing water table.

FAIRBANKS-MORSE
Deep Well Turbine Pumps
Sizes 4" to 20"
Capacities 20 to 3000 G.P.M.

Fairbanks - Morse turbine pumps are essentially vertical multi-stage centrifugal pumps for pumping considerable quantities of water from deep wells. They are simple but sturdily built to withstand severe service. Only the highest grade of materials are used, being chosen and proportioned for mechanical strength in excess of requirements as well as for wear and corrosion - resisting qualities. Their efficiency is high but without sacrifice of wearing qualities. These pumps are compact, dependable units, made in a range of sizes

The turbine is highly flexible without changing the size of the well. Just up-grade the motor horsepower and add more turbine stages. The introduction of pumps like this made electrification of the farm an imperative. (Fairbanks-Morse)

Eventually the motor would have to be upgraded to a larger horsepower rating, but these costs were a fraction of drilling a new well. These pumps became very popular during and after the war and continue to be used, on the majority of farms that irrigate.[7]

Siphon Tubes

Once the irrigating farmer gets the water out of the ground, he needs to move it to the fields. The standard practice for centuries has been to construct a network of ditches and channels to allow the water to run freely. These channels are placed at the edges of the fields, separated by embankments of dirt. The commonly used method of delivering the water to the field was to knock a hole through the bank, letting the water flow onto the field. Not only was this time-consuming, requiring rebuilding of the banks, but also the water volume delivered to the center of the field was far less than that nearest the channels.

Farmhand in central Arizona is setting siphon tube over the field berm. It is clear how easy they set, which is a good thing. Looking at the size of the fields, he's got plenty to do. (NARA)

When the war broke out, a shortage of farm labor became a chronic problem. It was no longer feasible to rebuild dikes every time a field was irrigated. One farmer, Harold Warp of Minden, Nebraska, devised the siphon- tube irrigation method. The tube's profile resembles a bicycle handlebar, a shallow double S shape. Made of salvaged electrical conduit forty inches long, it had an eleven-inch radius bend in the center and smaller counter-bends at each end. In this shape, water could be diverted from the main water channel and over the bank without damaging the embankment. The simple task of charging the siphon tube consisted no more than a simple flick of the wrist, which filled the tube with water. The resulting siphon effect would pull a steady stream onto the field until the tube was lifted, breaking the flow. One farmhand could start the flow and place the tubes at the rate of five a minute. By placing the tubes at every furrow, the volume of water delivered was equalized, netting an increased crop yield.

When the Nebraska Agriculture Service agent saw the tubes in operation, the innovative farmer was asked to produce them in volume. Skeptical about the demand, Warp reluctantly began production. Time has proved his cynicism to be unfounded, as millions of these simple tubes have been sold and are still used today.[8]

Hydroponics

Growing food without dirt. This concept became popular in the late 1960s as the farm of the future. Some of the benefits touted were that pests could be effectively controlled, seasonal produce would be available year-round, and crop yields would be greatly enhanced. Additionally, the dangers of soil contaminants could be strictly regulated, as only the nutrients for optimum growth would be introduced into the growth medium.

Surprisingly, this was not a new concept. In 1860, research into plant nutrients showed that the necessary chemicals were absorbed through the roots after being dissolved in water. The plant could then separate the nutrients within its structure as needed. The development of artificial fertilizers at the turn of the century was a direct outcome of this early research into botanical nutrition. It led to a standard chemical formula that is still very much in use today.

In 1936, two scientists at the University of California published a report on growing tomatoes in a water/nutrient solution. Their method relied on the plants growing on a mesh screen set over the nutrient-enriched water. The root mass would then grow through the screen to reach the water. By adjusting the space between the water and the screen, the researchers could control the amount of oxygen getting to the roots. The technique they proposed could be duplicated only with some difficulty, however, and it got little attention. A few commercial farmers attempted the system, as did several agricultural colleges in the desire to improve upon it.[9]

One modification came from Purdue University, where gravel was used as a replacement for the screen. The first large farms using this method, called Nutriculture, were built for the military as a test program on the Ascension Islands in the Atlantic. This barren rock was an important waypoint for transporting troops to Africa and the Mediterranean. The large contingent of service personnel stationed there required large quantities of foodstuffs that had had to be brought in by plane or ship. Working with the Department of Agriculture, the test program was expanded. Hydroponic gardens were constructed in several selected bases overseas, Okinawa and Iwo Jima among others, supplying the men with badly needed fresh vegetables.[10]

Immediately after the war, the largest hydroponics facility built to date was constructed in Japan. The Japanese custom of fertilizing the crops with human excreta made the American occupation troops ill from bacterial contamination. These new facilities provided the soldiers with a safe supply of vegetables, freeing the Japanese farmers to grow enough to feed their starving countrymen in the traditional way.[11]

Post-war American hydroponics became quite popular in the Deep South, mainly around Florida. But these facilities struggled with exposure to the weather, poor management, and shoddy construction. The materials used, even on the well-built ones, became a source of trouble. Chemicals in the concrete and pipes leached into the nutrient solution, poisoning the crops. But even with the problems, hydroponics gained favor, especially in situations where produce was economically unavailable from other sources.

Over the years, solutions for the different obstacles have been implemented. The few die-hard individuals who could see the benefits of hydroponics have made steady strides towards making the idea economical. One great advance came with the introduction of plastics. Tanks, pipes, pumps and weather shields made from the novel new materials reduced the incidence of contamination. The birth of electronic controls made managing the nutrient levels and atmosphere within the plastic hothouses easier to monitor and manipulate. Although many of our foodstuffs are still grown in the traditional manner, hydroponics has made the availability of fresh food in quantity, regardless of the weather or other conditions, a real possibility.

Aerial Spraying

As new chemical pesticides became available and gained acceptance, methods of dispersing them had to be developed. The Department of Agriculture developed a practical method of dusting cotton fields with calcium arsenate for boll weevil in 1922. Even though the test was successful, spraying from low-flying airplanes

An A-20 Intruder dumping pesticide, probably DDT, on the island of Corsica. Note how the chemical is dropping in one large clump, instead of diffusing over a wide area. This is one of the military's early attempts to dust for mosquitos from the air. Later, dusting spray bars would have far better results. (NARA)

411

continued to be the exception to the rule. Farms during the pre-war years were small—averaging 157 acres—a fact which made the technique uneconomical. In addition, skeptical farmers worried that the noise of the airplane buzzing low overhead would spook the animals, often their only means of working the fields.

With the outbreak of war, aerial spraying got renewed interest, but not for crops. The military had a vested interest in eradicating the mosquito in the South Pacific. Casualties from malaria were decimating the ranks, making the disease more dangerous than the Japanese army. The British campaign in Burma faced enormous losses to several jungle diseases, the most common being malaria. In 1943, they had to evacuate 120 ill men for every one wounded soldier. Similar experiences for the Americans occurred. On Guadalcanal, 10,206 U.S. Army cases were reported between March and December 1943. Hospitalization was the fate 80% of the First Marine Division that same period. The Mediterranean Theater was no better. For the same 1943 period, there were more than 69,000 cases of malaria requiring treatment. 1.2% were evacuated to Stateside hospitals.[12]

Spray units were shipped to the affected areas and adapted to fit available airplanes. Scouts and light trainers had the first nozzle bars fitted. Capable of slow flight at grass-top heights, the light planes carried a militarized version of a commercial spray rig. Subsequent trials were made using B-25 Mitchell and A-20 Havoc light bombers. This original design featured a wind-driven pump that pressurized a chemical solution tank. Liquid insecticide from the tank flowed through a set of pipes placed under the wings of the plane. Forced through a series of nozzles in the pipes, the fluid was atomized to drop to the ground. Results were moderately satisfactory, but complaints about weight, drag, and uneven application were voiced.[13]

The small planes were too underpowered to spread the insecticide effectively, especially in wooded swamps. The downdraft was found to be insufficient to drive the vapor through the brush into the water where it could do the most good. A lighter, more aerodynamic spray bar was built, and this design has lasted, pretty much unchanged, until the present day.

The modified bar was built in the Pacific theater with the aid of the U.S. Navy. Two tubes, set several feet apart, are attached to the bottom of the front wings. Tiny holes allow the fluid to spray out as before, but instead of nozzles, the spray strikes a solid concave surface that causes the spray to disintegrate into a uniformly fine mist. Turbulence from the air flowing past the wings spreads the micro-droplets out into a fan-shaped fog. By carefully regulating the airspeed, solution flow, and spray-hole sizes, a precise dosage of pesticide can be delivered with predictable results. Small aircraft were used in certain circumstances but C-47s had spray equipment fitted so that large flat areas, such as Manila, could be treated faster.[14]

Even before the end of the war, this new spray bar had been placed into service on American farms. A campaign to promote the benefits of aerial spraying was undertaken by federal, state, and county agriculture agencies to sell the concept. The few commercial sprayers who were available were recruited to train more pilots in low altitude maneuvers, sometimes measured in just a few feet. Precious aircraft and fuel were released to augment the spraying fleet. Yet newer formulations were created to deal with pests that damaged the forests, a problem that had been virtually ignored until the war.

A C-47 sprays for mosquitos over Manila. This is during summer 1945; the Japanese have been largely chased out of the Philippine capital. Compare the previous photo of the A-20 clump bombing the bugs and the good aerosolized spray emanating from this plane. (U.S. Army/NARA)

Although aerial spraying is not a panacea, it constitutes a major development for the control of a great many insects. The primary pesticide used during and in the years after the war, DDT, has been removed from use. Environmental concerns are now limiting the use of wholesale spraying. New classes of chemicals are being sought that do not destroy wildlife which eventually consumes the poisons. Regardless of the chemical, aerial spraying as a method of delivery is just another tool we have today as a result of the Second World War.[15]

Ground-Based Insecticide Blowers

Like its aerial cousin, the ground blower was first developed in 1922. This work actually was an outgrowth of the aerial spraying program when it was realized that airdropped insecticides could not reach under the dense canopy of trees and certain crops. Using aircraft engines mounted on trailers, engineers attempted to blow liquefied chemicals onto a variety of plants under differing conditions. The tests culminated in a few machines that did a mediocre job. The idea was dropped because the equipment was too bulky, required too much water, and the results were too uncertain. A number of machines were again introduced during the Depression to spray chemicals into the air from the ground. Similarly, these all proved to be woefully inadequate.

In 1940, a machine that used high-velocity, low-pressure air held promise. It took another three years of work— more important war work interrupted the project—to perfect it. Utilizing a tractor, the chemical, either dust or liquid, was shot through a three-and-a-half-inch hose. A fan, spinning at 4,000 RPM, creates the 160 MPH draft necessary to eject the atomized pesticide over 70 feet. Later development work showed that a larger volume of air at greater velocity would drive the chemicals further. Additionally, the atomizing would be more complete, and the area covered would be greater.

A post-war axial blower can get any pesticide into the thickest foliage.at the far end of this machine is a tractor, the driver's head is just visible. (Dept. of Agriculture)

This inspired the creation of the axial-flow blower. Cheaper to build and operate, the air blower could now hit vegetation from 125 feet away. At 100 feet, the chemical fan was eighteen to twenty feet wide. In one instance, a droplet cascade was catapulted more than three hundred feet by a blower using a twenty-five horsepower engine.

Development work continued after the war. The axial flow fan has now been replaced by the jet engine. (More on this in Chap. 2.) Beginning in the late 1950s, small turbo-jets became available that out-performed the early models.[16]

Organo-Phosphates: The Insecticide from Hell

DDT, a chlorine-based chemical, was synthesized in 1939. Hailed as a wonder weapon in the war on insects, it would be pitched about during the Second World War with reckless abandon. By the 1970s, the environmental effects had become all too evident and DDT was removed from the market. However, another class of insecticides was discovered just prior to DDT. Not only do these chemical compounds, called organo-phosphates, survive until the present, but under a different name, they tend to chill the hearts of all humankind: Tabun and Sarin nerve gases.

In a laboratory of the I.G. Farben chemical company, German scientist Dr. Gerhard Schrader was investigating a new line of research. His goal had been insecticides when he accidentally created a complex ester—ethyl NN-dimethyl-phosphoramidocyanidate. He originally did not appreciate the gravity of his serendipitous discovery, though an initial test on leafhoppers showed that a dilution of one part in 200,000 immediately killed an entire colony of the insects.

By January 1937, barely one month after the first test, Dr. Schrader and his assistants noticed that the poison had unpleasant effects on humans. Exposure to the slightest quantity caused contractions of the pupils and night blindness. Suffering from acute breathing difficulties, nausea, and with their hands and feet tingling, the entire laboratory staff retreated to their beds for three weeks of convalescence. This fortunate group was the first ever to be exposed to a nerve agent and, remarkably, some of the very few that lived to talk about it.

Recovered from the ordeal, the German scientists resumed studying the chemical. Offering up an insect to test the effectiveness, Schrader was amazed to discover that a minute smear, no more than a trace, killed in moments. Furthermore, the chemical continued to kill days after the initial application. Tests on animals showed that the toxicity was greater than any other poison ever seen. Dr. Schrader named his find Tabun.

The idea behind his original research was sound. German medical science had discovered that when an impulse travels though a nerve junction, acetylcholine transmits the signal and acetylcholinesterase is released to stop the impulse. If a chemical could be found that acts to stop the formation of acetylcholinesterase, then an unbelievably effective poison would be at hand. Organo-phosphates such as Tabun did just that with horrific efficiency.

Absorbed through the skin or the mucous linings of the respiratory tract, Tabun blocks acetylcholinesterase. When the body's ability to produce this vital enzyme is halted, the nervous system can no longer control the activation of muscles. Without this biochemical antagonist, all of the muscles violently contract. The heart stops in one violent contraction and breathing is arrested. Death is inevitably due to asphyxiation. Before that occurs, though, the entire skeleton is tortured by unremitting muscle contractions. Bones snap from muscle tension and the abdominal walls squeeze internal organs to a pulp. Now fully aware of what had been discovered, the Farben scientists informed the German military.

Impressed, they gave Dr. Schrader new facilities and all the support that he required. In this new lab, his ongoing research revealed a chemical related to Tabun that is ten times as toxic. Methylisopropoxy fluorophosphine oxide, also simply named Sarin, could kill a man with just one fiftieth of a drop. Both Sarin and Tabun were given priorities for immediate production and field-testing. Studies to find antidotes for the victims of nerve agents were begun. Methods of dispersion were tried—one of which led to the discovery of a solvent that played a role in the development of the Biro ballpoint pen—and perfected. Chemical troops were even trained in the use of Sarin and Tabun.

It remains debatable to this day why the German High Command (Oberkommando der Wehrmacht [OKW]) never fielded the chemical weapons. Germany had wholeheartedly participated in chemical warfare in the previous war. They had shown remarkable inventiveness when, in 1917, they introduced phosgene gas—aerosolized hydrochloric acid—in retaliation for the Allied use of mustard gas and other, less-lethal compounds. It is known that a production facility was established in at least one location. Speculation that Hitler himself refused to use the weapon are likely—he had been gassed near the end of the First World War.

In spite of the Nazis' reputation, the German Army still was commanded by old-school Prussian generals who had retained some vestiges of honor. It is possible that they blocked the usage of nerve gas as well. Late in the war, large quantities were shipped to front-line units but never used. Albert Speer, Hitler's Minister of Production, reputedly stated that Allied retaliation should poison gas be used would be a "most terrible catastrophe."

The war over, the western Allies discovered the massive amounts of chemical agents and swiftly seized them for their own arsenals. Fearing that the other side—the Soviets—had gained an upper hand in advanced weaponry, research into the nerve gases began in earnest. Soon, VX—which is an improved Sarin—GB, BZ, and S-341 were being stockpiled along with Tabun in shelters around the world. Modern chemical technology had made the nerve agents deadlier, with less dosage required to kill faster, and the chemicals were capable of surviving the effects of weather, making them more persistent. This very feature made the general use of organo-phosphate nerve agents too risky to be used as insecticides.

However, there is a group of commonly used insecticide that is closely related to the nerve agents. Malathion, Parathion, and Diazinon are organo-phosphates that have gained wide use. They differ from their wartime and Cold War cousins by their dosage weakness and their sensitivity to the weather. In spite of this, environmental issues have been raised over their use in aerial spraying for Mediterranean fruit flies. Experts insist that there is no danger, although doubts linger.

A Herbicide from Hell: Agent Orange

Like its organo-phosphate counterpart, the use of Agent Orange began innocently enough. Actually, the chemical compound did not get its infamous name until near the end of World War Two when equal quantities of two separate defoliants, 2,4-D and 2,4,5-T were combined. The two individual chemicals had proven themselves by controlling heavy vegetation in forestry work all through the Depression. Only with the building of the Burma Road in 1944-45 was Agent Orange sprayed with reckless abandon. A few health problems began to show up in the Allied troops, but the war ended before the substantial medical perils became evident. Throughout the 1950s, the herbicide was used indiscriminately around the world to clear road rights-of-ways, forests, and fields.

Vietnam circa 1968. American aircraft spray Agent Orange on the thick vegetation to render the enemy's hiding places barren. The true cost of this is still being tallied. Hundreds of American service-people have died from exposure.(DoD/NARA)

Sprayed in its undiluted form from aircraft flying in formation and from helicopters, Agent Orange became an image for the farcical tragedy that was the Vietnam War. American troops and Vietnamese, North and South, civilian or not, regularly got a thorough drenching with up to twice the recommended concentrations. Records show that several areas were sprayed up to 25 times in a period of months. Empty drums, still tainted with dioxin—one of the most toxic materials known and a key ingredient in Agent Orange—were used for a multitude of housekeeping devices from water barrels to rough-and-ready barbecues. Uninformed about the dangers, mechanics, technicians, and service personnel were exposed to the chemical whenever they touched any clothing, equipment or aircraft that had been contaminated. The total physiological effects of dioxin and Agent Orange are still not known, though at least 30 diseases are attributed to dioxin, which the Veterans Administration has acknowledged and now compensates veterans, a small victory from the war in Vietnam.[17]

A New Poison for Rat and Man

During the war, farmers were beginning to adopt less conventional feeds for their stock and develop storage methods to keep them during the winter months. Among these newer feeds was clover, commonly used as ground forage up until the war. However, improper clover storage techniques led to several dozen head of valuable stock to dying suddenly and rather gruesomely.

The discovery of Dicoumerol and its allied drugs was fortuitous. Variations of this drug eventually had other names: Coumadin, Warfarin.

At first, livestock experts and officials from the USDA thought there was either a new infection emerging or that an unknown chemical agent had poisoned the animals, accidentally or deliberately. The latter was especially on everyone's mind as the threat of Japanese attack in the weeks after Pearl Harbor had everyone on edge. As this farm was less than one hundred miles from the Pacific coast, the possibility of enemy action was even more certain.

Necropsies had shown that every internal organ had freely bled. Tests of the animals' body fluids showed that their blood's ability to clot had been reduced to negligible levels. The poison was finally traced to the clover. It had been put up while still damp and a natural substance called coumarin had fermented out of the clover. When ingested, coumarin destroys vitamin K, which is a vital substance to control bleeding. Within weeks of the first poison cases being reported, all clover was being inspected and any that had turned bad was promptly destroyed. Coumarin, however, was to prove to be a godsend for the overworked farmers and the entire war effort.

Rats constituted the greatest threat to grain crops after harvesting. Worldwide, it was estimated that rats were responsible for consuming almost one-quarter of the supply of food grains. A number of solutions had been offered up over the several millennia that mankind had been battling rats. The rat problem was partially responsible for the domestication of cats and for many of the breeds of dogs that we share our homes with today. Previously, the only rat poisons available were arsenic or strychnine. Although effective, they had unpleasant side effects. When a rat died of poisoning, it was typically in the most inaccessible nooks and crannies of a home. The rotting carcass would send up a horrible stink, necessitating some unlucky soul to search out and retrieve the body. Or the previously mentioned pets would discover the carcass, eat of the carcass and ingest the poison with sad but predictable results.

With coumarin, the rat died by internally bleeding to death. Even though it sounds unpleasant, the exsanguination dehydrated the body; hence there was no moisture to promote bacterial growth and no resulting stench. Additionally, coumarin poisoning is easily reversible in cases of accidental ingestion; so domesticated animals and children were less likely to become fatally poisoned by the rat bait.

In 1947, Warfarin—the name was derived from the organization that sponsored the original research: the Wisconsin Alumni Research Foundation—was introduced by University of Wisconsin biochemist Karl Paul Link. It featured coumarin-saturated grains that could be placed around the home or farm. Coumarin-based drugs were also introduced into medicine as anti-coagulants. This was particularly important to the hundreds of thousands of service personnel that required surgery or extended bed rest for their injuries. In either case, blood clots are a serious consequence and before this drug became available, there was very little the doctors could do. Often, if the clot passed into the lungs, heart or brain, it proved fatal.[18]

The results of one night of rat hunting at a Colorado Army camp's waste dump. It is clear from this display that rat populations are directly affected by the presence of large groups that do not dispose of their wastes properly. This was another reason a rodent poison such as Coumarin is so important. (U.S. Army)

New Plant Varieties

The coming war provided an increased awareness of food production. The American farm had languished during the Depression, and Roosevelt's revival plans had only just begun to show results. The United States was looked to as a gigantic breadbasket that could feed the Allied nations, even before Pearl Harbor. Shipments of grain, meat, and dairy products went overseas along with packaged and tinned foods.

Farmers are always searching for new crop variations that offer improved yields and better resistance to drought, pests, disease and weathering. Soils, differing according to geographical regions, were a factor in the success of a given crop. Another factor that drove agro-scientists to create new varieties was the popularity of the Victory Garden. The Department of Agriculture, and later the National Wartime Nutrition Program, promoted the idea of planting vegetables in small patches of ground for home consumption. By 1943, thirty-three percent of all of the vegetables grown in the United States were raised in more than 20,000,000 plots of fractional acreage.[19]

Wheat

One of the best examples of improving a staple crop was the case of wheat. Led by the USDA, fifty new varieties were created and distributed to farmers in the United States. Between the years 1942 and 1946, wheat harvests increased by eight hundred million bushels.[20]

Corn

Other crops enjoyed comparably enhanced production. Corn was hybridized to prosper in the southern and eastern states. Having unique soil, weather, and growing seasons, these regions did not typically have corn crops compared to the central midwestern corn belt. By 1946, the thirteen states of the Deep South had increased corn acreage fivefold, an increase of nearly five and a half million acres.

This amount does not seem significant until a historical perspective is taken. Over the three years of the First World War, the United States produced eight billion bushels of corn on 311 million acres (Average Yield; 25.72 Bushels/ acre.) In comparison, the corn crop for 1942-44 totaled 9.3 billion bushels on 281 million acres (Average Yield; 33.09 Bushels/acre.). The majority of this corn went to feed livestock, which in turn produced an extra five billion pounds of meat, enough to feed American consumers an additional thirty-eight pounds a year. Considering the wide-spread rationing—the allotment for meat was down to 115 pounds per person a year by 1943—that occurred in America during the Second World War, the added supply was truly a blessing.[21]

Oats

Long a staple for baking, breakfasts, and livestock feed, oats had been evolving with USDA attention since 1929. Diseases had repeatedly devastated oat crops and a new resistant variety became available in small quantities by 1940. By 1945, further enhancements had made the stalwart oat a favored crop for mechanized farming. The new oat with superior qualities had become an important cash crop for farmers, who now had a surplus.[22]

Rice

A major dietary component for much of the world, rice has been grown primarily in Southeast Asia. When Japan seized these areas, ninety percent of the world's rice supply was gone to the Allies. In response, the American farmer was asked to fill the need. Grain production jumped by seventy-five million bushels, to 225 million, by 1945. Grown mainly in California, Louisiana, Arkansas, and Texas, rice became the main cash crop for the area. The grain thrives where wet soils and high temperatures abound, although it tends to deplete the soil's nutrient levels rapidly. A great deal of work went into determining the methods to return to the soil the fertilizers and organic materials so badly needed for high yields.[23]

Through experimentation, it was discovered that a rice field would produce better if allowed to grow fertilized pasture grasses with grazing cattle on alternate years. Not only was the rice yield better from the recycled organics, but also the land could feed more cattle that then produced more calves.

Fruits, Vegetables, and Grasses

Grains were not the only crop that got a boost from war needs. Tomatoes, green beans, onions, potatoes, peaches, watermelons, blueberries, and strawberries all gained attention from agronomists to improve production. Grasses, clover, alfalfa, and hay were all refined through selective breeding to increase their output for animal feed.[24]

Sugar

Another staple item that was severely rationed during the war, sugar comes from three main plants: cane, beet and sorghum. Much of the cane sugar used in the United States had come from the Philippines, which fell to the Japanese. Sugar beets, grown in the western states since the First World War, had languished as uneconomical because of a viral disease. One expert suggested that fields contaminated with the virus be abandoned.

Fortunately, this was not done and the sugar beet now stands as a major American crop. Cross- and selective-breeding of beets led to the introduction of hardy varieties. New machinery, perfected during the war, mechanized planting and harvesting. One unique problem facing sugar beet production was determining the vector by which the virus was spread. Poor weed management, along with overgrazing, had knocked the natural foliage back and more vigorous plants had taken their place. A strain of leafhopper, feeding on the new weeds, carried the virus into the beet fields, infecting the crop.[25]

Managing the hoppers with pesticides, removing the objectionable weeds that they favored, and replanting the natural growth that they found unpalatable could control the virus. Cattle had been blamed for the overgrazing but the real culprits were hordes of jackrabbits and rats eating the vegetation. By excluding the rabbits—through traps and shooting—the natural growth would spontaneously return, whereas the rats, eliminated by poison, would no longer eat the dispersed grass seeds.

Sugar cane was also mechanically harvested during the war. Previously, the cane had been cut and gathered by hand, but wartime manpower shortages made machine harvesting essential. A number of alternate cane varieties, some developed long before the war, were released to plantations for field studies. Erect stalks with easily shed outer skins and high sucrose content were the selection factors for the new varieties. The yield per acre increased by 394 pounds in the war years, mostly due to new machinery practices.[26]

Coming from Africa, sugar sorghum was a prime source of molasses and sugar syrup used in early processed foods. Industrial alcohol, necessary for manufacturing explosives, was also derived from sorghum, and so, began an emergency program to develop strains of sorghum that would thrive in the United States. Seeds were collected from central African farm areas and shipped to America. After intense testing, the collected specimens were interbred with native species and, in 1942, a quarter of a million gallons of alcohol were produced from American sorghum.[27] Other plants from Ethiopia and India were crossbred to establish sorghum as a sugar producer. This second generation was still under development at the end of the war and has undergone continual improvement since.

New Farm Machinery

A new shortage resulted as men left the farm to join the military or to work in the factories. Farm labor, long the work of young men, fell to the few remaining farmers and what warm bodies could be conscripted for the job. This, along with the call to increase food production, provided motivation to develop machines to do the work.

The tractor was just coming into common use during the Depression, but many other tasks were done by hand. Very few farm machines were actually produced during the war as military equipment took priority because of scarce resources. In spite of the limitations, the machines that were made went a long way towards improving the efficiency of the American farmer.[28]

Georgia, 1940. Here again is a subsistence farm, this time in the Deep South. The war did a number of things for farmers like this: electrified home and outbuildings, mechanization, better crop stock, better healthcare for animals and people, more education. (NARA)

Potato Harvester

This machine, towed behind the tractor, dug up the tuber, cleaned off the excess dirt and sacked the potatoes all in one operation. Operated by two men, the picker could process four hundred bushels an hour according to the manufacturer.

The Combine

This essential farm equipment has been around since the mid-1800s in one form or another. Early models were pulled by draft animals and operated by means of chains turned by the wheels. Heavy and expensive, the combine was a rare sight on most farms.

The combine of the 1940s was actually adapted from the tractor. The Massey Harris Company introduced the first self-propelled combine in 1938. With a removable front cutter bar measuring seven to fourteen feet wide, this machine could harvest any threshable crops. Different cutter heads could be installed for the various duties and planting styles encountered.

Cotton Picker

Here is a machine that replaced innumerable laborers in a tedious job that formerly could be done only by hand. The first machine was patented in 1850 and more than 1,800 modifications of dubious value had been offered on the original idea. Only the labor shortage of World War Two provided the impetus to build a practical machine. Self-propelled, the picker could pick, remove dirt and pre-bale five hundred pounds of cotton in little more than an hour.

Cane Harvesters

Another variation on the combine, this machine eliminated two-thirds of the harvesting hand labor. It cuts the cane, strips off the outer leaves, and prepares bundles for transport to the mill.

Corn Pickers

After cutting cornstalks at the base, the ears of corn are picked, husked, and discharged into an attached trailer. Meanwhile, the stalks are shredded back onto the ground where they will decompose and return valuable nutrients to the soil. As an added benefit, pesky corn borers are killed in the process.

Hay Balers and Storage Equipment

Pulled by a tractor, the hay baler cuts, compresses, and wire-ties the hay into geometric, eighty-five pound bales that facilitate stacking. Baled hay is only one method of storage. Loose, bulk hay can be stored in silos where it is allowed to dry, preserving the precious vitamins it contains.

A whole range of new equipment manages the hay. After being cut in the field, it is allowed to dry. Then a tractor-driven pickup chopper shreds the hay where it is then taken to the silo. A screw conveyor lifts the dry fodder into a storage silo tower. Later, when the fodder is needed, an unloader suspended from the ceiling of the silo scrapes the hay up and sends it through the discharge pipe by means of air pressure.

Bulk hay can also be placed into the loft of the barn as it has been for years. Getting it there, however, became much easier in the 1940s. Implement manufacturers began to offer a modified tractor with a stout metal articulating frame hinged to it. With tines on the end of the frame, the machine, with its hydraulic cylinders doing the heavy work, could lift the hay up to the doors of the second-story loft. Not restricted to lifting baled hay, farmers found dozens of chores for this handy machine, mostly for lifting jobs around the farm.

Off-Road Tires

Prior to 1936, tractors came from the factory with steel wheels. In that year, the Firestone Tire Company introduced the first pneumatic rubber tires with lugs on the outer circumference. Able to gain traction in soft dirt or mud, the tire also shed mud spontaneously. The new tires, being inflated with low air pressure, not only resisted sinking into boggy areas but also gave a much smoother ride. In addition, the rubber tires did not tear up the county roads, as did the steel-lugged wheels of old. When farmers discovered that the herringbone-shaped lugs improved performance by nearly half, the tires were soon offered as standard.[29]

War needs for rubber severely curtailed the production of the tractor tires, the War Production Board determined that rubber tires were essential for military vehicles. Much to everyone's dismay, steel wheels with steel lugs came back as standard equipment on the rare new tractor. Replacements for the rubber style tire were restricted to retread, if the casing—the inner construct of the tire, also called the carcass—was not damaged, or the much-hated steel wheels had to be used.

Based on the experience of the rubber farm tire, the military adopted similar tread patterns for their wheeled vehicles. Several variations were experimented with to determine the best balance for the mud, sand, cobbles, snow and hard pavement, all of which the tires would be expected to encounter.

An early type of off-road tire that saw service was one which a sharp chevron-shaped lug that had to be installed in the proper direction to be effective. It worked well in the sands of North Africa, but the Russians, who got them as Lend-Lease supplies, thought little of the American tire. They installed the tires with no regard

Rubber tractor tires were a great improvement over the older steel wheels. Within months of their introduction, war-inspired rubber restrictions came. After the war, the tire companies began a heated competition over their tread variations. These two ads are a good representation of the typical competition. (Firestone/Goodyear) to the special mounting requirements. As a result, half of them were installed backwards, negating any enhancements gained by the tread. Later tire designs featured lugs that alternated from side to side on the face of the tread with no rotation preference. These became the standard tire used by the Allied armies for the rest of the war and for years after.[30]

With the war over, the lugged rubber tractor tire returned to the farm, this time to stay. Besides its obvious and logical uses with the construction and mining industries, off-road tire designs have revolutionized the consumer market. The successful wartime off-road tread has evolved, adapted, and modified to fit the role for contemporary sport utility vehicles, and quite a large market for the tire exists today for off-road adventurers. Taken to the extreme, lugged tires can be found on the giant trucks of monster truck exhibition shows.

Veterinary Drugs

Like their human counterparts, domesticated animals have enjoyed the fruits of the new biochemical age. Many of the human medicines recently discovered were subsequently found to be effective against animal diseases since numerous afflictions are shared between man and beast. For example, veterinarians adopted the revolutionary antibiotics as fast as the pharmaceutical experts could prove their efficacy in animals. But there were more than just antibiotics that applied to our animal partners.

Phenothiazine

Better known by its trade name Thorazine, phenothiazine was found to be a wonder drug of sorts in treating parasitic infections in swine. First discovered by synthesis in 1885, it remained a laboratory curiosity until 1938 when it was found to be especially potent against the intestinal roundworms that caused poor growth and lowered life expectancy among swine. Mixed with salt in hog feed, the drug became widely used during the war. By 1944, consumption of phenothiazine was up to nearly three million pounds a year, compared to nine hundred pounds used in 1939.[31]

Still used today, phenothiazine serves as an anti-parasitic for animals and man. Derivatives of it are used as an anti-psychotic drug, as an antihistamine in treating allergic reactions, and for reducing the symptoms of motion sickness.

Hog Cholera Vaccine

The economic effects of cholera on American swine herds by 1940 totaled more than sixty-five million dollars a year. A vaccine was introduced that same year, giving farmers new hope of avoiding financial collapse. A killed-virus serum, its value came into doubt when impurities began to create new medical problems. Spoilage rendered a number of doses impotent, and the lessened strength was undetectable. Strict limitations on the drug's use were set up as questions concerning its effectiveness were addressed.

Wartime food requirements and obvious need provided the impetus to improve the vaccine. Using recently developed sterile techniques; a joint government and industry effort re-introduced the vaccine with much more success. As the reputation of the vaccine among the dubious farmers grew, demand led to the creation of commercial production facilities. By 1944, restrictions were completely lifted. Shipped to Allied nations, the vaccine's efficacy was confirmed. The drug, essentially its latter form, is still in use today. Hog cholera is far from being eradicated, although it is nearly so in most of the agriculturally advanced countries.[32]

Required Rabies Vaccinations and Animal Licensing

Rabies, a viral infection, was undoubtedly one of the most feared scourges of the early twentieth century. Communicated by the bite or body fluids of a diseased animal, the virus attacks the central nervous system, eventually killing its victim. Before this happens, the patient suffers extreme pain accompanied by fever. The muscles of the throat become paralyzed, making swallowing difficult. The patient is unable to drink, and intense thirst only adds to the mental derangement beginning to overtake consciousness. The only known alleviation for an advanced case, even today, is to sedate the sufferer into a coma with death mercifully coming in three to five days.[33]

Louis Pasteur developed his rabies vaccination for humans in 1885, using attenuated rabbit cells. The inoculation was also effective on animals, but widespread use in this manner did not occur until the late 1930s. Under the guidance of the Department of Agriculture, veterinarians began prophylactic Pasteur treatments of all dogs and cats, the primary vector of the virus to humans. This program led to the requirement of licensing domestic pets and periodic re-immunization. It was not until the winter of 1945-46 that the Army Veterinary Service required all military dogs returning from overseas duty be vaccinated for rabies.[34] Agents trapped skunks, foxes, bats, and other animals known to carry rabies. This multi-prong attack on the rabies virus led to the present situation in which it is fairly rare for a human to encounter a rabid animal in the United States.

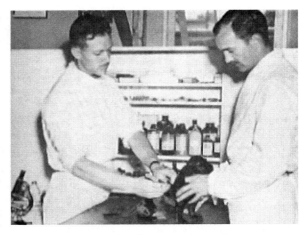

An Army veterinarian examines the newest member of the Canine Corps. Dogs became a part of the military for guard duty and then were found helpful in sniffing out the enemy. The problem came from the fact that most of the areas combat occurred were rife with rabies. Although Pasteur shots (anti-rabies) were available for years, it took the war dogs to force required rabies shots and licensing to keep track of the inoculations. (U.S. Army Veterinarian Corps)

Artificial Insemination

Stockbreeders are by necessity a choosy bunch. The economics of their business require them to want the best and most productive animals available. For centuries, cattle, sheep, goats, horses, and hogs have been selectively mated to acquire the finest traits of the parents in the offspring. It was an agonizingly slow process, and the results were less than satisfactory more often than not. One prized bull could service 30 to 50 females a year, if all went well. Out of this, only about three-quarters of the unions would result in successful births. Of that lot, statistically, there was only a one-in-four chance that the desired traits would be passed on to the offspring. Although the natural process worked rather well, breeders wanted faster results with better stock. Artificial insemination was the answer.

Originally demonstrated on a dog in 1780, the idea of manually injecting semen into the reproductive tract of the female did not take hold until 1919, when Russian Professor Elie Ivanov perfected his technique after twenty years of work. His project came to an abrupt halt when the Soviet revolution erupted.

Ivanov's principal techniques made their way into America where they had a mixed reception. Older farmers tended to be against the idea of meddling with nature, although a certain amount of reluctance could be attributed to Victorian mores. Progressive farmers, on the other hand, welcomed the opportunity to improve their stock and increase their yields. Early attempts were haphazard and clumsy, the donor sperm being mishandled and bulls poorly managed.

Artificial insemination was taught throughout the world during and after the First World War. The training of veterinarians in collecting the semen was primarily done while on the job with some remarkable gaffs. One memorable instance occurring soon after the Second World War is described by James Herriot (Nom de plume of James Alfred Wight, a Scottish vet working in England). Using a rubber double-walled tube with a glass collection tube mounted on the end, the vet was to fill the space between the rubber walls with warm water. When placed over the bull's erect penis, the rubber tube would act as an artificial vagina. A cow in heat was presented to the bull, and as he went to mount her, the veterinarian was to deftly direct the tube onto the bull's penis. This, of course put the doctor very near the center of action, so to speak.

The bull was quite affronted by the vet's interference and displayed his displeasure with a threatening shake of his horns. Bull and man both soon regained their composure and returned to the task at hand. The second attempt proved nearly disastrous when the bull flailed at the vet, knocking the artificial vagina to the ground. Knocked loose by the fall, the water plug fell out, draining away the water. The farmer volunteered to refill the tube for the now thoroughly flustered vet and did so—with nearly boiling water. Needless to say, the bull became intensely upset over this latest indignity when the well-stoked rubber sleeve managed to get placed over his not-so-tough penis. The whole fiasco with the artificial vagina came to a successful close after the fourth attempt, which had obtained a small but adequate sample. However, the bull apparently had had enough of the ham-fisted muddling about his loins, and his enraged response very nearly caused the glass collection receptacle to be shattered.[35]

Isolated problems with insemination as above being the exception, most of the wrinkles had been worked out of the artificial insemination program by the end of the Second World War. Now one prize bull could serve several hundred or even a thousand cows a year. In special circumstances, even more could be impregnated. With veterinarians using storage techniques such as freezing, a bull could continue to father offspring long after he became too old or had even died. In this manner, herds hundreds of miles distant could benefit from the new genetic influx without the dangers and expense of transporting the animal.

During the war, artificial insemination gained great favor as the need to increase stock production was obvious. Diluting the semen with egg white not only extended supplies of the best samples, but it was found to improve conception rates. Laboratory work to understand the physiology of sperm, especially in motility and cellular abnormalities, has led to new understandings that have crossed over into human medicine. New treatments for sterility in men are a direct result of the artificial insemination program.

Notes/Selected References

1   Statistics derived from USDA website: www.usda.gov/history2/text3.htm
2   The Good Earth Goes to Sea. *Popular Mechanics* magazine, July 1940. P. 82–85.
3   ibid. Pp 82–85.
4   ibid. Pp. 82–85. and Uhland, R. E. *Rotations in Conservation. The Yearbook of Agriculture 1943-1947.* 1947. Pp. 527-536. and Krimgold, D. B. *Managing Surface Runoff. The Yearbook of Agriculture 1943–1947.* 1947. Pp. 537–540.
5   *Universal Almanac* 1991. P. 294.
6   Clyde, George D. *Irrigation in the West. The Yearbook of Agriculture 1943–1947.* 1947. Pp. 602–607.
7   Molloy, E. *Pumps and Pumping.* 1941. Pp. 68–78.
8   Clyde, George D. *Irrigation in the West. The Yearbook of Agriculture 1943–1947.* 1947. P. 606.
9   Nicholls, Richard E. *Beginning Hydroponics.* 1977. Pp. 14–16. Revolution in Farming. *Popular Mechanics* magazine June 1942. Pp. 92-95.
10 Moore, Robert W. Greens Grow For G.I.s on Soil-less Ascencion. *National Geographic* magazine, August 45. Pp. 219–227.
11 Japanese agriculture suffered terribly during the war. The loss of labor, two bad harvest years, the Naval shipping blockade and government demands to feed the Army led the Japanese people to the brink of famine.
12 Havens, W. Paul Jr. MD. *The United States Army Medical Corps, Internal Medicine in WW II, Infectious Diseases.* 1963. P. 457.
13 Hoff, Ebbe Curtis, Ph. D., M.D. *The United States Army Medical Corps, Preventative Medicine in World War II, Environmental Hygiene Vol.2.* 1955. Pp. 222 – 224
14 ibid. Pp. 67–69.
15 Dunnigan, James F. and Nofi. Albert A. *Dirty Little Secrets of World War II.* 1994. P.101 and Stage, H.H. and Irons, Frank. *Air War Against Pests. The Yearbook of Agriculture 1943–1947.* 1947. Pp. 835–838.

16 Popham, W. L. *Blowers For Insecticides. Yearbook of Agriculture 1943–1947.* 1947. Pp. 839 – 842.

17 Freiman, Fran Locher et al. *Failed Technology Vol. 2.* 1995. Pp. 333–340.

18 Kalmbach, E.R. *Advances in Rodent Control. Yearbook of Agriculture 1943–1947.* Pp. 890 – 896.

19 Haskew, Michael E. *The World War II Desk Reference.* 2008. Pp. 388 – 389.

20 Bayles, B.B. *New Variety of Wheat. The Yearbook of Agriculture 1943-1947.* 1947. Pp. 379–384.

21 Jenkins, Merle T. *Corn Hybrids for The South. The Yearbook of Agriculture 1943-1947.* 1947. Pp. 389–394.

22 Stanton, T.R. *Disease Resistant Oats. The Yearbook of Agriculture 1943-1947.* 1947. Pp. 395 – 402.

23 Jones, Jenkin W. *New Rice; New Practices. The Yearbook of Agriculture 1943-1947.* 1947. Pp. 373 – 378.

24 Porte, William S. *Healthier Tomatoes.* Pp. 312 – 319. and Zaumeyer, W. J. *Control of Bean Diseases.* Pp. 333 – 337. and Jones, H.A. and A. E. Clarke. *Story of Hybrid Onions.* Pp. 320 – 326. and Stevenson F. J. and Robert V. Akeley. *Breeding Better Potatoes.* Pp. 327 – 332. and Havis, Leon, J.H.Weinberger and C.O.Hesse. *Better Peaches Are Coming.* Pp. 304 – 311. and Darrow, George M. *New Varieties of Blueberries.* Pp. 300 – 303. and ———— *Finer Strawberries.* Pp. 293 – 299. and Hein, M.A. *Grasses for Hay & Pasture.* Pp. 417 – 426. and Hollowell, E.A.. *More and Better Clover.* Pp. 427– 432. and Tysdal, H.M. *Breeding Better Alfalfa.* Pp. 433 – 438. *The Yearbook of Agriculture 1943-1947.* 1947.

25 Carsner, Eubanks and F.V. Owen. *Saving Our Sugar Beets. The Yearbook of Agriculture 1943-1947.* 1947. Pp. 357 – 362.

26 Sartoris, George B. *New Kinds Of Sugarcane. The Yearbook of Agriculture 1943-1947.* 1947. Pp. 353 – 356.

27 Brandes, E.W. *Progress With Sugar Sorgo. The Yearbook of Agriculture 1943-1947.* 1947. Pp. 344 – 352.

28 Gray, R.B. *Some New Farm Machines. The Yearbook of Agriculture 1943-1947.* 1947. Pp. 815 – 816. and Mechanizing the Small Farm. *Popular Mechanics* magazine, April 1940. Pp. 536 – 539.

29 Warp, Harold. *A History of Man's Progress.* 1978. P. 167.

30 Church, John. *Military Vehicles of World War* II, 1982. P. 16.

31 Schwartz, Benjamin. *Drugs to Control Parasites. The Yearbook of Agriculture 1943-1947.* 1947. Pp. 74-75.

32 Giltner, L.T. *Animal Diseases. The Yearbook of Agriculture 1943-1947.* 1947. Pp. 90-91.

33 Keane, Claire Brackman and Benjamin F. Miller. *Encyclopedia and Dictionary of Medicine and Nursing*. 1972. P. 812.

34 Miller, Everett B. Lt. Col. VC, USA. *United States Army Veterinary Service in World War II*. 1961. P. 637.

35 Herriot, James. *The Lord God Made Them All*. 1982. Pp. 235-243.

11

We're Going Places: Automobiles, Trains, Ships and What Makes Them Run

The Second World War occurred at a junction of time and circumstance where the old familiar ways of travel conflicted with the new. The automobile, just beginning its third decade, still had many of the features of its predecessor, the horse-drawn wagon. Much of the construction is wood, the wheels spoked, the manufacturers more often than not got their start in the time when horsepower meant just that; horse power. And yet, the new vehicles were fresh and exciting. Steel frames and body work that offered a permanence and durability that wood lacked. The unprecedented speed of modern transportation was thrilling, having almost a narcotic effect on the driver. Now, just about anybody with $550 could buy a new Ford V8 able to drive 60 MPH, granted one could find a suitable road built for such a speed. But even that was becoming commonplace. Large municipalities, plus state and federal road systems were being built and paved as a part of Depression recovery projects.

Much of this construction was done with business in mind. Prior to this time, the railroads had dominated the transportation industry, moving people and products at the railroad's price and schedule. With the growth of automobile driving, people were now getting used to the freedom, independence and economy of personal conveyance, if they could afford it. Businesses, too, were beginning to rely on the services of the cartage trucker, another relatively new concept. Instead of loading your goods into a box or flat car — given that your factory is serviced by a rail spur, most were then — to another siding where it would be unloaded and then onto the customer. Now, your product could be delivered direct to your customer's door, sometimes cutting days from delivery date. No more would a small start-up business be limited to the rail spurs, but could choose to work form a shed, a barn or even an open field could serve as a business location. This decentralization was contrary to the contemporary business where the huge, do-it-all behemoths like Ford's River Rouge plant was built. Encompassing 2,000 acres of riverside, semi-marshland, the factory featured coke ovens, blast furnaces for making their own steel, the world's largest foundry and a power plant capable of supplying the electric needs of town of 350,000. There were a total of 93 buildings on the site, containing fabrication, assembly, engineering and administration offices. In addition, there were laboratories for metallurgy, development engineering, paint, chemistry and plastics, a glass factory, cafeteria and medical offices.[1] Henry Ford's dream was to put "raw materials … in one end… and finished cars going out the other end." There certainly was output. His 75,000 employees could finish 4,000 cars a day.[2]

All of those cars had to go somewhere to drive. One new concept, the throughway, was on the horizon. Europe was the first with a network of high speed, all-weather roads linking the great cities of Germany together, An American clone, the Pennsylvania Turnpike, was completed about a year before the war. It was a good step towards an even more ambitious network to come.

One final example of old versus new is with the use of pack and draft animals. Prior to World War Two, all the major combatants in the coming conflict maintained formal mounted cavalry and thousands of pack/draft animals. Not much different than that from the Napoleonic wars. This was still the case despite the German boast and American stated goal of fielding fully mechanized armies.[3] This was declared at a time when the American artillery was 60% horse-drawn.[4] Dur-

Supply mules on the trail in the Philippine Islands circa. 1937. Although the American Army sought to be totally mechanized by 1943, the war, which redirected priorities, intervened. Fortunately, conditions in Italy and the Pacific meant that the pack animals did not get that last ride to the meat packer for dog food. (U.S. Army/NARA)

ing the Second World War, the U.S.Army purchased another 60,000 horses domestically, 6,000 more obtained in Australia and "many thousands …captured, requisitioned or received in China-Burma-India, the Mediterranean and European theaters."[5] These animals were found to of special use in mountainous terrain where even jeeps could not go.

German troops relied on pack animals more than the Allies. They had, according to one source, 750,000 horses for logistic and artillery draft on the Eastern Front alone. Their presence was probably fortunate because as the war turned against them, the Germans turned to eating the animals in the bitter cold winters.[6]

Happily, eating one's mode of transport was not one likely to happen to the post-war car owner. The automotive engine had far more desirable qualities that were only improved upon during the war. Most had been from small enhancements: a thicker casting here, a subtle change in metal content to delay wear, tightened dimensional tolerances for this or that, better corrosion resistance there, and so on. The war impelled improvements in engineering and manufacturing at an accelerated pace and the post-war world generally benefited from it.

Pneumatic Tools and Machinery

The success of the assembly line was based upon doing a given task faster. Time studies at Ford showed that the threaded fasteners, bolts, screws, and such required an excessive amount of effort merely to hand-tighten the threads. Shorter thread length was out of the question, as the strength of a thread is dependent on the length of engagement. Any time savings came from the fastener turning faster. This gave rise to the popularity of pneumatics; the power of air.

As with hydraulics, pneumatics did most of the work, since in both cases mechanical movement is being imposed by a displacement of fluid. Pneumatics uses compressed air, not generally regarded as fluid, but, as stated before, air behaves like a fluid in that it can be made to flow, it can be pressurized, and, most importantly, it can be regulated.

Probably the first crude step into the advantage of pneumatics came from the blow gun. The 1600s brought the first recorded studies of the phenomenon of air and its nature. This became vital to the invention of steam power and later, the internal combustion engine. The use of air power gradually became more common as machinery to compress air improved. The hard-rock miners of the late nineteenth century utilized air drills to bore blasting holes, a great improvement over the hand-held drill and sledgehammer.

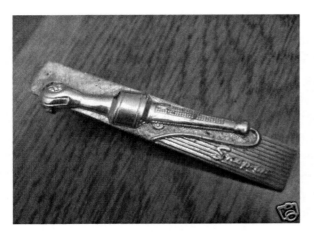

This is a very old Snap-On air ratchet. Tools as this made a huge time savings in the factories and at the front lines. Mechanic trucks all had small air compressors and a complete complement of air-drive tools. (Snap-on)

By the late 1920s, increasing speed in manufacturing processes, particularly in the automotive assembly plants, led to the invention of air-driven tools. The ability to quickly thread fasteners to a set torque greatly enhanced productivity on Henry Ford's assembly lines. Oil-driven tools were attempted for a time, but they were bulky and leaked terribly. Compressed air could run tools at high speed with no harmful residue. The pneumatic driving force, having completed its task, would simply return to the atmosphere.

Despite the success of air tools in Ford's plant, the air tool industry nearly self-destructed during the Depression. The technology was too new and industry in general had taken a major economic hit. However, air tools got a second opportunity with the defense industries starting up in 1939 and 1940.

Naturally, those pneumatic tools that applied to the automotive industry were the most in demand. Ratchets and nut runners were the first. Then, about 1936, the impact wrench came along. Soon after, a whole selection became available; air drill, rivet guns, buffers, grinders, sheet metal sheers, paint guns. Any tool that could be dreamed of could likely be converted to air.[7]

Air-Operated Automation

The desire to regulate machines of ever-increasing complexity led to the invention of automatic controls. The greatest need came from the rapidly expanding petroleum and chemical industries of the mid-1930s. Plant operators could manipulate an entire section of a processing area through one control station, minimizing risks and manpower. Furthermore, an automatic system could react to changes infinitely faster than humans could.

To turn electrical signals from the control panel into mechanical motion required a compact means of force and a way to control it. The environment, being hazardous, precluded the introduction of any foreign chemicals. It would not do to have a hydraulic cylinder leaking into chemicals that explode on contact with oil. Nor would an errant spark from an electric motor be acceptable around any stray fuel vapors that might detonate. The use of pneumatics fit the requirement perfectly. Components to control pressurized air were being improved upon, leading to simultaneous refinements of similar hydraulic elements such as valves, cylinders, regulators, and fittings.

At Massachusetts Institute of Technology, the Servomechanism Laboratory was established at the outbreak of war. The research and development done there laid the groundwork for modern automation. The present-day automobile, to name one example, would not be affordable without the advances made by this group. Air-actuated clamping devices hold the pieces in place for machining, welding, and assembly, while a variety of air-driven tools drill, tap, ream, and fasten. Furthermore, climate and emission controls on the typical car are mostly operated on vacuum, the inverse of compressed air. These components are all direct descendants of early pneumatic devices.

Today, other gases are used in conjunction with air—nitrogen, and argon being the most common. Instances of modern gas pneumatics are the cylinders that support the rear doors on many vehicles, the shock absorbers on mountain bicycles, and McPherson strut suspensions. And, of course, no self-respecting shade-tree mechanic would be without his (or her) compressor and a variety of air tools.

Diesel-Powered Trains

Once the trans-American railway was completed in 1868, the steam locomotive connected both coasts of the United States. For the next seventy-some years, steam power was the unrivaled king of the cross-country rails. Electricity brought the advent of the electric tram, used in inner cities for local commutes. Run by motors receiving power from overhead lines, these vehicles offered an inexpensive means of clean short-distance transportation. Electric power was also becoming commonplace on long-haul lines, especially in the industrialized northeastern United States. But the electric locomotive was an exception. The vast majority of rail traffic was pulled by the venerated steam engine, which had been around since the beginning of railroads in 1825.

There were a number of experimental Diesel or Diesel–type locomotives in America, Australia, and Western Europe beginning about 1895. None of these ever went into general use, even as late as 1926 when Westinghouse Electric Company engineers developed a reliable DC motor control. The Depression effectively ended any further work on Diesel powered locomotives in the United States. European rail companies did continue to use whatever prototype engines they had, but instead of DC motor drive, some engines were using hydrostatic and hydrokinetic drive coupled to Diesel power.

As the financial outlook began to improve in the late 1930s, General Motors, the largest manufacturer of automobiles, started to look at diversification. Claiming that steam had become an anachronism, GM set about to build the first cross-country (Class I) Diesel-electric locomotive. The Diesel was capable of generating an amazing amount of horsepower, but at a cost in weight. The GM locomotive subsidiary, Electro-Motive Division (EMD), set to work building a two-cycle Diesel engine. The engine would have no mechanical connection to the drive wheels. Rather, the wheels would be

Central England became a vast outdoor storage for the Allied build-up for the Normandy campaign. Here, a line of five Diesel-electric engines wait for their starring role on the Continent. The United States sent hundreds of new engines to aid in the eventual rebuilding of Europe. (WPB)

driven by small, powerful direct current (DC) motors running on current supplied by a generator driven by the Diesel engine.

The advantages of the Diesel-electric are manifold. Steam locomotives were, up to this time, primarily hand built, each having unique design features. As a result, the replacement parts supply was a logistical nightmare. Warehouses had to be maintained throughout the country for each railroad company stocking parts that may or may not get used. In the first hundred years of American railroad, dozens of companies built engines. Some were unique models. Some were of a dozen or less of the same design. Most of these companies went out of business or were swallowed by the bigger competitors. In these instances, factory replacement parts were out of the question. This forced railroads to equip and staff shops to fabricate the needed parts. GM's Diesel-electric locomotives were all new and made to one design. Spare parts would not be an issue.

Steam engines require solid fuel; preferably coal, to burn in the firebox. For lines in the eastern United States, this was not a problem as long as the coal miners did not strike, an event that occurred all too often in the early decades of the century. Coal was a burden for the trains in the west, though. Lacking convenient, local fuel supplies, carloads of coal had to be imported from mines in the Mid-west and from the east coast. Quite a bit of the fuel problem was avoided by turning to the forests of the western states. By the 1920s, however, the reserves of wood near the heavily traveled routes were nearly gone and natural fuel supplies were dwindling on the branch lines. Diesel fuel was widely available, easily transported in tank car or pipeline and inexpensive.

Public sentiment played a part in the demise of the steam engine as well. The smoke tended to be sooty, soiling anything downwind from the tracks. In larger towns that served as hubs for a number of different lines, the air would darken to a dusk-like hue that required that streetlights to be left on throughout the day. The situation was made worse by the need to have yard engines standing by with their boilers heated up in the event freight cars had to be moved. Standing at idle, the small switch machines would still be pouring out clouds of noxious smoke and cinders to rain down on the community.

Lack of versatility became another negative aspect against the steam power. The largest engine, used for hauling one hundred or more freight cars at high speed across country, was hardly the vehicle of choice as a switching engine in the rail yard. Nor was it economical to place a trans-continental engine on a small feeder line that hosted perhaps fifteen or twenty cars. In addition, the trestles of the small feeder line would not usually tolerate the enormous weight of the big freighters. To fulfill the differing roles, rail companies ordered a number of engines that would perform specific functions such as switching engines and light freighters.

GM's Diesel-electric locomotive, weighing in at 220,000 pounds, could be joined in tandem with a series of similar engines to provide greater power. This had an added benefit in that it was less stressful on the tracks, ties and roadbed than a half-million pound steamer. By coupling the Diesels together, the total tonnage being moved in one haul could be doubled and even tripled, cutting down the cost of tons per mile.

All these factors played a part in the demise of steam. EMD produced the first Diesel switch engines in 1935 and started delivering passenger train engines soon after. In a move that reflected the locomotive maker's heritage, EMD established a policy of building locomotives with interchangeable parts so that all railroads could eliminate the need for the expensive infrastructure that the steam engine required. EMD showed its heritage to the automotive business by setting up their factory in LaGrange, Illinois, on an assembly line basis.

EMD introduced their first long-haul freight locomotive, number 103, in 1940. Streamlined and sporting a snazzy yellow and green paint job, the 103 went to Pennsylvania on the first stop of a twenty-line tour where it immediately began breaking all previous tonnage records. Even though the Diesel-electric were well received, only a few rail companies considered buying the expensive machines.

In Europe after Hitler became Chancellor in 1933, German Reichsbahn (National Railway) engineers initiated the trial of a small Diesel-electric switching yard engine. Referred to as the WR 360, the little six-wheel machines did their duty through the war and on into the post-war rebuilding phase.

During the war, several dozen copies of the production version of the 103, renamed FT were built to replace tired steam engines and augment the already overworked American rail system. Several Diesel-electric engines were specially built on the rail spread, called the gauge, of European tracks. Better than a month after D-Day, two 150 H.P. locomotives and several flat cars were the first Allied rail stock landed on the Continent. They spearheaded an influx of another 48 Diesel-electric locomotives that would land by the end of July and spend the remainder of the war traveling the rails of France and Belgium, hauling supplies for the advancing Allied armies and returning with wounded troops and refugees.[8] Some of EMD's locomotives could also be found in the Middle East. The British had improved the existing rail lines of Iran and Iraq and had built several hundred miles of new track to provide an uninterrupted path for Lend/Lease materials to flow into Russia. Fifty-seven Diesels were imported to replace the worn-out steam engines of the Persian Gulf railroad systems between 1942 and 1944. During the war, a total of 3,066 new locomotives were placed into service; 1,891 of them being Diesel or Diesel-electric. As a result of all the attention and myriad minor improvements to the Diesel-electric locomotives over the course of the war, Diesel-electric power would have their true heyday afterwards.[9]

By 1947, orders for new steam locomotives plummeted while EMD and its competitor, American Locomotive Company, enjoyed a business boom. Focusing primarily on yard engines, the latter company would hardly be a match for EMD, which would dominate the market for years to come. The year 1953 saw the last new steam engine placed on the rails, and by the late 1960s steam had virtually disappeared from the American railroad. A few token steam machines still ply the tracks, mostly as nostalgic or tourist lines.

Another victim of the steam engine's passing is the job of the fireman. Originally hired to feed the fire under the boiler, the Diesel had no need for the fireman. Union contracts, though, stipulated their presence and it took court litigation and the intervention of President Kennedy to initiate the arbitration of a settlement, which led to the position's finally being eliminated in 1966.

Railroads are now used mostly for freight. Many freight lines have had to weather a series of setbacks. A few have gone bankrupt, only to be gobbled up by competitors. The advent of piggyback and containerized cargo has revolutionized the railroads by reducing the time needed to load and unload the rolling stock. Powerful new models of Diesel-electric locomotives have replaced the FTs. Strings of two hundred freight cars cruising at eighty MPH on the mainlines are not uncommon.

The nation's passenger train service was federalized in the 1970s under the name of Amtrak, but commercial airlines have taken the bulk of the traveling public away from trains. High-speed electric trains are now under development and are being considered for use in the United States. Already in use in Europe and Japan, these bullet trains rocket along at a breathtaking hundred-plus MPH. Electrically levitated trains, without the need for the steel rails, promise to be the train of the future. They are held inches above the roadbed by magnetic fields, and speeds approaching three hundred MPH have been achieved and may eventually displace the Diesel-electric locomotive.

Tractor-Trailer Trucks

As the railroads faced mounting competition from the airlines for passenger traffic, the trucking industry began to nibble into the railroad's cartage business. Early trucks were too small to carry great loads for long distances, mainly because the road system was a series of narrow, winding paths at the mercy of weather conditions. The trucks themselves were unable to match the load capacity that rail offered shippers. As a result, trucks were used to transport limited loads from farm or factory to or from rail sidings.

In the early 1930s, a few trucks began to run the road that had features still in use today. Companies such as Mack, International, Kenworth, and Diamond T all produced models to attract purchasers of their trucks. Kenworth offered tailor-made rigs while the others began to install doors, windows, lights, heaters, padded seats, speedometers and mirrors. Chrome bumpers began to show up in the mirrors of common automobiles as proud truck drivers dressed up their rigs. By the end of 1938, business necessities had essentially formed the tractor-trailer into its now familiar, modern form.[10]

From its inception, the trucking industry was a hodge-podge of independent truck owners hauling whatever they could get to wherever they managed to drive their trucks. There were no set limits on weight or content, nor were there any special license requirement for drivers. The industry became organized with the passage of the Motor Carrier Safety Act of 1935. Administered by the Interstate Commerce Commission, the act regulated rates and business practices concerning trucking and issued permits and licenses to carriers. With rules favoring the larger firms, the law changed the way manufacturers, drivers, and the public looked at trucking. Another law from these formative years place restrictions on the hours spent driving. From a study conducted in 1940, it was discovered that most accidents and mishaps occurred after drivers had been behind the wheel for more than ten hours. Truck drivers were then and still are limited to a ten-hour driving day, to be followed by an eight-hour break.

Another innovation, the sleeper unit, became more popular as many drivers could not afford lodging or it was inconvenient to use. An optional factory sleeper could be ordered from Kenworth beginning in 1936. Prior to that, drivers resorted to building their own. By 1941, the pace of industry in the United States had accelerated to the point that rail was beginning to achieve capacity without affecting passenger traffic. After the Pearl Harbor attack, the war effort hit fever pitch. Ever more trucks were required to move goods; the sleeper cab became

Poster produced by the War Production Board and Bendix Aviation Corp. These placards were disseminated to make drivers aware of the great importance of maintaining their equipment for the duration of the war. (NARA)

an absolute necessity as teams of drivers could spell each other for their ten- hour stretches, one driving with one napping in the bunk.

At this time, the general cab design copied the automotive industry, with enormous hoods stretching out far in front of the driver's seat. In a break with tradition, Ford came out with the cab-over truck. By eliminating the hood and raising the cab over the engine, the driver now had virtually unlimited visibility. Chevrolet, along with its parent company General Motors Co.(GMC), mimicked Ford with a semi cab-over featuring the short hood. Fire trucks built immediately after the war exhibited this design feature as well.

Engine and transmission combinations, the vital components of load hauling, had finally been perfected to give the driver the best control over mountain and desert terrain. The first Cummins Diesel was installed in a Kenworth body in 1932; Mack was the first to install its own Diesel in 1938.[11] More efficient than its gasoline counterpart, the Diesel engine offered more than twice the distance on equal amounts of fuel. Operating costs were further reduced as Diesel fuel cost per gallon was half that of gasoline.

Materials for building the big trucks evolved during the war. Cummins introduced the first Diesel engine made from aluminum in 1941. Installed in a Kenworth, it had cast iron cylinder sleeves, a forerunner of automotive blocks made in the 1980s. (In Germany, aluminum heads were also tried in the large Maybach engine of the Tiger tank). Aluminum became more common in frames, cabs and transmissions during the war in spite of its strategic importance. The reasoning behind the change was to lighten the truck weight without sacrificing strength. With every possible pound saved, one equivalent pound of payload could be hauled or equivalent fuel saved.

The introduction of tandem axle and dual tire arrangements to distribute the weight of the load went a long way toward increasing the effective payload. Cargo beds, previously limited by factors such as strength and maneuverability, began to grow longer. Mounting an articulating hinge at the union of the truck and the trailer solved the problem of maneuverability. It was first installed on the ladder trucks of city fire departments beginning about 1916. The ladder had to be steered independently from a station at the rear of the trailer, a task that required some practice. The forward hinge, called a fifth wheel, created the semi-trailer in which the frame and rear wheels formed a separate component. In the original design that lasted for about fifteen years, the trailer was permanently attached to the fifth wheel by means of a large retaining pin.

Subsequently, a notch in the pin and a mating groove in the fifth wheel allowed the trailer to be disconnected from the truck. By adding a set of landing legs to the forward section of the trailer to support the weight when separated from the truck, the modern tractor-trailer rig was created. In this form, the big rigs went to war carrying the massive amounts of supplies that a mobile army consumes.

From the start, the army was interested in working with the American Trucking Association (ATA) to stimulate the expansion of army highway transport and to eliminate any hindrances of that goal. The army recognized the potential of highway transport, the flexibility, availability, and expediency. At the time America entered the war, the stateside monthly amount of privately owned trucking amounted just over 44,000 tons shipped. By June 1945, that volume had swelled to 1,068,000 tons/month, capping off the wartime total of more than 26 million tons of cargo.[12] This logistics capability spelled doom to the German resistance.

Consider the "Red Ball Express." This was a circuit set up in the race across France to keep the Allied armies rolling against the retreating Germans. Lacking any port facilities east of the Normandy beachheads, the Allies were forced to establish a supply highway towards Germany. As the army moved, this road had to as well. The eventual ending area at Soissons, France was over two hundred miles away from the start. From the end of August to the middle of November, eighty-one days in all, about 412,193 tons were trucked to the front. That is an average of almost 5,089 tons a day. In one day, August 29, 5,958 trucks, mostly standard army 2-½ ton 6X6s, carried 12,342 tons.[13] Lacking a similar means of transport, the Germans were defeated by the endless stream of supplies shipped forward around the clock by truck after the French rail system had been destroyed by bombing and sabotage.

During the last days of the war, a limited experiment, called piggybacking, was undertaken. It was meant to eliminate the step of unloading a trailer's contents into boxcars, and then reloading trailers at the destination from the boxcars. The trailer, contents intact, was wheeled onto specially modified flatbed rail cars. A fitting, mounted on the car, replicated the fifth wheel to secure the entire load. This innovation reduced the time it took to transfer goods from one transport medium to another. Although the test was a success, the idea had few proponents because the rail industry misjudged the impact of the trucking industry. The railroads attempted to charge more for the piggyback loads than the trucking companies could to drive their own trailers. Then the coal strikes of 1947 practically paralyzed the American rail system—providing another reason to covert to Diesel locomotives, by the way—and undermined the railroad's ability to carry loads for the trucking industry. It was a breach of faith to the truckers.[14]

This was an experiment late in the European war where fuel supplies were brought forward in 750 gallon capacity palletized containers. This made every truck capable of transporting fuel without loading hundreds of Jerry cans. That too dispensed with the labor of filling, disbursing, and collecting the empties. Eventually, containerization would be mandated for other materials, including water. (U.S. Army/NARA)

The only saving grace for piggyback rail was the lack of an interstate highway system. Bad weather, narrow roads, accidents and improving railroad reliability all helped to restore the faith. Nearly half the goods shipped by truck from 1948 until the 1960s went at least part way on piggyback rail. When the states had constructed a substantial network of all-weather roads under the Federal Interstate Highway Act of 1956, truckers again began to haul their cargo by road.

But in 1973, the Arab oil embargo restricted shipments of oil to America. Fuel for the truckers was limited and, in some localities, rationed. Costs skyrocketed and piggyback had another chance at life. This time there was a twist. Reborn Asian industry, especially in Japan, had led to the invention of containerized shipping, an updated version of the piggyback. A sealed steel box, measuring the same as the standard trailer box, could be loaded onto a ship in stacks resembling a set of wooden blocks, then onto railcars and, finally, onto flatbed trucks to the ultimate destination. Being packed in the container, cargo had less chance of breakage and loss. The trucker and rail company did not lose the use of valuable rolling stock while the goods were packed. Being standard size, machinery to handle the containers was simplified.

Expanding into the containerized and piggyback cartage saved the rail industry. The rail, truck, and shipping industries have now reached a balance with these payload-handling systems. Some credit for the present global economy is due the same material methods, somewhat improved, that defeated the Axis.[15]

Specialized Trucks

Machinery Trucks

Every army needs to repair its weapons at some time. Roman Legionnaires were required to ensure that their personal equipment was in good condition under the penalty of death. Blacksmiths traveled with Napoleon's troops into Russia, fixing the wagons and arms. So too, did the

The vehicles in the center of the photo are shop trucks, two of a three vehicle unit. One truck carries a metal-cutting lathe, grinder, drill press, and a large variety of tools that any machine shop would have. The other truck carries a large milling machine and a wide assortment of cutting tools. The third is either a Jeep or a three-quarter-ton Dodge weapons carrier, either one towing a trailered electric generator. Together, the three vehicles set up not far from the front and provide any repairs that their equipment and training can fulfill. This is called a force-multiplier, as damaged equipment can be returned to the fight rapidly, often faster than the enemy can. (U. S. Army)

Allied and Axis men have personnel assigned to maintain their respective war machines.

A variety of light, medium, and heavy trucks were outfitted with machinery and tools to service everything from delicate optical instruments to artillery pieces. Specialist trucks were available to rebuild the thousands of vehicle engines that were wearing out through use, abuse, and misuse. Machine shop trucks had a selection of common industrial machines to fabricate new parts right on the battlefield. Each country had unique maintenance needs and they met these with typical ingenuity. The Japanese, having more cavalry than motorized vehicles, fielded special farrier trucks with a

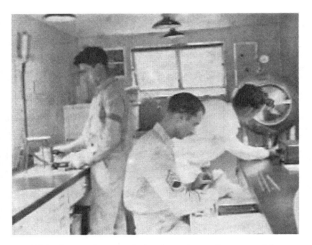

This is a photo of the interior of a portable medical laboratory. The military made an effort to make shop trucks as complete and ergonomic as possible. There were no less than 46 different shop or service truck beds during the war. (U.S. Army Medical Corps)

built-in forge furnace and a portable anvil. By war's end, American manufacturers had begun to build modular truck beds, with cabinets accessible through weatherproof doors that could be mounted onto a standardized truck frame. Ladder racks, frames to hold oxy-acetylene bottles, and so on, became commonplace. These designs went on to become the utility beds that are now built by the thousands with cubbyholes for all sorts of tools and parts.[16]

Septic Tank Delivery Trucks

When the bombing campaigns over Europe and Japan introduced the four-thousand-pound bomb to warfare, Army Air Force procurement officers commissioned a truck design capable of moving the high-explosive behemoth from storage fields to the waiting planes. Using a reinforced frame mounted on a standard two-and-a-half-ton truck, the bomb could be lifted and set on carts by means of a winch system driving a dolly that traveled on an overhead track. Hundreds of these trucks were built during the war, only to become surplus at the end of hostilities.

After the war, thousands of homes were being built in areas that would soon be

The post-war septic tank was little different from those of the present day. Cast concrete, it weighed between 600 to 2,000 pounds. Civilian vehicles did not have the capability to move that type of weight over the rough ground of a construction site. The War Department was holding a sale of surplus equipment at huge discounts. Light, demilitarized tanks went for $100 each. Bomb service trucks as above sold for $75 to $200. The trolley could lift 4,000 pounds and, with all wheel drive, get into the most rugged property. The Chevrolet version sold for about the same but could only lift 2,500 pounds. (U.S. Army Air Forces)

called the suburbs and the local municipalities did not have the resources to put in sewer systems. Instead, pre-cast concrete septic tanks became quite popular during this housing boom. The surplus bomb trucks became useful again to set the tanks into the ground. As the old war-era fleet began to wear out, new trucks based on commercial

The following picture is a modern septic tank delivery truck. It does not take much imagination to see the familial lines.

frames were built. Even today, one can see the heredity in the same winch/track and framework arrangement that obviously has World War Two inspiration.

Fire-fighting Equipment

More citizens were indirectly involved in the Second World War than in any other war in history. There was hardly a country in the Northern hemisphere that did not experience destruction of some magnitude. Neutral countries such as Switzerland and Sweden regularly had their borders violated and, inevitably, both were accidentally bombed. Even American shores were shelled by Japanese submarines and on at least one occasion, by Japanese aircraft. Later in the war, Japanese balloon bombs were randomly scattered all across North America, falling from Mexico well into Canada, and as far east as Michigan. In all these instances, fires were started as a result of the attacks. This was not accidental. By the Second World War, fire had reached its zenith as a weapon, and new equipment was developed to counter the threat.

The Hose Tender

Beginning in the spring of 1940, German bombers rained high explosives and incendiaries down on British factories and cities, in preparation of an invasion. Besides destroying structures above ground, some Second World War bombs were capable of piercing the ground, damaging infrastructure facilities such as gas and water lines. These same ruptured water lines were used to supply the hydrants for controlling the fires. Quite often, responding fire crews had to travel hundreds of yards to find a pressurized hydrant. To get the water to the fire, they developed a hose tender fire truck.

Carrying up to 2,000 feet of two-inch hose, the tender could also serve as a pumper, augmenting the available water pressure for the conventional fire apparatus. The hose tender is still in use, often assigned to work with a ladder truck, carrying the hoses and other tools that are needed.[17]

Foam Tankers

As described in Chapter 9, foam became an important firefighting tool for the military in dealing with the extreme heat and tenacity of high-octane fuel fires. Foam, as with any new material, required a certain amount of specialized equipment. In this case, foam trucks were outfitted with pumps and large tanks of foam concentrate. Early models were stationed at RAF airfields in England and when the Eighth Air Force made its debut in the summer of 1942; Reverse Lend-Lease ensured the Americans had the same advantage of foam.

However, the U.S.Navy was ahead of the Army Air Forces. The British had given samples in the early war years to U.S. Navy military observers and samples were sent to America. There, Naval scientists made major improvement to the foam and built the necessary vehicles to deliver the mixture of three gallons of foam concentrate and 97 gallons of water to produce 1,000 gallons of foam, more than enough to put out a sizable blaze.

High-Density Fog Systems

The U.S.Navy faced a very real threat of fire during the war. Shipboard fires accounted for the majority of the sinkings, whether touched off by enemy action or accidentally. There are hundreds of flammable chemicals and substances aboard a modern warship besides the obvious explosives-filled ordnance. Until the creation of sprayed fireproof insulation, most ships used thick sheets of cork to keep the chill of sea water out. Glued to the inner sides of the hull, cork and glue would burn like a torch, giving off deadly gases within the smoke.

It is particularly difficult to fight a fire in ships made of steel. Innumerable inaccessible nooks and crannies give the fire an opportunity to spread. Steel is an excellent conductor of heat, spreading the danger of fire well beyond the original site. Another danger in fighting a fire on a ship with conventional methods is that enormous amounts of water are typically used. Filling the hull with water may put out the fire, but that serves no purpose if the ship sinks from all the water pumped onboard to fight the fire. On-board pumps do no good either if the electricity is off, a common occurrence in fires.

To overcome the shortcomings of conventional fire-fighting techniques, the Navy developed the high-density fog system. A high-pressure mist of water is delivered to the fire through specially designed nozzles. The fog, really just finely atomized water, cools the surrounding air, which draws life-giving heat away from the fire. The fog also tends to capture the particulate matter that makes up the bulk of smoke, clearing the air faster. Fog machines used very little water in comparison to conventional fire-fighting equipment, so the flooding problems were greatly reduced.

The engine that produces the fog is quite a bit lighter than the large fire pumps found onboard ships, making it easier to carry into the lower decks, where fires often rage out of control. Blind compartments can be fitted with fog nozzles to remotely cool the steel plates, cutting off a fire's path. Best of all, the fog creates a wall of cooled air, protecting the firefighters from the fierce convection heat that typically comes from a fire, sapping their strength. Fog systems are still used for ships, commercial and military. Municipal departments have adopted fog nozzles as well.[18]

Community Fire Equipment

Many small communities in America had little, if any, organized fire protection before the Second World War. Times were tough and money was tight. Fire equipment was well out of the reach of most towns' budgets. With the war, jobs became available and tax revenues climbed, but now all the available fire equipment was going towards the war effort.

After the war, the American government declared thousands of military style fire trucks as surplus, to be sold off at a mere fraction of their original cost. Communities, their coffers swollen, went on a buying spree. Some towns, really just villages of two or three thousand people, found themselves in possession of the latest in fire protection technology. Volunteers enrolled in fire-fighting training classes, often taught by experienced veterans, who had been trained by the military to operate the very equipment they were now using on the local level.[19]

The Freeway System

In America, it was recognized since before the First World War that the ever-increasing numbers of cars would require better roads. At first individual states accepted the responsibility for road construction, leading to differences in quality from state to state and to outright fraud. Building roads of sub-standard quality and then rebuilding them a year later at the taxpayer's expense became almost a sport. State and county officials winked at the racket, knowing that their ill-gotten gains were secure.

To overcome this, the Federal government nationalized the states' road projects. Funds from Washington D.C. went to aid the states and to provide a rational basis for their engineering. A network of roads began to take shape across the nation, linking the opposite coasts. This system could hardly be compared to the modern interstate highways. They were narrow and offered little in the way of lane division. In the eastern United States, roads were paved with asphalt or concrete, but out west, most roads were built with clay or gravel.

In Germany, a concrete four-lane highway system, called the Autobahn, was rapidly linking major German cities together. The concept was originally suggested in 1921 and construction begun in 1928. The work progressed so slowly, though, that the Nazis were able to use the project for their own ends. Hitler gained the office of Chancellor largely on his promises to put the unemployed back to work and to return Germany's dignity. By claiming responsibility for the 2,000 miles of roadway, Hitler was able to show the German people, who conveniently overlooked the facts, that he had fulfilled both pledges.

Largely completed by 1938, the Autobahn provided the model for the interstate super-highway in other countries. The chief engineer of the American federal highway, Thomas H. MacDonald, toured the German system in 1936. Innovations such as the

This is one view of Hitler's precious Autobahn he never foresaw: tens of thousands of his soldiers walking in surrender as the enemy uses the all-weather highway to probe further into the German Reich. Actually, the Autobahn was a project already underway when Adolf came to power, he just usurped it for his purposes. (NARA)

limited access exit and entrance ramps, banked curves, multiple lanes widely separated by grass verges, channeling to control water flow, and reflective paints on road markings and signs were all impressive. The sophistication of the bridges and tunnels were equally magnificent, but MacDonald could not understand the justification for the grand scale of the Autobahn. Nevertheless, he returned to America with a new vision of the freeway of the future.

President Roosevelt wanted to begin to build a series of superhighways, and MacDonald was tapped to design and oversee the project. An abandoned rail bed, running roughly between Pittsburgh and Philadelphia, was chosen as the site for the first stretch of this new roadway. From the flatlands outside Philadelphia, the turnpike rose to pass over the Appalachian Mountains. Even though there was only eight hundred feet difference in elevation between the two cities, the road traversed six separate mountain ranges.

The construction contracts stipulated that the 160 miles of the Pennsylvania Turnpike would be completed in twenty months. Working twenty-four hours a day, crews blasted intervening ridges, using the waste to fill valleys. Partially built railroad tunnels were widened to accommodate the four lanes of the turnpike. The undulating route required 307 concrete monolithic culverts and bridges. The builders fought the weather as well as the terrain. Spring rains were followed by the worst summer weather—thunderstorms, hail, and, unbelievably, snow—in recent memory. Nevertheless, at 12:01 AM, October 1, 1940, the Pennsylvania Turnpike officially opened, only four months behind schedule.

The turnpike was an instant success. A convoy of fifty cars carrying members of Congress, reporters, highway department bureaucrats, military transportation experts, and representatives from automobile companies took a ride on it. Despite the fog and drizzle, the mile-long motorcade raced along at speeds up to 100 MPH. Thousands of motorists paid the toll to try their new road. Soon, it became common to stop along the way and break out a picnic basket for a noontime repast on the grassy median.

World War Two stopped all plans for other superhighways, though War Department officials, seeing the tactical advantages of high speed, all-weather roads traversing the country, fought for continued construction of the roadways. They were overruled and priorities were placed on other projects. Finally, in 1944, Congress appropriated $1.5 billion to initiate the Interstate and Defense Highway Act. Its purpose was to link the major industrial centers of the U.S. together and with the major highways of Canada and Mexico.[20] Once the war was over, highway projects gained popular support. Located mainly in the eastern states, state built, federally funded toll roads quickly became reality. Maine (1947), New York, and New Hampshire (1948), and New Jersey, (1949) all boasted their own toll roads. By 1955, a trip from Chicago to New York City could be made virtually non-stop.

The European war concluded with General Dwight Eisenhower commanding the victorious Allied armies. Eventually ascending to the Presidency, he recalled his tour in Germany and the important role the Autobahn had played in Allied movements. He knew that the United States, with its vast distances, would benefit from the commercial and military uses of such a road system. Eisenhower wanted his road system, but it took three attempts to get the legislation through Congress. Bickering over the costs, estimated to be five billion dollars a year for the next ten years, held the legislation up. On June 28, 1956, the President finally signed the Federal Interstate Highway Act.

Under the Act, the Federal government provided money to each state to construct freeways to a standardized set of plans furnished by the Department of Transportation. The states were required to kick in a small percentage of funds—ten percent—and the maintenance of the completed roads became the responsibility of the states. Federal funding continues to be given and the states generate much of the revenue through taxes on vehicle licenses, tires, batteries, and fuel. Now completed, the interstate highways are generally available on a no-charge basis, but there are a few stretches that are tolled. Much concern is now being voiced about the conditions of the bridges, especially in the northern states where salt has decayed the structures.[21]

Cable-stayed Bridges

German transportation systems were in shambles by the end of the war. They had borne the brunt of Allied air attacks, especially the numerous bridges across the major rivers of Europe. By all estimates there were more than fifteen thousand bridges of varying size to be rebuilt in West Germany alone.[22] This situation was viewed as an opportunity as well as a challenge by civil engineers. Materials, particularly steel and concrete were in short supply, so they were invited to apply new concepts to design and build lightweight bridges.

Prior to the Second World War, suspension bridges had evolved from iron cable and truss structures of nineteenth century England through John Roebling's massive brick and steel Brooklyn Bridge to the graceful span of the Golden Gate Bridge. Early British bridges first used a cable-stayed system of support, but the materials of the period were of such poor quality that cable-stayed bridges were soon discredited and fell into disuse. This however did not spell the demise of suspension bridges.

A suspension bridge like the Golden Gate Bridge or the Brooklyn Bridge typically uses a pair of swooping catenary cables anchored in enormous concrete casements on opposite shores to support the roadway. Tall towers, set into huge sunken foundations, bear the weight of the cables over the entire length of the span. The design is not only graceful to the eye but is immensely stable for extremely long spans.

A modern cable-stayed bridge, on the other hand, eliminates the concrete anchorage and the associated catenary cables. Instead, the suspension cables are strung to the tops of the towers from the deck, which is then supported by the towers. Because the cables extend equally to the deck on either side of the towers, the loads are evenly balanced. This balancing act requires careful considerations of all the load factors involved so that anticipated stresses can accurately be predicted. From the aesthetic point of view, the cable-stayed bridge is less graceful but makes a sharp and bold outline punctuated by the cables that form a series of equilateral triangles with the bridge deck.

Catenary suspension bridges that were built between 1883 — when the Brooklyn Bridge was opened — and 1935 pushed this theoretical frontier to new extremes. With each successive project, longer spans were achieved with fewer materials and less labor with a resulting reduction of cost per foot of span. Moreover, suspension bridges of the Golden Gate variety were highly regarded for their aesthet-

Cable-stayed structures extend beyond bridges for cars and people. This is a natural gas pipeline crossing the Rio Grande. The elegance of this design is that the load of the suspension is counterbalanced with a similar load on the other side of the tower. (Author's Collection)

ic attractiveness. This lightweight form reached its apogee in 1940 with the opening of the ill-fated Tacoma Narrows Bridge in Washington State. Within months, the lightly built "Galloping Gertie"—so called for its propensity of bucking up and down every time the wind blew—collapsed into the water during a stiff breeze.

Two years before the Tacoma Narrows Bridge fell, German engineer F. Dischinger was supervising the erection of a railroad bridge over the Elbe River near Hamburg. To compensate for the heavier-than-normal loading of rail traffic, Dischinger incorporated extra cables called stays extending from the towers to the bridge deck. The stays provided an unanticipated benefit of aerodynamic stability—the basic cause of the Tacoma bridge failure—and stiffness, far more than had ever been achieved in a suspension bridge before. This remarkable German engineer had rediscovered the cable-stayed bridge.

Dischinger survived the war and his achievement attracted the attention of Allied reconstruction advisors. During this period of reconstruction orthotropic deck designs gained high favor. Orthotropic plate construction—an engineering term used to describe the formation of the deck structure that is aligned in the longitudinal axis—was used in the Golden Gate Bridge and refined as a result of the Tacoma bridge disaster. Dischinger's cable design formulas and American orthotropic bridge building techniques had a post-war marriage that took a few years to come to fruition. By the early 1950s, shortly after Dischinger published a book detailing his work with cable-stayed bridges, several new bridges were in the design or development stages in West Germany and other European countries. The first was opened in 1955, the 1,085 feet long Strömsund bridge in Sweden. It is no small wonder that Dischinger, working in conjunction with the German engineering firm Demag got the contract.

As a direct result of Dischinger's work immediately before and after the war, cable-stayed bridges were springing up everywhere. By 1972, a total forty-three cable-stayed bridges had been constructed worldwide, thirteen of them in West Germany. After another five years, the number worldwide had grown to 62, Japan, another country ravaged by the war, accounting for eight.[23]

Carpooling

When the Japanese swept through the Malaysian peninsula, they managed to cut America off from her main supplies of natural rubber. As a result, the United States government, at that time on a total war footing, strove to limit the use of the remaining rubber. Domestic production of tires was severely curtailed and rationing of tires and fuel went into effect. A national speed limit of thirty-five MPH was imposed, as were mandatory tire inspections. Instructions were distributed for the care of precious tires, and multiple spares were seized.

All of this took place in a nation of car lovers, who were nonetheless expected to take up war work in the factories, often some distance from their homes. The apparent contradiction was handily met with the introduction of car-pooling. Buses were an option that met with success and hundreds of them, previously considered to be obsolete, were placed back into service. Bicycles were also in short supply, for vital metals were put to use. A few inspired individuals rode their horses to work, where employers obligingly supplied water troughs. The rest of the labor force was pressured to share the ride to and from work. Notices were posted on bulletin boards directing employees to sign up for car-pooling in offices set up to match riders.

A number of independent ideas were submitted to increase the capacity of the stock automobile. One such submission reorganized the seating of a four-door sedan—normally carrying up to six passengers—to seat ten adults or 16 children. The American population, spurred on by patriotic fervor, began to cram as many passengers as possible into their cars. Overloaded and running on tires that were already threadbare caused more than a few accidents, some ending in needless fatalities. Concerned with the overzealous behavior, local officials began to crack down on the worst offenders. Fortunately, the enthusiasm died down and further incidents were rare.

Not until the gasoline crisis in the 1970s did carpooling become popular again. When the Arab cartel reduced the supply of inexpensive petroleum to America, causing prices to skyrocket, driving became a luxury. Out of desperation, rides were sought, and companies aided by allowing work hours to be shifted to accommodate the employees' needs. An unexpected side benefit of the gas shortage was that the air began to clear, especially in larger cities that had pollution problems.

Locking Lug Nuts

Theft of precious tires during the Second World War was a constant problem. The Office of Price Administration (OPA), the government agency delegated to run the tire rationing program, established an inspection program that recorded the serial numbers of tires. If, on re-inspection, the numbers didn't match, serious trouble would ensue. The miscreant's tire and fuel rations could be revoked at the very least. Repeat

A close look at a Chrysler-designed wheel lock set. The round nuts have three holes that are uniquely spaced. A driver (in box at right) has pins that match the holes. On the car, the set also has a plate that fit over the center bearing cover so the tire thief could not remove the bearing nut to take the tire. (Chrysler)

offenders often had to pay hefty fines or serve jail sentences.

It became quite common to see cars festooned with chains and padlocks through the rims in an attempt to thwart thieves. The plan worked admirably until the car owner, in haste, forgot to unlock the chains. It is not hard to imagine the chagrin of the absent-minded driver, not to mention the very real damage done to the irreplaceable motorcar.

Pontiac introduced a novel solution. Two nuts, threaded to fit the lug studs, were supplied in a simple kit along with a sheet-metal shroud designed to fit over the wheel-bearing cap. Lacking the flats for the wrench, the new nuts have a large flat face with three holes drilled in at specific places. An accompanying wrench, with pins matching the hole pattern, was included. By replacing two of the standard lug nuts, the shroud and lock nuts would preclude the theft of the entire wheel assembly.

This unique solution is still an option. Tires are no longer rationed, but for some car enthusiasts, it is not unusual to spend hundreds of dollars for just one tire. For a few dollars at any auto parts store, a similar kit can be bought and installed in less than fifteen minutes.[24]

Solderless Electrical Fittings

Machinery became more electrified as the century progressed. Once lead-acid batteries were fitted into cars for lights, inventors began to devise more options that made driving safer and more reliable. By the 1930s, cars were regularly coming equipped with windshield wipers, brake lights, horns, and electrical starters. This meant that manufacturers spent more time installing not only the myriad of motors and switches that ran these items but the growing tangle of wiring that interconnected them.

A self-educated inventor named S.N. Buchanan invented a way for wires to be crimped into metal fittings without the benefit of solder in the mid-1930s. He hoped to sell his idea to the auto companies, who clung to their antiquated methods with uncustomary fervor. Solder was permanent and rarely failed to hold the wires securely. However, should the wire become overheated during the soldering process, there was a high likelihood that the wire would prematurely break. Buchanan's fitting eliminated that particular problem.

His method made the installation process faster as well. The fittings could be formed into flat plates—called spade terminals—that securely locked onto mated female fittings.

Frustrated by industry's intransigence, Buchanan teamed up with an electrical engineer from MIT named U.A. Whitaker. He had the experience to push Buchanan's ideas from the inventor's bench to commercial success. Besides his MIT training, Whitaker also held degrees in electrical engineering from Carnegie Mellon University and in law from the Cleveland School of Law.

Together, the two men opened their business, Aero-Marine Products Inc., in Newark, New Jersey on September 15, 1941. Their first contract was for making solderless electrical fittings for military aircraft and boats, which inspired the company to change its name to Aircraft-Marine Products in 1943.

The more technical the tools of war become, so too do the ways it can be disabled. Here we have two Signal Corps men stitching together a very large telephone cable. They are using a relatively new device; solderless electrical connectors. (Signal Corps/NARA)

During the course of the war, the company introduced several innovative lines of connectors, most of which served as initial models for present-day electrical fittings. There were open and closed stud fittings, snap-together bullet fittings, and clip-on styles, like those found on spark plug wires, for rapid factory assembly or repairs in the field. Under the military's guidance, Aircraft-Marine Products (AMP) produced a multiple-wire electrical connector encapsulated in an aluminum housing—called a cannon fitting, because it was first used for severe duty on artillery pieces—that threaded onto a matching fitting mounted on instrument packages. When assembled, the cannon fittings were nearly impossible to shake apart and retained water-tight integrity under all circumstances short of being completely destroyed.

In 1943, AMP introduced a hand-held tool that could replicate the special crimp that had previously been done only by machine. The company now began to sell packages of their terminal fittings and tools to industry and the military for maintenance purposes. That same year, the company posted $2.2 million in sales, indicating the massive popularity and usefulness of their product.

As the war drew to an end, AMP engineers began planning for a peacetime economy. Company representatives approached the hundreds of manufacturers using electrical components and offered to supply them with electrical wire harnesses and fittings. By using recently adopted plastic-injection molding techniques, AMP was soon making unitized electrical connectors for appliances, machinery and the automotive industry. As electronic hardware became more prevalent, AMP designed and fabricated the hundreds of customized fittings that were needed.[25]

The Quick-Change Windshield Wiper Blade

In the early 1920s, the driving public was introduced to an innovation from Detroit called the windshield wiper. Only one wiper was supplied, mounted on the driver's side and powered by hand. The invention reflected the rapidly changing nature of driving in inclement weather at higher speeds. By the end of the decade, vacuum- and electric-operated wipers were becoming standard, but the rubber strip that did the actual wiping still maintained its similarity to the common household squeegee. Changing the strip meant that a number of screws had to be removed, a new rubber blade carefully placed and the assembly put back together again. This was a time consuming and irritating chore for the typical American driver. Nevertheless, little was done to make changes to the wiper blade design until the Second World War.

Aircraft from that conflict needed to be maintained in the least amount of time, and it was not efficient to have a

This is a good example of the pattern of this war in particular; that the level of innovation was so pervasive, even the smallest details were studied for change and improvement. In addition, the level of engineering was so sophisticated that so many inventions have resisted the evolution process. (ANCO)

mechanic spend an hour changing the wiper blades of just one airplane. An American supplier of wiper blades to the military, the Anderson Company (Anco), introduced a new style of blade with a lock clip that snapped in place. No longer were tools required to remove the old blades, as they were released with a fingertip-activated latch.

After the war, Anco marketed the design under the name of "Dead-Locker," stressing the ease and convenience of the snap mechanism. Sixty years and millions of blades later, the Anco blade—and its imitators—are still being used.[26]

The Diaphragm Clutch

A clutch provides a breakable link between the engine and the wheels. The performance of a clutch is directly proportional to the engine's efficiency. Should the clutch be too weak, the car will be unable to ascend hills or negotiate muddy roads. An extra-strong clutch never slips, making hills or snowy lanes a snap, but the driver has to have the muscular build of Charles Atlas. A number of ideas were proposed to come to a happy medium. The majority had flaws that would eventually lead to their demise. Even the clutches on production cars had to be unnecessarily stiff to overcome slippage problems.

Then, in 1938, Chevrolet Motor Company introduced a revolutionary new clutch that was supposed to be easier to operate. Called the "Tiptoe-matic" clutch, it consisted of eighteen spring steel fingers that pressed against the throw-out bearing connected to the pedal. When depressed, the fingers levered the spring-loaded pressure plate away from the clutch disc, effectively disconnecting the engine from the wheels. According to an advertisement, it required only twenty-five pounds of pedal pressure to move the 1,100 pounds of spring.[27] (It requires about the same amount of the former to crush a modern soda can.)

The new clutch was revolutionary in that it enabled people of slighter stature and strength to operate a motor vehicle. This includes women, a segment of the American populace that had previously not

"TIPTOE-MATIC" CLUTCH IN 1938 CHEVROLETS HAS NEW, EASY-ACTING DIAPHRAGM SPRING

"You'll be AHEAD with a CHEVROLET!"

This type of clutch has become an industry standard for almost all passenger cars and light truck and many heavier vehicles too.

widely driven. During the war, women would be called upon to drive a wide variety of vehicles in the performance of their jobs. Without the new design, and its clones, their tasks would have been much more difficult.

The Constant Velocity (CV) Boot

The CV boot, an innocuous little item, hides beneath the modern front-wheel-drive car. The average consumer hardly knows it exists until informed by the mechanic that it needs replacement. A rupture in the cover, or in the common vernacular, the boot, allows all manner of dirt and water in to attack the precision-machined surfaces while allowing the lubricating grease out.

Actually, there are four boots on the typical front-wheel drive automobile. (Four-wheel drive automobiles may have four more on the rear drive axles.) The CV boots are located on pair of half-shafts that transmits power from the engine/transmission to the tires. Being on the front, these tires have to do triple duty; drive the car forward and articulate vertically to effect the ride and rotate side to side to accomplish the steering function. Because the power has to be continuously transmitted regardless of the wheel's position or the movement of the suspension, the shafts need to flex. The constant velocity joint accomplishes this.

An assembled Constant Velocity joint without the grease. The fits between the surfaces is close and very smooth. Even the smallest grain of sand will quickly devastate these surfaces. The rubber boot is the only protection.

The CV joint is a marvelous piece of engineering. It has three basic components: the outer shell, the balls, and the inner knuckle. The outer shell is forged from high-strength steel and machined to extremely tight tolerances. Depending on the size of the vehicle, the typical CV joint outer shell is about the size of a small coffee can. (See graphic) Within the shell are five or six concave grooves. Each groove is evenly spaced around the wall of the shell. In addition to their concave shape, the grooves are formed so that a ball rolling in the shell will describe an arc centered about an imaginary point exactly in its center.

The inner knuckle, about two inches in diameter and one inch thick, has similar grooves cut into its outer rim. They are machined so that a ball will follow the same arc as in the shell. Assembled, hardened steel balls, each approximately three-quarters of an inch diameter, ride in the grooves. Because the balls interlock between the inner and outer pieces, a mechanical link is made so that torque will be transmitted. The arc allows the joint to pivot into any angle or combination of angles, automatically compensating for driving conditions.

All the surfaces within the CV joint are finely ground so that there is absolutely no excessive clearance between the assembled parts, yet the elements all slide together smoothly. The friction-free action of the joint is aided by a surrounding bath of thick grease, contained by the boot. But, should the protective rubber boot tear or crack, the grease begins to leak and allows the joint to become contaminated. If permitted to remain, the dirt will simultaneously destroy the joint and the car owner's checking account.

An exploded veiw of a Constant Velocity joint. The boot is the large black item in the middle.

The most common type of CV joint was an invention of Alfred Hans Rzeppa, a Ford Motor Company engineer. Rzeppa's innovative mechanism was first used in a series of experimental four-wheel-drive racecars of the early 1930s. Drivers of this vehicle found that without CV joints, torque developed by the engine tended to pull the steering into the centralized, or straight-ahead, position. This phenomenon reportedly required incredible strength to overcome and exhausted all but the most robust drivers over the duration of a race. Naturally, this spelled an end to the experiment.

During the early days of the Nazi regime, Hitler began to rearm Germany and called upon the industrialists to start designing military equipment of unprecedented quality. One of their innovations was to adapt the Rzeppa CV joint. Although all-wheel-drive was not as important a feature of German war vehicles as it was for the Allies, the few models that were built were far advanced for their time, and the majority of these German vehicles used CV joints instead of the universal joint, primarily because the CV joint requires less maintenance.

To improve their idea even more, German engineers created a new seal of molded synthetic rubber to encase the joint. This was a great departure from the norm. Many manufacturers in many countries were using Rzeppa CV joints, but they used felt or leather seals. The German design, however, proved to be far superior to these traditional materials. The rubber boot was shaped roughly like a funnel. Pleats, as on an accordion, allowed free flexure while excluding all foreign debris. The ends were attached to the outer shell and the half-shaft respectively by stout stainless-steel bands.

The British early in the war captured samples of the seals and joints. It was common policy for Allied forces to send experts to review and inspect captured enemy equipment to gather intelligence about advances made in materials and manufacturing. At the time, the Allied experts disparaged the German CV boot design, which precluded its general adoption by the Allies. Only later, with the coming popularity of front-wheel-drive cars did the CV joint and rubber boot find their true calling.[28]

The Automatic Transmission

Driving an early automobile was work, regardless of how carmakers touted the entertainment value of driving. A great deal of the driver's time was spent shifting gears as road conditions changed. This condition was somewhat ameliorated by the introduction of synchronized gear sets. No longer did the driver have to double clutch and listen to the gears clashing. General Motors had a particular interest in reducing the amount of effort it took to drive because the company hoped to capture the one remaining, untapped market of drivers-to-be: the ladies. One example of this strategy is the "Tiptoe-matic" clutch. (See above.)

In 1938, GM introduced the first production version of the automatic transmission. Offered as an option only in Oldsmobile, the innovative gearbox had major teething problems. It was another two years before reliability had improved enough to gain grudging public acceptance. Even so, the automatic transmission was viewed as an extravagance that the average auto buyer was willing to forgo.

One of the reasons for skepticism was that the drive relied on a fluid coupling. The engine had no connection to the drive wheels as it would have when normally connected to the transmission and then to the wheels mechanically. Rather, a torque converter was bolted to the crankshaft. Vanes, similar to those in a waterwheel, took the rotating energy from the engine and imparted the power through a viscous fluid. Because the of the fluid's tendency to resist flow, it would hydrodynamically drive a second set of vanes, transmitting the power through a small hydraulic pump and into the transmission. Clutches within the gearbox used hydraulic pressure to engage the proper gears depending on the engine speed and loads. A set of valves in the transmission sensed the changing conditions and automatically selected the clutches. The seemingly complex mechanism was a major deviation from the safe and reliable manual unit.

Early wartime models of American tanks often had to slow down or even come to a complete stop to change gears, making them an easy target for the enemy's guns. Even moving could be dangerous as huge clouds of blue-black smoke from the over-worked engines, the driver having the transmission in the wrong gear, gave away the tank's position. When the American government began shopping to supply its new mechanized armies with updated equipment, it naturally approached General Motors. Specifically interested in armored fighting vehicles, GM proposed improving the drive train using their automatic transmission.

Through the winter of 1940, GM engineers feverishly worked long hours designing and redesigning the transmission. Often, the schedule demanded that metal for a new modification was being cut before the design prints had been completed. It was not unusual that components from other transmissions be salvaged and incorporated, albeit temporarily, to prove a technical point.

The greatest challenge was with the complex and little-understood fluid dynamics. One member of the staff stood out, mathematician Fred Ullery strove to define the complicated intricacies of how fluid behavior could be converted into subjective mathematical construct. Achieving this goal did not always follow a scholarly approach. Members of the engineering team utilized a free-running stream behind a colleague's home where a variety of model turbine blades could get raw data on the effects of fluid flow over different pinwheel shapes.

In all, there were at least 23 prototype versions of the Hydra-matic transmission that failed acceptance for a multitude of reasons, but all this labor was not in vain. The army agreed to try the transmission in an improved version of their M3 light tank. Coupled to twin Cadillac V-8s, the four-speed Hydra-matic proved a surprising success. The advanced model, now des-

This is a M-24 Chaffee. Its is classified as a light tank but carries a heavy-punching 75 mm gun. Drivers loved this tank for its speed, responsiveness and ease of operation.

ignated as the M5 light tank, went into production in February 1942.[29]

The U.S. Army was not alone when it came to automatic transmissions in vehicles. The infamous German 60-ton Tiger and King Tiger tanks had an eight speed, hydraulically shifted pre-selector transmission. The machine's enormous weight proved to be the weak spot in the drive train. Transmissions and final drives—the gears directly behind the sprockets that drove the treads— most commonly failed. Of the more than 1,300 Tigers built, more than half had to be destroyed by their own crews due to drive train breakdowns.[30]

Hydra-matic transmissions appeared in the American M24 Chaffee light tank, developed in March 1943. Similar to the M5 light tank in that they both had Cadillac engines, they served as the test bed for post-war engineers. Due to changes in the gearbox design, the M24 showed a 22% improvement in grade climbing and towing. Surveys by the army showed that drivers preferred the automatic to the standard shift transmission, citing smoothness of shift and responsiveness. Crewmembers liked the

fact that the automatic transmission did not toss them about the fighting compartment—like being bounced around the interior of a very roomy car without seats or restraints, but with a large variety of sharp corners and invariably hard surfaces.

With the success of GM's automatic transmission, other manufacturers began to make their own. The principle of hydraulic drive would go into the M6 and the M26 heavy tanks. The latter, weighing forty-six tons had been originally built with electric drive. This was abandoned later in favor of the Chrysler Torqmatic automatic

An M-26 Pershing heavy tank, new to the Americans early in the spring of 1945. In the design process for three years, it had a beefed-up three-speed Torq-Matic automatic transmission, a larger version than that in the M-24 Chaffee. (U.S. Army/NARA)

transmission. Chrysler had been working on the components of automatic transmission—overdrive, clutches, and shifting—but GM beat them to a production-worthy unit. Nevertheless, the war gave Chrysler the opportunity to perfect its automatic transmission.

After the war, the big three auto companies resumed auto production, but the designs were rehashed models mostly based on pre-war engineering. This was partly due to management's inability to abandon the path of automotive styling that had served them well prior to the war. But the larger hindrances were retooling from wartime to peacetime production and material restrictions. It would be well into the 1950s before these factors in the limited offerings completely ended. Chrysler's Power-Flite (1953) and Ford's Ford-o-matic (1951) automatic transmissions ended GM's stranglehold on the automatic transmission market. But even GM did not reintroduce their popular torque-converter transmission until 1948. When they did, more than three-quarters of all cars sold came with Hydra-matic.[31]

The British, however, were well aware of the postwar importance of the automatic transmission. In the spring of 1945, a British delegation in America asked for meetings and tours of American automakers regarding automatic transmissions. This was not an unusual request. There was a policy in place for much of the war that gave free access between the two Allies as to manufacturing, research, engineering, or supplies. This proved to be a little different though. The British paid little attention to any information regarding ordnance—war making—materials, but were eager to ask questions about intentions for the civilian market. Piqued, the American hosts asked for reciprocation about English transmissions and were rebuffed. Unable to do anything about it, it was clear that our "ally" had nefarious intentions.[32]

Presently, automatic transmissions dominate the driving world. Now offered as standard equipment, it is used in cars, trucks, buses, and military vehicles. Ironically, it is only the odd factory model that even has the conventional shift transmission, usually only as an option.

Cruise Control

The development of this product was a result not only of the Second World War but also of the bad driving habits of a lawyer and the queasy stomach of his remarkable client, Ralph Teetor. An engineer by training, Ralph was blinded at the age of five in an accident but was nonetheless drawn to anything mechanical. He developed a gift for visualizing whatever he happened to be working on to such an extent that his father—the owner of a prosperous manufacturing company—set up a complete machine shop for the youngster when he was only ten years old. Ralph worked in his shop whenever possible, in both wood and metal. At the age of twelve, he and his cousin manufactured their first car, featuring a one-cylinder engine made from a junked-out block. His talent went beyond the shop, though. There is one tale that relates how Ralph, when he was in high school, helped fabricate and set up the basketball hoops in the school gym. So certain of his memory and visualization prowess, he promptly and repeatedly sank basket after basket to everyone's amazement.

After high school, Ralph naturally gravitated towards mechanical engineering. Most schools turned him away when they learned of his handicap. Only one, the University of Pennsylvania, accepted him with a little help from Ralph's cousin, who happened to be enrolled there.

After completing his requirements for a degree, Ralph went to work in a steam engine department of a large marine equipment company. There he discovered a way to balance the rotors of steam turbine engines used in World War One torpedo boat destroyers. This feat alone is notable in that no one had ever been able to devise such a method before. It had taken the highly sensitive touch of a blind man to be successful.

One of his more advanced developments was an automatic transmission for automobiles. It was so far-reaching in its design that the motor companies shunned it, voicing concerns about its reliability. Only years later, after the patent had expired, did the automotive industry model the first automatic transmissions on a design very similar to that of Ralph's.

Ralph also invented whenever he saw a need, regardless of how whimsical. Once, his wrist became painful from the repeated flicking of his fly fishing rod. He made and patented a totally new type of fishing rod and reel. When the Second World War broke out, Ralph was overseeing engineering at the family business, the Perfect Circle Corporation, which made piston rings for most of the larger automobile companies. The war was generally good for the business and the company flourished.

In 1942, the Federal government decreed that the national speed limit would be a sluggish thirty-five MPH. This was intended to conserve not just on gasoline, which was rationed, but to save the virtually irreplaceable rubber of the tires. Ralph promptly saw the need for a device that could act as an "auto pilot" for the gas pedal. However, the pressures of the war industry pushed the idea aside. That is, until he took the fateful trip with his chatty lawyer in 1945.

History never recorded anything else about the attorney except that he had one bad habit. When he talked, he became very animated and lost focus on his driving. When he listened, he would realize that he had slowed down and would speed up; evidently with some fervor. Naturally, this driving style was very rough and the unfortunate Ralph would soon became carsick.

His discomfort motivated him, and before the end of the war, Ralph had developed the first form of cruise control, marketed under a variety of names including such memorable names as: "Controlmatic," "Touchomatic," "Pressomatic" and "Speedostat." It was thirteen years before the first production model, with the name of "Cruise Control," showed up as a factory option, on the 1958 Chrysler Imperial, New Yorker, and Windsor car models.

The Hemi Engine

During the war, Chrysler Corporation engineers tried their hand at designing a better aircraft engine. This was before the jet engine had been perfected; the reciprocating engine still commanded the air. As in all the other attempts to wring more power out of a fixed space, the Chrysler engine would bring about a far-reaching innovation.

Begun in 1941, Project XI-2220 showed its maker's relationship to the automotive industry. Basically, it was two V-8 engines mounted nose to nose and inverted. Capable of producing 2,500 horsepower, the propeller was driven via a reduction gearbox from the middle of the assembly, where the two engines were joined. Although it never flew except in trials, the XI-2220 was the first Chrysler engine to have hemispherical combustion chambers. The dome-shaped cavity took advantage of the scientific principle of the shaped charge. Fuel and air would enter and swirl around, following the half-round contour. A spark plug mounted at the apex of the chamber would then fire. The resulting explosion would reflect away from the concavity and be focused on the piston.

At the end of the war, all Chrysler projects concerning the war were dropped or cancelled, the XI-2220 included. However, the lesson learned about the amazing efficiency of the hemispherical engine was not forgotten. In 1951, Chrysler introduced the 330-cubic-inch Hemi engine. Offered as an option in the Imperial, the Saratoga, and the New Yorker, the Hemi would go on to become one of the most famous "muscle car" engines ever built. In the early 1970s, Chrysler discontinued the Hemi for a number of years but reintroduced the engine towards the end of the twentieth century. Now enhanced with the latest in computer-controlled fuel injection, electronic transmission output, and digitally monitored ignition, the engine is capable of producing up to 500 horsepower.[33]

"Jerry Can" Fuel Canisters

No World War Two movie worth its salt was without a Jeep somewhere in the story. And always, mounted on the back was a five-gallon can, purportedly carrying gasoline. These canisters, nicknamed "jerry cans" by the British, were, indeed, a German innovation.

The British, fighting in the North African desert, used a four-gallon tin to transport fuel. Lacking the specialized tank trucks so common today, logistic convoys streamed across the desert delivering their precious cargo. The square tins, called "flimsies" by the troops because they were made of thin sheet metal, tended to get punctured quite frequently. If they were stacked one upon another, their own weight would buckle the sides and crash over, usually spilling the contents through ruptured walls. Transport ships were known to have as much as sixteen inches of gasoline in the bilges from punched cans. One ship is known to have exploded and sunk from this problem. Even if the can remained liquid-tight, heat and sloshing caused the gasoline to vaporize, leaking out past the ineffective cork cap seal. It was quite possible for a four-gallon tin to have only one or two gallons left at the end of a thousand-mile journey. Even General Ritchie, commander of the British Eighth Army, bemoaned the obvious inferiority of the four-gallon tin to the German five-gallon canister.[34]

The German can did not suffer the same troubles. More rectangular in shape and deeper; it did not allow the gas to splash about as much. Made from heavier-gauge steel, the container was nearly impervious to all but small arms fire or worse. German engineers had perfected a synthetic rubber seal that expanded upon exposure to gasoline, creating an ever-tightening seal. An integrated handle made the can easier to grab and move about. Each can came with a pour spout that fit into the receiving vehicle to minimize loss due to spillage.

Jerry cans were captured by the British in 1940 and sent back home. Seeing the relative merits of the German design, an immediate program to manufacture and distribute the cans was set in motion. The Americans received samples from the British, the latter asking her ally to join in manufacturing the containers. Soon, hundreds of thousands of the cans were in shipment. To give an idea of the scope of the anticipated demand, the Allied effort to invade southern France, Operation Anvil, had 250,000 cans of gasoline and another 5,000 of Diesel fuel filled for the landing alone. In total, the Quartermaster ordered over 18 million cans for the war.[35]

All of those cans rode into combat on racks bolted or welded in place. Cans were hung from tank turrets, truck running boards, outside of armored cars, under truck beds and from the rear of Jeeps. Anywhere one could be fit in it was because no one was sure when the next refill would come. Eighty-eight percent of the gas used in Allied vehicles came from the five-gallon can. Often containing water, cans were marked to differentiate the contents. However, care was not always exercised when filling the cans with water. Veterans often tell stories where their only water supply was tainted by gasoline because the cans were not properly cleaned.

During the Normandy invasion, American discipline slipped badly when it came to fuel cans. The policy stated that one empty would be exchanged for a full one. Instead, the empties were strewn about countryside to such an extent that the Quartermaster resorted to engaging French youngsters to return the cans for a bounty. This shortage was to lead to a near disaster in September. The supply of cans became so desperate that as Patton's Third Army poised the break into Germany, a fuel crisis struck. Combat troops turned on their own supply forces and hijacked a column trucks loaded with ammo and their accompanying bulk fuel trucks meant for the column's return trip. This led to further supply disruptions because of the loss of a large number of trucks. The remedy was to fly fuel to both the quartermaster column and Patton's men.[36]

A trailer full of Jerry cans destined for the front, filled with potable water, not gasoline. Fresh drinkable water was a commodity in short supply almost always because of constant demand and limited sources. Fall 1944 NWE. (U.S. Army/ NARA)

The jerry can is still a fixture in America. Most commonly seen on popular sport utility vehicles, the five-gallon can is often more of a prop than a functional piece of equipment. Quite a few are used to carry liquids—water, oils, and fuels—mainly in industrial service vehicles. The German can, so blatantly copied, has become an American icon.

Motor Scooters

At the end of the war, Italy lay in ruins. Even though Italy had surrendered to the Allies in 1943, German resistance forced the fighting to continue until the very end. To resurrect the Italian economy, experts came from the Allied countries to help. They toured existing factories and evaluated factors such as the remaining work force, material supplies, and domestic needs. Clearly, Italy most needed employment and transportation.

At the Piaggio factory in Pontadora, 10,000 employees were instantly unemployed when the factory was flattened by Allied bombers. During the war, Piaggio had focused on making aircraft parts. Allied peace terms with Italy in 1943 restricted the manufacture of aircraft or component parts, but the reconstruction advisors suggested that the company rebuild their plant and manufacture some as yet determined consumer product. Concerned about his employees' welfare, company president Enrico Piaggio earnestly began to do precisely that.

The first motor scooter was an American idea, developed in Lincoln, Nebraska, at the Cushman Company in the late 1930s. Intended for youngsters, the little machine became the pattern for several different makes, replacing the automobile somewhat in the fuel and tire rationing years. America fell out of love with the small motorcycle as soon as the war and shortages ended. In other countries, scooters had held momentary attention. The Italians had built one disastrous scooter during the war for the military. Meant to be dropped by parachute, the Aermoto cycle was underpowered, unstable, and almost useless for cross-country travel. Nevertheless, the motor scooter concept sparked the inspiration of Enrico Piaggio.

With the close of World War Two, the Italian situation was indeed desperate. All the automobile factories had been converted to war manufacture, and subsequently bombed to rubble. Petrol products were scarce in post-war Italy for similar reasons. In addition, the Italian people, already experienced with a low standard of living in the years before the war, were now faced with the additional loss of their homes, land and possibly even family members dead from the war. With all of this in mind, Enrico believed that an inexpensive, reliable, low-maintenance, easy-to-drive vehicle was part of the answer in Italy's recovery.

After a false start with an inferior preliminary design, Enrico conceived the Vespa. At its debut in 1946, the Vespa—wasp in the native Italian—revealed its heritage. The Vespa had a stressed sheet-metal body built with aircraft monocoque assembly techniques. The suspension replicated landing gear mechanisms, again borrowed from the company's aircraft experience.

A Vespa scooter: light, nimble, economical. A good deal for post-war Europe, not such a bad idea now. (VESPA)

A number of inspired innovations not connected to aircraft designs were also included in the Vespa. Handlebar controls, including gearshift and clutch, gave the driver added safety in crowded urban traffic. The comfortable saddle seat was patterned after successful motorcycle components. Interchangeable front and rear wheels simplified production, replacement parts availability, and repairs by the side of the road. The Vespa had storage space dedicated to the tools and the parts needed to change the occasional flat, a first for any two-wheeled vehicle. Fenders, bodywork, an enclosed engine compartment, and unique floor pan all served to protect the driver from splashes of engine dirt and road debris.

Incredibly, the Vespa's 98cc, single-cylinder two-stroke engine got 100 miles to the gallon. Performance was far from meteoric. Top speed of the Vespa was a sedate 35 MPH, even with a three-speed gearbox. Because of the low speed, motorcycle purists regaled the Vespa with ridicule. It was declared unsafe and dismissed as a joke.

In spite of the criticism, Piaggio prevailed. Italian women liked the tiny scooter for its step-through frame, which respected their modesty. The gasoline economy, far surpassing anything else on the road, had its benefits in a time of extreme shortages. Maneuvering through rubble-strewn avenues was simplified by the scooter's small size and hand controls. The Vespa had come to stay. Now, a number of motorscooter manufacturers build the diminutive cycles. They are much more popular in Europe and Asia, what with their crowded roads. In America, the motorscooter serves as cheap transportation, particularly on university campuses.

The Jeep

In 1941, the United States Army Quartermaster Corps approached Willys-Overland Company to design and build a revolutionary new field car. In a matter of months, the prototype rolled out the door and a legend was born.

One of the most outstanding and popular developments of the war, the four-wheel-drive Jeep served as light reconnaissance vehicle, ambulance, general transport, command car, and anything else that the ingenious troops could find it useful for. A few were outfitted with machine guns—similar to the popular 1960s television show *The Rat Patrol*—to harass German troops, but the great majority of armed Jeeps were actually modified to act as antiaircraft support vehicles or reconnaissance in the Mediterranean theater.

The Jeep was a robust machine in spite of its relative lightweight of 3,253 pounds. Powered by a 355-pound four-cylinder engine, it was quite well received for its cross-country ability and reliability. One technical design factor built into the Jeep was the requirement that it be able to tow the 9,600-pound 155 mm howitzers in tandem with another Jeep. Many light trucks and even heavy civilian cars used by the Allies were withdrawn from service as Jeeps became available. Shipped in large quantities to the Russians, the Jeep was claimed by that country's politically sensitive officers to have been built at the fictitious Soviet city of Willys-Overland. The British, too, received a large share of Jeeps under the Lend-Lease. Most were utilized in the normal roles, but at least two met their end during trials of a rocket-propelled airdropped platform that was less than a smashing success, although that is exactly what happened to the Jeeps.[37]

Giving this Jeep the total workout. Most commanders would see this type of driving as a need for discipline. Many men coming into the service were unfamiliar with driving and needed training for the great swarm of vehicles that the military was purchasing. (FDRLPD/ NARA)

The small size of the Jeep made it the perfect choice when it came time to start designing transport aircraft. Both the CG-4 Waco assault glider and the C-47 cargo aircraft could accommodate a fully assembled Jeep. In Italy, the mountainous terrain was classified by the troops in one of two ways. Either the ground was steep enough to use a Jeep for resupply, or it was left to the pack animals. Nothing else, except for the troops themselves could conquer the steep, rocky ground.[38]

The Jeep inspired generations of similar vehicles. Some would not measure up to the original, but the value of the design has lived on to the present day in the form of the sport utility vehicle. The contemporary Jeep has only a faint resemblance to its noble ancestor. Now equipped with air-conditioning and stereo radio, the top-line Jeep is more of a status symbol for Yuppies. And the military, in its infinite wisdom, phased the Jeep out some years back in favor of the Humvee.

The Volkswagen

Germany had a two-wheel-drive vehicle that performed many of the tasks that the Jeep did and, like the Jeep, the design lasted long after the war ended. Hitler, in his desire to promote nationalistic goodwill amongst the populace, declared that Germans should be able to own individual cars as in America. Possibly visualizing himself as another Henry Ford, and perhaps to provide a credible excuse for building the Autobahn, Hitler requested that Ferdinand Porsche design an economical car that got good gas mileage and could seat a family of five.

Porsche's little car was truly unique. A rear-mounted, four-cylinder engine gave it a maximum speed of sixty-two MPH while getting 36 miles to the gallon. With a rearward-sloping roof, the car was an odd-looking machine that resembled an enormous ladybug. From this feature, the German public gave it the nickname of "Kafer," literally "Beetle," and it stuck. The official name, *Volkswägen*—later changed to the Anglicized *Volks Wagen*—literally translates to people's car, in light of the Nazi dream that every driver would own one.

Post-war Europe, probably Switzerland. Besides Displaced Persons, one of the first products made in Germany after the war was the Volkswagen. The factory was badly hit but through determination (and impending starvation) the workers got it back into production to become one of the best-selling cars in the world.

Meant to be sold by subscription and installment payments made through payroll deductions of five marks a week, the Beetle never got to the public before the war began. The factory in Wolfsburg was converted shortly after being built in 1938, for production of a military car of similar design. Having the identical frame of stamped sheet metal, as well as the suspension and engine that was the "Bug," the slab-sided "Kubelwagen" began to roll off the assembly lines and into the army. Just like the Jeep, the Kubelwagen performed yeoman duties wherever the Germans went and was greatly favored in the African campaign for its air-cooled engine that never seemed to die.

After the war, the stalwart Germans reopened the bombed-out plant and began to make the original Beetles again. Skeptical automotive executives like Ford's Ernie Breech told his boss Henry Ford II, upon being offered to buy the company, "What we're being offered here isn't worth a damn!"[39] They were certain that the weird little car would be a total failure in the sophisticated post-war market. Needless to say, they were wrong. The VW, as it became known from the imprint on the cars' front deck ornament, became the most successful car ever built, surpassing even the Model T in sales. In the mid-1970s, VW began to sell another model, simply called The Thing. Not nearly as well received as the Beetle, it was appreciated by World War Two re-enactors because it was virtually identical to the Kubelwagen.

The Beetle did not adapt well to the new emission restrictions that swept America in the 1970s. Taken out of the American showroom floor for some years, it has recently made a comeback. Although thoroughly redesigned for the 1990s with front-wheel drive, transverse-mounted engine, air conditioning, and so on, the new Bug is again enjoying brisk sales.[40]

Streamlining and Auto Racing

After the Second World War, those men who so readily abandoned their fast cars to go to war were now coming back to them, older and a little wiser. Quite a few benefited from comprehensive training, whether it was the physics of flight and engine power or the intricacies of turbo-superchargers and state-of-of-the-art electronic engine controls. To some, returning to the comparative sedate civilian life was just too mundane. These self-described "speed junkies" found an outlet for their energy and passion and revolutionized American sports racing.

Streamlining

In the period following the First World War, aviation was regarded as wondrous and just short of miraculous. The appearance of an airplane, especially in rural areas, was an event that made headlines in the local papers and was a reason for all work to come to a halt. Achievements of notables such as Charles Lindbergh and Amelia Earhart were cause for celebration. They were the rock stars of the time. New technologies and advancements were always reported in major magazines like *National Geographic*. Thus, when the government opened the new wind tunnel research facility at Langley Field, Virginia, it made the newsreels at theaters like the Bijou. Pretty soon, everybody was talking about streamlining.

The first to adopt streamlining concepts were the railroads. Even in 1935, the Diesel-electric locomotive loomed over the ubiquitous steam engine. Rail companies realized that Langley derived wind tunnel test results could be the savior of the steam engine by cutting its costs. By using plates to smooth over projections and facets that create drag, air resistance could be reduced. Less resistance meant that either less fuel was consumed or more work with equivalent fuel quantities was achieved. Of course, the principle of the public image of advanced technology and modernity was not lost on the rail company executives.

Massive public relations campaigns to advertise the latest innovations in railroad streamlining filled the papers and newsreels. Much to the dismay of the rail tycoons, General Motors announced that their new Diesel locomotives would also be streamlined, obviating the one hope of salvaging steam's future. The battle between the streamlined Diesels and the steam locomotives, which were sporting all manner of fairings and plates meant to reduce drag, would continue unabated throughout the 1930s. Only the bigger, worldwide war interrupted the battle of railroad streamlining, but the notoriety caused the concept to take hold.

While the public was closely following the steam/Diesel war of the railroads, Detroit automakers were well aware of the effects of airflow on their cars for years. But until the 1930s, streamlining had seemed an unnecessary expense. Contemporary roads were hardly capable of allowing any speeds of consequence—the average speed limit nationwide was a creeping 17 MPH. There were a few roads that could be sped on, but they did not warrant the costs of re-tooling the manufacturing lines. The concept of streamlining was not lost on the automobile racers. They embraced it.

Low slung and powerful, the early racecars were just barely aerodynamic as measured by any standards. Attempts to create a smooth front profile were defeated by the slab-sided radiators and exposed suspension of the Barney Oldfield era. A few hand-built cars achieved a measure of streamlining and they usually found themselves in the winners' circle. The popularity of racing, especially because of America's tendency to build large tracks such as the Indianapolis raceway, only served to promote more recreational involvement in the sport, and a number of gifted amateurs were discovered. They, in turn, made their contributions to the sport and, slowly, the face of racing changed.

Detroit began to refine its body styles in response to the public demand, which was inspired by the appearance and performance of these racecars. Fenders became long and gradually sloped to the rear. Fairings dropped down to cover the rear tires. Windshields and grills became rakish; if not actually creating better aerodynamics, at least giving the impression of it. One Ford executive said of the new style in 1932, "The new look was slanted backward, like something wind blown and fast moving. Streamlining hadn't quite arrived. But the slanted look was distinctly part of the transition."[41]

For every transportation mode of the 1930s, streamlining had remarkable repercussions. For aircraft, dozens of changes were instituted to reduce drag. Manufacturing processes such as flush rivets, high-precision assembly to tightly fit joints of the skin together, and polished aluminum skins went a long way to making World War Two military aircraft faster than ever before. Streamlined trains went farther, faster, and with bigger loads. The automotive industry, of course, had only begun to adopt streamlining, creating some of the most exciting and profound designs to ever come out of Detroit. War requirements put an end to the line, but even better was to come afterward. Driven by new progressive thinking inspired by the latest aircraft, including jets, new aerodynamic features—at least they were supposed to appear aerodynamic—like fins, air scoops, shiny nose cones and jet exhaust cones appeared. True aerodynamics, the functioning kind, would come to the family car when the 1973 oil embargo occurred.

National Stock Car Auto Racing (NASCAR)

In the southeastern United States, the Depression only increased incentive for moonshiners and their illicit stills. When Ford introduced the V-8 in 1932, this gave the "shiners" a new weapon in their perpetual dispute with law enforcement. Nightly, the cars would set out with a load of "hootch" and prepare for encounters that would end with either the smuggler racing away in a cloud of dust or piled up in a ditch at the side of the road, police nearby. Naturally, someone would start bragging about how fast their car was and the inevitable "put up or shut up" race would result. These races became a weekly event. There were no tracks; they would drive in a circle until the field was denuded of grass and the dirt was visible. Occasionally, someone would knock some stands together and sell tickets and offer a purse for the winners. Not surprisingly just as often the "promoter" would disappear before the end of the race. Or the prize would be a fraction of the offered purse. No one could complain; the promoter was usually packing a gun. This was the state of affairs in pre-war American racing.[42]

Junior Johnson is one of these pre-war drivers. He earned quite a reputation for his fearlessness on the "whiskey highway." He claimed to never have been caught behind the wheel of a smuggler car.[43] Smokey Yunick grew up on a Pennsylvania farm during the Depression. He once cobbled together a tractor from a one-ton pickup rear end and the front half of a Dodge six-cylinder auto. Before he joined the Army Air Forces, he worked in a machine shop.[44] Bud Moore was in the service, too. He went ashore on D-Day and captured a German field headquarters. Later, after fighting his way across France and into Germany, he got wounded. By the time he returned home to Spartanburg, S.C., he had earned five Purple Hearts and two Bronze Stars. He and a buddy started a used-car business where, taking a '39 Ford in trade, they got their start in racing.[45] The commonality behind these men, and several dozen others, was their passion for racing cars. One more man would set in motion the deeds that brought them together and made history.

William "Bill" H.G. France, worked as a mechanic in Washington, D.C. The winters eventually became too much for him, so he took his wife and young son and headed south. Arriving at a Florida beach, just over the line from Georgia, the family went swimming. It was there in Daytona Beach, in 1934, they decided to settle. On a breezy day in March 1935, Bill watched as Sir Malcolm Campbell set a new world speed record—276 MPH—on the beach with a supercharged V-8. Although he was successful, Sir Malcolm determined that the beach was too unsafe for further trials. Town officials who saw the loss as a hit to local businesses—it was still the Depression—expressed an interest in hosting something similar. Within a year, a 250-mile race on the beach was scheduled. It was a fiasco. Cars sank into the sand and got stuck. Others drove too fast, slid on the wet, and flipped their cars. It took so long to clean up the field that the high tide came in and forced the cancellation of the race. It took the better part of a week to declare a winner. Bill France received $375.[46] This too was the status of auto racing in pre-war America.

After the Pearl Harbor attack, racing came to a halt. No one could afford to risk an irreplaceable car, not to mention that gas and tires were rationed. In the immediate post-war period, the situation was not much better. Tires were still scarce and the cars had received very little maintenance for four years. Humpy Wheeler said of his youth in 1953, "When I was 15, I raced old stock cars, '37 Ford coupes. Back then it didn't cost much money to race. All you had to do was to take a stock '32, '34, or '37 Ford coupe, which you could buy for a couple hundred dollars, and rebuild the engine. We'd buy a seat belt from an F-6F Wildcat fighter at the surplus store."[47] It was nice to see the war inspired safety practices.

Situations like this disturbed Bill France. On December 12, 1947, he convened a meeting with like-minded racers at the Ebony Bar inside the Streamline Inn in Daytona Beach. His proposal was simple: to create an organization of drivers, mechanics, race promoters, and interested individuals to bring some sanity to auto racing. His vision included set safety rules, rules for keeping the competition and cars fair and equal, insurance for the drivers, and a point system to determine championship status. Moreover, France wanted an association that was distinct from any other so a nationwide venue could eventually form. Someone offered the name the National Stock Car Racing Association, but that was rejected because a group in Georgia was already using it. Local mechanic/driver "Red" Vogt suggested dropping the last two words and change the A to "Auto" to make National Stock Car Auto Racing. NASCAR was born.[48]

It would be another eighteen months before the first official NASCAR event took place in Charlotte Speedway. Now NASCAR is far more than Bill France ever dreamed of. It is America's number one spectator sport and number two for televised regular season sport, and it has more Fortune 500 companies involved than in any other sport. The NASCAR home office is still in Daytona Beach, far bigger than the Ebony Bar. There are nine different racing forums, international, national, regional, and even a grassroots series, in honor of their roots. In a year, NASCAR sponsors 1,200 races on 100 tracks in 30 states, Mexico, and Canada. Junior, Smokey, Bud, and all the others found a home.[49]

National Hot Rod Association (NHRA)

As already stated, the war put an end to all car-racing for the duration. Like their southeastern brethren, the hot-rodders of the southwest went off to fight. Not surprisingly, many of them opted for pilot training. The skills they had honed on the racetrack now came in handy and surely saved some lives.

After the war, these same men returned home to pick their lives back up. After four long years flying the best performance aircraft the American government could devise, returning to sedate civilian life seemed, to many, to be too mundane. These self-titled "speed junkies" found a new outlet for their passion and, in the meanwhile, revolutionized sports car racing.

Surplus drop tanks, lying about by the thousands, proved to be perfect ready-made bodies for racing. Designed for optimum airflow, the aluminum disposable tanks were carried under the wings of fighters to give added range. An elongated teardrop in shape, the tank held a rubber bladder that contained the gasoline. Removing the bladder gave the amateur racers an empty shell that measured perfectly the dimensions of a Ford flat-head V-8. Cutting a few holes for the rear drive axle, exhaust pipes, front suspension, and for the driver was all the bodywork that was needed. Because the driver was taller than the engine, he sat forward in the widest part of the tank. A racing drop-tank car sat just inches from the ground, and the rear-mounted engine placed the bulk of the weight nearest the center of gravity. These two design characteristics, accidental by necessity, would give the best stability for high-speed racing. And these cars did go fast.

Indianapolis Raceway speeds rarely topped 150 MPH, even in the post-war years. Meanwhile, drop-tank racecars, running on California dry lakebeds, were pushing 200 MPH regularly with 1932 Ford engines. One car with one of the new Chrysler Hemi engines, recorded an official speed of 292 MPH. Impressive as the speeds were, there was inherent danger, too.

The racing surface was far from smooth. Ridges, bumps, and holes made driving a drop-tank car similar to riding a manic jackhammer in hurricane force winds. Even though the cars had excellent aerodynamics, the only force holding the car to the ground was its own weight. Furthermore, the cars were extraordinarily loud. Open exhaust pipes, straight-cut gears, and vibration noise made tank-car racing a sport for the stout of heart or the profoundly deaf.[50]

Tank-car racing died out in the 1960s. The drivers drifted away. Some moved on to join the Formula I racing series. Others stayed closer to home where they formed the National Hot Rod Association (NHRA).

In the same dry lakebeds of California that the tank racers would eventually run, a group of car owners began to race the clock. Giving themselves the title of the Road Runners Club in 1937, they held regular time trials until the war intervened. 1947 saw a resurgence of the desert racing. One driver, Wally Park, stepped forward to be an organizer. A tank test driver for GM in the daytime, he foresaw the need to band together all of the desert racers to create a set of rules for their type of racing. He proposed a name—the Southern California Timing Association (SCTA). They changed their venue to an abandoned runway that had a computerized timing system. Moving closer to the city improved their attraction. In 1951, the SCTA became the National Hot Rod Association (NHRA), America's premier drag racing sanctioning body. Two years later, they moved to the parking lot of the Los Angeles County Fairgrounds for their first official race. Now, the association has 80,000 members, 35,000 licensed competitors appearing in over 5,000 track events on 140 member tracks.[51]

The Bulbous Bow

As has been said a number of times already, there are many ways water and air behave alike. One similarity is that they can both create drag. This was an amazing concept realized by the Japanese engineers during their shipbuilding frenzy in the 1930s.

The Washington Conference on Naval Limitation (referred to here as the Washington Treaty of 1921-22) gave the Japanese, as a member of the victorious alliance of First World War, a smaller share of parity as measured against the American and British navies. This came about because the Japanese navy had enormous growth before and during that war and the British were concerned about Japanese intentions regarding China and British colonies such as Hong Kong, Malaysia, Singapore, and the Australian archipelago. Reluctantly, the Japanese accepted the 5:5:3: ratio of capitol ships, Japan getting the latter portion. This was just one more insult that the Japanese felt the Allies, in particular the Americans, had perpetrated on Japan. There had been the annexation of Hawaii, the U.S. long-term policy of limiting Japanese immigration to a small quota, restrictions on Japanese inhabiting the West Coast, especially in California, and prohibitive taxes imposed on imported Japanese products.

The treaty did more than limit the number of military hulls. It restricted displacement weight, type, and size of weapons and types of ships. At first, the Japanese navy gave the treaty terms an honest effort. However, the goals of the builders were in a contradictory position. They wanted ships that would be superior in every way it mattered to the other navies, but that was impossible with the terms of the treaty. The ships that were built by the Japanese had major faults. Rather than scrap what was already built, they attempted to fix them. This, naturally, caused the ships to exceed the weight limits. Oddly, none of the Allied observers noticed the growing girth of the vessels. The Japanese were not talking but they did give the required two-year notice that they were dropping out of the treaty in 1934. Certain parts of the treaty had to stay in effect until 1940, mainly weight and numerical restrictions. This did not preclude the design phase from starting. The super battleship *Yamato* was born.

The design phase took more than a year. Fully loaded, she was just shy of 70,000 tons displacement, 863 feet long and 127 feet 9 inches in the beam. *Yamato* began with four unique Diesel/turbine drives but had to resort to the more conventional steam turbine plants due to manufacturing limitations. The original engine installation was slatted to give her incredible speed, but with the change, drag was going to be an issue for the engineers. This was not a surprise; plans called for making the smoothest hull possible to accommodate the enormous bulk to keep up with the rest of the fleet. Now the new steam plant would put out a 150,000-shaft horsepower; respectable but about two-thirds of the original plan.

The architects and engineers found no way around it; they had to find out how much drag there was and how to eliminate it. They built a large tank of water and mounted a dolly above the water to tow scale models of the hull. After months of negative results, one engineer consulted a marine biologist friend. After hearing the problem, the biologist suggested using the example of the bottlenose dolphin. He observed that they regularly keep pace with the navy's small coastal patrol boats and they are capable of more than 35 knots.

The two proceeded to craft a scale snout that fit the model's bow. The first try showed a small but significant improvement. After a week of trials, they had the answer. Back at dockside, shipbuilders fabricated the piece, not sure of its purpose. Nevertheless, when sea trials were performed, *Yamato*, with 35 feet of draft, practically raced through the sea. At the bow, there was no wave, an unheard of phenomenon. The elongated attachment stuck out forward of the bow about five meters (16 feet). Although it was actually under the surface of the water, underway it was barely submerged. The water hitting the foremost part of the bulge rolled away left and right, leaving a hollow space immediately in front of the bow that was lower than sea level. The engineers at first could not believe it when the bridge reported they were going slightly under 30 knots.

This is a 370 ton fishing boat and it has the bulbous bow inspired by the experience of the Yamato. Engineers state that the construct improves fuel economy by as much as 28%. The circular screened hole in the side is a bow thruster. (Author's Collection)

This was better speed than the current best American battleship, the *South Dakota* class, could do and *Yamato* weighed almost twice as much. Eventually all three of the Yamato-class hulls, the *Musashi* and the unnamed and unfinished third hull had bow bulges. *Yamato* was sunk in April 1945 while on a one-way suicide mission to disrupt the Okinawa landings.

Bow bulges are now standard on every ship above 250-ton displacement. They are shown to give 12% to 15% improvement on hull efficiency, which translates to better fuel economy, better speed, and improved maneuverability.[52]

Notes/Selected References

1   Brinkley, Douglas. Wheels *for the World: Henry Ford, His Company and A Century of Progress.* 2003. P. 283.
2   ibid. P. 282.
3   Risch, Erna. *The Quartermaster Corps, Organization, Supply and Services. Vol. 1.* 1953. Pp. 18 - 21.
4   Green, Constance McLaughlin, et al, *The Ordnance Department: Planning Munitions for War.* 1955. P. 203.
5   Miller, Everett B. Lt. Col. VC, USA. *United States Army Veterinary Service in World War II.* 1961. Pp. 489 - 490.
6   Bethall, Nicholas. *Russia Besieged.* 1980. Pp. 12- 13, 170.
7   Air Drive Operates Tools Forward or Backward. *Popular Mechanics* magazine. April 1934. P. 528. and Versatile Repair Tool Cuts Metal and Irons Out Car Fender. *Popular Mechanics* magazine. April 1942. P. 48.
8   Bykofsky, Joseph and Harold Larson. *The Transportation Corps: Operations Overseas.* 1957. *Pp.* 242 - 244, 285 - 287, 409.
9   Wardlow, Chester. *The Transportation Corps: Responsibilities, Organization and Operations.* 1951. P.332. and Bykofsky, Joseph and Harold Larson. P. 387.
10 Freight Trains of the Highway. *Popular Mechanics* magazine. Oct. 1940. Pp. 562 - 65, 116a-118a.
11 Thirteen Day Non-Stop Trip Tests Diesel Truck. *Popular Mechanics* magazine. Mar. 1932. P .403.
12 Wardlow, Chester. Pp. 359 – 359.
13 Bykofsky, Joseph and Harold Larson. Pp. 331- 337.
14 There is evidence that a similar plan was used in1934. A photo shows a truck removing what is stated as a 2,400-gallon milk tank from a rail flatbed. The caption says the operation is pushbutton controlled. I have not been able to find anything else about it. Freight Trains of the Highway *Popular Mechanics* magazine. Oct. 1940. P. 564.
15 Ewens, Graeme and Michael Ellis. *The Cult of the Big Rigs.* 1977. Pp. 33 - 57. Ryan, Keith. *The Illustrated History of Fire Engines.* 1998. P.142.
16 U.S. Army Manual of Standard Ordnance. Reprinted as *The American Arsenal.* 1996. Pp. 96 - 99.
17 Ryan, Keith. *The Illustrated History of Fire Engines.* 1998. Pp. 135 - 136.
18 ibid. P. 146.
19 ibid. P. 141.
20 Brinkley, Douglas. P. 538. and Wardlow, Chester. P.366.

21 Lewis, Tom. *Divided Highways*. 1997. Pp. 3-69. and Whiting, Charles. *The Home Front: Germany*. 1982. P. 27. and Patton, Phil. A Quick Way From Here to There Was Also a Frolic. *Smithsonian magazine*. October, 1990. Pp. 96 –108.

22 Podolny, Walter, and John B. Scalzi. *Construction and Design of Cable-Stayed Bridges*. 1986. Pp. 7- 8.

23 ibid. Pp. 3 - 16. and Troitsky, D.S. Pp. 6 - 21.

24 Lock Nuts on Auto Wheels Help Prevent Theft of Tires Popular *Mechanics* magazine. June, 1942. P. 45. Chaining Tires and Wheels Helps to Foil Thieves. *Popular Mechanics* magazine. June,1942. P. 50.

25 AMP Incorporated Website; http://www.amp.com/about/amp_profile.html AMP Incorporated Annual Report. 1968.

26 Advertisement in *Life magazine* May 13, 1946. P. 110. and Bolan, Nelson. *How Detroit Changed History*. 1987. Pp. 199 - 202.

27 Advertisement for Chevrolet. *Popular Mechanics* magazine. May, 1938. P. 113A.

28 Church, John. Pp. 118 - 119. Ellis, Chris. *Directory of Wheeled Vehicle of the Wehrmacht 1933-45*. 1974. Pp. 8 – 9. Schmelz, F., Seherr-Thoss, H.-Chr. and Aucktor, E. *Universal Joints and Driveshafts*. 1992. Pp. 12 - 26.

29 U.S. Army Manual of Standard Ordnance. Reprinted as *The American Arsenal*. 1996. Pp. 14-17, 20-21 and 32-35. Gott, Philip G. *Changing Gears*. 1991. Pp. 153 –155.

30 Schneider, Wolfgang. *Tigers in Combat Vols. 1 & 2*. 1998& 2000.

31 Wise, David Burgess. *The New Illustrated Encyclopedia of Automobiles*. 1997. Pp. 112, 122, 172, and 256.

32 Green, Constance McLaughlin, et al, P. 271, note 74.

33 Berkowitz, Bruce D. Monster Engines. *Air and Space magazine*. December 1997, January 1998. Pp. 85 – 86.

34 Bower, Tom. *The Paperclip Conspiracy*. 1987. P. 48. and Ross, William F and Charles F. Romanus. *The Quartermaster Corps: Operations in The War Against Germany*. 1965. Pp.162 –165.

35 ibid. P. 165. and Scott, Beth F. et al. *The Logistics of War*. 2000. P. 107.

36 ibid P. 165.

37 Pawle, Gerald. *Secret Weapons of World War II*. 1957. Pp. 209 –217.

38 Church, John. P.151.

39 Brinkley, Douglas. Pp. 544-545.

40 Boyne, Walter J. *Power Behind the Wheel*. 1988. Pp.110-113.

41 Brinkley, Douglas. P. 428.

42 Breaking Into Dirt Track Racing. *Popular Mechanics magazine*. April 1934. P.562-64, 126a.

43 Brinkley, Douglas. N. P.17.

44 ibid. P. 52.

45 ibid. P. 147.

46 ibid. Pp. 74 -75.

47 ibid. P. 39.

48 ibid. P .72.

49 NASCAR material derived from: Nascar.com/guides/about/nascar/

50 Wilkinson, Stephan. Tanks, Hot Rods and Salt. *Air & Space magazine*. April/May 1997. Pp. 60 - 63.

51 NHRA details derived from nrha.com/nhra101/history/.aspx

52 Mayer,S.L. Editor. *The Rise and Fall of Imperial Japan*. 1984. Pp. 7, 20-23, 78, 80, 83, 189, 201. and Bishop, Chris, Editor. *Encyclopedia of Weapons of WW II*. 1998. Pp. 483 - 485.

12

Leftovers: Stuff that Did Not Fit Anywhere Else

A book like this would hardly be complete if there were no "misfits." Research has taken me into the most unlikely places, where I have heard the most outlandish tales. Most of them were unverifiable through second and third sources or so out of the context of the book that they could not be included. However, articles in this section are more or less true. The Second World War was a serious business, but that doesn't mean a whole book on the subject has to reflect the heroic stoicism of the war. Laughter makes the serious more tolerable, as such; the articles in this final chapter are for fun.

Unidentified Flying Objects (UFO)s

Strange lights in the sky. Mystery craft hovering over farms, winching helpless cattle into cigar-shaped fuselages. These details are from some of the earliest reports of UFOs, dating back into the mid-nineteenth century. Although they were never explained, the accounts were novel for their originality and rarity. Fifty years later, other strange sightings would not be as unusual but just as original.

Throughout the Second World War, an increasing number of sightings of strange lights following Allied aircraft were reported. On more than one occasion, pilots and crewmen saw glowing objects moving unlike any conventional craft. At least one witness saw a gleaming disc that flew at tremendous speeds come to a dead stop and then shot off at eye-popping velocity in a new direction. Reports of strange craft trailing bombers reached epic proportions. Fighter pilots pursued these craft but were never able to get close enough to get good descriptions, much less shoot one down. American fliers were not the only witnesses to the phenomena. Japanese, Russian, German, British, and Italian pilots had similar experiences.

Naturally, military intelligence personnel took the reports and diligently processed them. Speculation raged that they were some sort of radio controlled drone. A small British office within the Air Ministry was reportedly set up to investigate the sightings in 1943. The project lasted only a year because intelligence sources determined that the Germans were as perplexed as the Allies. Medical officers made light of the claims, excusing them as symptoms of war-weariness or fatigue. The unidentified craft got stuck with a name: Foo-fighters.

They remain a mystery to this day. Some UFOlogists maintain that the Germans developed a remote-controlled jet aircraft with the ability to emit an electromagnetic pulse that interfered with the ignition systems of the bomber fleet. Some credence may be allowed for this as Allied reports did mention an inexplicable loss of power and rough-running engines. Furthermore, post-war documents written by Allied technical treasure hunters are allegedly still kept highly secret. In these papers are supposed to be the details of secret facilities discovered in the Bavarian Alps and in Czechoslovakia that were used to build these "fireballs." In recent years, details of a craft called the "Bell" that was allegedly capable of flight utilizing gravity drive that fits some of the descriptions. There is just enough recovered enemy material to create curiosity and fodder for cable TV true mystery shows.[1]

The "Bird Gun"

One invention of the war came as a result of the rapid increase in aircraft performance. Speeds had dramatically increased and the numbers of these high-performance craft were increasing precipitously. There were fears that the incidence of bird-plane collisions would increase as well. The Civil Aeronautics Administration insisted on developing windshields that could withstand impacts from large birds. Getting a bird to commit suicide against a speeding airplane was obviously out of the question, but there had to be some way to replicate the impact realistically. CAA officials turned to Westinghouse in late 1942.

The engineers abandoned any standard approach to the problem as impossible. Instead, they built a large "shotgun" that was capable of firing real birds. Powered by compressed air from an enormous storage tank, the gun had two barrels. Both were twenty feet long and respectively measured five and ten inches in diameter. The smaller was designed to propel chickens while the larger one accepted turkeys as large as 15 pounds. By varying the air pressure and aim, the birds could be hurled with scientific accuracy at specific points of the plane. Tests could run with any speed between 75 to more than 300 miles per hour.

Hundreds, if not thousands of tests were performed with the gun on all sorts of military aircraft and, after the war, civilian aircraft as well. The gun was also used on jet engines to determine the engine's ability to digest a struck bird without tearing the turbine blades into plane-wrecking junk. As high-speed trains became more common in the post-war world, the "bird gun" was used to test their windshields. As for the birds, they met their fate through electrocution first. Fresh birds, feathers and all, were preferred as they represented the closest to actual conditions as possible. (Actually, the frozen ones pack a much more intense punch, throwing the results into chaos and tearing through the toughest windscreens with impunity.)[2]

A Raccoon's Tale (and Two Other Stories of War-Driven Ecological Disasters)

Herman Göering, the overweight, heavy-handed Vice-Fuehrer, had a decided penchant for fancy clothing and uniforms. Besides being Hitler's heir apparent and commander of the Luftwaffe, he was responsible for thirteen other official posts, including Reich game warden. At some time before the war, he took an interest in raccoon coats. Believing that the German populace would fall in love with such garments, he envisioned becoming a furrier. He imported four raccoons from the United States and began a breeding program. When the venture flopped, he was stuck with several of the lively animals. Rather than destroy them, he released them into the German wilds that he was responsible for. There, they began to do what comes naturally to any healthy animal. Only long after the war was over did Europeans realize that they were beginning to be overrun with raccoons. Having no natural predators, the critters have flourished.[3]

The Brown Tree Snake of Guam

A major island of the Mariana Island chain, Guam was for centuries famous for its wide variety of birds. The United States gained the island after the Spanish-American War, and it became an important military post in the pre-World War Two era. In December 1941, Japanese invaders overwhelmed the American defenders of Guam and the island fell to the troops of the Emperor until a reconstituted American force could retake it in the summer of 1944. Placed strategically between the main air and sea route to and from the Philippines and ideally placed within bomber range of the Japanese homeland, Guam quickly became a bustling military base. Much equipment was shipped from Australia and New Guinea, which had been until then the locations of Allied military bases.

Unwittingly, the thousands of wooden crates that came from "down under" contained more than machinery, vehicles, and the vast items of hardware that the American military used. No one knows for sure how many hitchhiked their way onto Guam. However, from within these innocuous crates came poisonous—and amorous—brown tree snakes. Prior to this time Guam had been as snake-free as Ireland, and they consequently had no natural enemies. Native birds had no experience protecting their nests and young. Predation became the norm and bird was the main fare. As the years passed, the brown tree snakes became the dominant species. Without rivals to keep their population in check, the snakes reached densities of 13,000 per square mile. Their propensity for climbing led to more than 2,000 electrical outages when they got tangled in distribution equipment. Untold hundreds of islanders have been bitten. But the greatest damage has been done to the bird population. Eight of the eleven original native species of forest birds have been wiped out by the snakes, and experts see no way to avert destruction of the remaining species. As for the snakes, they are a permanent fixture of what once was a tropical paradise for birds.[4]

The "Mile-a-Minute" Weed of India

In the early days of America's involvement in the Pacific war, India provided advanced bases to stop or delay the progress of the Japanese hordes as they marched across China and Burma. The end strategy for the Nazi-allied Japanese was to cut off the remaining Chinese resistance and to force the withdrawal of the British from India. Once that was done, there was a real threat that Japanese forces could proceed to cross the lower Asiatic continent, cut through the Middle-East states of Iran and Iraq—who were known to be sympathetic to the Axis—and link up with German forces coming out of the Caucasus or from the North African deserts. Once this was done, Russia and China would be isolated from the south, cutting a major pipeline for Allied Lend-Lease materials. In addition, the Nazis and Japanese would hold the huge oil reserves of Arabia. Furthermore, these new territories would give the Germans an immense new reserve of men, from amongst a vast Muslim population, who had a millennia-long incentive to see to the extermination of the world's Jewish population. Clearly, the Allied cause was best served by stopping the Japanese on the eastern border of India.

That was a tough call, though. The Japanese had the superior aircraft in their nimble fighter, the Zero. American fighters could not dogfight successfully with them, even if they could get enough planes to overcome the 5-to-1 ratio of Japanese to Allied aircraft. Bombers were even more difficult to get. Whenever a base was established, the Japanese frequently strafed and bombed the airfields into ruin.

This is where the "mile-a-minute" weed came into play. Better known by its Latin name of *Mikania micrantha*, it was felt by American engineers charged with constructing the bases that Japanese attacks on the Indian airfields would be stymied if the aprons, runways, and aircraft parking areas could be camouflaged with the fast-growing weed native to Central and South America. As the common name implies, its characteristic fast growth was desirable to gain the maximum coverage in the shortest time. However, it was not foreseen that subtle differences in the weather patterns between the two regions would be disastrous. The rainfall patterns of the home territory of *Mikania micrantha* and the native animals that feasted on it served to control its growth. Once it was transplanted onto the Indian subcontinent, all natural controls were missing and the weed soon became rampant. Sixty years later, a thick green carpet of *Mikania micrantha* has ravaged whole forests and arable lands alike. Scientists doubt that it will ever be brought under control.[5]

Gremlins

A B-17 bomber returns to base with its high-explosive load intact. The crew reports that the bomb bay doors opened inexplicably while over the English Channel but the bombs would not drop. After the bomb bay is carefully unloaded, operational tests show that all is normal. This event repeats itself three consecutive times and, just as suddenly, the fault disappears, never to return. Barring any logical explanation, gremlins get the blame.

Gremlins seem to have appeared in military lore sometime after the First World War at the hands of the RAF as a way to explain the inexplicable. The creatures remained an isolated joke until the next war. With thousands of American fliers coming to England in late 1942, the joke expanded and spread. Suspicious and somewhat superstitious crews encountered faulty equipment on nearly every flight. Mechanics could pinpoint the majority of the troubles and repair them without any fuss. Even the most stubborn and puzzling failures were usually tracked down in time. However, a random few were to remain mysterious. Now only half joking, the crews and mechanics claimed they were the work of gremlins.

The gremlins are reputed to be gnome-like creatures, green, gray, or a dusky brown and about a foot tall. They wear little pointed shoes and have, by all accounts, snow-white hair. Capable of moving rapidly, they have the enviable ability to travel on the outside surfaces of airplanes, unheeding of the frigid, 200-MPH draft. Naturally, they have families and the females and children reportedly have been seen. The lady gremlins were called Finella and Widgets were the offspring. Do they exist? Ask any crewmember that has flown in combat, especially during World War Two, and the likely answer will be an emphatic yes.

The gremlin has entered the twentieth-century lexicon and myth. American Motors Corporation produced a car sporting the gremlin moniker. This may have inspired the critter to respond to AMC unkindly, for the car did not do well and AMC folded a few years later. Gremlins seem to have a penchant for the movies though. At least three movies have been released featuring the pesky creatures and they did very well. Maybe their egos need stroking.[6]

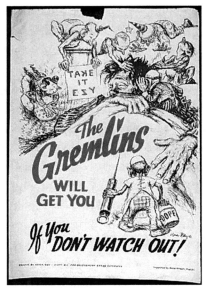

The American government had a vested interest in seeing the everyone with a job to show up on time and ready to work. This poster is unusual in that it admits that Americans may have a problem with drugs (the figure in front with the needle). This is a departure from the classic film Reefer Madness, where a select few get hooked on marijuana and ruin their lives. (OWI)

The Predecessor to the ZIP Code

For two hundred years, the Federal Postal Department ensured that the mail always got through. When the railroads began to spread out across the nation in an ever-widening spider-web of track, mail was aboard. Airplanes began to carry letters under contract, and America's airlines became established businesses as a result. So by 1942 the Postal Department had solved transportation problems with new technologies. But what about delivering mail to the recipients?

In years past, local men or women handled mail delivery. These folks were from the towns or neighborhoods they served and they were familiar with their customers. The local carrier, who often took part in celebrating, grieving, or commiserating, noticed all births, deaths, marriages, and family strife. If a family moved, the carrier

A sample from a selection of contemporary advertisements showing the presence of pre-ZIP code numbering for selected cities. Those include Chicago, New York, Detroit, Baltimore, San Francisco, Washington D.C., Los Angeles, Seattle, Cincinnati, and Minneapolis, and more. Note that El Paso, Texas and Sandusky, Ohio do not have them.

knew of the change and saw to it that the mail was forwarded properly.

By the beginning of the Second World War, the Postal Department had begun to see an enormous increase in the number of mailings. Families, torn apart as war factories attracted laborers from distant states, wrote home to longed-for relatives. Soldiers joining the service added to the increase of social correspondence as well. With money flowing again in the revitalized economy, business fliers, bills, statements, magazines, insurance premiums, mortgage billings, payments, dividends, and Social Security checks traveled through the mail. The combination of increased bulk and all the new faces—and for the first time quite a few were to stay strangers as unusual work hours precluded getting to know the residents—began to exclude the postal carrier as a person "in the know." There was just too much to do.

To combat the ensuing burden, federal mail officials began to consider a coding scheme to direct the mail with less chaos. The principle was simple. Each geographic area, such as a large city, would be assigned a code. Any mail destined for addresses within the area would have that code written on the outside of the envelope. The first of these systems was instituted in 1943, limited to the ten largest municipalities. The coding system worked rather well, especially in congested central districts. A number of attempts to extend the codes to smaller towns failed, primarily because the population was in post-war flux and new housing developments were throwing the codes into bedlam.

Mail volume continued to increase at a frightening pace. Railroads had been replaced by the growing interstate highway system, providing a new means of mail transportation. Computers became an essential business tool, generating reams of mostly unwanted advertisements delivered through the mail. With manpower costs on the rise, mechanical sorting was beginning to look attractive to the post office. But this would require a comprehensive and expandable nationwide code.

President John F. Kennedy appointed an advisory board to consider the options. Based on the board's recommendations, the Zone Improvement Program came to be adopted. With a typical government passion for acronyms, the title was reduced to the ZIP code, which began on July 1, 1963.[7]

Smokey (the) Bear

During the Second World War, every resource was seen as a strategic material, even the untouched millions of acres of American forest. In 1944, the United States Forest Service (USFS) adopted the image of a cute brown bear cub as a symbol for its "Protect the Forests" campaign. Children were specifically targeted by Smokey Bear—the "the" was added in the 1950s—and with the message to help prevent forest fires. Now familiar slogans such as "DON'T PLAY WITH MATCHES" and "ONLY YOU CAN PREVENT FOREST FIRES" were coined. Few know that Smokey Bear led the second campaign to protect the forests and the animals within. An earlier crusade featuring Disney's "Bambi" character from the movie of the same name was the first icon for the USFS anti-fire campaign in 1942. This received a lukewarm response, as war restrictions on travel limited the opportunities for children to be exposed to camping in the forest. After the war, vacations and camping trips became more popular. As children saw the wonders of the forest and animal life, Smokey Bear began to gain real impact.

It took a devastating fire in the Lincoln National Forest of New Mexico in 1950 to bring Smokey Bear to life. A five-pound bear cub was found clinging to a tree,

Fires destroyed prime timber, a necessary and irreplaceable war material. Wood became as scarce as copper or canvas when it came to providing enough for military and public projects. (USDA:Forest Service/NARA)

scared, scorched, and hungry. He evidently had found himself surrounded by the fire, separated from his mother. With nowhere to run, he climbed the tree and, by some miracle, survived. There, firefighters found him and cared for his needs. Without a mother, his only chance at survival was to be hand-raised. The future Smokey was sent by plane to the National Zoo in Washington, D.C. The attending publicity made him the most popular animal there. The zoo soon became inundated with mail from school children. The volume grew to such proportions that Smokey was assigned his own ZIP code, 20252.

Smokey lived out the rest of his life in pampered splendor. He died in 1976 and was buried in the forest where he was found near Capitan, New Mexico. The townspeople erected a stone memorial marker and a museum in his honor. Although the bear cub has passed on, his story and message live, protecting the forests.[8]

La Tomatina

As a truck, loaded with tomatoes fresh from the vine, crawls slowly down the narrow main street in the eastern Spanish town of Bunòl, men and women begin to pelt each other with the ripe fruit. Gleefully, a crowd of several thousand dive into piles of tomatoes to gather ammunition in what is probably the world's largest food fight. After two hours, the revelry stops at the sound of a large firecracker exploding. Volunteers sweep the rem-

Buñol Spain celebrates the day they ran off Facsist dictator Franco with a barrage of ripe tomatoes. Called Tomatina, thousands come to enjoy what could be called the world's biggest food fight.

nants of 50,000 pounds of crushed tomatoes down the storm drains. Residents and storekeepers wash the splattered walls and walkways clean and remove the plastic sheeting that has been hung to safeguard their windows. Participants, soaked to the skin in tomato juice, rinse off under public showers or in a nearby stream. This unusual and much-publicized ritual occurs every year on the last Wednesday of August. The tomato ritual in Bunòl, locally called La Tomatina, is a tradition that dates back to World War Two.

In 1944, Spanish dictator Francisco Franco visited the region. His Fascist policies had upset the generally liberal population, particularly his demand for more agricultural production to be sent to Germany. During this trip, rebellious townspeople shouted insults and catcalls during his speech. The mood of the crowd grew more menacing, and before long, Franco became the target of a barrage of tomatoes. Unhurt but humiliated, Franco and his entourage departed in haste. History does not record whether the police ever detained any suspects from the attack or whether there was any retaliation, but the town continues to honor the tradition.

The Hell's Angels

Immediately following the war, most returning American servicemen were busy rebuilding their lives with homes and families. There were others though, who yearned for the excitement and action that had become part of everyday life in the military. The mundane repetition of going to work and raising families chafed at their youthful energy.

Motorcycles proved to be one outlet for this group. Before the war, there were fewer than 200,000 motorcycles in America. Production of the machines was vastly increased for the military during the war and as a result, there was a huge surplus of practically new, high performance motorcycles available at war's end. Many of them were bought by newly domesticated veterans for weekend cruising and gathering with like-minded friends for an afternoon of wheeling through the mud or cruising the highways during the warm months. Soon, these loose associations organized into clubs with chosen leadership and closer social ties among club members. It was not long before these new motorcycle clubs began to form under the aegis of the American Motorcycle Association (AMA), which organized meets and events.

Some clubs adopted names that reflected a more rebellious spirit, such as "The Pissed-off Bastards" and the "Booze Fighters." These clubs naturally attracted the more anti-social types and rowdies. In 1947, there was what is now considered to be a classic clash, the infamous Hollister riot, between the two rival groups. It all started during the AMA's annual meet in Hollister, California, over the Fourth of July. Outlaw bikers from the Pissed-off Bastards club began the mayhem by racing through the town's streets, ignoring traffic signals, and riding on the sidewalks. Alcohol consumption was prodigious, and as a result, anyone who dared to venture outside was endangered. Traffic misdemeanors soon grew to felonious vandalism when businesses were targeted, furniture and glass being favored. Once the business district had been ravaged, the action moved into the residential streets. By now the booze had begun to take its toll and most of the bikers sought quiet places to sleep their drunk off. Locals woke the next morning to find half-drunken bikers sleeping on their lawns, many of them ill from their alcohol consumption. The smell of vomit filled the early morning air. As they began to awake, the bikers resorted to using nearby bushes for toilets. There were numerous arrests for public drunkenness and indecent exposure, leading the police chief to state, "It was one hell of a mess."

The Hell's Angels name actually goes back to a squadron in the First World War. Howard Hughes used the name for a movie in 1930. Now this crew has honored the name on their B-17. It was the post-war bikers that have made the name, for better or worse, memorable. (U.S. Army Air Force)

The AMA immediately tried to disassociate itself from the unruly pack and the activities of the holiday, proclaiming, "99 percent of motorcycle riders were decent, law-abiding people." That remaining "one percent" would become a badge of honor. The following year, 1948, the Pissed-off Bastards motorcycle club splintered into two different factions after a series of internal squabbles. This breakaway group adopted the name of a World War Two fighter squadron, The Hell's Angels. The "one-percenters" as they proudly referred to themselves, would become the core of the notorious motorcycle gangs of the fifties and sixties.

Molotov Cocktails

In one of the sideline wars overshadowed by the bigger conflict called World War Two, a weapon for the truly desperate was given its famous moniker. On November 30, 1939, Russia began a lopsided war against its miniscule neighbor to the west, Finland. Six weeks earlier, Stalin had pressured Finland to open negotiations for a land swap. For woodlands of dubious value in the north, near Murmansk on the Kola Peninsula, Finland would release the land that encompassed the Karelian peninsula in the south. Furthermore, the Soviets would build a naval base on the Finnish Gulf, giving the Soviet Navy a second port into the Baltic Sea. Stalin also wanted to gain some extra territory to act as a buffer from Hitler's troops—the two European powers had carved Poland up the previous fall under a secret agreement—but Stalin was wary of Hitler's intentions. The talks broke down when the Finnish delegation refused to acquiesce to the pressures of Soviet Foreign Minister Vyacheslav Molotov. The Soviets reacted by invading Finland.

For three and a half months the Finnish army held off the vastly superior Russian forces. The war was marked by equal amounts of Finnish tenacity and Soviet ineptitude. Finally and predictably, the Finns were over-powered by the brute vastness of Soviet resources. Near the end, supplies of ammunition, guns and food were running low. Desperately, the Finns resorted to using gasoline bombs first devised during the Spanish Civil War of 1935.

This explosion was brought about by a single Molotov Cocktail. After the disaster of Dunkirk, where the British lost the greatest bulk of their heavy weapons and military transport, the Army relied on the easiest weapons possible until the factories could get working. One weapon was the bottle filled with gasoline, wicked with a rag, and named after a Russian diplomat. These recruits are learning that it was effective and dangerous. From the trails of white smoke, this one looks like it contained some white phosphorus. (IWM)

Poorly made, Russian armored vehicles proved to be extremely vulnerable to the flowing fire from the gasoline-filled glass bottles. Thrown against the hull of a tank, the burning gasoline would seep into cracks and crevices, killing the occupants in a most grisly manner. Cynically, the Finns called their gasoline bombs Molotov Cocktails in honor of the despised Russian diplomat who had engineered the treaty meetings. The name stuck and ever since, dissidents, rioters, and violently militant protestors have turned to the Molotov cocktail as one of the few weapons of minor mass destruction available to them.

Sex and the Second World War

World War Two occurred during the greater time period of the sexual revolution that began in the late 1880's. Decade by decade, sexual mores in the United States eroded with appalling consistency. The last decade of that century saw the popularity of Freud and his analysis of revealing sexual fantasies. Ten years later, Margaret Sanger was deliberately peddling her illegal latex condoms and diaphragms in New York. The First World War saw a greater availability of condoms and acceptance of birth control—a new phrase that was coined during this time. The 1920s were the era of flappers and F. Scott Fitzgerald's "naughty novels" that glamorized the loose lifestyles of the young.

Some more posters using fear or humor to get the point across. "Pro" or prophylaxis was a medical treatment meant to flush any bacterial infection from the male. The Army used a three stage protocol for the prevention of infection; condom, flush, prophylaxis. Until penicillin, it was better to abstain. (OWI/U.S. Army)

As America entered into the Depression, movies, which reflected and set the standard by which Americans lived, became more explicit. This "poor man's sex education" forced the wholesale adoption of the Hays Code of Standards, outlining what and was not acceptable, particularly on the subject of sex. Another means of illicit titillation was the introduction of "one penny books" or "eight-pagers." These diminutive pamphlets featured popular cartoon characters such as Popeye and Olive Oyl in dramatic sexual positions that left nothing to the imagination. All manner of sexual variations were treated equally. Homosexuality, bestiality, male and female masturbation, sadism, masochism; nothing was taboo.

Such was the sexual atmosphere when America went to war, and the distractions of war kicked open the door of sexual freedom. In the first few months, the marriage rate went up over twenty percent. The American soldier adopted the persona of the rogue, predatory wolf. Young girls, besotted with patriotic fervor and a newfound freedom as their parents went to work in the factories, gave of themselves willingly. The U.S. Army and Navy, in a reversal of past policy,

This was a real breakthrough. The staid Army actually admitted their female members partook of the intimate. Regulations still called for the expulsion for women members if they got pregnant or, for a time, married. There was still the rule that female officers could not have any off-duty contact with the enlisted. Some things still have not changed. (OWI/U.S. Army)

began a program to teach troops about venereal disease and sex. Another break from tradition was that condoms were made available to the volume of fifty million a month. The sexual predatory nature of the Americans inspired their British hosts to complain, "The problem with you Yanks is that you are over paid, over sexed, and over here." A suggested ad campaign tag line for a new line of ladies underwear read, "One Yank and they're off." But that was just the tip of the iceberg. Consider the following entries that show the American casual attitudes towards sex reflected in a war era.

Pinup Art

American troops, stationed so far from home, had few diversions for their free time. One such mode of entertainment was the pinup girl. This art form traces its ancestry back to turn-of-the-century Paris. During the period now referred to as the Gay '90s, French women rebelled against strict social moral codes and were doffing their lacy underthings to pose for artists and a new medium, photography. By 1910, 100 million postcards featuring these nude buxom beauties had been printed and distributed worldwide. During the First World War, American troops bought the titillating novelties to bring home. But public mores in America were still rooted in the Victorian era, and most of the war souvenirs remained hidden away.

Throughout the 1920s and '30s, popular entertainment such as the Ziegfield Follies with its scantily clad women began to erode strict, puritanical attitudes. Moviemaker Mack Sennett introduced his "Bathing Beauties" to America, showing their exposed bodies in skimpy, tight swimming suits. Movie studios began to promote their wares with less and less modesty, outraging the puritans. With one loud cry of dismay, the movie studios came under the authority of censorship in the guise of the Hay's commission. This proved to be a rocky relationship, with constant wars of words being exchanged.

Then suddenly, America was really at war again and just as quickly, sexually explicit artwork became legitimized. Except for a few weak voices, there was hardly anything more said about the eroding morality of America's young men. Pinups—the word formally entered the lexicon in 1942—appeared nearly everywhere. Dozens of movie starlets clamored for their pictures to be taken in the most suggestive, seductive poses possible. The military itself joined the fray when it used a popular photo of Betty Grable, overlaid with a grid pattern, as a tool to teach cadet pilots the basics of coordinate map reading. Publications such as *Yank* and *Esquire*, containing fresh photos on a regular basis, were distributed all the

Boys will be boys. Even in the landing craft headed to the beach, the pin-up girl will be there. Actually, this group of Marines is going to the beach for bivouac or shore leave. If this had been a combat landing, they would be ducking low below the gunwale, armed to the teeth and tense. Pinups inspired a heated debate on the propriety of that type of art. (U.S. Navy/OWI)

way up to the front lines, sometimes to the exclusion of the mail.

An extension of pinup art went into battle, proudly displayed across the noses of the hundreds of bombers. Nearly every base had one or two men who had been professional artists in civilian life. These talented individuals made a comfortable living by offering their services for a fee—typically, a bottle of hard-to-get Scotch—painting lavish nudes and semi-nudes. After some of the more "overexposed" examples of the nose art received the attention of the commanding officers in Washington D.C., unequivocal orders came down to put clothes on the worst of the risqué illustrations.

Pinups, however, became an American icon. When the men returned home after the war, they still demanded their pinups. Madison Avenue advertising had made near-nudity commercially acceptable with actresses posing for linen, clothing, and personal products advertisements. Companies found that giving away free calendars featuring scantily clad women made for good business.

In 1953, Chicago publisher Hugh Hefner began circulating his new *Playboy* magazine. He broke all of society's rules by offering professionally photographed, totally nude models, and inventing the centerfold, thereafter bringing pinup art to an all time high of acceptability.

Shaken, Not Stirred: James Bond

This fictional character, which has come to epitomize the ideal spy, is, in part, a reflection of his creator's own experiences during the war. Writer Ian Fleming imparted his own love of fast cars, gambling, golf, and adventure to his character. But there is more of the Second World War in the Bond adventures than first meets the eye.

Fleming was born into a well-to-do Scottish family extensively involved in business and politics. He attended Eton where he excelled at golf and shooting. He then entered Sandhurst, the British equivalent of America's Army Academy at West Point, but Army life disillusioned him. Ian then entered into universities on the Continent where he learned German, French and a smattering of Russian. His studies finished, he went to work at Reuter's news agency where he was assigned to work as a roving reporter back across the Channel. In 1933, he was sent to Moscow to cover the espionage trial of six British technicians. They had been sent to Russia on contract to assist in the installation and repair of industrial machinery but had been accused of paying bribes to gain information regarding Soviet industrial secrets and of sabotaging the very equipment they were working on. With the British engineers was Anna Sergeevna Kutusova, a beautiful, doe-eyed, twenty-something Russian secretary who stood as co-defendant. Clearly, the unfolding drama and its female participant was one of the earliest models that Fleming would draw upon as a plot device for his future spymaster.

In 1939, Fleming was once again dispatched to Russia as a correspondent for *The Times* to cover a trade mission. It's curious that he returned from Moscow, weeks before Germany and Russia opened their mutual war on Poland, to be immediately recruited as a full-fledged member of British intelligence. It has been reported that years later Moscow Radio called Ian Fleming "a former spy."[9]

As an agent, now sporting the rank of Lieutenant R.N.V.R.,[18] he battled the Axis with never-ending streams of reports, dockets, and signals, the minutia of operating

18 R.N.V.R. Royal Navy Volunteer Reserve, equal to the U.S. Naval Reserve.

a network of intelligence agents. From these documents he drew the 007 prefix. The number series denoted a type of communication within the Royal Navy Intelligence Department.

Over time, though, Fleming was assigned tasks away from the tedium of office work. In 1941, he accompanied his chief, Admiral John Godfrey to Lisbon, Portugal en route to Washington, D.C. While waiting for their flying boat connection, Fleming inveigled Godfrey to enter the local casino. Once there, Fleming, experienced in *chemin de fer*, encountered three German agents who were up for a game. Fleming could not resist visualizing the embarrassment that the Germans would suffer should the British win their money. However, these three, who were later determined to be local Nazi intelligence agents, soon had relieved the British agent of his fifty-pound travel money. It was fortunate that the good Admiral was along to clear the way for replacement funds to be made available. In later years, this episode was used in Fleming's first book *Casino Royale*. However, in the book, our hero Bond humiliated the villainous Russian by taking his money.

Another incident used in *Casino Royale* was inspired by a more gruesome incident from the war. Two Bulgarians, in the pay of the Russians, stationed themselves outside the apartment block inhabited by the British Embassy staff in Ankara, Turkey. Their intended target was no other than the German Ambassador to Turkey, Fritz von Papen and his wife. The plan was for the two to set off a small bomb set inside a box. To affect their escape and to create confusion, they were then to set off a similar-sized smoke bomb. However, the two assassins suspected that their sponsors were not necessarily playing fair. As the Papens approached, the assassins decided to set off the smoke bomb first. One can imagine the shock of the Papens as the two men suddenly exploded just yards away. The "smoke" bomb was actually a second bomb designed to destroy the assassins after the deed was done. Fleming could hardly resist using such a device.

Fleming was not shy about using personalities as prototypes for later characters. Admiral Godfrey was the model for Bond's stiff, impersonal director "M." There is speculation that the character of "Honey Ryder"—played by Ursula Andress—in the movie *Dr. No* was inspired by Anna Sergeevna Kutusova, the beautiful Russian spymistress.

Nor were names off limits. Fleming's Jamaican getaway home where he wrote every one of his Bond novels was named with the romantic *Goldeneye*, derived from the title of the operation planned by Winston Churchill to seal off the bastion of Gibraltar should Franco join the war on the side of the Axis. The reason Fleming had the property on Jamaica in the first place was as a result of the war. In early 1942, he attended an important meeting between American and British planners of anti-submarine warfare to present a strategy for the coming year and, although the weather was hideous, Fleming fell in love with the exotic island and pledged to return.

Speaking of Words

Every decade adds more words to the English language, reflecting the social character of contemporary people and events. Wartime amplifies the growth of vocabulary as the conflict arbitrarily throws individuals from diverse backgrounds and cultures together where they unwittingly exchange ideas and language. Remarkable moments gain a notoriety of their own, and, to mark the occasion, an accompanying set of idioms is invented that set the incident apart forever.

The Holocaust

No event did more to shape the image of World War Two than the deliberate wholesale destruction of European Jews and Slavic peoples. Originally, the word came from the Greek *holokauston* meaning a burnt sacrificial offering. In the interim centuries, it came to refer to large-scale slaughter, particularly where masses of humans were destroyed by fire. Although *holocaust* has retained that definition, the word has largely fallen into general disuse, while in its capitalized form it evokes visceral reactions that are sure to last for generations, if not eternity.[10]

Genocide

Over the course of history, there have been other attempts to exterminate the entire populations of opposing religious, ethnic, or political beliefs. However, in their twelve years of power the Nazis reached a pinnacle of brutality that required a whole new word. The term *genocide*—from the Greek *genos,* meaning race, and the Latin *cide,* "killing"—is attributed to Raphael Lemkin, a Jewish law professor from Yale University. He had set out to study and document discriminatory laws, especially Germany's racist legislation. In his book, *Axis Rule in Occupied Europe*—published in 1944—he coined the term genocide. Two years later, the newly formed United Nations gave definition to the term as the systematic annihilation of racial or national groups.[11]

Gestapo

An abbreviated word for *Geheime Staats Polizie* (Secret State Police), the Gestapo was one of the many police organizations of the Nazi party and probably the most notorious for its treatment of political prisoners, captured resistance fighters, and POWs. Volumes have been written about the brutal tortures, mutilations, and loathsome cruelty of the Gestapo. In addition to this popular perception, the Gestapo was also known for its authoritative presence and threatening omnipotence. The latter nomenclature has become part of contemporary vernacular as a descriptive insult for authority, particularly when attached to sinister conspiracy theories or intrusive government officials and their dour treatment of the citizenry.[12]

Swastika

Although this symbol is ancient, the Nazis forever corrupted its use and meaning when they officially adopted it as their party emblem in 1935 after having used it in several forms since the 1920s. Ancient swastika-shaped crosses, though, have been found in China, Japan, India, and Bronze Age Europe. North American Indigenous People held the symbol as a sign of good luck. The word swastika is an old Sanskrit word meaning "good fortune."

Blitz

This term, literally meaning "lightning" in its native German tongue, has come to signify a sudden and irrepressible offensive tactic in the American sport of football. In law enforcement, a "blitz attack" has the meaning of an fast, violent assault. It was first used by the Oberkommando der Wehrmacht [OKW] (Military High Command) in the mid-1930s to describe their new military tactics of overpowering the enemy with the combined forces of armor, aircraft and infantry supported by massed artillery. *Blitz* became part of the English language during the spring and summer of 1940, when Hitler's Luftwaffe attempted to bomb England into submission, all as a part of a planned invasion in the early fall of 1940.

Blackout

During the blitz, British citizens were ordered to install special curtains and covers to eliminate any lights shining through to the outside. This was meant to deprive German bomber navigators of any landmarks while they were wandering about in the dark English nights. The term's widespread use is indicative of the proliferation of electric power—hence lights—since the First World War. At the present, it still means total darkness. However, it is less often voluntary and more commonly a result of a failure in the electric distribution system.

Flak

Ask almost any one what this word means and they will most likely think back to what they received when they neglected to let their spouse know that they were going to be late for dinner or reported a mistake to their boss. Originally, the name came from the German *Flieger Abwehr Kanonen,* or anti-aircraft cannon. During the war, the concentrated air defenses over German cities and factories were responsible for losses of sometimes as high as 45% of Allied aircraft. The phrase "taking intense flak" came to mean being in the crosshairs with little chance of escape without damage.

Brownout

This word came into popular use when new industrial plants or equipment demanded more energy than the system was capable of delivering. The problem was worldwide; a rumor has it that Philadelphia suffered a brownout when the ENIAC computer was first started in 1945. In Iran, whenever a heavy cargo crane unloading Lend-Lease supplies bound for Russia was used it caused random brownouts in the nearby town of Ahwaz.

Automation

A Ford Motor Company engineer, Delmar S. Harder, coined this word in 1946 to describe the system the company had devised to machine and assemble vehicle engines automatically. Using electro-hydraulic controls and air-driven tools, the process required fewer than twenty people to operate and could produce an engine every 14 minutes.

Bottleneck

This descriptive noun came to mean a hindrance to production from any means; shortages, absenteeism, poor workmanship, labor interference (strike or walkout). Bottlenecks were constantly being sought out and eliminated to increase the delivery of goods to support the war effort. Employees were enticed to identify stoppages and potential bottlenecks with cash awards, prizes, and paid vacations.

Crash Production

Originally British, this phrase was adopted by Americans soon after their entry into the war. There were times when special equipment such as electronic counter-measures was so in demand that the developing laboratory would be tasked with the initial production run. Later in the war there was no way this action could be tolerated: crash production is extremely wasteful of mass-production capacity and laboratory resources and was done only in the most severe instances of need.[13]

Dear John

This was the infamous opening of the dreaded letter informing the recipient that the woman at home was no longer chastely waiting for him. The results of getting a Dear John letter could be devastating. It is unknown how many men were killed by carelessness while in the throes of depression brought on by such missives. The problem became so severe at one point that a government campaign to explain the effects of the morale-destroying letters to stateside women was undertaken. Officers and chaplains also received special training to identify and intercede with the men who had gotten Dear John letters.

With the great influx of women into the service, a feminine version—Dear Jane—was also coined, but it did not receive nearly as much usage as its masculine counterpart. This was probably due to the military's strict regulations about accepting and retaining women who were married and also to the fact that the women who were serving overseas usually had left few romantic ties behind.

Quisling (Norway)

Former Minister of Defense and frustrated Norwegian politician Vidkun Quisling sold out his country to the Germans in 1940. In return, the Germans allowed Quisling to form his own government based on National Socialist (Nazi) ideologies. Even though he rose to the post of Minister President in 1942, both the German occupation forces and most Norwegians found Quisling's activities to be laughable as well as sad. When the war ended, Quisling was tried, convicted, and executed by his fellow countrymen for treason, leaving the legacy of a name synonymous with "collaborator."

Fifth Column(ists)

The Spanish Civil War, long seen by historians as a dress rehearsal for the Second World War, was the birthplace for this phrase that has come to represent an infiltrated group in sympathy with the enemy. Fifth columnists are suspected of participating in espionage, sabotage, and to spread propaganda, which is exactly what happened in Spain.

In the summer of 1936, the rebellious Army General Emilio Mola directed his troops to march on Madrid in a coordinated attack with Francisco Franco. In preparation of this action, Franco and Mola had successfully infiltrated the capitol city with sympathizers who organized a large contingent of locals who were also on the Fascist's side. Mola was asked which of his four separate armies, split into columns approaching from different directions, would be the first to capture the city. With airy confidence, he replied, "The Fifth Column."

Despite support from Germany and Italy, Franco and Mola failed immediately to gain the capitol. The city endured more than two years of siege, eventually surrendering in March, 1939. As Franco's forces marched through the streets of Madrid, thousands of Fifth columnists cheered and shouted with joy.

World War Two

Obviously, this phrase would not have existed had it not been for the widespread conflict that occurred in the third and fourth decades of the 20th century. The declared war was only eight days old when the term *World War Two* was coined in an article in *Time* magazine, released on September 11, 1939. Although the phrase received immediate and widespread usage, President Roosevelt hated it. He preferred *The War for Survival* and resolutely refused to use that other, less poetic term. Only after his death and the ascendancy of Harry Truman, did *World War Two* become the official name of the recently ended conflict.

Place Names

World War Two opened new geographical horizons for a large segment of the world's population. Maps were a big seller in America during the war, as families charted the progress of the war or the travels of their loved ones. Newspaper reports and newsreels presented a weekly travelogue of strange new lands with funny-sounding names, often in connection with American troops fighting and dying. Place names such as Guadalcanal, Tarawa St. Lô, and Remagen—all scenes of epic battles—will be remembered only by historians and the dwindling number of men who courageously fought there. However, there are other places that will never be forgotten or lost to history.

Pearl Harbor

This small city next to a naval base gained new significance with the attack on December 7, 1941. Before that date, the minority of the population who had even heard the name regarded it as a romantic tropical paradise with a few navy ships stationed somewhere nearby. An indication of the isolation of Pearl Harbor is expressed in the amusing tale that none of the officers of the German High Command had a clue where Pearl Harbor was on the news of the Japanese attack, provoking Adolph Hitler into a hysterical tirade for their ignorance and obvious incompetence.

Auschwitz, Treblinka, Bergen-Belsen Concentration Camps

Unlike Pearl Harbor, the names of all of the concentration camps were not in general usage, at least in the West, until well after the war was over. The above named camps are only three of several hundred that dotted the European continent. There are perhaps no other words in the English language that awaken such horror as the evil perpetrated by the Nazi Party and the SS.

Normandy

The long-awaited invasion of France took place on the beaches of Normandy on June 6, 1944. When the news broke, civilians were generally unclear as to where Normandy was in relation to England.

Viet Nam

Until the Japanese invaded the land east of present-day Thailand, the region was commonly referred to as French Indochina. Japan utilized the country's rice and agriculture production to bolster their own needs, but when they surrendered in 1945, it left a power vacuum in the area. When an indigenous communist leadership, led by Ho Chi Minh, arose to proclaim their independence, they adopted the name of *Vietnam*.

Hiroshima and Nagasaki

Until August 1945, Hiroshima and Nagasaki were, in the minds of most westerners, quaint little towns somewhere in Japan, far from the beaten path of tourists. Dropping the atomic bombs on these two heavily industrialized Japanese cities ensured that both of them would have a permanent place in the language of the world.

The Age of Acronyms

The first known acronym is from Cesarean Roman when the address; "Senatus Populusque Romanus" (the Senate and the People of Rome) got shortened to SPQR. When Morse code started to be used for radio signals at sea, single letters would adopt the place of entire words. An early example of this is the distress signal: SOS. The commonly held belief at the time was that it stood for "Save Our Ship" or "Save Our Souls," when in reality it was used because of the simple three dots and dashes denoting those letters were easiest to remember in an emergency.

Beginning around the time of FDR's inauguration, the American people started to see a proliferation of capitalized letters in their conversations and newspapers. Agencies such as the Agricultural Adjustment Administration were shortened to the AAA. So many new agencies, administrations and bureaucracies were formed that a veritable alphabet soup had to be created to save space on editorial pages. Even the President-elect was sporting a foreshortened three letter moniker.

The PWA, WPA, CCC, and the NRA joined the language alongside NAACP, the AMA and the AFL/CIO. It became so bad that the average listener practically required a game card to translate the conversation. It got worse when the CWA (Civilian Works Administration) became entangled with the CCC (Civilian Conservation Corps) and the PWA (Public Works Administration). This was especially confusing because all three organizations were doing similar work. Sometimes, two organizations with the same acronym for a name had nothing in common. The National Recovery Act (the NRA) did not mean the National Rifle Association (the NRA) and the more modern Equal Rights Amendment (ERA) is a long stretch of the imagination from baseball's ERA (Earned Run Average).

Manufacturers used a system of designating their products based on the alphabet. General Motors identified production versions and types with a four- or five-letter system beginning in 1939. The amphibious two and one-half ton truck, the Duck, got its name from the fortunate combination of GM model numbers: DUKW. Individually, the letters decode as 1942 manufacture (D), Utility (U), all-wheel drive (K), six-wheeled (W). GIs claimed that the name was appropriate however. Just like its animal namesake, the DUKW crossing the water was serene on the surface and paddling like hell underneath.

The military also joined the abbreviation fray. The U.S.Navy, in particular, liked acronyms, sometimes with horribly ironic results. The commanding officer of the fleet stationed at Pearl Harbor sported the title of "Commander in Chief, United States." Shortened to CinCUS, it was pronounced—with the unintentional dare—"Sink US." The title was changed just days after the Pearl Harbor attack to Commander, US Pacific Fleet (ComUSPacFlt).

The military has had a reputation for its incomprehensible methods, In the Navy and the Army, it was the catch-all; "Hurry up and Wait." This led to the young recruits to adopt language that was not necessarily used at home. As a result, the men adopted several permutations of a less-than-acceptable-in-public phrase to express exasperation. Some examples: Situation Normal, All F***ed Up (SNAFU), F***ed Up Beyond All Redemption (FUBAR), and a Joint Army/ Navy; F***-Up (JANFU) were just a few of the superlatives adapted for different situations.[14]

Even Allied POWs used acronyms to torment their German captors. The British adopted the derogatory term "goon" from a large, stupid character in the Popeye cartoon strip to apply to any German. Early on, POWs explained to their curious targets that goon was an acronym for "German officer or non-commissioned officer." To the amazement and awe of the prisoners responsible for this deception some German officers strictly required the use of the slur until they were informed of the true meaning.

Notes/Selected References

1   McCombs, Don, and Fred Worth. *World War Two, 4139 Strange and Fascinating Facts.*

1983. P.194. and Vesco, Renato, and David Hatcher Childress. *Man-made UFOs, 1944-1994*. 1994. Pp. 156 –159. and Good, Timothy. *Above Top Secret, The Worldwide UFO Cover-up*. 1988. Pp.18 -19.

2 Woodbury, David O. *Battlefronts of Industry: Westinghouse in World War II*. Pp. 188 -189.

3 McCombs, Don, and Fred Worth. P. 222.

4 McGrath, Susan Attack of The Alien Invaders; National Geographic magazine, March 2005. P. 97.

5 ibid. P. 98.

6 McCombs, Don, and Fred Worth. P. 230. and Brewer, Ebenezer Cobham. Brewers Dictionary of Phrase and Fable: 14th Ed. 1989. P. 502.

7 Information on the history of the ZIP Code and ZIP +4 is from the USPS websites: www.usps.gov/history/his3_5.htm#ZIP4 and # ZIP: www.usps.gov/history/his2_75.htm

8 United States Department of the Interior, Forest Service: www.r8web.com/texas/ smokey.htm www.smokeybear.com/cgi-bin/rbox/fr.cgi

9 Gant, Richard. *Ian Fleming, The Man With the Golden Pen*. 1966. P. 29. and *Current Biography: 1964*. Pp. 123 – 125.

10 Gutman, Israel. *The Encyclopedia of the Holocaust*. 1990. P. 681.

11 Lifton, Robert Jay. *The Nazi Doctors*. 1986. P. 466. Gutman. *The Encyclopedia of the Holocaust*. 1990. Pp. 860 - 861.

12 Butler, Rupert. *An Illustrated History of the Gestapo*. 1993. and Williamson, Gordon. *The SS: Hitler's Instrument of Terror*. 1998. Pp. 86 – 87.

13 Thompson, George Raynor and Dixie R. Harris. *The Signal Corps: The Outcome (Mid-1943 Through 1945.)* 1966. P. 302, footnote #3.

14 A respectable-sized list of superlatives is found in McCombs, Don, and Fred Worth. P. 567.

Guide to Photo Credits:

ALCo American Locomotive Company
ANCo Anderson Company
FDRLPDC Franklin D. Roosevelt Library and Public Document Center
INCo International Nickel Company
IWM Imperial War Museum
LANL Los Alamos National Laboratories
NAA North American Aviation
NARA National Archives and Records Administration
NASA National Aeronautics and Space Administration
OSRD Office of Scientific Research and Development
OWI Office of War Information
TVA Tennessee Valley Authority
USAAF United States Army Air Force
USSBS United States Strategic Bombing Survey
WPB War Production Board
USHMM United States Holocaust Memorial Museum

Index

Symbols

A

B

H

I

K

L

M

N

nitrogen 373, 406, 437
nitrogen narcosis 352
nitrous oxide 213
Nobel Prize 130, 225
Nordhausen 104
Normandy 21, 376, 444, 469, 507
North Africa 23, 96, 126, 169, 170, 204, 309, 312, 371, 425, 468, 488
North American Indigenous People 503
North Carolina 32
Northern hemisphere 447
Northern Regional Research Laboratory 210
North Korea 192
Northrop Aircraft 286
Norway 72, 102, 505
Nose Wheel 92
nuclear 241
nurses 79, 80, 150, 199, 228, 234, 312
nylon 81, 226, 229, 301, 302, 368
Nysander, Marie 202

O

Oak City 58
Oak Ridge 57, 58, 375
oats 420
Oberkommando der Wehrmacht 416, 503
Oberweisenfeld 104
Occupational Safety and Health Administration 262
Ocean 404
Office of Civil Defense 77
Office of Price Administration 264, 455
Office of Production Management 380
Office of Scientific 21
Ohio 396
Ohl, Russell 130
oil 28, 62, 91, 98, 123
Okinawa 410, 481
Oklahoma 404
Oklahoma City 317
Oldfield, Barney 475
Oldsmobile 462
Opelika, Alabama 144
Open pit mining 41
Operation Anvil 468
Operation Aphrodite 349

Q

R

S

Bibliography

Ahnfeldt, Arnold Lorentz, MC, USA. *Radiology in World War II*. Washington, DC: Office of the Surgeon General, Department of the Army. 1966.

Aly, Götz, Peter Chroust, and Christian Pross. *Cleansing the Fatherland: Nazi Medicine and Racial Hygiene*. Baltimore: The Johns Hopkins University Press. 1994.

The American Arsenal. Mechanicsburg, PA: Stackpole Books. 1996. Originally issued by Office of the Chief of Ordnance, Technical Division, U.S. Army. Washington, DC: 1944.

Anastasi, Anne. *Psychological Testing*. New York: Macmillan Publishing. 1988.

Anderson, Robert S. Col. MC, USA. *Army Medical Specialist Corps*. Washington, DC: Office of the Surgeon General, Department of the Army. 1968.

Anderson, Robert S. Col. MC, USA. *Physical Standards in World War II*. Washington, DC: Office of the Surgeon General, Department of the Army. 1967.

Andrus, E. C., D.W. Bronk, et al. editors. *Advances in Military Medicine, Vols. 1 and 2*. Boston: Little, Brown and Company. 1948.

Armstrong, Harry G., MD, F.A.C.S. MC, USA. *Principles and Practices of Aviation Medicine*. Baltimore, MD: Williams and Wilkins Co. 1939.

Asbell, Bernard. *The Pill: An Autobiography of the Drug That Changed the World*. New York: Random House. 1995.

Bailey, Ronald H. *World War II: The Home Front: USA*. Alexandria, VA: Time-Life Books. 1981.

Balzer, Gerald H. *American Secret Pusher Fighters of World War II*. North Branch, MN: Specialty Press. 2008.

Barber, Bernard, John, J., Lally, Julia Loughlin Makarushka, and Daniel Sullivan. *Research on Human Subjects: Problems of Social Control in Medical Experimentation*. New York: Russell Sage Foundation. 1973.

Barger, Harold, and Sam H. Schurr. *The Mining Industries, 1899-1939*. New York: Arno Press. 1972.

Bateman, Alan M. *Economic Mineral Deposits*. New York: John Wiley and Sons. 1942.

Beeson, Walter J. and R.B. Scott. *The Oxford Companion to Medicine*. New York: Oxford University Press. 1986.

Bell, Mary T. *Mary Bell's Complete Dehydrator Cookbook*. New York: William Morrow and Company. 1984.

Benjamin, Ludy T. *A History of Psychology in Letters*. Dubuque, IA: Brown and Benchmark. 1993.

Benford, Timothy B. *The World War II Quiz and Fact Book*. New York: Galahad Books. 1993.

Berenbaum, Michael. *The World Must Know*. New York: Little, Brown and Company. 1993.

Berkow, Robert. editor. *The Merck Manual of Diagnosis and Therapy 16th Ed.* Rahway, NJ: Merck Research Laboratories. 1992.

Bethall, Nicholas. *Russia Besieged.* Alexandria, VA: Time-Life Books. 1980.

Beyers, James C. Major, MC, USA. *Wound Ballistics.* Washington, DC: Office of the Surgeon General, Department of the Army. 1962.

Bijker, Weibe E. *Of Bicycles, Bakelite and Bulbs.* Cambridge, MA: MIT Press. 1995.

Blair, Clay. *Hitler's U-Boat War, the Hunted: 1942-1945.* New York: Random House. 1998.

Blair, Thomas A. *Weather Elements.* New York: Prentice-Hall, Inc. 1944.

Blay, John S. *The Civil War: A Pictorial Profile.* New York: Bonanza Books. 1958.

Bolan, Nelson. *How Detroit Changed History.* Lawrenceville, VA: Brunswick Publishing. 1987.

Borkin, Joseph. *The Crime and Punishment of I.G. Farben.* New York: Barnes and Noble Books. 1978.

Borkin, Joseph, and Charles A. Welsh. *Germany's Master Plan.* New York: Duell, Sloan, Pearce Inc. 1943.

Botting, Douglas. *From the Ruins of the Reich: Germany 1945-1949.* New York: Crown Publishing. 1985.

————— *World War II, the Aftermath: Europe.* Alexandria, VA: Time-Life Books. 1981.

Bowen, Ezra, editor. *This Fabulous Century 1930-1940.* Alexandria, VA: Time-Life Books. 1971.

Bower, Tom. *The Paperclip Conspiracy.* Boston: Little, Brown and Company. 1987.

————— *Nazi Gold.* New York: Harper Collins. 1997.

Boyce, Joseph. *New Weapons for Air Warfare.* Boston: Little, Brown and Co. 1947.

Boyne, Walter J. *Power Behind the Wheel.* New York: Stewart, Tabori & Chang. 1988.

Breuer, William. *Geronimo! American Paratroopers in World War II.* New York: St. Martins Press. 1989.

Brickhill, Paul. *The Dam Busters.* New York: Ballantine Books. 1957.

Brinkley, Douglas. *Wheels For the World: Henry Ford, His Company and A Century of Progress.* New York: Viking Press. 2003.

Broomfield, Lewis. *Out of the Earth.* New York: Harper & Bros. Publishing Co., Inc. 1950.

Brophy, Leo P., Wyndham D. Miles, and Rexmond C. Cochrane. *The Chemical Warfare Service: From Laboratory to Field.* Washington, DC: Office of the Chief of Military History, Department of the Army. 1959.

Brown, D. Clayton. *Electricity for Rural America.* Westport, CT: Greenwood Press. 1980.

Bruun, Erik, and Keith Buzzy. *Heavy Equipment.* New York: Black Dog & Leventhal Publishers, Inc. 1997.

Bryan, John L. *Fire Suppression and Detection Systems.* New York: Macmillan Publishing Company. 1993.

Buderi, Robert. *The Invention That Changed the World.* New York: Simon and Schuster. 1996.

Bullock, Barbara L., Pearl Philbrook and Rosendahl,. *Patho-Physiology, Adaptations and Alterations in Function*. Boston: Little, Brown & Co. 1984.

Burgett, Donald R. *Currahee: A Screaming Eagle at Normandy*. Novato, CA: Presidio Press. 1967.

Burkhart, Bryan, and David Hunt. *Airstream: History of the Land Yacht*. San Francisco, CA: Chronicle Books. 2000.

Burns, James MacGregor. *Roosevelt: The Soldier of Freedom*. New York: Harcourt Brace Jovanovich, Inc. 1970.

Burton, Jerry. *Zora Arkus-Duntov: The Legend behind the Corvette*. Cambridge, MA: Bentley Publishers. 2002.

Butler, Rupert. *An Illustrated History of the Gestapo*. Osceola, WI: Motorbooks International. 1992.

Bykofsky, Joseph, and Harold Larson. *The Transportation Corps: Operations Overseas*. Washington, DC: Office of Chief of Military History, Department of the Army. 1957.

Campbell-Kelly, Martin, and William Aspray. *Computer: A History of the Information Machine*. New York: Basic Books. 1996.

Carper, Robert S. *American Railroads in Transition*. New York: A.S. Barnes and Co. 1968.

Cartwright, Frederick F. *The Development of Surgery*. New York: Thomas Y. Crowell Company. 1967.

The Chemical Warfare Service in World War II: A Report of Accomplishments. New York: Reinhold Publishing Corp. 1948.

Church, John. *Military Vehicles of World War II*. New York: Sterling Publishing Co., Inc. 1982.

Clancy, Tom. *Submarines*. New York: Berkeley Books. 1993.

Coakley, Robert W., and Richard M. Leighton. *Global Logistics and Strategy; 1943-1945*. Washington, DC: Center of Military History, Department of the Army. 1999.

Cohen, Stan. *V for Victory, America's Home Front during World War II*. Missoula, MT: Pictorial Histories Publishing Co., Inc. 1991.

Coll, Blanche D, Jean E. Rosenthal. *The Corps of Engineers: Troops and Equipment*. Washington, DC: Office of Chief of Military History, Department of the Army. 1958.

Collison, Thomas. *The Superfortress Is Born*. New York: Duell, Sloan & Pearce. 1945.

Condon-Hall, Mary Ellen, and Albert E. Cowdry. *The Medical Department: Medical Service in the War against Japan*. Washington, DC: Center of Military History, Department of the Army. 1998.

Conn, Stetson, Rose C. Engelman and Byron Fairchild. *The Western Hemisphere: Guarding the United States and Its Outposts*. Washington, DC: Office of the Chief of Military History, Department of the Army. 1964.

Cornwell, John. *Hitler's Scientists: Science, War and the Devil's Pact*. New York: Viking. 2003.

Cowdrey, Albert E. *Fighting for Life, American Military Medicine in World War II*. New York: Free Press. 1994.

Craven, Wesley Frank, and James Lea Cate. *The Army Air Forces in World War II Vol. Six*. Chicago: University of Chicago Press. 1955.

Crismon, Fred V. *U.S. Military Wheeled Vehicles*. Osceola, WI: Crestline Books. 1994.

David, Jay. Ed. *Growing Up Black*. New York: Avon Books. 1992.

Davis, Franklin M. Jr. *Across the Rhine*. Alexandria, VA: Time-Life Books. 1980.

Davis, Kenneth S. *F.D.R. The New Deal Years: 1933-1937*. New York: Random House. 1986.

DeNevi, Don, and Bob Hall. *United States Military Railway Service*. Toronto: Stoddart Publishing Co. Ltd. 1992.

Denison, Merrill. *Bristles and Brushes*. New York: Dodd, Mead and Co. 1949.

Distel, Ruth, and Ruth Jakusch, editors. *Concentration Camp Dachau, 1933-1945*. Munich: Comité International de Dachau. 1978.

Dix, Keith. *What's a Coal Miner to Do?* Pittsburgh, PA: University of Pennsylvania Press. 1988.

Dod, Karl C. *The Corps of Engineers: The War against Japan*. Washington, DC; Office of the Chief of Military History, Department of the Army. 1966.

Donaldson, Cyril, and George LeCain. *Tool Design*. New York: Harper & Bros. 1943.

Downs, L. Vaughn. *The Mightiest of Them All*. Fairfield, Washington: Ye Galleon Press. 1986.

DuBois, Josiah E. Jr. *The Devil's Chemists*. Boston: Beacon Press. 1952.

Dunnigan, James F. *Dirty Little Secrets of the Twentieth Century*. New York: Quill. 1999.

Dunnigan, James F., and Albert A. Nofi. *Dirty Little Secrets of World War II*. New York: William Morrow and Company. 1994.

Eden, Paul, and Soph Moeng, general editors. *Aircraft Anatomy of World War II*. Edison, NJ: Chartwell Books, Inc. 2003.

Eiler, Mary Ann. editor. *Specialty Profiles*. Chicago: Department of Physician Data Services, Survey and Data Resources, AMA. 1988.

Ellis, Chris. *Directory of Wheeled Vehicles of the Wehrmacht 1933-45*. London: Ducimus Books Ltd. 1974.

Engelmann, Bernt. *In Hitler's Germany*. New York: Pantheon Books. 1986.

Ewens, Graeme, and, Michael Ellis. *The Cult of Big Rigs*. Secaucus, NJ: Chartwell Books. 1977.

Fahey, James J. *Pacific War Diary: 1942-1945*. Boston: Houghton Mifflin Company. 1991.

Fairchild, Byron and Jonathon Grossman. *The Army and Industrial Manpower*. Washington, DC: Center of Military History, Department of the Army. 1988.

Fenichell, Stephen. *Plastic: The Making of a Synthetic Century*. New York: Harper Collins Publishers. 1996.

Fermi, Rachel and Esther Samra. *Picturing the Bomb: Photographs from the Secret World of the Manhattan Project*. New York: Harry Abrams Publishing, Inc. 1995.

Fine, Lenore and Jesse Remington. *The Corps of Engineers: Construction in the United States*. Washington, DC: Center of Military History, U.S. Army. 1989.

Fisher, David E. and, Jon Marshall. *Tube: The Invention of Television*. Washington, DC: Counterpoint. 1996.

Fodor, Denis J. *World War II, the Neutrals*. Alexandria, VA: Time-Life Books. 1981.

Fowler, William. *The Jeep Goes to War*. New York: PRC Publishing. 1994.

Francher, Raymond E. *Pioneers of Psychology*. New York: W. W. Norton Publishing. 1979.

Freeman, Frank S. *Theory and Practice of Psychological Testing; revised edition*. New York: Henry Holt and Company. 1957.

Freiman, Fran Locher, and Neil Schlager. *Failed Technology, Vol. 2*. New York: Gale/Cengage. 1995.

Gant, Richard. *Ian Fleming: The Man with the Golden Pen*. New York: Lancer Books. 1966.

Garcia, Juan Ramon. *Operation Wetback*. London: Greenwood Press. 1980.

Giddings, W. Philip, M.D., et al. *Surgery in World War II: General Surgery, Vol. II*. Washington, DC: Office of the Surgeon General, Department of the Army. 1955.

Ginn, Richard V.F. *The History of the U.S. Army Medical Service Corps*. Washington, DC: Office of the Surgeon General and the Center of Military History, United States Army. 1997.

Glass, Albert J., Col. MC, USA, (Ret.) and Lt. Col. Robert Bernucci, MC, USA, (Ret.). *Neuropsychiatry in World War II: Vol. I. Zone of Interior*. Washington, DC: Office of the Surgeon General, Department of the Army. 1966.

Glass, Albert J., Col. MC, USA, (Ret.). *Neuropsychiatry in World War II: Vol. II. Overseas Theaters*. Washington, DC: Office of the Surgeon General, Department of the Army. 1973.

Glasser M.D., Ronald J. *365 Days*. New York: George Braziller, Inc. 1996.

Goldstein, Donald M., Katherine V. Dillon, and J. Michael Wenger. *Rain of Ruin: A Photographic History of Hiroshima and Nagasaki*. Washington, DC: Brassy's. 1995.

Good, Timothy. *Above Top Secret, the Worldwide UFO Cover-up*. Toronto: McClelland & Stuart. 1988.

Gott, Philip G. *Changing Gears*. Warrendale, PA: Society of Automotive Engineers. 1991.

Greenwald, Robert A., Mary Kay Ryan, and James E. Mulvihill. eds. *Human Subjects: A Handbook for Institutional Review Boards*. New York: Plenum Press. 1982.

Greenwood, Ivan A. Jr., J. Vance Holdam and Duncan Macrae. *Electronic Instruments*. New York: McGraw-Hill Book Co. 1948.

Gutman, Yisrael, and Michael Berenbaum, editors. *Anatomy of the Auschwitz Death Camp*. Bloomington, IN: Indiana University Press. 1998.

Halle, Kay. *Irrepressible Churchill*. London, Robson. 1985.

Hampton, Oscar P. Jr. M.D., F.A.C.S., Col., MC, USAR. *Surgery in World War II: Orthopedic Surgery in the Mediterranean Theater of Operations*. Washington, DC: Office of the Surgeon General, Department of the Army. 1957.

Harris, Jack C. *Plastic Model Kits*. New York: Crestwood. 1993.

Havens, Thomas R.H. *Valley of Darkness*. New York: University Press of America. 1986.

Havens, W. Paul, editor. *Internal Medicine in World War II: Activities of Medical Consultants, Vol. I*. Washington, DC: Office of the Chief of Military History, Department of the Army. 1961.

Havens, W. Paul, editor. *Internal Medicine in World War II: Infectious Diseases, Vol. II*. Washington, DC: Office of the Chief of Military History, Department of the Army. 1963.

————— *Internal Medicine in World War II: Infectious Diseases and General Medicine, Vol. III*. Washington, DC: Office of the Chief of Military History, Department of the Army. 1968.

Herriot, James. *The Lord God Made Them All*. New York: Bantam Books. 1982.

Higonnet, Margaret Randolph, et al, editor s. *Behind the Lines, Gender and the Two World Wars*. New Haven CT: Yale University Press. 1987.

Hillel, Marc and Clarissa Henry. *Of Pure Blood*. New York: McGraw-Hill. 1976.

Hoff, Ebbe Curtis, Ph. D., M.D. editor. *Preventive Medicine in World War II: Vol. II. Environmental Hygiene*. Washington, DC: Office of the Surgeon General, Department of the Army. 1955.

————— *Preventive Medicine in World War II: Vol. III. Personal Health Measures and Immunization*. Washington, DC: Office of the Surgeon General, Department of the Army. 1955.

————— *Preventive Medicine in World War II: Vol. V. Communicable Diseases, Transmitted Through Contact or By Unknown Means*. Washington, DC: Office of the Surgeon General, Department of the Army. 1960.

————— *Preventive Medicine in World War II: Vol. VI. Communicable Diseases, Malaria*. Washington, DC: Office of the Surgeon General, Department of the Army. 1963.

————— *Preventive Medicine in World War II: Vol. VII. Communicable Diseases*. Washington, DC: Office of the Surgeon General, Department of the Army. 1964.

————— *Preventive Medicine in World War II: Vol. IX, Special Fields*. Washington, DC: Office of the Surgeon General, Department of the Army. 1969.

Hogg, Ian V. *German Secret Weapons of World War II*. London: Greenhill Books. 1999.

Holley, Irving Brinton Jr. *Buying Aircraft: Material for the Army Air Forces*. Washington, DC: Center of Military History, Department of the Army. 1989.

Hoopes, Roy. *Americans Remember The Home Front*. New York: Berkley Publishing. 2002.

Infield, Glenn B. *Disaster at Bari*. New York: The Macmillan Company. 1971.

Innes, Sherri, A. editor. *Delinquents and Debutantes*. New York: New York University Press. 1998.

Italia, Robert. *Great Auto Makers and Their Cars*. Minneapolis, MN: Oliver Press, Inc. 1993.

Ivens, Bryna, editor. *The Seventeen Reader*. New York: J.B. Lippincott Co. 1951.

Jamieson, Elizabeth M., B.A. R.N. and Mary F. Sewall. B.S. R.N. *Trends in Nursing*. Philadelphia. W.B. Saunders Co. 1949.

Jamieson, John. *Books for the Army*. New York: Columbia University Press. 1950.

Jeffcott, George F. *A History of the United States Army Dental Service in World War II*. Washington, DC: Office of the Surgeon General, Department of the Army. 1955.

Jones, Vincent C. *The United States Army in World War II: Special Studies: Manhattan, the Army and the Atomic Bomb*. Washington, DC: Office of the Chief of Military History, Department of the Army. 1985.

Kalmbach, A.C. *Railroad Panorama*. Milwaukee, WI: Kalmbach Publishing Co. 1944.

Kendrick, Douglas B., Brigadier General MC, USA. *Blood Program in World War II*. Washington, DC: Medical Department, USA, Office of the Surgeon General, Department of the Army. 1989.

Kevles, Bettyann Holtzmann. *Naked to the Bone*. New Brunswick, NJ: Rutgers University Press. 1997.

Kindleberger, Charles. *The World in Depression*. Berkeley, CA: University of California Press. 1975.

Kirk, John and Robert Young Jr. *Great Weapons of World War II*. New York: Walker and Company. 1990.

Kleber, Brooks E. and Dale Birdsell. *The Chemical Warfare Service: Chemicals in Combat*. Washington, DC: United States Army. 1990.

Klee, Ernst. *Auschwitz: die NS-Medizin und ihre Opfer*. Frankfurt am Main: S. Fischer Verlag GmbH. 1997.

Krawiec, T.S. editor.*The Psychologists*. *Vol. 2*. London: Oxford University Press. 1974.

Leahey, Thomas Hardy. *A History of Psychology*. Englewood Cliffs, NJ: Prentice Hall. 1980.

Lem, James, Cay Beardsley, and Paul Beardsley. Home Hydroponics. Pasadena, CA: Ward Ritchie Press. 1977.

Lewis, Brenda Ralph. *Hitler Youth: The Hitlerjugend in War and Peace: 1933-1945*. Osceola, WI: MBI Publishing Co. 2000.

Lifton, Robert Jay. *The Nazi Doctors, Medical Killing and the Psychology of Genocide*. New York: Basic Books, Inc. 1986.

Lingeman, Richard R. *Don't You Know There's a War On?* New York: G .P. Putnam's Sons. 1970.

Lucas, James. *World War II through German Eyes*. London: Arms and Armor Press. 1987.

Lyons, Albert S. and Joseph R. Petrucelli. *Medicine: An Illustrated History*. New York: Harry N. Abrams Inc. 1987.

McClelland, Bramlette, and Michael D. Reifel. *Planning and Design of Fixed Offshore Platforms*. New York: Van Nostrand Reinhold Company. 1986.

McCombs, Don, and Fred Worth. *World War Two: 4139 Strange and Fascinating Facts*. New York: Wings Books. 1983.

McCraw, Thomas K. *TVA and the Power Fight: 1933-1939*. New York: J.B. Lippincott Company. 1971.

McDermott, Kathleen. *Timex: A Company and Its Community, 1854-1998*. Middlebury, CT: Timex Corporation. 1998.

McGurn, Barrett. *Yank: The Army Weekly, Reporting the Greatest Generation*. Golden CO: Fulcrum Publishing. 2004.

Maisel, Albert Q. *Miracles of Military Medicine*. Garden City, NJ: Garden City Books. 1943.

Maloney, Dennis M. *The Protection of Human Research Subjects*. New York: Plenum Press. 1984.

Marshall, Chester W. and Warren Thompson. *Final Assault on the Rising Sun*. North Branch MN: Specialty Press Publishers and Wholesalers. 1995.

Mayer, S. L., editor. *Signal: Years of Triumph 1940-1942*. Englewood Cliffs, NJ: Prentice-Hall, Inc. 1979.

Mayer, S. L. *The Rise and Fall of Imperial Japan*. New York: Military Press. 1984.

Mayo, Lida. *The Ordnance Department: On the Beachhead and Battlefront*. Washington, DC: United States Army. 1968.

Metzger, H. Peter. *The Atomic Establishment*. New York: Simon and Schuster. 1972.

Miller, David. *Fighting Men of World War II: Axis Forces Uniforms, Equipment and Weapons*. Mechanicsburg, PA: Stackpole Books. 2007.

Miller, Everett B. Lt. Col. VC, USA. *United States Army Veterinary Service in World War II*. Washington, DC: Office of the Surgeon General, Department of the Army. 1961.

Mollo, Andrew. *A Pictorial History of the SS*. New York: Stein and Day Publishers. 1977.

Molloy, E. *Pumps and Pumping*. Brooklyn, NY: Chemical Publishing Company, Inc. 1941.

Monohan, Evelyn and Rosemary Neidel-Greenlee. *And If I Perish: Frontline Army Nurses in World War II*. New York: Knopf. 2003.

Montgomery, M.R. and Gerald Foster. *A Field Guide to Airplanes: 2nd Edition*. Boston: Houghton Mifflin Company. 1992.

Motley, Mary Penick. Ed. *The Invisible Soldier, the Experience of the Black Soldier in World War Two*. Detroit, MI: Wayne State University Press. 1987.

Munson, Richard. *Cousteau, the Captain and His World*. New York: William Morrow and Company, Inc. 1989.

Myrdal, Gunnar. *An American Dilemma, the Negro Problem and Modern Democracy*. New York: Pantheon Books. 1972.

Neufeild, Michael J. *The Rocket and the Reich*. Cambridge, MA: Harvard University Press. 1995.

Nicholls, Richard E. *Beginning Hydroponics*. Philadelphia, PA: Running Press. 1977.

Nijboer, Donald. *Graphic War: Secret Aviation Drawings and Illustrations of World War II*. Ontario: Boston Mills Press. 2005.

Nye, David E. *Electrifying America*. Cambridge, MA: MIT Press.1991.

Ohly, John. *Industrialists in Olive Drab*. Washington, DC: Center for Military History. United States Army. 1999.

O'Reilly,Maurice. *The Goodyear Story*. Elmsford, NY: Benjamin Books. 1983.

Osborne, Charles, and Sheldon Cotler. editors. *World War II, The Aftermath: Asia*. Alexandria, VA: Time-Life Books. 1981.

Otfinoski, Steven. *Alexander Fleming: Conquering Disease with Penicillin*. New York: Facts on File. 1992.

Panati, Charles. *Extraordinary Origins of Everyday Things*. New York: Harper & Row Publishing. 1987.

Pawle, Gerald. *Secret Weapons of World War II*. New York: Ballantine Books. 1957.

Pernkopf, Eduard. *Atlas of Topographical and Applied Human Anatomy*, *Vols. 1& 2*. Philadelphia: W.B. Saunders Co. 1963.

Pitzer, Paul. *Grand Coulee*. Pullman, WA: Washington State University Press. 1994.

Podolny, Walter, and John B. Scalzi. *Construction and Design of Cable-Stayed Bridges*. New York: John Wiley and Sons. 1986.

Poolman, Kenneth. *The Winning Edge*. Annapolis, MA: Naval Institute Press. 1997.

Porter, Roy. *The Greatest Benefit to Mankind*. New York: W.W. Norton Press. 1997.

Pringle, Heather. *The Master Plan: Himmler's Scholars and the Holocaust*. New York: Hyperion. 2006.

Rader, Benjamin G. *Baseball: A History of America's Game*. Chicago: University of Illinois Press. 1992.

Reiser, Stanley Joel. *Medicine and the Reign of Technology*. Cambridge, England: Cambridge University Press. 1979.

Reuben, Carolyn. *Antioxidants, Your Complete Guide*. Rocklin, CA.: Prima Publishing. 1995.

Reynolds, A.K., and Lowell O. Randall. *Morphine and Allied Drugs*. Toronto: University of Toronto Press. 1957.

Reynolds, Clark G. *America at War: 1941-1945: The Home Front*. New York: Gallery Books. 1990.

Rhodes, Richard. *The Making of the Atomic Bomb*. New York: Simon and Schuster. 1988

Rigge, Simon. *The War in the Outposts*. Alexandria, VA: Time-Life Books. 1980

Riordan, Michael, and Lillian Hoddeson. *Crystal Fire, the Birth of the Information Age*. New York: W.W. Norton Company. 1997

Risch, Erna. *The Quartermaster Corps: Organization Supply and Services, Vol. I.* Washington, DC: Office of the Chief of Military History, Department of the Army. 1953.

Risch, Erna, and Chester L. Keiffer. *The Quartermaster Corps: Organization Supply and Services. Vol. II.* Washington, DC: Chief of Military History, Department of the Army. 1955.

Rochow, Eugene G. *Silicon and Silicones.* Berlin: Springer-Velag Publishers. 1987.

Ross, William F., and Charles F. Romanus. *The Quartermaster Corps: Operations in the War against Germany.* Washington, DC: Office of Chief of Military History, Department of the Army. 1965.

Russell, Francis. *World War II, The Secret War.* Alexandria, VA: Time-Life Books. 1981.

Ryan, Keith, *The Illustrated History of Fire Engines.* Edison, NJ: Chartwell Books. 1998.

Salvati, Raymond E. *Island Creek.* New York: The Newcomen Society in North America. 1957.

Schmelz, Friedrich, Count Hans-Christoph Seherr-Thoss, and Erich Aucktor *Universal Joints and Driveshafts.* Berlin:Springer-Verlag. 1992.

Schmidt, Jacob Edward. *Medical Discoveries.* Charles C. Thomas, Publisher: 1959.

Schurcliff, William A. *Polarized Light.* Princeton, NJ: D. Van Nostrand. 1964.

Schneider, Wolfgang. *Tigers in Combat, Vols. 1 & 2.* Mechanicsburg, PA: Stackpole Books. 2000, 1998.

Scott, Beth F., Lt. Col. James C. Rainey, and Capt. Andrew Hunt. *The Logistics of War.* Maxwell AFB, Alabama: The Air Force Logistics Management Agency. 2000.

Serling, Robert J. *When the Airlines Went to War.* New York: Kensington Books. 1998.

Shachtman, Tom. *Terrors and Marvels.* New York: Harper-Collins. 2002.

Shawcross, William. *Rupert Murdoch.* London: Chatto & Windus. 1992.

Shermer, David. *World War I.* Secaucus, NJ. Derby Books. 1973.

Shields, Bert. *Air Pilot Training.* New York: McGraw Hill Book Co. 1942.

Simonds, Herbert R., M.H Bigelow, and Joseph V. Sherman. *The New Plastics.* New York: D. Van Nostrand Company, Inc. 1945.

Simonson, R.D. *The History of Welding.* Morton Grove, IL: Monticello Books. 1969.

Skolnick, Jerome H., and Elliott Currie. editors. *Crisis in American Institutions: 4th Ed.* Boston: Little, Brown and Company. 1979.

Smith, Clarence McKittrick. *The Medical Department: Hospitalization and Evacuation, Zone of Interior.* Washington, DC: Office of the Chief of Military History, Department of the Army. 1956.

Soled, Julius. *Fasteners Handbook.* New York: Reinhold Publishing. 1957.

Spencer, William. *Germany: Then and Now.* New York: Franklin Watts. 1994.

Spielberger, Walter J. and Hilary Doyle. *Tigers I and II: and Their Variants.* Atglen PA: Schiffer Publishing Ltd. 2000.

Spilling, Michael, editor. Luftwaffe Squadrons: 1939-1945. London: Amber Books. 2006.

Spurling, R. Glen, M.D. and Barnes Woodhall, M.D. *Surgery in World War II: Neurosurgery, Vol. II*. Washington, DC: Office of the Surgeon General, Department of the Army. 1959.

Stack, Barbara. *Handbook of Mining and Tunneling Machinery*. New York: John Wiley and Sons. 1982.

Staerk, Chris, editor. *Allied Photo Reconnaissance of World War II*. San Diego, CA: Thunder Bay Press. 1998.

Starr, Douglas. *Blood: An Epic History of Medicine and Commerce*. New York: Alfred A. Knopf. 1998.

Stauffer, Alvin P. *The Quartermaster Corps: Operations in the War against Japan*. Washington, DC: Office of the Chief of Military History, Department of the Army. 1956.

Stefferud, Alfred, editor. *The Yearbook of Agriculture 1943-1947: Science in Farming*. Washington, DC: U.S. Government Printing Office. 1947.

Steinhoff, Johannes, Peter Pechel and Dennis Showalter. *Voices from the Third Reich: An Oral History*. Washington, DC: Regnery Gateway. 1989.

Stern, Robert C. *Type VII U-Boats*. Annapolis, MD: Naval Institute Press. 1991.

Stevens, Joseph. *Hoover Dam*. Norman, OK: University of Oklahoma Press. 1988.

Stokely, James. *Science Remakes Our World*. New York: Ives Washburn Publishers. 1946.

Stout, Wesley W. *Great Engines and Great Planes*. Detriot, MI: Chrysler Corp. 1947.

Strandh, Sigvard. *A History of the Machine*. New York: A&W Publishers, Inc. 1979.

Suits. C. G., George Harrison, and Louis Jordan. editors. *Applied Physics, Electronics and Metallurgy*. Boston: Little Brown and Company. 1948.

Sullivan, John, W. W. *The Story of Metals*. Ames, IA: American Society for Metals. Iowa State College Press. 1951.

Sulzberger, C. L. *The American Heritage Picture History of World War II*. New York: American Heritage Publishing Co. Inc. 1966.

Sweeting, C.G. *Combat Flying Equipment*. Washington, DC: Smithsonian Institution Press. 1989.

Taylor, John R., editor. *Combat Aircraft of the World*. New York: G.P. Putnam's Sons. 1969.

— — — — *The Lore of Flight*. New York: Crescent Books. 1978.

Teller, Edward. *The Legacy of Hiroshima*. Garden City NJ: Doubleday. 1962.

Terkel, Studs. *The Good War, an Oral History of World War Two*. New York: Pantheon Books. 1984.

Terret, Dulany. *The Signal Corps: The Emergency (To December 1941)*. Washington, DC: Office of the Chief of Military History, Department of the Army: 1956.

Thiesmeyer,Lincoln R., and John E. Burchard. *Combat Scientists*. Boston: Little, Brown and Company. 1947.

Thompson, George Raynor, and Dixie R. Harris. The Signal Corps: The Outcome, (Mid-1943 Through 1945). Washington, DC: Office of the Chief of Military History, Department of the Army. 1966.

Thompson, George Raynor, et al. *The Signal Corps: The Test (December 1941to July 1943)*. Washington, DC: Office of the Chief of Military History, Department of the Army. 1956.

Thomson, Harry C., and Lida Mayo. *The Ordnance Department: Procurement and Supply*. Washington, DC: United States Army. 1960.

Thomson, Harry C., and Peter C. Roots. *The Ordnance Department: Planning Munitions for War*. Washington, DC: United States Army. 1955.

Thomson, James E.M. editor. *Lectures on Peace and War, Orthopedic Surgery: Instructional Courses from the 11th Annual Assembly of the American Academy of Orthopedic Surgeons*. Ann Arbor, MI: American Academy of Orthopedic Surgeons. 1943.

Travers, Bridget, and Jeffrey Muhr. *A World of Invention*. Detroit: Gale Research Corporation. 1994.

True, Webster P. editor. *Smithsonian Treasury of 20th Century Science*. Washington, DC: Simon and Schuster. 1966.

Tuve, Richard L. *Principles of Fire Chemistry*. Boston: National Fire Protection Association. 1976.

U.S. War Department Handbook on German Military Forces. Baton Rouge, LA: Louisiana State University Press. 1995.

Vesco, Renato, and David Hatcher Childress. *Man-Made UFOs: 1944-1994*. Stelle, IL: Adventures Unlimited Press. 1994.

Voss, Frederick S. *Reporting the War: Journalistic Coverage of World War II*. Washington, DC: Smithsonian Press. 1994.

Walton, Mary. *The Deming Management Method*. W. Element Stone OR: Dodd, Mea and Co. 1986.

Ward, Geoffrey C. *Baseball: An Illustrated History*. New York: Alfred A Knopf Publishing. 1994.

Wardlow, Chester, *The Transportation Corps: Movements, Training and Supply*. Washington, DC: United States Army. 1956.

Warp, Harold. *A History of Man's Progress*. Minden, Nebraska: The Harold Warp Pioneer Village. 1978.

Warrick , Dr. Earl L. *Forty Years of Firsts*. New York: McGraw-Hill Publishing Company. 1990.

Warshofsky, Fred. *The Rebuilt Man: The Story of Spare Parts Surgery*. New York: Thomas Y. Crowell Company. 1965.

Watson, J.B. *Psychological Care of Infant and Child*. New York: W. W. Norton Publishing. 1928.

Watterson, John Sayle. *College Football: History, Spectacle, Controversy*. Baltimore: John Hopkins University Press. 2000.

Weal, Elke, and John Weal. *Combat Aircraft of World War Two*. New York: Macmillan Publishing Co., Inc. 1977.

Weatherford, Doris. *American Women and World War Two*. New York: Facts on File, Inc. 1990.

Weinreich, Max. *Hitler's Professors*. New Haven CT: Yale University Press. 1999.

Whayne, Tom F. Col. MC, USA. (Ret.) and Micheal DeBakey, M.D. *Cold Injury, Ground Type*. Washington, DC: Office of the Surgeon General, Department of the Army. 1958.

Wheeler Keith. *Bombers over Japan*. Alexandria, VA: Time-Life Books. 1982.

Wheeler, Keith. *War under the Pacific*. Alexandria, VA: Time-Life Books. 1981.

White, Richard. *The Organic Machine*. New York: Hill and Wang. 1995.

Whiting, Charles. *World War II, the Home Front: Germany*. Alexandria, VA: Time-Life Books. 1981.

Williams, Trevor I. *A History of Technology. Vol. VI, parts 1&2*. Oxford: Clarendon Press. 1978.

————— *Science: A History of Discovery in the Twentieth Century*. London: Oxford University Press. 1990.

Williamson, Gordon. *The SS: Hitler's Instrument of Terror*. Osceola WI: MBI. 1998.

Wills, Clint. editor. *The War: Stories of Life And Death From World War II*. New York: Thunder's Mouth Press/ Balliett & Fitzgerald Inc. 1999.

Wiltse, Charles M. *The Medical Department: Medical Service in the Mediterranean and Minor Theaters*. Washington, DC: Office of the Chief of Military History. 1965.

Wolf, William. *Endocrinology in Modern Practice*. Philadelphia, PA: W.B. Saunders Company. 1937.

Woodbury, David O. *Battlefronts of Industry: The Westinghouse Story*. New York. John Wiley and Sons. 1948.

Wyman, Carolyn. *I'm a SPAM Fan: The Stories behind America's Favorite Foods*. Stamford, CT: Longmeadow Press. 1993.

Yellin, Emily. *Our Mother's War*. New York: Free Press. 2004.

Specialty Reference; Textbooks & Compendiums

Air Force ROTC. Foundations of Air Power. Maxwell Air Force Base. AL: United States Air Force. 1958.

Bishop, Chris, editor. *The Encyclopedia of Weapons of World War II*. New York: Barnes and Noble Books. 1998.

Brewer, Ebenezer Cobham, *Brewer's Dictionary of Phrase and Fable: 14th Edition*. New York: Harper & Row. 1989.

Carts before Shoppers. Southern Living magazine. May 1990.

Chamberlain, Peter, and Hilary L. Doyle. *Encyclopedia of German Tanks of World War II*. New York: Arco Publishing. 1978.

Compton's Summary of The Second World War and Its Consequences. Chicago: F.E. Compton and Co. 1947.

Cummins, Lyle. editor. *History of Aircraft Lubricants*. Warrendale PA: Society of Automobile Engineers. 1997.

Day, Lance, and Ian McNeil, editors. *Biographical Dictionary of the History of Technology*. London: Routledge. 1996.

Dictionary of Literary Biography Vol. 46.

Frankenfield, Tom. *Using Industrial Hydraulics*: Cleveland, OH: Rexroth Corporation. 1984.

Guttman, Israel. *The Encyclopedia of the Holocaust*. New York: Macmillan Publishing. 1990.

International Directory of Company Histories, Volumes 1- 8. Chicago: Reference Publishers International, Inc. 1988.

Isaacs, Allen. *Dictionary of Physics, Third Ed*. New York: Oxford University Press. 1996.

Katz, Ephraim. *The Film Encyclopedia*. New York: Harper-Perennial. 1994.

Keane, Claire Brackman, and Benjamin F. Miller. *Encyclopedia and Dictionary of Medicine and Nursing*. Philadelphia: W.B. Saunders Co. 1972.

Klinghoff, Robert W. *Introduction To Fire Protection*. New York: Delmar Publishing, Inc. 1997.

Kroschwitz, Jacqueline and Winokur, Melvin. *Chemistry, General, Organic, Biological: 2nd Ed*. New York: McGraw-Hill, Inc. 1990.

Kurian, George Thomas. editor. *Datapedia of the United States*. Lanham, MD: Bernan Press. 1994.

Kurtz, Edwin B. *The Lineman's and Cableman's Handbook 4th Edition*. New York: McGraw-Hill Book Company.1964.

McCarthy,Willard J. and Robert E. Smith. *Machine Tool Technology*. Bloomington Il. McKnight & McKnight Publishing. 1968.

McNeil, Ian. *An Encyclopedia of the History of Technology*. New York: Routledge. 1990.

Manly, H.P. *Heating, Cooling and Air Conditioning Handbook*. Chicago, Frederick J. Drake and Co. 1945.

Manual of Flight, Cessna Integrated Flight Training System. USA: Jeppesen & Company. 1976.

Melick, Dermott Wilson, MD. *Nylon Sutures*. Unpublished thesis manuscript, 1941. In possession of The University of Arizona College of Medicine rare document library.

Oberg, Erik and Franklin D Jones. *Machinery's Handbook 11th Edition*. New York: Industrial Press. 1941.

Oberg, Erik, Franklin D. Jones, and Holbrook L. Horton. *Machinery's Handbook 23rd Edition*. New York: Industrial Press. 1988.

PDR; Physician's Desk Reference, 37th Edition. Oradell NJ: Medical Economics Co. 1983.

Parrish, Thomas. editor. *The Simon and Schuster Encyclopedia of World War II*. New York: Simon and Schuster Corporation. 1978.

Reader's Digest Association Stories behind Everyday Things. White Plains NY: Reader's Digest Association. 1980.

Smithsonian Institution, Annual report of the Year End, June 30, 1942. Washington, DC: U.S. Government Printing Office. 1942.

United States Air Force Museum Catalog. Dayton, OH: Wright-Patterson AFB. Air Force Museum Foundation. 1982.

United States Bureau of the Census. *Historical Statistics of the United States: Colonial Times to 1970*. Washington, DC: Government Printing Office. 1975.

Veatch, Henry C. *Transistor Circuit Action*. New York: McGraw-Hill Book Co. 1968.

Wise, David Burgess. *The New Illustrated Encyclopedia of Automobiles*. Edison, NJ: Quarto, Inc. 1997.

World Education Encyclopedia. New York: Facts on File Publications. 1988.

Zeigler, Paul F. *Textbook on Sutures*. Walpole, MA: Lewis Manufacturing Co. 1936.

Periodical Articles

Berkowitz, Bruce D. *Monster Engines*. Washington, DC: *Air & Space* magazine. December 1997/ January 1998.

D'Alto, Nick. *Above It All*. Washington, DC: *Air & Space* magazine. September 2009.

Duffy, Tom, and Alec Foege. *Jimmy Found* New York: *People Magazine*. Time Inc. Publishers. 1998.

Ford, Daniel. *Gentlemen, I Give You the Whittle Engine*. Washington, DC: *Air & Space* Magazine. October/ November 1992.

Ford, Daniel. *B-36: Bomber at the Crossroads*. Washington, DC: *Air & Space* magazine. April/May 1996.

Ford, Daniel. *The Sorry Saga of the Brewster Buffalo*. Washington, DC: *Air & Space* magazine. June/July 1996.

Garrison, Peter. *Model Behavior*. Washington, DC: *Air & Space* magazine. February/March 2007.

Hoover's Handbook of World Business. Hoover's Inc. 1991.

Huntington, Tom *One Good Year*. Washington, DC: *Air & Space* magazine. February/ March 1997.

Industrial Engineering Chemistry. May 1939.

Israel, Howard A. and William E. Seidelman. *Nazi Origins of an Anatomy Text: The Pernkopf Atlas. Journal of the American Medical Association*. 11/27/96.

Keister, Edwin. *A Curiosity Turned Into the First Silver Bullet Against Death*. Washington, DC: *Smithsonian* magazine. November 1990.

Kuznik, Frank. *Hover Dance*. Washington, DC: *Air & Space* magazine. October/November 1997.

Life magazine.

Lightbody, Howard D. and Harry L. Fevold. *Biochemical Factors Influencing the Shelf Life of Dried Whole Eggs and Means for the ir Control*. Printed in *Advances In Food Research, Vol. 1*. E. M. Mrak and George F. Stewart: editors. 1948.

McCaul, editor, *The Ingenious Maunsell Forts Defended the British Coastline against Marauding German Aircraft and E-boats*. Leesburg, VA: *World War II* magazine. March 1996.

McGrath, Susan. *Attack of the Alien Invaders*. Washington, DC: *National Geographic* magazine. March 2005.

Michel, Sonya. *American Women and the Discourse of the Democratic Family in World War II. Behind the Lines*. New York: *The Journal of Modern History*. Vol. 61, December 1989.

Moore, Robert W. *Greens Grow For G.I.s on Soil less Ascension*. Washington, DC: *National Geographic* magazine. Vol. 88, No. 2, August 1945.

Palmer, Katherine Bell. *Flying Our Wounded Veterans Home*. Washington, DC: *National Geographic* magazine. Vol. 88, No. 3, September 1945.

Pappalardo, Joe. *Swing Wings*. Washington, DC: *Air & Space* magazine. August/September 2006.

Patton, Phil. *A Quick Way From Here To There Was Also A Frolic*. Washington D.C: *Smithsonian* magazine. October/November. 1990.

Posey, Carl. *Out of Thin Air*. Washington, DC: *Air & Space* magazine. October/November 1996.

Posey, Carl. *In The Grip of the Whirlwind*. Washington, DC: *Air & Space* magazine. October/November 1992.

Reed, John C. *Petroleum Possibilities in Alaska. Bulletin of the American Association of Petroleum Geologists*. Vol.30, No. 9. September 1946.

Scammell. Henry. *Across the Atlantic*. Washington, DC: *Air & Space* magazine. April/ May 1996

Scully, Michael. *A Look Back*. New York: *Your Company* magazine. December 1998-January 1999.

Slattery, Chad. *The Model Man*. Washington, DC: *Air & Space* magazine. October/ November 1996.

Sotham, John. *Bigfoot*. Washington, DC: *Air & Space* magazine. February/ March 1998.

Tenner, Edward. *Hardheaded Logic. Invention and Technology* magazine.

Vol. 19, No.1, Summer 2003.

U.S. Bureau of Mines Informational Circular #7417. Annual Report of Research and Technologic Work on Coal. 1946.

Vosburgh, Frederick G. *Metal: Sinews of Strength. National Geographic* magazine. Vol. 81, No.4, April 1942.

Walker, Lester. *Secrets by the Thousands.* New York. *Harper's Magazine.* Aug. 1946.

Weeks, L.G. *Developments in Foreign Petroleum Fields. Bulletin of the American Association of Petroleum Geologists.* Vol.32, No. 6. June 1946.

Weinberg, Gerhard. *Hitler's Image of the United States.* New York. *American Historical Review.* #69. July 1964.

Wilkinso, Stephan. *Tanks, Hot Rods and Salt.* Washington DC: *Air & Space* magazine. April/ May 1997.

Wright, John. W. editor. *Universal Almanac 1991.* Kansas City: Andrews and McNeil.1990.

Army Medical Bulletin. Washington, DC: Department of the Army, Office of the Surgeon General. 1939-1947.

Thirteen Day Non-stop Trip Tests Diesel Truck. Popular Mechanics magazine. March 1932.

Air Drive Operates Tools Forward or Backward. Popular Mechanics magazine. April 1934.

Breaking Into Dirt Track Racing. Popular Mechanics magazine. April 1934.

Radio-Driven Model Plane is the Target for Guns. Popular Mechanics magazine. May 1935.

Homes Assembled Like Autos Would Cost Two-Thirds Less. Popular Mechanics magazine. February 1937.

Life Saving Inventions Pay Dividends. Popular Mechanics magazine. May 1938.

Mechanizing the Small Farm. Popular Mechanics magazine. April 1940.

The Good Earth Goes To Sea. Popular Mechanics magazine. July 1940.

110 Foot Laminated Wood Beam Supports Vast Load. Popular Mechanics magazine. July 1940.

Baby's Tags and Footprints Prevent Hospital Mix-ups. Popular Mechanics magazine. October 1940.

Flying Nurses. Popular Mechanics magazine. October 1940.

Freight Trains of the Highway. Popular Mechanics magazine. October 1940.

Mobile Catastrophe Hospital Handles Major Operations. Popular Mechanics magazine. April 1942.

Gateway to the World. Popular Mechanics magazine. April 1942.

Versatile Repair Tool Cuts Metal and Irons out Car Fender. Popular Mechanics magazine. April 1942.

Chaining Tires and Wheels Helps Foil Thieves. Popular Mechanics magazine. June 1942.

Lock Nuts on Auto Wheels Help Prevent Theft of Tires. Popular Mechanics magazine. June 1942.

New Disguises of the Demon Fire. Popular Mechanics magazine. June 1942.

New Landing System OK'd. Impact: The Army Air Forces "Confidential" Picture History of World War II. July 1944. Reprinted 1980.

Revolution in Farming. Popular Mechanics magazine. June 1942.

The Paste That Welds Anything. Popular Mechanics magazine. July 1959.

Op. Ed. Minneapolis Star Tribune. Aug. 4, 1997Metro Edition: News, P.5A.

Industry Supplied Material

General Foods Press Release: *The Extraordinary Mr. Durrani*. Ca. 1951
Ibid. GF Newsletter: *Launching a Bestseller*. Vol. X, No. 9, September 1949
Kennametal, Inc. *Properties and Proven Uses of Kennametal Hard Carbide Alloys*. 1977.
Miles Laboratories Information Brochure. 1978.

World Wide Web (WWW) Resources.

AMP Inc.: www.amp.com/about/amp_profile.
Ampex Company History: www.fundinguniverse.com/company-histories/ Ampex-Corporation-company-history.
Bridgeport Machine: www. "http://www.fundinguniverse.com/company-histories/ Bridgeport" fundinguniverse.com/company-histories/ Bridgeport-Machines-Inc-Company-history
Civil Air Patrol: "http://www.caphistory.org/museum" www.caphistory.org/museum
Chiquita Bananas:www.fundinguniverse.com/company -histories/Chiquita-Brands-International-Inc-Company-History.
Johnson Publishing: www.ebony.com/historya.
Kaiser-Permenante History: www.kaiserpermenante.org/about/50years.
Kodak: www.kodak.com/aboutkodak/kodakhistory/milestones33to79.
Morton, David. The Chronology of Recording Tape: "http://www.rci.rutgers.edu/~dmorton/minifon" www.rci. rutgers.edu/~dmorton/minifon. And
www.rci. rutgers.edu/~dmorton/wire.
Morton, David. John Herbert Orr, tape recording pioneer, and founder of Orradio Industries, Inc.: "http://www.rci.rutgers.edu/~dmorton/orradio" www.rci.rutgers. edu/~dmorton/orradio.
NASCAR: www.nascar.com/guides/about/nascar.
NHRA: www.nhra.com/nhra101/history/
Oshkosh Trucks: www.fundinguniverse.com/company-histories/Oshkosh-Truck-Corporation-Company-history
Silly Putty: www.courant.com/entertainment/xroads/pleasure/putty.
Smoke Jumpers: www/fs.fed.us/fire/operations/jumpers/redding/history.
U-Haul: "http://www.u-haulinternational.co/history" www.u-haulinternational.co/history And: "http://www.fundinguniverse.com/company-histories/AMERCO-Company-history" www.fundinguniverse.com/company-histories/AMERCO-Company-history.
USDA: "http://www.usda.gov/history2/text3" www.usda.gov/history2/text3.
U.S. Dept. of Interior, Forest Service: "http://www.r8web.com/texas/smokey" www.r8web. com/texas/smokey. and
www.smokeybear.com/cgi-bin/rbox/fr.

ZIP Code: "http://www.usps.gov/his3_5" www.usps.gov/his3_5. and
www.usps.gov/his2_75.

Videos

Burke, James. *The Long Chain*. New York: Ambrose Video BBC-Time/Life. 1978

CPSIA information can be obtained at www.ICGtesting.com
261832BV00002B/53-300/P